Jurisprudence of International Criminal Justice

Jurisprudence of International Criminal Justice

Farhad Malekian

CAMBRIDGE
SCHOLARS
PUBLISHING

Jurisprudence of International Criminal Justice
By Farhad Malekian

This book first published 2014

Cambridge Scholars Publishing

12 Back Chapman Street, Newcastle upon Tyne, NE6 2XX, UK

British Library Cataloguing in Publication Data
A catalogue record for this book is available from the British Library

F.Malekian.in.crim.l@telia.com

ISBN (10): 1-4438-5360-7, ISBN (13): 978-1-4438-5360-6

To my wife the basic chamber of my heart and brainpower
– Kerstin Nordlöf

The only woman I will ever love

The first thing we do, let's kill all the lawyers.
Henry the Sixth, Part II, IV, ii
Shakespeare from the law of the land

TABLE OF CONTENTS

ABSTRACT

This challenging volume examines the jurisprudence and the essence of international criminal justice from various points of view. The philosophy of justice may vary from time to time and from nation to nation, depending on prevailing attitudes towards the substantive rules which deal, in one way or another, with cultural norms. In the national and international area, the principles of criminal justice have a key role in the abolition, elimination, prohibition, prevention, extradition, prosecution, jurisdiction, judgment or punishment of international crimes. In particular, the principles are effective in examining the scope of the most serious violations of international criminal law. It is on the basis of appropriate judgment that these principles may be accumulated and achieved for the future conduct of man. This volume, therefore, examines the principles and dimensions of the constitutions of various international criminal tribunals such as Nuremberg, the ICTY, the ICTR, the Sierra Leone Court, non-trial justice, with particular focus on the Statute of the International Criminal Court (ICC). As such, the volume offers a comprehensive evaluation of the rule of law and criminal justice and their legal tasks within the complementarity system of international criminal jurisprudence. This includes such as *de lege lata, nullum crimen sine lege, nulla poena sine lege*, non-retroactivity *ratione personae*, jurisdiction *ratione temporis* or *materiae*, criminal responsibility and *ne bis in idem.*The volume emphasises the prosecution and punishment of all those who may successfully escape from the proceedings of national and international criminal courts because of their juridical, political, religious, economic or military power. It also demands the implementation of international law of *jus cogens*. The provisions of the Statute should not be deduced in contradiction to the norms from which no derogation is possible, such as prohibitions governing crimes against humanity, torture, apartheid, rape, war crimes, genocide and aggression. This means that all international relations between international legal persons including states or entities and even groups or individuals are subject to the realm of peremptory norms and they should not violate the fundamental principles of justice. If the value of the task of the Court is to be realised by the majority of states in the international community, the cycle of impunity has to be abolished in the case of all states including the five permanent members of the Security Council of the United Nations.

Key words: international, law, crime, equality, justice

INTRODUCTION

Farhad Malekian, a distinguished scholar of international law has now authored a comprehensive work on *Jurisprudence of International Criminal Justice*. The absence of agreement among leading decision makers for maintaining peace has led to endless suffering and destruction of humankind; and the absence of a permanent international criminal court to deter aggression, genocide, crimes against humanity and massive war crimes has been a missing link in the world legal order.

In his scholarly chapter-by-chapter analysis, Malekian notes the cultural, economic and legal diversities that need to be harmonized in order to protect universal human rights. Although punishment will not prevent all international crimes,it will help to deter some of them if perpetrators know they will be brought to justice. He calls for a global vision that will recognize the legal and moral obligations of states as well as individuals and the rights of victims.

The author traces the development of international criminal law from the Nuremberg and Tokyo trials through to the existing ad hoc tribunals created by the United Nations to deal with the massive human rights violations in the former Yugoslavia, Rwanda, and other areas.

He notes the importance of respect for established principles of fair trial, non-retroactivity and the avoidance of double jeopardy. He welcomes the growth of national jurisdictions to cope with international crimes. He recognizes that in certain situations it may be necessary in the interests of peace to forego legal prosecutions in favor of non-legal solutions by reconciliation commissions.

In his historical analysis, the author sketches the evolutionary movement from the early United Nations General Assembly Resolutions in 1946 to the culmination in Rome in 1998 when the idea of a permanent international criminal tribunal was resoundingly endorsed by most nations. A Review Conference that took place in Kampala, Uganda in June 2010, agreed on a new definition of the crime of aggression but was unable to agree that it should be punishable by the ICC. As was done in Rome, the problem has been deferred for further consideration until sometime after 2017. Malekian's books, which analyze the Rome Statute and the activities of the International Criminal Court, offer very timely reference points.The author wisely expresses the hope that the Court will end the existing impunity of those leaders who are responsible for the supreme international crime of aggression. He looks forward to the implementation of criminal justice

The new legal body is in its infancy. That is why the Assembly of States Parties iscontinuously taking those important problems of the Court into consideration. However, one cannot deny that the text on the Elements of Crimes greatly aids understanding of the Statute and its main functions. Nevertheless, the Statute presents a mixture of adversary-accusatorial and inquisitorial methods including criminal procedures which may, in particular situations, prevent access to peace and justice relatively slow because of differences between those methods. The Court hopefully prevents impunity of those who are personally responsible for transgressions, in particular, those who are responsible for grave violations of international humanitarian law of armed conflicts or genocide. This is the minimum hope for the implementation of criminal justice and the prevention of grave violations of international legal and moral law.

Malekian concludes that the principles of international criminal justice in the Court are, sooner or later, an integral part of international law of jus cogens. He bases this on the fact that war crimes, crimes against humanity, genocide and aggression are not only contrary to the basic elements of international human rights law, but also violations of those norms which infringe human civilization as a whole. These are accepted by the international community of states as peremptory or jus cogens norms from which no derogation is permitted under international law and are to be respected by all states irrespective of whether they have signed or ratified: a state is not permitted to make a reservation to those crimes which are against humankind. According to him, those norms encourage the international legal community to pay special attention to certain civilized values: these are the safeguarding and maintenance of security and peace, as well as the respect of certain fundamental common human values.

Prof. Farhad Malekian has produced a much needed comprehensive survey showing the evolution of international criminal law and international courts from the Nuremberg Tribunals following World War Two to the most recent problems confronting the International Criminal Court in The Hague. The prolific author takes the reader through the maze of new international courts that are still in formative stages.

His clear and scholarly analysis depicts the problems and gradual movement towards the criminalization of human rights violations still taking place throughout the world. The slow process toward a more rational and humane world under the rule of law binding all states, groups and individuals is a work still in progress.

Prof. Malekian's important contribution offers new insights into a rapidly expanding field of law that hopefully points the way toward a more humane and peaceful future.

The book constitutes a prized addition to the literature of international criminal justice. It presents an unbiased and significant facet of international jurisprudence. It should be read eagerly by those who are searching for a new analysis of the rule of law.

New Rochelle, New York
Professor Benjamin B Ferencz[1]

[1] Professor Benjamin B Ferencz, J.D. Harvard 1943, a former Nuremberg war crimes prosecutor who has written extensively on the subject.http://www. benferencz.org. He was awarded Erasmus Prize together with Antonio Cassese in 2009.

FOREWORD

The body of international criminal law is growing rapidly and has become one of the most important parts of international legislation. This is especially apparent in the case of the jurisprudence of international criminal justice, which has a long history of legislative development. In fact, international criminal law cannot function properly without an effective understanding of its norms and rules, as well as the philosophy behind the implementation of its theory. A body of law may not be taken seriously if its provisions or norms are not protected by a system of jurisdiction that executes justice based on genuine adherence to the principle of equal treatment. Moreover, at the national and international levels, the principles of justice play the most significant role governing the abolition, elimination, prohibition, prevention, extradition, prosecution, jurisdiction, judgment and punishment of international crimes. Whilst the principles of justice may never convince the victims of crime, they represent to the people of the world the message of peace, security, humanity, common understanding of international problems and respect for the rule of law. If such principles could be successfully upheld, atrocities and antagonisms between the nations of the world might be reduced and harmonious relations between nations developed and strengthened.

In recognition of the growing number of international conventions which recognize and analyse international crimes, the focal point in the development of the system of international criminal law in recent decades has been the establishment of international criminal courts. Nevertheless, what the philosophy of justice is, and what its functions, aims, purposes and, principles are, continue to constitute some of the most important elementary questions of international criminal jurisprudence. The tradition of criminal law provides for four discrete authorities for the implementation of the philosophy and principles of criminal justice, namely, national, regional, hybrid and international criminal courts. These authorities have been exercised and consolidated within the civilizations of different states and constitute today integral parts of the legislative framework of human rights law. The constitutions of the *ad hoc* tribunals, including those of Nuremberg, Yugoslavia and Rwanda, as well as the Sierra Leone Court, and even the procedures of non-trial justice, imply the chronological improvement of the jurisprudence of criminal justice. The provisions of the 1998 Statute of the International Criminal Court (ICC) also empower the jurisprudence of justice. A milestone of the Statute is the creation of a framework for a code of international crimes recognising the concept of the international criminal responsibility of individuals. The crimes identified in the code are genocide, crimes against humanity, war crimes and aggression.

This volume consists of twelve chapters. The first chapter deals with the philosophy of international criminal justice, the reason for its existence, and the need for the equal application of its principles. To a great extent the problems faced by the international political and legal community in applying international criminal justice are related to the distribution of unequal power in the world, as well as the fact that the implementation of many principles of criminal justice depends on a concern to uphold a proper relation between different subjects of international law. The chapter focuses on the solution of these problems at a theoretical level and calls for the equal application of the philosophy and principles of international criminal law, as well as the enforcement of justice and the elimination of impunity.

Chapters two and three focus on the formation, creation and operation of the international criminal tribunals and courts established under the authority of the victorious states of the Second World War, the United Nations and the international legal community as a whole. These are the Nuremberg Tribunal, the Tokyo Tribunal, the ICTY, the ICTR, the SCSL, and the ICC. It is impossible to understand the development of the jurisprudence of international criminal law and justice without first analysing the fundamental role played by the creation of the tribunals and courts and their operation. These chapters examine many of the key principles which have had an important function in the progressive evolution of the system of international criminal law and the establishment of a number of temporary tribunals around the world. The chapters also analyse the legal characteristics of these tribunals and the *raison d'être* of their applications.

Chapters four, five and six relate to three core principles of international criminal justice: international crimes, international legal procedures and the various concepts pertaining to the international criminal responsibility of individuals. Taken together, these three chapters prove that neither the official position of individuals who have committed crimes, nor the fact that they acted pursuant to orders from their governments or a superior can be sufficient reason to escape international prosecution and punishment.

Chapters seven to ten set out the *conditio* sine qua non or the practical value of the development of international criminal justice. They contain detailed presentations of the Statute of the permanent International Criminal Court (ICC) and its recent development during the Review Conference on the Rome Statute of the International Criminal Court (ICC) in Kampala, Uganda from 31 May to 11 June 2010. It is worth mentioning here that the Statute of the ICC is based on substantive law and elaborates the provisions of *de lege lata, nullum crimen sine lege, nulla poena sine lege*, non-retroactivity *ratione personae*, jurisdiction *ratione temporis* or *materiae*, criminal responsibility and *ne bis in idem.*

The ICC, in fact, exercises an extraordinary function for the domestic criminal courts, as it authorizes recourse to the enforcement system of international criminal law when the courts are, for one reason or another, unable to exercise jurisdiction over accused persons. As a result, it is the legal duty of the Court to wait for a clear decision by the national authorities of a state concerning the investigation of a case. If the authorities avoid serious criminal investigation of the case, the principle of complementarity may empower the Court to evaluate and apply the provisions of the Statute. The Court may also, in certain circumstances, act in accordance with a decision of the Security Council concerning one of the major crimes. The Council can empower the Court to examine a criminal case, even where violations of the provisions of the Statute are committed by individuals of those states which have not signed or ratified the Statute of the ICC. This is based on the protection of the integrity of the international human community as a whole. However, this presents its own serious juridical and legal predicaments.

Chapters seven to ten deal with many questions relating to this dilemma of legal authority.My purpose is to offer a comprehensive evaluation of the rule of law and criminal justice and their legal operation within the complementarity system of international criminal jurisdiction. Chapter ten, in particular, examines certain cases heard by the international criminal tribunals and the courts.

Chapter eleven addresses the use of non-trial justice, including truth commissions and amnesties, to deal with serious offenders. The intention is to highlight that the strength of international criminal justice does not rest solely on the procedures of criminal courts, but also on forgiveness. The chapter aims to analyse how the integration and reconciliation of offenders and victims can be achieved.

The twelfth chapter concludes the whole volume. It underlines that the jurisprudence of international criminal law strongly condemns impunity for *jus cogens* crimes. It consequently calls upon the implementation of the *jus cogens* principles of international criminal law in the ICC and the prosecution and punishment of all those who have seriously violated the provisions of international criminal law, humanitarian law, human rights law and criminal justice. I have therefore argued that the goals and values of international criminal jurisprudence should not be dismissed on the grounds of non-ratification of international criminal conventions.

Although each chapter of this volume has its own legal philosophy and is independent of the other chapters, the volume taken as a whole contributes to one legal discipline.Throughout the chapters of this work, we look into the principles of jurisdiction and its proceedings, which have been adopted for the protection of the rights of man, but which are violated by individuals, groups or governments. The argument of all chapters is based on the idea of individual criminal responsibility, which constitutes the principal theory within the statutes of international criminal tribunals or the ICC.

F. Malekian
Director
Institute of International Criminal Law
Uppsala, Sweden

CHAPTER ONE

THE ORIGIN OF INTERNATIONAL CRIMINAL JUSTICE

1. Introduction

International criminal justice is the fruit of transcultural morality, cooperation, assistance, reciprocity, mutual and multilateral tolerances, and a combination of different political necessities. It is, moreover, inspired by ideals of fairness, reparation and rehabilitation. When we talk about the principles of international criminal justice, we do not necessarily mean only the judgments that may be delivered by international criminal courts, but also the living structure of international criminal law as it exists in the international relations of states. International criminal justice is therefore not just a matter of criminal jurisdiction. The term has its own framework of recognition of what is right and what is wrong between different nations. That is why we talk about the general principles of law and their effects in the system of international criminal law. The rights secured by the principles of criminal law obviously should not be subject to political interference by any state or authority. As a recognised principle of justice, criminal rules should be applied equally to all individuals, whether they are weak or powerful. The rationale behind these principles is to provide effective measures against violators of international law and to consolidate the principle of non-impunity. This philosophy should be followed within national or international criminal jurisdictions.

2. The Philosophy of Law

2.1. Spirit

A law is the command of social order.[1] By "order" we mean the rules of relationships which have been agreed upon. The members of a community may expect that the law, *inter alia*, creates freedom, equality, assistance,

[1] Lord Lloyd of Hampstead, Introduction To Jurisprudence (4th ed. 1979).

justice and peace. When theorising law and order we are looking to find the most practical and convincing way of regulating the relations between the members of one society, and also of those members with members of other societies.[2] This is the simple aspect of the law and the normal expectation behind the creation and establishment of new norms of legislation. As society continues to evolve, it also develops the scope and the perspective of the law. In other words, a law is the language of the development of relations between its members. One of the final stages of these developments is the creation and evolution of the system of customary and conventional international criminal law in order to protect the purposes of societies, including their legal as well as moral aspirations. However, what the command of social order is, or who or what the principal inspiration of this order is, varies from one legal system to another and from one society to another. This is because a law lacks the obvious biological systems of the human body consisting of different organs such as the heart or brain. In other words, a law is not a material or tangible product of our social environment, like, for instance, a package wrapped up in Christmas paper. Rather, a law is the consequence of the circumstances of a given social order, whether derived from monarchy, dictatorship, religion, democracy or other such social phenomena.[3]

Although most of the subjects of most social sciences may be observed and recorded by one means or another, this is not possible in the case of law or the social legal order. In another sense, a law does not exist as do other material objects until it has been created by human agents through their attention in terms of political science. Thus, a law is tied into human thoughts, human understanding and misunderstanding; human interpretation, inspiration, instigation; human will and resistance; human tolerance and intolerance; and also, human physical and moral capability.[4] In the final stages of its creation, the law is bound by material—i.e., visible—subjects of our social environment, transferred from a piece of paper to physical violence.

---

[2] Brian Tamanaha, A General Jurisprudence Of Law And Society (2001).

[3] For a discussion on what the nature of law is, See Cairns Huntington, *Plato's Theory of Law*, 56 Harvard Law Review 359-387 (1942).

[4] See *also* M.J. Detmold, The Unity of Law And Morality: A Refutation Of Legal Positivism (1984); Natural Law (John Finnis, Ed., 1991); Lon Luvios Fuller, The Morality Of Law (2 Ed., 1969); The Autonomy Of Law: Essays On Legal Positivism (Robert P. George, Ed., 1995); Robert P. George, Natural Law Theory: Contemporary Essays (1994); Law, Morality and Society: Essays in Honour of H.L.A. Hart (P.M.S. Hacker And J. Raz, Eds., 1977); John Finnis, Natural Law and Natural Rights (1980); John Finnis, Fundamentals of Ethics, (1983); John Finnis, Aquinas: Moral, Political and Legal Theory (1998).

Consequently, talking about a law is similar to talking about the nature of a human being, his or her habits and the borderline of his or her understanding of the surrounding environment. For example, a person who lives in a rainforest, and is free to feed himself/herself by whatever is available, has quite a different understanding of the law compared with a person who lives inside a zone of armed conflict. Similarly, a person who has grown up in a rich family has quite a different understanding of the law compared with someone from a poor family. They see the law from different aspects and different angles. They may reach similar conclusions, but with different perceptions, views and frameworks. There are further factors that also affect our personal understanding of the law. These may be religions, politics, theories, philosophies, ideologies, cultural flexibilities, economic variations or the historical description of the development of social expectations of sadness and happiness. In other words, a law may be defined in terms of individual tolerance. This means the tolerance to accept a different understanding of the law and its interpretation from one's own.[5] Thus, a law is a form of integration and disintegration of the will of a human being regarding what is recognised by him or her to be reasonable and not reasonable.[6] The law should therefore represent the principle of give and take and, more obviously, the framework of duties and responsibilities of persons to recognise the existence of other theories.[7]

2.2. Respect

In one word, the basic philosophy of the law is "respect". What is meant by "respect" is securing the will of human beings in their social interactions.[8] The framework of an accurate and equal law is thus the

---

[5] According to J. Shklar the law "relies on what appears already to have been established and accepted." J. Shklar, *Legalism,* in Lord Lioyd of Hampstead note 11, at 24.

[6] Brian Barry, *Justice as Reciprocity* in JUSTICE (Eugene Kamenka and Alice Erh-Soon Tay, eds., 1979), at 58, 73, 76.

[7] Eugene Kamenka, *What is Justice?* in JUSTICE (Eugene Kamenka and Alice Erh-Soon Tay, eds., 1979), at 4-5.

[8] But see also Issues in Contemporary Legal Philosophy: The Influence of H.L.A. Hart (Ruth Gavison, ed., 1987); Heidi Hurd, *Challenging Authority,* 100 Yale Law Journal 1611 (1991); G. Hughes, *Validity and the Basic Norm,* 59 California Law Review695 (1971); H.L.A. Hart, Essays in Jurisprudence and Philosophy (1983); Joseph Raz, The Morality of Freedom (1986); J.W. Harris, Legal Philosophies, 2nd edn. (1997); John Austin, The Province of Jurisprudence Determined and the Uses of the Study of Jurisprudence (1954); Postema, Gerald J, Bentham and the

framework of an individual mechanism, which should normally be respected by all individuals. By the term "individual" we mean not only the individual who has taken part in the formulation of the law, but also the individual who has not, for one reason or another, been able to take part in its drafting. Although the basic construction of a law may be re-examined by a new generation for various necessary modifications and alterations, its essence is generally the same.[9] This is because, as long as modifications of the law are not dictatorial or fanatical, they may simply polish its legal effect and modify it according to the new requirements of the time.[10] This is what we have become used to through the adoption of a number of international conventions within the system of international law and international criminal law.[11] But certain modifications or

---

Common Law Tradition (1986); Julie Dickson, Evaluation and Legal Theory (2001); H.L.A. Hart, The Concept of Law (1961); H.L.A. Hart, The Concept of Law, 2nd edn., (P.A. Bulloch and J. Raz eds., 1994).

9 See Joseph Raz, The Authority of Law (1979); Joseph Raz, Practical Reason and Norms (1999); Paul Phillips, Marx and Engels on Law and Laws (1980); M.J. Detmold, The Unity of Law and Morality: A Refutation of Legal Positivism (1984); J. Rawls, A Theory of Justice (1971); G. MacCormack, *Scandinavian Realism* Juridical Review 33 (1970); G. MacCormack, *Hägerström on Rights and Duties,* 59 Juridical Review (1970); Karl Olivecrona, Law as Fact, 2nd edn. (1971); W.J. Waluchow, Inclusive Legal Positivism (1994); Karl Olivecrona, Law as Fact (1939); Donald Black, The Behavior of Law (1976); Roscoe Pound, Jurisprudence(1959); Karl Olivecrona, *The Imperative Element in Law,* 18 Rutgers Law Review 794 (1964); Perry Anderson, Arguments within English Marxism (1980).

10 But read also Ian Ward, An Introduction to Critical Legal Theory (1998); Richard Rorty, Philosophy and the Mirror of Nature (1990); Mark Kelman, A Guide to Critical Legal Studies(1987); Anne Barron, *(Legal) Reason and its "Others": Recent DevelopmentinLegal Theory,* in Introduction to Jurisprudence and Legal Theory: Commentary and Materials (Schiff Penner, and Nobles, eds., 2002), 1038-63; Peter Goodrich, Reading the Law: A Critical Introduction to legal Method and Techniques (1986); *Legal Coherence,* 103 Yale Law Journal105 (1993); F. Ewald, *Unger's Philosophy: A Critical Legal Study* 5 Yale Law Journal 665(1988); The Politics of Law: A Progressive Critique (David Kairys, ed., 1982).

11 The development of international criminal law has been so great and effective that it has come to occupy an important place in the literature of international law. For an analysis of this law and its scope On international criminal law see Georg Schwarzenberger, 'The Problem of an International Criminal Law,' 3 *Current Legal Problems* (1950) 263; Edward M. Wise, 'Prolegomenon to the Principles of International Criminal Law,' 16 *New York University Law Review* (1970) 562; Farhad Malekian, *International Criminal Law: The Legal and Critical Analysis of International Crimes* (2 vols. 1991); Farhad Malekian, *Principles of Islamic International Criminal Law: A Comparative Search* (2011); Farhad Malekian, *The*

interpretations of the system of international criminal law may be so serious and dangerous that they create international annoyance, disagreement and, finally, war.[12] This is because the system of

---

Monopolization of International Criminal Law in the United Nations: A Jurisprudential Approach (2 ed, 1995); M. Cherif Bassiouni (ed.), *International Criminal Law* (3 vols., 1999); Farhad Malekian, *International Criminal Responsibility,* in M. Cherif Bassiouni (ed.), *International Criminal Law*, (1999) 153; Michael Bachrach, 'The Protection and Rights of Victims under International Criminal Law,' 34(1) *The International Lawyer* (2000); M. Cherif Bassiouni, 'International Recognition of Victims' Rights,' in Bassiouni (ed.), *International Criminal Law,* vol. III, 635-701 (2008); Boas Gideon and William A. Schabas (eds.), *International Criminal Law Developments in the Case Law of the ICTY* (2003); Yoram Dinstein, *'International Criminal Law,'* 20 *Israel Law Review* 206 (1985); Robert A Friedlander, 'The Foundations of International Criminal Law: A Present-Day Inquiry,' 15 *Case Western Reserve Journal of International Law* 13 (1983); M. Cherif Bassiouni, *Introduction to International Criminal Law* (2003); M. Cherif Bassiouni, 'The Discipline of International Criminal Law,' in M. Cherif Bassiouni (ed.), *International Criminal Law*, vol. 1 (2008) pp.3-40; M. Cherif Bassiouni, 'The Subjects of International Criminal Law: Ratione Personae' in M. Cherif Bassiouni (ed.), *International Criminal Law*, vol. 1 (2008) pp.41-70; Robert Cryer, 'The Doctrinal Foundations of International Criminalization,' in *International Criminal Law*, Vol.1 (M. Cherif Bassiouni, ed. 2008) pp. 107-128. Vespasian V. Pella, *Plan for World Criminal Code*, 17 Revue Internationale de Droit Penal (1946); Vespasian V. Pella, *Fonctions Pacificatrices du Droit Pénal Supranational et Fin du Système Traditionnel des Traités de Paix*, Le Droit Internazional Public 1 (1947); Edward M. Wise, *Prolegomenon to the Principles of International Criminal Law*, 16 New York University Law Review 562 (1970); Quincy Wright, *The Scope of International Criminal Law: A Conceptual Framework,* 15 Virginia Journal of International Law (1975); L.C. Green, *An International Criminal Code - Now?*, 3 Dalhousie Law Journal 560 (1976); Farhad Malekian, Principles of International Criminal Law (2011); Farhad Malekian, *International Criminal Responsibility,* in International Criminal Law 153 (M. Cherif Bassiouni ed., 1999); M. Cherif Bassiouni, *The Discipline of International Criminal Law, in* International Criminal Law, vol I (M. cherif Bassiouni, ed. 2008) pp.3-40; M. Cherif Bassiouni, *The Subjects of International Criminal Law: Ratione Personae in* International Criminal Law, vol i (M. cherif Bassiouni, ed. 2008) pp.41-70; Robert Cryer, *The Doctrinal Foundations of International Criminalization, in* International Criminal Law, vol i (M. cherif Bassiouni, ed. 2008) pp. 107-128.

[12] For international criminal law one can also see the followings: Robert A. Friedlander, *The Foundations of International Criminal Law: A Present-Day Inquiry*, 15 Case Western Reserve Journal of International Law 13 (1983); Gerhard O.W. Mueller, *International Criminal Law: Civitas Maxima,* 15 Case Western Reserve Journal of International Law (1983); Yoram Dinstein, *International Criminal Law*, 20 Israel Law Review 206 (1985); E.M. Wise, *International Crimes*

international criminal law guarantees the application of the law and this principle should not be modified or interpreted without a considerable amount of thought.[13] Thus, one should not undermine the power of justice as a consequence of dispositions of law.

3. The Power of Criminal Justice

There are no special rules for the interpretation of the principle of justice in international criminal law, but the interpretation indicates the way in which the terminology of justice is discussed and explained by different

---

and Domestic Criminal Law, 38 DePaul Law Review 923 (1989); Julio Barboza, *International Criminal Law*, 278 Recueil des cours 9-200 (1999-2000); David, Eric, Principes de Droit des Conflits Armés (2nd ed. 1999). There are many different views concerning the position and function of international criminal law. They base the development of international criminal law on various reasons. In one view "International criminal law, though not quite as comprehensively codified or as widely ratified by States as international human rights obligations, is relevant to the study and protection of international human rights because it, generally, is aimed at punishing acts which affect fundamental human rights, namely: life, liberty, and security. The codification of international criminal law can also make sense in light of the fact that this body of law aims to punish actions which may have been carried out as part of a broader State policy—meaning they are perhaps unlikely to be punished at the domestic level for as long as the responsible administration retains power—and/or which may threaten the sovereignty of another State—meaning the international community has an added interest in their prosecution. Although States' international human rights obligations would also require investigation and prosecution of such crimes, the international criminal law conventions and tribunals may be seen as particularly necessary with regard to States that refuse to comply with these obligations and/or are not (or were not at the relevant time) party to a binding mechanism for the adjudication of international human rights violations (namely, the Inter-American, European or African systems). Like criminal law generally, international criminal law prohibits certain actions by individuals and establishes the sanctions applicable when an individual commits those actions. In this regard, criminal law (whether domestic or international) differs from human rights law and international law generally, in that those held accountable are individuals, rather than governments. …International criminal law can be distinguished from domestic criminal law in that the former penalizes crimes which are particularly egregious and capable of producing wide-scale harm (such as crimes against humanity or genocide) and those crimes that can be thought of as 'international' in that they involve actions traditionally carried out by States or their agents (war crimes, acts of aggression) or are of a trans-national, or multi-jurisdictional, nature (terrorism, drug trafficking, piracy, slave trade). http://www.ijrcenter.org/ihr-reading-room/international-criminal-law/.

[13] See ibid.

nations in the international legal community as a whole.[14] The distribution of international criminal justice or fairness must be the same for all states,

---

[14] International criminal law is that part of international law which deals exclusively with criminal violations. The framework of international criminal law is essentially based on conventional and customary laws which have been formulated and practised in the international relations of states. The basic function of international criminal law is to identify and prevent international crimes and to extradite, prosecute or punish the perpetrators of such crimes. International criminal law is thus based on a policy of the prevention of the commission of international crimes and, if possible, the prosecution and punishment of the individuals responsible. "The first purpose of international criminal law is to secure the international legal order and therefore to maintain international perpetual peace. Consequently, international criminal law is a body of law which is attributable to wrongful conduct which violates international public regulation and endangers the maintenance of international legal order and peace. The second aim of international criminal law is to secure domestic legal systems where they are unable to implement their own legal systems. In this case international criminal law can be defined as a body of rules cooperating in criminal matters with domestic legal systems for the effective prosecution of criminals. International criminal law therefore has two characteristics. The first being international criminal laws arising from international criminal conventions having more or less international legal enforceability. The other is to regulate rules between municipal criminal legal systems for the enforcement of national criminal court decisions. Two examples of this are extradition and information gathering. The difference between the former and the latter is that the former is enforceable internationally, while the latter is only enforceable among a certain number of states. The former may, in certain situations, be considered as a principle of *jus cogens* and therefore creates obligations for all states regardless of their participation in an international criminal convention - such as the convention on genocide. The latter's enforceability is regional. Nevertheless, both concepts of international criminal law are correlative and have a more or less similar aim in the maintenance of a particular legal system. However, in the final analysis the enforceability of international criminal law of both types depends upon political considerations. This is because the structure of international criminal law depends at present upon national provisions, which means the concept of violation varies from one nation to another." Farhad Malekian., *I International Criminal Law* (1991), pp. 9-10.Although the burden of proof for international crimes is juridical, the final phase of criminalizing and punishing an internationally criminal wrongful conduct depends on political considerations and consequently on the various interpretations presented by different states. However, it cannot be ignored that the prevention, prosecution and punishment of some international crimes are not only stated by international conventional and customary law, but also by the domestic criminal legislation of most states, such as piracy, narcotic offences and falsification of currency to note but a few. These international crimes are treated by the universality principle, which means that the perpetrators of these international

without any regard to their political, juridical, economic or cultural aspects, or to language or religion, or to the size of their population.[15] If a just verdict for a specific crime is recognised and properly acknowledged by the criminal law of an overwhelming majority of states, it may be expected that justice has been carried out when that law is applied to a particular case. This is true when states have given democratic rights and duties to their people to participate in the construction of national and international legislation, human rights, humanitarian law and the application of their norms and provisions.[16] This is because the concept of justice may vary from time to time and from nation to nation depending on attitudes towards certain substantive rules dealing in one way or another

---

crimes can be punished by any state under the jurisdiction of which the accused is arrested. Two of the basic aspects of international criminal law are that it protects both the provisions of international human rights law and the international humanitarian law of armed conflict, both of which are recognised as an integral part of its framework and development. For this reason, the function of international criminal law is to protect human beings from various types of suffering, in both peace and war. The system of international criminal law is thus applicable even to the activities of states which are not at war, but which have undertaken different criminal, legal and political activities against their own and other countries' populations, the final stages of which violate the provisions of international criminal law and open the door to international criminal jurisdiction.

[15] But *also* read Hans Kelsen, *What is Justice?* Justice, Law and Politics in the Mirror of Science (1957); Hans Kelsen, Pure Theory of Law (transl Maz Knight, 1967); Legal Positivism (Mario Jori, ed., 1992); C Sypnowich, The Concept of Socialist Law (1990); C. Perelman, The Idea of Justice and the Problem of Argument (1963); Douzinas Costas, Peter Goodrich and Yifat Hachamovitch, Politics, Post modernity and Critical Legal Studies (1994); Legality, Ideology and the State(David Sugarman, ed., 1983); Critical Legal Studies (James D.A. Boyle, ed., 1992); Peter Goodrich, Languages of Law (1990); D. Kennedy, *Law and Ideology'* 3 Tikkun (1988); R. Unger, *The Critical Legal Studies Movement,* 96 Harvard Law Review 561 (1983); J. Derrida, *Force of Law: Mystical Foundation of Authority,* 11 Cardozo Law Review 919 (1990); James Boyle, *Is Subjectivity Possible? The Postmodern Subject in Legal Theory,* 62 University of Colorado Law Review 489 (1991); Dangerous Supplements: Resistance and Renewal in Jurisprudence (P. Fitzpatrick, ed., 1991); S. Fuller, *Playing Without a Full Deck: Scientific Realism and the Cognitive Limits of Legal Theory,* 97 Yale Law Journal 549 (1988); Alasdair MacIntyre, *After Virtue: A Study in Moral Theory,* (1982); Postmodernism and Law (Dennis Patterson, ed., 1994).

[16] M. Cherif Bassiouni, *Enforcing Human Rights through International Criminal Law and through an International Criminal Tribunal*, in Human Rights: An Agenda for the Next Century (Louis Henkin & John Lawrence Hargrove eds., 1994) (Studies in Transnational Legal Policy, no. 26) 524p.

with their cultural norms.[17] Understanding criminal law is not therefore an easy task.[18]

Moreover, international criminal justice arises not just from the accumulation of international legal instruments and cases, but also from the examination of the principle of equality in the application of international provisions.[19] Thus, when we speak of the special conditions for the application of international criminal justice, we do not necessarily mean that certain specific norms or provisions have to be implemented by international judges in an international court; rather, we ask whether the implementation of those provisions fulfils their application on an equal footing.[20] This is because the purpose of international criminal justice is not necessarily the satisfying of international conventions but the application and protection of fundamental rules and principles arising from the recognition of the equality of all human beings formulated into the documents on the principles of international human rights law.[21] By this we mean that human beings are born in the same way and with the same equal natural conditions: there is no difference in the nature of a man born in poverty in Africa and a man born into a wealthy family in Hawaii. Both have the same rights and obligations from the natural point of view, if not

---

[17] See John Rawls, A Theory of Justice (1999); *The Dynamics of International Criminal Justice - Essays in Honour of Sir Richard May* (Hirad Abtahi & Gideon Boas eds., 2005); International Human Rights in Context (Alston & Steiner eds., 2000); Association internationale de droit pénal/International Association of Penal Law, *International Criminal Justice: Historic and Contemporary Perspectives* (1996); H. Ball, Prosecuting War Crimes and Genocidee: The Twentieth Century Experince (1999); Farah Hussain, *A Functional Response to International Crime: An International Justice Commission*, St. John's Law Review (1996).

[18] Joshua Dressler, Understanding Criminal Law (1998). See *also* Thomas L. Friedman, The Lexus and the Olive Tree: Understanding Globalism (1999).

[19] See M. Cherif Bassiouni, From Versailles to Rwanda in Seventy-Five Years: The Need to Establish a Permanent International Criminal Court, 10 Harvard Human Rights Journal 11-62 (1997).

[20] Id.

[21] Farhad Malekian, Documents on the Principles of International Human Rights (2007). See also Werner Feld, *The Court of the European Communities: New Dimension in International Adjudication* (1964). See also Amnesty International, *The International Criminal Court: Making the Right Choices-Part V* (1998); Richard J. Goldstone, *For Humanity: Reflections of a War Crimes Investigator* (2000); The Law of the International Criminal Tribunal for the Former Yugoslavia (M. Cherif Bassiouni and Peter Manikas, 1996); International Humanitarian Law: Origins, Challenges and Prospects (John Carey and John R. Pritchard, eds., 2000); George A. Bermann et al., *Cases and Materials on European Community Law* (1993); Thomas M. Franck, *Fairness in International Law and Institutions* (1997).

from the juridical point of view. This means that the natural rights of man are integral parts of his existence, the proof of his integrity and his/her living conditions in international society. In other words, they are an integral part of his/her dignity and are protected and supported by the international legal community. Serious violations of these rights may be recognised as crimes[22] and condemned as such by the United Nations Organization.

Thus, when an international criminal court is established for the implementation of the rule of law and the prosecution and punishment of perpetrators of international crimes, the purpose of the court should be essentially the application of international provisions protecting the rights of man from the unlawful and inhuman conduct of governments or states.[23] Furthermore, the court must be independent and impartial—for example, Article 14 of the International Covenant on Civil and Political Rights states that all persons are entitled to a fair and just trial.[24] Similarly,

---

[22] This is regardless of against whom and where we have committed the criminal acts. For instance, the serious crimes committed against Palestinian civilians in Sabra and Shatila in Beirut in 1982. See the Security Council Resolution 521 (1982), which reads, "*Condemns* the criminal massacre of Palestinian civilians in Beirut". Similar reaction can be seen in the General Assembly Resolution (37/123D). It reads that the General Assembly: "*Recalling* its resolution 95 (I) of 11 December 1946, *Recalling* also its resolution 96 (I) of 11 December 1946, in which it, inter alia, affirmed that genocide is a crime under international law which the civilised world condemns, and for the commission of which principals and accomplices - whether private individuals, public officials or statesmen, and whether the crime is committed on religious, racial, political or any other grounds - are punishable, *Referring to* the provisions of the Convention on the Prevention and Punishment of the Crime of Genocide, adopted by the General Assembly on 9 December 1948, *Recalling* the relevant provisions of the Geneva Convention relative to the Protection of Civilian Persons in Time of War, of 12 August 1949, *Appalled* at the large-scale massacre of Palestinian civilians in the Sabra and Shatila refugee camps situated at Beirut, *Recognising* the universal outrage and condemnation of that massacre, *Recalling* its resolution ES-7/9 of 24 September 1982,

1. Condemns in the strongest terms the large-scale massacre of Palestinian civilians in the Sabra and Shatila refugee camps;

2. Resolves that the massacre was an act of genocide."

[23] See also Pierre Sob, The Dynamics of International Criminal Tribunals: Perspectives on Achieving Effective Human Rights Protection, 67: 2 Nordic Journal of International Law (1998), pp. 139-163.

[24] The article provides that "1. All persons shall be equal before the courts and tribunals. In the determination of any criminal charge against him, or of his rights and obligations in a suit at law, everyone shall be entitled to a fair and public

---

hearing by a competent, independent and impartial tribunal established by law. The Press and the public may be excluded from all or part of a trial for reasons of morals, public order (ordre public) or national security in a democratic society, or when the interest of the private lives of the parties so requires, or to the extent strictly necessary in the opinion of the court in special circumstances where publicity would prejudice the interests of justice; but any judgment rendered in a criminal case or in a suit at law shall be made public except where the interest of juvenile persons otherwise requires or the proceedings concern matrimonial disputes or the guardianship of children.
2. Everyone charged with a criminal offence shall have the right to be presumed innocent until proved guilty according to law.
3. In the determination of any criminal charge against him, everyone shall be entitled to the following minimum guarantees, in full equality:
1. To be informed promptly and in detail in a language which he understands of the nature and cause of the charge against him;
2. To have adequate time and facilities for the preparation of his defence and to communicate with counsel of his own choosing;
3. To be tried without undue delay;
4. To be tried in his presence, and to defend himself in person or through legal assistance of his own choosing; to be informed, if he does not have legal assistance, of this right; and to have legal assistance assigned to him, in any case where the interests of justice so require, and without payment by him in any such case if he does not have sufficient means to pay for it;
5. To examine, or have examined, the witnesses against him and to obtain the attendance and examination of witnesses on his behalf under the same conditions as witnesses against him;
6. To have the free assistance of an interpreter if he cannot understand or speak the language used in court;
7. Not to be compelled to testify against himself or to confess guilt.
4. In the case of juvenile persons, the procedure shall be such as will take account of their age and the desirability of promoting their rehabilitation.
5. Everyone convicted of a crime shall have the right to his conviction and sentence being reviewed by a higher tribunal according to law.
6. When a person has by a final decision been convicted of a criminal offence and when subsequently his conviction has been reversed or he has been pardoned on the ground that a new or newly discovered fact shows conclusively that there has been a miscarriage of justice, the person who has suffered punishment as a result of such conviction shall be compensated according to law, unless it is proved that the non-disclosure of the unknown fact in time is wholly or partly attributable to him.
7. No one shall be liable to be tried or punished again for an offence for which he has already been finally convicted or acquitted in accordance with the law and penal procedure of each country."

judges of the court must preserve their judicial impartiality regarding the case.[25] This is in order to ensure objectivity in judicial decisions.[26]

Here, the word "justice" may mean the respect of the fundamental rights of man recognised and acknowledged by the body of international human rights law as a whole.[27] It also means understanding the position of victims who have been subjected to mutilation, humiliation, violations or degrading circumstances.[28] The first condition for the application of the pure theory of justice may therefore be the way in which we understand the nature and spirit of human beings in connection with positive and unlawful acts or omissions.[29] In other words, it is of "fundamental importance that justice should not only be done, but should manifestly and undoubtedly be seen to be done."[30] The value of justice depends on its purely practical application.

---

[25] William A. Schabas, 'The Banality of International Justice', 11 *Journal of International Criminal Justice* (2013), pp.545–551.

[26] Judicial impartiality means "there is a general rule that a Judge should not only be subjectively free from bias, but also that there should be nothing in the surrounding circumstances which objectively gives rise to an appearance of bias. On this basis, the Appeals Chamber considers that the following principles should direct it in interpreting and applying the impartiality requirement of the Statute:
A. A Judge is not impartial if it is shown that actual bias exists.
B. There is an unacceptable appearance of bias if:
i) a Judge is a party to the case, or has a financial or proprietary interest in the outcome of a case, or if the Judge's decision will lead to the promotion of a cause in which he or she is involved, together with one of the parties. Under these circumstances, a Judge's disqualification from the case is automatic; or
ii) the circumstances would lead a reasonable observer, properly informed, to reasonably apprehend bias.
In terms of the second branch of the second principle, the Appeals Chamber adopts the approach that the 'reasonable person must be an informed person, with knowledge of all the relevant circumstances, including the traditions of integrity and impartiality that form a part of the background and apprised also of the fact that impartiality is one of the duties that Judges swear to uphold.'"*Furundzija*, (IT-95-17/1-A), Judgement, 21 July 2000, paras.189-190.

[27] See also William A. Schabas, Justice, Democracy and Impunity in Post Genocide Rwanda: Searching for Solutions to Impossible Problems, 7 *Criminal Law Forum* (1996), p. 523.

[28] See also ibid.

[29] For a useful examination of the development of the principles of international criminal courts within international criminal law see A Draft International Criminal Code and Draft Statute for an International Criminal Tribunal (2nd rev. ed. 1987). (2nd rev. & updated ed.1987).

[30] This is the well-known maxim of Lord Hewart CJ. See *R v. Sussex Justices ex parte McCarthy* [1924] 1 KB 256 at p. 259.

4. Core Principles of Criminal Justice

International criminal justice is based on the fulfilment of certain principles, which are vitally important for the safeguarding of the fundamental rights of man.[31] An appropriate international justice system must therefore seek to protect and implement the relevant principles of the machinery of justice. These are listed below.

4.1. The Principle of *de lege lata*

Law must always be enforceable consistently. This means that an international criminal court has to base its judgment on rules or provisions which were already in force at the time an international crime was committed.[32] The court must always avoid the application of the principle of *ex post facto* law or retroactivity. The law in force is thus the expression of the principle of *de lege lata,* which relates to the value of the existing law in contrast to what the law *ought* to be in its future aspects.[33]

A simple explanation of the principle of *de lege lata* is that it should represent the total sum of norms and rules that have been nominated by all the people of our international legal and political community. They should represent those norms of international behaviour that nations have acknowledged as their values. Here we seek the recognition of an appropriate initial *status quo* in order to ensure that the principles of justice are based on the fundamental elements of criminal law. In order for the role of international criminal justice to be fulfilled correctly, it should be united with the juridical values of the principle of *de lege lata*. The implementation of the principle of equality may scarcely fulfil its function, if the fundamental intentions of the principle dismiss the reasons for the existence of the law.[34]

---

[31] See William A. Schabas, *Sentencing by International Tribunals: For a Human Rights Approach,* 7:2 Duke Journal of Comparative & International Law (1997), pp. 461-518.

[32] For a new collection of conventional international criminal law see Eric David and Pascale Heirman, Code de Droit International Pénal 2009 (2e edition, 2009).

[33] Historical legal systems such as Roman law also clearly prohibited the application of retroactive punishment.

[34] The principle of equality constitutes one of the significant principles of justice. This principle is also stated in Article 21(1) of the Statute of the ICTY: "All persons shall be equal before the International Tribunal." The Appeals Chamber of the ICTY has describes the above provision. According to it "This provision reflects the corresponding guarantee of equality before the law found in many international instruments, including the 1948 Universal Declaration of Human

4.2. The Principle of *Nullum Crimen Sine Lege*

The principle of legality or *de lege lata* protects individuals from being subject to arbitrary civil or criminal jurisdiction,[35] and argues for the principle of *nullum crimen sine lege* or *nulla poena sine lege*, which means that there is no crime without a definite law.[36] There is a similar

---

Rights, the 1966 International Covenant on Civil and Political Rights, the Additional Protocol I to the Geneva Conventions, and the Rome Statute of the International Criminal Court. All these instruments provide for a right to equality before the law, which is central to the principle of the due process of law. The provisions reflect a firmly established principle of international law of equality before the law, which encompasses the requirement that there should be no discrimination in the enforcement or application of the law. Thus Article 21 and the principle it embodies prohibit discrimination in the application of the law based on impermissible motives such as, *inter alia*, race, colour, religion, opinion, national or ethnic origin. The Prosecutor, in exercising her discretion under the Statute in the investigation and indictment of accused before the Tribunal, is subject to the principle of equality before the law and to this requirement of non-discrimination." Zejnil Delalic (IT-96-21-A), Judgement, 20 February 200, para.605.

[35] It is important to quote Article 7 of the European Convention on Human Rights here:
"1. No one shall be held guilty of any criminal offence on account of any act or omission which did not constitute a criminal offence under national or international law at the time when it was committed. Nor shall a heavier penalty be imposed than the one that was applicable at the time the criminal offence was committed.
2. This article shall not prejudice the trial and punishment of any person for any act or omission which, at the time when it was committed, was criminal according the general principles of law recognised by civilized nations."

[36] Article 5 of the European Convention on Human Rights contains important matters concerning the suspect or detainee and their civil and criminal rights. In fact, the article aims at the protection of several principles of criminal law, criminal procedure and fundamental rights of a person who has, for one reason or another, been arrested by the legal authorities. It states:
"1. Everyone has the right to liberty and security of person.
No one shall be deprived of his liberty save in the following cases and in accordance with a procedure prescribed by law:
(a) the lawful detention of a person after conviction by a competent court;
(b) the lawful arrest or detention of a person for non-compliance with the lawful order of a court or in order to secure the fulfilment of any obligation prescribed by law;
(c) the lawful arrest or detention of a person effected for the purpose of bringing him before the competent legal authority of reasonable suspicion of having

maxim embodying the basic principle of criminal law which holds that conduct cannot be punished as criminal unless some rule of law has already declared that conduct to be criminal and punishable as such.

This principle constitutes an important guarantee of the implementation of appropriate justice. In other words, no international criminal court may apply the provisions of international criminal law to the conduct of a person when such conduct was not characterized as criminal before it was committed.[37] There must therefore be an intention

---

committed and offence or when it is reasonably considered necessary to prevent his committing an offence or fleeing after having done so;
(d) the detention of a minor by lawful order for the purpose of educational supervision or his lawful detention for the purpose of bringing him before the competent legal authority;
(e) the lawful detention of persons for the prevention of the spreading of infectious diseases, of persons of unsound mind, alcoholics or drug addicts, or vagrants;
(f) the lawful arrest or detention of a person to prevent his effecting an unauthorized entry into the country or of a person against whom action is being taken with a view to deportation or extradition.
2. Everyone who is arrested shall be informed promptly, in a language which he understands, of the reasons for his arrest and the charge against him.
3. Everyone arrested or detained in accordance with the provisions of paragraph 1(c) of this article shall be brought promptly before a judge or other officer authorized by law to exercise judicial power and shall be entitled to trial within a reasonable time or to release pending trial. Release may be conditioned by guarantees to appear for trial.
4. Everyone who is deprived of his liberty by arrest or detention shall be entitled to take proceedings by which the lawfulness of his detention shall be decided speedily by a court and his release ordered if the detention is not lawful.
5. Everyone who has been the victim of arrest or detention in contravention of the provisions of this article shall have an enforceable right to compensation."

[37] See Vespesian V. Pella. *Plan d'un Code Répressif Mondial,* 6 Rewe International de Droit Pénal 1948 (1935); United Nations War Crimes Commssion, History of the United Nations War Commission and the Deveelopment of the Laws of War. 443-50 (1949); Vespesian V. Pella. *Towards an International Criminal Court,* 44 American Journal of International Law 37 (1950); A. Sowilet, Sowilet A., The Problem of the Creation of a Permanent International Criminal Court (1951); Yeun-Li Liang, *The Establishment of an International Criminal Jurisdiction: The First Phase,* 46 American Journal of International Law (1952); Quincy Wright, *Proposal for an International Criminal Court,* 46 American Journal of International Law 60 (1952); Bienvenido C. Ambion, *Organization of a Court of International Criminal Jurisdiction,* 29 Philippine Law Journal 345 (1954); Fannie Klein & Daniel Wilkes, *United Nations Draft Statute for an International Criminal Court: An American Evaluation, in* International Criminal Law 526 (Gerhard O.W. Mueller & Edward M. Wise eds., 1965); Stone Julius and Robert Woetzel, Toward

by the legislature to make an act a crime before it is committed. In other words, when an international court is examining whether the actions or omissions of a person constitute a crime, it must base its judgment on definitions of crimes that were consolidated before the court came into existence. For this reason, the court should take into deliberation various important principles which are themselves part of the principle of *nullum crimen sine lege*. These are studied in the following sections.

4.2.1. Classification of the Principle

1. The court must not ignore the principle of *nullum crimen, nulla poena sine lege praevia*. This means that there are strict prohibitions against the application of retroactive, or *ex post facto*, law. Nor is an international court permitted to retroactively introduce more severe sanctions against the convicted person. This is also called the principle of non-retroactivity.

2. The court must also respect the principle of *nullum crimen, nulla poena sine lege scripta.* This means that the court must be extremely cautious when applying punishment which is the consequence of unwritten law or the customary law of different nations. The law must clearly be identified by the principle of legality.[38] If, however, the relevant applicable provisions are to count as an integral part of international customary law, they should be systematically recognised in the practice of the overwhelming majority of nations. The principle may also be called the principle of identified punishment.

---

a Feasible International Criminal Court (1970). Jean Dautricourt, *The Concept of International Criminal Court Jurisdiction-Definition and Limitations of the Subject*, in1 A Treatise on International Criminal Law 636 (M.C. Bassiouni & V.P. Nanda eds., 1973); *La Créationd'une Juridiction Pénale Internationale et la Coopération Internationale en Matière Pénale,* 45 Revue Internationale de Droit Penale 435 (1974); Louis Kos-Rabcewicz-Zubrowski, *The Creation of an International Criminal Court, in* International Terrorism and Political Crimes 519 (M. Cherif Bassiouni ed., 1975); Ferencz Benjamin, International Criminal Court (2 vols. 1980); M. Cherif Bassiouni & Daniel Derby, *Final Report on the Establishment of an International Criminal Court for the Implementation of the Apartheid Convention and Other Relevant Instruments,* 7 Hofstra Law Review 523 (1981).

[38] M. Cherif Bassiouni, *Principles of Legality in International and Comparative Criminal Law, in* International Criminal Law, vol i (M. cherif Bassiouni, ed. 2008) pp. 73-105; M. Cherif Bassiouni, *The Ratione Materiae of International Criminal Law, in* International Criminal Law, vol i (M. cherif Bassiouni, ed. 2008) pp. 129-203.

3. *Nullum crimen, nulla poena sine stricta* is another principle of criminal justice relating to the prohibition of the use of legal analogy in the recognition of the criminality of the accused, or with the intention of applying severe punishment. However, the employment of this principle may be permitted in international criminal law in favour of the accused, which may mitigate his or her punishment.

4. There is a further principle of criminal justice implying the prohibition of the recognition of an act as a crime when its elements are not clearly identified by the criminal justice system. This is the principle of *nullum crimen, nulla poena sine lege certa*, which speaks of the application of specific definitions of crimes and punishment. The principle is also known as the principle of definite elements. A clear example is the elements of crimes within the Statute of the ICC.

4.3. Proper Distribution of Justice

The fulfilment of the principles of *de lege lata* and *nullum crimen sine lege* in international criminal law is crucially important in ensuring the proper distribution of the system of international criminal justice.[39] Thus, when one criticises international criminal norms or certain international criminal judgements, one may point to the criteria of the application of the principle of *nullum crimen sine lege* in certain situations.[40] Furthermore, it is clear that any international criminal violation must be prosecuted and punished without any political, juridical, economic or military discrimination between legal and physical persons, as this violates the

---

[39] See Hans Kelsen, *What is Justice?* Justice, Law and Politics in the Mirror of Science (1957); HANS Kelsen, Pure Theory of Law (transl. Maz Knight, 1967); egal Positivism (Mario Jori, ed., 1992).

[40] Examine David Wippman, *Atrocities, Deterrence, and the Limits of International Justice*, 23 Forham International Law Journal 473 (1999); Vladan A. Vasilijevic, *Crimes Against Peace: Between the Past and the Future,* 43 Jugoslovenska Revija Za Medunarodno Pravo 425 (1996); Egon Schwelb, *Crimes Against Humanity,* British Yearbook of International Law (1946) 178; Mark J. Osiel, *Why Prosecute? Critics of Punishment for Mass Atrocity,* 22 Human Rights Quarterly 118 (2000); Naomi Roht-Arriaza, *State Responsibility to Investigate and Prosecute Grave Human Rights Violations in International Law,* 78 California Law Review 451 (1990); D.W. Bowett, *Jurisdiction: Changing Patterns of Authority over Activities and Resources,* British Year Book of International Law 1 (1982); Bruce Broomhall, International Justice and the International Criminal Court: Between Sovereignty and the Rule of Law (2003).

provisions of international criminal law. This is the basic theory of criminal justice.[41]

The principle of *nullum crimen sine lege* became one of the most important questions faced by international criminal jurisdictions after the Second World War. The question was mostly considered in the case of war crimes, crimes against peace and crimes against humanity.[42] These three categories of international crimes which were drafted in the London Agreement started a very serious conflict between national and international jurists concerning the legal validity of the jurisdiction of the tribunals.[43] Many writers were of the opinion that most of the three categories of international crimes created in the London Agreement were retroactive law and therefore could not correspond to existing law, i.e., *de lege lata*.[44] The conflict was fiercely contested among the international legal community, with even the United Nations Commission for the affirmation of the principles of the Nuremberg Tribunal unable to resolve this controversial judicial issue.[45] The question raised in the United Nations was that if the principles of the Charter of the International Military Tribunal were an integral part of the system of international law or *nullum crimen sine lege*, why was it necessary to reaffirm them again under the authority of the United Nations Organization?[46] Therefore, one of the essential reasons for the reconsideration of the principles of the

---

[41] It must however be noted that the system of international criminal law within different international courts deals solely with the notion of individuals' criminality and does not, for instance, deal in the Statute of the ICC, with the concept of the criminal responsibility of legal persons or entities.

[42] See Article 6 of the Charter of the International Military Tribunal annexed to the London Agreement of 8 August 1945.

[43] See for instance, Ian Brownlie, International Law and the Use of Force by States, at 201; M. R. Garcia-Mora, *Crimes Against Peace*, 34 Fordham Law Review (1965), at 6; F. B. Schick, *The Nuremberg Trial and the International Law of Future* 41 American Journal of International Law (1947).

[44] Georg Finch, *The Nürenberg Trial and International Law*, 41 American Journal of International Law (1947), at 20-37, see particularly p.33 and 35; F.J. Berber, *Some Thoughts on the Laws of War and the Punishment of War Crimes* in Essays on International Law (M. K. Nawaz, ed., 1976), at 260-5.

[45] See Year Book of International Law Commission (vol.1, 1950), at 111; The GAR. 488 (V), Suppl.20 (A/1775), at 77.

[46] No answer was given to the question, and the consequence was that the question of the legality of the principles of the Charter of the Nuremberg Tribunal has stagnated in the United Nations ever since.

Charter of the Military Tribunal in Nuremberg by the United Nations may be said to be the principle of *nullum crimen sine lege*.[47]

5. The Statute of Criminal Law

Criminal law constitutes one of the oldest subjects of human civilization and it has also had a direct effect on the development of international relations. Generally speaking, criminal law consists of two parts: one is the substantive part that discusses what actions or omissions constitute crimes or offences, and the other is the procedural part that deals with the machinery for implementing and enforcing criminal law when it is violated by individuals. The system of international criminal law also consists of two similar parts, with the caveat that it has a wider scope than the application of different criminal laws, which are combined for a common end. In international procedural law, a court may hear cases and deliver verdicts regarding the commission of criminal conduct.[48]

By comparison with the system of international criminal law, the burden of proof in international criminal procedure rests on the prosecution. This means that the defendant is innocent until the prosecution proves the contrary. This means that the prosecution must adduce corroborative evidence for each case. Thus, one of the principles of justice in international criminal law is the presumption of innocence. However, this may function in different ways in different countries depending on their legislative attitudes. Article 6 of the European

[47] It was obvious that many of the provisions of the Tribunal were not compatible with the principle of *nullum crimen sine lege*. In fact, it was argued by many international lawyers that the provisions of the Tribunal violated the juridical character of the principle. It was strongly believed that the question was not whether the German military authorities had violated international criminal law or had committed crimes against Jewish nationals of the states of Europe. Obviously, most of the acts committed by Germany or other nations against these Jewish nationals could be brought to justice and be recognised as grave violations of international criminal law by many European States if they had been committed under the contemporary system of international criminal law. But the serious problem was that the crimes recognised by the Tribunal in Nuremberg were not yet drafted under the system of international criminal law. Thus, the question was not the legality or the illegality of the acts of the German military authorities but the very significant character of the principle of *nullum crimen sine lege*.

[48] The difference between national criminal law and civil law is that the former protects social legal order and the latter applies to disputes between two or several parties. In other words, a civil law may deal with actions that are not of importance for public apprehension.

Convention on Human Rights, which is accepted by the great majority of members of the Council of Europe, clearly defends the rights of the accused.[49]

In the system of international criminal justice, as we will see later, the defendant has the right to counsel and to not receive the death penalty.[50] These rights have been consolidated since the creation of the Nuremberg Tribunal and developed in the statutes of other international criminal courts. A defendant who cannot afford to have his/her own lawyer must, as a general rule, be given a court-appointed lawyer at public expense.[51]A defendant also has the right to be defended in person and to receive judicial assistance during the trial.[52] Basically, in order to find the defendant guilty of the crime charged, a criminal trial must prove his/her criminality beyond reasonable doubt. An international criminal court may find the accused not guilty if there is insufficient evidence for the proof of criminality. In fact, international criminal law simultaneously protects individuals from unlawful charges.International criminal law has therefore

---

[49] It states that: "1.In the determination of his civil rights and obligations or of any criminal charge against him, everyone is entitled to a fair and public hearing within a reasonable time by an independent and impartial tribunal established by law. Judgement shall be pronounced publicly by the press and the public may be excluded from all or part of the trial in the interest of morals, public order or national security in a democratic society, where the interests of juveniles or the protection of the private life of the parties so require, or the extent strictly necessary in the opinion of the court in special circumstances where publicity would prejudice the interests of justice. 2. Everyone charged with a criminal offence shall be presumed innocent until proved guilty according to law. 3. Everyone charged with a criminal offence has the following minimum rights: (a) to be informed promptly, in a language which he understands and in detail, of the nature and cause of the accusation against him; (b) to have adequate time and the facilities for the preparation of his defence; (c) to defend himself in person or through legal assistance of his own choosing or, if he has not sufficient means to pay for legal assistance, to be given it free when the interests of justice so require; (d) to examine or have examined witnesses against him and to obtain the attendance and examination of witnesses on his behalf under the same conditions as witnesses against him; (e) to have the free assistance of an interpreter if he cannot understand or speak the language used in court."

[50] William A. Schabas *War Crimes, Crimes Against Humanity and the Death Penalty,* 60:3 Albany Law Review (1997), pp. 733-770; see also William A. Schabas, The Abolition of the Death Penalty in International Law (2002 and 2003).

[51] See Stuart Beresford & Hafida Lahiouel, The Right to be Defended in Person or Through Legal Assistance and the International Criminal Court, 13 Leiden Journal of International Law 949 (2000).

[52] Ibid.

different functions including prosecution, jurisdiction, punishment, prohibition, prevention, deterrence, rehabilitation, as well as protecting individuals from any criminal intrigue and accusation. With the implementation of international criminal law, the aim is to achieve justice through international criminal tribunals or courts. That is why the establishment of the Court has been seen a necessary condition in the development of the new international legal order.[53]

[53] M. Cherif Bassiouni& Christopher L. Blakesley, *The Need for an International Criminal Court in the New International World Order*, 25 Vanderbilt Journal of Transnational Law 151-182 (1992).

CHAPTER TWO

THE CREATION OF INTERNATIONAL CRIMINAL TRIBUNALS AND THE COURTS

1. Overview of the Nuremberg Tribunal

The economic recession and depression of the 1920s and 30s, combined with many other political and juridical factors, led to the outbreak of the Second World War. These factors also ultimately led to the creation of the Nuremburg Tribunal. Millions of innocent people, mostly European Jews, were murdered during the war, but one should not overlook the millions of people in other parts of the world, for example in the USSR, murdered not only by Hitler's genocide machine, but also by Stalin's communist regime – Stalin having been one of those who signed and ratified international conventions for the establishment of justice, equality and humanity by peace-loving states.[1] Yet these figures cannot be considered comprehensive without taking into account the Japanese murdered in the dropping of the atomic bombs on Hiroshima and Nagasaki.[2] In addition, one should emphasise that millions of civilians in China, North Korea, South Korea, the Philippines and other East Asian countries were murdered or brutally mistreated by the Japanese themselves, both before and during the Second World War. Also, thousands of women and girls were systematically raped and abused by Japanese troops, while prisoners of war were tortured and murdered in order to destroy proof. A clear example of this is the Nanjing Massacre of 1937, carried out by the Japanese armed forces. All of these events attest to the commission of war crimes by the Japanese armed forces.[3]

---

[1] See Donald Bloxham, Genocide on Trial: War Crimes Trials and the Formation of Holocaust History and Memory (2001).

[2] See The Atomic Bombs: Voices From Hiroshima and Nagasaki (Japan in the Modern World), (Kyoko Selden, Mark Selden and Robert Jay Lifton, eds., 1997); Richard Rhodes, the Making of the Atomic Bomb (1995).

[3] "It may be pointless to try to establish which World War Two Axis aggressor, Germany or Japan, was the more brutal to the peoples it victimised. The Germans killed six million Jews and 20 million Russians; the Japanese slaughtered as many

The figures above demonstrate that millions of people became the victims of World War II because of international political relations.[4] Despite this, the international community was unable to reach a decision in order to create an international criminal court.[5]

1.1. Preparations

The extreme nature of the inhuman and immoral actions committed and the slaughter of the civilian populations of different countries on the basis of race, culture, religion, language and economy during World War II, caused the Allied Powers to decide to bring the perpetrators of the war before an international criminal tribunal for prosecution and punishment. The leading political powers considered it necessary to prepare certain rules and provisions, which could be implemented in the procedures of an international criminal tribunal. For this reason, alongside their discussions concerning the strategies of war during their different meetings in Moscow, London, New York and Tehran, the Allied Powers examined different views concerning the establishment of the tribunal. It would have the power to bring the perpetrators of different crimes to public trial where their actions could be deemed to be violations of the provisions of international law.

---

as 30 million Filipinos, Malays, Vietnamese, Cambodians, Indonesians and Burmese, at least 23 million of them ethnic Chinese. Both nations looted the countries they conquered on a monumental scale, though Japan plundered more, over a longer period, than the Nazis. Both conquerors enslaved millions and exploited them as forced labourers – and, in the case of the Japanese, as prostitutes for front-line troops. If you were a Nazi prisoner of war from Britain, America, Australia, New Zealand or Canada (but not Russia) you faced a 4 per cent chance of not surviving the war; the death rate for Allied POWs held by the Japanese was nearly 30 per cent." Chalmers Johnson, Looting of Asia (2003).

[4] There is not yet a reliable statistic concerning the number of persons who were killed in different countries as a consequence of the Second World War.

[5] See, H.L. Bellot Hugh, *Draft Statute for the Permanent International Criminal Court,* in International Law Association, Report of the Thirty-Third Conference Held at the Riddarhuset and at the Riksdaghuset, Stockholm 8th to 13th September 1924, 75 (1925); H.L. Bellot Hugh, *A Permanent International Criminal Court*, The International Law Association, Report of the Thirty-First Conference Held at the Palace of Justice, Buenos Aires, 24th August-30th August, 1922 49 (1923).

1.2. Moscow Declaration

The Moscow Declaration, which was signed before the end of World War II in 1943, is one of the most significant instruments of international criminal law.[6] It is called the Declaration of the Four Nations on General Security and consists of four separate parts.[7] The Declaration aimed at the consolidation of several principles, which were fundamentally important for the future of international relations.[8] One of these principles affirmed the importance of the prosecution and punishment of the perpetrators of World War II.[9]

The relevant part of the Declaration states that "At the time of granting any armistice to any government which may be set up in Germany, those German officers and men and members of the Nazi party who have been responsible for or have taken a consenting part in the above atrocities, massacres and executions will be sent back to the countries in which their abominable deeds were done in order that they may be judged and punished according to the laws of these liberated countries and of free governments which will be erected therein." This term of the Declaration was supplemented by others focusing on prosecution and punishment, which were put into practice with the creation of the Nuremberg Tribunal. On this point the Declaration states that "The above declaration is without

---

[6] Parties to the Declaration were the governments of the United States of America, the United Kingdom, the Soviet Union and China.

[7] "The Moscow Declaration was significant for several reasons. It recognised, among other things, China's role in both waging the war and making the desired peace. By the Declaration, the four Governments publicly committed themselves to continue the fight against Germany, Italy and Japan until the Axis Powers "laid down their arms on the basis of unconditional surrender". *Towards a "general international organization." - UN commemorates 50th anniversary of the Declaration of the Four Nations on General Security, October 30, 1943, Moscow, Soviet Union,* findarticles.com/p/articles/mi_m1309/is.../ai_14879138/.

[8] "The Declaration was not seen by the Allies as the ruling out an executive decision to punish them. Churchill's original view was that extrajudicial firing squads were the best option, and it was only because of an unlikely alliance between the United States and the USSR that he was persuaded otherwise... The ambiguity did not prevent the Moscow Declaration providing the political backdrop to the creation of the Nuremberg IMT, and it was cited in the latter's founding instrument." Accordingly, the policy of the declaration was rather mixed. In the same opinion "Minor offenders were to be sent back for trail in the *locus delicti*, whereas major offenders, or those whose offences were not geographically limited, were to be dealt with by joint action." Cryer Robert, Prosecuting International Crimes: Selectivity and the International Regime (2005), p.37.

[9] See *infera.*

prejudice to the case of German criminals whose offenses have no particular geographical localization and who will be punished by the joint decision of the government of the Allies." The final development of the provisions of the Declaration may be seen through an examination of the London Agreement and the establishment of the international criminal tribunal.[10]

1.3. The London Agreement

In response to the grave violations of the law of war, the Allied Governments issued a number of declarations concerning the prosecution and punishment of the war criminals of World War II. It was decided in 1942 that a United Nations War Crimes Commission should be created in order to investigate questions concerning war crimes. The Commission was created in 1943 and began accumulating and listing the acts which should be recognised as war crimes. Finally, the London Agreement was signed on 8 August 1945 by the Allied Governments and came into force on the same day. The content of this agreement relates to the creation of the Charter of the Nuremberg Tribunal and its duties and tasks were to bring accused persons under the Tribunal's jurisdiction for prosecution and punishment. The agreement consists of an introduction and 30 articles which had an important role in the consolidation of the Tribunal.[11]

[10] In particular the Declaration has stated some of the important principles of human rights. It reads that "In furtherance of this policy in the future the Foreign Secretaries of the three governments are agreed that the following measures are important and should be put into effect: 1. It is essential that the Italian Government should be made more democratic by inclusion of representatives of those sections of the Italian people who have always opposed Fascism. 2. Freedom of speech, of religious worship, of political belief, of press and of public meeting, shall be restored in full measure to the Italian people, who shall be entitled to form anti-Fascist political groups. 3. All institutions and organizations created by the Fascist regime shall be suppressed. 4. All Fascist or pro-Fascist elements shall be removed from the administration and from institutions and organizations of a public character. 5. All political prisoners of the Fascist regime shall be released and accorded full amnesty. 6. Democratic organs of local government shall be created. 7. Fascist chiefs and army generals known or suspected to be war criminals shall be arrested and handed over to justice."

[11] See also chapter three.

2. Overview of the Tokyo Tribunal

The Allied Powers during World War II divided the work of prosecuting and punishing war criminals between two different courts based on geo-political considerations: the Nuremberg Tribunal and the International Military Tribunal for the Far East.[12] The former was run by the Allied powers whilst the government of the United States established the second Tribunal.[13] The latter is also known as the Tokyo War Crimes Tribunal.[14] It operated from May 1946 to November 1948.[15]

The Charter of the International Military Tribunal for the Far East was declared in a Special Proclamation by General Douglas MacArthur of the United States on 19 January 19, 1946. MacArthur, as Supreme Commander for the Allied Powers in Japan, had the responsibility for carrying into effect the general surrender of the Japanese armed forces due to the authority given to him by the governments of the United States, Great Britain and the Soviet Union at the Moscow Conference of December 1945. MacArthur had the authority to select members of the tribunal from names given to him by the US government.[16] These can be seen from the articles of the constitution of the Tribunal:

---

[12] For an historical analysis see Robert Cryer and Neil Boister (eds.), Documents on the Tokyo International Military Tribunal: Charter, Indictment and Judgments (2008), at 1-3 and 4 12.

[13] *Id.*, at 28-30.

[14] *Id.*, at 31.

[15] For the work of the Tokyo Tribunal and its judgment see *id.*, at 74-88.

[16] For further discussions see Appleman, John Alan, Military Tribunals and International Crimes (1954); Ushimura, Kei Beyond the "Judgment of Civilization": The Intellectual Legacy of the Japanese War Crimes Trials, 1946–1949, trans. Steven J. Ericson. Tokyo: LTCB International Library Trust/ International House of Japan (2003); Blewett, George F., "Victor's Injustice: The Tokyo War Crimes Trial." American Perspective 4(3) (1950), pp. 282–292; United Nations War Crimes Commission, Law Reports of Trials of War Criminals, 15 volumes (1947–1949); Hankey, Lord, Politics, Trials, and Errors, (1950); Pritchard, R. John, "International Military Tribunal for the Far East and the Allied National War Crimes Trials in Asia in International Criminal Law (vol.3,1998); Keenan, Joseph B., and Brendan F. Brown, Crimes against International Law (1950); Piccigallo, Philip R., The Japanese on Trial: Allied War Crimes Operations in the East, 1945–195 (1979); Minear, Richard H., Victors' Justice: The Tokyo War Crimes Trial. Ann Arbor: Center for Japanese Studies (2001); Brand George (ed.), United Nations War Crimes Commission History of the United Nations War Crimes Commission and the Development of the Laws of War (1948) Whitney, Courtney The Case of General Yamashita: A Memorandum. Tokyo: Supreme Commander for the Allied Power (1950).

> Article 1: Tribunal Established. The International Military Tribunal for the Far East is hereby established for the just and prompt trial and punishment of the major war criminals in the Far East. The permanent seat of the Tribunal is in Tokyo.
>
> Article 2: *Members*. The Tribunal shall consist of not less than six members nor more than eleven members, appointed by the Supreme Commander for the Allied Powers from the names submitted by the Signatories to the Instrument of Surrender, India, and the Commonwealth of the Philippines.

The Tokyo Tribunal has been criticised because of the monopolization of its power by the United States government. It has been argued that its power, authority, procedures, judgements, and punishments were all the workings of "victor's justice" and were not based on international legal standards.[17]

3. Overview of the ICTY

Whilst the system of international criminal law has been extensively developed since the outbreak of World War II and has become one of the most important parts of international legislation, especially with the development of the international humanitarian law of armed conflicts, the system has in recent years been violated more often than ever before by states, groups and individuals. There is, however, almost no logical reason behind these violations and most of them have been carried out in order to dispute the territorial independence of states, to gain money, or to violate the integrity of individuals or groups. Some of the clearest examples of these inhuman actions were carried out during the war in the territory of the Former Yugoslavia, which caused the deaths of a large number of people and was characterised by grave violations of the laws governing armed conflicts.[18]

---

[17] However, for the support of the jurisdiction of the Tokyo Tribunal in its political and historical context see Boister, Neil and Cryer, Robert, The Tokyo International Military Tribunal - A Reappraisal (2008).

[18] The Kingdom of Yugoslavia was proclaimed in 1943 and became the Democratic Federal Yugoslavia. Later, it became the Federal People's Republic of Yugoslavia. Subsequently, it became the Socialist Federal Republic of Yugoslavia in 1963.The SFRY depended politically on the Soviet Socialist Republic. The atrocities during the recent wars caused the disintegration of the Yugoslav state by the beginning of 1990. The Yugoslav state was a combination of the present states

3.1. The Establishment of the ICTY

One of the most unlawful and immoral actions to take place during the war in the territory of the former Yugoslavia was the systematic rape of a large number of women including females of very young ages.[19] These violations were seen as so harmful and shameful that the United Nations, for the first time in the history of international criminal justice, was compelled to arrange high-level meetings with the intention of creating an international criminal court.[20] The aim was to bring the violators of international criminal law before a criminal jurisdiction.

Obviously, the establishment of such a court which could have jurisdiction over criminals including the heads of states was not easy.[21] The idea of an international criminal court having power over states was certainly seen as controversial.[22] The problem was not the drawing up of a draft proposal for the court but the disinclination of the most powerful states to establish a court which could be a model for the creation of other international courts and in the development of case law.[23] As usual, the system of international criminal justice was not only short of criminal jurisdiction, but also struggled with the accumulation of power-politics into one integral system. The United Nations' task was therefore very difficult. It had to deal with the question of international criminal justice while remaining neutral in its aims and this was in reality impossible since

---

of Bosnia and Herzegovina, Croatia, Republic of Macedonia, Montenegro, Serbia and Slovenia.

[19] Kelly Dawn, Askin, War Crimes against Women: Prosecution in International War Crimes (1997).

[20] N. Kandic, The ICTY Trials and Transitional Justice in Former Yugoslavia, 38 (3) Cornell International Law Journal (2005), pp. 789-792; J. Post and L. Panis, Tyranny on Trial: Personality and Courtroom Conduct of Defendants Slobodan Milosevic and Saddam Hussein, 38 (3) Cornell International Law Journal (2005), pp. 823-836; William A. Schabas, The UN International Criminal Tribunals: the Former Yugoslavia, Rwanda and Sierra Leone (2006).

[21] There were in fact many conflicts concerning the establishment of the tribunal. In addition, the creation of the tribunal was very strongly influenced by the fact that politically more powerful nations were behind its establishment. The tribunal also needed to have good financial support in order to be able to bring the perpetrators to trial. See Pierre Hazan, Justice in a time of War, the true story behind the International Criminal Tribunal for the Former Yugoslavia (James Thomas Snyder, translator, 2004).

[22] See *also* Gary Jonathan, Bass, Stay the Hand of Vengeance: The Politics of War Crimes Tribunals (2000), pp. 48-54.

[23] International Criminal Law Developments in the Case Law of the ICTY (Gideon Boas & William A. Schabas, eds., 2003).

most states involved in the creation of the tribunal were NATO member countries.[24]

Since the United Nations' permanent members, particularly the United States and its allies, had several purposes simultaneously, the problem was not only the creation of the international criminal tribunal for the former Yugoslavia, but also, the division of the former Yugoslavia into a number of states. The interests of the United States and its allies, such as Great Britain, France and Germany, had to be fulfilled in one way or another.

The work of the United Nations was finally completed with the adoption of Resolutions 808 and 827 in 1993. The resolutions aimed at the establishment of an international tribunal for the prosecution of persons responsible for the serious violations of international humanitarian law which had been committed in the territory of the Former Yugoslavia since 1991. In the pursuance of the above resolutions, many other resolutions were also accepted for the creation of the tribunal.

After a succession of meetings and gatherings concerning the establishment of the tribunal, the Security Council of the United Nations accepted the establishment of the International Tribunal for the Prosecution of Persons Responsible for Serious Violations of International Humanitarian Law Committed in the Territory of the Former Yugoslavia

---

[24] Some of the criticisms of the ICTY were submitted by Hans Köchler to the Security Council in 1999. These were *inter alia* "1. The "indictment" issued by the "Chief Prosecutor" of the so-called "International Criminal Tribunal for the Former Yugoslavia" is legally invalid because this "Tribunal" has no jurisdiction whatsoever in the present or any other case … 3. When adopting the above resolution, the Security Council acted *ultra vires*. According to the provisions of the U.N. Charter, the Council has no competence whatsoever in judicial matters. The provisions of Chapter VII determine the Council's competence in matters of international security but not in matters of criminal justice or other judicial matters. The sole authority in international judicial matters rests with the International Court of Justice. …4. The "determination," in the preamble of Security Council resolution 827, paragraph four, that the "widespread and flagrant violations of international humanitarian law" on the territory of the former Yugoslavia "constitute a threat to international peace and security" does not provide a sound legal basis for the Security Council acting as a surrogate judicial authority or establishing an international court with jurisdiction in this or any other case….5. It is regrettable that the institution of the Security Council, while being unable to stop the undeclared war waged by NATO countries against Yugoslavia in violation of international law, and while being prevented, because of the veto power of countries conducting the present war, from restoring international peace and security in Yugoslavia, is now being used to take a so-called "judicial" action against the legitimate Head of State and other high officials of the country under attack …" http://i-p-o.org/yu-tribunal-memo1999.htm, visited on 2009-06-30.

(ICTY). This was presented in its Resolution 827 on 25 May 1993. As the Tribunal was established on the basis of this resolution,[25] the ICTY is not established by treaty.[26]

3.2. Reasons for the Creation of the ICTY

There are many reasons why the ICTY had to be created for the prosecution and punishment of criminals. Some of the reasons for the development of the ICTY are the following:

- The numerous statements and reports of widespread and systematic violations of international humanitarian law and human rights taking place within the territory of the former Yugoslavia, and especially in Bosnia and Herzegovina;
- The wrongful imprisonment and the systematic violation of the dignity and rights of civilians in detention centres;
- The intentional attacks on hospitals and humanitarian transportation in order to prevent the delivery of food and medical supplies to the civilian population;
- The systematic attacks on Red Cross facilities;
- The mass forced deportation and expulsion of civilians;
- The deliberate attacks on non-combatants including those on the inhabitants of villages with the sole purpose of killing civilians and destroying their houses;
- The systematic practice of "ethnic cleansing" in the territories of the Former Yugoslavia, especially against the Muslim population;
- The systematic rape of women and girls of a very young age, especially in Bosnia Herzegovina;
- The deliberate and wanton destruction and devastation of property including villages, schools, historical monuments, bridges and so forth;
- The non-compliance of the military forces with the provisions of the Charter of the United Nations and international criminal law.

The above were some of the reasons for the creation of the ICTY. There were also other reasons such as the need for the implementation of the provisions of international criminal law and prevention of further genocide. The Tribunal's work also implies this. In fact, the establishment

---

[25] See *infera*.

[26] See also Farhad Malekian, The Monopolization of International Criminal Law in the United Nations (1995).

of the Tribunal and the intensive efforts of various states in the United Nations and Europe finally brought an end to the grave violations of human rights in the territories of the former Yugoslavia.[27]

4. Overview of the ICTR

The Rwanda genocide is essentially based on several centuries' ethnic antagonism between two regional groups namely the minority Tutsi and the majority Hutus. They made up about 15 and 80 percent of the population of Rwanda. Therefore, the serious and systematic violations of the system of international criminal law in Rwanda have been the subject of discussions within various international meetings.[28] As a result of these criminal actions, approximately over one million Tutsis and moderate Hutus were inhumanly murdered.[29] These systematic killings were carried out in 1959, 1963, 1966 and 1973 and from 1990.[30] Killings were committed each year and were intensified in 1994.[31] These barbarous

---

[27] For the development of the ICTY see International Criminal Law: Developments in the Case Law of the ICTY (Gideon Boas & William A. Schabas, eds., 2003); John Ackerman, Eugène O'Sullivan Practice and procedure of the International Criminal Tribunal for the Former Yugoslavia (2000); William Schabas, The UN international criminal tribunals: the former Yugoslavia, Rwanda and Sierra Leone (2006); Gabrielle Kirk McDonald, Olivia Swaak-Goldman, Substantive and Procedural Aspects of International Criminal Law: Commentary (2000); Yusuf Aksar, Implementing International Humanitarian Law: From the Ad Hoc Tribunals to a Permanent International Criminal Court (2000); Salvatore Zappalà, Human rights in international criminal proceedings (2003); Herwig Roggemann, Petar Šarčević,National security and international criminal justice (2002); Christoph Johannes, Maria Safferling, Towards an international criminal procedure (2001); Rachel R. Kerr, The International Criminal Tribunal for the Former Yugoslavia: an exercise in law, politics and diplomacy (2004); Richard May, David Tolbert, John Hocking, Ken Roberts; Bing Bing Jia, Daryl Mundis, Gabriel Oosthuizen, Essays on Icty Procedure and Evidence in Honour of Gabrielle Kirk McDonald (2000); L. Vierucci, *The First Steps of the International Criminal Tribunal for the Former Yugoslavia,* 6 European Journal of International Law 134 (1995).

[28] Peter Uvin, Difficult Choices in the New Post-Conflict Agenda: The International Community in Rwanda after the Genocide, 22: 2 Third World Quarterly (2001), pp. 177-189.

[29] See *also* Paul Webster, *France Denies Arming Hutus for Genocide*, Guardian Weekly, London, (18.1.1998), p. 3.

[30] See also *Id.*

[31] See Genocide in Rwanda (John A. Berry & Carol Pott Berry, eds., 1999); Roman Boed, *The International Criminal Tribunal for Rwanda, in* International Criminal Law, vol iii (M. cherif Bassiouni, ed. 2008) pp. 103-116; The path of a genocide:

actions were also carried out in the territories of neighbouring states from 1 January up to 31 December 1994. These were such as Burundi and Uganda. Much of the slaughter was carried out during a particularly violent three-month period. The situation was highly controversial and there was much criticism because of the fact that no international intervention was organised by the United Nations during these criminal actions.[32] The Security Council, which is politically and juridically responsible for the maintenance of international peace, security and justice, did not take any action either.[33]In other words, the politicians in Belgium,[34] France and the United States who were aware of the plans of crime of genocide and crimes against humanity in the region, deliberately or mistakenly failed to prevent their commission.

The Rwanda Crisis, from Uganda to Zaire (Howard Adelman, & Astri Suhrke, eds., 1999); Colette Braeckman, Rwanda: Histoire d'un genocide (1994); Colette Braeckman, Terreur africaine. Burundi, Rwanda, Zaïre: Les racines de la violence (1996); Christopher Browning, The path to genocide: Essays on launching the final solution (2002); *Genocide in Rwanda,* Africa Research & Information Centre, (Napoleon Abdulai, ed., 1994); African Rights, *Rwanda: Death, Despair and Defiance* (1995); Amnesty International, *United Nations International Criminal Tribunal for Rwanda: Trials and tribulations*, AI Index IOR 40/03/98, (1998); Amnesty International, *Rwanda: The troubled course of justice*, AI Index AFR 47/10/00, (2000); J. E. Ackerman & E. O'Sullivan, Practice and procedure of the International Criminal Tribunal for the Former Yugoslavia; with selected material from the International Criminal Tribunal for Rwanda (2000); Michael N. Barnett, Eyewitness to a Genocide: The United Nations and Rwanda(2002); Belgian Senate, *Parliamentary Commission of Inquiry concerning Rwanda / Commission d'enquête parlementaire concernant les événements du Rwanda*, Report/Rapport, Brussels/Bruxelles, 6.12.1997. Laurence Burgorgue, Larsen (ed.), *La repression internationale du genocide rwandais,* (2003); Jacques Castonguay, *Les Casques Bleus au Rwanda*,(1998); Jean Pierre Chrétien, *Le défi de l'ethnisme: Rwanda et Buruni, 1990 - 1996,* (1997);Jean Pierre Chrétien., *The Great Lakes of Africa: Two thousand years of history*, (2003).

[32] See *also* Makau Wa Mutua, *The Rwanda Tribunal: A critical Assessment*, Africa Legal Aid Quarterly, April-June (2001), pp. 6.

[33] For some problems of the ICTR see *Id.*

[34] The Belgium had the Rwanda mandate under the provisions of the League of Nations after World War I.

4.1. Motives for the Establishment of the ICTR

The Rwandan criminal justice system was incapable of bringing accused persons before its jurisdiction.[35] Many of those who had committed crimes against humanity and genocide and had violated the humanitarian law of armed conflicts could therefore flee to other countries without any restriction. The effect was that their impunity could not be brought to an end and many individuals escaped prosecution and punishment. In fact, the international response was fragile and inconsistent.[36]

Another serious problem was that the United Nations had not yet established a permanent international criminal court. The world was busy with the initiation and creation of the ICTY, but the world also had to give time to the serious violations of the system of international criminal law in Rwanda. In response to a request by the Rwandan government, the Security Council adopted Resolution 935 in which the Secretary General was requested to create a commission of experts in order to present a report on the violence in Rwanda. According to the report of the Commission, grave violations of the international humanitarian law of armed conflicts were committed. The report led to the setting up of a tribunal for Rwanda.

The situation for the drafting of a statute for the prosecution and punishment of the criminals and perpetrators of Rwanda was not as difficult as the situation in which the ICTY was created. This was because the International Criminal Tribunal for the Prosecution of Persons Responsible for Genocide and Other Serious Violations of International Humanitarian Law Committed in the Territory of Rwanda and Rwandan Citizens Responsible for Genocide and Other Such Violations Committed in the Territory of Neighbouring States (ICTR) takes into consideration and duplicates in many aspects the Statute of the ICTY.[37] Finally, the Security Council adopted Resolution 955 according to which the ICTR was established.[38] The text of the Statute of the tribunal was therefore

---

[35] See A, de Waal, *The Genocide in Rwanda and the International Response,* Current History94:591 (1995), pp. 156-161.

[36] See *id.*

[37] Final Report of the Commission of Experts established pursuant to Security Council Resolution 935 (1994), UNSC, UN Doc. S/1994/1405 (1994).

[38] Some of the reasons of the adoption of the resolution were the followings: "*Expressing once again* its grave concern at the reports indicating that genocide and other systematic, widespread and flagrant violations of international humanitarian law have been committed in Rwanda, *Determining* that this situation continues to constitute a threat to international peace and security, *Determined* to put an end to such crimes and to take effective measures to bring to justice the

annexed to this resolution. This means that the ICTR was not created by treaty but was established as an *ad hoc* tribunal by an authoritative resolution of the Council.

5. Overview of the Special Court for Sierra Leone

In March 1991 the West African state of Sierra Leone became embroiled in a civil war, which took hold after the invasion on the basis of intervention of forces led by Charles Taylor, the leader of the neighbouring state of Liberia. The killing, sexual abuse, forced labour, amputation and cannibalisation inflicted upon civilians and the destruction of their property was mainly carried out with the intention of taking possession of diamond resources in the territory of Sierra Leone. Both of these African countries are the creation of the colonial rule of western states.

The Special Court for Sierra Leone (SCSL) is one of the four courts set up under the authority of the United Nations in order to investigate the serious crimes committed in violation of international criminal law and Sierra Leonean law since 30 November 1996.[39] The Special Court is empowered to deal with the appropriate prosecution and punishment of those who have violated the basic principles of the international humanitarian law of armed conflicts during the Sierra Leone Civil War.[40] The Court is an independent juridical body located in Freetown, the capital of Sierra Leone. The Court is, in fact, the third *ad hoc* court created by the United Nations, following the creation of the international criminal

---

persons who are responsible for them, *Convinced* that in the particular circumstances of Rwanda, the prosecution of persons responsible for serious violations of international humanitarian law would enable this aim to be achieved and would contribute to the process of national reconciliation and to the restoration and maintenance of peace, *Believing* that the establishment of an international tribunal for the prosecution of persons responsible for genocide and the other above-mentioned violations of international humanitarian law will contribute to ensuring that such violations are halted and effectively redressed."

[39] The Court did not receive authority over crimes that had been committed since the start of the civil war in 1991.

[40] C. Sriram, Wrong-sizing International Justice? The Hybrid Tribunal in Sierra Leone, 29 (3) Fordham International Law Journal (2006), pp.472-506; Konstantinos D. Magliveras, The Special Court for Sierra Leone: A New Type of Regional Criminal Court for the International Community? 17 International Enforcement Law Rep. (Feb. 2001); David M. Crane, The Special Court for Sierra Leone, in International Criminal Law, Vol. III (M. Cherif Bassiouni, ed. 2008) pp. 195-218.

tribunals for the former Yugoslavia (ICTY) in 1993 and Rwanda (ICTR) in 1994.[41]

5.1. Background

The civil war in Sierra Leone was initiated by the Revolutionary United Front (RUF) under the control of Foday Sankoh.[42] He was also the founder of the RUF and one of the key instigators of the development of the civil war and the killing of almost 75, 000 people. Approximately two million people were displaced and took asylum in the territories of neighbouring countries. The Civil War began on 23 March 1991 and finished on January 18, 2002. Most shockingly, the recruitment of children as soldiers was one of the first strategies adopted at the beginning of the war.[43] The war ended after years of atrocities and brutality against civilians as well as the destruction of civilian services, for instance, 1270 schools were destroyed. During the civil war, the government of Sierra Leone did not have much capacity to fight against the rebels. This was due to the fact that the rebels were receiving help and weapons from neighbouring Liberia, whose president was intent on gaining control of the diamond resources.[44]

---

[41] According to some writers a hybrid court holds 'a good deal of promise and actually offers an approach that may address some of the concerns about purely international justice, on the one hand, and purely local justice, on the other.' L. Dickinson, *The Relationship between Hybrid Courts and International Courts: The Case of Kosovo*, New England Law Review 1059-1072 (2003), at 1060; Suzanne Katzenstein, *Hybrid Tribunals: Searching for Justice in East Timor*, Harvard Human Rights Journal245-278 (2003); L. Dickinson, *Transitional Justice in Afghanistan: The Promise of Mixed Tribunals*, Denver Journal of International Law and Policy 23-42 (2002).

[42] For some introduction to the history of Sierra Leone see www.historyworld.net/wrldhis/PlainText Histories.asp?historyid=ad45-45k; www.britannica.com/EBchecked/topic/543389/history-of-Sierra-Leone-45k-; www.infoplease.com/ce6/world/A0861084.html-40k.Visited on 10/11/2008.

[43] See Alison Smith, *Child Recruitment and the Special Court for Sierra Leone*, 2 Journal of International Criminal Justice 1141-1153 (2004).

[44] For further consideration on Sierra Leone's history of development and the struggles within the country see A. P. Kup, A Histoy of Sierra Leone 1400-1787 (1961); Johan L Hirsch, Sierra Leone: Diamonds and The Struggle For Democracy (2001); Banton Michael, West African City: A Study of Tribal Life in Freetown (1957). Bound to Cooperate, Conflict, Peace and People in Sierra Leone (Anatole Ayissi and Robin-Edward Pulton, eds), (2000).

5.2. Formulating a Peace Treaty

The mass killings of civilians and the destruction of civilian property and services were two strong motivations leading to the conclusion of the peace treaty in Sierra Leone. The rebel Revolutionary United Front (RUF) army committed such crimes, but it is also true that the pro-government Civil Defence Force under the supervision of Sam Hinga Norman was also responsible for committing similar crimes.[45] These events finally led to the intervention of the United Nations and its contribution to the formulation of the Lome Peace Accord between both conflicting parties in 1999.[46] These parties were the government of President Ahmed Tejan Kabbah and the RUF, under the leadership of Foday Sankoh. The Special Representative of the United Nations Secretary General also signed the Lome Peace Accord.

The Peace agreement granted amnesty to members of the RUF and also created a Truth Commission in order to record the violations of the international humanitarian law of armed conflict.[47] Despite this, the RUF

---

[45] For the Norman case see section 8. Recruitment of Children.

[46] Two of the most significant articles of the agreement concern cease-fire. They read, "The armed conflict between the Government of Sierra Leone and the RUF/SL is hereby ended with immediate effect. Accordingly, the two sides shall ensure that a total and permanent cessation of hostilities is observed forthwith." (Article 1) "1. A Cease-fire Monitoring Committee (hereinafter termed the CMC) to be chaired by the United Nations Observer Mission in Sierra Leone (hereinafter termed UNOMSIL) with representatives of the Government of Sierra Leone, RUF/SL, the Civil Defence Forces (hereinafter termed the CDF) and ECOMOG shall be established at provincial and district levels with immediate effect to monitor, verify and report all violations of the cease-fire. 2. A Joint Monitoring Commission (hereinafter termed the JMC) shall be established at the national level to be chaired by UNOMSIL with representatives of the Government of Sierra Leone, RUF/SL, CDF, and ECOMOG. The JMC shall receive, investigate and take appropriate action on reports of violations of the cease-fire from the CMC. The parties agree to the definition of cease-fire violations as contained in Annex 2 which constitutes an integral part of the present Agreement. 3. The parties shall seek the assistance of the International Community in providing funds and other logistics to enable the JMC to carry out its mandate." (Article 2).

[47] Article 6 of the Peace agreement reads that: "1. In order to bring lasting peace to Sierra Leone, the Government of Sierra Leone shall take appropriate legal steps to grant Corporal Foday Sankoh absolute and free pardon. 2. After the signing of the present Agreement, the Government of Sierra Leone shall also grant absolute and free pardon and reprieve to all combatants and collaborators in respect of anything done by them in pursuit of their objectives, up to the time of the signing of the present Agreement.. 3. To consolidate the peace and promote the cause of national

violated the provisions of the treaty and the killing of civilians and civilian refugees continued. However, government forces finally captured Foday Sankoh and he was taken into custody in the capital of Freetown in order to be prosecuted and punished for serious violations of the international humanitarian law of armed conflict.[48]

5.3. The Establishment of the Special Court

The Special Court is one of the most important organs of the United Nations in working to bring the perpetrators of killings, amputations, mass rape, sexual violence and other atrocities under an official jurisdiction.[49] In order to put an end to continuous violations and also to begin the reconciliation process, the government of Sierra Leone requested that the United Nations establish an international criminal court for the prosecution and punishment of criminals. Thus, pursuant to Resolution 1315 (2000) of the Security Council, which mandated the creation of the statute of the court, the Secretary General was requested to take responsibility for this important task in order to create an independent special court consistent with the provisions of the resolution.

The resolution specifically recommended that three important principles be taken into account in the formulation of a statute for a special

---

reconciliation, the Government of Sierra Leone shall ensure that no official or judicial action is taken against any member of the RUF/SL, ex-AFRC, ex-SLA or CDF in respect of anything done by them in pursuit of their objectives as members of those organisations, since March 1991, up to the time of the signing of the present Agreement. In addition, legislative and other measures necessary to guarantee immunity to former combatants, exiles and other persons, currently outside the country for reasons related to the armed conflict shall be adopted ensuring the full exercise of their civil and political rights, with a view to their reintegration within a framework of full legality."

[48] Foday Sankoh died of a heart attack before his case was heard in the hybrid court.

[49] The international crime of rape has also been committed during armed conflict in other parts of the world. These include Aceh, Afghanistan, Algeria, Angola, Azerbaijan, Bosnia, Bougainville, Chad, Chechnya, Croatia, Cyprus, East Timor, Georgia, Guatemala, Haiti, India, Indonesia, Iran, Jaya, Kashmir, Kosovo, Liberia, Mozambique, Myanmar (Burma), Namibia, Palestine territories, Persian Gulf Conflict (1990-91), Peru, Philippines, Rwanda, Sierra Leone, Somalia, during the apartheid in South Africa, Sudan, Tibet, Uganda, and West Papua. See Gardam Judith G. and Michelle J. Jarvis, Women, Armed Conflict and International Law (2001), at 27.

court.[50] Firstly, it sets out the importance of the recognition of various violations and categories of crimes committed during the civil war. It says that "the subject matter jurisdiction of the special court should include notably crimes against humanity, war crimes and other serious violations of international humanitarian law, as well as crimes under relevant Sierra Leonean law committed within the territory of Sierra Leone;"[51] Secondly, it puts a heavy weight on the concept of criminal responsibility. This responsibility is to be recognised without regard to the concept of official rank. For this reason, it recommends that "the special court should have personal jurisdiction over persons who bear the greatest responsibility for the commission of the crimes referred to in paragraph 2, including those leaders who, in committing such crimes, have threatened the establishment of and implementation of the peace process in Sierra Leone."[52] The third principle of the resolution is that the accused should be subject to a fair and just trial conducted according to international standards of criminal justice. It therefore underlines "the importance of ensuring the impartiality, independence and credibility of the process, in particular with regard to the status of the judges and the prosecutors."[53] An examination of the Statute of the Special Court demonstrates that all of these principles have been formulated into its structure.[54]

Thus, after many international political discussions, especially between the permanent members of the Security Council, such as the United States and the United Kingdom, the Special Court for Sierra Leone was created in 2002 on the basis of a joint Agreement on the Establishment of a Special Court for Sierra Leone[55] between the United Nations and the Government of Sierra Leone.[56] It must be underlined that the grave

[50] Resolution 1315 (2000) has given a number of duties to the Secretary General of the United Nations so that the Security Council be aware of the situation. For example, the Secretary General was responsible for writing a report concerning the establishment of the court based on relations and negotiations with the government of Sierra Leone. For this purpose, he was asked to send a team of experts to Sierra Leone. He was also requested to address in his report *inter alia* the questions of the temporal jurisdiction of the special court and the creation of an appeals chamber.

[51] Resolution 1315 (2000), para.2.

[52] *Id.*, para.3.

[53] *Id.*, para.4.

[54] See also www.un.org/Depts/dpko/missions/unamsil/spcourt.htm - 8k -, visited on 10/11/2008.

[55] Report of the Secretary-General on the Establishment of a Special Court for Sierra Leone, 4 October 2000, U.N. Doc. S/2000/915.

[56] For the consent of the Government of Sierra Leone see Betsy Pisik, *Annan Proposes a Joint Tribunal,* The Washington Times, October 6, 2000, at A13.

violations of the system of international criminal law and the serious infringement of the principles of human rights law that took place during the civil war are two of the most important reasons for the creation of the SCSL.[57] Since the opening of the trials on June 3, 2004, the Special Court has been the subject of various discussions in the international legal and political community. On the whole, the jurisdiction of the Special Court has been appreciated for its achievements in re-establishing justice and providing some satisfaction for the victims. However, there have also been some criticisms of the framework of the Court, including its jurisdiction and enforcement powers. It has been argued that certain provisions of its Statute may undermine the ability of the Court to deliver appropriate justice, such as its political and legal control by the Security Council.[58]

5.4. Differences between the SCSL and the Tribunals

Whilst one cannot deny the fact that the ICTY and the ICTR have followed similar policies in their application of international criminal law and justice, they are to some extent different from the SCSL.[59] There are therefore still further differences between the establishment of the Nuremberg Tribunal, the ICTY, the ICTR and SCSL.[60] The following are some of the differences which may be observed between the three above-mentioned juridical bodies:

- Formally, the ICTY and the Special Court deal with conflicts which are of an international character while the ICTR is concerned with conflicts which are of a national character. However, this difference is superficial given that the conflict in Rwanda was also a threat to peace and stability in the wider region.[61]

---

[57] For the whole agreement see Report of the Secretary-General on the Establishment of a Special Court for Sierra Leone, 4 October 2000, U.N. Doc. S/2000/915.

[58] See infera.

[59] But see also the differences between the ICTY and the ICC in Gideon Boas, *Comparing the ICTY and the ICC: Some Procedural and Substantive Issues*, 47 Netherlands International Law Review 267-292 (2000).

[60] For some difference between ICTY and ICTR consult Mark R. von Sternberg, *A Comparison of the Yugoslav and Rwandan War Crimes Tribunals: Universal Jurisdiction and the Elementary Dictates of Humanity*, 22 Brooklyn Journal of International Law, (1966), p.111.

[61] In the Joseph Kanyabashi case, the Trial Chamber for the ICTR did not accept the argument that the Security Council had no legal power to establish the Tribunal. It therefore declares that "While it is true that the conflict in Rwanda was

- The Special Court is an organ under the supervision of the Secretary General of the United Nations while the ICTY and ICTR are the result of the relevant Security Council resolutions.[62]
- While the Sierra Leonean government requested the creation of the Special Court, the ICTY and ICTR were largely established at the request of the international community as a whole. This means that the last two tribunals opened the door to the former.

---

internal in the sense that it emerged from inherent tensions between the two major groups forming the population within the territory of Rwanda and otherwise did not involve the direct participation of armed forces belonging to any other State, the Trial Chamber cannot accept the Defence Counsel's notion that the conflict did not pose any threat to international peace and security. The question of, whether or not the conflict posed a threat to international peace and security is a matter to be decided exclusively by the Security Council. The Trial Chamber nevertheless takes judicial notice of the fact that the conflict in Rwanda created a massive wave of refugees, many of whom were armed, into the neighbouring countries which by itself entailed a considerable risk of serious destabilization of the local areas in the host countries where the refugees had settled. The demographical composition of the population in certain neighbouring regions outside the territory of Rwanda, furthermore, showed features which suggest that the conflict in Rwanda might eventually spread to some or all of these neighbouring regions. …The Trial Chamber concludes that there is no merit in the Defence Counsel's argument that the conflict in Rwanda did not pose any threat to international peace and security and holds that this was a matter to be decided exclusively by the Security Council." Furthermore, "the establishment of the ICTR was called for by the Government of Rwanda itself, which maintained that an international criminal tribunal could assist in prosecuting those responsible for acts of genocide and crimes against humanity and in this way promote the restoration of peace and reconciliation in Rwanda." Joseph Kanyabashi, Decision on the Defence Motion on Jurisdiction, (*ICTR-96-15-T,* 18), June 1997.

[62] While, there are differences between the ICTY, the ICTR and the Special Court, the Court is of the view that it is of the same quality to other courts. "Although the Special Court was established by treaty, unlike the ICTY and ICTR which were each established by resolutions of the Security Council in the exercise of powers by virtue of Chapter VII of the UN of Charter, it was certain that the power of the Security Council to enter into an agreement for the establishment of the court was derived from the Charter of the United Nations both in regard to the general purposes of the United Nations as expressed in Article 1 of the Charter and the specific powers of the Security Council in articles 39 and 41. These powers are wide enough to empower the Security Council to initiate, as it did by Resolution 1351, the establishment of the Special Court by Agreement with Sierra Leone." *Taylor* (SCSL-03-01-I), Decision on Immunity from Jurisdiction, 21 May 2004, para.37.

- The Special Court was established by an agreement between the government of Sierra Leone and the United Nations while the ICTY and ICTR are not based on agreements between the United Nations and the relevant states or governments but were initiated on the initiative of the international legal and political community as a whole. The latter were established as a result of the provisions of Chapter VII of the United Nations which are based on the resolutions of the Security Council.[63]

---

[63] However, there have been objections to the legal validity of the ICTY. These objections claim that the establishment of the ICTY was illegal, in that the United Nations Organization has not received, under its Charter, any authority to establish such a body. Accordingly, international criminal courts, *ad hoc* or permanent, have to be established by the provisions of a treaty. These objections came from British and Dutch criminal lawyers. The objections were however rejected by the Trial Chamber on 10 August 1995. The Court provides that "There are clearly enough matters of jurisdiction which are open to determination by the International Tribunal, questions of time, place and nature of an offence charged. These are properly described as jurisdictional, whereas the validity of the creation of the International Tribunal is not truly a matter of jurisdiction but rather the lawfulness of its creation [...]" (Decision at Trial, at para.4.) It goes further and states that "[I]t is one thing for the Security Council to have taken every care to ensure that a structure appropriate to the conduct of fair trials has been created; it is an entirely different thing in any way to infer from that careful structuring that it was intended that the International Tribunal be empowered to question the legality of the law which established it. The competence of the International Tribunal is precise and narrowly defined; as described in Article 1 of its Statute, it is to prosecute persons responsible for serious violations of international humanitarian law, subject to spatial and temporal limits, and to do so in accordance with the Statute. That is the full extent of the competence of the International Tribunal." (Decision at Trial, at para.8.) Decision on the Defence Motion for Interlocutory Appeal on Jurisdiction. According to the Chamber, in a similar case, in its advisory opinion on the *Effect of Awards of the United Nations Administrative Tribunal,* the International Court of Justice clearly points out that "[T]he view has been put forward that the Administrative Tribunal is a subsidiary, subordinate, or secondary organ; and that, accordingly, the Tribunal's judgments cannot bind the General Assembly which established it. [...] The question cannot be determined on the basis of the description of the relationship between the General Assembly and the Tribunal, that is, by considering whether the Tribunal is to be regarded as a subsidiary, a subordinate, or a secondary organ, or on the basis of the fact that it was established by the General Assembly. It depends on the intention of the General Assembly in establishing the Tribunal and on the nature of the functions conferred upon it by its Statute. An examination of the language of the Statute of the Administrative Tribunal has shown that the General Assembly intended to establish a judicial body." (Effect of Awards of Compensation Made by the United Nations

- The Special Court may only prosecute crimes that have been committed since 30 November 1996. This means that its jurisdiction is restricted to a particular period of a conflict which actually lasted from 1991 to 2002. The ICTY and ICTR have jurisdiction over the whole period in which atrocities took place, namely, since 1991 for the ICTY and during 1994 for the ICTR.
- The Special Court has primacy over domestic prosecutions in Sierra Leone. This means that the Special Court may issue orders which are binding for the government of Sierra Leone. Consequently, the Special Court has concurrent jurisdiction. The national courts have the right to hear a case but must hand it over to the Special Court if this is requested.[64]
- When seeking to bring an accused under its own jurisdiction, the Special Court does not have primacy of jurisdiction over national courts of a third state to require the surrender of the accused. This is not the case for the ICTY and ICTR, which have primacy of jurisdiction over the domestic courts of other states for the prosecution and punishment of criminals. Thus, if a suspected person is under the territorial jurisdiction of a third state, the Sierra Leonean government has to make a request for his/her return or extradition.
- The jurisdiction of the Special Court is exclusively over crimes that have occurred in the territory of Sierra Leone. The jurisdiction of the ICTY is over several states constituting the former Yugoslavia.
- There are some very slight differences between the sources of the ICTY, the ICTR and the sources of the Special Court. This is because the latter also partly relies on the internal criminal code of Sierra Leone. Nevertheless, all of these courts are heavily based on provisions of treaty law[65] and also follow the norms of customary

---

Administrative Tribunal, 1954 I.C.J. Reports 47, at 60-1 (Advisory Opinion of 13 July) (hereinafter *Effect of Awards*)).

[64] See the following paragraph.

[65] For instance, the Appeal Chamber in the Tadic case explicates that "Before both the Trial Chamber and the Appeals Chamber, Defence and Prosecution have argued the application of certain agreements entered into by the conflicting parties. It is therefore fitting for this Chamber to pronounce on this. It should be emphasised again that the only reason behind the stated purpose of the drafters that the International Tribunal should apply customary international law was to avoid violating the principle of *nullum crimen sine lege* in the event that a party to the conflict did not adhere to a specific treaty (Report of the Secretary-General, at para.34.) It follows that the International Tribunal is authorised to apply, in addition to customary international law, any treaty which: (i) was unquestionably

international law and the international humanitarian law of armed conflicts.[66] They are also bound by general principles of international law[67] and certain judiciary decisions. However,

---

binding on the parties at the time of the alleged offence; and (ii) was not in conflict with or derogating from peremptory norms of international law, as are most customary rules of international humanitarian law. This analysis of the jurisdiction of the International Tribunal is borne out by the statements made in the Security Council at the time the Statute was adopted. As already mentioned above (paras.75 and 88), representatives of the United States, the United Kingdom and France all agreed that Article 3 of the Statute did not exclude application of international agreements binding on the parties." Tadic, (IT-94-1-AR72), Decision on the Defence Motion for Interlocutory Appeal on Jurisdiction, 2 October 1995, para.143.

[66] For instance, the ICTY explains this fact. It says that "The Appeals Chamber deems it fitting to specify the conditions to be fulfilled for Article 3 to become applicable. The following requirements must be met for an offence to be subject to prosecution before the International Tribunal under Article 3: (i) the violation must constitute an infringement of a rule of international humanitarian law; (ii) the rule must be customary in nature or, if it belongs to treaty law, the required conditions must be met (see below, para.143); (iii) the violation must be "serious", that is to say, it must constitute a breach of a rule protecting important values, and the breach must involve grave consequences for the victim. Thus, for instance, the fact of a combatant simply appropriating a loaf of bread in an occupied village would not amount to a "serious violation of international humanitarian law" although it may be regarded as falling foul of the basic principle laid down in Article 46, paragraph 1, of the Hague Regulations (and the corresponding rule of customary international law) whereby "private property must be respected" by any army occupying an enemy territory; (iv) the violation of the rule must entail, under customary or conventional law, the individual criminal responsibility of the person breaching the rule. It follows that it does not matter whether the "serious violation" has occurred within the context of an international or an internal armed conflict, as long as the requirements set out above are met." *id*., para.94.

[67] *Kupreski*, (IT-95-16-T), Judgment, 14 January 2000, para.677. Two of the judges of the Appeals Chamber in *Erdemovic* case have clearly pointed out the value of the general principle of law. According to them "although general principles of law are to be derived from existing legal systems, in particular, national systems of law, it is generally accepted that the distillation of a "general principle of law recognised by civilised nations" does not require the comprehensive survey of all legal systems of the world as this would involve a practical impossibility and has never been the practice of the International Court of Justice or other international tribunals which have had recourse to Article 38(1)(c) of the ICJ Statute. Second, it is the view of eminent jurists, including Baron Descamps, the President of the Advisory Committee of Jurists on Article 38(1)(c), that one purpose of this article is to avoid a situation of *non-liquet*, that is, where an international tribunal is stranded by an absence of applicable legal rules. Third, a "general principle" must

general principles of law and judiciary decisions are considered the subsidiary sources of the tribunals and the court and as such are accorded a different value.[68]

---

not be confused with concrete manifestations of that principle in specific rules. As stated by the Italian-Venezuelan Mixed Claims Commission in the *Gentini* case: A rule … is essentially practical and, moreover, binding; there are rules of art as there are rules of government, while a principle expresses a general truth, which guides our action, serves as a theoretical basis for the various acts of our life, and the application of which to reality produces a given consequence. In light of these considerations, our approach will necessarily not involve a direct comparison of the specific rules of each of the world's legal systems, but will instead involve a survey of those jurisdictions whose jurisprudence is, as a practical matter, accessible to us in an effort to discern a general trend, policy or principle underlying the concrete rules of that jurisdiction which comports with the object and purpose of the establishment of the International Tribunal." *Erdemovic*, (IT-96-22-A), Joint Separate Opinion of Judge McDonald and the Vohrah, 7 October 1997, para.57.

[68] The ICTY has stated this fact. According to it "Being international in nature and applying international law *principaliter*, the Tribunal cannot but rely upon the well-established sources of international law and, within this framework, upon judicial decisions. What value should be given to such decisions? The Trial Chamber holds the view that they should only be used as a 'subsidiary means for the determination of rules of law' (to use the expression in Article 38(1)(d) of the Statute of the International Court of Justice, which must be regarded as declaratory of customary international law). Hence, generally speaking, and subject to the binding force of decisions of the Tribunal's Appeals Chamber upon the Trial Chambers, the International Tribunal cannot uphold the doctrine of binding precedent (*stare decisis*) adhered to in common law countries. Indeed, this doctrine among other things presupposes to a certain degree a hierarchical judicial system. Such a hierarchical system is lacking in the international community. Clearly, judicial precedent is not a distinct source of law in international criminal adjudication. The Tribunal is not bound by precedents established by other international criminal courts such as the Nuremberg or Tokyo Tribunals, let alone by cases brought before national courts adjudicating international crimes. Similarly, the Tribunal cannot rely on a set of cases, let alone on a single precedent, as sufficient to establish a principle of law: the authority of precedents (*auctoritas rerum similiter judicatarum*) can only consist in evincing the possible existence of an international rule. More specifically, precedents may constitute evidence of a customary rule in that they are indicative of the existence of *opinio iuris sive necessitatis* and international practice on a certain matter, or else they may be indicative of the emergence of a general principle of international law. Alternatively, precedents may bear persuasive authority concerning the existence of a rule or principle, i.e. they may persuade the Tribunal that the decision taken on a prior occasion propounded the correct interpretation of existing law. Plainly, in this case prior judicial decisions may persuade the court that they took the correct

- Another difference is the composition of the Special Court. While the judges of the ICTY and ICTR are solely composed of international judges elected by The General Assembly of the United Nations., the judges of the Special Court are composed of both international and Sierra Leonean judges.
- The prosecutors for the ICTY and the ICTR are elected by the Security Council, while, for the Special Court, the chief prosecutor is elected by the Secretary-General and a deputy prosecutor by the Sierra Leonean authorities in consultation with the United Nations.[69]
- The Statutes of the ICTY and the ICTR, which deal with several categories of international crimes, include genocide among them, while the Statute of the Special Court does not. The crime of genocide was not entered into the Statute of the Special Court because the crimes, which were committed during the civil war, were not perpetrated against an identifiable ethnic, racial, religious or national group.[70] In short, the Special Court deals with war crimes, crimes against humanity and violations of Sierra Leonean

---

approach, but they do not compel this conclusion by the sheer force of their precedential weight. Thus, it can be said that the Justinian maxim whereby courts must adjudicate on the strength of the law, not of cases (*non exemplis, sed legibus iudicandum est*) also applies to the Tribunal as to other international criminal courts."Kupreskic, (IT-95-16-T), judgement, 14 January 2000, para.540. According to the ICTY, there are also different values between the decisions of national criminal courts with that of international criminal courts. Due to the Trial Chamber, there should be "a stricter level of scrutiny to national decisions than to international judgements, as the latter are at least based on the same *corpus* of law as that applied by international courts, whereas the former tend to apply national law, or primarily that law, or else interpret international rules through the prism of national legislation." Id., para.542.

[69] Article 15.

[70] "In its resolution 1315 (2000), the Security Council recommended that the subject-matter jurisdiction of the Special Court should include crimes against humanity, war crimes and other serious violations of international humanitarian law. Because of the lack of any evidence that the massive, large-scale killing in Sierra Leone was at any time perpetrated against an identified national, ethnic, racial or religious group with an intent to annihilate the group as such, the Security Council did not include the crime of genocide in its recommendation, nor was it considered appropriate by the Secretary-General to include it in the list of international crimes falling within the jurisdiction of the Court." Report of the Secretary-General on the Establishment of a Special Court for Sierra Leone, UN Doc. S/2000/915, para.13.

law. The last category does not exist within the Statutes of ICTY and ICTR.
- The key objective of all three tribunals is the restoration and maintenance of peace and there is not therefore any difference between them concerning this matter.[71] The deterrence of further violations is commonly stated as one of the primary objectives of the courts. For instance, the Chamber of the ICTY elucidated this fact in the Momir Nikolic case.[72]

6. Overview of the ICC

The creation of a permanent international criminal court has been one of the long-term aspirations of the system of international criminal justice.[73]

---

[71] For instance, the first annual report of the ICTY reads that "it would be wrong to assume that the Tribunal is based on the old maxim fiat justitia et pereat mundus (let justice be done, even if the world were to perish). The Tribunal is, rather, based on the maxim propound by Hegel in 1821: fiat justitia ne pereat mundus (let justice be done lest the world should perish). Indeed, the judicial process aims at averting the exacerbation and aggravation of conflict and tension, thereby contributing, albeit gradually, to a lasting peace." Final Annual Report of the ICTY, UN Doc.A/49/342-S/1994/1007, annex, para.18.

[72] It stated that "The Tribunal was to achieve justice through criminal proceedings. The purpose of such proceedings was multi-fold: the primary objective was to convict – and punish – those individually responsible for their crimes. The suffering and loss of the victims of such crimes would thereby be internationally recognised and acknowledged. Furthermore, through criminal proceedings, the Security Council intended to send the message to all persons that any violations of international humanitarian law – and particularly the practice of "ethnic cleansing" – would not be tolerated and must stop. It was further hoped that by highlighting breaches of obligations under international humanitarian law, and in particular the Geneva Conventions, that the parties to the conflict would recommit themselves to observing and adhering to those obligations, thereby preventing the commission of further crimes. Finally, it was hoped that this commitment to end impunity in the former Yugoslavia would promote respect for the rule of law globally." Momir Nikolic, (IT-02-60/1-S), Sentencing Judgment, 2 December 2003, para.59.

[73] For an examination of the principles of the International Criminal Court see Manley O. Hudson, *The Proposed International Criminal Court,* 32 American Journal of International Law 549 (1938); Benjamin B. Ferencz, An International Criminal Court, A Step Toward Peace: A Documentary History (1980); M. Cherif Bassiouni, The statute of the International Criminal Court: a Documentary History (1998); The International Criminal Court: Observations and Issues before the 1997-98 Preparatory Committee and administrative and financial implications (1997), The Rome Statute of the International Criminal Court: a commentary

Achieving its creation was not, however, particularly easy because of the circumstances at the time,[74] including grave atrocities[75] and the force of

---

(Antonio Cassese and Albin Eser, eds., 2002); Essays on the Rome Statute of the International Criminal Court (Lattanzi, Flavia and Santori Valeria, eds., 2004);The International Criminal Court: the Making of the Rome Statute: Issues, Negotiations, Results (R.S. Lee, ed., 1999);The International Criminal Court: Recommendations on Policy and Practice: Financing, Victims, Judges, and Immunities, (T. Ingadottir, ed., 2003); The Prosecution of International Crimes: a Practical Guide to Prosecuting ICC Crimes in Commonwealth States (Ben Brandon, ed., 2005); The International Criminal Court: Global Politics and the Quest for Justice (W. Driscoll, ed., 2004);The Definition of Aggression and the ICC (W. Michael Riesman, ed., 2002), pp. 181-192; Commentary on the Rome Statute of the International Criminal Court, (O. Triffterer, ed.,1999); Observations on the Consolidated ICC text before the final session of the Preparatory Committee (Leila Sadat Wexler and M. Cherif Bassiouni, eds., 1998);Y. Aksar, Implementing international humanitarian law: from the ad hoc tribunals to a permanent International Criminal Court (2004);The Permanent International Criminal Court: Legal and Policy Issues (Dominic Mac Goldrick, ed., 2004); From Nuremberg to The Hague: the future of international criminal justice (P. Sands, ed.,2003); The International Criminal Court and the Crime of Aggression (M. Politi, ed., 2004);The Rome Statute of the International Criminal Court: a Challenge to Impunity (M. Politi and G. Nesi, eds., 2004); The United States and the International Criminal Court: national security and international law (S.B. Sewall, ed., 2000);The International Criminal Court: Global Politics and the Quest for Justice (Suzette Zompetti, Joseph P. Zompetti and William Driscoll, eds., 2004); *La Corte Penale Internazionale* (G. Tisci, ed., 2003); D.M. Amann and M.N.S. Sellers., *The United States of America and the International Criminal Court,* American Journal of Comparative Law (2002), pp. 381-404; D. Akande, *The jurisdiction of the International Criminal Court over Nationals of Non-Parties: Legal Basis and limits,* Journal of International Criminal Justice (2003), pp. 618-650; D Akande, *International Law Immunities and the International Criminal Court*, American Journal of International Law (2004), pp. 407-433; R.T. Alter, *International Criminal Law: A Bittersweet Year for Supporters and Critics of the International Criminal Court,* The International Lawyer (2003), pp. 541-550; William Bourdon, La Cour penalE internationale (2000); Daniel H. Derby, *An International Criminal Court for the Future,* 5 Transnational Law and Contemporary Problems 307 (1995); George E. Edwards, *International Human Rights Law Challenges to the International Criminal Court: Right to Privacy in the Search and Seizure Context,* 26 Yale Journal of International Law 1 (2001); Lord Phillimore, *An International Criminal Court and the Resolutions of the Committee of Jurists*, British Yearbook of International Law 79 (1922-23).

[74] Mark Osiel, Mass Atrocity, Collective Memory, and the Law (1997); M. Cherif Bassiouni, *The Time Has Come for an International Criminal Court*, 1 Indiana International and Comparative Law Review1-43 (1991).

[75] Id.

the political realities in the world.[76] The international legal community has long struggled against the political power of states wishing to exercise their own authority on law making decisions.[77] Alongside this struggle,[78] the development of the machinery of justice[79] and its rules and provisions

[76] For instance, the United States government was continuously against the establishment of the Court. The debates were very heated and very problematic. The treaty was not welcome in the Senate. This should be examined in conjunction with the fact that the Senate has constitutionally several extraordinary powers not granted to the House. For example, the consent of the Senate is a necessary precondition for the ratification of international treaties. In addition, consent for the appointments of Federal judges and Cabinet Secretaries relies also on the Senate. According to one of the Senate's reports, the Secretary of State should give assurances that "1. The United States will never vote in favour of the Security Council referring a case to the ICC under Article 13(b). 2. The United States will not provide any assistance to the ICC -- or to any other international organization in support of the ICC -- either in funding, in-kind contributions, or other legal assistance. 3. The United States will not extradite any individual to the ICC, or directly or indirectly refer a case to it. 4. The United States will include in all of its bilateral extradition treaties a provision that prohibits a treaty partner from extraditing U.S. citizens to the ICC. 5. The United States will renegotiate all of its status of forces agreements to include a provision that prohibits a treaty partner from extraditing U.S. soldiers to the ICC, and will not station American forces in any country that refuses to accept such a prohibition. 6. The United States will not permit a U.S. soldier to participate in any NATO, U.N., or other international peacekeeping mission until the United States has reached agreement with all of our NATO allies, and the U.N., that no U.S. soldier will be subject to the ICC's jurisdiction." Hearing on the United Nationals International Criminal Court before the Subcommand on Int'l Operations of the Senate Commission on Foreign Relations, 105th Cong. (1998) (statement of Sen. Jesse Helms); Quoted in Patricia McNerney., *The International Criminal Court: Issues for Consideration by the United States Senate*, 64 Law & Contemporary Problems.181(Winter 2001). See also www.law.duke.edu/shell/cite.pl?64+Law+&+Contemp.+Probs.+181+(Winter +2001)- 43k.

[77] William A., Schabas An Introduction to the International Criminal Court (2ed, 2004); William A., Schabas, The UN International Criminal Tribunals: the former Yugoslavia, Rwanda and Sierra Leone (2006); Atrocities and International Accountability: Beyond Transnational Justice (William A. Schabas, Ramesh Thakur, and Edel Hughes,, eds.), (2007).

[78] See Sandra L. Jamison, *A Permanent International Criminal Court: A Proposal that Overcomes Past Objections*, 23 Denver Journal of International Law and Policy 419 (1995).

[79] See Benjamin B. Ferencz, An International Criminal Court, 2 vols. (1980); Human Rights Watch, Commentary to the Preparatory Commission on the International Criminal Court, Elements of Crimes and Rules of Evidence and Procedure (June 2000); Lawyers Committee for Human Rights, The International

has been progressively extended.[80] This can especially be examined in the works of the United Nations and observations of the discussions in the Preparatory Committee[81] encouraging the establishment of an international criminal court[82] which finally ended in the formulation of one of the most significant multilateral treaties which has ever been ratified in the history of international civilisation.[83] This is the Statute of the ICC in 1998. As a whole, the ICC meets certain needs of the international legal community:[84] "A cet égard, on peut distinguer trois attitudes possibles, qui ne désignent pas nécessairement trois catégories d'Etats définitivement fixées, car leurs attitudes pourront évoluer en fonction des circonstances: ceux qui rejettent l'existence de la CPI telle qu'elle résulte de la Convention de Rome; ceux qui l'acceptent pleinement; ceux qui l'acceptent avec un ensemble de restrictions explicites ou implicites, et pourraient bien n'y voir qu'une institution de caractère symbolique."[85] Although a large number of states have ratified the Statute of the ICC, these states vary drastically in their views and attitudes, and subjectivity matters a great deal in international criminal cases.[86]

Criminal Court Trigger Mechanism and the Need for an Independent Prosecutor (July 1997).

[80] J. Holmes Armstead Jr., *The International Criminal Court: History, Development and Status,* 38 Santa Clara Law Review 745-835 (Summer 1998).

[81] See the relevant section below.

[82] For an historical evolution of the framework of the court in Rome see Mahnoush H. Arsanjani, *The Rome Statute of the International Criminal Court,* 93 American Journal of International Law, 22 (1999).

[83] See J. Holmes Armstead Jr., The International Criminal Court: History, Development and Status, 38 Santa Clara Law Review 745-835 (Summer 1998).

[84] See M. Cherif Bassiouni, From Versailles to Rwanda in Seventy-Five Years: The Need to Establish a Permanent International Criminal Court, 10 HARVARD HUMAN RIGHTS JOURNAL 11 (1997); M. Cherif Bassiouni, *Negotiating the Treaty of Rome on the Establishment of an International Criminal Court,* 32 Cornell International Law Journal 443 (1999); M. Cherif Bassiouni, *The Time has come for an International Criminal Court,* 1 Indiana International and Comparative Law Review (1991); Christopher L. Blackesley, *Obstacles to the Creation of a Permanent War Crimes Tribunal,* 18 Fletcher Forum of World Affairs, 77 (1992).

[85] Serge Sur., Le Droit International Pénal entre l'État et la Société Internationale, Rapport Présentélors du Colloquesur "l'internationalisation du droit pénal" qui s'esttenu à la Faculté de droit de l'Université de Genève les 16 et 17 mars 2001.*www.ridi.org/adi/200110sur.htm.*

[86] A clear example is the Gaza Strip Case and murdering of approximately 1500 Palestinians by Israeli military forces in 2008-2009.

Up until today, some of the most important cases brought before the jurisdiction of the ICC are the cases of Thomas Lubanga Dyilo,[87] Germain Katanga,[88] Mathieu Ngudjolo Chui[89] and Bosco Ntaganda,[90] who are accused of committing crimes against humanity and war crimes including rape and torture in the Democratic Republic of the Congo; Joseph Kony,[91] Vincent Otti,[92]Okot Odhiambo,[93] Dominic Ongwen[94] and Raska Lukwiya[95] who are accused of committing war crimes and crimes against humanity in Uganda; and Ahmad Muhammad Harun ("Ahmad Harun"),[96] Ali Muhammad Ali Abd-Al-Rahman ("Ali Kushayb"),[97] Omar Hassan

---

[87] *Thomas Lubanga Dyilo*, (ICC-01/04-01/06),Warrant of Arrest, 10 February 2006.

[88] *Germain Katanaga* (ICC-01/04-01/07), Situation in the Democratic Republic of Congo, 2 July 2007.

[89] *Mathieu Nagudjolo (*ICC-01/04-02/07), Situation in the Democratic Republic of the Congo, 6 July 2007.

[90] *Bosco Ntaganda*(01/04-02/06), Situation in the Democratic Republic of the Congo, 7 August 2006.

[91] *Joseph Kony* (ICC-02/04-01/05), Warrant of Arrest for *Joseph Kony* issued on 8 July 2005 as amended on 27 September 2005. *Joseph Kony* was the alleged Commander-in-Chief of the Lord's Resistance Army. He is accused of thirty-three counts of crimes against humanity and war crimes. The Lord's Resistance Army "is an armed group carrying out an insurgency against the Government of Uganda and the Ugandan Army (also known as the Uganda People's Defence Force ("UPDF")) and local defence units ("LDUs") since at least 1987; that over this time, including the period from the 1st day of July 2002, the LRA has been directing attacks against both the UPDF and LDUs and against civilian populations; that, in pursuing its goals, the LRA has engaged in a cycle of violence and established a pattern of "brutalization of civilians" by acts including murder, abduction, sexual enslavement, mutilation, as well as mass burnings of houses and looting of camp settlements; that abducted civilians, including children, are said to have been forcibly "recruited" as fighters, porters and sex slaves to serve the LRA and to contribute to attacks against the Ugandan army and civilian communities." See *Joseph Kony* case (ICC-02/04-01/05), Warrant of Arrest for *Joseph Kony* issued on 8 July 2005 as amended on 27 September 2005.

[92] *Vincent Otti*(ICC-02/04), Warrant of Arrest, 8 July 2005. He is accused of thirty-three counts of crimes

[93] *Okot Odhiambo*(ICC-02/04), Warrant of Arrest, 8 July 2005. He is accused of nineteen counts crimes.

[94] *Dominic Ongwen* (ICC-02/04), Warrant of Arrest, 8 July 2005. He is accused of thirty-three counts crimes.

[95] *Raska Lukwiya* (ICC-02/04), Warrant of Arrest, 8 July 2005. He is accused of nine counts crimes.

[96] *Muhammad Harun* (ICC-02/05-01/07) Warrant of Arrest, 27 April 2007.

[97] *Ali Abd-Al-Rahman* (ICC-02/05-01/07), Warrant of Arrest, 27 April 2007.

Ahmad Al Bashri[98] and Bahar Idriss Abu Garda[99] accused of committing war crimes and crimes against humanity in Darfur, Sudan. Consequently, the aims of the ICC are *inter alia* to prevent the commission of international crimes, implement the provisions of international criminal law, put an end to impunity and create justice.

6.1. The Draft Code of Crimes for a Court

6.1.1. Historical Review

Whilst the conflicts surrounding the drafting of a Code of Crimes against the Peace and Security of Mankind (Code) need not be discussed at great length, a short consideration of its period of preparation may be useful for understanding the background of the ICC in the United Nations. This is because the aim of the UN was to draft a Code and a Court to be used in conjunction with each other. The preparation of a Draft Code of Offences against the Peace and Security of Mankind was originally suggested in the United Nations in order to indicate "clearly the place to be accorded to the principles of international law recognized in the Charter of the Nuremberg Tribunal."[100] Although there was a long debate concerning the scope of definition of the Code and whether it was the duty of the International Law Commission (ILC) to investigate the subject with due regard to the basic principles of the Nuremberg Tribunals, it was nevertheless clear that the subject of the Code was constituted by the main points in the progressive development of international law.[101] Thus, the proposals for the Code were principally brought to the United Nations as a result of the Second World War, but it later appeared that a draft code must not only take into consideration the former provisions of international criminal law, but should also present the progressive development of the law for the future international relations of states. The aim was to have a clear system of

---

[98] *Omar Hassan Ahmad Al Bashir* (ICC-02/05-01/09), Warrant of Arrest, 4 March 2009.

[99] *Bahar Idriss Abu Garda* (Summons to Appear issued under seal by the ICC), 7 May 2009. This is for the first time in the history of the ICC that the Court judges did not issue a warrant for arrest but a summons to appear. The underlying reason was that the Pre-Trial Chamber I was of the view that the accused would appear before the ICC.

[100] Y.B.I.L.C., 1949, p.216. The preparation of a Draft Code of Offences against the Peace and Security of Mankind was originally addressed by GA Res.177 (II) (item 3(b) of the agenda) (A/CN.4/25).

[101] Y.B.I.L.C., 1949, pp.216-50.

legislation for an international criminal court. Therefore, the actual scope of the Code to be used in an international criminal court was eventually the most important question considered during the drafting of the Code. A profound discussion thus ensued during the early meetings of the ILC concerning the scope of the definition of the offences against the peace and security of mankind.

6.1.2. Codification of a Code of Crimes

The first attempt to establish a code regarding certain crimes in international criminal law in the United Nations was made by the General Assembly in Resolution 95 (I) of 11 December 1946, at its first session.[102] In this resolution the Assembly affirmed the principles of international law recognized by both the Charter of the Nuremberg Tribunal and the Judgment of the Tribunal and directed the Committee on the Codification of the Principles of International Law established by Resolution 94 (I) "to treat as a matter of primary importance plans for the formulation, in the context of a general codification of offences against the peace and security of mankind or of an International Criminal Code, of the principles recognized in the Charter of the Nuremberg Tribunal and the Judgement of the Tribunal."

In the course of its work, the Committee suggested to the Assembly the creation of an International Law Commission for the codification and formulation of different topics.[103] In response, the General Assembly of the United Nations established the International Law Commission by Resolution 174 (II), on 21 November 1947. The General Assembly also directed the Commission by Resolution 177 (II) to "'*(a)* Formulate the principles of international law recognized in the Charter of the Nuremberg Tribunal and in the Judgement of the Tribunal,' and '*(b)* Prepare a draft code of offences against the peace and security of mankind, indicating clearly the place to be accorded to the principles mentioned in subparagraph *(a)* above'."

The International Law Commission examined the subject of Resolution 177 (II) at its first session in 1949. The Commission also appointed Mr. Jean Spiropoulos as Special Rapporteur in order to work with the relevant sections of the resolution concerning the draft code. As a result of a report by Mr. Spiropoulos on the formulation of the Nuremberg Principles at its

---

[102] Affirmation of the Principles of International Law Recognized by the Charter of the Nuremberg Tribunal, U.N.G.A. Res.95(I), U.N.Doc. A/64/Add.1 (1946).

[103] Official Records of the General Assembly, Second Session, Sixth Committee, Annexed No. 1, document A/331.

second session, the Commission adopted a formulation of the principles of international law recognized in the Charter of the Nuremberg Tribunal and in the Judgement of the Tribunal. Additionally, on the basis of a report by the Special Rapporteur on the draft Code, the Commission examined paragraph (b) of Resolution 177 (II) and the replies received from governments to its questionnaire relating to the Code.

6.1.3. Formation of a Code

The General Assembly in its Resolution 488 (V) invited governments of member states to furnish their observations on the formulation of the principles of international law recognized in the Charter and Judgement of the Nuremberg Tribunal. It also requested the Commission, in preparing a draft Code of Offences against the Peace and Security of Mankind, to take account of observations made on that formulation by delegations during the fifth session of the General Assembly and of any observations which might be made by governments. In 1951, following the completion of this procedure and at the request of the General Assembly for the continuation of the work on the draft, the second report on the draft Code was submitted by the Special Rapporteur to the ILC.

The Commission, after examining the report of the Rapporteur, a memorandum on the draft by Professor Pella, as well as the observations received from Governments on the formulation of the Nuremberg Principles, adopted a draft Code of Offences against the Peace and Security of Mankind which consists of five articles with their relevant commentaries.[104]

This draft was submitted to the General Assembly in 1951. In the same year, however, the consideration and examination of a draft code was postponed by the General Assembly and there was no further draft code until 1954. The new draft code took into account the comments and observations received from governments and consisted of four articles dealing with some of the important principles of international criminal law governing international crimes. This Code was adopted by the International Law Commission in 1954.

6.1.4. The Code and a Court

Although some agreements were made regarding the question of the application and definitions of the Code, the discussion of certain relevant

[104] For an earlier work of Pella see Vespasien V. Pella, La Codification du Droit Penal International (1922).

questions had to be postponed until future meetings of the ILC. Among the reasons for this were:

i) The General Assembly had already entrusted to a special committee the task of preparing a report on a draft definition on aggression and, as the Code raised the same issues concerning the definition of aggression, it seemed unnecessary for the Code to deal with these issuesbefore the Special Committee on the Question of Aggression had completed its task;

ii) There was scarcely any agreement on the question of what does and does not constitute international crime;

iii) Powerful states would not give their consent to the adoption of a code governing the principles of international criminal law and international crimes under which they might legally be found guilty according to the statement of an international criminal court;

iv) The adoption of a draft code would most probably provide a strong argument for the creation of an international criminal court, for the establishment of which no state was prepared; and

v) It was impossible to reflect both political realities and international legal standards in the Code and the Court.

6.1.5. Modification of a Code of Crimes

The General Assembly did not consider it wise to make any further considerations of the draft Code as long as the task of defining "aggression" was not completed by the Special Committee. The question of the drafting of a code on offences against the peace and security of mankind was therefore not raised again until 1974 when the General Assembly adopted the resolution on the Definition of Aggression.Up to this point, the preparation of a draft statute for an international criminal court was not possible due to the non-existence of a draft code on the definition of serious international crimes. Since the above resolution had already been approved by the General Assembly, there was no longer any obstacle to the reconsideration and re-examination of a draft code and a court.

From 1974 onwards, the question of the codification of a draft code was raised both in the General Assembly and in the International Law Commission. The General Assembly, by its resolution 33/97 of 16 December 1978, invited Member states and relevant international intergovernmental organizations to submit their observations and comments on the draft code.[105] Afterwards, on the basis of comments received from member states, the General Assembly adopted Resolution

---

[105] See also General Assembly Resolution 35/49 of 4 December 1980.

36/106 on 10 December 1981 entitled *Draft Code of Offences against the Peace and Security of Mankind*. This resolution invited the International Law Commission once again to consider and examine the drafting of a new code on the relevant subject. The aim was to reach agreement on a final version of the code and then to create an international criminal court in order to deal with the violators of that code.

6.1.6. Controversial Questions raised by the Code

Between 1982 and 1991 the Commission worked on the draft of the Code of Offences against the Peace and Security of Mankind and received observations and comments from member states on the draft on several occasions. The reports to the Commission were prepared by the Special Rapporteur, Mr. Doudou Thiam and were subsequently taken into consideration and examined by the Commission. Two of the most controversial questions raised in the meetings of the International Law Commission relevant to the draft Code of Offences against the Peace and Security of Mankind were; i) which international crimes should be dealt with in the Code? And; ii) who are the subjects of responsibility and liability for the violation of the provisions of the Code? On the whole, the first question has been limited to the most serious international crimes, while the second has been restricted to the criminal responsibility of individuals and/or the civil liability of states.

The provisional adoption of the Draft Code of Crimes by the ILC in 1991 led to the creation of the Working Group, whose task it was to work for the creation of an international criminal court. Accordingly, the Working Group produced a report concerning different questions relevant to the creation of an international court. The ILC then put forward some basic propositions for the Working Group. These were *inter alia:*

a) an international criminal court established by a statute in the form of a treaty agreed to by States Parties;
b) in the first phase of its operations, at least, (the court) should exercise jurisdiction only over private individuals. Its jurisdiction should be limited to crimes of an international character defined in specified international treaties in force, including, but not limited to, the crimes defined in the draft Code of Crimes against the Peace and Security of Mankind upon its adoption and entry into force;
c) It should be possible for a State to become a party to the statute without thereby becoming a party to the Code;
d) The court would be a facility for States Parties to its statute (and also, in clearly defined terms, for other States) which could be called into operation as and when required;

e) In the first phase of its operation, at least, it should neither have compulsory jurisdiction nor be a standing full-time body;

f) Whatever the precise structure of the court or of any of the other mechanisms which were suggested and considered, it must guarantee due process, independence and impartiality in its procedures.[106]

Although the above provisions were outlined by the ILC, they did not produce any particular result. However, the Draft Statute was adopted by the ILC in 1994. The Draft Statute suggested that the Court should consist of four organs: judicial body, registry, procuracy and a presidency. Meanwhile, in 1996, the ILC completed the Draft Code and the term "offences", which was used in the earlier draft, was from this time officially replaced with the term "crimes." It is called the Draft Code of Crimes against the Peace and Security of Mankind. The Code contains many articles concerning international crimes and it deals exclusively with the international criminal responsibility of individuals. At the request of the General Assembly, the Preparatory Committee took into account the Draft Code in order to prepare a Draft Statute for the International Criminal Court. Thus, the Draft Code of Crimes has had a significant role in the creation and the development of the International Criminal Court (ICC). As has been rightly asserted, "The very success of the ILC in preparing the Draft Statute lies partly in the de-linking of it from the long and complex codification efforts relating to the Draft Code of Crimes against the Peace and Security of Mankind, to which it had formerly been tied. From this point of view, it might be far better to keep the Draft Statute entirely procedural."[107] It has been further asserted that "Regardless, the ILC should be asked to proceed on a priority basis with the codification process, so that the ICC's Statute may eventually incorporate by reference a Code of Crimes. Such incorporation should be provided for in the text of the Statute."[108]

A serious question for the Commission has been the level and the degree of penalties applicable to perpetrators of international crimes who have been found guilty by an international criminal court. This question has been examined by the Commission in accordance with different systems of prosecution and punishment. The question, however, is even more pressing when an international criminal court wants to deal with the crimes in the Code, since such a court ought to apply an international

---

[106] Yearbook of International Law Commission (1992), vol. II (Part Two), paras.11 and 104.

[107] Daniel C. Prefontaine, The Proposed International Criminal Court, www.icclr.law.ubc.ca/Publications/Reports/propicc.PDF visited on 2009-07-06.

[108] Id.

standard of penalties - a standard which does not exist at the present time. This is today one of the most serious problems faced by the ICC, which has to work in accordance with the principle of complementarity at the same time as the states which exercise their jurisdiction over the accused persons have different levels of punishment.

The majority of the crimes enumerated in the Code have a long history within conventional or customary international criminal law and some of these crimes, such as genocide, apartheid and war crimes, are today considered an integral part of the international law of *jus cogens* and the Statute of the ICC, including the *ad hoc* tribunals such as the ICTY, the ICTR and the Special Court for Sierra Leone.[109] This means that the legal characterization of these international crimes cannot be modified by the terms of an agreement, but only by the expression of subsequent provisions of general international law having the same character. The provisions governing these international crimes are enforceable not only against the contracting parties to the relevant international conventions but are also binding for all other states which have not directly expressed their consent to the relevant international conventions.

---

[109] See the relevant chapters *supra.* Further types of courts have also been established under the authority of the United Nations. The key instance is the Extraordinary Chambers in the Courts of Cambodia. In 1975, the Khmer Rouge came into power in Cambodia in 1975. During the following four years, approximately 1.7 million civilians were killed by various means. Finally, in 1979, the Khmer Rouge lost power because of the assistance provided by armed forces from Vietnam. However, the United States continued its support for the Khmer Rouge by different means including its seat in the United Nations. This meant in practice that no criminal justice could be established for the prosecution of criminals. While formulation of an agreement for the punishment of criminals was necessary, the political reality prevented its conclusion. It was only in 2003 that the United Nations, after years of negotiations, concluded an agreement with the Cambodian government in order for an international criminal tribunal to be established for the prosecution and punishment of the leaders of the former Khmer Rouge. See also David Scheffer, *The Extraordinary Chambers in the Courts of Cambodia, in* International Criminal Law, Vol. III (M. Cherif Bassiouni, ed. 2008) pp. 219-255.

CHAPTER THREE

THE MECHANISM OF INTERNATIONAL CRIMINAL TRIBUNALS AND THE COURTS

1. The Constitution of the Nuremberg Tribunal

The Charter of the Nuremberg Tribunal is conventionally divided into five parts. The first part is the constitution of the International Military Tribunal in Nuremberg (IMT), which presents its most important principles. These principles are as follows:

1. There should be an agreement that permits the establishment of a tribunal;[1]
2. The purpose of the establishment of the tribunal must be clear. This is in order to define clearly the scope of the applicability of the rules of the tribunal. The purpose of the Nuremberg Tribunal was to prosecute and punish the major war criminals of the European Axis Powers;[2]
3. The number of the members of the tribunal must be clearly set out. The Tribunal in Nuremberg consisted of four members, each with an alternate;[3]
4. The alternate should, as far as possible, be present at all sessions of the Tribunal;[4]
5. If any member of the Tribunal could not be present, his alternate would take his place;[5]
6. The Tribunal's character was fixed. The defendants or their counsel could therefore make no objection to its legal existence;[6]

---

[1] Article 1.
[2] Article 1.
[3] Article 2.
[4] Article 2.
[5] Article 2.

7. The presence of all four members, or their alternates in case of absence, was necessary to constitute a quorum;[7]
8. The presidency of the Tribunal had to be selected by the members of the Tribunal;[8]
9. The decision of the Tribunal had to be taken by a majority vote, with the President exercising the deciding vote in cases where the votes were evenly divided;[9]
10. When (it was) necessary, other tribunals could also be established in accordance with the Charter of the Nuremberg Tribunal.[10]

1.1. Constitutional Approach to Indictment

The Nuremberg Constitution's rules regarding the submission of an inducement are among its most significant features. This was dealt with, *inter alia*, within articles 9, 14, 15, 16 and 24. The rules of the procedures of the tribunal also made reference to this matter.[11] "Indictment" means the formal accusation of a person of the commission of certain crime(s). It also refers to an application issued by a jury having sufficient evidence to prove that the defendant has committed the relevant crime. According to the constitution of the Tribunal, the chief prosecutor, who was responsible for the investigation of the charges against major war criminals and their prosecution, had the authority to approve the indictment.[12]

The United States, United Kingdom, France and the Soviet Union made the indictments against the Nazi war criminals. The Nuremberg

---

[6] Similar measures can be found under the provisions of the tribunal monopolised by the United States for the prosecution of the dictator of Iraq.

[7] Article 4.

[8] Article 5.

[9] *Id.*

[10] *Id.*

[11] For instance, Article 9 of the Constitution stated that "At the trial of any individual member of any group or organization the Tribunal may declare (in connection with any act of which the individual may be convicted) that the group or organization of which the individual was a member was a criminal organization. After receipt of the Indictment, the Tribunal shall give such notice as it thinks fit that the prosecution intends to ask the Tribunal to make such declaration and any member of the organization will be entitled to apply to the Tribunal for leave to be heard by the Tribunal upon the question of the criminal character of the organization. The Tribunal shall have the power to allow or reject the application. If the application is allowed, the Tribunal may direct in what manner the applicants shall be represented and heard."

[12] See Article 14 of the Constitution.

Tribunal had jurisdiction over twenty-two individual Nazi officials[13] who were members of different groups or organizations.[14] The role of these organizations was to carry out the Nazi programs. According to the rules of the International Military Tribunal (IMT), defendants were charged with three categories of international crimes. These were war crimes, crimes against humanity, and crimes against peace or conspiracy against peace.

The implementation of the judgments of the Tribunal was not as easy as the victorious states had expected. This was because some of the accused committed suicide and others were freed from prosecution and punishment for various reasons. For instance, although Gustav Krupp was named in the indictment, he was found physically not strong enough to stand trial. Robert Ley was charged as a defendant but committed suicide before the trial. Borman was tried in absence. Many other leaders of the Nazi Party, such as Hitler, Himmler, and Goebbels, could not be brought under the judgment of the Nuremberg Tribunal because they committed suicide at the end of the war.

1.2. Constitutional Approach to Trial

The Constitution of the Nuremberg Tribunal was, however, the first international constitution for the prosecution of international criminals. It was significantly based on the categorization of the different criminal acts committed by the perpetrators of international crimes. Therefore, the scope

[13] There were many lawyers from different countires. One of the most known of these was Robert H Jackson. It is interested to note that "Jackson "Played an important role in not only the trial itself, but also in the creation of the International Military Tribunal, as he led the American delegation to London that, in the summer of 1945, argued in favour of prosecuting the Nazi leadership as a criminal conspiracy. According to Airey Neave, Jackson was also the one behind the prosecution's decision to include membership in any of the six criminal organizations in the indictments at the trial, though the IMT rejected this on the grounds that it was wholly without precedent in either international law or the domestic laws of any of the Allies. Jackson also attempted to have Alfried Krupp be tried in place of his father, Gustav, and even suggested that Alfried volunteer to be tried in his father's place. Both proposals were rejected by the IMT, particularly by Lawrence and Biddle, and some sources indicate that this resulted in Jackson being viewed unfavourably by the latter." http://en.wikipedia.org/wiki/Nuremberg Trials.

[14] These groups had very active role in the preparation of criminal acts. These were recognized criminal organizations which were planning or preparing certain criminal decisions against the Jews. They followed different criminal policies and unjustified behaviours.

of the Nuremberg Tribunal was not unlimited. It worked under certain statutes, which specified what actions, or omissions should be recognised as crimes under international law. Therefore, the trial of the German war criminals established several important principles by the opening of the main trial. The Tribunal began its jurisdiction with the reading of indictments which had four significant divisions. These were:

> Division one: "conspiracy to wage aggressive war," which addressed crimes committed before the war officially began.
>
> Division two: "waging an aggressive war," which addressed the undertaking of war in violation of international treaties.
>
> Division three: "war crimes," which addressed more traditional violations of the laws of war, including the killing or mistreatment of prisoners of war, and the use of outlawed weapons.
>
> Division four: "crimes against humanity," which addressed the crimes committed against Jews, ethnic minorities, physically and mentally disabled persons, civilians in occupied countries, and others.

The above four divisions became the most important guidelines of the Charter of the Nuremberg Tribunal.[15] Ever since the creation of the Nuremberg Tribunal, these division have been regarded as the most important phenomena in the development of the system of international criminal law.[16] They were the justification based upon which the Tribunal referred to a number of international conventions which had been violated during World War II.[17]

---

[15] See the following sections

[16] See chapter seven.

[17] Some of these conventions are: Convention for the Amelioration of the Condition of the Wounded in Armies in the Field, 22 August 1864; Additional Articles Relating to the Condition of the Wounded in War, Geneva on 20 October 1868; Declaration Renouncing the Use, in Time of War, of Explosive Projectiles Under 400 Grams Weight (St. Petersburg Declaration), 11 December 1868; Declaration Concerning the Prohibition, for the Term of Five Years, of the Launching of Projectiles and Explosives from Balloons or Other New Methods of a Similar Nature (First Hague, IV, 1), 29 July 1899; Declaration Concerning the Prohibition of the Use of Projectiles Diffusing Asphyxiating Gases (First Hague, IV, 2), 29 July 1899; Hague Declaration of 1899; Hague Convention II with Respect to the Laws and Customs of War on Land, 29 July, 1899; Hague Convention III for the Adaptation to Maritime Warfare of the Principles of the Geneva Convention of 22 August 1864, 1899; Geneva Convention for the Amelioration of the Condition of the Wounded and Sick in Armies in the Field, 6

2. The Constitution of the Tokyo Tribunal

The Tokyo Tribunal had a very limited Constitution due to the fact that it was written by a United States general and was not therefore discussed by the members of the Allied Powers. Obviously, all terms of jurisdiction and its methods of application were decided by the Supreme Commander of the United States. According to the Charter of the Tribunal, there were three recognised categories of international crimes which were, in some respects, similar to the crimes recognised by the Nuremberg Tribunal. The Charter of the Tokyo Tribunal made it clear that the Tribunal had authority solely over individuals. According to the first two articles of the Constitution, the aims of the Tribunal and its members were specified. They read that:

> Article 1: Tribunal Established. The International Military Tribunal for the Far East is hereby established for the just and prompts trial and punishment of the major war criminals in the Far East. The permanent seat of the Tribunal is in Tokyo.
>
> Article 2: *Members.* The Tribunal shall consist of not less than six members nor more than eleven members, appointed by the Supreme Commander for the Allied Powers from the names submitted by the Signatories to the Instrument of Surrender, India, and the Commonwealth of the Philippines.

July 1906; Convention IV Respecting the Laws and Customs of War on Land, 18 October, 1907; Convention X for the Adaptation to Maritime Warfare of the Principles of the Geneva Convention, Hague, 18 October 1907; Convention IX Concerning Bombardment by Naval Forces in Time of War, 18 October 1907; Convention XI Relative to Certain Restrictions with Regard to the Exercise of the Right of Capture in Naval War, Hague, 18 October 1907; Declaration Prohibiting the Discharge of Projectiles and Explosives from Balloons, 18 October 1907; Fourth Hague Convention Regarding the Laws and Customs of Land Warfare, 18 October 1907; Declaration Relative to Prohibiting the Discharge of Projectiles and Explosives from Balloons (Second Hague, XIV), 18 October 1907; Declaration (XIV) Relative to Prohibiting the Discharge of Projectiles and Explosives from Balloons, 1907; Treaty of Versailles, 28 June 1919; Geneva Protocol for the Prohibition of the Use in War of Asphyxiating, Poisonous or Other Gases, and of Bacteriological Methods of Warfare, 17 June 1925; Geneva Convention for the Amelioration of the Condition of the Wounded and Sick in Armies in the Field (Red Cross Convention), 27 July 1929; Geneva Convention for the Relief of Wounded and Sick in Armies in the Field of 1929 and Geneva Convention Relative to the Treatment of Prisoners of War, 27 July, 1929.

The legitimacy of the Tokyo Tribunal mostly depended on the number of states that participated in the trial and also on the political and military power of the states which took part in the trial. In any event, the constitution formulated certain rules applicable in the case of the absence of members of the court and regarding what could be recognised as a fixed minimum number of members of the court. It declared that:

> *(a) Convening and Quorum.* When as many as six members of the Tribunal are present, they may convene the Tribunal in formal session. The presence of a majority of all members shall be necessary to constitute a quorum.
>
> *(b) Voting.* All decisions and judgments of this Tribunal, including convictions and sentences, shall be by a majority vote of those Members of the Tribunal present. In case the votes are evenly divided, the vote of the President shall be decisive.
>
> *(c) Absence.* If a member at any time is absent and afterwards is able to be present, he shall take part in all subsequent proceedings; unless he declares in open court that he is disqualified by reason of insufficient familiarity with the proceedings which took place in his absence.[18]

Despite the above provisions, the Supreme Commander of the United States, General MacArthur, was given full power over the judgement and sentences of the Tribunal. This meant that although the Constitution of the Tribunal had formulated certain rules, their implementation could be affected by political reality. The judgment and sentences were confirmed on 24 November 1948. As a result of political negotiations, a decree was issued by the Supreme Commander in 1950 which reduced the judgement and sentence based on political agreement.

3. Dimensions of the Statute of the ICTY

Security Council Resolution 808 of 22 February 1993 decreed that an international tribunal should be established for the prosecution of persons responsible for serious violations of international humanitarian law committed in the territory of the former Yugoslavia since 1991. This marked the beginning of the creation of international criminal trials for the prosecution and punishment of individuals who had seriously violated the international humanitarian law of armed conflicts.[19] In fact, the resolution

[18] Article 4 of the International Military Tribunal for the Far East.

[19] The resolution may therefore be asserted to be one of the most effective instruments of the United Nations that may open the door for the prosecution and

became a model for the creation of subsequent courts in order to put an end to impunity.[20]

Pursuant to Resolution 808, the International Tribunal for the Prosecution of Persons Responsible for Serious Violations of International Humanitarian Law Committed in the Territory of the Former Yugoslavia (ICTY) since 1991 was finally established in accordance with Resolution 827.[21] The Tribunal is a body of the United Nations and its duties and tasks

---

punishment of individuals of powerful states under the proceedings of the permanent International Criminal Court (hereafter ICC).

[20] According to the resolution, the General Secretary of the United Nations became responsible for a quick investigation into the question of the establishment of the Tribunal. The Secretary was requested "to submit for consideration by the Council at the earliest possible date, and if possible no later than 60 days after the adoption of the present resolution, a report on all aspects of this matter, including specific proposals and where appropriate options for the effective and expeditious implementation of the decision [to establish an international tribunal], taking into account suggestions put forward in this regard by Member States."

[21] Resolution 827 was adopted on 25 May 1993 (S/RES/827, 1993). Since the content of the resolution has had an important function in the development of international criminal justice after the creation of the Nuremberg Tribunal, the resolution is reproduced here.

The Security Council,

Reaffirming its resolution 713 (1991) of 25 September 1991 and all subsequent relevant resolutions,

Having considered the report of the Secretary-General (S/25704 and Add.1) pursuant to paragraph 2 of resolution 808 (1993),

Expressing once again its grave alarm at continuing reports of widespread and flagrant violations of international humanitarian law occurring within the territory of the former Yugoslavia, and especially in the Republic of Bosnia and Herzegovina, including reports of mass killings, massive, organized and systematic detention and rape of women, and the continuance of the practice of "ethnic cleansing", including for the acquisition and the holding of territory,

Determining that this situation continues to constitute a threat to international peace and security,

Determined to put an end to such crimes and to take effective measures to bring to justice the persons who are responsible for them,

Convinced that in the particular circumstances of the former Yugoslavia the establishment as an ad hoc measure by the Council of an international tribunal and the prosecution of persons responsible for serious violations of international humanitarian law would enable this aim to be achieved and would contribute to the restoration and maintenance of peace,

Believing that the establishment of an international tribunal and the prosecution of persons responsible for the above-mentioned violations of international humanitarian law will contribute to ensuring that such violations are halted and effectively redressed,

Noting in this regard the recommendation by the Co-Chairmen of the Steering Committee of the International Conference on the Former Yugoslavia for the establishment of such a tribunal (S/25221),

Reaffirming in this regard its decision in resolution 808 (1993) that an international tribunal shall be established for the prosecution of persons responsible for serious violations of international humanitarian law committed in the territory of the former Yugoslavia since 1991,

Considering that, pending the appointment of the Prosecutor of the International Tribunal, the Commission of Experts established pursuant to resolution 780 (1992) should continue on an urgent basis the collection of information relating to evidence of grave breaches of the Geneva Conventions and other violations of international humanitarian law as proposed in its interim report (S/25274),

Acting under Chapter VII of the Charter of the United Nations,

1. *Approves* the report of the Secretary-General;

2. *Decides* hereby to establish an international tribunal for the sole purpose of prosecuting persons responsible for serious violations of international humanitarian law committed in the territory of the former Yugoslavia between 1 January 1991 and a date to be determined by the Security Council upon the restoration of peace and to this end to adopt the Statute of the International Tribunal annexed to the above-mentioned report;

3. *Requests* the Secretary-General to submit to the judges of the International Tribunal, upon their election, any suggestions received from States for the rules of procedure and evidence called for in Article 15 of the Statute of the International Tribunal;

4. *Decides* that all States shall cooperate fully with the International Tribunal and its organs in accordance with the present resolution and the Statute of the International Tribunal and that consequently all States shall take any measures necessary under their domestic law to implement the provisions of the present resolution and the Statute, including the obligation of States to comply with requests for assistance or orders issued by a Trial Chamber under Article 29 of the Statute;

5. *Urges* States and intergovernmental and non-governmental organizations to contribute funds, equipment and services to the International Tribunal, including the offer of expert personnel;

6. *Decides* that the determination of the seat of the International Tribunal is subject to the conclusion of appropriate arrangements between the United Nations and the Netherlands acceptable to the Council, and that the International Tribunal may sit elsewhere when it considers it necessary for the efficient exercise of its functions;

7. *Decides also* that the work of the International Tribunal shall be carried out without prejudice to the right of the victims to seek, through appropriate means, compensation for damages incurred as a result of violations of international humanitarian law;

are to prosecute grave breaches of the Geneva Conventions of 1949, violations of the laws and customs of war, genocide and crimes against humanity committed in the territories of the former Yugoslavia. The Tribunal has jurisdiction only over persons and not organizations or governments.

For the effective implementation of its provisions and in order to decrease criticisms of the power of the jurisdiction of the tribunal, the tribunal is essentially based on the principle of *nullum crimen sine lege*. This means that the court applies the rules that are already accepted in customary and conventional international criminal law and which are considered an important part of the international humanitarian law of armed conflict. This embodies a considerable number of international conventions such as the 1899 Hague Convention (IV) Respecting the Laws and Customs of War on Land and the Regulations annexed thereto of 18 October 1907, the 1949 Convention for the Amelioration of the Condition of the Wounded and Sick in Armed Forces in the Field, the 1949 Convention for the Amelioration of the Condition of the Wounded, Sick and Shipwrecked Members of Armed Forces at Sea, the 1949 Convention Relative to the Treatment of Prisoners of War, and the 1949 Convention Relative to the Protection of Civilian Persons in Time of War including their 1977 Protocols.

It must be emphasised that the adoption of the relevant resolution of the Security Council for the creation of the ICTY is not an innovation in the recognition of the system of conventional international criminal law. This is because most of the provisions of conventional international criminal law governing the rules of armed conflicts were already an integral part of customary international criminal law. This is amply demonstrated by the provisions of the United Nations Charter which call on all states to respect international law at all times. This means that the function of the ICTY is the *implementation* of international criminal law and not the creation of its rules and provisions. However, one of the basic problems of the ICTY is that its creation was a result of the order of the Security Council and not the international legal community as a whole. The tribunal has therefore a somewhat retroactive character.[22]

---

8. *Requests* the Secretary-General to implement urgently the present resolution and in particular to make practical arrangements for the effective functioning of the International Tribunal at the earliest time and to report periodically to the Council;
9. *Decides* to remain actively seized of the matter.

[22] According to one view "It would be fitting that the so-called 'Tribunal'– if it wants, at least, to prove its credibility in terms of basic moral standards, in spite of its legal incompetence as explained above – should also turn its attention to the

3.1. The Scope of Jurisdiction

The ICTY has been given a wide-ranging authority in order to carry out its functions and to bring the perpetrators of international crimes under its jurisdiction. The authority and the power of the Tribunal arise from its 1993 Statute. This has however been amended in order to make the provisions of the Statute more practically relevant to the needs of the Tribunal.

Questions have often been raised regarding the date from which the ICTR could initiate a criminal investigation. In response to which there have been different views expressed. In the *Nsengiyumva* case, the Trial Chamber stated that the "Trial Chamber accepts the Prosecution's submission that allegations dating before 1994 do not constitute independent crimes. These allegations merely represent what the Prosecution intends to offer as relevant and admissible evidence of crimes occurring in 1994, or relate to the continuation of events, clarify, and are supplementary to the substantive charges."[23] For the above reasons, the Trial Chamber does not set a time limit for the discovery of offences and concerning certain matters such as conspiracy, provides a highly flexible date of recognition. For instance, the Trial Chamber "finds that the limited temporal jurisdiction of the Tribunal does not bar evidence of an alleged

---

practices applied by the NATO coalition in its undeclared war against the people of Yugoslavia (including the province of Kosovo). The provisions of Article 3 of the so-called 'Tribunal' identify, among others, the following practices as 'violations of the laws or customs of war': (a) 'employment of poisonous weapons or other weapons calculated to cause unnecessary suffering;' (c) 'attack, or bombardment, by whatever means, of undefended towns, villages, dwellings, or buildings;' etc. NATO's use of depleted uranium missiles and of cluster bombs, NATO's attacks on villages, civilian buses etc. fall clearly within the definition of 'violations of the laws or customs of war' as given in the Statute of that very 'Tribunal' not to speak of the numerous grave breaches of the Geneva Conventions of 1949 committed by the NATO alliance, for which the 'Tribunal' also claims to be competent according to Article 2 of its Statute. As long as the 'Tribunal' does not take action against those NATO politicians and military officers responsible for these grave breaches of international humanitarian law, the 'Tribunal' can only be considered as one more futile exercise in the political use of judicial procedures within the framework of a 'policy of double standards' which seems to be the essence of power politics in NATO's 'New World Order.'" http://i-p-o.org/yu-tribunal-memo1999.htm. Visited on 2011-06-30.

[23] *Nsengiyumva* (ICTR-96-12-I), Decision on the Defence Motions Objecting to the Jurisdiction of the Trial Chamber on the Amended Indictment, 13 April 2000, para.27

conspiracy of which the agreement was made before 1994."[24] It goes further and states that "to the contrary, evidence of a pre-1994 conspiracy may be admissible and relevant in showing the commission of a conspiracy in 1994."[25] According to this statement, conspiracy constitutes a 'continuing crime.' For this reason, if it "is a continuing crime, then events that took place outside the period of the Statute can be taken into account if it can be shown that the conspiracy continued into the relevant period of the Statute. Evidence before 1994 may show when the conspiracy actually commenced. All activities prior to 1 January 1994, so far as they related to the conspiracy, may be relevant."[26] The statement of the ICTR has obviously created a norm according to which certain criminal conducts may be investigated retroactively for the proof of guilt.

From the earliest stages in the Tribunal's creation, questions have been raised about the legal scope of its jurisdiction and the borderline of its powers under the provisions of the system of international criminal law. Article 1 of the Statute of the Tribunal clearly outlines its competency by stating its power to prosecute persons responsible for serious violations of international humanitarian law committed in the territory of the former Yugoslavia from the initiation of the war in 1991.

The scope of the authority of the Tribunal concerning the prosecution and punishment of certain international crimes is stated in Articles 2, 3, 4 and 5. According to these articles, the Tribunal has jurisdiction over four categories of international crimes. These are grave breaches of the 1949 Geneva Conventions,[27] violations of the laws and customs of war,[28] genocide[29] and crimes against humanity.[30] The jurisdiction of the Tribunal is, of course, over natural persons.[31]

The provisions of the Statute of the ICTY are not original but have long been recognised under the principles of customary and conventional international criminal law. In the jurisprudence of international law, the provisions of customary international criminal law may or may not be found within conventional criminal law and each may borrow rules or provisions from the other. Some rules of customary international criminal law may also be formulated into the body of conventional law. This means

---

[24] *Id.*, para.28.
[25] *Id.*, para.28.
[26] *Id.*, para.28.
[27] Article 2 of the Statute.
[28] Article 3 of the Statute.
[29] Article 4 of the Statute.
[30] Article 5 of the Statute.
[31] Article 6 of the Statute.

that the Tribunal's authority governing the prosecution of the accused persons was not retroactive. Both sources of international criminal law imply this fact.

3.2. Elements of Jurisdiction

The jurisdiction of the ICTR is based on several principles of jurisdiction, which are considered the basic elements of its competence. These are the following:

- The Tribunal has the subject-matter jurisdiction or *ratione materiae*. This means simply that the tribunal has a legal right to hear a case before its jurisdiction by reason of the nature of the criminal acts involved.
- The Tribunal has jurisdiction over persons or *ratione persona*, which relates to the concept of the international criminal responsibility of individuals. This means that the Tribunal has a legal right to jurisdiction over those who have violated the provisions of international criminal law. In other words, participating in, preparing or committing grave breaches of international humanitarian law in the former Yugoslavia is a matter of individual responsibility.Accused persons cannot escape from the jurisdiction of the Tribunal by referring to the order of superiors or acts carried out under the international legal personality of the state.
- Another principle is territorial jurisdiction or *ratione loci* which constitutes one of the oldest principles of jurisdiction. This principle refers to the relevant territory in which the criminal acts have been planned and committed by the perpetrators. According to the Statute, "The territorial jurisdiction of the International Tribunal shall extend to the territory of the former Socialist Federal Republic of Yugoslavia, including its land surface, airspace and territorial waters"[32]
- The jurisdiction of the ICTY is based on temporal jurisdiction or *ratione temporis*. This principle clarifies from which particular time the Tribunal has jurisdiction over the acts of criminals. This means that the Tribunal must have a definite starting time in order to prosecute the acts of the accused under its jurisdiction. The

---

[32] Article 8 of the Statute.

temporal jurisdiction of the ICTY is therefore extended to a period beginning on 1 January 1991.[33]

- Another important principle governing the competence of the Tribunal is that its character is temporary and not permanent. This means that the Tribunal will function for a period of time to prosecute and punish those who have committed international crimes. That is why the Tribunal has an *ad hoc* character. Although the Tribunal will end its jurisdiction, this will not prevent other tribunals in the territories of the former Yugoslavia and other parts of the world from prosecuting and punishing those who have for one reason or another escaped from the jurisdiction of the tribunal.
- The ICTY and national courts have been given concurrent jurisdiction over persons who have committed international crimes. This means that both have been given rights and duties to prosecute and punish criminals. However, the ICTY has primacy over national courts whenever it is deemed necessary for the implementation of its provisions and rules.[34] It may therefore formally ask national courts to wait for its primacy over the case to be determined, in order for the Tribunal to take precedence.[35] But

---

[33] Article 8 of the Statute.

[34] However, in certain situations the ICTY has exercised cooperative jurisdiction with national courts. In the Novislav Djajic and Nikola Jorgic cases, the prosecutor clarifies the relationship between the prosecutor of the ICTY and the German legal authorities with the following words "Justice Arbour points out that reports that these cases are being prosecuted in Germany because the ICTY's court case-load is too heavy are simply not correct. Equally erroneous are press suggestions that the International Tribunal has somehow "failed" to prosecute these cases itself. The true position is that the International Tribunal and national courts have concurrent jurisdiction, and that such cases can be properly prosecuted in either forum. The establishment of the International Tribunal has not affected the obligation under international law for national authorities to apprehend and prosecute, under their own domestic legislation, persons who have committed serious violations of international humanitarian law. The prosecution of such cases is not the exclusive domain of the ICTY, although the Tribunal can exercise primacy over national court. The Djajic and Jorgic cases were initiated and investigated by the German authorities, who Seed with the Office of the Prosecutor of the International Tribunal. The Prosecutor assessed that it was not appropriate to seek a deferral of these cases, and the decision was made that they continue to be prosecuted by the German authorities. There is on-going co-operation between the Prosecutor and the German authorities on these and other cases." CC/PIO/171-E, The Hague, 19 March 1997, *www.icty.org/sid/7565. Visited on 2009-11-09.*

[35] Article 9 of the Statute has clearly stated that "1. The International Tribunal and national courts shall have concurrent jurisdiction to prosecute persons for serious

this does not prevent national courts from prosecuting persons for serious violations of international humanitarian law committed in the territory of the former Yugoslavia when it has not been requested that a case be deferred to the competence of the ICTY or when they are dealing with two different cases of persons having been accused of committing crimes enumerated in Articles 2 to 5. In this way, some persons have been prosecuted within the national jurisdiction of other states, for instance, in Sweden.

3.3. The Machinery of the ICTY

The ICTY is one of several temporary organs acting under the provisions of the United Nations. It is composed of different parts responsible for carrying out its functions: chambers, prosecutors and a registry.[36] The latter serves both of the former. The chambers are divided into three trial chambers and an appeals chamber. The conditions for the composition of the chambers are:

1. Chambers are composed of sixteen permanent independent judges. The judges must not be of the same nationality;
2. A maximum at any one time of twelve *ad litem* independent judges are to be appointed in accordance with article 13 ter, paragraph 2, of the Statute;
3. No two judges may be nationals of the same State;
4. Three permanent judges and a maximum at any one time of nine *ad litem* judges shall be members of each Trial Chamber;
5. Each Trial Chamber to which *ad litem* judges are assigned may be divided into sections of three judges each, composed of both permanent and *ad litem* judges, except in the circumstances specified;
6. A section of a Trial Chamber shall have the same powers and responsibilities as a Trial Chamber under the Statute and shall render judgement in accordance with the same rules;
7. Seven of the permanent judges shall be members of the Appeals Chamber;
8. The Appeals Chamber shall, for each appeal, be composed of five of its members;

---

violations of international humanitarian law committed in the territory of the former Yugoslavia since 1 January 1991. 2. The International Tribunal shall have primacy over national courts. At any stage of the procedure, the International Tribunal may formally request national courts to defer to the competence of the International Tribunal in accordance with the present Statute and the Rules of Procedure and Evidence of the International Tribunal."

[36] Article 11 of the Statute.

9. A person who for the purposes of membership of the Chambers of the International Tribunal could be regarded as a national of more than one State shall be deemed to be a national of the State in which that person ordinarily exercises civil and political rights;
10. In accordance with the request of the President of the International Tribunal, the Secretary-General may appoint, from among the *ad litem* judges, reserve judges to be present at each stage of a trial to which they have been appointed and if necessary to replace a judge if that judge is unable for one reason or another to continue sitting;
11. In the event that exceptional circumstances require a permanent judge in a section of a Trial Chamber to be replaced resulting in a section solely comprising of *ad litem* judges, that section may continue to hear the case without prejudice, notwithstanding that its composition no longer includes a permanent judge.

4. Dimensions of the Statute of the ICTR

The competence or the legal personality of the ICTR can be found within two articles.[37] The Tribunal has thus, similarly to the ICTY, a temporary character such that its international legal validity is limited to specified territories and periods. In other words, it is an *ad hoc* Tribunal. According to its Statute, the ICTR is authorized to punish individuals who have committed crimes against humanity, genocide and serious violations of the international humanitarian law of armed conflicts.[38] This means that the Tribunal has no legal power to prosecute or punish organizations.[39] Its power is over the individuals who have committed crimes in the territories of Rwanda. The scope of the jurisdiction of the Tribunal is also clearly described as the territory of Rwanda including its land and airspace.[40] The borderline of the functions of the Tribunal concerning the prosecution of individuals may also be extended to include Rwandan citizens found responsible for such violations committed in the territory of neighbouring states.[41] This means that it has concurrent jurisdiction to prosecute persons for various crimes.[42] This concurrent jurisdiction is also given to national courts to prosecute and punish those who are accused of committing

[37] The Statute, Articles 1 and 5.
[38] Article 5.
[39] Article 1.
[40] Article 7.
[41] Id.
[42] Alexander Zahar, *Command Responsibility of Civilian Superiors for Genocide*, 14 (3) Leiden Journal of International Law, Hague International Tribunals (2001), pp. 591-616.

genocide, crimes against humanity and serious violations of the humanitarian law of armed conflicts.[43] However, it must be emphasised that the Tribunal has priority of jurisdiction over accused persons and it may, if necessary, request national courts to defer to its competence in the Statute and the Rules of Procedure and Evidence.[44]

4.1. Mechanism of the Tribunal

The ICTR has different organs fulfilling different functions. These are the Chambers, comprising the three Trial Chambers and the Appeals Chamber, the Prosecutor and the Registry. The Chambers consist of sixteen judges possessing the necessary qualifications. In the composition of the Chambers and sections of the Trial Chambers, special attention is given to judges who have experience in criminal law, international law, international humanitarian law and human rights law.

The Office of the Prosecutor is the organ of the Tribunal responsible for the investigation of all aspects of the crimes with due regard to the jurisdiction of the Tribunal. Similarly, the Registry is another organ of the ICTR. It has a duty concerning the administration and management of the Tribunal. It gathers information for legal and judicial support services to the Prosecutor and the Trial Chambers. It also makes arrangements for contact with witnesses and victims. As part of this function, the Registry organises the Witnesses and Victims Support Section as well as obtaining and managing information regarding witnesses' identity, location, and so on.The Registry arranges access to witnesses and victims before, during and after proceedings as well as protecting their anonymity.

The Registry is also responsible for providing defence counsel.[45] However, the situation varies regarding the accused persons. They may themselves obtain counsel of their own choice.[46] In certain situations where they cannot afford counsel, the Tribunal may assist them. In any event, the Registry may assist them in selecting counsel in accordance with their own wishes.

---

[43] Id.

[44] Article 8.

[45] See *also* Michail Wladimiroff, *The Assignment of Defence Counsel before the International Criminal Tribunal for Rwanda*, 12 (4) Leiden Journal of International Law (1999), pp. 957-968.

[46] Id.

5. Competence of the SCSL

The SCSL operates with the status of a hybrid court. This means that it has a mixed jurisdiction consisting of national and international provisions, principles and judges. The Court is authorized under the legal and political sponsorship of the United Nations. Among the strongest reasons for the creation of this category of court was the need to resolve the problems of the transportation of victims and witnesses, the issue of arrest warrants for the prosecution of accused persons and access to evidence.

According to the Statute of the Special Court, the Court consists of trial chambers, appeals chamber, prosecutor and registry.[47] Each of these organs has their own specific function. The Statute also requires that the judicial staff of the Special Court is comprised of a combination of international and domestic judges. They should be persons of high moral character and integrity, and should possess the qualifications required in their respective countries. In particular, they should be independent and should not accept any instruction from any source for the treatment or implementation of a case.[48]

As a whole, the competence of the jurisdiction of the Special Court is dealt with in Article 1 of its Statute. The relevant article consists of three subparagraphs. The first concerns the power of the Special Court to prosecute persons who have the heaviest responsibility for serious infringements of international humanitarian law and certain rules or provisions of Sierra Leonean law carried out and committed in the territory of Sierra Leone. The bearers of this responsibility are also those leaders who, in connection with violations of international humanitarian law, have threatened the process of peace in Sierra Leone. The competence of the Special Court is not unlimited since it does not cover the majority of the period of conflict between 1991 and 1996 but starts on 30 November 1996. This means that the Special Court has no legal power over any person who has committed acts against its Statute before that date.

The second sub-paragraph emphasises that the Special Court has no jurisdiction over peacekeepers who have acted wrongly in the territory of Sierra Leone.[49] It reads that "Any transgressions by peacekeepers and

---

[47] Article 11 of the Statute of the SCSL.

[48] Article 13.

[49] The question of the jurisdiction of a court over peacekeepers has been discussed in several ways in international meetings. The United States has not taken a positive view regarding this question and has tried to ignore any such jurisdiction. For example, it has long opposed the establishment of an international criminal court. The reason is that it does not want its peacekeepers to face politically

related personnel present in Sierra Leone pursuant to the Status of Mission Agreement in force between the United Nations and the Government of Sierra Leone or agreements between Sierra Leone and other Governments or regional organizations, or, in the absence of such agreement, provided that the peacekeeping operations were undertaken with the consent of the Government of Sierra Leone, shall be within the primary jurisdiction of the sending State." According to this sub-paragraph, the Special Court is not permitted to deal with the criminal wrongful conduct of a peacekeeper. He/she may only be prosecuted under the jurisdiction of their own state.[50]

The provisions of sub-paragraph 2 have however, in certain situations, been modified by the provisions of sub-paragraph 3. Accordingly, the Special Court may exercise jurisdiction over such a person accused of committing crimes under the Statute if the sending State does not want or does not have the capability to carry out an investigation or prosecution. In this case, the competence of the Special Court has to be authorized by the Security Council.[51]

5.1. Limitation of Jurisdiction

The Special Court and national courts have concurrent jurisdiction over the crimes listed in the Statute, with the reservation that the Special Court

---

motivated prosecutions. For the same reason, the Special Court in Sierra Leone did not receive any power of jurisdiction over the peacekeepers of any state, who had acted wrongly during their mission. For instance, in Sierra Leone, two Ukrainian soldiers raped a women and a Guinean soldier raped a 12 year old girl. Another example is the sexual exploitation and abuse perpetrated by the Indian peacekeepers in Congo. See www.guardian.co.uk/world/2003/ jan/16/sierraleone. west Africa - 70k; zero_tolerance_for_sexual.../3363294.cms - 39k, visited on 20/11/2008. For some measures against sex abuse by the United Nations peacekeepers urged by the United States See www.america.gov/st/ washfile-english/2005/July/20050727185147adynne d0.469494.html.Visited on 20/11/2008.

[50] It seems that states which have contributed to the peacekeeping process do not want their individuals, even if their actions are against the Statute of the Special Court, to be brought before the jurisdiction of the Court. They have fought to keep the rights of jurisdiction over their nationals.

[51] The Security Council has, therefore, legal and political control over the Special Court in this matter. Whilst the policy of the United Nations is understandable because of the circumstances of its peacekeepers, it seems that the prosecutor of the Court is forced to put a different weight on crimes that have been carried out at the time of armed conflict. The rape of civilians should be treated by the same regulations, as long as an armed conflict has not come to an end.

has primacy of jurisdiction over the national courts of Sierra Leone.[52] A national court should therefore defer its competence if the Special Court formally requests this.[53] This means that all the crimes within Article 2, 3, 4 and 5 are under the concurrent jurisdiction of the Special Court.[54]

Although the Special Court takes decisions over all matters of jurisdiction, its jurisdiction is limited to persons who are over 15 years old. Thus, the Special Court does not have any jurisdiction over persons who are under the age of 15. They are considered children.[55] This means that if a person at the time of the alleged commission of the crime was under the age of 15, the Special Court exercises no criminal jurisdiction.[56]

Furthermore, the Statute restricts the authority of the Special Court over those who at the time of the alleged commission of the crime were between 15 and 18 years of age. It clearly states that the Court shall treat him/her "with dignity and a sense of worth, taking into account his or her young age and the desirability of promoting his or her rehabilitation, reintegration into and assumption of a constructive role in society, and in

---

[52] For an examination of the principle of primacy of jurisdiction See generally Frédéric Mégret., *In Defense of Hybridity: Towards a Representational Theory of International Criminal Justice,* 38-3 Cornell International Law Journal 725-751 (2005).

[53] See generally *ibid.*

[54] Article 8.

[55] For an examination of the prohibition of the use of children in the time of armed conflict see Farhad Malekian., *Prohibition Governing Child Soldiers Constituting an Integral Part of Jus Cogens and Obligatio Erga Omnes,* XVII World Congress of the International Association of Youth and Family Judges and Magistrates, Belfast, Northern Ireland, 27 August – 2 September, 2006. http://www.youthandfamily2006.com/welcome.htm.

[56] This rule has today become one of the most important principles in the protection of the rights of children and the protection of arrested, detained and even unlawfully convicted children. This principle speaks about the protection of persons who are at the time of the commission of crimes under the age of 15. Although the respect of this principle is very important for the maintenance of justice, the practice of some states demonstrates that their authorities often violate its implementation. Although the execution of juveniles is an abolished institute in international law, some states, such as Iran and the United States, execute juveniles. See Kerstin Nordlöf, Unga Lagöverträdare i Social, Straff- och Processrätt (2005); Kerstin Nordlöf, Straffprocessuella Tvångsmedel: Gripande, Anhållande och Häktning (1987); Kerstin Nordlöf, The Legal Philosophy of Protecting a Suspect Child, Journal of the XVII World Congress of the International Association of Youth and Family Judges and Magistrates in Belfast, Northern Ireland, 27 August – 1September 2006; Kerstin Nordlöf, Straffrättens Processer för Unga Lagöverträdare (1991).

accordance with international human rights standards, in particular the rights of the child."[57]

The above provisions are strengthened with further provisions in order to guarantee a minimum standard of justice for juveniles. Specifically, the Special Court has a duty of care regarding the juvenile offender and as such may be required to order any of the following: foster care; care guidance and supervision orders; correctional, educational and vocational training programmes; community service orders; counselling; approved schools and, where appropriate, programmes of disarmament, demobilization and reintegration or programmes of child protection agencies.[58]

5.2. The Mixed Policy

The Statute of the SCSL is different from that of other *ad hoc* tribunals because of its mixed policy regarding the jurisdiction of international and national criminal courts. Nevertheless, in many other aspects it follows the policy of other tribunals. The Special Court, like its predecessors, the ICTY and the ICTR, has a combination of Trial Chambers and Appeals Chambers. The Special Court consists of eleven judges. There are three judges in each of the two Trial Chambers and five in the Appeals Chambers. The United Nations has two appointed judges in each Trial Chamber and three judges in the Appeals Chamber. The remaining four judges are from Sierra Leone and are divided between seats in the Trial Chambers and the Appeals Chamber. The Trial Chamber II also has an alternative judge who is appointed by the government of Sierra Leone.[59]

The judgment of the Special Court should be rendered by a majority of the judges.[60] The penalties may include imprisonment for a specific number of years.[61] The term of imprisonment may be served in Sierra Leone or in the states with which the ICTR and the ICTY have an agreement for the enforcement of sentences.[62]

The Trial Chamber is advised to have recourse to the same practices concerning the setting of prison sentences as the ICTR and national courts

[57] Article 7 (1).

[58] Article 7 (2).

[59] One serious problem faced by the Special Court is its funding which is based on direct voluntary contributions by different states. Approximately 80% of the voluntary funding is granted by Canada, Great Britain, the Netherlands and the United States.

[60] Article 18 of the Statute of the SCSL.

[61] This is not however for the juvenile cases.

[62] Article 22 of the Statute of the SCSL.

of Sierra Leone. Additionally, the penalty of imprisonment may be supplemented by the forfeiture of property, the proceeds of crime and any assets acquired illegally, in order for them to be returned to their rightful owner. The severity of the sentence imposed should be proportional to the gravity of the offence and take into account the circumstances of the convicted person.[63]

The Statute has also provided for an Appeals Chamber, which hears appeals from convicted persons. This may be on the basis of a procedural, legal or factual error. The judges of the Appeals Chamber may take into consideration the decisions of the ICTY and the ICTR. When applying the laws of Sierra Leone, they should take into consideration the decisions of the Supreme Court of Sierra Leone.[64] To ensure the appropriate implementation of justice, the Statute allows for review proceedings to take place when a new fact has been discovered which could have had a significant effect on the decision of the trial. In such cases the convicted person or the prosecutor may submit an application for a review of the judgment. It must be noted that review proceedings may only take place in cases where there is a fact that was not known about at the time of the proceedings. In any event, it is the Appeals Chamber which decides about the validity or the merit of the new fact and which may reject or accept the case for a review proceeding.[65]

6. The Framework of the Statute of the ICC

6.1. Formation

The Statute of the International Criminal Court (ICC) or *Cour pénale internationale*[66] was worked out and drafted under the auspices of the General Assembly of the United Nations Organization.[67] This significant

[63] Article 19.
[64] Article 20.
[65] Article 21.
[66] It was signed on 17 July 1998 and came into force on 1 July 2002.
[67] For the earlier works of the General Assembly see for instance the Memorandum entitled "Historical survey of the question of international criminal jurisdiction" (document A/CN.4/7/Rev.1 published in United Nations publication, Sales No. 1949.V.8) and bibliography on International Criminal Law and International Criminal Court (document A/CN.4/28). See further M. Cherif Bassiouni, *Policy Perspectives Favouring the Establishment of the International Criminal Court,* 52 Journal of International Affairs 795 (1999); Fanny Benedetti and John L. Washburn, *Drafting the International Criminal Court Treaty: Two Years to Rome and an Afterword on the Rome Diplomatic Conference,* 5 Global Governance 1

work was based on the draft Statute of the International Law Commission in 1994[68], which has been evaluated from different aspects.[69] On the basis of a General Assembly decision, an Ad Hoc Committee was created and met on two occasions in 1995.[70] During these significant meetings, representatives of states expressed different opinions regarding the creation of the ICC.[71] Controversies arose concerning the scope and the

---

(1999); M. Bachrach, *The Permanent International Criminal Court: An Examination of the Statutory Debate*, 5 ILSA Journal of International and Comparative Law 139 (1998).;Jose A. Baez, *An International Crimes Court: Further Tales of the King of Corinth,* 23 Georgia Journal of International and Comparative Law 289 (1993); Kofi Annan, *Advocating for an International Criminal Court,* 21 Fordham International Law Journal 363 (1997); J. Holmes Jr. Armstead, *The International Criminal Court: History, Development and Status,* 38 Santa Clara Law Review 745 (1998); Kelly Dawn Askin, *Crimes Within the Jurisdiction of the International Criminal Court*, 10 Criminal Law Forum 33 (1999); L. S. Bickley, *US Resistance to the International Criminal Court: Is the Sword Mightier than the Law,* 14 Emory International Law Review 159 (2000); J. R. Bolton and K. Roth, *Toward an International Criminal Court? A Debate,* 14 Emory International Law Review 159 (2000); Audrey I. Benison, *International Criminal Tribunals: Is There a Substantive Limitation on the Treaty Power?,* 37 Stanford Journal of International Law 75 (2001); Bradley E. Berg, *The 1994 ILC Draft Statute for an International Criminal Court: A Principled Appraisal of Jurisdictional Structure,* 28 Case Western Reserve Journal of International Law 221 (1996); Bruce Broomhall, *The International Criminal Court: A Checklist for National Implementation,* 13 *Quarter* Nouvelles etudes pénales 113 (1999); Bruce Broomhall, *Looking Forward to the Establishment of an International Criminal Court: Between State Consent and the Rule of Law,* 8 Criminal Law Forum 317 (1997).

[68] But for an earlier draft Statute for an International Criminal Court see Official Records of the General Assembly, Seventh Session, Supplement No. 11 (A/2136). For more discussion see also Official Records of the General Assembly, Twenty-ninth Session, Annexes, agenda item 86, document A/9890, para.2.

[69] See Bradley E. Berg, The 1994 I.L.C. Draft Statute for an International Criminal Court: A Principled Appraisal of Jurisdictional Structure, 28 Case Western Reserve Journal of International Law 221 (Spring 1996).

[70] See also Fanny Benedetti & John L. Washburn, *Drafting the International Criminal Court Treaty: Two Years to Rome and an Afterward on the Rome Diplomatic Conference*, 5 Global Governance: 1 A Review of Multilateralism and International Organizations 1-37 (1999).

[71] See Bruce Broomhall, International Justice and the International Criminal Court: Between Sovereignty and the Rule of Law (2003). This book goes through the historical evolution of international criminal justice from the Nuremberg Tribunal to The Hague and the reasons for the basic tensions between the international justice and sovereignty interests.

power of the Court.[72] In particular, questions were raised as to which crimes should be considered as international crimes and dealt with by an international criminal court.[73] This was based on the fact that there were many instruments.[74] Consequently, negotiations and discussions were very heated and had significant consequences.[75]

There was also a serious question concerning the structure of the Court.[76] This was because many states were reluctant to agree to a treaty, which could limit their territorial criminal jurisdiction over various crimes.[77] The question was debated from different aspects and different opinions were expressed.[78] One of the most practical solutions to the problem was based on the concept of the "complementarity" principle.[79]

---

[72] See *id.*

[73] Model Draft Statute for the International Criminal Court Based on the Preparatory Committee's Text to the Diplomatic Conference, Rome, June 15 – July 17, 1998 (Association Internationale de Droit Pénal, Nouvelles Études Pénales No. 13ter) (Leila Sadat Wexler, ed., 1998).

[74] Bassiouni M. Cherif., The Statute of the International Criminal Court and Related Instruments: Legislative History, 1994-2000 (2001).

[75] Id. See also Philippe Kirsch and John T. Holmes, The Rome Conference on an International Criminal Court: The Negotiating Process, 93 American Journal of International Law 2 (1999); Hans-Peter Kaul, Towards a Permanent International Criminal Court: Some Observations of a Negotiator, 8 Human Rights Law Journal 169 (1997); Philippe Kirsch and John T. Holmes, The Rome Conference on an International Criminal Court: The Negotiating Process, 93 American Journal of International Law 2 (1999); Philippe Kirsch and V. Oosterveld, Negotiating an Instrument of the Twenty-First Century: Multilateral Diplomacy and the International Criminal Court, 46 McGill Law Journal 1141 (2001).

[76] Mahnoush H. Arsanjani, *The Rome Statute of the International Criminal Court*, 93 American Journal of International Law 22-43 (1999).

[77] *Id. At* 23-25.

[78] See also Shabtai Rosenne, The World Court: What it is and how it works (1989); The International Criminal Court: The Making of the Rome Statute(Roy S. Lee, ed., 1999).

[79] For some more discussions and analysis see Christopher Keith Hall, The First Proposal for A Permanent International Criminal Court, 322 International Review of the Red Cross (1998); Jamison, Sandra L., A Permanent International Criminal Court: A Proposal that Overcomes Past Objections, 23 (2) Denver Journal of International Law & Policy (1995); Broomhall, Bruce, International Justice and the International Criminal Court: Between Sovereignty and the Rule of Law (2003); Lippman, Matthew., Towards an International Criminal Court, 3 (1) San Diego Justice Journal (1995); MacPherson, Bryan F., *Building an International Criminal Court for the 21st Century*, 13 (1) Connecticut Journal of International Law (1998); International Criminal Law Reports (Malcolm, Helen and Rodney Dixon, eds., 2000); Maogoto, Jackson Nyamuya, State Sovereignty and International

This means that an international criminal court should have general supremacy over cases where the domestic courts are, for one reason or another, unable or unwilling to take the case under their jurisdiction.[80] In other words, the complementarity principle refers to the prosecution and punishment of criminals at a different level to national courts. This means that there are first and second class priorities, i.e., national and international ones. Both of these are, however, independent from one another. It also means that the new international criminal court has to wait to see how domestic courts react to the prosecution and punishment of specific crimes.[81] This suggestion was rather different from the proposals of International Law Commission draft articles.[82]

Another suggestion was that international crimes should be defined in the constitution of the Court. This suggestion was also at variance with the International Law Commission draft that enumerated the crimes. This suggestion increased the power of the Court and reduced the potential for any future conflicts over the interpretation of the scope of enumerated

---

Criminal Law: Versailles to Rome (2003); O'Connor, Gerard E., The Pursuit of Justice and Accountability: Why The United States Should Support the Establishment of an International Criminal Court, 27 (4) Hofstra Law Review (1999); Schabas, William A., An Introduction to the International Criminal Court (2001); Best, Geoffrey, Peace Conferences and the Century of Total War: The 1899 Hague Conference and What Came After, 75 (3) *International Affairs* (1999); Bos, Adriaan, The International Criminal Court: A Perspective, in *The International Criminal Court: The Making of the Rome Statute: Issues, Negotiations, Results* (Roy S. Lee, ed., 1999); Latore, Roseann M., Escape Out the Back Door or Charge in the Front Door: U.S. Reactions to the International Criminal Court, 25 (1) *Boston College International & Comparative Law Review (*2002); Levie, Howard S., History of the Law of War on Land,838 International Review of the Red Cross (2000).

[80] See Bartram S. Brown, Primacy or Complementarity: Reconciling the Jurisdiction of National Courts and International Criminal Tribunals, 23 Yale Journal of International Law 383 (Summer 1998).

[81] See Leila Sadat Wexler, *The Proposed Permanent International Criminal Court: An Appraisal,* 29 Cornell Journal of International Law 665 (1996); Leila Sadat Wexler and S. Richard Carden, *The New International Criminal Court: An Uneasy Revolution,* 88 Georgetown Law Journal 381 (2000); Leila Sadat Wexler, *The Establishment of the International Criminal Court: From The Hague to Rome and Back Again,* 8 DET. Journal of International Law and Practice 97 (1999).

[82] The draft was requested as a matter of priority by the General Assembly in 1993 in its resolution 48/31. It consists of 60 articles. It dealt with genocide, apartheid, exceptionally serious war crimes, aggression, torture, systematic or massive violations of human rights, hijacking, hostage taking and illicit trafficking in narcotic drugs.

crimes. The Ad Hoc Committee also suggested that the statute of the new court should have provisions concerning the application of a high standard of justice and respect for the fundamental principles of human rights law.

6.1.1. Preparatory Committee

Although efforts were made by the Ad Hoc Committee in order to reconcile the differing opinions of states into one single instrument for adoption, this was not successful.[83] In 1995, the General Assembly convened a Preparatory Committee in order to reconsider the drafting of a statute.[84] The Assembly invited member states and international and non-governmental organizations. Meetings were held in 1996, 1997 and

---

[83] M. Cherif Bassiouni, The International Criminal Court: Observations and Issues before the 1997-98 Preparatory Committee, and Administrative and Financial Implications (Toulouse: Chicago: Érès; International Human Rights Institute, DePaul University, 1997)(Nouvelles Études Pénales13) (Joint project of: International Association of Penal Law, International Human Rights Law Institute, DePaul University, International Institute of Higher Studies in Criminal Sciences, International Law Association, American Branch, Committee on ICC); M. Cherif Bassiouni, *Observations Concerning the Structure of the (Zutphen) Consolidated Text,* 13*bis*NouvellesÉtudesPénales 5 (1998). See *also* Jordan J. Paust, Leila Sadat Wexler and Edward M. Wise, *Commentary on Part 2 of the Zutphen Intersessional Draft: General Principles of Criminal Law,* 13*bis*NouvellesÉtudesPénales 27 (1998); James Crawford, *The ILC's Draft Statute for an International Criminal Tribunal,* 88 American Journal of International Law 140 (1994); Dorean M. Koenig, *Commentary on Parts 7 and 8 of the Zutphen Intersessional Draft: General Principles of Criminal Law,* 13*bis*NouvellesÉtudesPénales 95 (1998); Sien Ho Yee, *A Proposal to Reorganize Article 23 of the ILC Draft Statute for an International Criminal Court,* 19 Hastings International and Comparative Law Review 529 (1996);Christopher Keith Hall, *The Fifth Session of the UN Preparatory Committee on the Establishment of an International Criminal Court,* 92 American Journal of International Law331-339 (1998).

[84] *Id.* Adriaan Bos, *The Experience of the Preparatory Committee, in* The Rome Statute of the International Criminal Court: a Challenge to Impunity (Mauro Politi and Giuseppe Nesi, eds., 2004) pp.17-28; Jordan J. Paust, *The Preparatory Committee's 'Definition of Crimes' – War Crimes* 8 CRIMINAL LAW FORUM 431 (1997); Dorean M. Koenig and Christopher C. Joyner, *Model Draft Statute for the International Criminal Court Based on the Preparatory Committee's Text to the Diplomatic Conference, Rome, June 15 – July 17, 1997, Parts 7 and 8,* 13*ter*NouvellesÉtudesPénales 111 (1998); Christopher Keith Hall, *The First Two Sessions of the UN Preparatory Committee on the Establishment of an International Criminal Court,* 91 American Journal of International Law 177 (1997).

1998.[85] The most important of all these meetings and negotiations[86] resulted in the "Zutphen draft" in the Netherlands. The Diplomatic Conference finally recorded this draft for examination. From 1995 to 1998, the Preparatory Committee (which became known as PrepCommand), which was working with the questions of the establishment of the court, resolved the most serious issues relating to the juridical effect of the power of the Court on national legal systems.[87]

At the General Assembly's request, in its resolutions adopted in 1996 and 1997, the United Nations Diplomatic Conference of Plenipotentiaries on the Establishment of an International Criminal Court assembled in Rome on 15 June 1998.[88] It was the first time in the history of international criminal law that an overwhelming majority of states of the world had gathered to discuss the establishment of an international criminal court.[89] There were 160 delegations from different states of the world in the headquarters of the Food and Agricultural Organization. There were also other bodies, including international and non-governmental organizations. The time was ripe for the adoption of the constitution of an international criminal court. Among the most important reasons for why participating states supported the idea of the establishment of the court were probably the on-going armed conflicts in different parts of the world and the existence already of two *ad hoc* tribunals, the ICTY

---

[85] Id.

[86] John Washburn, The Negotiation of the Rome Statute for the International Criminal Court and International Lawmaking in the 21st Century, 11 Pace International Law Review 361 (1999).

[87] See The Rome Statute of the International Criminal Court: a Challenge to Impunity (2004), note 1.

[88] Hereafter referred to as "Diplomatic Conference".

[89] For some examinations of international criminal law and its machinery of enforcement see Beth Van Schaack and Ronald C. Slye, International Criminal Law and its Enforcment: Cases and Matterials (2007); M. Cherif Bassiouni, International Criminal Conventions and their Penal Provisions (1997); Ronald C. Slye and Beth Van Schaack, International Criminal Law: The Essentials (2008); Young Sok Kim, Law of the International Criminal Court (2007); Lyal Sunga, The Emerging System of International Criminal Law: Developments in Codification and Implementation(1997); Edwin Shorts, International Criminal Law and Human Rights (2003);Gerhard Werle, Völkerstrafrecht (2007); Jann K. Kleffner, Complementarity in the Rome Statute and National Criminal Jurisdictions: International Courts and Tribunals, (2009); Antonio Cassese, The Oxford Companion to International Criminal Justice (2009); Nancy Combs, Guilty Pleas in International Criminal Law: Constructing a Restorative Justice Approach (2006).

and the ICTR.[90] All of these contributed to the adoption of the Statute of the ICC in 1998.[91]

6.1.2. Positive Reasons

There were several reasons for the positive participation of different states in the continuation of the work on the establishment of an international criminal court.[92] Some states were interested in the structure of the new draft, such as the inherent jurisdiction of the court concerning the core crimes,[93] namely, genocide, crimes against humanity, war crimes and

---

[90] For instance, for an examination of the opinion of African states concerning the creation of ICC see Mohamed Aref, *La Cour Pénale Internationale: une Nouvelle Perspective Pour le Continent Africain,* 1 International Law Forum Du Droit International 30 (1999).

[91] According to one opinion "the Court broadly reflected the aspirations and objectives of the international community." Philippe Kirsch, *The International Criminal Court: A New and Necessary Institution meriting Continued International Support* 28 (2) Fordham International Law Journal (2005), p. 294.

[92] M. Cherif Bassiouni, *Policy Perspectives Favoring the Establishment of the International Criminal Court,* 52 Journal of International Affairs 795-810 (No.2, Spring 1999).

[93] See *Id.* For further discussions and analysis see *also* George Finch, *Draft Statute for an International Criminal Court,* 46 American Journal of International Law 67(1990);M. Cherif Bassiouni, *Draft Statute International Criminal Tribunal,* 9 Nouvellese Etudes Penales (1993); M. Cherif Bassiouni, *A Comprehensive Strategic Approach on International Cooperation for the Prevention, Control and Suppression of International and Transnational Criminality, Including the Establishment of an International Criminal Court,* 15 Nova Law Review 353 (1991); Benjamin Ferencz, *An International Criminal Code and Court: Why They Stand and Where They're Going,* 30 Columbia Journal of Transnational Law 375 (1992); International Courts for the Twenty-First Century (Mark W. Janis ed., 1992); M. Cherif Bassiouni & Christopher Blakesley, *The Need for an International Criminal Court in the New International World Order* 25 V. and J. Transnat'l 151 (1992); Peter Burns, *An International Criminal Tribunal: The Difficult Union of Principle and Politics,* 5Criminal Law Forum 341 (1994); James Crawford, *The ILC's Draft Statute for an International Criminal Tribunal, 88* American Journal of International Law140 (1994); Timothy C. Evered. *An International Criminal Court: Recent Proposals and American Concerns,* 6 Pace International Law Review 121 (1994); Sandra L. Jamison, *A Permanent International Criminal Court: A Proposal that Overcomes Past Objections,* 23 Denver International Law and Policy 2 (1995); James Crawford, *Prospects for an International Criminal Court,* 48 Current Legal Problems 303 (1995); Henri D. Bosly, *Actualité du Tribunal International Pénal, 1-2* h's.4 Les Droit de Lowain 3 (1995); Brigitte Stern, *La Cour Criminelle Internationaledans le Projet de la*

aggression.[94] They appreciated above all that the principle of complementarity created for states the primary right of jurisdiction over international crimes.[95] This meant that they did not need to mobilize themselves against the establishment of the Court.[96] Their domestic systems were given priority before international systems so that they would not refuse to sign and ratify the statute. It was also argued that an independent prosecutor with the power to initiate proceedings against the alleged perpetrators of crimes would help the functioning of an independent international jurisdiction.[97] Another important matter was that it became obvious in the drafting of the statute that the court could not be established if the Security Council could not obtain certain rights concerning the description of international crimes.[98]

Commission du Droit International, in International Legal Issues Arising Under United Nations Decade of International Law 739-60 (1995); Substantive and Procedural Aspects of International Criminal Law: The Experience of International and National Courts, Documents 3 vols. (Gabrielle Kirk McDonald, Olivia Swaak-Goldman, eds., 2002).

[94] For an earlier discussion concerning the need for the creation of an international criminal court see Jeffrey L. Bleich, *Problems Facing The War Crimes Tribunal And The Need For A Permanent International Criminal Court*, 16 Whittier Law Review 404 (1995).

[95] See Jennifer J. Llewellyn, A Comment on the Complementary Jurisdiction of the International Criminal Court: Adding Insult to Injury in Transitional Contexts? 24 Dalhousie Law Journal 192 (2001); William A. Schabas., Complementarity in Practice: Creative Solutions or a Trap for the Court in The Rome Statute of the International Criminal Court: a Challenge to Impunity (Mauro Politi and Federica Gioia, editors, 2001), 25-48, at 31; Frédéric Mégret., In Defense of Hybridity: Towards a Representational Theory of International Criminal Justice, 38-3 Cornell International Law Journal 725-751 (2005); International Crimes, Peace and Human Rights: The Role of the International Criminal Court(Dinah Shelton ed., 2000); M. Cherif Bassiouni, Mixed Models of International Criminal Justice, in International Criminal Law, Vol iii (M. Cherif Bassiouni, ed. 2008) pp. 155-194; M. Cherif Bassiouni, The Making of the International Criminal Court, in Bassiouni above, pp. 117-154.

[96] Frédéric Mégret, *id.*, at 726.

[97] See also Antonio Marchesi, *initiation of Proceedings before the International criminal Court, in* The International Criminal Court: Comments on the Draft Statute (Flavia Lattanzi, ed. 1998) pp. 121-38.

[98] That is why the Statute does not define the international crime of aggression. See *infera.* However, the new modification will alter the position of the crime of aggression.

The remaining tasks were how to convince the participating states to agree with the statute and how to define aggression clearly.[99] These questions were extremely sensitive and not easy to answer on account of the fact that the attitude of states varied from one another and the issues needed more consideration. As for aggression, when considered as a recognized international crime under the provisions of the Statute, it was impossible to define it and include it in any political and juridical understanding of the question. It was for these reasons that the question was not resolved and it was left up to the authority of the Security Council of the United Nations to decide about any given situation. As for capital punishment, the argumentation in favour of it did not carry any weight and therefore capital punishment is prohibited under the provisions of the Court.[100] One essential reason for the elimination of capital punishment is that the existing instruments of international human rights law do not give any permission to states to exercise capital punishment.[101] The practice is also prohibited under the law of the Statute in order to harmonise its provisions in accordance with the instruments of human rights law. This policy of the Statute has also opened the door to the abolition of capital punishment within the law of other states in the world. It also encourages its abolition within the legislations of other states which still have their own provisions governing the application of the death penalty.

---

[99] See Jacob Katz Cogan, *International Criminal Courts and Fair Trials: Difficulties and Prospects,* 27 Yale Journal of International Law 111-41 (2002); Antonio Cassese, The Statute of the International Criminal Court: Some Preliminary Reflections, 10 European Journal of International Law 158 (1999); Bruce Broomhall, The International Criminal Court: Overview and Cooperation with States, 13 Quarter Nouvelles Etudes Pénales 45 (1999); Marie-Claude Roberge, The New International Criminal Court: A Preliminary Assessment, 325 International Review of the Red Cross 671 (1998); Sharon A. Williams, The Rome Statute on the International Criminal Court: From 1947-2000 and Beyond, 38 Osgood Hall Law Journal 297 (2000); Patrick Zahnd, How the International Criminal Court Should Help Implement International Humanitarian Law, in International cCimes, Peace and Human Rrights: The Role of the International Criminal Court (Dinah Shelton, ed., 2000) pp.35-42; Andreas Zimmermann, The Creation of a Permanent International Criminal Court, 2 Max Planck Yearbook of United Nations Law 169 (1998).

[100] *Id.*

[101] Examine Farhad Malekian Documents on hte Principles of International Human Rights (2007).

6.1.3. Development of Other Agreements

When the Statute of the International Criminal Court was adopted, the Diplomatic Conference also adopted a Final Act on 17 July 1998, which supported the establishment of a Preparatory Commission by the General Assembly of the United Nations. The Commission had different duties, two of which had a more significant role for the jurisdiction of the Court. One was the drafting of the Rules of Procedure and Evidence, which concerns the evidentiary and procedural matters. The other was the drafting of the Elements of Crimes, which essentially concerns the core crimes in the Statute, namely Articles 6, 7 and 8.

The Commission also had other duties such as submitting proposals for a treaty between the United Nations and the ICC in order to formulate their future relations. This was because the ICC is an independent international organization having an international legal personality of its own. The Commission also prepared an agreement between the host state, the Netherlands, and the Court. The seat of the Court is at The Hague and this has to be regulated for the future relations of the parties. The Commission also prepared an agreement on the budget of the Court and on the Privileges and Immunities of the International Criminal Court.[102] The latter agreement has been ratified by a considerable number of states and is an important agreement in securing immunities for the personnel of the Court.[103]

The Statute was signed promptly, but the 60 instruments of ratification or accession were not signed until 11 April 2002.[104] This is because the

[102] See P. Mochochoko, The Agreement on Privileges and Immunities in the International Criminal Court, 25 Fordham International Law Journal 638 (2002).

[103] The Agreement entered into force on 22 July 2004.

[104] See Bassiouni, M. Cherif., Negotiating the Treaty of Rome on the Establishment of an International Criminal Court,43 (2) Cornell International Law Journal (1999); Bassiouni, M. Cherif., From Versailles to Rwanda in Seventy-Five Years: The Need to Establish a Permanent International Criminal Court, 10 Harvard Human Rights Journal 1 (1997); Bassiouni, M. Cherif., Establishing an International Criminal Court: Historical Survey, 149 Military Law Review (1995); Bassiouni, M. Cherif., The Time has Come for an International Criminal Court, 1 (1) Indiana International and Comparative Law Review (1991); Allmand, Warren., The International Criminal Court and the Human Rights Revolution, 46 (1) McGill Law Journal, (2000); Andreasen, Scott W., The International Criminal Court: Does the Constitution Preclude Its Ratification By the United States? 85 (2) Iowa Law Review (2000); Arnaut, Damir., When in Rome? The International Criminal Court and Avenues for U.S. Participation, 43 (2) Virginia Journal of International Law (2003); Arsanjani, Mahnoush H., The Rome Statute of the International Criminal

Statute is essentially based on the complementarity principle and consequently the states were not domestically ready to ratify the treaty.[105] They needed to go through their national legal systems and make sure that they were able to prosecute and punish the perpetrators of war crimes, crimes against humanity and genocide under their own legislations.[106]

The Assembly of States Parties gathered on 3 to 10 September 2002. It discussed various questions, and on the 10th of September, it adopted the following documents: the Rules of Procedure and Evidence and the Elements of Crimes; the Relationship Agreement between the UN and the Court; the Financial Regulations of the Court and the Agreement on Privileges and Immunities of the International Criminal Court. The election of the Judges of the Court took place in February 2003 and the first Prosecutor was elected in April of the same year.

6.1.4. The Hague Invention Act

When the Statute came into force, it caused difficulties for the United States.[107] Its government was not of the opinion that it should ratify the

---

Court, American Journal of International Law, Vol. 93, Issue 1, (1999); Askin, Kelly Dawn, Crimes within the Jurisdiction of the International Criminal Court, 10 (1) Criminal Law Forum (1999); Bachrach, Michael., The Protection and Rights of Victims under International Criminal Law, 34 (1) *The International Lawyer* (2000).

[105] Id.

[106] Id.

[107] David J. Scheffer, *The United States and the International Criminal Court*, 93 American Journal of International Law 12-22 (1999); Henry T. Jr King, and T.C. The of rastous, *From Nuremberg to Rome: A Step Backwards for US Foreign Policy,* 31 Case Western Reserve Journal of International Law 47 (1999); Ruth Wedgewood, *Fiddling in Rome: American and the International Criminal Court,* 77:6 Foreign Affairs 20 (1998); Ruth Wedgewood, *The International Criminal Court: An American View,* 10 European Journal of International Law 93 (1999); Aryeh Neier, *Waiting for Justice: The United States and the International Criminal Court*, 15 World Policy Journal 33 (Fall 1998); Marten Zwanenburg, *The Statute of an International Criminal Court and the United States: Peace without Justice?*, 12 Leiden Journal of International Law 1-8 (no. 1, 1999); Douglass Cassel, *Empowering United States Courts to Hear Crimes Within the Jurisdiction of the International Criminal Court*, 35 New England Law Review 421-445 (2001); The International Criminal Court: Protecting American Servicemen and Officials from the Threat of International Prosecution: Hearing before the Committee on Foreign Relations, United States Senate, One Hundred Sixth Congress, Second Session, June 14, 2000 (Washington, D.C.: U.S. Government Printing Office, 2000). S. Hrg. 106-769. 44-page PDF file; The United States and the International Criminal

Statute of the Court.[108] It therefore reported to the Secretary-General of the United Nations its unwillingness to remain a signatory state to the Statute. Meanwhile, it formulated international agreements with several states in order to protect its nationals from different types of accusation, prosecution and punishment.[109] The agreements between the United States government and these other states were so controversial and juridically outlandish and unreasonable that the European Parliament of the European Union opposed all of those bilateral immunity arrangements.[110] According to the European Parliament, they were against the provisions of the Statute.[111] Consequently, it condemned the American Service-Members' Protection Act in several resolutions.[112]

Court: National Security and International Law (Sarah B. Sewall & Carl Kaysen eds., 2000).

[108] See *id.*

[109] For some examination of the United States opinion see *The United States and the International Criminal Court* (Sarah B. Sewall and Carl Kaysen, eds., 2000).

[110] Rosanne van Alebeek, From Rome to the Hague: Recent Developments on Immunity Issues in the ICC Statute, 13 Leiden Journal of International Law 485 (2000).

[111] The 2 July 2002 European Parliament resolution on the draft American Service members' Protection Act (ASPA) reads in part that "D. noting that, in Rome in 1998, 120 nations voted to create the Court, while only seven nations opposed it, including China, Israel and the US, E whereas the then President Clinton signed the Rome Statute, thus allowing for substantial US participation in secondary legislation under the Statute, but recommended that his successor should not forward the Treaty to the Senate for advice and consent for ratification, F. noting that both Houses of the US Congress have now passed legislation which seeks, inter alia, to:
- prohibit US participation in UN or other peacekeeping missions unless US personnel are exempted from ICC jurisdiction;
- insist that any Security Council resolution authorising peacekeeping should give US personnel permanent exemption from ICC jurisdiction;
- prohibit cooperation by any US public body in ICC investigations;
- prohibit intelligence cooperation with any country that has signed the Rome Statute;
- prohibit military assistance to any country (except NATO members and seven others) which has ratified the Rome Statute;
- authorise the US President to use all necessary and appropriate means to free US or allied personnel detained by or on behalf of the ICC,
G. noting that, by already taking national judicial action itself, the US can prevent its citizens from being brought before the International Criminal Court, H. deeply deploring the fact that on 30 June 2002 the US vetoed in the Security Council the extension of the mandate of the UN Mission in Bosnia and Herzegovina (UNMIBH) beyond 3 July 2002, arguing that peacekeepers should be exempted

from prosecution by the ICC, I. believing that those guilty of war crimes or crimes against humanity should know that they will be brought to justice no matter who they are or which nationality they have, …
5. Calls on the US Congress to reject the unilateralism which the ASPA represents, and to embrace in deeds as well as rhetoric the reality that only the common endeavour of the international community will bring to justice tyrants and perpetrators of genocide or other crimes against humanity, including terrorists; 6. Points out that the new bill strongly contrasts with the founding treaties of NATO and the WEU, which have been built on unreserved partnership and solidarity between the partners in case of armed attack on one of the signatories, and on abstention from violence in resolving conflicts between the partners …" P5_TA-PROV(2002)0367, Consequences for transatlantic relations of law on the protection of US personnel European Parliament resolution on the draft American Service members' Protection Act (ASPA). See *also* Marten Zwanenburg, *The Statute for an International Criminal Court and the United States: Peacekeepers under Fire?,* 10 European Journal of International Law 124 (1999).

[112] The 26 September 2002 European Parliament Resolution on the ICC condemning UN Security Council Resolution 1422 and asking Member States not to sign bilateral agreements with the US provides very important and valuable principles. It reads that:
The European Parliament,
- having regard to its previous resolutions on the International Criminal Court, in particular those of 19 November 1998, 18 January 2001, 28 February 2002 and its resolution of 4 July 2002 on the draft American Service members' Protection Act (ASPA),
- having regard to the Rome Statute of the International Criminal Court and in particular Articles 16, 86 and 98 thereof,
- having regard to the declaration of 1 July 2002 on the International Criminal Court by the Council Presidency on behalf of the EU,
A. whereas a positive development in transatlantic relations could reinforce the convergence between the European Union and the USA as regards the major values and objectives of democracy and the rule of law and should take place in the framework of a strong commitment to a multilateral approach to problems,
B. whereas the Rome Statute makes a decisive contribution to the implementation of international law and justice and can thus be seen as part of the Copenhagen political criteria,
C. regretting UN Security Council Resolution 1422 adopted on 12 July 2002 on operations established or authorised by the United Nations, whereby the ICC shall not commence or proceed with investigation or prosecution of any case of acts or omissions by current or former officials or personnel from a contributing State not a party to the Rome Statute for a twelve-month period starting on 1 July 2002, with the possibility of renewal each 1 July for a further twelve-month period,
D. whereas the current worldwide political pressure being exerted by the government of the United States to persuade States Parties and Signatory States of the Rome Statute, as well as non-signatory states, to enter into bilateral immunity

agreements which seek, through misuse of its Article 98, to prevent US government officials, employees, military personnel or nationals from being surrendered to the International Criminal Court should not succeed with any country, in particular with the Member States, the candidate countries, the countries involved in the Stabilisation and Association Process, the countries associated with the EU in the Euro-Mediterranean partnership, the Mercosur, Andean Pact and San José Process countries or the ACP countries,
E. regretting that the Council and the Commission did not address clear political guidelines in this regard to the candidate countries, as well as to all the other countries associated with the EU under various agreements,
F. deeply disappointed by the decision of the Romanian government to sign an agreement with the United States contradicting the spirit of the status of the ICC and worried that three other candidate countries - the Czech Republic, Lithuania and Malta - have not yet ratified the treaty,
G. taking the view that Turkey's failure even to sign the Treaty is unacceptable,
H. deeply concerned at the approach to the ICC expressed by representatives of some of the governments of Member States during the informal meeting of the EU foreign ministers in Helsinki on 29 and 30 August 2002 and at the lack of clear information on the outcome of the meeting held in New York on 13 September 2002 between the US Administration and the Foreign Affairs Ministers of the Member States,
I. whereas the independent prosecutor may prosecute criminal acts before the ICC which are not prosecuted in the State Party whose national has committed the crime,
J. insisting that the common guidelines that the Council is to adopt on 30 September 2002 should not represent any step backwards in EU support for the full effectiveness of the ICC and should respect the letter and spirit of the EU common position already adopted in this regard,
1. Underlines that no immunity agreement should ever afford the possibility of impunity for any individual accused of war crimes, crimes against humanity or genocide;
2. Underlines the heavy US involvement in peacekeeping operations and considers that the credibility of the EU position vis-à-vis the United States could be strengthened by accepting a proportionate contribution to peacekeeping operations;
3. Firmly believes that the ICC States Parties and Signatory States are obliged under international law not to defeat the object and purpose of the Rome Statute, under which, according to its Preamble, - the most serious crimes of concern to the international community as a whole must not go unpunished - and that States Parties are obliged to cooperate fully with the Court, in accordance with Article 86 of the Rome Statute, thus preventing them from entering into immunity agreements which remove certain citizens from the States' or the International Criminal Court's jurisdictions, undermining the full effectiveness of the ICC and jeopardising its role as a complementary jurisdiction to the State jurisdictions and a building block in collective global security;

4. Stresses that the Rome Statute was ratified by all Member States as an essential component of the democratic model and values of the European Union and calls upon the Member States to make the Rome Statute a part of the Community acquis;
5. Expects the governments and parliaments of the Member States to refrain from adopting any agreement which undermines the effective implementation of the Rome Statute; considers in consequence that ratifying such an agreement is incompatible with membership of the EU;
6. Addresses the same request to the candidate countries, the countries associated with the EU in the Euro-Mediterranean partnership, the Mercosur, Andean Pact and San José Process countries, the countries involved in the Stabilisation and Association Process and the ACP countries which are parties or signatories to the Statute; encourages the parliaments of Romania, Israel, Tajikistan, East Timor, Honduras, India, Uzbekistan, Mauritania, Palau, the Marshall Islands and the Dominican Republic not to ratify the agreements signed by their governments with the United States, under Article 98 of the Rome Statute;
7. Invites all Signatory States to ratify the Statute and calls in particular on the Czech Republic - currently in the chair of the UN General Assembly -, Lithuania and Malta to do so as a matter of the utmost urgency in order to prevent any delay in the on-going process of EU accession;
8. Is convinced that the Member States and candidate countries should act as a single block in the establishment of the ICC in order to commit fully to it and to enable it to succeed in preserving its independence, impartiality and integrity, in particular by:
- reinforcing the EU political dialogue with the United States, inside and outside the Transatlantic Dialogue, with the purpose of persuading its government to change its attitude towards the ICC,
- reinforcing EU financial support for the ICC through the funding of actions under the European Initiative for Human Rights,
- adopting a common approach to the future appointment of its judges, prosecutor and staff; respecting the principles of transparency and full consistency with the criteria of the Rome Statute, in particular on gender equality;
9. Invites the Conference of European Affairs Committees (COSAC) to examine, at its next meeting in October 2002, the current situation regarding the ICC and the possible violation of the Rome Statute by the bilateral agreements proposed by the USA government under its Article 98;
10. Invites the governments and national parliaments of the candidate countries and all other countries associated with the EU under various agreements respectively to sign and ratify the ICC Treaty immediately;
11. Recalls its request to the Council to present to the European Parliament a progress report on the ICC before the next Copenhagen European Council in December 2002; is of the opinion that this report should identify any international agreement related to the ICC and evaluate its compatibility with the Rome Statute, and therefore with the Community acquis; 1 Under points II 5 and 6 of the

The situation became even more embarrassing when the United States proclaimed that it would veto all resolutions of the Security Council governing peacekeeping and collective security operations if the Council did not pass a resolution granting the members of those operations certain immunities from the jurisdiction of the ICC.[113] The United States even

---

Protocol to the Treaty of Amsterdam on the "role of National Parliaments in the European Union".
12. Urges Member States, candidate countries and all other countries associated with the EU under various agreements to undertake an analysis of the legal implications of Security Council Resolution 1422, and calls for strong action against the renewal of the UN Security Council Resolution in July 2003;
13. Reminds Member States of their obligations regarding the prohibition of the death penalty and the European Arrest Warrant, and calls for an in-depth analysis of the legal implications of Article 98 in this area;
14. Instructs its President to forward this resolution to the Council, the Commission, the parliaments of Romania, Israel, Tajikistan and East Timor, Honduras, India, Uzbekistan, Mauritania, Palau, the Marshall Islands and the Dominican Republic the government and Congress of the United States, the UN Secretary-General, COSAC, the national parliaments of the candidate countries and the abovementioned countries associated with the EU under various agreements, and the President of the Assembly of States Parties to the Rome Statute of the ICC." P5_TA-PROV(2002)0449, European Parliament resolution on the International Criminal Court (ICC). Footnotes omitted.

[113] For further examination of the United States' position concerning the ICC see J. L. Talbee, A Call to Arms Declined: The United States and the International Criminal Court, 14 Emory International Law Review 105 (2000); Mohamed El Zeidy, The United States Dropped the Atomic Bomb of Article 16 of the ICC Statute: Security Council Power of Deferrals and Resolution 1422, 35 Vanderbilt Journal of Transnational Law 1503 (2002); D.W. Cassel, *Empowering United States Courts to Hear Crimes Within the Jurisdiction of the International Criminal Court*, 35 New England Law Review 421 (2001); A. Ward, *Breaking the Sovereignty Barrier: The United States and the International Criminal Court*, 41 Santa Clara Law Review 1123 (2001); Christopher Joyner and Christopher C. Posteraro, *The United States and the International Criminal Court: Rethinking the Struggle Between National Interest and International Justice,* 10 Criminal Law Forum 359 (1999); S. W. Krohne, *The United States and the World Need an International Criminal Court as an Ally in the War Against Terrorism,* 8 Indiana International Comparative Law Review 159 (1997); Aryeh Neier, *Waiting for Justice: The United States and the International Criminal Court,* 15 World Policy Journal 33 (1998); Shannon K. Supple, *Global Responsibility and the United States: The Constitutionality of the International Criminal Court*, 27 Hastings Constitutional Law Quarterly 181 (1999); Marten Zwanenburg, The Statute of an International Criminal Court and the United States: Peace Without Justice?, 12 Ledien Journal of International Law 1 (1999); John P. Murphy, *The Quivering*

warned that it would withdraw peacekeeping troops from East Timor.[114] The United States signed into law the American Service-Members' Protection Act, which was supported and passed by the American Congress, in order to strengthen its power over the Court's law and jurisdiction. The Act grants the United States government a status beyond the authority of the United Nations and allows the US, if necessary, to take military or other measures against the Court in order to release United States nationals or other allied personnel detained or imprisoned at The Hague.

The Act has even authorized the President of the United States "to use all means necessary and appropriate to bring about the release of any person … who is being detained or imprisoned by, on behalf of, or at the request of the International Criminal Court." The Act's notoriety was manifest in the name often informally given to it: the "Hague Invasion Act". The purpose of the Act was very clear and in some aspects it went against the basic principles of human rights law. It legally permitted and encouraged persons who had committed criminal acts to go free and not to be prosecuted or punished by the Court. This included not only the past but also the present and the future authorities of the United States government.

These problems aside, the Court is already established and is working on some of the most serious cases concerning violations of international criminal law and core crimes under its jurisdiction. It will, in the near future, hopefully bring the individuals of those states who have managed to escape prosecution and punishment thus far, under international jurisdiction. When the time comes for this type of prosecution, no legislation or act may circumvent the jurisdiction of the Court.

Gulliver: US Views on a Permanent International Criminal Court 34 International Lawyer 45 (2000).

[114] East Timor, a Portuguese colony since the 16th century, declared its independence in 1975. In the same year, the Indonesian government occupied the country as an integral part of its own country. In 1999, a UN-sponsored agreement between Timor, Indonesia, Portugal and the United States, required East Timor to choose between Special Autonomy within Indonesia and independence. The majority of the population voted for independence, but this resulted in violence and atrocities against civilians. It was led by the Indonesian military and aided by Timorese pro-Indonesia militias. Serious crimes against humanity were committed, and this resulted in the United Nations' contributing peacekeeping soldiers.

6.1.5. The *Raison d'être*

All attempts at creating a permanent international criminal court have been motivated by the need to respond to the devastating armed conflicts of the twentieth century[115] in which millions of people perished and were the targets of the use of force, atrocities and inhuman actions of governments.[116] The Statute of the ICC was created in order to put an end to such impunity and injustices.[117] The Preamble of the ICC clearly points out this fact, stating that the states parties to the Statute are "mindful that during this century millions of children, women and men have been victims of unimaginable atrocities that deeply shock the conscience of humanity."

In addition to the above, there are also significant codes relating to the problems arising from those atrocities and the protection of humanity.[118] According to the Statute, one of the necessary conditions for the maintenance of justice and prevention of crime is the establishment of an international criminal court having the authority to prosecute and punish criminals. Accordingly, "the most serious crimes of concern to the international community as a whole must not go unpunished and that their effective prosecution must be ensured by taking measures at a national level and by enhancing international cooperation." Without such measures, serious international crimes are a threat to international peace, security and the wellbeing of the world.[119]

The above codes set out some of the most essential reasons for the creation of the ICC and for its jurisdiction over individuals who have seriously violated the system of international criminal law. They constitute in fact the *raison d'être* for the implementation of the provisions of international treaties which have been seriously violated under the international legal personality of different states. Therefore, the ICC

---

[115] M.Cherif Bassiouni, The Statute of the International Crime Court, (1998).

[116] Priscilla B. Hayner, Unspeakable Truths: Confronting State Terror and Atrocity (2001); Eric David, Principes de droit des conflits armés, (2d ed), (1999); Green, Leslie C. The Contemporary Law of Armed Conflict (2d ed.) (2000).

[117] Adriaan Bos, *The International Criminal Court: A Perspective, in* The International Criminal Court: The Making of the Rome Statute 470 (Roy S. Lee, ed., 1999).

[118] Examine *also* Michael D. Greenberg, *Creating an International Criminal Court*, 10 Boston University International Law Journal 119 (1992); Christopher Keith Hall, *The First Proposal for a Permanent International Criminal Court*, 322 International Review of the Red Cross 75-74 (1998).

[119] See International Criminal Law (M. Cherif Bassiouni, ed., 2nd ed. 3 vols., 1999).

basically upholds five important principles. These are i) implementation of the law, ii) the necessities of accountability, iii) prosecution of the guilty, iv) punishment of criminals and v) prevention or deterrence of the commission of the same crimes in the future international relations of states.

Whilst the *raison d'être* for the creation of the ICC is obvious, the implementation of the law and the accountability of individuals before an international criminal jurisdiction depend on various circumstances.[120] The Court has also dealt with human rights issues[121] at a national and international level.[122]

The question is as always whether the international political community genuinely wants to create a criminal jurisdiction over all the perpetrators of serious international crimes, including genocide, torture, rape, crimes against humanity, war crimes, disappearance of persons, violations of the principles of humanitarian law and serious infringements of the principles of human rights law.[123] The reason for this being that the pure theory of justice is sometimes not workable and many individuals may go without prosecution and punishment.[124] Truth commissions and amnesties may grant impunity by various means of forgiveness and by making use of different forms of political asylum due to the non-existence of extradition treaties. This means that although the *raison d'être* for the establishment of the ICC is clear, there are other factors and political aspirations that have to be worked out in order for the Court to exercise appropriate criminal jurisdiction.[125] Although one may celebrate the creation of such a court for the purpose of the elimination of atrocities, the

---

[120] Audrey I. Benison, War Crimes: A Human Rights Approach to a Humanitarian Law Problem at the International Criminal Court, 88 Georgetown Law Journal 141-176 (1999).

[121] See i*d.*

[122] Kenneth S. Gallant, Sovereignty, Judicial Assistance and Protection of Human Rights in International Criminal Tribunals, 9 *National Law School Law Review* 20 (1997); George E. Edwards, International Human Rights Law Challenges to the New International Criminal Court: The Search and Seizure Right to Privacy, 26 *Yale* Journal of International Law323-412 (2001).

[123] David. S Mitchell, The Prohibition of Rape in International Humanitarian Law as a Norm of Jus Cogens: Clarifying the Doctrine, 15 Duke Journal of Comparative & International Law 219 (2005).

[124] Sometimes the perpetrator of serious violations may also be responsible for the administration of justice *Id.*, at 219.

[125] Questions have often been asked about what is wrong with the Statute of the ICC. See John R. Bolton, *Courting Danger: What's Wrong with the International Court*, The National Interest, No. 54, Winter 1998, at 60-71.

proper implementation of the provisions of the ICC is not a given.[126] This is especially so when one considers that the Statute of the ICC did not examine the question of self-determination. This creates a serious contradiction between the provisions of the ICC and the United Nations Charter and also other relevant international documents.[127] The decisions

---

[126] Adriaan Bos, Dedicated to the Adoption of the Rome Statute of the International Criminal Court 1948-1998: The Universal Declaration of Human Rights and the Statute of the International Criminal Court, 22 Fordham International Law Journal 229 (December 1998). The ICC already faces a serious problem in arresting Sudan's President Omar al-Bashir for genocide in Darfur.

[127] The principle of self-determination, which constitutes one of the most important principles of international law, has not been entered into the Statute of the ICC. The principle may apply *inter alia* to the political, legal and cultural self-determination of peoples. The term "self-determination" was originally used to denote the struggle of a group or a people who have been forced to follow the political and legal conditions of a stronger political party. In addition, the term basically applies to two concepts. The first concept covers those groups, nations and populations which are forced to bind themselves to certain legal, political and economic obligations by a state or a group of states. The second concept relates to the independent characterisation of every nation.

The principle of self-determination has been especially well supported in the Charter of the United Nations and has also been recognized as one of the integral purposes of the Organization. Article 1 (2) of the Charter in particular reads that the purpose of the United Nations is "To develop friendly relations among nations based on respect for the principle of equal rights and self-determination of peoples, and to take other appropriate measures to strengthen universal peace." This principle has also been supported in other articles of the Charter and there are indeed a great number of instruments adopted by the Organization applicable to the principle of the self-determination of peoples. The principle of self-determination has also been recognized in the contents of a number of instruments applicable to international crimes. This has been for several essential reasons. One of the most important of these has been to protect the territorial integrity and political independence of every nation and also to emphasize that no international criminal conventions or any other criminal instruments can be a reason for preventing the struggle of peoples who are fighting for the independence of their traditional legal rights, including those which have been recognized under the constitution of the United Nations Organization. This means that certain correctly struggles by certain recognized peoples for the purpose of self-determination cannot be treated under the provisions of international criminal instruments applicable to international crimes. *Farhad Malekian, II International Criminal Law (1991)* p.105. For example, the legality of the struggle of peoples for the re-establishment of their rights is stated in a resolution concerning the Convention on the Prevention and Punishment of Crimes Against Internationally Protected Persons, Including Diplomatic Agents adopted by the General Assembly of the United Nations in

of the ICC may go against certain established rules of international criminal law.[128] They may also, in connection with certain cases, violate the United Nations Charter.[129]

1973. See General Assembly Official Records: 28th Session, Supplement No.30 (A/9030), Resolution 3166 (XXVIII), 14 December 1973, at pp.146-9. Although the Convention has prohibited acts against internationally protected persons, it has nevertheless stipulated that the provisions of the Convention are not applicable to acts which are carried out for the purpose of self-determination. It recognises that: "the provisions of the annexed Convention could not in any way prejudice the exercise of the legitimate right to self-determination and independence, in accordance with the purposes and principles of the Charter of the United Nations and the Declaration on Principles of International Law concerning Friendly Relations and Co-operation among States in accordance with the Charter of the United Nations, by peoples struggling against colonialism, alien domination, foreign occupation, racial discrimination and *apartheid*." *Id.,* paragraph 4 of the resolution, p.147.

[128] For example, one of the resolutions of the General Assembly reads that, "The General Assembly … *Recognizing* that the Palestinian people are entitled to self-determination in accordance with the Charter of the United Nations, *Expressing its grave concern* that the Palestinian people has been prevented from enjoying its inalienable rights, in particular its right to self-determination, *Guided* by the purposes and principles of the Charter, *Recalling* its relevant resolutions which affirm the right of the Palestinian people to self-determination, 1. *Reaffirms* the inalienable rights of the Palestinian people in Palestine, including: *(a)* The Right to self-determination without external interference; *(b)* The right to national independence and sovereignty; 2. *Reaffirms also* the inalienable right of the Palestinians to return to their homes and property from which they have been displaced and uprooted, and calls for their return; 3. *Emphasizes* that full respect for and the realization of these inalienable rights of the Palestinian people are indispensable for the solution of the question of Palestine; 4. *Recognizes* that the Palestinian people is a principal party in the establishment of a just and lasting peace in the Middle East; 5. *Further recognizes* the right of the Palestinian people to regain its rights by all means in accordance with the purposes and principles of the Charter of the United Nations; 6. *Appeals* to all States and international organizations to extend their support to the Palestinian people in its struggle to restore its rights, in accordance with the Charter; 7. *Requests* the Secretary-General to establish contacts with the Palestinian Liberation Organization on all matters concerning the question of Palestine …" General Assembly Official Records: 29th Session, Supplement No.31 (A/9631), at p.4, Resolution 3236 (XXIX), 22 November 1974.

[129] The types of provisions detailed above are also formulated in Resolution 3314 (XXIX) of the General Assembly on the Definition of Aggression and the 1966 Code of Crimes against the Peace and Security of Mankind. The resolution reads that: "Nothing in this article could in any way prejudice the right to self-determination, freedom and independence, as derived from the Charter, of peoples

forcibly deprived of that right and referred to in the Declaration on Principles of International Law concerning Friendly Relations and Co-operation among States in accordance with the Charter of the United Nations, particularly peoples under colonial and racist regimes or other forms of alien domination; nor the right of these peoples to struggle to that end and to seek and receive support, in accordance with the principles of the Charter and in conformity with the above-mentioned Declaration." One must, however, be very cautious when applying the provisions of the above paragraph. This is because not all conflicts or struggles necessarily come under the term self-determination. Any conflict by any nation can in general easily be defined under the principle of self-determination and, as a result, the provisions of international criminal conventions can be difficult to implement against various criminal activities by nations or political groups. This means that, while the principle of self-determination is broad enough to protect struggles by peoples for their rights in conformity with the principles of the Charter of the United Nations, this principle cannot be a sufficient reason to neglect international criminal law and violate it in the international relations of states. The ICC will be highly responsible for prosecuting the relevant individuals. The principle of self-determination must therefore first of all be employed in connection with peoples existing under colonial and occupied territories, racist regimes or other forms of alien domination. Indigenous people may also come under the statute of self-determination. Therefore, the legal right to self-determination is also applicable to peoples who have quite a different ethnical, cultural, linguistic or political background. (For example, one can examine the Declaration on Principles of International Law concerning Friendly Relations and Co-operation among States in accordance with the Charter of the United Nations. Approved by the General Assembly Resolution 2625 (XXV) of 24 October, 1970. U.N. Gen. Ass. Off. Rec., Suppl. No. 28, A/8028). This does not necessarily mean that the Security Council of the United Nations must confirm the struggle of a people for self-determination. Recognition of the self-determination of a people can be granted in several ways, such as opening communications with the relevant people under the authority of the United Nations, defending their rights in different international meetings, financial support, accepting their government in exile, giving direct political and legal support and providing any other assistance in order to help them achieve the right of self-determination. Obviously, all this must be done within the framework of the United Nations Charter and should not violate its principles. There are a number of examples denoting the legality of the self-determination of a number of peoples without any need for the recognition of these struggles by permanent members of the United Nations in the Security Council. For instance, the struggles of the Palestinians and of the black population in South Africa and Namibia were repeatedly recognized in the General Assembly of the United Nations, even though some of the permanent members did not support these cases.

6.2. The International Legal Personality of the ICC

Creating the ICC has been the most complicated challenge facing international criminal law and justice.[130] It needed a range of negotiations and decisions between various states. This was in order to conclude an international treaty which would be acceptable to most states of the world and could meet almost all aspects of international customary and conventional criminal law.[131] At the beginning, a number of states were not in favour of the creation of the ICC. This was based on the fact that it could limit their sovereign independence. One of the important questions around the creation of the ICC was its legal scope and character. The founders of the ICC were requested to create a statute which was not based on common law or civil law systems, but which was instead a statute governing the requirements of both systems of jurisdiction. This would mean creating an entity which would really consist of two national and international legal systems and which could fulfil the requirements of the international legal and political community. Finally, the Statute integrated all these facts. Thus, the institutional structure of the ICC is based on a new system of jurisdiction or on a character of complementarity.[132] This is illustrated by the following words:

> An International Criminal Court ("the Court") is hereby established. It shall be a permanent institution and shall have the power to exercise its jurisdiction over persons for the most serious crimes of international concern, as referred to in this Statute, and shall be complementary to national criminal jurisdictions. The provisions of this Statute shall govern the jurisdiction and functioning of the Court.[133]

Since the ICC has a range of duties and responsibilities to fulfil in carrying out its provisions, the founders had to give it the full capacity to act freely without partisan political interference. It was on this basis that the contracting parties to the Statute of the ICC permitted it to have full *international legal personality*. This was crucial for the future work of the ICC and its progressive development. Therefore, the Statute of the ICC deals with this important principle.

---

[130] See generally International Criminal Law for an International Criminal Court, Phillipe Kirsch, Alain Pellet and Bert Swart, eds., 2001).

[131] See The International Criminal Court: The Making of the Rome Statute—Issues, Negotiations, Results (Roy S. Lee, ed., 1999).

[132] See *infera*.

[133] Article 1.

Article 4 of the Statute concerns the legal status and powers of the Court *inter alia* to conclude international treaties.[134] The provisions of this article underline several important matters concerning the legal scope of the Court. These are:

i) The Court has international legal personality, which means it is an international person having rights and duties;
ii) The Court is entitled to legal capacity;
iii) The Court has full capacity to exercise its functions;
iv) The Court is permitted to enter into the formulation and ratification of international treaties by any state;[135]
v) The Court is entitled to have jurisdiction on the territory of any other state by special agreement;
iv) The Court is permitted to achieve its purposes by means of implementing its Statute.[136]

---

[134] For instance see Theodoor C. van Boven, *The European Union and the International Criminal Court*, 5 Maastricht Journal of European and Comparative Law 325-327 (no.4, 1998); Teresa Maria Moschetta, *Cooperation Between the European Union and the International Criminal Court: Legal Basest and Opportunities for Implementation* in The International Criminal Court and National Jurisdications (Mauro Politi and Federica Gioia, editors, 2008), pp.121-130

[135] It is based upon this important provision that the Court has entered into the formulation and ratification of international treaties with other states and international entities. For instance, the Agreement between the International Criminal Court and the European Union on Cooperation and Assistance was signed on 10th April 2006 and was ratified on 1st May 2006. The agreement opens an important door to future cooperation between the contracting parties. Article 12 of the agreement relates to privileges and immunities. It reads that "If the Court seeks to exercise its jurisdiction over a person who is alleged to be criminally responsible for a crime within the jurisdiction of the Court and if such person enjoys, according to the relevant rules of international law, any privileges and immunities, the relevant institution of the EU undertakes to cooperate fully with the Court and, with due regard to its responsibilities and competencies under the EU Treaty and the relevant rules there under, to take all necessary measures to allow the Court to exercise its jurisdiction, in particular by waiving any such privileges and immunities in accordance with all relevant rules of international law."

[136] For the full text of Article 5 see Appendix *infera.*

6.3. The Relationship between the ICC and the United Nations

6.3.1. Independence

From both a juridical and a political point of view, the ICC removes, in part, the power of the permanent members of the United Nations concerning the control of its jurisdiction.[137] The Court does not, therefore, depend on the decisions of the United Nations.[138] This is because the Court is an international legal person having rights and duties independent of the legal personality of the United Nations. The international personality of the Court means that its bureaucratic foundations, procedures, power and authority are wholly independent of the United Nations. Although the administration of the Court is rather expensive, it has its own financial plans. This independence was one of the most important reasons for the acceptance and the creation of the Court by the majority of states participating in the discussions.

This independence was not welcomed by the United States government because of its loss of political and legal power over the jurisdiction of the Court.[139] Nevertheless, the majority of the delegates in the Diplomatic Conference appreciated the basic conditions for the establishment of the Court.[140]

Another reason for the independent character of the Court is that the constitution of the Court may be modified to meet the needs of the time and may even be altered, in practice, without necessarily any need for the modification of the Statute of the Court.[141] This was not easy to bring about under the United Nations Charter as its modification could then

---

[137] This is mostly in the case of the question of aggression as an international crime.

[138] See Roger S. Clark, The Proposed International Criminal Court: Its Establishment and Its Relationship with the United Nations, 8 Criminal Law Forum 411 (1997).

[139] The United States was disappointed with the character of the Court. This was due to the fact that the Court was not under the control of the Security Council of the United Nations.

[140] It has to be emphasised here that the independence of the Court should not be interpreted as implying that the United Nations was not in favour of the creation of the Court. On the contrary, the United Nations had a significant role in the creation of the Court. For example, the United Nations contributed to the continuation of the Diplomatic Conference. Its moral and technical support was therefore crucial for the establishment of the Court.

[141] See infera.

depend on the juridical or political circumstances of certain permanent members. Moreover, it would create a complicated situation because of controversies regarding the interpretation of the provisions of the Charter and tense or chilly political relations between the members. Therefore, the international legal personality of the ICC helps the Court to be more concrete in its decisions and not to have to wait for any small decisions on the bureaucratic details of the provisions of the Charter.

The Statute of the ICC has consequently formulated a separate article governing the future international relations of the Court and the United Nations. This is stated in Article 2 of the Statute, which clarifies the relationship between the two entities, "The Court shall be brought into relationship with the United Nations through an agreement to be approved by the Assembly of States Parties to this Statute and thereafter concluded by the President of the Court on its behalf." The provisions entered into Article 2 of the ICC became the foundation for the future development of international relations between the United Nations Organization and the permanent International Criminal Court. Consequently, pursuant to the requirements of Article 2, both entities assembled and worked on the drafting of a treaty, finally resulting in the formulation of the Negotiated Relationship Agreement between the International Criminal Court and the United Nations in 2004.[142] According to this agreement, the International Criminal Court has been established as an independent permanent institution in relationship with the United Nations system.

---

[142] The agreement was adopted and entered into force on 4th October 2004. ICC-ASP/3/Res.1. For the clarification of the position of the ICC to the United Nations Organization, it is important to mention two of the articles of the Agreement here. Article 2 concerning Principles reads "1. The United Nations recognizes the Court as an independent permanent judicial institution which, in accordance with articles 1 and 4 of the Statute, has international legal personality and such legal capacity as may be necessary for the exercise of its functions and the fulfilment of its purposes. 2. The Court recognizes the responsibilities of the United Nations under the Charter. 3. The United Nations and the Court respect each other's status and mandate." Article 3 concerns the Obligation of cooperation and coordination. It states "The United Nations and the Court agree that, with a view to facilitating the effective discharge of their respective responsibilities, they shall cooperate closely, whenever appropriate, with each other and See each other on matters of mutual interest pursuant to the provisions of the present Agreement and in conformity with the respective provisions of the Charter and the Statute."

6.3.2. Dependency

According to Article 3 of the Negotiated Relationship Agreement between the International Criminal Court and the United Nations, the Court and the United Nations have agreed to work closely. Although they encourage cooperation between the two entities, the provisions of this article may be monopolized by the United Nations permanent members because of their powerful authority under the provisions of Chapter VII of the Charter. This is because Article 3 concerning the Obligation of Cooperation and Coordination reads that the "United Nations and the Court agree that, with a view to facilitating the effective discharge of their respective responsibilities, they shall cooperate closely, whenever appropriate, with each other and consult each other on matters of mutual interest pursuant to the provisions of the present Agreement and in *conformity with the respective provisions of the Charter and the Statute.*"[143] The last words of Article 3 openly refer to the provisions of Chapter VII of the United Nations which give an extraordinary authority to certain members of the United Nations to veto certain decisions of the majority of the states of the world. Article 3 also refers to the provisions of the Statute concerning its limited jurisdiction in the case of international crime of aggression.[144] However, this position of the Statute of the ICC may be changed as, due to the new modification by the 2010 Review Conference, there is still a lack of clarity regarding the position of the Court vis-à-vis the Security Council.[145]

The Court has to cooperate with the United Nations with due regard to the provisions of Article 3, but this is done on the basis of the provisions of the Charter alone. On a close reading, the provisions of Article 3 and Chapter VII of the Charter mean that the Court cannot act without due regard to the politico-legal opinions of the permanent members, even though the new modification of Article 3 has altered its provisions. Moreover, certain members of the United Nations will not take any decision which may limit their powers and authority under the Charter. According to the provisions of Articles 5 and 16, the Security Council has the right to interfere in certain matters, which are of primary importance for the recognition of breaches of peace, threats against peace and acts of aggression. The Security Council has the right to put off the proceedings

---

[143] Italics added.
[144] See *infera* the relevant section.
[145] See *infera* sections on the 2010 Review Conference.

of the Court's hearing until a later date, if it considers this necessary.[146] This can, however, be done only at certain times and under certain conditions.[147] Article 5 of the Statute of the ICC provides that "The Court shall exercise jurisdiction over the crime of aggression once a provision is adopted in accordance with articles 121 and 123 defining the crime and setting out the conditions under which the Court shall exercise jurisdiction with respect to this crime. *Such a provision shall be consistent with the relevant provisions of the Charter of the United Nations.*"[148] In contemporary international relations there have been several suggestions for how to define the term "aggression" and an amendment of the Statute of the ICC is therefore seriously recommended.[149] However, one cannot

---

[146] But for some aspects of the relations between the Security Council and the Court See Morten Bergsmo, Occasional Remarks on Certain State Concerns about the Jurisdictional Reach of the International Criminal Court, and Their Possible Implications for the Relationship between the Court and the Security Council, 69 Nordic Journal of International Law 87-113 (no.1, 2000); Vera Gowlland-Debbas, The Relationship Between the Security Council and the Projected International Criminal Court, 3 Journal of Armed Conflict Law97 (1998); Elizabeth Wilmshurst, The International Criminal Court: The Role of the Security Council, in The Rome Statute of the International Criminal Court: a Challenge to Impunity (Mauro Politi and Giuseppe Nesi, eds., 2004) pp. 39-42.

[147] Id.

[148] Article 5 (2). Emphasis added.

[149] For instance, according to the new suggestion, the definition of aggression is mostly taken from the earlier definition of aggression. Based on the Report of the Special Working Group on the Crime of Aggression, the crime in Article 8 of the Statute should be modified in the following way:

1. For the purpose of this Statute, "crime of aggression" means the planning, preparation, initiation or execution, by a person in a position effectively to exercise control over or to direct the political or military action of a State, of an act of aggression which, by its character, gravity and scale, constitutes a manifest violation of the Charter of the United Nations.

2. For the purpose of paragraph 1, "act of aggression" means the use of armed force by a State against the sovereignty, territorial integrity or political independence of another State, or in any other manner inconsistent with the Charter of the United Nations. Any of the following acts, regardless of a declaration of war, shall, in accordance with United Nations General Assembly resolution 3314 (XXIX) of 14 December 1974, qualify as an act of aggression:

(a) The invasion or attack by the armed forces of a State of the territory of another State, or any military occupation, however temporary, resulting from such invasion or attack, or any annexation by the use of force of the territory of another State or part thereof;

(b) Bombardment by the armed forces of a State against the territory of another State or the use of any weapons by a State against the territory of another State;

(c) The blockade of the ports or coasts of a State by the armed forces of another State;
(d) An attack by the armed forces of a State on the land, sea or air forces, or marine and air fleets of another State;
(e) The use of armed forces of one State which are within the territory of another State with the agreement of the receiving State, in contravention of the conditions provided for in the agreement or any extension of their presence in such territory beyond the termination of the agreement;
(f) The action of a State in allowing its territory, which it has placed at the disposal of another State, to be used by that other State for perpetrating an act of aggression against a third State;
(g) The sending by or on behalf of a State of armed bands, groups, irregulars or mercenaries, which carry out acts of armed force against another State of such gravity as to amount to the acts listed above, or its substantial involvement therein.
3. The following text is inserted after article 15 of the Statute: which clarifies exercise of jurisdiction over the crime of aggression. These are: Article 15 bis: Exercise of jurisdiction over the crime of aggression
1. The Court may exercise jurisdiction over the crime of aggression in accordance with article 13, subject to the provisions of this article. 2. Where the Prosecutor concludes that there is a reasonable basis to proceed with an investigation in respect of a crime of aggression, he or she shall first ascertain whether the Security Council has made a determination of an act of aggression committed by the State concerned. The Prosecutor shall notify the Secretary-General of the United Nations of the situation before the Court, including any relevant information and documents. 3. Where the Security Council has made such a determination, the Prosecutor may proceed with the investigation in respect of a crime of aggression.
4. (Alternative 1) In the absence of such a determination, the Prosecutor may not proceed with the investigation in respect of a crime of aggression,
Option 1 – end the paragraph here.
Option 2 – add: unless the Security Council has, in a resolution adopted under Chapter VII of the Charter of the United Nations, requested the Prosecutor to proceed with the investigation in respect of a crime of aggression.
4. (Alternative 2) Where no such determination is made within [6] months after the date of notification, the Prosecutor may proceed with the investigation in respect of a crime of aggression,
Option 1 – end the paragraph here.
Option 2 – add: provided that the Pre-Trial Chamber has authorized the commencement of the investigation in respect of a crime of aggression in accordance with the procedure contained in article 15;
Option 3 – add: provided that the General Assembly has determined that an act of aggression has been committed by the State referred to in article 8 bis;
Option 4 – add: provided that the International Court of Justice has determined that an act of aggression has been committed by the State referred to in article 8 bis.

deny the fact that the legal position of the Statute will be modified by the ratification of the new regulations, especially with regard to the definition of aggression, at the 2010 Review Conference. The new situation will still perhaps have to be examined in the light of further changes to circumstances after 2017.

The content of Article 5 outlined above states that even if a clear definition of the crime of aggression is recognized, the Security Council still has the ultimate authority to decide on the scope of the accountability of an individual for the international crime of aggression.[150] Article 16 of the Statute, in particular, has strengthened the provisions of Article 5. It is, in reality, the monopolization of one of the most important questions of international criminal law with reference to the provisions of Article 3 of the Negotiated Relationship Agreement Between the International Criminal Court and the United Nations in 2004. Article 16 of the Statute of the ICC relating to the deferral of investigation or prosecution reads that "No investigation or prosecution may be commenced or proceeded with under this Statute for a period of 12 months after the Security Council, in a resolution adopted under Chapter VII of the Charter of the United Nations, has requested the Court to that effect; *that request may be renewed by the Council under the same conditions*."[151] This means that the work of the

---

5. A determination of an act of aggression by an organ outside the Court shall be without prejudice to the Court's own findings under this Statute. 6. This article is without prejudice to the provisions relating to the exercise of jurisdiction with respect to other crimes referred to in article 5.
4. The following text is inserted after article 25, paragraph 3 of the Statute:
3 bis.In respect of the crime of aggression, the provisions of this article shall apply only to persons in a position effectively to exercise control over or to direct the political or military action of a State.
5. The first sentence of article 9, paragraph 1 of the Statute is replaced by the following sentence:
1. Elements of Crimes shall assist the Court in the interpretation and application of articles 6, 7, 8 and 8 bis.
6. The chapeau of article 20, paragraph 3 of the Statute is replaced by the following paragraph; the rest of the paragraph remains unchanged:
3. No person who has been tried by another court for conduct also proscribed under article 6, 7, 8 or 8 bis shall be tried by the Court with respect to the same conduct unless the proceedings in the other court:
Assembly of States Parties, International Criminal Court, Seventh session (second resumption), New York 9-13 February 2009 (ICC-ASP/7/SWGCA/2); See also http://www.icc-cpi.int/iccdocs/asp_docs/ ICC-ASP-7-SWGCA-2%20English.pdf.

[150] Examine A.C. Carpenter, *The International Criminal Court and the Crime of Aggression,* 64 Nordic Journal of International law 223 (1995).

[151] Emphasis added.

Court may be interrupted on several occasions according to the interests of the permanent members of the United Nations.

Even the new draft proposal of 2009 concerning the definition of aggression, which is based on the United Nations General Assembly resolution 3314 (XXIX), does not guarantee any non-political decision. Similar views may be asserted regarding the provisions of the new amendment formulated during the 2010 Review Conference in Kampala, Uganda. Although one cannot deny that these documents establish criminal responsibility for those who have engaged in aggressive conduct, the attribution of responsibility is tied up with the Security Council's decision. That is why three divergent views have been expressed concerning the question of the prosecution of crime. According to the first view, the prosecutor should proceed with an investigation relating to a crime of aggression only if the Security Council has previously determined that a state has committed an act of aggression. According to the second view, when nothing has been determined by the Security Council of the United Nations, the prosecutor may only proceed with an investigation if:

(a) The Security Council has adopted a resolution under Chapter VII of the Charter requesting the Prosecutor to proceed with an investigation;
(b) The Pre-Trial Chamber has authorized the commencement of the investigation in accordance with the procedure contained in article 15;
(c) The United Nations General Assembly has determined that an act of aggression has been committed; or
(d) The International Court of Justice has determined that an act of aggression has been committed.[152]

According to the third view held by some of the delegations, when no such act of aggression has been determined by the Security Council, this should not be reason enough to prevent the Prosecutor from proceeding with an investigation.[153]

Whilst we do not deny that a strong relationship between the United Nations and the International Criminal Court is logical and necessary, this does not necessarily mean that the formula which is used in the convention

---

[152] www.icc-cpi.int/Menus/Go?id=a0c1c6e6-40ff-4eda-be9e-ab68caf67ed4&lan=en-GB - 22k -.Visited on 2009-04-22.

[153] The new regulations suggested in the 2010 Review Conference have aimed to solve all these issues. See the new modification *infera* chapter nine on The Review Conference in Kampala.

is correct.[154] The reason for this is that individuals who have committed serious international crimes, including aggression, may easily escape from prosecution and punishment because of the circumstances of the time and the conventional obligation of the ICC to act in conformity with the provisions of the Charter of the United Nations, which may be renewed by the Security Council under the same conditions. In other words, the relevant articles may encourage impunity and not non-impunity.

6.4. The Incorporated Character of the ICC

6.4.1. Taking Account of Juridical Systems

Creating a system of international criminal justice which could be seen to represent the interests of all nations was very difficult and problematic.[155] Naturally, the different national legislations do not have one legal system. Different nations have different cultures and different social attitudes towards the implementation of criminal justice. Some acts, which are recognized by some nations as wrong or as serious violations of the fundamental principles of human rights law, may scarcely be identified as violations by other nations. This is also true in the case of the application of laws, including the proceedings of their implementation.

In order both to respect the different cultures of the world and to prevent them from ignoring one another, many rules have been formulated in the Rome Statute. They especially emphasise the validity of different elements for the presentation of its jurisdiction. When selecting judges the states parties to the Statute have to take into account the juridical systems of different states. The principles to be followed include i) The representation of the principal legal systems of the world; ii)equitable geographical representation; and iii)a fair representation of female and male judges.[156]

---

[154] But See Franklin Berman, *The Relationship Between the International Criminal Court and the Security Council, in* Reflections on the international criminal court: Essays in Honour of Adriaan Bos, (Herman von Hebel, Johan G. Lammers and Jolien Schukking, eds. 1999) pp. 173-80.

[155] Broomhall Bruce, International Justice and the International Criminal Court: Between Sovereignty and the Rule of Law (2003).

[156] Article 36 (8) of the Statute.

6.4.2. Models of Jurisdiction

The ICC has based its jurisdiction on two widely recognized models of jurisdiction. These are common law[157] and civil law[158] systems.[159] Both systems basically constitute the legacy of Western classical jurisdictions.[160] The principal elements of both systems are comprised by the Rome Statute. It has therefore benefited both models of jurisdiction. This establishes new procedural methods for the future conduct of the Court's jurisdiction where neither of the systems may be ignored during the procedures of the Court. In any event, the Court has to safeguard the rights

---

157 In the common law system the decisions of judges have an important function for the development of the law. The common law system originated and grew in England. The judges in fact have the authority to decide what the purpose of law is where there is no authoritative description of the relevant law. This means that abstract rules in common law are drawn from given cases in the court. When an appellate court has already decided what the nature and character of the law is, that decision or the precedent set is binding for the future conduct of that appellate court. This means that the decision binds all lower courts examined by that appellate court empowered to review juridical decisions when the basic facts of a case are similar to the earlier decision. These decisions are binding and cannot be altered as long as there is no other authoritative statement of the law by a higher court or legislator. In other words, the decisions of the courts in a common law system are considered as laws, just like statutes. Rules of common law are therefore developed from usages and customs of the court decisions rather than on legislative rules. Consequently, the decisions of a prior court may be recognized by common law as precedents due to the conditions of the case law. The latter is also called *stare decisis.*

158 Civil law has developed from Roman law, Canon law and the enlightenment. It constitutes one of the oldest systems of the world. The civil law system is originally based on rules and regulations that are adopted by the legislators as laws. Consequently, abstract rules are, contrary to those of the common law system, already codified by the legislators. Two well known civil law systems are the Swiss Civil Code and the German BGB/Bürgerliches Gesetzbuch.

159 It is worth mentioning here that the Common Law system is, in some ways, the technique of jurisdiction used in the Islamic juridical system. The judges in both systems may represent decisions that are valuable and may be used in other judgements of a similar character. Thus, such an interpretation is accepted and the law may be developed where it was previously silent. See Farhad Malekian, The Principles of Islamic International Criminal Law (2011); Farhad Malekian, *The Homogeneity of International Criminal Court with the Islamic Jurisprudence*, 9 International Criminal Law Review (2009), 1-27 pp.

160 There were serious controversies regarding the legal statute of both systems. Countries representing the civil law system could not accept the argument of the Common law system and the contrary was also true.

of the accused, witnesses and victims and to create the right balance between the requisite independence of the ICC and the self-governing sovereignty of states parties.

6.4.3. Organs of the Court

The administration of the International Criminal Court consists of four organs each having different functions and power. These are i) the Presidency, ii) the Judiciary composed of three different sub-organs: Pre-Trial Divisions, Trial and Appeals, iii) the Office of the Prosecutor, and iv) the Registry. The work of all these organs must be in conformity with the provisions of the Court and should not violate the essence of the jurisdiction of the Court. According to the Court's Statute, the judges,[161] prosecutor, deputy prosecutor[162] and registrar[163] should be elected and serve on a full-time basis. Moreover, the contracting parties may establish an Assembly of States Parties in order to directly or indirectly assist the organs of the Court. This Assembly has already been established.

6.4.4. Victims and Witnesses Unit

The Statute of the ICC aims to protect the rights of victims and if possible to redress damages.[164] A significant feature of the system of international criminal jurisdiction under the Rome Statute is the inclusion of the Victims and Witnesses Unit created with reference to meetings with the Office of the Prosecutor. According to the Statute of the ICC, the Unit shall provide, in consultation with the Office of the Prosecutor, protective measures and security arrangements, counselling and other appropriate assistance to witnesses and victims who appear before the Court. It may also take such measures where necessary for others who are at risk on account of testimony given by witnesses. The Unit shall include staff with expertise in trauma, including trauma related to crimes of sexual violence.[165]

---

[161] Article 35 (1).
[162] Article 42 (2).
[163] Article 43 (5).
[164] See Bottigliero Ilaria, Redress for Victims of Crimes under International Law (2004).
Ilaria Bottingliero., Redress for Victims of Crimes under International Law (2004); M. Cherif Bassiouni, *International Recognition of Victims' Rights, in* International Criminal Law, Vol iii (M. Cherif Bassiouni, ed. 2008) pp. 635-701; M. Cherif Bassiouni, *Issues Pertaining to the Evidentiary Part of International Criminal Law, in* Bassiouni, above pp. 581-602.
[165] Article 43 (6).

The Statute also strengthens the provisions of the Court governing sexual violence in order to protect females, and particularly children.[166] It is thus the duty of the prosecutor to appoint advisers with legal expertise on specific issues, including violations against women.[167] This includes but is not limited to sexual and gender violence and violence against children.[168]

6.4.5. Gratis Personnel

The prosecutor may, in exceptional circumstances, employ the expertise of gratis personnel offered by non-governmental or intergovernmental organizations and state parties. The prosecutor may accept any such offer

---

[166] The system of international law has struggled in different ways to protect women and children from unlawful and inhuman sexual exploitation. Respect for the integrity of women and children has been stated especially within the Declaration on Social Progress and Development, 1969, Universal Declaration on the Eradication of Hunger and Malnutrition, 1974, Declaration on the Elimination of All Forms of Intolerance and of Discrimination Based on Religion or Belief, 1981, Declaration on the Human Rights of Individuals Who are not Nationals of the Country in which They Live, 1985, Vienna Declaration and Program of Action: World Conference on Human Rights, 1993, Draft United Nations Declaration on the Rights of Indigenous Peoples, 1994, Cairo Declaration of Human Rights in Islam, 1990, American Convention on Human Rights, 1969,African Charter on Human and Peoples' Rights, 1981, Arab Charter on Human Rights, 2004, European Convention for the Protection of Human Rights and Fundamental Freedoms of 1950 as amended by Protocol No. 11 of 1998, Charter of Fundamental Rights of the European Union, 2000,Convention on the Reduction of Statelessness, 1961, Supplementary Convention on the Abolition of Slavery, the Slave Trade, and Institutions and Practices Similar to Slavery, 1956, Declaration on the Protection of Women and Children in Emergency and Armed Conflict, 1974, International Covenant on Civil and Political Rights, 1966, International Convention on the Protection of the Rights of All Migrant Workers and Members of Their Families, 1990.

[167] Concerning crimes against women see Kelly Dawn Askin, War Crimes Against Women (1997).

[168] Article 42 (9). See also Rhonda Copelon, Gender Crimes as War Crimes: Integrating Crimes against Women into International Criminal Law, 46 McGill Law Journal 217 (2000). Farhad Malekian, Kerstin Nordlöf., Prohibition of Sexual Exploitation of Children Constituting Obligation Erga Omnes (2013).

on behalf of the Office of the Prosecutor. This type of personnel should be employed according to the guidelines of the Assembly of States Parties.[169]

Although the receiving of gratis personnel is a benefit, it does, however, have certain disadvantages. The reason for this is that gratis personnel are mainly offered by wealthy states, as illustrated by the practices of the International Criminal Tribunal for the Former Yugoslavia (ICTY)[170] and the International Criminal Tribunal for Rwanda (ICTR).[171] In other words, the organs of the Court or the Office of the Prosecutor may be monopolized by the greater political and juridical strength of the rich nations.

In practice, gratis personnel whose government is accused of committing crimes against humanity, war crimes and genocide may occupy the Court. Even states offering gratis personnel who are not suspected of violations of the fundamental principles of international criminal law, may still have good political relations with governments notorious for the violation of the basic rules of international human rights law. Thus, the Court has to be careful when it comes to the use of gratis personnel in order for its machinery not to be involved in international intrigues leading to impunity.

Although the jurisdictional machinery of the ICC has been intended to present a more comprehensive means of justice and jurisdiction compared with the ICTY and the ICTR, it has indeed greater problems of its own.[172] This is because the ICC operates on the basis of the complementarity principle while the other two aforementioned tribunals operate on the basis of primacy of jurisdiction.[173] The consequence is that both *ad hoc* tribunals may require states to extradite the accused under their jurisdiction while the ICC, due to its legal position, cannot enforce such a requirement. In practice, the Court has to take other legal measures in order to deliver defendants.[174]

---

[169] See generally Guido Ruegenberg, The Independence and Accountability of Prosecutor of a Permanent International Criminal Court, Zeitschrift Fur Rechtspolitik 68 (1999).

[170] International Criminal Tribunal for the Former Yugoslavia. World Wide Web document, 2001. http://www.un.org/icty. Judgments and other documents.

[171] International Criminal Tribunal for Rwanda. World Wide Web document, 2001. http://www.ictr.org. Judgments and other documents.

[172] See Frédéric Mégret., In Defense of Hybridity: Towards a Representational Theory of International Criminal Justice, 38-3 Cornell International Law Journal 725-751 (2005)., at 744-745.

[173] *Id.*, at 751.

[174] See infera.

6.4.6. The Judiciary

6.4.6.1. Qualification

One of the most important parts of the machinery of justice of the permanent International Criminal Court is its judiciary system governing the qualifications, nomination and election of judges for the implementation of the provisions of the Statute. The Court consists of eighteen judges,[175] although this number may be increased according to the needs of the Court. The President of the Court is responsible for giving a proposal on this matter to the states parties explaining why it is necessary to increase the number of judges.[176]

The Statute clearly points out that the persons who are nominated as judges for the Court should be of "high moral character, impartiality and integrity who possess the qualifications required in their respective States for appointment to the highest judicial offices."[177] The persons who are elected to the Court should have the relevant knowledge of criminal law, criminal procedures, international law, or humanitarian law.[178] When a person has fulfilled the conditions of the Court, he may be elected by secret ballot at a meeting of the Assembly of States Parties.[179]

The Court does not disqualify judges on the basis of their nationality. It specifically points out that a judge shall not participate in any case in which his/her impartiality might reasonably be doubted on any ground. Accordingly, a judge may be disqualified from a case due to the fact that the judge has previously been involved in some capacity in that case before the Court or in a related criminal case at the domestic level involving the person being investigated or prosecuted. A judge may also be disqualified on other grounds provided for in the Rules of Procedure and Evidence.[180] According to the Statute, no two judges may be nationals of the same state. A person who has two nationalities should be deemed to be

---

[175] Article 36 (1).

[176] Article 36 (2).

[177] Article 36 (3). However, the wording of Article 36 (3) concerning "the qualifications required" is subject to very strong criticism. This is because such qualifications may vary from state to state depending on their national legislations and whether legislation is itself violating the fundamental principles of human rights. A condition, which may be recognized as qualification in one state, may be in contradiction with the conditions of another state. This means that the ICC may have differently qualified judges who do not fulfil the qualification of each others' states.

[178] Article 36 (3) (a, b, c).

[179] Article 36 (6).

[180] Article 41 (2), (a)

a national of the state in which that person exercises his/her social rights including civil and political ones. The period for which the judges are in charge of the Court varies between three, six and nine years.[181]

6.4.6.2. Unanimity

The Statute encourages the judges to achieve unanimity in their decision. If the trial fails in this matter, the majority of the judges may take the decision.[182] The decision of the Court must be in writing and should contain the reasons for the statement of the Trial Chamber relating to the findings of the evidence and conclusions. The Trial Chamber is also allowed to issue a decision. If there is no such unanimity between the judges, the Trial Chamber's decision should contain not only the views of the majority but also the minority of judges. Thereafter, the decision or a summary of the decision should be delivered in an open court.[183]

The Statute goes further and permits the statement of majority and minority views in the Appeals Chamber. Accordingly, the judgment may be taken by a majority of the judges in the Appeals Chamber and may be delivered in an open court. The judgment has to state the reasons for the verdict. If there is no unanimity concerning the case, the judgment of the Appeals Chamber should present the views of the majority and the minority. A judge is also allowed to submit a separate or dissenting opinion concerning the relevant question of law and his precise view concerning the whole case.[184]

6.4.6.3. Dissenting Opinion

As may be seen, the Statute has permitted the presentation of the decisions of both the majority and minority in the Trial and Appeals Chambers whenever there is no unanimity concerning the conclusion of a given case. It has also permitted the issuance of separate views concerning the question of law in the Appeals Chamber.[185] The policy of the Court can thus balance different views, which may be useful for the jurisdiction of the Court with regard to its power, authority, integrity and credibility. Although the Court, by establishing the right to dissenting opinion,

---

[181] Article 36 (9).
[182] Article 74 (3).
[183] Article 74 (5).
[184] Article 83 (4).
[185] Examine Hans-Jörg Behrens, Investigation, Trial and Appeal in the International Criminal Court Statute (Parts V, VI, VIII), 6 European Journal of Crime and Criminal Justice 113 (1998); Claus Kress, Investigation, Trial and Appeal in the International Criminal Court Statute (Parts V, VI, VIII), 6 European Journal of Crime, Criminal Law and Criminal Justice 126 (1998).

advocates directly against the legal machinery of some of the signatory parties to the Statute, the permission to express a dissenting opinion may be to the advantage of the criminal justice system when it comes to the development, modification and creation of new rules.[186]

The problem of the model which is offered by the Statute of the ICC may be that it may lead to controversy between the judges. It might have been better for the Court to adopt a method that relied on the majority decisions of the judges. This is because the problem will be more serious when several judges have the same nationality or different nationalities where they have social or political activities in common. This means that we may have two judges with different nationalities but who also share the nationality of a third state. Moreover, the first nationality (original) of X and Y may be E, but X may also have the nationality of S, where he has social and political activities, and Y may also have obtained the nationality of S, but without social activities. How can we believe that those two judges are not simultaneously influenced by their own first nationality, while one speaks for the original and the other for the adopted nationality? Moreover, the transparency, integrity and independence of a judge is not guaranteed by rules or by their being a specific sex, but through a full understanding of humanity, of the ethical and philosophical reasons for the existence of the law and, not least, of justice as a norm of human nature and a reliable social phenomenon.

6.4.6.4. Divisions of Judges

The judges of the ICC are, after their election, requested to make decisions concerning several matters.[187] They are requested to elect the holders of the Presidency.[188] The ICC also has an Appeals Division consisting of one appeals chamber with five judges including the President. Similarly, the Trial division, which consists of at least six judges, is further divided into Trial Chambers consisting of three judges each. There is also a Pre-Trial Division consisting of six judges which is further divided into Pre-Trial Chambers consisting of one or three judges.[189] These divisions may vary

[186] However, it is asserted that one of the strong reasons for the successful development of the European Court of Justice is that it does not allow the judges to submit a separate or dissenting opinion concerning the relevant question of law. The International Criminal Court and the Transformation of International Law: Justice for the New Millenium (2002). This may, however, be very hazardous for the development of the principles of international criminal justice and may prevent the development of international human rights law.

[187] Article 39(1).

[188] Article 38 (1).

[189] Article 34 (b).

depending on the functions of the pre-trial chambers.[190] The Statute clearly indicates that the functions of the Pre-Trial Chamber shall be performed either by three judges of the Pre-Trial Division or by a single judge of that division with due regard to the provisions of the Statute and the Rules of Procedure and Evidence.[191] As a whole, the function of all these divisions is to speed up the procedure of the Court and to prevent longer procedures which may occur when there are only two trial chambers. They are in fact based on the body of international procedural criminal law.[192]

The functions of the Pre-Trial Division are to supervise each case, which is brought before it, and from the beginning, to consider whether it shall initiate an investigation. According to the Statute, if the Pre-Trial Chamber, based on the examination of the request and the supporting material, finds that the case comes under the jurisdiction of the Court and there is reason to start an investigation, it should approve the initiation of the investigation. This should be without any prejudice to subsequent determinations by the Court, regarding the jurisdiction and admissibility of a case.[193] These proceedings are pursued until the confirmation of charges for which the accused may be submitted to a Trial Chamber.[194] If the Pre-Trial Chamber refuses to authorise an investigation concerning the case, this should not prevent the prosecutor from subsequently presenting a request concerning evidence dealing with the same case.[195]

---

[190] Article 39 (1), 39(2) (b).

[191] Article 39(b) (iii).

[192] "International procedural criminal law can be described as a body of international rules promulgated to regulate and implement international substantive criminal law. It is also meant to set the rules according to which individuals may be prosecuted and tried for international crimes and subjected to an international penal system. In other words, international procedural criminal law contemplates that part of international criminal law that governs international criminal proceedings." See Geert-Jan G. J. Knoops, Theory and Practice of International and Internationalized Criminal Proceedings 1 (2005). For further analysis of criminal procedures see Mirjan Damaska, *Structures of Authority and Comparative Criminal Procedure,* 84 Yale Law Journal 480 (1974); Jean Pradel, Procedure pénale (1997); Lawyers Committee for Human Rights, *Report Issues of Jurisdiction and Admissibility in the Rules of Procedure and Evidence* (2000); Rudolf B. Schlesinger, *Comparative Criminal Procedure: A Plea for Utilizing Foreign Experience,* 26 Buffalo Law Review 361 (1977).

[193] Article 15(4). Lawyers Committee for Human Rights, *Issues of Jurisdiction and Admissibility* (2000).

[194] Article 61(7).

[195] Article 15(5).

It is also necessary to emphasise that a prosecutor may have a different opinion concerning the case and the continuation of the investigation. Therefore, the prosecutor may initiate investigations *propriomotu* on the basis of information about crimes which fall under the jurisdiction of the Court.[196] Nevertheless, the prosecutor has a duty to follow the Statute and should not take any action in violation of its provisions.[197] His/her investigation must consequently be reliable and should take account of all evidence. One strong reason for this is that the Pre-Trial Chamber bases its warrant of arrest on the prosecutor's investigation and takes a decision accordingly regarding the continuation of the case.[198]

---

[196] See also section on Prosecutor.

[197] See J. D. van der Vyver, Personal and Territorial Jurisdiction of the International Criminal Court, 14 Emory International Law Review 1 (2000).

[198] A clear instance is the *Germain Katanaga*case. Accordingly, the Pre-Trial Chamber asserted that "CONSIDERING that, on the basis of the evidence and information submitted by the Prosecution CONSIDERING that there are reasonable grounds to believe that from July 2002 until the end of 2003, there was a protracted armed conflict on the territory of Ituri involving armed groups based thereon and having a hierarchical organisation and the ability to plan and carry out sustained military operations, including the *Front des nationalistes et intégrationnistes* [National Integrationist Front] "the FNI", the *Force de résistance patriotique en Ituri* [Patriotic Resistance Force in Ituri] ("the FRPI"), the *Union des patriotesCongolais*[Union of Congolese Patriots] ("the UPC")/the *Forces patriotiques pour la libération du Congo* [Patriotic Forces for the Liberation of Congo] ("the FPLC") and the *Parti pour l'unité et la sauvegarde de l'intégrité du Congo* [Party for Unity and Safeguarding of the Integrity of Congo] ("the PUSIC"); CONSIDERING that there are reasonable grounds to believe that the Uganda People's Defence Force ("UPDF") allegedly also participated in the above-mentioned armed conflict; CONSIDERING, therefore, that there are reasonable grounds to believe that a protracted armed conflict took place during the said period and that it may be characterised as being of a non-international, or alternatively, as being of an international character; CONSIDERING that there are reasonable grounds to believe that in the context of this armed conflict, the FNI and the FRPI, acting with a common purpose, carried out an attack on the village of Bogoro which started on or around 24 February 2003; CONSIDERING that there are reasonable grounds to believe that the attack directed against the village of Bogoro was indiscriminate, and that during, and in the aftermath of, the attack, members of the FNI and FRPI committed several criminal acts against civilians primarily of Hema ethnicity, namely i) the murder of about 200 civilians; ii) causing serious bodily harm to civilians; iii) arresting, threatening with weapons and imprisoning civilians in a room filled with corpses; iv) pillaging and v) the sexual enslavement of several women and girls; CONSIDERING also that there are reasonable grounds to believe that members of the FNI and FRPI used children under the age of fifteen years to participate actively in this attack;

6.5. The Prosecutor

6.5.1. The Power

One of the problems which arose during the drafting of the ICC Statute was defining the power of the prosecutor.[199] A particularly important question was whether he/she should be able to act *propriomotu* or *ex officio* based on his/her own suggestion to submit a case to the Court. There were different opinions during the formation of the statute concerning the power of the prosecutor. Most of the five permanent members of the United Nations were against an independent prosecutor while some other countries were not.[200] The issue was finally resolved in the interest of fair jurisdiction.

The office of the prosecutor constitutes an independent organ of the ICC.[201] It has an effective function in the 1998 Statute. The office of the

---

CONSIDERING, therefore, that there are reasonable grounds to believe that, during, and in the aftermath of, the attack on the village of Bogoro, war crimes within the jurisdiction of the Court pursuant to articles 8(2)(a)(i), 8(2)(1)(ii), 8(2)(b)(i), 8(2)(b)(xvi), 8(2)(b)(xxii), 8(2)(b)(xxvi), 8(2)(c)(i), 8(2)(e)(i), 8(2)(e)(v), 8(2)(e)(vi) and 8(2)(e)(vii) of the Statute, as described in the Prosecution Application, were committed; CONSIDERING that there are reasonable grounds to believe that between January 2003 and at least March 2003, the FNI and FRPI carried out an attack directed against the civilian population of certain parts of the territory of Ituri, primarily of Hema ethnicity; that the attack was of a systematic or widespread nature; and that during such a systematic or widespread attack, on or around 24 February 2003, during, and in the aftermath of, the attack on the village of Bogoro, the following crimes were committed: the murder of about 200 civilians, causing serious bodily harm to civilians and the sexual enslavement of several women and girls; CONSIDERING, therefore, that there are reasonable grounds to believe that during the attack on the village of Bogoro, crimes against humanity within the jurisdiction of the Court pursuant to articles 7(1)(a), 7(1)(g) and 7(1)(k) of the Statute, as described in the Prosecution Application, were committed."*Germain Katanaga* (ICC-01/04-01/07), Situation in the Democratic Republic of the Congo, 2 July 2007, pp.3-7. See *also* warrant of arrest concerning *Mathieu Nagudjolo (*ICC-01/04-02/07), Situation in the Democratic Republic of the Congo, 6 July 2007; *Bosco Ntaganda* (01/04-02/06), Situation in the Democratic Republic of the Congo, 7 August 2006.

[199] The first prosecutor of the ICC was Luis Moreno Ocampo who was presented by the Assembly of States Parties on 21 April 2003. He was a deputy prosecutor in the former Military Junta Trials in Argentina.

[200] These were China, France, Russia and the United States; the position of the United Kingdom was not clear. Some other states, which also opposed the independent prosecutor, were Israel, India, Malaysia, Egypt and Syria.

[201] Article 42 (1).

Prosecutor is responsible for receiving any substantiated information concerning the crimes which are under the jurisdiction of the Court. The prosecutor also has the responsibility of examining the information and beginning investigations within the jurisdiction of the Court. Moreover, the members of the office of the prosecutor should not in any way seek or act on the orders of, or according to instructions from, any external source.[202]

The Assembly of States Parties shall elect the prosecutor. The prosecutor is supposed to have full control over his/her office. Deputy prosecutors may assist the prosecutor in his duties, but they should all have different nationalities.[203] They should also be persons of high moral character and competent in the trial of criminal cases.[204] The prosecutor or deputy prosecutor should not engage in activities which may interfere with their functions. The impartiality of the prosecutor and deputy prosecutor is therefore very important for discovery of the truth. Questions regarding the disqualification of the prosecutor or a deputy prosecutor may be considered by the Appeals Chamber. In any case, the Presidency of the ICC has the right to excuse the prosecutor or a deputy prosecutor, with due regard to his/her request, from engaging in the process of a particular case.[205]

The prosecutor has, in particular, been authorized to appoint advisers with legal expertise on specific issues which are relevant to certain activities. These include such as sexual and gender violence and violence against children.[206] This means that the prosecutor ought to base the proceedings of investigations on the substantive knowledge of persons who are specialists in the relevant areas of the law.

6.5.2. Reasonable Basis

In general, the prosecutor is responsible for investigating the reliability of the information received from states. If the information is insufficient, he/she is responsible for informing those who have provided the information that it cannot be submitted to the Pre-Trial Chamber.[207] However, if the prosecutor considers the evidence important for the investigation of the case in the Pre-Trial Chamber, she/he must also seek

---

[202] Article 42(1).
[203] Article 42(2).
[204] Article 42(3).
[205] Article 42(3 to 8).
[206] Article 42(9).
[207] Article 15(6).

extra or supplementary information from different entities. These include states, organs of the United Nations, intergovernmental or non-governmental organizations, or any other reliable source that seems appropriate according to the prosecutor.

The prosecutor may also receive oral or written testimony at the seat of the Court.[208] With these preliminary authorisations, the prosecutor is responsible for submitting a case to the Pre-Trial Chamber for investigation if he/she considers that there are reasonable grounds for the case to proceed to the Chamber.[209]

The Pre-Trial Chamber is responsible for taking the investigation of the prosecutor and his/her decision concerning the arrest of a person seriously.[210] In a situation where the Pre-Trial Chamber does not consider the presented evidence sufficient for investigation, the prosecutor may subsequently resubmit the case to the Pre-Trial Chamber if he/she has received new information and evidence concerning the case which has significant value for the representation of the case and proof of the guilt of the accused in the Pre-Trial Chamber.[211]

Although the Statute does not define the term "reasonable basis", the prosecutor may only start the proceeding when he/she and the Pre-Trial Chamber composed of three judges have understood that there is already a reasonable basis for beginning the investigation.[212] While the Statute does not enter into the definition of the term, it offers different channels for finding a reasonable basis for the initiation of an investigation.

Accordingly, the prosecutor must take different matters into consideration which are deemed essential for the initiation of an

---

[208] Article 15(2).

[209] Article 15(3).

[210] A clear example is the Thomas Lubanga Dyilo case at the ICC. The crimes were committed in the territory of the Democratic Republic of Congo. The Prosecutor of the ICC initiated investigations in the Democratic Republic of Congo in 2004. Thereafter, Lubanga, the leader of the Union des Patriotes Congolais (UPC) was arrested and transferred with the French government's assistance to the ICC in 2006. The prosecutor found that there were sufficient reasons to believe that Lubanga had especially committed the conscripting and enlisting of children under the age of fifteen and of making them actively take part in the conflict. For further examination of the case and its rejection in 2008 and its further investigation in 2009 see *infera* chapter ten. Warrants for arrest have also been issued by the Pre-Trial Chamber against four senior commanders of Uganda's Lord's Resistance Army. None of them have appeared in the Court at The Hague. Arrest warrants have also been issued against leaders of Darfur.

[211] Article 15 (4 and 5).

[212] Article 15(3).

investigation. This is because the key principle for investigation is the interest of justice and more importantly the interest of the victim, or victims, who have suffered on account of unjustified actions. Thus, the prosecutor should evaluate the case to find out if: (a) there is reason to believe that a crime within the jurisdiction of the Court has been or is being committed; (b)the case is or would be admissible under article 17; or (c) there is reason to believe that an investigation would not serve the interests of justice with regard to the gravity of the crime and the interests of the victims.[213]

Furthermore, the prosecutor may, after investigation, conclude one or several of the following: that there is no reliable basis for prosecution on the grounds that there is not a satisfactory legal or factual basis to ask for a warrant or summons under article 58; that the case is inadmissible due to the provisions of Article 17 or that a prosecution is not, generally speaking, in the interests of justice.[214] Nevertheless, the Statute gives permission to the Pre-Trial Chamber to thoroughly review the decision of the prosecutor not to proceed if it is discovered that the decision regarding the case does not serve the interests of justice due to the circumstances surrounding it. Here, the questions of the interests of justice may be analysed differently by the Trial Chamber and may be a reason for prosecuting the accusers. The reasons that are therefore presented by the prosecutor must be clear and guarantee the interests of justice. The Statute has consequently tried to give priority to these interests according to the circumstances arising around a case and the conditions of the present time.

6.6. Presidency

There have been several discussions concerning the power, authority and functions of the presidency of the ICC. The drafters of the Statute of the ICC had envisioned many functions being assigned to the Presidency of the Court but these were reduced by the creation of the Pre-Trial Division. The Presidency of the Court has been nominated to fulfil certain requirements. According to the Statute, the president and the first and second vice-presidents are elected by an absolute majority of the judges. Presidents may serve for a term of three years or until the end of their respective terms of office as judges. This also depends on which term expires earlier. They may be re-elected only once.[215]

---

[213] Article 53(1).
[214] Article 53(2).
[215] Article 38(1).

According to the Statute, the first vice president is required to act in place of the president if he/she is not available for one reason or another, for example, if the president is unavailable or disqualified. The second vice-president may also perform duties in place of the president if neither the president nor the first vice-president is available or if they are disqualified from a case for one reason or another in accordance with the provisions of the Statute.[216]

In general, the three presidents, that is, the president and the first and second vice-presidents, have certain responsibilities. One of the most important responsibilities of the Presidency is the proper administration of the Court, with the exception of the Office of the Prosecutor.[217] For this purpose, the Presidency, which is acting on behalf of the Court authority, may suggest the number of judges be increased in accordance with the provisions of the Statute.[218] The Presidency may also have other functions recognized by the Statute.[219]

6.7. Registry

The Statute of the ICC has created the Registry as an important organ of the Court, although it does not have a judicial function.[220] The Registry has different functions for facilitating the tasks of the Court. The Registry is consequently responsible for having sufficient personnel for the variety of duties of the Court and for ensuring that these duties are carried out without prejudice to the functions and powers of the Prosecutor in accordance with article 42.[221]

---

[216] Article 38(2).

[217] Article 38(3)(a).

[218] Article 36 (2) (a).

[219] Article 38(3)(b).

[220] The Registry's functions are very important for the proper implementation of the Statute. The hope is that the Registry will not face the problems that were faced within the proceedings of the ICTY and the ICTR. The members of other organs of these two tribunals sought to exercise the administrative functions of their Registrars. This means that there was a special control of the tasks of the registrars of both tribunals in order to increase the value of their functions. See Comments on the Report of the Expert Group to Conduct a Review of the Effective Operation and Functioning of the International Tribunal for the Former Yugoslavia and the International Criminal Tribunal for Rwanda (UN Document A/54/850) dated 27 April 2000, paras 164 – 174 regarding Recommendation 43 of the Report of the Expert Group, and paras 190 – 207 regarding Recommendation 45 of the Report of the Expert Group.

[221] Article 43(1). See *also* Article 44.

The Registrar, who is the principal administrative officer of the Court, directs the Registry. Judges may elect both the Registrar and the Deputy Registrar.[222] But, the Registrar is only elected by an absolute majority of the judges. His/her functions are carried out under the authority of the President of the Court.[223] It is important that the Registrar and the Deputy Registrar are persons of high moral character. They should also be competent and have the knowledge necessary for carrying out their duties.[224] According to the provisions of the Statute, the Registrar is responsible for the establishment of a Victims and Witnesses Unit within the Registry.[225] The Registry also has a duty concerning the assignment of the defence counsel of the international criminal court.[226] Thus, they should strive to make these matters function smoothly.[227] This is in order to promote the effective implementation of the function of the ICC regarding different questions which may crop up during the investigation of a case. On account of this, the Registrar and Deputy Registrar have a

---

[222] Article 43(4).

[223] Article 43(2).

[224] Article 43(3).

[225] Article 43(6).

[226] The system of Registry of the ICC has actually been criticised by Adama Dieng, the United Nations Assistant Secretary-General and Registrar in the International Criminal Tribunal for Rwanda. According to him "It appears from the Rome Statute that not enough reflection was given to the role of the Registrar of the Court, while much – and appropriate – attention was paid to the institutional role of the Presidency and the other judges, on the one hand, and the Prosecutor on the other. But the experience of the International Criminal Tribunal for Rwanda shows conclusively that the Registrar has a crucial operational role to play in the effectiveness of any international criminal court. Is the lack of such recognition of this reality in the Statute an oversight? Or have the wrong lessons been drawn from the experience of the *ad hoc* tribunals? … It may ultimately not be helpful to be offering lessons to the future Registrar of the International Criminal Court if he is not in an institutional position to make a significant contribution to tasks that are not assigned to him or are truncated among several organs, but which, by their very definition in the context of an international criminal jurisdiction and with benefit of experience, no one else is better placed to perform."Adama Dieng, The International Criminal Court: Lessons From the International Criminal Tribunal for Rwanda - Potential Problems for the Registrar, paper presented at the Conference on "Towards Global Justice: Accountability and the International Criminal Court" held at Wilton Park, Sussex, United Kingdom 4 – 8 February 2002, www.unictr.org /ENGLISH/speeches/adwiltonpark020202.htm - 40k. Visited on 30/10/2008.

[227] Kenneth S. Gallant, The Role and Powers of Defense Counsel in the Rome Statute of the International Criminal Court, 34 International Law Lawyer 21 (2000).

heavy responsibility concerning the protection of victims and witnesses. The purpose is not to "take any risks nor have even the slightest possibility that the identity of the witness could be revealed."Consequently, it is possible that the hearings in the Court may be closed.[228]

6.8. Assembly of States Parties

The Assembly of States Parties consists of the representatives of the states parties to the Court. It is not an organ of the Court but it has a very substantial function for the task of the Court. We can deduce from the provisions of the Statute that it has a vital role in many important decisions and especially in the carrying out of the work of the organs of the Court. Originally, the suggestion concerning the creation of the Assembly of States Parties came from the French delegation and the idea took its place in the Draft Statute submitted to the Diplomatic Conference in 1998.

The Assembly of States Parties was established in accordance with the provisions of the Statute.[229] It is at the heart of the Statute and at the root of the effective implementation of justice under the supervision of the Court. The Assembly of States Parties has a variety of functions including the conduct of administrative matters. It gives the officers of the Court a great deal of advice and a general policy for the implementation of the provisions of the Statute. The decisions of the Assembly are to be taken by consensus, unless otherwise stated by the Statute.

The Assembly of States Parties is also responsible for the establishment of the Bureau. The Bureau consists of a President, two Vice-Presidents and eighteen members elected by the Assembly for three-year terms.[230]

The meetings of the Assembly may be at the seat of the Court or Headquarters of the United Nations.[231] The Statute clearly states that each state party should have one representative in the Assembly and this representative may be accompanied by alternates and advisers. Other states which have signed the Statute but are not party to the Statute may be observers in the Assembly.[232] As a whole, the Assembly of States Parties considers and adopts, as appropriate, recommendations of the Preparatory

---

[228] article.wn.com/view/2009/03/20/Registrar_of_the_ICC_It_is_Not_Acceptable_to_Interrupt_Justi/.
[229] Part 11, Article 112.
[230] Article 112(3).
[231] Article 112(6).
[232] Article 112(1).

Commission.[233] It is the duty of the Assembly to provide management oversight for the Presidency, the Prosecutor and the Registrar in matters relating to the administration of the Court.[234] It is also responsible for the reports and activities of the Bureau,[235] the budget for the Court,[236] the number of judges[237] and any question relating to non-cooperation.[238] The Assembly may additionally perform any other function consistent with the provisions of the Statute or the Rules of Procedure and Evidence.[239] It may also formulate its own rules of procedure.[240]

One significant task of the Assembly of States Parties is to decide about the alteration of the number of judges. This function of the Assembly may make the provisions of the Statute more efficient. The Assembly has the right to create subsidiary bodies whenever this is needed by the Court. This includes, *inter alia*, an independent oversight mechanism for evaluating and investigating the Court. This is in order to make it more efficient and economical.[241]

The Assembly and the Bureau are responsible for organizing at least one meeting a year relating to different matters of interest. During the meetings of the Assembly and the Bureau, not only the representatives of states parties, but also the President of the Court, the Prosecutor and the Registrar or their representatives may participate in discussions.[242] The Assembly may take decisions by consensus within the Assembly and in the Bureau.[243] Whenever it is impossible to reach consensus, the decision

---

[233] Article 112(2)(a). On preparatory committee see Knut Döhrmann, *Preparatory Commission for the International Criminal Court: The Elements of War Crimes,* 82 International Review of the Red Cross 771 (2000); Knut Döhrmann, *The First and Second Sessions of the Preparatory Commission for the International Criminal Court,* 2 Yearbook of International Humanitarian Law 283 (1999); Philippe Kirsch and V. Oosterveld, *The Preparatory Commission for the International Criminal Court,* 25 Fordham International Law Journal 563 (2002); Christine Byron and David Turns, *The Preparatory Commission for the International Criminal Court,* 50 International and Comparative Law Quarterly Law 420 (2001).

[234] Article 112(2)(b).

[235] Article 112(2)(c).

[236] Article 112(2)(d).

[237] Article 112(2)(e).

[238] Article 112(2)(f).

[239] Article 112(2)(g). See also Richard May and Marieka Wierda, International Criminal Evidence(2002).

[240] Article 112(9).

[241] Article 112(4).

[242] Article 112(5).

[243] Article 112(7).

may be taken on matters of substance by a two-thirds majority of those present and taking part in the voting in the Assembly.[244] It may also take decisions in matters of procedure by a simple majority of the states parties present and taking part in the voting.[245] The right to vote may be rescinded if a state party has not for one reason or another paid the financial contributions which are necessary for meeting the costs of the Court.[246] It must, however, be stated that the Assembly of States Parties cannot in any way obstruct the judicial functions of the ICC. Disputes relating to the judicial functions of the Court can only be resolved by a decision taken by the Court itself.

The President of the Court, the prosecutor and the registrar or their representatives, each has the right to take part in the meetings of the Assembly. The first Assembly of States Parties gathered in New York City, at the United Nations, headquarters on 3 September 2002.[247] On 13 February 2009, the Assembly of States Parties resumed and concluded the second resumption of its seventh session. One of the main tasks of the Assembly was to examine the Special Working Group's work on the Crime of Aggression which had been in progress since 2003.[248]

---

[244] Article 112(7) (a).
[245] Article 112(7) (b).
[246] Article 112(8).
[247] At the first Assembly of States Parties, it was stated that "States parties to the treaty creating the International Criminal Court (ICC), which came into force on 1 July of this year, began their one week session this morning to formally adopt the legal agreements that will enable the Court to function, and to finalize the procedure for beginning the nomination and election process for the Court's judges and Prosecutor." The Assembly elected Zeid Ra'ad Zeid Al-Hussein (Jordan) as President of the First Session of the Assembly of States Parties. According to him the world's achievements in international criminal jurisdiction were only possible "because the position of the international community was unshakeable in its support for the Court, anchored in the conviction that humanity will never truly advance, rest with its conscience, find comfort or peace, unless we do what we hitherto have been unable to do: provide a global juridical instrument to deter those persons seeking to commit the gravest of crimes, prosecute those accused of having already brought enormous suffering on the innocent, and offer truth and justice to the victims and to ourselves collectively." International Criminal Court, Assembly of States Parties, First Session, 1st and 2nd Meetings (AM & PM), Press Release L/3012.
[248] For further consideration see chapter nine on the development of the Statute of the ICC in Kampala. The last meeting of the Assembly of states parties was on 18 Novermber 2013. It took many significant questions *inter alia* regarding budget, a quid line to achieve an operational tool to enhance expeditious execution of arrest

---

and surrender orders, and facilitation of exchange of information on states and organization concerning to their complementarity related activities.

CHAPTER FOUR

CATEGORIZATION OF CRIMES IN THE INTERNATIONAL CRIMINAL TRIBUNALS AND THE COURTS

1. Categories of Crimes in the Nuremberg Tribunal

The Nuremberg Tribunal mainly dealt with three categories of international crimes recognised and set out in the London Agreement concerning the prosecution of those who had violated the system of international law.[1] Article 6 of the Constitution of the International Military Tribunal related to this important question.[2] The classification of crimes under the Constitution of the Tribunal still constitutes an important part of international criminal law and is a basis for the development of the law in the contemporary statute of the International Criminal Court (ICC).[3] Moreover, the categories of crimes under Article 6 became the basic ground for the judgment of the Nuremberg Tribunal. Article 6 reads that:

> The Tribunal established by the Agreement referred to in Article 1 hereof for the trial and punishment of the major war criminals of the European Axis countries shall have the power to try and punish persons who, acting in the interests of the European Axis countries, whether as individuals or as members of organizations, committed any of the following crimes.
>
> The following acts, or any of them, are crimes coming within the jurisdiction of the Tribunal for which there shall be individual responsibility:
>
> (a) Crimes against peace: namely, planning, preparation, initiation or waging of a war of aggression, or a war in violation of international treaties, agreements or assurances, or participation in a common plan or conspiracy for the accomplishment of any of the foregoing;

---

[1] The agreement was signed on August 8th 1945.

[2] The article contains the key principles for the recognition of international crimes.

[3] See Chapter seven.

(b) War crimes: namely, violations of the laws or customs of war. Such violations shall include, but not be limited to, murder, ill-treatment or deportation to slave labour or for any other purpose of civilian population of or in occupied territory, murder or ill-treatment of prisoners of war or persons on the seas, killing of hostages, plunder of public or private property, wanton destruction of cities, towns or villages, or devastation not justified by military necessity;
(c) Crimes against humanity: namely, murder, extermination, enslavement, deportation, and other inhumane acts committed against any civilian population, before or during the war; or persecutions on political, racial or religious grounds in execution of or in connection with any crime within the jurisdiction of the Tribunal, whether or not in violation of the domestic law of the country where perpetrated.

Although all three categories of international crime specified under the Constitution of IMT have their own legal characterizations,[4] their use overlapped when applied in practice to certain actions or omissions during the war.[5] Thus, the Tribunal could clarify that crimes against humanity could, at the same time, be recognised as war crimes.[6]

1.1. The General Principles of the Charter

The Charter of the Nuremberg Tribunal was basically established with the purpose of the attribution of the concept of international criminal responsibility to those who had seriously violated the law of armed conflict or committed one or several of the crimes recognised by the constitution of the tribunal. It means that crimes against peace, war crimes, and crimes against humanity have received very strong recognition within the provisions of the Charter.[7] The creation of the Nuremberg Tribunal essentially aimed to bring the relevant individuals under jurisdiction for prosecution and punishment.[8] The second part of the Charter deals, therefore, with some of the most important principles of international

[4] See M. C. Bassiouni., Crimes Against Humanity in International Criminal Law (1999).

[5] Id.

[6] Id.

[7] Horst Fischer., *Grave Breaches of the 1949 Geneva Conventions* in Substantive and Procedural Aspects of International Criminal Law: The Experience of International and National Courts, Documents 3 vols. (Gabrielle Kirk McDonald, Olivia Swaak-Goldman, eds., 2002), 67.

[8] The Tribunal became the foundation for the development of the law of armed conflicts and the formulation of the 1948 Geneva conventions including the recognition of grave breaches. *Id.*

criminal justice which have had a significant function in the recognition and consolidation of the categories of international crimes. It declared *inter alia*:

1. International criminal responsibility applies to individuals without regard to their official position including heads of state or responsible officials in government departments.[9]
2. The position of an individual does not mitigate his/her punishment before the system of international criminal justice.[10]
3. Following the orders of a superior does not free a defendant from criminal responsibility but may mitigate his punishment if the conditions of justice so require.[11]
4. The Nuremberg Tribunal had the right in connection with the conviction of an individual to declare an organization or a group as a criminal organization or having criminal character.[12]
5. If a group or organization was declared criminal, the national authority of the signatory powers had the right to bring the individuals of the organization to trial under their own military or occupation courts.[13]
6. The punishment imposed by the military or occupation courts could be additional to the punishment imposed by the Tribunal.[14]
7. The Nuremberg Tribunal had the right in the interests of justice to take proceedings against an absent person charged with categories of crimes. His absence could not free him from prosecution and punishment.[15]
8. The Tribunal had the right to adopt rules for its procedure but they should not be inconsistent with the rules of the Charter of the Tribunal.[16]

[9] Article 7.
[10] Article 7.
[11] Article 11
[12] Article 9.
[13] Article 10.
[14] Article 11.
[15] Article 12.
[16] Article 13.

1.2. Formulation of the Principles of the Nuremberg Tribunal

The international criminal military tribunals in Nuremberg and Tokyo based their judgments on their charters establishing the criminal responsibility of individuals for the commission of war crimes, crimes against peace and crimes against humanity. In Resolution 95 (I), the General Assembly affirmed the 'principles of the international law recognised by the Charter of the Nuremberg Tribunal and the Judgment of the Tribunal.'[17] In 1947, the General Assembly established the International Law Commission with another resolution to formulate the principles of international law recognised in the Charter of the Nuremberg Tribunal. In 1950, the Commission formulated the following crimes in international law:

> Principle I
> Any person who commits an act which constitutes a crime under international law is responsible therefore and liable to punishment.
>
> Principle II
> The fact that internal law does not impose a penalty for an act which constitutes a crime under international law does not relieve the person who committed the act from responsibility under international law.
>
> Principle III
> The fact that a person who committed an act which constitutes a crime under international law acted as Head of State or responsible Government official does not relieve him from responsibility under international law.
>
> Principle IV
> The fact that a person acted pursuant to order of his Government or of a superior does not relieve him from responsibility under international law, provided a moral choice was in fact possible to him.
>
> Principle V
> Any person charged with a crime under international law has the right to a fair trial on the facts and law.
>
> Principle Vl
> The crimes hereinafter set out are punishable as crimes under; international law:

---

[17] This was adopted in 1946. See also *inera* chapter five.

a. Crimes against peace:
i. Planning, preparation, initiation or waging of a war of aggression or a war in violation of international treaties, agreements or assurances;

ii. Participation in a common plan or conspiracy for the accomplishment of any of the acts mentioned under (i).

b. War crimes:
Violations of the laws or customs of war which include, but are not limited to, murder, ill-treatment or deportation to slave-labour or for any other purpose of civilian population of or in occupied territory, murder or ill-treatment of prisoners of war, of persons on the seas, killing of hostages, plunder of public or private property, wanton destruction of cities, towns, or villages, or devastation not justified by military necessity.

c. Crimes against humanity:
Murder, extermination, enslavement, deportation and other inhuman acts done against any civilian population, or persecutions on political, racial or religious grounds, when such acts are done or such persecutions are carried on in execution of or in connection with any crime against peace or any war crime.

Principle VII
Complicity in the commission of a crime against peace, a war crime, or a crime against humanity as set forth in Principles VI is a crime under international law.

2. Categories of Crimes in the Tokyo Tribunal

The Tokyo Tribunal, like the Nuremberg Tribunal, had several important functions for the prosecution of criminals in the Far East. It recognised three classes of crimes committed during World War II. These were crimes against peace, war crimes and crimes against humanity.[18] The relevant article of the constitution of the Tribunal states that:

Jurisdiction Over Persons and Offences. The Tribunal shall have the power to try and punish Far Eastern war criminals who as individuals or as members of organizations are charged with offences which include Crimes against Peace. The following acts, or any of them, are crimes coming

---

[18] Pritchard R.J. (ed.), The Tokyo Major War Crimes Trial. The Records of the International Military Tribunal for the Far East with an Authorized Commentary and Comprehensive Guide (1998-2005, 124 volumes).
(R.J. Pritchard, ed., 124 volumes 1998-2005).

> within the jurisdiction of the Tribunal for which there shall be individual responsibility:
>
> *(a) Crimes against Peace:* Namely, the planning, preparation, initiation or waging of a declared or undeclared war of aggression, or a war in violation of international law, treaties, agreements or assurances, or participation in a common plan or conspiracy for the accomplishment of any of the foregoing;
>
> *(b) Conventional War Crimes:* Namely, violations of the laws or customs of war;
>
> *(c) Crimes against Humanity:* Namely, murder, extermination, enslavement, deportation, and other inhumane acts committed against any civilian population, before or during the war, or persecutions on political or racial grounds in execution of or in connection with any crime within the jurisdiction of the Tribunal, whether or not in violation of the domestic law of the country where perpetrated. Leaders, organizers, instigators and accomplices participating in the formulation or execution of a common plan or conspiracy to commit any of the foregoing crimes are responsible for all acts performed by any person in execution of such plan.[19]

The Tribunal in the Far East prosecuted twenty-five Japanese political and military leaders for committing crimes against peace.[20] Curiously enough, the Japanese Emperor Hirohito[21] and Prince Asaka were not brought before the jurisdiction of the Tribunal in Tokyo for alleged offences committed during World War II.[22]

---

[19] Article 5.

[20] See Cryer Robert and Neil Boister (eds.), Documents on the Tokyo International Military Tribunal: Charter, Indictment and Judgments (Robert Cryer and Neil Boister, eds., 2008).

[21] There were in fact many arguments for his immunity from prosecution and punishment. *Id.*, at 638-639.

[22] Even suspected criminals were released for one reason or another. The system of international criminal justice, which was supposed to be implemented by the Tribunal, did not function. For instance, the Tribunal in Tokyo did not try Kishi Nobusuke, who was suspected of crimes against peace. Instead, he later became the Japanese prime minister. In general 300,000 Japanese nationals were charged with three classifications of violations. These were crimes against humanity, war crimes and abuse of prisoners. Moreover, the Far East Tribunal did not carry out any procedure concerning violations, which were committed by the Japanese troops in Korea and China. However, the Chinese authorities had thirteen tribunals against the Japanese who had committed serious crimes in their territories. Under Chinese jurisdiction, 504 persons were convicted and 149 persons were executed.

Juridically, the position of the Tokyo Tribunal compared with the Nuremberg Tribunal was much weaker in the system of international criminal law. This relative weakness results from several facts that are indispensable when analysing both tribunals.[23] One chief difference between these two tribunals is their international legal personality within international law. As a whole, the Nuremberg Tribunal had a well-recognised international political-legal personality by the standards of the time. By contrast, the personality of the Tokyo Tribunal was very narrow or, one may say, local.

3. Categories of Crimes in the ICTY

The ICTY is the first international Criminal Tribunal to have been established under the authority of the United Nations since the creation of the Nuremberg Tribunal. From the beginning, it was intended that the Tribunal should have jurisdiction over several international crimes. This was in order not to restrict the scope of jurisdiction of the tribunal and to prevent the individuals responsible from fleeing from punishment for their criminal acts because of the non-applicability of certain international crimes under its jurisdiction. Consequently, the tribunal has been given a range of powers in order to put an end to impunity.

The tribunal therefore has jurisdiction over several international crimes. These include grave breaches of the Geneva Conventions of 1949, violations of the laws and customs of war, genocide and crimes against humanity. Each one of these crimes is also divided into many other classifications which overlap with the definitions of other international crimes. For instance, the term "crimes against humanity" is invoked in many different contexts in order to satisfy its conventional or customary requirements. Similar conclusions can also be argued for other crimes classified by the Statute of the Tribunal.

3.1. Grave Breaches

The ICTY has been given the authority to prosecute those who have committed acts against the provisions of conventional international criminal law governing the regulation of armed conflicts. Thus, the jurisdiction of the court is based on two important sources of international criminal law, namely, conventional and customary law. This is to guarantee the legal position of the Tribunal in order to give it the basic

---

[23] M.C. Bassiouni, Nuremberg Forty Years After, 1986 Proc ASIL, 64.

capacity to bring the perpetrators of crimes under its jurisdiction and prevent impunity.

According to the Statute, the Tribunal has the power to prosecute persons who have seriously violated the system of conventional criminal law governing the regulation of armed conflicts. The Tribunal is therefore authorized to implement the provisions of the Geneva Conventions of 1949 which are an integral part of the international humanitarian law of armed conflicts. This body of law applies to armed conflict and, to some extent, to the period following armed conflict. This is clearly stated under the provisions of Article 2 of the Statute concerning the implementation of the provisions of international criminal law. In other words, atrocities committed in wartime are treated within the framework of international humanitarian law and may be recognised as war crimes. In 1995, the Appeals Chamber of the ICTY unmistakably referred to this fact.[24] This

[24] The *Tadic* case is a clear example referring to the violations of the international humanitarian law of armed conflicts by the Serbian authorities. Therefore, the Appeals Chamber has taken into serious examination the provisions of the humanitarian law of armed conflicts. According to it "On the basis of the foregoing, we find that an armed conflict exists whenever there is a resort to armed force between States or protracted armed violence between governmental authorities and organized armed groups or between such groups within a State. International humanitarian law applies from the initiation of such armed conflicts and extends beyond the cessation of hostilities until a general conclusion of peace is reached; or, in the case of internal conflicts, a peaceful settlement is achieved. Until that moment, international humanitarian law continues to apply in the whole territory of the warring States or, in the case of internal conflicts, the whole territory under the control of a party, whether or not actual combat takes place there. Applying the foregoing concept of armed conflicts to this case, we hold that the alleged crimes were committed in the context of an armed conflict. Fighting among the various entities within the former Yugoslavia began in 1991, continued through the summer of 1992 when the alleged crimes are said to have been committed, and persists to this day. Notwithstanding various temporary cease-fire agreements, no general conclusion of peace has brought military operations in the region to a close. These hostilities exceed the intensity requirements applicable to both international and internal armed conflicts. There has been protracted, large-scale violence between the armed forces of different States and between governmental forces and organized insurgent groups. Even if substantial clashes were not occurring in the Prijedor region at the time and place the crimes allegedly were committed - a factual issue on which the Appeals Chamber does not pronounce - international humanitarian law applies. It is sufficient that the alleged crimes were closely related to the hostilities occurring in other parts of the territories controlled by the parties to the conflict. There is no doubt that the allegations at issue here bear the required relationship. The indictment states that in

fact is moreover confirmed within the judgments of the Tribunal.[25] But it should be emphasised that crimes committed during armed conflict do not all constitute war crimes. In order for an act to constitute a war crime, the acts of the perpetrator should have a close relation to the acts involved in hostilities.[26] This is also confirmed in the jurisdiction of the ICTY.[27] In the

---

1992 Bosnian Serbs took control of the Opstina of Prijedor and established a prison camp in Omarska. It further alleges that crimes were committed against civilians inside and outside the Omarska prison camp as part of the Bosnian Serb take-over and consolidation of power in the Prijedor region, which was, in turn, part of the larger Bosnian Serb military campaign to obtain control over Bosnian territory. Appellant offers no contrary evidence but has admitted in oral argument that in the Prijedor region there were detention camps run not by the central authorities of Bosnia-Herzegovina but by Bosnian Serbs... In light of the foregoing, we conclude that, for the purposes of applying international humanitarian law, the crimes alleged were committed in the context of an armed conflict." *Tadic* (IT-94-1-AR72), Decision on the Defence Motion for Interlocutory Appeal on Jurisdiction, 2 October 1995, para.70.

[25] *Milosevic* (IT-02-54-T), Decision on Motion for Judgment of Acquittal, 16 June 2004, para.16 The judgment also refers to *Prosecutor v. Tadic*, Case No. IT-94-1-T, "Opinion and Judgement", 7 May 1997 ("*Tadic* Trial Judgement"), at paras.561, 628; *Prosecutor v. Delalic, et al.,* Case No.IT-96-21-T, "Judgement", 16 November 1998 ("*Delalic* Trial Judgement"), para.183; *Prosecutor v. Kunarac, et al.,* Case No.IT-96-23-T & IT-96-23/1-T, "Judgement", 22 February 2001, at para.412; *Prosecutor v. Kordi} & ^erkez*, Case No. IT-95-14/2-T, "Judgement", 26 February 2001, at para.24; *Prosecutor v. Naletili} & Martinovic*, Case No.IT-98-34-T, "Judgement", 31 March 2003, at para.177.

[26] See also Larissa Van Den Herik and Elies Van Sliedregt., Ten Years Later, the Rwanda Tribunal still Faces Legal Complexities: Some Comments on the Vagueness of the Indictment, Complicity in Genocide, and the Nexus Requirement for War Crimes, Leiden Journal of International Law, 17 (2004), pp. 537–557.

[27] In the *Kunara* case, the Appeals Chamber stated that "What ultimately distinguishes a war crime from a purely domestic offence is that a war crime is shaped by or dependent upon the environment – the armed conflict – in which it is committed. It need not have been planned or supported by some form of policy. The armed conflict need not have been causal to the commission of the crime, but the existence of an armed conflict must, at a minimum, have played a substantial part in the perpetrator's ability to commit it, his decision to commit it, the manner in which it was committed or the purpose for which it was committed. Hence, if it can be established, as in the present case, that the perpetrator acted in furtherance of or under the guise of the armed conflict, it would be sufficient to conclude that his acts were closely related to the armed conflict. The Trial Chamber's finding on that point is unimpeachable... In determining whether or not the act in question is sufficiently related to the armed conflict, the Trial Chamber may take into account, inter alia, the following factors: the fact that the perpetrator is a combatant; the fact

Tadic case the ICTY Trial Chamber stated that it would be enough to prove that the crime was committed in connection with the hostilities.[28]

Despite the above, the accused's awareness of their actions also appears to be one of the necessary elements in the commission of a war crime. However, the requirement of knowledge is accompanied by three other criteria according to the provisions of the ICC: "there is no requirement for a legal evaluation by the perpetrator as to the existence of an armed conflict or its character as international or non-international; In that context there is no requirement for awareness by the perpetrator of the facts that established the character of the conflict as international or non-international." But, it goes on to state, "there is only a requirement for the awareness of the factual circumstances that established the existence of an armed conflict that is implicit in the terms 'took place in the context of and was associated with'."[29] However, it must be stated that knowledge constitutes only one aspect of the 'mental element' of a criminal act. This is because the mental element not only consists of knowledge, but also, intent. Again, prosecution of an accused person for war crimes does not rest entirely on intent. This is because the nature of atrocities committed in the time of armed conflicts is sufficient without proof of intent.[30]

---

that the victim is a non-combatant; the fact that the victim is a member of the opposing party; the fact that the act may be said to serve the ultimate goal of a military campaign; and the fact that the crime is committed as part of or in the context of the perpetrator's official duties." *Kunarac et al.* (IT-96-23/1-A), Judgement, 12 June 2002, para.58-59.

[28] It says that "It would be sufficient to prove that the crime was committed in the course of or as part of the hostilities in, or occupation of, an area controlled by one of the parties. It is not however, necessary to show that armed conflict was occurring at the exact time and place of the proscribed act alleged to have occurred…nor is it necessary that the crime alleged take place during combat, that it be part of a policy or of a practice officially endorsed or tolerated by one on the parties to the conflict or that the act be in actual furtherance of a policy associated with the conduct of war or in the actual interest of a party to the conflict; the obligations of individuals under international humanitarian law are independent and apply without prejudice to any question of the responsibility of States under international law." Tadic (IT-94-1-T), Opinion and Judgement, 7 May 1997, para.573.

[29] See the final document in this book concerning the Elements of Crimes.

[30] In the Aleksovski case, the Appeals Chamber asserted that "The Trial Chamber concluded that the *mens rea* of the offence is the 'intent to humiliate or ridicule the victim' and did not refer to discrimination.50 There is therefore no basis for the contention that the Trial Chamber found that a discriminatory intent was a necessary element of the offence of outrages upon personal dignity. Counsel for the Appellant made the more general submission that an essential element of offences

The provisions of Article 2 are actually taken from the common article of the Geneva Conventions relating to their grave breaches.[31] In general, the common articles of the four Geneva Conventions protect four specific categories of victims. The Geneva Convention I relates to the protection of the wounded and sick in armed forces in the field. Convention II protects the wounded, sick and shipwrecked members of armed forces at sea. According to the provisions of Convention III, prisoners of war are protected from any armed attack. The protection of civilians is at the

---

under Article 3 of the Statute is that the perpetrator is 'motivated by a contempt towards other persons' dignity in racial, religious, social, sexual or other discriminatory sense'.51 However, he provided no authority to support this specific formulation or the existence generally of an international law requirement of discriminatory intent or 'motive' for war crimes. The only apparent legal basis put forward for the submission is that, because of the extreme gravity of the crimes which fall within Article 3 of the Statute, not every assault on physical integrity and personal dignity is criminal and only proof of a discriminatory intent in committing those acts will establish that the acts are of adequate gravity.52 20. The Appellant's argument is unfounded. There is nothing in the undoubtedly grave nature of the crimes falling within Article 3 of the Statute, nor in the Statute generally, which leads to a conclusion that those offences are punishable only if they are committed with discriminatory intent. The general requirements which must be met for prosecution of offences under Article 3 have already been clearly identified by the Appeals Chamber in the *Tadic* Jurisdiction Decision, and they do not include a requirement of proof of a discriminatory intent or motivation. The Appeals Chamber recognised there that the relevant violation of international humanitarian law must be 'serious' in the sense that it 'must constitute a breach of a rule protecting important values and the breach must involve grave consequences for the victim.' This in no way imports a requirement that the violation must be committed with discriminatory intent." Aleksovski (IT-95-14/1-A), Judgement 24 March 2000, paras.18-20.

[31] The concept of grave breaches arises from the Geneva Conventions. "The grave breaches provisions of the Geneva Conventions of 1949 have a unique role in the criminalization of international atrocities. The different grave breaches provisions do not only contain the basic manifestation of the international community's will to criminalize certain serious violations of international humanitarian law.... While the basis of the grave breaches system of the Geneva Conventions of 1949 has been reaffirmed in the recent past, the jurisprudence of the ICTY has developed our understanding of certain problems related to its concrete application. In particular, the ICTY has shed light on the difficulties in applying the grave breaches of the Geneva Conventions to so-called internationalized armed conflicts." Horst Fischer., *Grave Breaches of the 1949 Geneva Conventions* in Substantive and Procedural Aspects of International Criminal Law: The Experience of International and National Courts, Documents 3 vols. (Gabrielle Kirk McDonald, Olivia Swaak-Goldman, eds., 2002), 93.

centre of Convention IV. These four categories of victim are regarded as 'protected persons' and prosecution of a grave breach of the four Geneva Conventions demands, explicitly or implicitly, proof that the criminal actions were committed against such a protected person. The article clearly states that the Tribunal has the authority to prosecute those who have committed or have received orders to commit grave breaches of the Geneva Conventions of 1949.[32] These include acts against persons or property protected under the provisions of the relevant four Geneva Conventions.[33] The followings acts are listed in the contents of Article 2:

(a) wilful killing;
(b) torture or inhuman treatment, including biological experiments;
(c) wilfully causing great suffering or serious injury to body or health;
(d) extensive destruction and appropriation of property, not justified by military necessity and carried out unlawfully and wantonly;
(e) compelling a prisoner of war or a civilian to serve in the forces of a hostile power;
(f) wilfully depriving a prisoner of war or a civilian of the rights of fair and regular trial;
(g) unlawful deportation or transfer or unlawful confinement of a civilian;
(h) taking civilians as hostages.

The above provisions aim at the protection of several subjects of war which should be respected during armed conflicts.[34] These include, as a whole, human beings who are recognised as the victims of war and their property.[35] The above provisions are also considered an integral part of customary international criminal law that has long been recognised in international criminal law.[36] Thus, the instructions which are given to the Tribunal by the Statute concerning the grave breaches of the Conventions are not new and they were formulated into the Geneva Conventions to evade any further difficulties at the time of their application. Therefore, the provisions of Article 2 of the Statute overlap, in many instances, with the provisions of Article 3 of the same Statute.[37] Their interpretation and application depend therefore on the circumstances and the position of each case investigated under the jurisdiction of the Tribunal. Another difference

---

[32] Id, at 69. Even if they disobeyed the orders but their acts still resulted in the commission of crimes, they are to be brought before the jurisdiction of the tribunal.
[33] *Id.,* at 69 and 71.
[34] *Id,* at 70.
[35] *Id,* at 71.
[36] *Id,* at 71.
[37] See the next section.

between these two articles is also the gravity of the crimes committed by the conflicting parties.

3.2. Violations of the Laws or Customs of War

The ICTY has been authorized to deal with other types of violation, which may not necessarily come under the provisions of Article 2 concerning grave breaches. These are dealt with in Article 3 of its Statute. The article concerns two important areas of the system of international criminal law. These are conventional and customary law.[38] It points also to the fact that the Tribunal is permitted to use both sources for proof of the violations of the laws or customs of war. The violations listed within the article are not exhaustive.[39]

Both parts of the article are subject to each other and cannot easily be separated. The first part is the law of war. In the legal sense, this implies the existing legislation enforceable in the clash of armed forces between subjects of international law. This includes states, organizations, groups or individuals. The legislation of the law of war also applies in cases of the occupation of foreign territories by the armed forces of one of the conflicting parties. The relevant rules of the laws of armed conflict should also be respected when one of the conflicting parties does not meet any armed resistance in the territory of another conflicting party. This means that the ICTY is not limited by the terminological definition of armed conflict, whether international or national, or any other such excuse in order not to prosecute criminals for their military criminal conducts.

The second part of the article presents the same provisions of the laws of armed conflict but in the form of customs of war. In fact, the laws of war and customs of war complement one another within the provisions of Article 3. The term "customs of war" deals with actions or omissions which are in accordance with customary international criminal law and have to be respected by the conflicting parties. The reason for the combination of the laws of war and customs of war in a single article is to disallow any interpretation or reasoning against the laws of war by conflicting parties claiming not to be a party to the relevant international conventions.

The provisions of Article 3 have therefore empowered the Tribunal to prosecute persons committing acts or omissions against the laws and

---

[38] See Thomas Merton., The Normative Impact on International Law of the International Tribunal for the Former Yugoslavia, Israel Yearbook on Human Rights 1994, pp. 163-82.

[39] *Id.*, at 77.

customs of war. The article lists the following as violations of its provisions:

(a) employment of poisonous weapons or other weapons calculated to cause unnecessary suffering;
(b) wanton destruction of cities, towns or villages, or devastation not justified by military necessity;
(c) attack, or bombardment, by whatever means, of undefended towns, villages, dwellings, or buildings;
(d) seizure of, destruction or wilful damage done to institutions dedicated to religion, charity and education, the arts and sciences, historic monuments and works of art and science;
(e) plunder of public or private property.

The enumerations of different sub-sections in the above are only an exemplification of the laws and customs of war and are not therefore exhaustive of what does and does not constitute the violations of the laws and customs of war.[40] The scope of the jurisdiction of the ICTY is consequently not limited to the above provisions and they may be enlarged according to the requirements of the jurisdiction and the judgment of the Tribunal based on consolidated customary international criminal law.

In connection with the above, one of the most significant achievements of the ICTY was the recognition of the application of the provisions of grave breaches to internal armed conflicts. For instance, the Trial Chamber in the *Celebici* judgment stated the absolute consolidation of the principle of attribution of criminal responsibility for grave breaches which have occurred during internal conflicts. According to this judgment "the majority of the Appeals Chamber (in the *Tadic* Case) did indeed recognise that a change in the customary law scope of the grave breaches regime in this direction might be occurring. This Trial Chamber is also of the view that the possibility that customary law has developed the provisions of the Geneva Conventions since 1949 to constitute an extension of the system of 'grave breaches' to internal armed conflicts should be recognised."[41] The ICTY, in the application of the provisions of Article 3, has also referred to the theories of the International Military Tribunal in Nuremberg and the Nigerian Courts concerning the international criminal responsibility of individuals who engaged in wanton or unjustifiable activities.[42]

---

[40] See *also* the above paragraphs.

[41] Prosecutor V. Delalic & Others, Judgment, ICTY Case No.IT-96-21-T, T.CH. Haguater, 16 No.1998, para.202.

[42] The ICTY stated that "Even if customary international law includes certain basic principles applicable to both internal and international armed conflicts, Appellant

The ICTY has consequently concluded that the provisions of Article 3 of its Statute are equivalent to the provisions of Common Article 3 of the Geneva Conventions. This means that they are the presentation of customary international criminal law. Although the above statement clearly refers to the application of the provisions of the humanitarian law of armed conflicts to internal or international conflicts, the policy of the ICTY has not been followed by the ICC creating some controversy.[43]

---

argues that such prohibitions do not entail individual criminal responsibility when breaches are committed in internal armed conflicts; these provisions cannot, therefore, fall within the scope of the International Tribunal's jurisdiction. It is true that, for example, common Article 3 of the Geneva Conventions contains no explicit reference to criminal liability for violation of its provisions. Faced with similar claims with respect to the various agreements and conventions that formed the basis of its jurisdiction, the International Military Tribunal at Nuremberg concluded that a finding of individual criminal responsibility is not barred by the absence of treaty provisions on punishment of breaches. The Nuremberg Tribunal considered a number of factors relevant to its conclusion that the authors of particular prohibitions incur individual responsibility: the clear and unequivocal recognition of the rules of warfare in international law and State practice indicating an intention to criminalize the prohibition, including statements by government officials and international organizations, as well as punishment of violations by national courts and military tribunals. Where these conditions are met, individuals must be held criminally responsible, because, as the Nuremberg Tribunal concluded: '[c]rimes against international law are committed by men, not by abstract entities, and only by punishing individuals who commit such crimes can the provisions of international law be enforced.' Applying the foregoing criteria to the violations at issue here, we have no doubt that they entail individual criminal responsibility, regardless of whether they are committed in internal or international armed conflicts. Principles and rules of humanitarian law reflect 'elementary considerations of humanity' widely recognised as the mandatory minimum for conduct in armed conflicts of any kind. No one can doubt the gravity of the acts at issue, nor the interest of the international community in their prohibition. Furthermore, many elements of international practice show that States intend to criminalize serious breaches of customary rules and principles on internal conflicts. As mentioned above, during the Nigerian Civil War, both members of the Federal Army and rebels were brought before Nigerian courts and tried for violations of principles of international humanitarian law." *Tadic* (IT-94-1-AR72), Decision on the Defence Motion for Interlocutory Appeal on Jurisdiction, 2 October 1995, paras.128-129.

[43] Horst Fischer, *Grave Breaches of the 1949 Geneva Conventions* in Substantive and Procedural Aspects of International Criminal Law: The Experience of International and National Courts, Documents 3 vols. (Gabrielle Kirk McDonald, Olivia Swaak-Goldman, eds., 2002).

3.3. Genocide

During the war in the territories of the former Yugoslavia, a large number of criminal acts were perpetrated against different ethnic groups. Some of these acts not only constituted grave violations of the humanitarian laws of armed conflict but beyond any doubt also constituted violations of the provisions of the genocide convention. This was because these violations were systematically planned and committed against particular groups, such as the Muslim inhabitants of Herzegovina, on grounds of religion and/or ethnicity.

The Statute of the ICTY therefore in Article 4 empowered the Tribunal to bring any person who has committed genocide under its jurisdiction for prosecution and the application of appropriate punishment.[44] The provisions of Article 4 are taken from the provisions of the Convention on Genocide of 1948. "Genocide" is defined as any of the following acts committed with intent to destroy, in whole or in part, a racial, ethnical, religious or national group such as:

(a) killing members of the group;
(b) causing serious bodily or mental harm to members of the group;
(c) deliberately inflicting on the group conditions of life calculated to bring about its physical destruction in whole or in part;
(d) imposing measures intended to prevent births within the group;
(e) forcibly transferring children of the group to another group.

3. The following acts shall be punishable:

(a) genocide;
(b) conspiracy to commit genocide;
(c) direct and public incitement to commit genocide;
(d) attempt to commit genocide;
(e) complicity in genocide.

Although many international lawyers criticize the shortcomings of the definition of genocide in the 1948 Convention, the definition of genocide in the Statute of the ICTY is similar to that of the Convention. One of the reasons for this was to avoid any controversy, which may have prevented the adoption of the Statute of the Tribunal. Another reason was to bring justice rapidly into force and to put an end to the war and to impunity. Furthermore, for the first time in the history of the legislation of

---

[44] M. Cherif Bassiouni and P. Manikas, The Law of the International Criminal Tribunal for The Former Yugoslavia (1996).

international criminal courts, a tribunal could bring persons before its jurisdiction for the violations of the provisions of the Convention on Genocide. Even though the crime had previously been committed during various international armed conflicts, it was impossible to judge it because of the non-existence of an international criminal court.

The ICTY has further developed the definition of genocide and has tried to prevent any complication of its definition. For instance, the *Sikirica* Trial Chamber spoke against the ICTY's Prosecutor who had unnecessarily complicated the definition of intent in genocide. The Chamber stated that "the first rule of interpretation is to give words their ordinary meaning where the text is clear. Here, the meaning of intent is made plain in the chapeau to Article 4(2). Beyond saying that the very specific intent required must be established, particularly in the light of the potential for confusion between genocide and persecution, the Chamber does not consider it necessary to indulge in the exercise of choosing one of the three standards identified by the Prosecution. In the light, therefore, of the explanation that the provision itself gives as to the specific meaning of intent, it is unnecessary to have recourse to theories of intent."[45]

Although the ICTY has dealt with different cases regarding the matter of genocide and intent, it has clearly stated that the intention to commit genocide must involve a substantial or reasonably substantial number. This means that the crime of genocide must involve the intent to destroy a *substantial part* if not a *very important part*. The ICTY has also employed the term a *reasonably substantial number* governing a special group.[46] For instance, relating to the Bosnian Muslims of Srebrenica, the *Krstic* Trial Chamber stated that "the victims of genocide must be targeted *by reason* of their membership in a group … The intent to destroy a group as such, in whole or in part, presupposes that the victims were chosen by reason of

---

[45] Sikirica et al. (IT-95-8-T), Judgement on Defence of Motions to Acquit, 3 September 2001, para.60.

[46] In one of the cases, the Trial Chamber states that "The evidence must establish that it is the group that has been targeted and not merely specific individuals within that group. That is the significance of the phrase 'as such' in the chapeau. Whereas it is the individuals that constitute the victims of most crimes, the ultimate victim of genocide is the group, although its destruction necessarily requires the commission of crimes against its members, that is, against individuals belonging to that group. This is what differentiates genocide from the crime against humanity of persecution. Even though they both have discriminatory elements, some of which are common to both crimes, in the case of persecution, the perpetrator commits crimes against individuals, on political, racial or religious grounds." *Sikiricaet a.* (IT-95-8-T), Judgement on Defence of Motions to Acquit, September 3, 2001, para.89.

their membership in the group whose destruction was sought. Mere knowledge of the victims' membership in a distinct group on the part of the perpetrators is not sufficient to establish an intention to destroy the group as such."[47] The Chamber goes further and states that:

> … the intent to destroy a group, even if only in part, means seeking to destroy a distinct part of the group as opposed to an accumulation of isolated individuals within it. Although the perpetrators of genocide need not seek to destroy the entire group protected by the Convention, they must view the part of the group they wish to destroy as a distinct entity which must be eliminated as such. A campaign resulting in the killings, in different places spread over a broad geographical area, of a finite number of members of a protected group might not thus qualify as genocide, despite the high total number of causalities, because it would not show an intent by the perpetrators to target the very existence of the group as such.[48]

The Chamber expressed that "the intent to kill all the Bosnian Muslim men of military age in Srebrenica constitutes an intent to destroy in part the Bosnian Muslim group within the meaning of Article 4 and therefore must be qualified as a genocide."[49] Consequently, the Chamber came to the conclusion that the international crime of genocide had been committed against the Bosnian Muslim population at Srebrenica in July 1995.[50]

---

[47] *Krstic (*IT-98-33-T), Judgment, 2 AUGUST 2001, para.561.
[48] *Krstic (*IT-98-33-T), Judgment, 2 AUGUST 2001, para.590.
[49] *Id.*, 598.
[50] The Chamber explains that "595. Granted, only the men of military age were systematically massacred, but it is significant that these massacres occurred at a time when the forcible transfer of the rest of the Bosnian Muslim population was well under way. The Bosnian Serb forces could not have failed to know, by the time they decided to kill all the men, that this selective destruction of the group would have a lasting impact upon the entire group. Their death precluded any effective attempt by the Bosnian Muslims to recapture the territory. Furthermore, the Bosnian Serb forces had to be aware of the catastrophic impact that the disappearance of two or three generations of men would have on the survival of a traditionally patriarchal society, an impact the Chamber has previously described in detail. The Bosnian Serb forces knew, by the time they decided to kill all of the military aged men, that the combination of those killings with the forcible transfer of the women, children and elderly would inevitably result in the physical disappearance of the Bosnian Muslim population at Srebrenica. Intent by the Bosnian Serb forces to target the Bosnian Muslims of Srebrenica as a group is further evidenced by their destroying homes of Bosnian Muslims in Srebrenica and Poto~ari and the principal mosque in Srebrenica soon after the attack. 596. Finally,

As a whole, the work of the ICTY has been useful in the recognition of the international crime of genocide and its recent development in the system of international criminal law. For instance, the Appeals Chamber has maintained that there is no requirement to establish a "plan" to commit the international crime of genocide. In other words, it is sufficient to establish the commission of the crime of genocide without any evidence of the engagement of state or entity machinery. The ICTY has even stated that it is possible to establish genocide when an individual is acting alone. The *Jelisic* case merely implies this fact.[51] Although, this must be proved in substance, the possibility always exists.[52] It must however be underlined

---

there is a strong indication of the intent to destroy the group as such in the concealment of the bodies in mass graves, which were later dug up, the bodies mutilated and reburied in other mass graves located in even more remote areas, thereby preventing any decent burial in accord with religious and ethnic customs and causing terrible distress to the mourning survivors, many of whom have been unable to come to a closure until the death of their men is finally verified. 597. The strategic location of the enclave, situated between two Serb territories, may explain why the Bosnian Serb forces did not limit themselves to expelling the Bosnian Muslim population. By killing all the military aged men, the Bosnian Serb forces effectively destroyed the community of the Bosnian Muslims in Srebrenica as such and eliminated all likelihood that it could ever re-establish itself on that territory… 599. The Trial Chamber has thus concluded that the Prosecution has proven beyond all reasonable doubt that genocide, crimes against humanity and violations of the laws or customs of war were perpetrated against the Bosnian Muslims, at Srebrenica, in July 1995."*Krstic* (IT-98-33-T), Judgment, 2 August 2001.

[51] According to the Appeals Chamber, "Such a case is theoretically possible. The murders committed by the accused are sufficient to establish the material element of the crime of genocide and it is *a priori* possible to conceive that the accused harboured the plan to exterminate an entire group without this intent having been supported by any organisation in which other individuals participated. In this respect, the preparatory work of the Convention of 1948 brings out that premeditation was not selected as a legal ingredient of the crime of genocide, after having been mentioned by the *ad hoc* committee at the draft stage, on the grounds that it seemed superfluous given the special intention already required by the text and that such precision would only make the burden of proof even greater. It ensues from this omission that the drafters of the Convention did not deem the existence of an organisation or a system serving a genocidal objective as a legal ingredient of the crime. In so doing, they did not discount the possibility of a lone individual seeking to destroy a group as such." *Jelisic* (IT-95-10-T), Judgment, 14 December 1999, para.100.

[52] The Appeals Chamber clarifies that "As to proof of specific intent, it may, in the absence of direct explicit evidence, be inferred from a number of facts and circumstances, such as the general context, the perpetration of other culpable acts systematically directed against the same group, the scale of atrocities committed,

that the development of the scope of the international crime of genocide was not particularly welcomed by many states, and therefore the Statute of the ICC, by contrast, requires a plan or policy as an element for the recognition of the crime of genocide.

The commission of the crime of genocide has also been recognised within other cases by the ICTY. The ICTY is the first international criminal tribunal which has closely dealt with the crime of genocide since its formulation in 1948. The Tribunal is also continuing its work in other cases for the recognition of the commission of the crime of genocide and prevention of its development. One of the most well-known cases is the case of Radovan Karadzic who has been brought to trial in The Hague. His trial started in autumn 2009. The case involves 1.2 million pages of evidence and a considerable number of crime scenes including hundreds of witnesses. The victims have been waiting for this historical event for many years. However, in the beginning, Karadzic failed to attend the Court. Finally, on 3 November, he appeared in the Court but asked for more time. He has refused to accept the time limit. He is probably using the tactic which proved successful enough for Milosevic which means not accepting the legal forum or any acts taken on behalf of the tribunal. Milosevic died before any judgment was delivered against him by the ICTY. This means that Milosevic was never legally found guilty of the commission of international crimes during the four-year trial against him.

3.4. Crimes against Humanity

Another category of crime, which is addressed by the Statute of the ICTY, is crimes against humanity. The relevant definition for these crimes derives essentially from the provisions of the International Military Tribunal in Nuremberg, the Principles of the Charter of the Nuremberg Tribunal accepted in the General Assembly of the United Nations and the Draft Code of Crimes against the Peace and Security of Mankind.

The presentation of crimes against humanity in the Statute of the ICTY is strongly influenced by the extreme barbarism of the many acts carried

---

the systematic targeting of victims on account of their membership of a particular group, or the repetition of destructive and discriminatory acts. … The Appeals Chamber is of the opinion that the existence of a plan or policy is not a legal ingredient of the crime. However, in the context of proving specific intent, the existence of a plan or policy may become an important factor in most cases. The evidence may be consistent with the existence of a plan or policy, or may even show such existence, and the existence of a plan or policy may facilitate proof of the crime." *Jelisic* (IT-95-10-T), Judgment, 5 July 2001, paras.47 and 48.

out during the conflict in violation of the fundamental rights of man. These rights were recognised by different instruments of international human rights law or the international humanitarian law of armed conflicts.

Article 5 of the Statute permits the Tribunal to have jurisdiction over persons who have committed acts constituting crimes against humanity. These imply murder, extermination, enslavement, deportation, imprisonment, torture, rape, persecution on political, racial and religious grounds, and any other inhuman actions. With its use of the last term, the Statute gives broad authority to the Tribunal to examine the character of unspecified inhuman acts with due regard to the other acts listed above and to determine whether such inhuman acts fall within the realm of crimes against humanity. The fundamental aim of this definition is to protect any civilian population from any unlawful and illegal behaviour. This category of international crime has also been widely recognised by the ICTY and has been one of the leading principles within its procedures. The Tribunal has, to some extent, succeeded in prosecuting individuals who committed crimes against humanity during the war in the territories of the former Yugoslavia. The Tribunal has strongly emphasised the importance of the "knowledge" of the accused in taking part in the implementation of a certain ideology.[53] However, the ICTY judgments have also based the recognition of crimes against humanity on two other important principles, namely, widespread attack and systematic attack. The term "widespread" refers to the measure and the degree of acts perpetrated and the number of victims of criminal acts. This means that the attack must be systematic or widespread. Taken as a whole, for the commission of crimes against humanity, the state legal personality may be used.

One serious flaw in the Statute of the ICTY governing crimes against humanity is that an exhaustive list of punishable acts is stated within its provisions. This means that it creates some form of limitation on the

---

[53] For instance, in the *Tihomir Blaskic* case, the Trial Chamber asserted that "It follows that the *mens rea* specific to a crime against humanity does not require that the agent be identified with the ideology, policy or plan in whose name mass crimes were perpetrated nor even that he supported it. It suffices that he knowingly took the risk of participating in the implementation of the ideology, policy or plan. This specifically means that it must, for example, be proved that: - the accused willingly agreed to carry out the functions he was performing; - that these functions resulted in his collaboration with the political, military or civilian authorities defining the ideology, policy or plan at the root of the crimes; - that he received orders relating to the ideology, policy or plan; and lastly - that he contributed to its commission through intentional acts or by simply refusing of his own accord to take the measures necessary to prevent their perpetration." *Tihomir Blaskic* (IT-95-14-T), Judgement, 3 March 2000, para.257.

aspects of crimes against humanity. Although the ICTY cannot include new categories of punishable acts to the list, it may consider “other inhuman acts” as crimes against humanity. This “makes the substantive content of crimes against humanity illustrative rather than exhaustive.”[54] In other words, the language of the Statute of the ICTY has two different interpretations. Consequently, the legal language of the Statute may go against the principle of *nullum crimen sine lege*. In response to this situation, the ICTY has endeavoured to define the term “other inhuman acts”. The position is clarified with reference to the definition of the term by the 1996 Draft Code of Crimes against the Peace and Security of Mankind. The Draft illustrates that the term “other inhuman acts” means “acts which severely damage physical or mental integrity, health or human dignity, such as mutilation and severe bodily harm.”[55] This definition has been used and enlarged by the ICTY in the *Tadic* case. According to the judgment:

> The findings of fact about the acts of the accused relevant to this count are those concerning beatings and acts of violence referred to in dealing with Count 10. The Trial Chamber finds beyond reasonable doubt that those beatings and other acts of violence which were suffered by the six victims there named, who are Muslims, constitute inhumane acts and are crimes against humanity committed during an armed conflict as part of a widespread or systematic attack on a civilian population and that the accused intended for discriminatory reasons to inflict severe damage to the victims' physical integrity and human dignity. The Trial Chamber further finds that the accused in some instances was himself the perpetrator and in others intentionally assisted directly and substantially in the common purpose of inflicting physical suffering upon them and thereby aided and abetted in the commission of the crimes and is therefore individually responsible for each of them as provided by Article 7, paragraph 1, of the Statute. The Trial Chamber accordingly finds beyond reasonable doubt that the accused is guilty as charged in Count 11 of the Indictment in respect of each of those six victims.[56]

The Trial Chamber went even further and stated that *a)* beating a person, *b)* forcible removal of a person from one area to another, *c)* widespread attack on a civilian population, *d)* systematic attack on a civilian population, *e)* severe physical damage to a civilian and, *f)* severe damage to a civilian's personality all constitute, without doubt, crimes

---

[54] Yusuf Aksar, Implementing International Humanitarian Law: From the AD Hoc Tribunals to a Permanent International Criminal Court (2004), p.262.
[55] Article 18 (k) of the Draft Code.
[56] *Tadic* (IT-94-1-T), Judgement, 7 May 1997, para.730.

against humanity. Accordingly, the Trial Chamber concluded that "the accused intended thereby for discriminatory reasons to inflict severe damage to the physical integrity and human dignity of the victims. The Trial Chamber, accordingly finds beyond reasonable doubt that the accused is guilty" of crimes against humanity. Consequently, the accused, by his participation in illegal acts during the relevant armed conflict, had committed criminal acts falling under the jurisdiction of the ICTY.[57] In the *Drazen Erdemovic* case, the Trial Chamber goes even further and defines crimes against humanity as 'very grave crimes' or, a violation of the collective conscience of the international human community as a whole.

Generally speaking, crimes against humanity are recognised as very grave crimes which shock the collective conscience. The indictment supporting the charges against the accused at the Nuremberg Trial specified that the crimes against humanity constituted breaches of international conventions, domestic law, and the general principles of criminal law as derived from the criminal law of all civilised nations. The Secretary-General of the United Nations, in his report which proposed the Statute of International Tribunal, considered that 'crimes against humanity refer to inhumane acts of *extreme gravity*, such as wilful killing, torture or rape, committed as part of a widespread or systematic attack against any civilian population on national, political, ethnic, racial or religious grounds.' In 1994, the International Law Commission asserted that 'the definition of crimes against humanity encompasses inhumane acts of a *very serious character* involving widespread or systematic violations aimed at the civilian population in whole or in part.' Crimes against humanity are serious acts of violence which harm human beings by striking what is most essential to them: their life, liberty, physical welfare, health, and or dignity. They are inhumane acts that by their extent and gravity go beyond the limits tolerable to the international community, which must perforce demand their punishment. But crimes against humanity also transcend the individual because when the individual is assaulted, humanity comes under attack and is negated. It is therefore the concept of humanity as victim which essentially characterises crimes against humanity.[58]

The ICTY has also within many other cases dealt with the concept of crimes against humanity regarding murder, extermination, enslavement, deportation, imprisonment, torture, persecution and rape. All of these actions have been recognised as serious violations of international criminal

[57] *Id.*, para.764.

[58] *Drazen Erdemovic*, Sentencing and Judgement, 29 November 1996, paras.27-28.

law and have given rise to the concept of the international criminal responsibility of the perpetrators.

The term "murder" refers to the act of killing with the intention of premeditated murder.[59] But, the premeditation is not a necessary requirement.[60] The word "extermination" refers to acts of killing with the purpose of destroying the characteristics of a population.[61] The Statute of the ICTY by the term "enslavement" denotes the status of a person over whom the rights of ownership are exercised.[62] The expression

---

[59] *Kupreskic* et al. (IT-96-16-T), Judgment, 14 January 2000, para.561.

[60] *Kordic, et al.* (IT-95-14/2-T), Judgment 26 February 2001, para.235-236.

[61] In the *Vasiljevic* case, the Trial Chamber explains the condition of extermination. It says that "This Trial Chamber concludes from the material which it has reviewed that criminal responsibility for "extermination" only attaches to those individuals responsible for a large number of deaths, even if their part therein was remote or indirect. Responsibility for one or for a limited number of such killings is insufficient. The Trial Chamber also concludes that the act of extermination must be collective in nature rather than directed towards singled out individuals. However, contrary to genocide, the offender need not have intended to destroy the *group* or part of the group to which the victims belong. It is also apparent from the material reviewed that it is not sufficient to establish extermination for the offender to have intended to kill a large number of individuals, or to inflict grievous bodily harm, or to inflict serious injury, in the reasonable knowledge that such act or omission was likely to cause death as in the case of murder. He must also have known of the vast scheme of collective murder and have been willing to take part therein. As opposed to persecution pursuant to Article 5(h) of the Statute, it need not be established that he acted on any discriminatory grounds. Also, the ultimate reason or motives – political or ideological – for which the offender carried out the acts are not part of the required *mens rea* and are, therefore, legally irrelevant. The Trial Chamber therefore finds that the elements of the crime of "extermination" are as follows: 1. The material element of extermination consists of any one act or combination of acts which contributes to the killing of a large number of individuals (*actusreus*). 2. The offender must intend to kill, to inflict grievous bodily harm, or to inflict serious injury, in the reasonable knowledge that such act or omission is likely to cause death, or otherwise intends to participate in the elimination of a number of individuals, in the knowledge that his action is part of a vast murderous enterprise in which a large number of individuals are systematically marked for killing or killed (*mens rea*)." *Vasiljevic* (IT-98-32-T), Judgment, 29 November 2002, paras.227-229.

[62] In the case of *Kunarac,* the Appeals Chamber also recognised that the notion of slavery had developed beyond chattel slavery. It stated that "the chief thesis of the Trial Chamber that the traditional concept of slavery, as defined in the 1926 Slavery Convention and often referred to as 'chattel slavery', has evolved to encompass various contemporary forms of slavery, which are also based on the exercise of any of or all of the powers attaching to the right of ownership. In the

"deportation" implies the forcible transfer of population.[63] By the word "imprisonment", the Statute refers to cases where a person is arbitrarily deprived of liberty. This means that there is no legal reason for the detention of a person.[64] "Torture" implies where physical or mental pain or suffering is inflicted on a person in order to obtain information.[65] By the term "rape", the Statute refers to sexual penetration of another person without obtaining her/his actual consent.[66] The language "persecution"

---

case of these various contemporary forms of slavery, the victim is not subject to the exercise of the more extreme rights of ownership associated with 'chattel slavery,' but in all cases, as a result of the exercise of any or all of the powers attaching to the right of ownership, there is some destruction of the juridical personality; the destruction is greater in the case of 'chattel slavery' but the difference is one of degree. The Appeals Chamber considers 20 that, at the time relevant to the alleged crimes, these contemporary forms of slavery formed part of enslavement as a crime against humanity under customary international law." *Kunarac*, et al. (IT-96-23/1-A), Judgement, 12 June 2002, para.117. The Appeals Chamber went further and reached the conclusion that "... the law does not know of a right of ownership over a person". Article 1(1) of the 1926 Slavery Convention speaks more guardedly "of a person over whom any or all of the powers attaching to the right of ownership are exercised." That language is to be preferred ... The question whether a particular phenomenon is a form of enslavement will depend on the operation of the factors or indicia of enslavement identified by the Trial Chamber. These factors include the "control of someone's movement, control of physical environment, psychological control, measures taken to prevent or deter escape, force, threat of force or coercion, duration, assertion of exclusivity, subjection to cruel treatment and abuse, control of sexuality and forced labour". Consequently, it is not possible exhaustively to enumerate all of the contemporary forms of slavery which are comprehended in the expansion of the original idea; this Judgement is limited to the case in hand." *Kunarac*, et al. (IT-96-23/1-A), Judgement, 12 June 2002, paras.118-119.

[63] The crime against humanity of deportation is not recorded in the judgements of the ICTR and SCSL. The position has also been controversial regarding the judgements of the ICTY. The policy has been very slow. Nevertheless, the ICTY Appeals Chamber has more or less accepted the concept and employed it in its judgments. *Krnojelac* (IT-97-25-A), Judgement, 17 September 2003, paras.222-223.

[64] *Kordic*et el. (IT-95-14/2-T), Judgement, 26 February 2001, para.302.

[65] *Krnojelac* (IT-97-25-T), Judgement, 15 March 2002, para.182.

[66] The definition of rape which was stated by the ICTY has become one of the most significant definitions in the system of international criminal law. It has been taken into serious examination in the Elements of Crimes adopted by the General Assembly of States Parties of the International Criminal Court (ICC). The Chamber stated that "the sexual penetration, however slight, either of the vagina or anus of the victim by the penis of the perpetrator, or any other object used by the

implies the denial of a fundamental right or rights of a person.[67] Finally, the term "other inhuman acts", as we have mentioned above, refers to any act which may fall under the definition of crimes against humanity. These are acts such as sexual assault, enforced prostitution, sexual slavery and forced pregnancy. The term "sexual assault" within the Rules of Procedure and Evidence of the ICTY means to use by one means or another sexual

---

perpetrator, or of the mouth of the victim by the penis of the perpetrator, where such penetration is effected by coercion or force or threat of force against the victim or a third person." Furundzija (IT-95-17/1-T), Judgment, 10 December 1999, para.185. In another case, the Chamber stated that rape "the sexual penetration, however slight: (a) of a vagina or anus of the victim by the penis of the perpetrator or any other object used by the perpetrator; or (b) the mouth of the victim by the penis of the perpetrator; where such sexual penetration occurs without the consent of the victim. Consent for this purpose must be consent given voluntarily, as a result of the victim's free will, assessed in the context of the surrounding circumstances. The *mens rea* is the intention to effect this sexual penetration, and the knowledge that it occurs without the consent of the victim."*Kunarac, Kovac, & Vukovic*, (IT-96-23-T & IT-96-23/1-T), Judgment, 22 February 2001, para.460.

[67] In the *Kupreskic* case, a good statement concerning the scope of persecutions was formulated. It was asserted that "The Trial Chamber, drawing upon its earlier discussion of 'other inhumane acts', holds that in order to identify those rights whose infringement may constitute persecution, more defined parameters for the definition of human dignity can be found in international standards on human rights such as those laid down in the Universal Declaration on Human Rights of 1948, the two United Nations Covenants on Human Rights of 1966 and other international instruments on human rights or on humanitarian law. Drawing upon the various provisions of these texts it proves possible to identify a set of fundamental rights appertaining to any human being, the gross infringement of which may amount, depending on the surrounding circumstances, to a crime against humanity. Persecution consists of a severe attack on those rights, and aims to exclude a person from society on discriminatory grounds. The Trial Chamber therefore defines persecution as the gross or blatant denial, on discriminatory grounds, of a fundamental right, laid down in international customary or treaty law, reaching the same level of gravity as the other acts prohibited in Article 5. In determining whether particular acts constitute persecution, the Trial Chamber wishes to reiterate that acts of persecution must be evaluated not in isolation but in context, by looking at their cumulative effect. Although individual acts may not be inhumane, their overall consequences must offend humanity in such a way that they may be termed 'inhumane'. This delimitation also suffices to satisfy the principle of legality, as inhumane acts are clearly proscribed by the Statute." *Kupreskic* et al. (IT-95-16-T) Judgement, 14 January 2000, paras.621-622.

violence against the integrity of a person.[68] Similarly, the phrase "enforced prostitution" denotes the involvement of a person in sexual activities under conditions of coercion or intimidation.[69] The phrase "sexual slavery" denotes the position of a person who has lost her/his liberty and where acts of purchasing, selling or lending are exercised upon her/him.[70] Lastly, the expression "enforced pregnancy" denotes the position of a female forcibly made pregnant.[71] However, it must be asserted that these definitions are illustrative and not exhaustive.

4. Categories of Crimes in the ICTR

The Statute of the ICTR takes into recognition the three categories of international crimes that have been progressively recognised in international criminal law since 1945, 1948, 1949 and 1977. These crimes are also recognised and formulated into the Statute of the ICTY. They are genocide, crimes against humanity and grave breaches of the Geneva Conventions. The role of the legislator has therefore been, more or less, to apply the concept of crimes that have been recognised in the former *ad hoc* tribunals. The definition and scope of categories of crimes listed in the Statute of the ICTR are also taken from relevant international conventions that have been recognised in international criminal law. These are, for example, the Convention on Genocide, the four Geneva Conventions and their Protocol II.[72] The provisions of the conventions have created serious discussions to be brought before the ICTR.[73]

---

[68] In the *Miroslav Kvocka* case, the Appeals Chamber stated that "The *Akayesu* Trial Chamber defined sexual violence as 'any act of a sexual nature which is committed on a person under circumstances which are coercive.' Thus, sexual violence is broader than rape and includes such crimes as sexual slavery or molestation. Moreover, the *Akayesu* Trial Chamber emphasised that sexual violence need not necessarily involve physical contact and cited forced public nudity as an example.' *Kvocka* et al. (IT-98-30-/1-T), Judgement, 2 November 2001, para.180.

[69] According to the Appeals Chamber, "Sexual violence would also include such crimes as sexual mutilation, forced marriage, and forced abortion as well as the gender related crimes explicitly listed in the ICC Statute as war crimes and crimes against humanity, namely 'rape, sexual slavery, enforced prostitution, forced pregnancy, enforced sterilization' and other similar forms of violence." *Kvocka*et al. (IT-98-30/1-T), Judgement, 2 November 2001, footnote 343 (para.180).

[70] Id.

[71] Id.

[72] According to a report by the Secretary General of the United Nations published after the adoption of the Statute of the ICTR, the provisions of the common Article

4.1. Genocide: Crime of Crimes

The Statute of the ICTR takes into serious consideration the international crime of genocide. Genocide is referred to as 'the crime of crimes' by the ICTR because of its extreme criminal character. The definition of genocide in the Statute is borrowed from the Genocide Convention which defines it as acts committed with intent to destroy in whole or in part, a national, ethnic, racial or religious group. Acts of genocide include, for example,killing members of such a group and causing serious bodily or mental harm to members of such a group among many other acts.[74]

---

3 of Protocol II were recognised as part of customary international law. The Secretary General clarified in the report that the "Security Council elected to take a more expansive approach to the choice of the applicable law than the one underlying the Statute of the International Criminal Tribunal for the former Yugoslavia, and included within the subject-matter jurisdiction of the ICTR international instruments regardless of whether they were considered part of customary international law or whether they have customarily entailed the individual criminal responsibility of the perpetrator of the crime. Article 4 of the Statute, accordingly, includes violations of Additional Protocol II, which, as a whole, has not yet been universally recognised as part of customary international law, and for the first time criminalizes Common Article 3 of the four Geneva Conventions." UN Doc. S/1995/134, Para.12.

[73] *William A.* Schabas, *International Decisions: Barayagwisav. Prosecutor* (ICTR Appeals Chamber, 3 November 1999 & 31 March 2000), 94: 3 American Journal of International Law 563-571 (2000).

[74] Rape and sexual violence were considered as constituting genocide in certain situations by the ICTY. This was proved in the Trial Chamber in *Akayesu* case. The Chamber stated that "With regard, particularly, to the acts described in paragraphs 12(A) and 12(B) of the Indictment, that is, rape and sexual violence, the Chamber wishes to underscore the fact that in its opinion, they constitute genocide in the same way as any other act as long as they were committed with the specific intent to destroy, in whole or in part, a particular group, targeted as such. Indeed, rape and sexual violence certainly constitute infliction of serious bodily and mental harm on the victims and are even, according to the Chamber, one of the worst ways of inflict harm on the victim as he or she suffers both bodily and mental harm. In light of all the evidence before it, the Chamber is satisfied that the acts of rape and sexual violence described above, were committed solely against Tutsi women, many of whom were subjected to the worst public humiliation, mutilated, and raped several times, often in public, in the Bureau Communal premises or in other public places, and often by more than one assailant. These rapes resulted in physical and psychological destruction of Tutsi women, their families and their communities. Sexual violence was an integral part of the process of destruction, specifically targeting Tutsi women and specifically contributing to their destruction and to the destruction of the Tutsi group as a whole. The rape of Tutsi women was

According to the provisions of the Statute, the Tribunal has the power to bring those who have committed genocide under its jurisdiction for prosecution and punishment.[75] The judgments of the ICTR recognise genocide as 'the crime of crimes' which has to be prosecuted and punished appropriately. The Tribunal clarifies that "the Chamber is of the opinion that genocide constitutes the crime of crimes, which must be taken into account when deciding the sentence."[76] One of the most important motivations for declaring genocide to be the crime of crimes is the application of an equivalently heavy penalty for the guilty person as well as emphasizing the serious criminal character of the conduct constituting genocide.

The ICTR has therefore put a heavy emphasis on the term 'serious bodily and mental harm' within the definition of the crime of genocide. In

---

systematic and was perpetrated against all Tutsi women and solely against them. A Tutsi woman, married to a Hutu, testified before the Chamber that she was not raped because her ethnic background was unknown. As part of the propaganda campaign geared to mobilizing the Hutu against the Tutsi, the Tutsi women were presented as sexual objects. Indeed, the Chamber was told, for an example, that before being raped and killed, Alexia, who was the wife of the Professor, Ntereye, and her two nieces, were forced by the *Interahamwe* to undress and ordered to run and do exercises "in order to display the thighs of Tutsi women". The Interaham we who raped Alexia said, as he threw her on the ground and got on top of her, "let us now see what the vagina of a Tutsi woman takes like". As stated above Akayesu himself, speaking to the *Interahamwe* who were committing the rapes, said to them: "don't ever ask again what a Tutsi woman tastes like". This sexualized representation of ethnic identity graphically illustrates that Tutsi women were subjected to sexual violence because they were Tutsi. Sexual violence was a step in the process of destruction of the Tutsi group - destruction of the spirit, of the will to live, and of life itself. On the basis of the substantial testimonies brought before it, the Chamber finds that in most cases, the rapes of Tutsi women in Taba, were accompanied with the intent to kill those women. Many rapes were perpetrated near mass graves where the women were taken to be killed. A victim testified that Tutsi women caught could be taken away by peasants and men with the promise that they would be collected later to be executed… In light of the foregoing, the Chamber finds firstly that the acts described *supra* are indeed acts as enumerated in Article 2 (2) of the Statute, which constitute the factual elements of the crime of genocide, namely the killings of Tutsi or the serious bodily and mental harm inflicted on the Tutsi. The Chamber is further satisfied beyond reasonable doubt that these various acts were committed by Akayesu with the specific intent to destroy the Tutsi group, as such." Consequently, the Chamber finds Akayesu individually criminally responsible for genocide." *Jean-Paul Akayesu* (ICTR-96-4-T), Judgement, 2 September 1998, paras.731-734.

[75] Article 2.

[76] *Jean Kambanda* (ICTR 97-23-S), Judgment, 4 September 1998, para.16.

doing so, the Tribunal wishes to underline that genocide as the crime of crimes is not just the act of killing, but also includes other acts. For this reason, the term 'serious bodily and mental harm' has received different definitions. According to one of the Trial Chambers,

> Causing serious bodily or mental harm to members of the group does not necessarily mean that the harm is permanent and irremediable. In the Adolf Eichmann case, who was convicted of crimes against the Jewish people, genocide under another legal definition, the District Court of Jerusalem stated in its judgment of 12 December 1961, that serious bodily or mental harm of members of the group can be caused "by the enslavement, starvation, deportation and persecution [...] and by their detention in ghettos, transit camps and concentration camps in conditions which were designed to cause their degradation, deprivation of their rights as human beings, and to suppress them and cause them inhumane suffering and torture". For purposes of interpreting Article 2 (2)(b) of the Statute, the Chamber takes serious bodily or mental harm, without limiting itself thereto, to mean acts of torture, be they bodily or mental, inhumane or degrading treatment, persecution.[77]

Another Trial Chamber with reference to the above case defines the term 'serious bodily harm' by saying that:

> In the *Akayesu* Judgement, it was held that serious bodily harm does not necessarily mean harm that is permanent or irremediable. The *Akayesu* Judgement further held that acts of sexual violence, rape, mutilations and interrogations combined with beatings, and/or threats of death, were all acts that amount to serious bodily harm. The Trial Chamber concurs with these determinations. It is the view of the Trial Chamber that, to large extent, "causing serious bodily harm" is self-explanatory. This phrase could be construed to mean harm that seriously injures the health, causes disfigurement or causes any serious injury to the external, internal organs or senses.[78]

The same Chamber also clarifies the effects of serious mental harm in the commission of the crime of genocide. It states that:

> The Prosecution submits that there is no prerequisite that mental suffering should be the result of physical harm. The Prosecution relies upon the commentary offered in the Preparatory Committee's Definition of Crimes that suggests that serious mental harm should include 'more than minor or temporary impairment on mental faculties.' The Prosecution suggested that

---

[77] *Akayesu* (ICTR-96-4-T), Judgement, 2 September 1998, paras.502, 503 and 504.
[78] *Clement Kayishema* (ICTR-95-1-T), Judgement, 21 May 1999, paras.108-109.

> the inflicting of strong fear or terror, intimidation or threat may amount to serious mental harm. The Defence teams submitted that the serious bodily and mental harm alleged by the Prosecution was merely a consequence of attempts to kill and did not amount to genocidal offences in themselves. It argued that the Prosecution witnesses who had been wounded did not demonstrate that the perpetrators had intention to cause serious bodily or mental harm. The Defence contends therefore, that there was intention to cause murder and not to cause serious bodily or mental harm. The Chamber considers that an accused may be held liable under these circumstances only where, at the time of the act, the accused had the intention to inflict serious mental harm in pursuit of the specific intention to destroy a group in whole or in part.[79]

4.2. Crimes against Humanity

The concept of crimes against humanity within the practice of the ICTR is taken from its predecessors such as the Nuremberg Tribunal, the Tokyo Tribunal, Control Council No 10 and the ICTY. Crimes against humanity are also prosecutable and punishable crimes under the provisions of the Statute of the ICTR. In order for an act to constitute a crime against humanity, it has to be part of a widespread or systematic attack against any civilian population on national, political, ethnic, racial or religious grounds. Such attacks include enslavement, extermination, murder, deportation, torture, rape, imprisonment, persecution on political, racial and religious grounds, and also any other similar inhuman acts.[80]

The ICTR has dealt with all the concepts listed above. According to it, they are punishable acts. The list is, however, exhaustive and the ICTR may not add new classifications to the list. The relevant article of the Statute has, nevertheless, used the term 'other inhuman acts.' This means that the restrictive definition of the Statute may be enlarged in the practice of the Tribunal. Furthermore, the ICTR has sincerely stated that a crime against humanity violates the fundamental values of the international community. According to it, both accused, namely *Elizaphan Ntakirutimana* and *Gérard Ntakirutimana,* "have been found guilty of genocide and crimes against humanity. These crimes are of an utmost gravity; they are shocking to the conscience of mankind, in view of the fundamental human values deliberately negated by their perpetrators and the sufferings inflicted. These crimes threaten not only the foundations of the society in which they are perpetrated but also those of the international

[79] *Clement Kayishema* (ICTR-95-1-T), Judgement, 21 May 1999, paras.110-112

[80] Article 3.

community as a whole."[81] For this reason, the Tribunal has taken into account the gravity of the crimes committed. It says that the seriousness and the "gravity of the offences shall therefore be reflected primarily in the Chamber's decision on the sentence to be inflicted upon the Accused, in order to serve such primary purposes as retribution, deterrence, protection of society, stigmatization and public reprobation of international crimes."[82] Furthermore, according to the ICTR "deterrence is particularly emphasised in this respect, so as to demonstrate 'that the international community [is] not ready to tolerate serious violations of international humanitarian law and human rights.'"[83]

Consequently, the ICTR Trial Chamber has held that beyond any reasonable doubt extermination, murder, enslavement, deportation, torture, rape, imprisonment, prosecution on political, racial and religious grounds as well as any other similar inhuman acts are crimes against humanity and perpetrators must be held criminally responsible accordingly.[84]

---

[81] *Elizaphan Ntakirutimana* and *Gérard Ntakirutimana* (ICTR-96-10 & ICTR-96-17-T), Judgement and Sentence, 21 February 2003, paras.881.

[82] *Id.*, 882.

[83] Id.

[84] According to the ICTR Trial Chamber in *Jean Paul Akayesu*, extermination and killing constitute crimes against humanity. The judgement explains "Count 3 of the indictment charges the Accused with crimes against humanity (extermination), pursuant to Article 3(b) of the Statute, for the acts alleged in paragraphs 12 to 23 of the indictment. The definition of crimes against humanity, including the various elements that comprise the enumerated offences under Article 3 of the Statute have already been discussed. The Chamber finds beyond a reasonable doubt that during his search for Ephrem Karangwa on 19 April 1994, the Accused participated in the killing of Simon Mutijima, Thaddée Uwanyiligra and Jean Chrysostome, by ordering their deaths and being present when they were killed. The Chamber finds beyond a reasonable doubt that on 19 April 1994, the Accused took eight detained refugees and handed them over to the local militia, known as the *Interahamwe* with orders that they be killed. The Chamber finds beyond a reasonable doubt that the *Interahamwe* and the local population, acting on the orders of the Accused killed five teachers namely; a professor known as Samuel; Tharcisse who was killed in the presence of the Accused; Theogene, Phoebe Uwineze and her fiancé. The Chamber finds beyond a reasonable doubt that the eight refugees as well as Simon Mutijima, Thaddée Uwanyiligra, Jean Chrysostome, Samuel, Tharcisse, Theogene, Phoebe Uwineze and her fiancé were all civilians, taking no active part in the hostilities that prevailed in Rwanda in 1994 and the only reason they were killed is because they were Tutsi. The Chamber finds beyond a reasonable doubt that in ordering the killing of the eight refugees as well as Simon Mutijima, Thaddée Uwanyiligra, Jean Chrysostome, Samuel, Tharcisse, Theogene, Phoebe Uwineze and her fiancé, the Accused had the requisite intent to cause mass destruction,

4.3. Violations of Article 3 Common to the Geneva Conventions

The third category of crimes under the Statute of the ICTR is called violations of Article 3, a category common to the Geneva Conventions and the additional Protocol II. Therefore, much emphasis has been put on Article 3. The Tribunal has the power to prosecute persons committing or ordering certain acts to be committed that are recognised as grave violations of the Geneva Convention of 12 August 1949 for the Protection of War Victims and of Additional Protocol II of 8 June 1977. The Tribunal is empowered to prosecute any acts of violence that are listed in its Statute but the relevant provisions do not prevent the Tribunal from listing also other acts which may be considered violations of Article 3. These acts are, for example, violence to life, murder, torture, mutilation, collective punishments, acts of terrorism, the taking of hostages, and the execution of persons in the absence of a judgement delivered by an authorized court.[85]

Article 4 of the Statute of the ICTR has received particular recognition in the practice of the ICTR. It has therefore a significant function in the case of the attribution of the concept of international criminal responsibility to the accused. According to the Appeals Chamber, "there is no explicit provision in the Statute that individual criminal responsibility is restricted to a particular class of individuals. In actuality, articles of the Statute on individual criminal responsibility simply reflect the principle of

---

directed against certain groups of individuals, as part of a widespread or systematic attack against the civilian population of Rwanda on ethnic grounds. The Chamber finds beyond a reasonable doubt that in ordering the killing of the eight refugees as well as Simon Mutijima, Thaddée Uwanyiligra, Jean Chrysostome, Samuel, Tharcisse, Theogene, Phoebe Uwineze and her fiancé, the Accused is individually criminally responsible for the death of these victims, pursuant to Article 6(1) of the Statute. The Chamber finds beyond a reasonable doubt that there was a widespread and systematic attack against the civilian population in Rwanda on 19 April 1994 and the conduct of the Accused formed part of this attack. Therefore the Chamber finds, beyond a reasonable doubt that the killing of the eight refugees as well as Simon Mutijima, Thaddée Uwanyiligra, Jean Chrysostome, Samuel, Tharcisse, Theoge ne, Phoebe Uwineze and her fiancé, constitute extermination committed, as part of a widespread or systematic attack on the civilian population on ethnic grounds and as such constitutes a crime against humanity. Accordingly, the Chamber finds beyond a reasonable doubt that the Accused is guilty as charged in count 3 of the indictment." *Jean-Paul Akayesu* (ICTR-96-4-T), Judgement, 2 September 1998, paras.735-744.

[85] Article 8.

individual criminal responsibility as articulated by the Nuremberg Tribunal."[86]

The Appeals Chamber of the ICTR has also clarified that Article 4 applies to all individuals belonging to the armed forces of either of the belligerent parties and includes all those who have, by one means or another, participated in the commission of war crimes, crimes against humanity and genocide. According to the Appeals Chamber, "Article 4 makes no mention of a possible delimitation of classes of persons likely to be prosecuted under this provision. It provides only that the Tribunal 'shall have the power to prosecute persons committing or ordering to be committed' in particular, serious violations of Article 3 common to the Geneva Conventions." According to the Appeal Chambers, an examination of the provisions of Article 4 in conjunction with other provisions of the Statute also connotes this fact.[87]

In fact, there is no legal obstacle in international criminal law to charging a civilian with a crime where questions of crimes against humanity, genocide, war crimes and aggression are concerned. Therefore, the definitions of the terms relevant to armed conflicts should not restrict the accountability of civilians for war crimes. In the *Musema* case, the Appeals Chamber, with reference to other judgements, stated that:

> a too restrictive definition of these terms would dilute the protection afforded by these instruments to the victims and potential victims of armed conflicts. Hence, in the opinion of the Trial Chamber, the categories of persons covered by these terms should not be limited to individuals of all ranks belonging to the armed forces under the military command of either belligerent parties but should be interpreted in their broadest sense, to include individuals who are legitimately mandated and expected as public officials or agents or persons otherwise holding public authority *de facto* representing the Government to support or fulfil the war efforts. This was affirmed in both the *Rutaganda* Judgement and the *Kayishema* and *Ruzindana* Judgement.[88]

The historical evolution as well as evaluation of the concept of the international criminal responsibility of individuals, within the jurisprudence of the international criminal tribunals, also implies the above development. In other words, the provisions of Article 4 of the Statute do not put any limitation on the ICTR's authority to identify civilians who are

[86] *Jean-Paul Akayesu*, (ICTR-96-4-A), Judgement, 1 June 2001, para.436.
[87] *Id.*, para.435.
[88] Alfred Musema (ICTR-96-13-T), Judgement, 27 January 2000, para.266.

guilty of war crimes. The Appeals Chamber of the ICTR has confirmed that:

> ... it is well-established that the post-World War II Trials unequivocally support the imposition of individual criminal liability for war crimes on civilians where they have a link or connection with a Party to the conflict. The principle of holding civilians liable for breaches of the laws of war is, moreover, favoured by a consideration of the humanitarian object and purpose of the Geneva Conventions and the Additional Protocols, which is to protect war victims from atrocities. Therefore, the Chamber concludes that the Accused could fall in the class of individuals who may be held responsible for serious violations on international humanitarian law, in particular serious violations of Common Article 3 and Additional Protocol II.[89]

4.4. Nexus to War

One of the most significant questions for the ICTR has been the concept of *nexus*.[90] The word *nexus* denotes a link between two or more concepts in law. Based on this definition, one might assume that there are various types of *nexus* between war crimes and internal armed conflict. However, the Chambers of the ICTR made it clear that there is no positive concept of *nexus* between internal armed conflict and war crimes. The Trial Chamber of the ICTR clarifies that when "the country is in a state of armed conflict, crimes committed in this period of time could be considered as having been committed in the context of armed conflict. However, it does not mean that all such crimes have a direct link with the armed conflict and all the victims of these crimes are victims of armed conflict."[91] Moreover, due to the ICTR, it is also a function of the Prosecution to provide facts beyond a reasonable doubt. Consequently, "the term nexus should not be understood to be something vague and indefinite. A direct connection between the alleged crimes, referred to in the Indictment, and the armed conflict should be established factually. No test, therefore, can be defined in abstract to."[92] The Tribunal goes further and asserts that it is the duty of the "Trial Chamber, on a case-by-case basis, to judge on the facts, submitted as to whether a nexus existed. It is incumbent upon the

[89] Alfred Musema (ICTR-96-13-T), Judgement, 27 January 2000, paras.274-275.

[90] This question has also been raised in the procedure of the ICTY.

[91] Clément Kayishema and Obed Ruzindana (ICTR-95-1-T), Judgement, 21 May, 1999, para.600.

[92] *Id.*, para.188.

Prosecution to present those facts and prove, beyond a reasonable doubt, that such a nexus exists."[93]

Obviously, a sufficient link must be established between the offences that were carried out in a region and the provisions of international armed conflict which are assumed to be violated. However, this does not necessarily mean that the crimes must all have been committed in that particular region. In other words, crimes committed by the accused, must have some connection with the foregoing war or acts of hostilities and rules applicable to international armed conflict. According to the Trial Chamber of the ICTR:

> It is important to establish whether all the crimes committed during the non-international armed conflict should be considered as crimes connected with serious violations of Common Article 3 and Protocol II. The Chamber is of the opinion that only offences, which have a nexus with armed conflict, fall within this category. If there is not a direct line between the offences and the armed conflict there is no ground for conclusion that Common Article 3 and Protocol II are violated. The jurisprudence in this area of the law requires such a link between the armed conflict and the offence. The ICTY Trial Chamber… stated that 'there must be an obvious link between the criminal act and the armed conflict.'… Such a conclusion means that, in the opinion of that Chamber, such a connection is necessary.[94]

The above conclusion means that according to the ICTR, in the *Rwanda* internal armed conflict, the murders and atrocities committed against a large number of *Tutsi* civilians under the orders of the leaders of the *Interahamwe* imply a *nexus* between war crimes and internal armed conflict. Consequently, these acts constituted war crimes. However, the killing of other *Tutsi* civilians with the purpose and intention of their elimination by various means may constitute not war crimes, but rather genocide and crimes against humanity. Nevertheless, all three categories of crime, namely, crimes against humanity, genocide and war crimes, may have different characteristics and, at the same time, overlap one another.

It must be stipulated here that the *nexus* to war does not constitute a rule for the recognition of crimes against humanity or genocide.[95] Both

---

[93] *Id.*

[94] *Id.*, paras.185-186.

[95] The ICTY states that "the next issue which must be addressed is the required nexus between the act or omission and the armed conflict. The Prosecution argues that to establish the nexus necessary for a violation of Article 5 it is sufficient to demonstrate that the crimes were committed at some point in the course or duration of an armed conflict, even if such crimes were not committed in direct

these categories of international crimes may be committed in connection with an armed conflict or otherwise. Thus, *nexus* to war is not a pre-requisite for the recognition of the relevant crimes. However, one cannot deny that the International Military Tribunal required a *nexus* to war for the identification of crimes against humanity, which limited in practice the punishment of this category of crimes. The Control Council Law No. 10 did not, however, include the *nexus* to war in the definition of crimes against humanity. However, the term *nexus* to war was formulated again in the Statute of the ICTY in Article 5. According to this new formulation the Tribunal has the authority to prosecute persons responsible for certain crimes "when committed in armed conflict, whether international or internal in character, and directed against any civilian population". Nevertheless, the requirement of Article 5 was interpreted differently by the ICTY with reference to the Statute of the ICTR which has omitted the term "nexus to war" or "when committed in armed conflict". On this interpretation, the ICTY makes it clear that the relevant function of the ICTR is clearly in conformity with latest developments in international customary and conventional law. It says that:

> Article 5 of the Statute, addressing crimes against humanity, grants the International Tribunal jurisdiction over the enumerated acts 'when committed in armed conflict'. The requirement of an armed conflict is similar to that of Article 6(c) of the Nürnberg Charter which limited the Nürnberg Tribunal's jurisdiction to crimes against humanity committed "before or during the war", although in the case of the Nürnberg Tribunal jurisdiction was further limited by requiring that crimes against humanity be committed "in execution of or in connection with" war crimes or crimes against peace107. Despite this precedent, the inclusion of the requirement of an armed conflict deviates from the development of the doctrine after the Nürnberg Charter, beginning with Control Council Law No. 10, which no longer links the concept of crimes against humanity with an armed conflict. As the Secretary-General stated, 'Crimes against humanity are

---

relation to or as part of the conduct of hostilities, occupation, or other integral aspects of the armed conflict. In contrast the Defence argues that the act must be committed "in" armed conflict. The Statute does not elaborate on the required link between the act and the armed conflict. Nor, for that matter, does the *Appeals Chamber Decision,* although it contains several statements that are relevant in this regard. First is the finding, noted above, that the Statute is more restrictive than custom in that "customary international law no longer requires any nexus between crimes against humanity and armed conflict". Accordingly, it is necessary to determine the degree of nexus which is imported by the Statute by its inclusion of the requirement of an armed conflict. This, then, is a question of statutory interpretation." *Tadic* (IT-94-1-T), Judgement, 7 May 1997, paras.629-630.

aimed at any civilian population and are prohibited regardless of whether they are committed in an armed conflict, international or internal in character.' In the Statute of the International Tribunal for Rwanda the requirement of an armed conflict is omitted, requiring only that the acts be committed as part of an attack against a civilian population. The Appeals Chamber has stated that, by incorporating the requirement of an armed conflict, "the Security Council may have defined the crime in Article 5 more narrowly than necessary under customary international law"110, having stated earlier that 'since customary international law no longer requires any nexus between crimes against humanity and armed conflict … Article 5 was intended to reintroduce this nexus for the purposes of this Tribunal.'[96]

5. Categories of Crimes in the SCSL

The Statute of the SCSL has some similarities with other international criminal tribunals concerning the recognition of certain international crimes. These are, for example, crimes against humanity, violations of the common articles of the Geneva instruments and violations of the international humanitarian law of armed conflicts. To this list, the statute adds other crimes that are recognised under the national law of Sierra Leone. It is therefore mostly under the last heading and the crime of genocide that the Statute of the Special Court differs from other international criminal tribunals that have been established under the supervision of the United Nations organization, such as the ICTY and the ICTR.

5.1. Crimes against Humanity

Among the most serious categories of crimes to have been recognised by the Statute of the Special Court is "crimes against humanity". Article 2 of the Statute relates to this category of crimes. According to the article, the Special Court should have power to prosecute persons who have committed one of the following crimes. These are:

(a) Murder;
(b) Extermination;
(c) Enslavement;
(d) Deportation;
(e) Imprisonment;
(f) Torture;

[96] *Tadic* (IT-94-1-T), Judgement, 7 May 1997, para.627.

(g) Rape, sexual slavery, enforced prostitution, forced pregnancy and any other form of sexual violence;
(h) Persecution on political, racial, ethnic or religious grounds;
(i) Other inhumane acts.

The provisions of Article 2 state that in order for an act to constitute a crime against humanity it should have one of the accepted characteristics for the recognition of the relevant crime. These are the characteristics of being widespread or systematic. This means that the relevant crime must be a part of a widespread or systematic attack against the civilian population. Consequently, the article emphasises that an act may not constitute a crime against humanity, if it is not directed against the civilian population.

5.2. Violations of Article 3 common to the Geneva Conventions

Article 3 of the Statute of the SCSL relates to the violations of Article 3 common to the 1949 Geneva Conventions and their 1977 Additional Protocol II. The purpose of the legislator is the protection of war victims, something which was promised under the relevant conventions and protocol. This was in order not to give any accused person the possibility of escaping from his/her criminal responsibility by invoking reasons of military strategy. Therefore, Article 3 of the Statute recognises the following violations as constituting the violation of its framework:

(a) Violence to life, health and physical or mental well-being of persons, in particular murder as well as cruel treatment such as torture, mutilation or any form of corporal punishment;
(b) Collective punishments;
(c) Taking of hostages;
(d) Acts of terrorism;
(e) Outrages upon personal dignity, in particular humiliating and degrading treatment, rape, enforced prostitution and any form of indecent assault;
(f) Pillage;
(g) The passing of sentences and the carrying out of executions without previous judgement pronounced by a regularly constituted court, affording all the judicial guarantees which are recognised as indispensable by civilized peoples;
(h) Threats to commit any of the foregoing acts.

Obviously, the provisions above have been borrowed from the provisions of the Geneva Conventions and their Protocol II. More significantly, these provisions constitute a part of customary international criminal law and a part of the international law of *jus cogens*. This means that in the application of the provisions of Article 3 of the Statute of the Special Court, the Court has far-reaching powers in the case of certain violations that overlap with *jus cogens* norms. The Special Court clearly has to act within the limitations of its Statute, but this does not necessarily mean that the Court can ignore the relevant provisions of *jus cogens* which speak of similar criminal violations.

5.3. Serious Violations of Humanitarian Law

The Statute of the SCSL has dealt very extensively with violations of the provisions of the international humanitarian law of armed conflicts. This is considered one of the most significant factors of its legal personality in its struggle against international crimes. The provisions of Article 4 of the Statute have in fact strengthened Article 3 of the same Statute. This can be seen when the relevant provisions of both articles are examined. In other words, the provisions of Article 3 emphasise the important recognition of Article 3 common to the Geneva Conventions concerning the protection of civilians.[97] The provisions of Article 4 have broadened the definition of criminal acts both within and without conjunction to the provisions of Article 3 of the Statute. Thus, the content of Article 4 concerns other serious violations of the international humanitarian law of armed conflicts, which may not necessarily come under the provisions of Article 3 common to the Geneva Conventions or the Statute of the Special Court. Article 4 refers to three serious violations. These are:

(a) Intentionally directing attacks against the civilian population as such or against individual civilians not taking direct part in hostilities;
(b) Intentionally directing attacks against personnel, installations, material, units or vehicles involved in a humanitarian assistance or peacekeeping mission in accordance with the Charter of the United Nations, as long as they are entitled to the protection given to civilians or civilian objects under the international law of armed conflict;
(c) Conscripting or enlisting children under the age of 15 years into armed forces or groups or using them to participate actively in hostilities.

Paragraphs (a), (b) and (c) state important principles which are not only interdependent, but which are also complementary to one another.

[97] See the above section.

Paragraph (b) aims specifically at protecting various United Nations peacekeeping missions, the tasks of which are to protect civilians or civilian property and installations as a whole. This paragraph was specifically drafted into the content of Article 4 to ensure the punishment of those who have been aggressive towards United Nations missions when they were carrying out certain duties within the territory of Sierra Leone. More significant are the provisions of paragraph (c) concerning the protection of children under the age of 15. The central aim of the paragraph is to criminalize the employment of children in armed forces or hostile engagements in order for the Special Court to have the authority to bring the responsible persons under its jurisdiction. The paragraph has obviously taken into consideration the provisions of the Convention on the Rights of the Child and its relevant protocols.

5.4. National Criminal Code

The SCSL has somewhat different legislation by comparison to the Nuremberg, the ICTY, and the ICTR. In fact, the SCSL is the first court in the history of international criminal courts which has taken into effective and practical recognition the criminal legislation of the country in which the criminal acts were carried out. For this reason, Article 5 of the Statute deals with the criminal provisions of Sierra Leonean law. This is one of the reasons why some of the judges of the Special Court are also chosen from Sierra Leone. In particular, Article 5 is divided into two paragraphs and some sub-paragraphs. Paragraph (a) of the article concerns the protection of females of young age. It has three sub-paragraphs dealing with different issues concerning the abuse of girls younger than 13 or between 13 and 14 years of age. The paragraph reads:

> (a) Offences relating to the abuse of girls under the Prevention of Cruelty to Children Act, 1926 (Cap. 31):
> (i) Abusing a girl under 13 years of age, contrary to section 6;
> (ii) Abusing a girl between 13 and 14 years of age, contrary to section 7;
> (iii) Abduction of a girl for immoral purposes, contrary to section 12.

Paragraph (b) of the Article relates to offences dealing with non-movable objects that have certain significant functions for civilians and are considered of fundamental importance for the daily life of civilian persons. This means that the provisions of the paragraph aim at the protection of civilian installations, houses and facilities. The paragraph has in fact focused on the protection of public and even non-public buildings. These include all types of buildings such as schools, hospitals, charity premises but also any other building that does not have a public function. It reads that:

> (b) Offences relating to the wanton destruction of property under the Malicious Damage Act, 1861:
> (i) Setting fire to dwelling-houses, any person being therein, contrary to section 2;
> (ii) Setting fire to public buildings, contrary to sections 5 and 6;
> (iii) Setting fire to other buildings, contrary to section 6.

One significant function of paragraph (b) in Article 5 is to complete the wording of Articles 3 and 4 regarding the common Article 3 in the Geneva Convention and the Statute of the Special Court and other serious violations of the international humanitarian law of armed conflict specified in Article 4. These three articles have more or less similar functions for the protection of civilians and civilian objects and it is therefore very difficult to apply them in isolation when their criteria, more frequently, overlap with one another.

6. Categories of International Crimes in the ICC

It is necessary to emphasise here that the Statute of the ICC constitutes one of the most recognised international treaties dealing with various concepts of international crime. It broadly identifies those offences documented as crimes under the system of international criminal law for which the concept of the international criminal responsibility of individuals is recognised. The aim of the Statute is to create a legal forum for the prevention of certain international crimes in the international legal community as a whole. The aim of the Statute although clear, is at the same time very complex. It is clear in the sense that certain criminal acts are conventionally recognised as international crimes, which are prosecutable as well as punishable before national and international criminal courts. The complexity of the law lies in the fact that different states have different attitudes towards the precise recognition of international crimes. The concept of international crime is further complicated by the fact that the Security Council has an authoritative position in the identification of international crimes because of its legal power under the provisions of Chapter VII of the Charter of the United Nations.

6.1. Principles of Expansion

6.1.1. Borders of Crimes

The system of international criminal law has been defined in different ways in order to meet the requirements of the time. It has, in fact, been one of the chief purposes of international criminal law to apply the law to conduct which was deemed to be dangerous for the maintenance of international peace, security, justice and above all humanity. It was upon these elementary principles of the international legal and political community that the system of international criminal law was developed during the establishment of the Nuremberg and Tokyo tribunals.[98] These developments were also effective in the creation of a number of other international criminal tribunals such as the ICTY, the ICTR and the permanent International Criminal Court.

The laws of all these international criminal tribunals and the Court have endeavoured to legalise the definitions of these crimes and their scope of applicability. The provisions, norms and terms of these crimes have been discussed in various meetings in order to prevent the possibility of impunity.[99] That is why most international crimes within the statutes of the tribunals have been treated with the aim of creating equitable norms for the future relations of the parties. Whilst crimes have been defined, the scopes of the definitions of international crimes have been modified from time to time, and this is even more tangible in the case of the definitions of crimes which are the cornerstones of the Rome Statute.

Some of the most important factors in the development of the definitions of certain substantive crimes, such as war crimes or crimes against humanity are the four Geneva Conventions of 1949 and their Protocols of 1977 and the ratification of a considerable number of international conventions prohibiting acts against humanity. Clear examples are the 1948 Convention on Genocide and the 1989 Convention

[98] Arnold C. Brackman, The Other Nuremberg (1987). James F. Willis, Prologue to Nuremberg: The Politics and Diplomacy of Punishing War Criminals of the First World War (1981); Cassese Antonio, Albin Eser, Giorgio Gaja and Robert E. Conor, Justice at Nuremberg (1980). The Laws of War: Constraints on Warfare in the Western World (George J. Andreopoulos and Mark R. Shulman, eds., 1994).

[99] But see Jessica Gavron, Amnesties in the Light of Developments in International Law and the Establishment of the International Criminal Court, 51 International and Comparative Law Quarterly 111 (2002).

on the Rights of the Child and its Protocols.[100] These and many other international legal instruments have been effective in the adoption of the definitions of crimes under the Rome Statute.

The Statute of the ICC recognises four types of crimes that are to be dealt with by the Court. They include crimes against humanity, genocide, war crimes and aggression.[101] These crimes have been the subject of many discussions during the proceedings of the formulation and adoption of the Statute. They were treated differently by different groups of states. Therefore, controversies over their attitudes, scopes, terms and recognition of criminality, including the power and the authority of the Court, have been very heated and critical. Some states have been of the view that the boundaries of their definitions should be increased and others have wished to limit their applications. Many others wanted to have clear definitions for all four categories of crimes. This was in order not to give any opportunity to any state party or the Court to put a different interpretation on the scope of the crimes, according to the political circumstances.

---

[100] Farhad Malekian, Kerstin Nordlöf., Confessing the International Rights of Chidren: the Basic Docuemtn with Analysing (2012).
The following articles of the Convention for the protection of children's rights have had an especially significant effect on the provisions of the Statute. Article 38 reads that "1. States Parties undertake to respect and to ensure respect for rules of international humanitarian law applicable to them in armed conflicts which are relevant to the child. 2. States Parties shall take all feasible measures to ensure that persons who have not attained the age of fifteen years do not take a direct part in hostilities. 3. States Parties shall refrain from recruiting any person who has not attained the age of fifteen years into their armed forces. In recruiting among those persons who have attained the age of fifteen years but who have not attained the age of eighteen years, States Parties shall endeavour to give priority to those who are oldest. 4. In accordance with their obligations under international humanitarian law to protect the civilian population in armed conflicts, States Parties shall take all feasible measures to ensure protection and care of children who are affected by an armed conflict." Article 39 of the same Convention provides that "States Parties shall take all appropriate measures to promote physical and psychological recovery and social reintegration of a child victim of: any form of neglect, exploitation, or abuse; torture or any other form of cruel, inhuman or degrading treatment or punishment; or armed conflicts. Such recovery and reintegration shall take place in an environment which fosters the health, self-respect and dignity of the child."

[101] For a recent examination of aggression as an international crime See Larry May, Aggresion and Crimes Against Peace (2008).

6.1.2. Treaty Crimes

The Rome Statute does not deal with treaty crimes such as terrorism, narcotic offences and crimes against the protected persons of the United Nations.[102] It concentrates on core crimes or substantive crimes, the

---

[102] Unfortunately, the Statute does not deal with all criminals. In practice, this means that there are certain limitations on the application of the law of the Statute. For instance, whether the law of the Statute applies to the crimes committed by the United Nations peacekeeping missions is very doubtful and creates controversy. This is because the examination of a large number of international legal material and documents proves that international crimes are not just committed by individuals or states but also by the personnel of the United Nations who enjoy protected status. Peacekeeping missions and various personnel of the organisation have been engaged in the sex trafficking and sexual exploitation of women and children. The Security Council and the Secretary General of the United Nations have strongly condemned these international criminal activities but without result. In other words, the zero tolerance policy of the organisation for the prevention and elimination of trafficking in persons by the United Nations missions has not generated any positive effect. Some of the regions in which sexual abuse and sex exploitation have occurred are Cambodia, Mozambique, Somalia, Bosnia and Herzegovina, Mozambique, Sierra Leone, Haiti, Iberia, Guinea, East Timor, Eritrea, Ethiopia, the Democratic Republic of Congo, Burundi, Bosnia, Macedonia and Kosovo. The Security Council in one of its resolutions emphasises that "12. *Expresses its serious concern* at the violence, particularly sexual violence, suffered by women and children during the conflict in Sierra Leone, and emphasizes the importance of addressing these issues effectively; 14. *Expresses its serious concern* at allegations that some United Nations personnel may have been involved in sexual abuse of women and children in camps for refugees and internally displaced people in the region, supports the Secretary-General's policy of zero tolerance for such abuse, looks forward to the Secretary-General's report on the outcome of the investigation into these allegations, and requests him to make recommendations on how to prevent any such crimes in future, while calling on States concerned to take the necessary measures to bring to justice their own nationals responsible for such crimes." Resolution 1400 (2002), adopted by the Security Council at its 4500th meeting, on 28 March 2002.In another resolution, it states that "*Requests* the Secretary-General to take the necessary measures to achieve actual compliance in UNMEE with the United Nations zero-tolerance policy on sexual exploitation and abuse, including the development of strategies and appropriate mechanisms to prevent, identify and respond to all forms of misconduct, including sexual exploitation and abuse, and the enhancement of training for personnel to prevent misconduct and ensure full compliance with the United Nations code of conduct, *requests* the Secretary-General to take all necessary action in accordance with the Secretary-General's Bulletin on special measures for protection from sexual exploitation and sexual abuse (ST/SGB/2003/13) and to keep the Council informed, and *urges* troop-contributing countries to take appropriate preventive

definition of which is the result of much debate.[103] The definitions of the crimes within the Statute are thus the result of rather recent combinations, innovations and the re-adoption of the previous provisions of international criminal law. This was because the International Law Commission did not define the relevant crimes and the Draft Code of Crimes against Humanity from 1996 was unsuccessful in achieving acceptable definitions.[104] The reasons for this were mainly political and the drafters of the Draft Code

---

action, including the conduct of pre-deployment awareness training, and *take disciplinary action* and other action to ensure full accountability in cases of such conduct involving their personnel." Security Council Resolution 1622 (2005). As is evident the United Nations Security Council does not confirm the power of the ICC but addresses member states to *take disciplinary action* against those international crimes committed by its missions. See Press Release, Secretary-General Kofi-Annan, Sexual Exploitation 'Utterly Immoral', Completely at Odds with United Nations Mission, says Secretary-General to New York Conference, U.N. Doc. SG/SM/10776 (Dec. 4, 2006), http://www.un.org/News/Press/docs/2006/sgsm10776.doc. htm.; Elizabeth F. Defeis, *U.N. Peacekeepers and Sexual Abuse and Exploitation*: *An End to Impunity*, 7 Washington University Global Studies Law Review,185-214 (2008); Anna Shotton, *A Strategy to Address Sexual Exploitation by U.N. Peacekeeping Personnel*, 39 Corrnel Law Review 97 (2006), 103; AvRay Murphy, UN peacekeeping in Lebanon, Somalia and Kosovo: operational and legal issues in practice (2007). See *also* David W. Wainhouse, International Peacekeeping at the Crossroads: National Support—Experience and Prospects (1973); The Evolution of UN Peacekeeping: Case Studies and Comparative Analysis (William J. Durch, ed., 1993); United Nations Department of Public Information, The Blue Helmets: A Review of United Nations Peace-keeping (3rd ed. 1997); David W. Wainhouse, International Peace Observation: A History and Forecast, (1986); Paul F. Diehl, International Peacekeeping (1993); Peacekeeping, American Politics and the Uncivil Wars of the 1990s (William J. Durch, ed., 1996); Barbara Benton, Soldiers for Peace: Fifty Years of United Nations Peacekeeping (1996);Peacekeepers and Their Wives: American Participation in the Multinational Force and Observers (David R. Segal and Mady W. Segal, 1993); AvRay Murphy, UN peacekeeping in Lebanon, Somalia and Kosovo: operational and legal issues in practice (2007); Understanding Peacekeeping (Alex J. Bellamy, Paul D. Williams and Stuart Griffin, eds., 2004), 10-13.

[103] See Machteld Boot, Genocide, Crimes Against Humanity, War Crimes: Nullum Crimen Sine Lege and the Subject of Maater Jurisdicton of the International Criminal Court (Series School of Human Rights Research, v. 12, 2002).

[104] It was consequently for these and many other reasons that treaties crimes did not enter into the structure of the Statute. The borderline of their definitions or non-existence of definitions concerning the relevant crimes and the unwillingness of the majority of states to deal with certain crimes prevented any development of the idea of legislating treaties crimes entering into the Statute of the ICC.

and the Statute of the Court in the International Law Commission were rather cautious in their definitions in order to avoid controversy between the states of the world.[105]

As mentioned earlier, the crimes defined within the Statute are crimes against humanity, genocide, war crimes and aggression.[106] All these crimes have certain elements that are jurisdictional in nature. Thus, the differences between these crimes and municipal crimes are essentially the scope of their applicability and nature, their recognition as international crimes and the grave hazard they pose to the philosophy of justice and the conscience of humanity.[107] However, this does not mean that the relevant international crimes cannot be found under national criminal jurisdictions. On the contrary, states should adopt certain penal measures for the penalisation of the above crimes and their prosecution and punishment on their territories.

6.1.3. Substantive Crimes

The system of international criminal law consists of a considerable number of international crimes that are recognized by conventional or customary international criminal law.[108] The conventions constitute an integral part of

---

[105] Fifteen years of work by the Commission therefore became ineffective. This problem was however solved in 1996 and during fourteen weeks preparatory sessions and five weeks of diplomatic negotiations, governments achieved not only the definitions of the core or substantive crimes but also the structure of the Court.

[106] Kelly D. Askin, Crimes within the Jurisdiction of the International Criminal Court, 10 Criminal Law Forum 33 (1999).

[107] Thus, certain crimes because of their nature may be considered as international crimes. This means that they may be committed within different countries and be recognized as trans-border crimes. They may also be carried out in international zones such as international airspace and the high seas. The sanctions for the recognition and punishment of these crimes may be found in conventional international law or customary obligations. For instance, piracy or slavery is punishable not only by the provisions of conventional international criminal law but also by customary law because of the long recognition or the consolidation of their definitions as constituting international crimes.

[108] There are approximately twenty eight international crimes which are identified by international conventional or customary criminal law. These crimes are: aggression, war crimes, unlawful use of weapons, theft of nuclear materials, slavery, crimes against humanity, genocide, racial discrimination/apartheid, torture, crime of unlawful medical human experimentation, piracy, hijacking, the taking of hostages, crimes against internationally protected persons, terrorism, drug offences, crimes against cultural property, crimes against the natural environment, unlawful acts against certain establishments on the sea and maritime navigations,

international legislation.[109] The substantive crimes or core crimes are those crimes that are, due to their nature and character, considered to be the most

---

mail offences, falsification and counterfeiting currency, obscene publications offences, mercenaries, recruitment, use, the financing and training of mercenaries, organized crime and the bribery of foreign public officials. For these international crimes see Malekian, I § II International Criminal Law (1991); M. C. Bassiouni Introduction to International Criminal Law (2003). There are also numerous international conventions applicable to these international crimes, a great number of which exclusively relate to the international humanitarian law of armed conflicts. Some of these international crimes do not, however, have a particular conventional definition. Clear examples of these are piracy, crimes against natural environments, postal offences and medical human experimentation. These crimes have no international criminal conventions of their own and therefore rely heavily on the provisions of other international criminal conventions.

[109] Some of these international criminal conventions are: International Agreement for the Suppression of White Slave Traffic, 1904; Convention for the Suppression of the White Slave Traffic, Paris, May 1910; International Opium Convention, Hague, 23 January 1912; International Convention for the Suppression of the Traffic in Women and Children, Geneva, 30 September 1921; International Convention for the Suppression of the Circulation of and Traffic in Obscene Publications, 12 September 1923; Agreement Concerning the Suppression of the Manufacture of, Internal Trade in, and Use of Prepared Opium, Geneva, 11 February, 1925; International Opium Convention, Geneva, 19 February 1925; Protocol to the International Opium Convention, Geneva, 19 February 1925; Convention of Slavery, 1824; Convention of Slavery, 25 September, 1926; Convention for Limiting the Manufacture and Regulating the Distribution of Narcotic Drugs, Geneva, 13 July 1931; International Convention for the Suppression of the Traffic in Women of Full Age, concluded at Geneva on 11 October 1933; Convention for the Suppression of the Illicit Traffic in Dangerous Drugs, Geneva, 26 June 1936; Convention for the Prevention and Punishment of Terrorism, 16 November 1937; Arrangement for the Suppression of the Circulation of Obscene Publications, 4 May 1910; Charter of the International Military Tribunal, 8 August 1945; International Convention for the Suppression of the Circulation of and Traffic in Obscene Publications, concluded at Geneva on 12 September 1923 and amended by the Protocol signed at Lake Success, New York, on 12 November 1947; Protocol Bringing under International Control Drugs Outside the Scope of the Convention of 13 July 1931 for Limiting the Manufacture and Regulating the Distribution of Narcotic Drugs, as Amended by the Protocol, Lake Success, New York, 11 December 1946, Paris, 19 November 1948; Agreement for the Suppression of the Circulation of Obscene Publications of 4 May 1910, amended by the Protocol of 4 May 1949; Protocol for Limiting and Regulating the Cultivation of the Poppy Plant, the Production of, International and Wholesale Trade in, and Use of Opium, New York, 23 June 1953; Supplementary Convention on the Abolition of Slavery, the Slave trade, and Institutions and Practices Similar to Slavery, Geneva, 1956; Protocol Amending the 1926

serious violations of the system of international criminal law.[110] These crimes are mostly committed with the complicity of the national government or individuals who have strong control over the sovereign power of a state. In other words, substantive crimes are planned, organised and directed under the international legal personality of the relevant state through the acts of its individuals. Instances of such acts are the

---

Convention on Slavery, 1953; Single Convention on Narcotic Drugs, New York, 30 March 1961; Treaty Banning Nuclear Weapons Tests in the Atmosphere, in Outer Space and Under Water, 5 August 1963; Convention on Offences and certain other Acts Committed on board Aircraft, 14 September 1963; International Convention on the Elimination of All Forms of Racial Discrimination, 7 March 1966; Treaty on the Non-Proliferation of Nuclear Weapons, 1 July 1968; UNESCO Convention on the Illicit Movement of Art Treasures, 14 November 1970; Convention for the Suppression of Unlawful Seizure of Aircraft, 16 December 1970; Convention to Prevent and Punish the Acts of Terrorism Taking the Form of Crimes Against Persons and Related Extortion that are of International Significance, 2 February 1971; Treaty on the Prohibition of the Emplacement of Nuclear Weapons and Other Weapons of Mass Destruction on the Seabed and the Ocean Floor and in the Subsoil Thereof, 11 February 1971; Convention on Psychotropic Substances, Vienna, 21 February 1971; Convention for the Suppression of Unlawful Acts Against the Safety of Civil Aviation, 23 September 1971; Protocol Amending the Single Convention on Narcotic Drugs, 1961, Geneva, 25 March 1972; International Convention for the Prevention of Pollution from ships, 2November, 1973; International Convention on the Suppression and Punishment of the Crime of Apartheid, 30 November 1973; Convention on the Prevention and Punishment of Crimes against Internationally Protected Persons, Including diplomatic Agents, 13 December 1973; Declaration on the Protection of All Persons from being Subjected to Torture and Other Cruel, Inhuman or Degrading Treatment or Punishment (1975); European Convention on the Suppression of Terrorism, 27 January 1977; Convention on Long-Range Trans boundary Air Pollution, 13 November 1979; International Convention Against Hostage Taking, 18 December 1979; Convention against Torture and Other Cruel, Inhuman or Degrading Treatment or Punishment (1984); Convention for the Suppression of Unlawful Acts Against the Safety of Maritime Navigation, Rome, 10 March 1988; Protocol for the Suppression of Unlawful Acts against the Safety of Fixed Platforms located on the Continental Shelf, Rome 10 March 1988; Protocol for the Suppression of Unlawful Acts of Violence at Airports Serving International Civil Aviation, Supplementary to the Convention for the Suppression of Unlawful Acts against Safety of Civil Aviation, Montreal, 24 February 1988; United Nations Convention Against Illicit Traffic in Narcotic Drugs and Psychotropic Substances, 1988; Convention on the Prevention and Punishment of the Crime of Genocide, 9 December 1948; Convention on the Rights of the Child, 20 November 1989.

[110] M. CHERIF BASSIOUNI, Crimes against Humanity in International Law, 2d ed. (1999).

commission of crimes against humanity against the Armenian people by the Turkish government in 1915-1917; the Jewish population in 1939-1945 in Europe by the German government with the complicity of other European states; the Vietnamese people during 1959-1975 by the United States Government; the Muslim population in Bosnia Herzegovina during 1990 and 1992-1995 by Serbian; the genocide against the Kurdish population in Iraq during 1980; in Rwanda in 1994; torture in Abu Ghraib in 2005-6 in Iraq and Isreal against Palestinians.[111] These were all directed and organized with the direct and indirect complicity of the high-ranking individuals of the relevant states.

In general, the victims of substantive crimes are sometimes the citizens of different states, but it is more often the criminal government's own population that becomes the target of inhuman violations. In this context, the core crimes or substantive crimes are not only grave violations of the provisions of international humanitarian law of armed conflicts but are also serious violations of the fundamental principles of international human rights law. This means that the substantive crimes under the Rome Statute also protect the implementation of the principles of human rights law.

Consequently, the term "substantive crimes" may denote the gravity and the seriousness of the crimes which are committed in combination with state personality and groups. In fact, the whole system of international criminal law, and particularly the substantive crimes, have been developed from several factors *inter alia* are i) the law of war or the law of armed conflicts, ii) international humanitarian law, iii) domestic criminal law, iv) the law governing human rights law, and v) the transitional justice movement.

The law of war denotes the conventional and customary rules of war which have to be respected during armed conflict. International humanitarian law implies the existence of certain consolidated international conventions that regulated the new rules of law in 1949 and 1977. Domestic criminal law is the combination of certain rules which criminalise certain acts as crimes and therefore make their perpetrators liable for punishment. Human rights law regulates the natural and positive rights of man within certain international documents. "Transitional justice" is the expression used by those countries that were moving from oppressive and tyrannical governments towards modern radical democratic

[111] See Judging International Criminal Justice in the Occupied Territories, *International Criminal Law Review* (2012), pp.827–869.

states.[112] These were regimes like the military dictatorships in Latin America, South Africa, many of the states of Africa under the dictatorship of a considerable number of European states like France, Great Britain and Spain,[113] and the former states of Eastern Europe. Transitional justice consists therefore of certain manifestations such as criminal prosecutions, reparations and truth commissions. As a result, the recognition of a substantive crime offers the eradication of acts or omissions whose aim is to destroy in whole or in part the essential principles of civilisations.

Some other criteria for the recognition of certain crimes as being substantive crimes are their involvement of massive destruction, large numbers of killings, heavy extermination, widely planned and organized atrocities, lack of respect for the provisions of the international humanitarian law of armed conflicts, the collective aim of humiliation, violations of the generally recognized principles of civilisation, violations of fundamental principles of criminal law, violations of the law of the United Nations and violations of the dignity of mankind. These criteria taken together or in isolation, and many others that we will discuss later, are some of the basic elements for the recognition of certain crimes as substantive crimes under the system of international criminal law or the law of the permanent International Criminal Court. In fact, the ICC bases its credibility on the nature of crimes and their prosecution as well as the punishment of those who have violated the law of the international community as a whole.

6.1.4. Dimensions of Crimes

The work behind the definitions of crimes and their structure has been one of the most difficult tasks in the creation of the ICC. This was because there was not a code of crimes which would be acceptable to all negotiating states. Many suggestions had to be discussed and analysed in the course of meetings. In addition, the dimensions of crimes had to be clear and not be liable to confusion in the course of proceedings.

The crimes, which are entered into the Rome Statute, are based on several significant principles that are of essential importance for the application of the rules of the Statute. Accordingly, the definitions of

---

[112] See International Internet Bibliography inuserpage.fu-berlin.de/~theissen/biblio/ - 2k, visited 2008-03-28.

[113] Although one cannot deny that most of the African states were monopolized under the dictatorship of many European states and were subjects of various international crimes, they could not, in reality, establish a criminal prosecution or truth commission against the governments of those states.

crimes must therefore coincide with the following principles that have particular functions in the recognition and application of their scope.

6.1.4.1. Seriousness

A close analysis of the Rome Statute implies the fact that the jurisdiction of the Court is mostly intended for the prosecution and punishment of those who have committed the gravest violations of the system of international criminal law. This means that those who are accused of the commission of crimes under the jurisdiction of the ICC may be brought to the Court. In other words, the Court deals solely with major criminals or those who are chiefly responsible for the commission of certain grave crimes. The subordinates and other minor criminals may be prosecuted and punished by national courts. Otherwise, it would be very problematic to bring all the perpetrators of substantive crimes under the jurisdiction of the ICC. A close reading of some of the pieces of the Statute confirms this fact. Accordingly, "most serious crimes of concern to the international community as a whole must not go unpunished".[114] Moreover, jurisdiction, admissibility and the applicable law of the Court stipulate a similar view.[115]

6.1.4.2. Non-Exhaustive Nature

The crimes listed in the Statute are not exhaustive and are only defined "for the purpose of this Statute."[116] This means that the Statute does not aim at giving particular definitions to the four categories of crimes that are enumerated within its articles. In other words, the definitions presented in the Statute are for the purpose of the application of the machinery of the Court and are not intended to affect the codification of the system of international criminal law itself.

Whilst one may easily understand the purpose of the drafters of the Statute in limiting its application, namely, to minimise political conflict and increase the likelihood of the acceptance of the provisions of the Statute, it is nevertheless the case that the provisions and definitions of the crimes within the Statute are based on the rules, norms and provisions of international criminal law. This means that the provisions of the Statute governing the definitions and scope of the crimes may in the very near future contribute to the consolidated rules of customary international criminal law. At the same time, it is impossible to assert that the rules and provisions of the Statute concerning those crimes are not taken from the

---

[114] The Preamble of the Statute.

[115] Article 5(1).

[116] See Articles 6, 7(1) and 8(2).

provisions of customary law, humanitarian law and more obviously from the norms of *jus cogens*.[117] This means that the formulation "for the purpose of this Statute" is more a matter of symbolism and semantics. The efficiency and the essence of the Statute is the basic background from which its framework arises.[118]

However, it is very doubtful for this writer whether the Court and its respected judges can, in certain circumstances, avoid referring to the principles of customary international criminal law when a reference is needed. Although the definitions of the crimes are intended for the purpose of the Statute, few judges can deliver an illustrative statement or dissenting view without reference to the provisions of customary law. Furthermore, other courts in the world may use the relevant definitions in order to provide a more comprehensive definition of the crimes in their own proceedings.

6.1.4.3. Non-Limitation

The definitions of crimes that are enumerated in the Statute do not, in any way, prevent the development of the system of international criminal law. This is clearly stated within the law of the Statute. It reads that "Nothing in this Part shall be interpreted as limiting or prejudicing in any way existing or developing rules of international law for purposes other than this Statute."[119] This means that the definitions within the Statute do not limit the development of international criminal law in certain relevant areas and suggests that the system must eventually be enlarged when it comes to crimes against humanity, war crimes, genocide and the crime of aggression.

The above provisions also suggest that the international legal and political communities are not under any obligation to restrict the definitions of future international agreements to the provisions of the ICC Statute. According to a radical interpretation of the above provisions, the development of the rules of international law may be grounds for the subsequent evolution of the scope of definitions of crimes within the Statute and its modification.

---

[117] Hilary Charlesworth and Christine Chinkin, *The Gender of Jus Cogens,* 15 Human Rights Quarterly 63 (1993).

[118] For instance, the judgment and the prosecution in the Special Court for Sierra Leone have already referred to the Statute of the ICC. See Chapter Five.

[119] Article 10. See also Leila Nadya Sadat, Custom, Codification and Some Thoughts about the Relationship Between the Two: Article 10 of the ICC Statute, 49 DePaul Law Review 909 (2000).

6.1.4.4. Non-Autonomous

A significant matter within the provisions of the Rome Statute is that the definitions, which are expressed in several articles, are not autonomous and therefore need to be completed by the States Parties. This is clearly stated in the Statute. It reads that the elements of crimes must "assist the Court in the interpretation and application" of the relevant article concerning the definitions of crimes within the Statute. The elements are to be formulated and adopted by a two-thirds majority of the members of the Assembly of States Parties.[120] These elements may even be modified at the request of a state party, judge or prosecutor.

Thus, the definitions of crimes are subject to the elements of crimes that are already accepted by the members of the Assembly of States.[121] These elements refer to the component elements of the crimes against humanity, genocide and war crimes under the jurisdiction of the Court and are applicable regulations for the proceedings of the ICC. Whilst the definitions of crimes within the Statute are subject to the elements of crimes, the relevant machinery of the Court must be very vigilant concerning the employment and interpretation of elements of crimes in any given case.[122]

One of the most problematic issues is that the Assembly of States Parties has not been able to take any decision relating to the elements of the crime of aggression, due to the fact that the Security Council has not defined the crime. When it does so, the Assembly of States Parties will have to formulate such elements.[123]

---

[120] Article 9(1).

[121] See appendix.

[122] See Larry May, Aggression and Crimes Against Peace (2008).

[123] See *id.* However, it is neither clear nor possible to assert that the Security Council will not monopolise the formulation of the elements of crimes for the crime of aggression. This is because it is logically and practically almost impossible to presume that the Security Council will define the term aggression, without drafting its elements, both of which are an integral part of each other. It is true that the question of the definition of the term aggression has not been solved since the establishment of the United Nations and the answer to this question rests entirely in the power of the Security Council of the United Nations. Curiously enough, although we have adopted the 1974 resolution on the definition of aggression in the General Assembly of the United Nations, the resolution does not have binding force because of Article 5 of the Statute. In other words, the Statute seriously interferes in the structure of the system of international criminal law. The Statute clearly ignores the definition of aggression which is presented in Resolution 3314 (XXIX). This means that the resolutions of the General Assembly do not have a law-creating power and the Statute implicitly and explicitly rejects

6.1.4.5. Respect of Principles

The Rome Statute makes it clear that the definition of crimes should not be read in isolation from the General Principles of Criminal Law.[124] This implies the fact that the Statute fully respects those generally accepted principles of criminal law. These include *nullum crimen sine lege*, *nulla poena sine lege*, non-retroactivity, *ratione personae*, individual criminal responsibility, exclusion of jurisdiction over persons under eighteen, irrelevance of official capacity, responsibility of commanders and other superiors, non-applicability of the statute of limitations, mental elements, grounds for excluding criminal responsibility, mistake of fact or mistake of law, superior orders and prescription of law.[125]

According to the Rome Statute, the judges of the Court should be very cautious in the application and the definition of the crimes. Accordingly, "(T)he definition of a crime shall be strictly construed and shall not be extended by analogy. In case of ambiguity, the definition shall be interpreted in favour of the person being investigated, prosecuted or convicted."[126] Consequently, the prosecutors and the judges of the ICC are required to apply the existing law, but they also have a duty in the case of ambiguity or uncertainty to interpret the law in favour of the person who is under investigation by the Court. The Court is not entitled to take into account new developments in conventional or customary international criminal law if the purpose of the legislator is not deemed reasonable. It has to define the law in the light of its aims and purposes and not give a stronger definition to the law in a particular case in order to find the accused guilty of committing certain crimes.

---

other relevant resolutions of the General Assembly which deal, in one way or another, with questions of international criminal law. The seriousness of the question becomes particularly clear when one realises that the resolution on the definition of aggression is the result of at least 36 years work by different organs of the United Nations. The hope is that the new definition of the crime of aggression entered into the resolution of the 2010 Review Conference will resolve all these issues.

[124] Antonio Cassese, *The Statute of the International Criminal Court: Some Preliminary Reflections*, 10 European Journal of International Law 144-171 (1999), at 153

[125] *Id.*

[126] Article 22(2).

6.2. Genocide

6.2.1. Legal Formation

The Rome Statute is the manifestation of the will of the international legal and political community to bring the perpetrators of heinous crimes under prosecution and punishment.[127] The Rome Statute recognizes the crime of genocide as one of the core crimes which has to be prosecuted and punished.[128] This can also be confirmed in its earlier drafts.[129]

Genocide, as an international crime, is as old as the existence of criminal law within different civilisations.[130] However, the crime was not identified until the establishment of the United Nations and the adoption of the International Convention on Genocide in 1948.[131] The Convention on Genocide is thus the response to the situation at the time of its creation, and a close examination of its provisions reveals the impact of the inhuman acts and atrocities which were committed against the Jewish population of Europe during World War II.[132]

---

[127] See section on Substantive Crimes.

[128] During the preparation of the Statute, the discussions concerning the recognition of the crime of genocide and concerning when a state party has to take the initiative to lodge a complaint regarding the commission of genocide were very heated. See Report of the International Law Commission on the Work of its Forty-Sixth Session, 2 May-22 July 1994, Chapter II, UN Doc. A/49/10.

[129] *Id.*, paragraphs 21-25.

[130] See W. Michael Riesman, Legal Responses to Genocide and Other Massive Violations of Human Rights, 59 Law and Contemporary Problems 75 (1996); William L. Hurlock, The International Court of Justice: Effectively Providing a Long Overdue Remedy for Ending State-Sponsored Genocide (Bosnia-Herzegovina v. Yugoslavia), 12 American University Journal of International Law and Policy 299 (1997); Beth van Schaack, The Crime of Political Genocide: Repairing the Genocide Convention's Blind Spot, 106 Yale Law Journal 2259 (1997);Martha Minow, Between Vengeance and Forgiveness: Facing History After Genocide and Mass Violence (1998); John D. van der Vyver, Prosecution and Punishment of the Crime of Genocide, 23 Fordham International Law Journal 286 (1999); Mary Robinson, Genocide, War Crimes, Crimes Against Humanity, 23 Fordham International Law Journal 275 (1999); William A. Schabas, Genocide in International Law (2000); Matthew Lippman, Genocide, in International Criminal Law, vol. i (M. cherif Bassiouni, ed. 2008) pp. 403-435.

[131] See also Symposium, The International Criminal Court: Consensus and Debate on the International Adjudication of Genocide, Crimes Against Humanity, War Crimes, and Aggression, 32 Cornell International Law Journal 437-541 (1999).

[132] *Id.* It was on this basis that the United Nations General Assembly drafted the 1948 International Convention on the Prevention and Punishment of the Crime of

As a whole, the definition of genocide as an international crime within the provisions of the 1948 convention is very restricted and does not take into recognition many acts which could easily be identified as genocide.[133] For instance, the provisions of the convention do not apply to crimes against political or social groups.[134] There have been attempts by certain

---

Genocide. The aim of this international crime is essentially the material destruction of a group or nation either by physical or biological means. It aims in essence, therefore, at the elimination of a group's rights. This can be carried out by either physically killing, sometimes through mass killings, but also by biological means, such as the prevention of birth, marriage and other forms of restrictions on the normal social life of the group.

[133] M. Cherif, Bassiouni, *Protection of Collective Victims in International law, New York Schoold Human Rights Annual* (1985); See *also* William A Schabas, Genocide in International Law, the Crime of Crimes (2000).

[134] The words of the provisions of the ICC are taken from the Convention on genocide and therefore do not present any new development to the international crime of genocide. It would be more useful if the Statute could overcome the shortcomings of the convention on genocide. The convention does not, for example, illustrate at any level under what conditions the crime of genocide may be recognised. The Convention and the Statute are both silent concerning this question. Furthermore, in connection with the definition of the Convention, it is argued that systematic material destruction, either physical or biological, is essential in order to recognise that the crime has been committed. While this argument sounds rather logical, it is controversial in practice. This is because the term "systematic" is itself subject to discussion. "Systematic" means the action or inaction is based on a regular plan for the purpose of a specific result without necessarily achieving that result. It may also mean an action or inaction which is essentially based on a fixed method in order to cause a definite result. Certainly the scope of systematic is not clear. Systematic action is an action which is carried out repeatedly, not occasionally. Apartheid in South Africa was systematic for example. Similarly the British policy of Irish integration was also systematic. Israeli actions against Palestinians were also systematic. This means that, in all the above examples, certain actions were based on a regular plan or fixed method in order to reach a particular result. They were carried out over a long period of time with due regard to their purposes. In other words, the length of time, degree and purpose of a regular fixed method must have a special link with one another. A systematic action carried out for the purpose of harming does not need to be carried out over a prolonged length of time. A person suffering from a systematic hooding, subject to continuous noise, deprived of sleep, food or drink may give information even though the length of the systematic action has not been long. In such cases a particular result has been reached without need for continuous repetition. Similarly, the systematic rape of women and children, for whatever purpose, does not need a prolonged period of time. Thus, the occupation of a village by the armed forces of a conflicting party and the killing, raping, destroying

international movements at solving these shortcomings of the convention, but these attempts have not been successful on account of the political interests of states.

6.2.2. Limitation

The problems of the 1948 Convention have also been dealt with in the inner structure of the Rome Statute. This was the only way of passing the ratification of the Statute of the ICC. States were not, as a whole, interested in the development of the scope and definition of the crime of genocide. Therefore, some of the acts which could easily be identified as genocide were incorporated into the structure of other crimes, such as persecution, and were on political grounds brought under the provisions of crimes against humanity. This was in order to avoid any controversy between the contracting parties. The Statute has, as a result, adopted a definition which is similar to that of the 1948 Convention on Genocide.[135]

It recognizes that for the purpose of the Statute, the crime of genocide is any of the acts enumerated below, which are committed with the intention of destroying a racial, religious, ethical or national group.[136]

---

and burning houses are all evidence of the commission of genocide by one conflicting party against another. The period of time for the proof of an apartheid system may, however, be much longer than in such a repetition. It may come under prolonged systematic action.

[135] See also David Wippman, *Can an International Criminal Court Prevent and Punish Genocide*?, in Protection Against Genocide: Mission Impossible?, (Neal Riemer, ed., 2000), 85-104.

[136] For a crime to be identified as genocide it must be based on a regular plan or fixed method pursued in order to obtain a certain result. On the one hand, length of time, degree and purpose are all essential factors in identifying an action as constituting genocide. On the other hand, genocide can be committed over a very short period of time depending on different causal factors. Bombing a particular civilian location in a time of war may constitute both a war crime and a crime against peace and may at the same time constitute genocide depending on the intent to destroy, in whole or in part, a national, ethnic, racial or religious group of that civilian location. This means that bombing in that area was deliberately planned and calculated to destroy a particular group. In certain situations one cannot draw the conclusion that the bombing of civilian people exclusively constitutes a war crime or a crime against peace; however, it may also constitute genocide. We have seen clear instances of this in the Yugoslavian war and the genocide committed by Serbian authorities against Muslims and Croatians. This means that although a systematic and regular method of action is essential for the commission of the crime of genocide, they are not necessarily essential for the fulfilment of an object. Consequently, to identify an act as genocide, a particular

Accordingly, genocide may be committed against those groups as a whole or in part. The following acts are identified as genocide:

(a) Killing members of the group;
(b) Causing serious bodily or mental harm to members of the group;
(c) Deliberately inflicting on the group conditions of life calculated to bring about its physical destruction in whole or in part;
(d) Imposing measures intended to prevent births within the group;
(e) Forcibly transferring children of the group to another group.

The inadequacy of the definition of the crime of genocide in the Statute is, however, not a fact which has only recently come to light. The provisions of the Convention were not employed until rather recently by the ICTR which delivered the decision of Prosecutor v. Jean-Paul Akayesu.[137] The decision stated that rape during war may also constitute genocide. It also clarified that "physical invasion of a sexual nature, committed on a person under circumstances which are coercive" constitutes a grave violation of the law of armed conflicts. In 2007, Bosnia Herzegovina brought the first case against the Federal Republic of Yugoslavia into the International Court of Justice in order to enforce the provisions of the Convention on Genocide. However, the Court did not deal with the question of the commission of genocide at length.[138]

---

systematic method is not needed. This situation arises from the special character of the crime of genocide, which depends on the variation of the systematic methods used by the perpetrators for the commission of genocide. Another problem with the definition of the crime of genocide in the International Convention on the Prevention and Punishment of the Crime of Genocide is that it does not cover new methods for the destruction of groups or nations used by different regimes. These are such things as cultural genocide, including national, linguistic and religious suppression, and so forth. Although its drafters took up this fault in the Convention in 1947, it was not resolved and has now caused a problem in the definition and interpretation of the Convention. Yet, the problem was neither solved by the International Law Commission in its draft Code of Crimes against the Peace and Security of Mankind in 1996 nor by the Statute of the ICC.

[137] Prosecutor v. Rutaganda (Case No.ICTR-96-4-T), Judgment (ICTR Trial Chamber I, Sept. 2, 1998.

[138] See Application of the Convention on the Prevention and Punishment of the Crime of Genocide (Bosnia and Herzegovina *v.* Serbia and Montenegro), See also: Application for Revision of the Judgment of 11 July 1996 in the Case concerning *Application of the Convention on the Prevention and Punishment of the Crime of Genocide (Bosnia and Herzegovina v. Yugoslavia), Preliminary Objections* (Yugoslavia *v.* Bosnia and Herzegovina), www.icj-cij.org/docket/index.php? Visited on 2008-03-22.As is rightly asserted "The ruling by the International Court

6.2.3. Scope

There are many questions relating to the scope of the international crime of genocide that are not easy to answer. The document attached to the Statute of the ICC concerning the element of crimes does not define many of its terms, such as the term "group". This has created great difficulty concerning what does or does not constitute a group. There is not yet any clear definition of the term "group" which may be acceptable in the practice of international tribunals. For instance, what constitutes a national, ethnic, racial or religious group is indeed ambiguous and needs definitions and interpretations. In 1998, the ICTR concluded that Hutu and Tutsi were two different ethnic groups, although they had the same race, religion, language, culture and nationality.[139] This means that a nation may be considered to have different ethnic groups although they have more or less similar statuses.[140]

The difficulty that may arise when a nation is divided into different ethnic groups is indeed unavoidable. Especially when a nation has, more or less, the same race, culture, religion and language backgrounds. However, the philosophy behind this division may not solely be juridical, and there may also be other important considerations, such as recognizing the basic principles of natural law more juridically. The purpose of this recognition may also, in certain situations, be the identification of the implementation of natural law principles over positive law. Providing a

---

of Justice (ICJ) in the case brought by Bosnia-Herzegovina against Serbia, delivered on 26 February 2007, is a compromise judgment, giving something to the Bosnian victims but largely denying the Bosnian genocide and exonerating the Serbian state of its role. Although seen by some western media as a progressive judgment, it is has largely been greeted with dismay by Bosnians and welcomed by apologists for the most reactionary Serbian forces, including those who seem to occupy the comment pages of the Guardian whenever Yugoslav war issues return to the headlines. … Genocide is widely acknowledged to be the supreme international crime, but for this very reason courts seem reluctant to recognise it, despite overwhelming evidence. It is not too strong to say that in this case, the International Court of Justice has engaged in systematic denial of the Bosnian genocide." By Martin Shaw, The International Court of Justice: Serbia, Bosnia, and Genocide,www.globalpolicy.org/intljustice/icj/2007/0228icjshaw.htm - 19k visited 2008-03-22.

139 Johan D. van der Vyver, *Prosecution and Punishment of the Crime of Genocide,* Fordham International Law Journal 286, 302-04 (1999).

140 The Tribunal sentenced Jean Kambanda, a former prime minister of Rwanda, to life imprisonment. He is the first person in the world to be convicted of genocide in an international criminal tribunal. Many others were also convicted for the same crime by the ICTR.

clear definition of an ethnic group may be very difficult in certain circumstances because of the limited scope of the positivist interpretation of the provisions of law or the genocide convention. It may, however, not be too difficult to say that the right to life and existence is the natural right of any human being and, for this reason, systematic violations of the rights of a group or part of a group, with the clear intention of killing, without doubt constitutes genocide; especially when it is carried out on a large scale, with intention, and with the direct or indirect complicity of governments.[141] This has often been proved to be the case.[142]

6.2.4. Subjectivity and Objectivity

Jurisdictional elements of a crime do not necessarily mean the juridical recognition of an action in the proceedings of criminal justice. The burden of proof of guilt may be combined with other circumstances, such as the ambition to carry out an identified criminal act in order to destroy evidence and confound the criminal justice system through very complicated criminal behaviour or fraud. The conclusion reached by the ICTR required the group to be "stable". This means that it must be determined by birth rather than be "mobile". While the description of the Tribunal may be useful and fundamental, the recognition of the subjective intent of a group may be more effective than the objective nature of the same group. In the same way, the philosophy of the identification of an act as genocide is clearly the prohibition of serious immoral actions pertaining to the destruction of a group in part or as a whole. A group may even have committed genocide against a part of its own group, where race, language, religion and cultural identity are the same. A part of a group, which is divided by adherence to different ethical or political views, may thus be the target of genocidal actions by a different part of a group. The motivation for this may be rooted in economic or ideological differences. Thus, identifying an act of genocide that is broader than positive international law cannot be interpreted as violation of the law, as long as the substance of the recognition of the act is the same. This means that the ICC is not limited to securing the definition because of its semantic nature. The actual facts must be the reason for its application.

[141] See Genocide, War Crimes and the West History and Complicity, (Adam Jones, ed.,2004).

[142] Id.

6.2.5. Elements of Genocide

When the Statute of the ICC was drafted, it was impossible at the time to draft the elements of crimes concerning genocide, war crimes and crimes against humanity. The Assembly of States Parties deferred this task to later meetings and decisions.[143] The elements of crimes were in fact formulated due to the requirements of Article 9. The purpose of the elements is to assist the Court in order to apply the provisions of articles 6, 7 and 8 properly.

Accordingly, among the most important purposes of the elements of crimes are the resolution of many interpretative difficulties and the reduction of any confusion that may arise in the proceedings of the Court. A clear example of this element is the term "in the context of", which is entered into Article 6 of the ICC, denotes the initial acts in an emerging pattern. Similarly, the term "manifest" is intended to have a requisite objective qualification.[144] According to the elements of crimes, the Court may decide on the requirements for mental elements which are provided in Article 30 of the Statute of the ICC for the proof of genocidal intent on a case-by-case basis.[145]

Article 6 of the ICC has, similar to the provisions of the Convention on Genocide, divided the crime into several parts. These are genocide *a)* by killing, *b)* genocide by causing serious physical or mental harm, *c)* genocide by deliberately inflicting conditions of life calculated to bring about physical destruction, *d)* genocide by imposing measures intended to prevent births, and *e)* genocide by forcibly transferring children. Each of these actions has its own elements of recognition for the proof of violations of the provisions of the Convention on Genocide or the Statute of the ICC.[146]

---

143 International Criminal Court, Elements of Crimes, U.N. Doc. PCNICC/2000/1/Add.2 (2000).

144 Guglielmo Verdirame., The Genocide Definition in the Jurisprudence of the ad hoc Tribunals, Vol. 49, No. 3 The International and Comparative Law Quarterly, (Jul., 2000), pp. 578-598.

145 See Mohamed Elewa Badar, *The Mental Element in the Rome Statute of the International Criminal Court: A Commentary from a Comparative Criminal Law Perspective,* Criminal Law Forum (2008); Roger S. Clark, The Mental Element in International Criminal Law: The Rome Statute of the International Criminal Court and the Elements of the Offences, 12 Criminal Law Forum 291 (2001).

146 International Criminal Court Act (Elements of Crimes, 2001).

6.2.6. Actual Killing

The elements of genocide by killing are: 1. The perpetrator has killed one or more persons. 2. The victims who were killed belonged to a particular national, ethnical, racial or religious group.[147] 3. The perpetrator had intended to destroy, in whole or in part, that racial, ethnical, national or religious group. 4. The conduct was carried out in connection with a manifest pattern of similar conduct directed against that group, or the nature of the conduct could also itself be a reason for destruction of a group.

Therefore, actual killing refers to intentions to kill which have been carried out or were intended to be carried out against a group.[148] This element is so clear and identifiable that it should not be confused with other international crimes. In other words, it is the intention of killing directed against a group which classifies the action as genocide.

6.2.7. Bodily Harm

According to the ICC, genocide by causing bodily or mental harm consists of four elements. These are 1. A person causes serious bodily or mental harm to one or more persons; 2. Persons who are the victims of the crimes are of a particular national, ethnical, racial or religious group; 3. The perpetrator had intended to destroy, in whole or in part, that racial, ethnical, national or religious group; 4. The conduct took place in the context of a manifest pattern of similar conduct directed against that group or was conduct that could itself effect such destruction.

---

[147] It must be emphasised that "A *national group* means a set of individuals whose identity is defined by a common country of nationality or national origin. An *ethnical group* is a set of individuals whose identity is defined by common cultural traditions, language or heritage. A *racial group* means a set of individuals whose identity is defined by physical characteristics. A *religious group* is a set of individuals whose identity is defined by common religious creeds, beliefs, doctrines, practices, or rituals." www.preventgenocide.org/genocide/officialtext.htm. Visited on 2009-07-11.

[148] "*Killing members of the group* includes direct killing and actions causing death. *Causing serious bodily or mental harm* includes inflicting trauma on members of the group through widespread torture, rape, sexual violence, forced or coerced use of drugs, and mutilation." www.preventgenocide.org/genocide/officialtext.htm. Visited on 2009-07-11.

6.2.8. Deliberately Inflicting

According to Article 6 (c) of the Statute of the ICC, genocide by deliberately inflicting conditions of life calculated to bring about physical destruction has been formulated into five elements of recognition.[149] These are: 1.The perpetrator has inflicted definite conditions of life on one or more persons who are the victims of the crime of genocide; 2. The person or persons belong to a particular racial, ethnic, national or religious group; 3.The perpetrator had intended to destroy, in whole or in part, that national, ethnic, racial or religious group; 4.The conditions of life were intended to cause the physical destruction of the group, in whole or in part; 5.The conduct took place in the context of a manifest pattern of similar conduct directed against that group or was conduct that could itself effect such destruction.

6.2.9. Prevention of Birth

Genocide by imposing measures intended to prevent births also consists of five significant elements of recognition.[150] These are the following: 1. The perpetrator has imposed certain measures by force on one or more persons; 2. The victims are considered an integral part of a particular racial, ethnic, national or religious group; 3. The perpetrator has intended to destroy, in whole or in part, that national, ethnic, racial or religious group; 4. The measures which were imposed were intended to prevent births within that particular group; 5. The conduct was carried out in the context of an obvious pattern of similar action directed against that group or was conduct that could itself effect such destruction.

---

[149] "*Deliberately inflicting conditions of life calculated to destroy a group* includes the deliberate deprivation of resources needed for the group's physical survival, such as clean water, food, clothing, shelter or medical services. Deprivation of the means to sustain life can be imposed through confiscation of harvests, blockade of foodstuffs, detention in camps, forcible relocation or expulsion into deserts." www.preventgenocide.org/genocide/officialtext.htm.Visited on 2009-07-11.

[150] "*Prevention of births* includes involuntary sterilization, forced abortion, prohibition of marriage, and long-term separation of men and women intended to prevent procreation." www.preventgenocide.org/genocide/officialtext.htm. Visited on 2009-07-11.

6.2.10. Forcibly Transferring

The ICC has also recognized certain provisions governing the forcible transfer of children.[151] The elements of genocide by forcibly transferring children are the following: 1. The perpetrator has forcibly transferred one or more persons; 2. Those persons belong to a particular national, ethnic, racial or religious group; 3. The perpetrator has intended to destroy, in whole or in part, that racial, ethnic, national or religious group; 4. The transfer of children was from that particular group to another group; 5. The person or persons who were the victims of transferral were under 18 years old; 6. The perpetrator had the information or should have realised that the victims were less than 18 years old; 7. The conduct was carried out in connection with an obvious pattern of similar conduct that was directed against that particular group or was conduct that could itself effect such destruction.

6.2.11. Requisite Intent

Since genocide constitutes a very serious international crime, there are certain conditions for its recognition that must not be ignored by the Court. In other words, the recognition of the crime of genocide is based on requisite intent which denotes the special intent known as *dolus specialis*. Any lack of requisite intent may be interpreted as lack of knowledge of the commission of the crime. This means that the existence of certain criteria for the commission of the crime of genocide will limit the discretion of the prosecutor in identifying an act under the scope of the definition of genocide. Thus, the Court has to prove that the offender had intended to destroy the target group in whole or in part. As a result, many of those who were actively involved in the commission of the crime of genocide will not be prosecuted and punished for the crime of genocide on account of lack of knowledge. Whilst it must be emphasised that the crime of genocide must be punished on the basis of obligations in the Genocide Convention,

---

[151] "*Forcible transfer of children* may be imposed by direct force or by fear of violence, duress, detention, psychological oppression or other methods of coercion. The Convention on the Rights of the Child defines children as persons under the age of 18 years." www.preventgenocide.org/genocide/officialtext.htm.visited on 2009-07-11.

which are obligations *erga omnes,*[152] this may not be carried out in full because of a lack of proof of requisite intent.

6.3. Crimes against Humanity

6.3.1. Recognition

The principles concerning the recognition of crimes against humanity that have been recorded in the Declaration of 1915, the Charter of the Nuremberg Tribunal, the ICTY and ICTR have also, more or less, been established in the Statute of the ICC.[153] The formulation of crimes against humanity in Article 7 of the Statute is therefore the development of the existing literature of international criminal law.[154] Whilst the crimes have been recognized internationally, the adoption of a definite formulation concerning what does or what does not constitute crimes against humanity presented some of the greatest difficulties at the Rome conference.[155] This is because the philosophy underlying a crime against humanity is very broad and requires an analysis of the different principles in international criminal law.[156] The prior definitions varied from one another and yet the concepts of crimes against humanity have increased in number enormously since the adoption of various definitions in different instruments.[157]

While there was no acceptable definition of crimes against humanity in conventional or customary international criminal law, the drafting of the Statute of the ICC faced more contradictions between the different ideas

---

[152] This means that each state and the Court are under an international obligation to prosecute and punish genocide. Ian Brownlie, Principles of Public International Law (6th, ed, 2003), 568.

[153] See Farhad Malekian, *Armenian Genocide and the Questions of Responsibility of the Turkish Government,* 31-9 (House of Commons Conference on the Armenian Genocide, Armenian Solidarity, British-Armenian All-Party Parliamentary Group, No Security Publication (2007).

[154] For a philosophical examination of crimes against humanity See Larry May, Crimes Against Humanity: A Normative Account (2004).

[155] M. Cherif Bassiouni, *Crimes Against Humanity, in* International Criminal Law, vol I (M. Cherif Bassiouni, ed. 2008) pp. 437-492; M. Cherif Bassiouni, *The Normative Framework of International Humanitarian Law: Overlaps, Gaps and Ambiguities, in* Bassiouni above, pp. 493-531.

[156] See *Id.*

[157] These are such as the Nuremberg and Tokyo Charters, Control Council Law No.10, ICTY and ICTR.

presented by the representatives of states.[158] One of the questions raised was whether the recognition of crimes against humanity requires *nexus* to armed conflict.[159] This question was finally answered negatively and it became clear that the recognition of a crime against humanity does not necessarily need connection to a state of armed conflict.[160]

Some of the conditions for the recognition of crimes against humanity that are recognized by the Statute are met when acts are committed as part of a *widespread* or *systematic attack* directed *against any civilian population* and with *knowledge of the attack.* These are acts such as murder, extermination, enslavement, deportation or the forcible transfer of population, imprisonment, severe deprivation of physical liberty, torture, rape, sexual slavery, enforced prostitution, forced pregnancy, sterilization, persecution against any identifiable group (including political, racial, national, ethnic, cultural and religious groups), the enforced disappearance of persons, apartheid, and other inhumane acts of a similar character causing serious suffering. Each of these terminologies is more specifically defined by paragraphs and subparagraphs of Article 7 in order to reduce the possibility of any misinterpretation of the article.[161]

6.3.2. Precondition

The Statute underlines four basic preconditions that must be fulfilled before its jurisdiction is to be exercised for the charges of crimes against humanity. These conditions are a compromise between different schools of thought: those who interpret crimes against humanity too widely and those who thought them too narrow. The conditions have two different characters, namely, jurisdictional and material. The jurisdictional elements imply the fact that once they have been settled in the proceedings of the Court, they do not any longer need to be proved in the case of each defendant. The material elements refer to the fact that the defendant had the necessary knowledge or intent to commit the relevant crimes.[162] These elements must be proved in the case of each defendant.

---

[158] Darryl Robinson, *Defining 'Crimes Against Humanity' at the Rome Conference*, 93 American Journal of International Law 43-57 (1999).

[159] *Id.*, 43.

[160] *Id.*, 43.

[161] *Id.*, 45.

[162] Article 30 of the Rome Statute.

6.3.3. Widespread

According to the Statute, crimes against humanity should be proved to be part of a "widespread or systematic attack." These conditions, having a jurisdictional character, were not made clear in the Statute of the ICTY, but they are also expressed in the Statute of the ICTR. Both terms, "widespread attacks" and "systematic attacks", have been defined broadly in the decisions of the ICTR.

The Statute of the ICC tried to reach a compromise between these two legal systems in order to avoid difficulties in the application of the concept of crimes against humanity. Thus, the terms "widespread attack" and "systematic attack" may have an almost identical character and their definitions may overlap one another when it comes to intention. In other words, one may refer to widespread intention and systematic intentional attack. This means that the relevant requirements may not be the necessary conditions for the recognition of crimes against humanity, but rather the way in which an attack directed against a civilian population is implicitly acknowledged as multiple commissions of acts listed in the Statute in respect to crimes against humanity.

6.3.4. Civilian Population

Another precondition for the recognition of crimes against humanity is that the attack must be carried out against a "civilian population". The inclusion of these two words, "civilian" and "population", has complicated the recognition of crimes against humanity. This is because the concept of crimes against humanity rests, in the first stage, on the concept of widespread or systematic attack/violation, which, to a large extent, means to carry out an action with clear intention. For example, the ICTR has defined the word "widespread" as "massive, frequent, large scale action, carried out collectively with considerable seriousness and directed against a multiplicity of victims."[163] The same Tribunal has defined the word "systematic" as "thoroughly organized and following a regular pattern on the basis of a common policy involving substantial public or private resources."[164] Thus, recognising "civilian population" as a juridical condition for charges of crimes against humanity, reduces the attribution of international criminal responsibility to those who have committed crimes against humanity.

---

[163] Prosecutor v. Akayesu (Case No.ICTR-96-4-T), Judgment, para.580 (ICTR Trial Chamber I, Sept.2, 1998).
[164] Id.

The term "civilian population" may, in the course of various actions, be interpreted differently.[165] One may identify certain people as constituting a civilian population and certain other people may not be included in the definition of the term. Furthermore, the term openly discriminates between civilian and non-civilian victims of great inhuman actions or suffering.[166] We should not forget that the distinction between civilian and non-civilian is very narrow and creates, in the case of crimes against humanity, great difficulties. In addition, the definition of the word "civilian" is itself subject to question and may be interpreted differently. But what we understand from the words "civilian population" in the Statute of the ICC includes without doubt any person, who has, for one reason or another, been the target of an attack constituting a crime against humanity. This includes, for example, nationals, foreigners, diplomats, protected persons, refugees and other persons. The distinction between civilian and non-civilian is solely juridical, but a juridical reason may also be considered simultaneously as material in that it focuses on the character of the criminal conduct. It may otherwise be taken to recommend that the interpretation of the term "civilian population" means, at the same time, the granting of permission to commit crimes against humanity.[167]

6.3.5. Knowledge

Another precondition for the application of the provisions of crimes against humanity is the existence of knowledge. Article 7 has clearly stated that crimes must be committed "with knowledge of the attack." This condition is also the material element of crimes against humanity and should be proven in each case to be true on the part of the defendant. Thus, the prosecutor or the trial chamber cannot draw a general conclusion against all defendants. The case of each individual must be examined separately with regard to intent and knowledge of attack.

---

[165] See Darryl Robinson, *Defining 'Crimes Against Humanity' at the Rome Conference*, 93 American Journal of International Law 43-57 (1999), at 48.

[166] *Id.*

[167] As has been stated long ago, the purpose of crimes against humanity "which either by their magnitude and savagery or by their large number or by the fact that a similar pattern was applied…endangered the international community or shocked the conscience of mankind." *History of the United Nations War Crimes Commission and the Development of the Laws of War,* 179 (1943).

6.3.6. Pursuant to Policy

Article 7 of the Statute emphasises that the attack must be "a course of conduct involving the multiple commission of acts … against any civilian population, pursuant to or in furtherance of a State or organizational policy to commit such attack."[168] Although we do not deny that the Statute exclusively deals with the notion of the criminal responsibility of individuals, this statement in Article 7 must be considered an important contribution of the Statute towards the concept of the international criminal responsibility of governments, states or entities. The article has actually two objects: "multiple commission of acts" and "a state or organization policy to commit such attack." The first focuses on the fact that, in order for an act to constitute a crime against humanity, it should be one of multiple commissions of an act or several acts of the same nature. The second requires that the multiple commissions of acts must be a part of a policy directed or instigated under a state or organizational power. Both parts are an integral part of the other.

Although the article might not suggest here the idea of the criminal responsibility of governments and their liability to punishment before the ICC, it certainly argues that government actions and policy may also be instrumental in the commission of crimes against humanity. One should, however, be very cautious in the case of crimes against humanity. This is because a crime may even have occurred under the authority of an organization or entity without necessarily a state being involved in the commission of the crime. In some situations, crimes against humanity may be committed within a state territory when an official government does not exist at all or there is a civil war within the territory of a state.[169] This may even be extended to the fact that a crime against humanity may equally be the result of state action or failure to prevent the crime. Therefore, the

---

[168] Article 7 (2) (a).

[169] However, a considerable degree of caution must be exercised in the situation where a state or government becomes involved in the performance of crimes and violates the system of international criminal law. A government may consider certain acts as civil war or acts of insurgents, rebels or revolutionaries and does not therefore accept its responsibility for crimes against humanity. For instance, crimes against humanity occurred in 1915 against the Armenian people on Turkish territory and were considered not to provide sufficient reason for the concept of criminal responsibility to apply to the Turkish government. Farhad Malekian, *Armenian Genocide and the Questions of Responsibility of the Turkish Government,* 31-9 (House of Commons Conference on the Armenian Genocide, Armenian Solidarity, British-Armenian All-Party Parliamentary Group, No Security Publication (2007).

elements of crimes emphasise that "The acts need not constitute a military attack. It is understood that "policy to commit such attack" requires that the State or organization actively promote or encourage such an attack against a civilian population."[170] In other words, crimes against humanity may be committed during war or peacetime.

6.3.7. Elements of Crimes against Humanity

6.3.7.1. The Boundaries of the Elements

The provisions concerning the recognition of crimes against humanity are of fundamental importance for the protection of the basic rights of man. They insist upon the international criminal responsibility of the relevant individuals who were engaged in the commission of crimes against humanity. In addition, these crimes are also recognised as among the most serious crimes concerning the international legal and political community as a whole.

Elements of various crimes against humanity have been based on two significant pillars which are necessary for the recognition of the relevant conduct. These are that the conduct was committed as part of a widespread or systematic attack directed against a civilian population and that the perpetrator knew about this matter. Accordingly, these elements denote both the existence of knowledge and the existence of a systematic attack against a civilian population. However, this must not be interpreted as requiring that the perpetrator knew about the precise details of the plan or policy of the state, but the existence of an emerging widespread or systematic attack against a civilian population and the participation of the perpetrator in the conduct suffice to prove his intent.

By the term "Attack directed against a civilian population" is meant a course of conduct involving the multiple commission of acts listed in Article 7 (1) of the Statute against any civilian population with the intention of fulfilling the policy of an organization or state. The acts in question do not necessarily need to be a military attack. The term "policy to commit such attack" means that the organization or state has actively encouraged and permitted such an attack against a civilian population.

The scope of crimes against humanity is also based on several other elements which are essential for the recognition of the crimes. For instance, the relevant rules recognize some of the necessary conditions for the identification of crimes against humanity in the enforced disappearance of persons. Accordingly, there some actions must have been

---

[170] International Criminal Court, Elements of Crimes, U.N. Doc. PCNICC/2000/1/Add.2 (2000).

taken leading to the policy of disappearance. Examples of these are where the perpetrator has arrested, detained or abducted one or more persons. He may also refuse to admit the arrest, detention or abduction and may fail to provide sufficient information regarding the location of such a person. This refusal by the perpetrator may be accompanied by other acts which help in carrying out his/her intentions concerning the enforced disappearance.

The perpetrator knew that the arrest, detention or abduction and the refusal to give information about the location of the person or deprivation of his freedom was planned or performed with the support, authorisation or the will of a state or a political organization. These denote his/her engagement in the commission of crimes against humanity. It may also be possible that the perpetrator has, for a long period of time, intentionally removed the person in question from legal protection and consequently deprived him/her of legal rights.

6.3.7.2. The Necessary Elements

There are different elements concerning different crimes in the category of crimes against humanity. Some of these elements may be summarized as:

- i) intention to carry out the conduct,
- ii) awareness of the criminality of the conduct,
- iii) violating the liberty or freedom of a person by various actions,
- iv) a policy of widespread and systematic attacks,
- v) a common policy involving substantial public or private policy,
- vi) killing or murdering one or several persons,
- vii) establishing ownership of a person,
- viii) forcible transferring of population based on organizational or state policy,
- ix) violating the fundamental principles of international law,
- x) awareness of the factual circumstances that established the gravity of the conduct,
- xi) severely depriving a person of fundamental rights,
- xii) depriving a person by reason of the identity of a group,
- xiii) deprivation for political, racial, national, ethnic, cultural, religious or gender reasons,
- xiv) arresting, detaining and abducting one or more persons,
- xv) refusing to acknowledge the arrest, detention or abduction and not providing information about the place of that person,
- xvi) deprivation of freedom,
- xvii) intention to remove the juridical protection of a person for a long period of time,

xviii) inflicting great suffering, serious injury to body or to mental or physical health, by means of an inhumane act,

xix) awareness of the factual circumstances causing the act.

The last two elements of each crime against humanity are highly problematic, which is provided for in the end of the description of the elements of each crime.[171] These elements make clear the requisite knowledge of a widespread or systematic attack and participation in this attack against a civilian population.

6.3.7.3. The Predominant Element

The complex question of what constitutes a civilian population has been debated in a variety of ways. The complexity lies in the fact that a civilian population may be considered differently depending on the circumstances and, as a whole, a population may fall into the definition of a civilian population, even though they are fighting against an unconventional armed attack. The *Tadic* case is an illustration of this position. The case focused on two significant matters: first, what the character of the targeted population must be for it to qualify as "civilian"; second, how it would decide "whether an individual victim qualifies as a civilian". This is when we want to identify acts committed against an individual victim which constitute crimes against humanity with due regard to that particular situation. The conclusion of the ICTY was very interesting. It stated that the "civilian population" has two characteristics. These are, on the one hand, a jurisdictional character that questions the nature of atrocities and, on the other hand, its particular material aspect that inquires into the nature of the act in combination with the status of the victim's position. Crimes against humanity concerning a civilian population may therefore be defined as "inhuman acts committed against civilians as opposed to members of the armed forces."[172] Here, this definition clearly separates those who are armed and engaged in armed conflicts from those who are not armed and do not take part in the actual armed conflict.

There is another possible definition of the term "civilian population" which can either give it a much clearer aspect, or present a more clarified

---

[171] These are "The conduct was committed as part of a widespread or systematic attack directed against a civilian population" and "The perpetrator knew that the conduct was part of or intended the conduct to be part of a widespread or systematic attack directed against a civilian population." See Elements of Crimes, crimes against humanity.

[172] Prosecutor v. Tadic (Case No.IT-94-1-T), Opinion and Judgement, paras.634, 640 (ICTY Trial Chamber II; May 7, 1997).

but different aspect of the term. On this definition, crimes against humanity are applicable in all possible cases where the perpetrators of the acts and the victims of the crimes have the same nationality. This is without regard to the fact that the victims are military personnel or civilians. In other words, the civilian population comprises all persons who are civilians. Therefore, the targeted population does not necessarily need to be entirely civilian in nature but rather predominantly civilian as a whole. This means that if the non-civilians are, for one reason or another, integrated into a civilian population, the character of the civilian population cannot be modified or defined differently because of this situation.[173] In certain cases when one does not know whether a person is a civilian, that person should nevertheless be recognized as a civilian. Furthermore, it must not be set aside that the families of the members of armed forces are certainly an integral part of the civilian population.

6.3.7.4. The Principles of Distinction

There are two principles that must be respected in the time of armed conflicts. These are the principle of proportionality and the principle of distinction. The first principle which is also an integral part of international customary law makes it clear that even if there is a definite military target, one should not attack it if there is a possibility that civilians or civilian property may be harmed more than the expected military target. Moreover, the term "military target" is very difficult to define when it is, in special circumstances, used for both civilians and military personnel. A clear example of this is a radio or TV station that may be regarded as a legitimate military target and also a public place for the broadcasting of information for civilians about matters other than the armed conflict. It may therefore not be easy to specify that a civilian is the subject of attack because of the circumstances of the relevant broadcasting stations. There must be full respect for the principle of proportionality. As a consequence, the conflicting parties are obliged to respect the principle of precaution in an attack. The principle calls upon the parties to supplement their general obligation to distinguish, at all times, between combatants and civilians and more clearly between military and civilian objects as a whole. Obviously, the combination of a military object and a civilian object, for the purpose of confusion during an armed conflict, creates a great responsibility for both conflicting parties. They should be clear in the case of both objects and should not use them for the purpose of attack.

---

[173] *Id.*, paras.636, 638.

6.4. War Crimes

6.4.1. Terminology

One of the core crimes within the provisions of the Statute is war crime.[174] The terminology of war crimes in the Statute of the ICC relies heavily on the existence of a large number of international criminal conventions that have been ratified during centuries of civilisation.[175] It is also recognised

---

[174] Thomas Graditzky, *War Crime Issues Before the Rome Diplomatic Conference on the Establishment of an International Criminal Court* 5 University of California at Davis Journal of International Law and Policy 199 (1999). But see *also* Lionel Yee Woon Chin, *Not Just a War Crime Court: The Penal Regime Established by the Rome Statute of the International Criminal Court,* 10 Singapore Academy of Law Journal 321 (1998).

[175] Some of these conventions are Agreement for the Prosecution and Punishment of Major War Criminals of the European Axis (London Charter), 8 August 1945; Geneva Convention for the Amelioration of the Condition of the Wounded and Sick in Armed Forces in the Field, 12 August 1949; Geneva Convention for the Amelioration of the Condition of Wounded, Sick and Shipwrecked Members of Armed Forces at Sea, 12 August 1949; Geneva Convention Relative to the Protection of Civilian Persons in Time of War, 12 August, 1949; Geneva Convention Relative to the Treatment of Prisoners of War, 12 August 1949; Control Council Law No, 10 (Punishment of Persons Guilty of War Crimes, Crimes Against Peace and Crimes Against Humanity), 20 December 1945; Charter of the International Military Tribunal for the Far East, 19 January, 1946; Special Proclamation: Establishment of an International Military Tribunal for the Far East, 19 January 1946; Affirmation of the Principles of International Law Recognized by the Charter of the Nuremberg Tribunal (United Nations General Assembly Resolution), 11 December 1946; Hague Convention for the Protection of Cultural Property in the Event of Armed Conflict, 14 May 1954; Convention on the Prohibition of the Development, Production and Stockpiling of Bacteriological (Biological and Toxin) Weapons and on Their Destruction, 10 April 1972; Convention on the Prohibition of Military or Any Other Hostile Use of Environmental Modification Techniques, 18 May 1977; Geneva Protocol I Additional to the Geneva Conventions of 12 August 1949, and Relating to the Protection of Victims of International Armed Conflicts, 12 December 1977; Geneva Protocol II Additional to the Geneva Conventions of 12 August 1949, and Relating to the Protection of Victims of Non-International Armed Conflicts, 12 December 1977; Convention on Prohibition or Restriction on the Use of Certain Conventional Weapons Which May be Deemed to be Excessively Injurious or to Have Indiscriminate Effects, 10 April, 1981; Protocol I of the Convention on Prohibition or Restriction on the Use of Certain Conventional Weapons Which May be Deemed to be Excessively Injurious or to Have Indiscriminate Effects, 10 April, 1981; Protocol II of the Convention of 1981 (above).

within customary international criminal law concerning certain conducts that are not permitted during an armed conflict. Thus, the regulations concerning war crimes are not an innovation; they have often been created after an armed conflict. Clear examples of these are the Four Geneva Conventions of 1949 and their two Protocols of 1977. These instruments have aimed at regulating certain rules that should be respected during war or armed conflict. Therefore, the regulations concerning war crimes entered into the Statute of the ICC are the integration of the previous rules governing the protection of individuals, groups and nations.[176]

6.4.2. List of Crimes

Article 8 of the Statute of the ICC lists a considerable number of actions that are recognised as war crimes.[177] The controversy over the list was

---

[176] Article 3 common to the Four Geneva Conventions of 1949 is relevant and is therefore presented here. The article reads that:
"In the case of armed conflict not of an international character occurring in the territory of one of the High Contracting Parties, each Party to the conflict shall be bound to apply, as a minimum, the following provisions:
(1) Persons taking no active part in the hostilities, including members of armed forces who have laid down their arms and those placed hors de combat by sickness, wounds, detention, or any other cause, shall in all circumstances be treated humanely, without any adverse distinction founded on race, colour, religion or faith, sex, birth or wealth, or any other similar criteria.
To this end the following acts are and shall remain prohibited at any time and in any place whatsoever with respect to the above-mentioned persons:
(a) violence to life and person, in particular murder of all kinds, mutilation, cruel treatment and torture;
(b) taking of hostages;
(c) outrages upon personal dignity, in particular humiliating and degrading treatment;
(d) the passing of sentences and the carrying out of executions without previous judgment pronounced by a regularly constituted court, affording all the judicial guarantees which are recognized as indispensable by civilized peoples.
(2) The wounded and sick shall be collected and cared for.
An impartial humanitarian body, such as the International Committee of the Red Cross, may offer its services to the Parties to the conflict.
The Parties to the conflict should further endeavour to bring into force, by means of special agreements, all or part of the other provisions of the present Convention.
The application of the preceding provisions shall not affect the legal status of the Parties to the conflict."

[177] See also Djamchid Momtaz, War Crimes in Non-International Armed Conflicts under the Statute of the International Criminal Court, 2 Yearbook of International

very intense. The list is, however, much more comprehensive than any of the previous documents.[178]

Some writers argue that the provisions of Article 8 do not apply to the conditions that may arise from the interpretation of Article 2(4) of the United Nations Charter. They advocate that the provisions of the article are only applicable to armed conflict and not to illegal use of force with due regard to the provisions of article 2(4).Accordingly, "the Statute does not appear to criminalize uses of force (which may nevertheless be illegal under article 2(4)... or under some other provision of international law that occur outside a state of armed conflict."[179]Although one may interpret the provisions of Article 8(2) as only applicable to armed conflicts due to their reference to "grave breaches of the Geneva Conventions of 12 August 1949", this interpretation may be too narrow and may make it possible for states to commit war crimes. The reason for this is that the definition concerning state of war or state of armed conflict applies, not only to the traditional concept of war, but also to any situation in which armed forces are engaged.

The applications of the Geneva Conventions are not limited to the violations of their provisions in wartime, but also to any illegal use of force by states. Otherwise, states may illegally use their armed forces against one another and violate the provisions of international law without accepting that they have committed war crimes. In addition, the Court is entitled to prosecute "the most serious crimes of concern to the international community as a whole."[180] This means that war crimes may also be committed under the provisions of Article 2(4) of the United Nations Charter because of special circumstances. Thus, legal or illegal use of force by states, even under the supervision of the United Nations, may call for the application of the relevant articles of the Statute. Any

---

Humanitarian Law 177 (1999); Hilaire McCoubrey, War Crimes Jurisdiction and a Permanent International Criminal Court: Advantages and Difficulties, 3 Journal of Armed Conflict 9 (1998); Jeffrey L. Bleich, Problems Facing the War Crimes Tribunal and the Need for a Permanent International Criminal Court, 16 Whittier Law Review 404 (1995); Darryl Robinson and Herman von Hebel, War Crimes in Internal Conflicts: Article 8 of the ICC Statute, 2 Yearbook of International Law 193 (1999); Darryl Robinson, Defining 'Crimes Against Humanity' at the Rome Conference, 93 American Journal of International Law 43 (1999).

[178] In general, some representatives were of the view that the list should be enlarged and some were against it.

[179] Sadat Leila Nadya., The International Criminal Court and the Transformation of International Law: Justice for the New Millenium (2002).

[180] Article 5 (1) of the Statute.

other interpretation may diminish the legal validity of the Statute of the ICC concerning the prosecution of certain international crimes.

6.4.3. Elements of War Crimes

6.4.3.1. Factual Circumstances

The elements of war crimes are fundamental to the structure of the Statute of the ICC. These elements have been formulated pursuant to the provisions of Article 9 of the Statute. The function of the elements of crimes is to assist the Court in the interpretation and application of crimes against humanity, genocide and war crimes.

According to the Elements of Crimes, the elements governing war crimes should be interpreted within the scope of the international law of armed conflict. According to these elements, the perpetrator does not need to a) evaluate the existence of an armed conflict; b) establish the character of an armed conflict as international or non-international; c) be aware of the facts that establish the character of the conflict. The perpetrator should, however, be aware "of the factual circumstances that established the existence of an armed conflict that is implicit in the terms 'took place in the context of and was associated with'".[181]

The elements of war crimes are very extensive and they are, generally speaking, a guideline for the application of Article 8 of the Statute of the ICC. The Court has to go through the whole submitted case and recognise whether acts suspected of constituting war crimes meet the primary requirements of the elements of war crimes for their application.

Article 8 of the Statute lists a large number of acts, the commission of which constitutes war crime. All of these acts come under the jurisdiction of the Court. This means that in case of the commission of these acts by a person, the Court may exercise its jurisdiction over the person accused of committing war crimes. Article 8 (2, a) is essentially concerned with the concept of Grave Breaches of the four Geneva Conventions of 1949. It may however be asserted that the list of grave breaches in the Statute is not illustrative but an extensive recognition of acts constituting war crimes. The article is therefore based on the definition of grave breaches already enumerated in the provisions of the Geneva Conventions. These are, *inter alia*, wilful killing, torture, wilfully causing great suffering, extensive destruction and appropriation of property, compelling a prisoner of war to serve in the forces of a hostile power, wilfully depriving a prisoner of war

---

[181] See Article 8 of the International Criminal Court, Elements of Crimes, U.N. Doc. PCNICC/2000/1/Add.2 (2000).

or other protected person of the right to a fair and regular trial, unlawful deportation and the taking of hostages.

6.4.3.2. The Civilian Position

Contrary to paragraph 8 (2, a), Article 8 (2, b) takes another position concerning the recognition of war crimes. It takes into account "other serious violations of the laws and customs applicable in international armed conflict, within the established framework of international law." The purpose of the legislator here is to emphasise the existence of other elements which call upon the responsibility of the perpetrators. The relevant provision in Article 8 (2, b) has therefore strengthened the concept of war crimes and their recognition as obvious violations of the international humanitarian law of armed conflicts. These are intentional attacks directed against the civilian population, objects, personnel, installations, material, buildings, or buildings dedicated to religion, education, art, science or charitable purposes, medical units, peacekeeping mission, attacking or bombarding, by whatever means, towns or villages, killing or wounding a combatant who has laid down his arms, making improper use of a flag of truce, the transferring directly or indirectly by the Occupying Power of parts of its own civilian population into the territory it occupies, destroying or seizing the enemy's property, compelling the nationals of the hostile party to take part in the operations of war directed against their own country, employing poison or poisoned weapons, employing poisonous or other gases, committing rape, sexual slavery, enforced prostitution, forced pregnancy, using starvation of civilians as a method of warfare, enlisting children under the age of fifteen years into the national armed forces or using them to participate actively in hostilities.[182] It appears that the status of civilians under the provisions of the Statute of the ICC involves significant considerations that cannot be left aside. We will discuss some of these aspects in the following subparagraphs.

6.4.3.3. Armed Conflicts

The provisions of Article 8 (2) (b) of the Statute complete the provisions of Article 8 (2) (a). This is in order to avoid any controversy regarding its

---

[182] See Farhad Malekian – *Prohibition Governing Child Soldiers Constituting an Integral Part of Jus Cogens and Obligatio Erga Omnes,* XVII World Congress of the International Association of Youth and Family Judges and Magistrates, Belfast, Northern Ireland, 27 August – 2 September, 2006. http://www.youthandfamily 2006.com/welcome.htm. Published also by the Institute of International Criminal Law, Uppsala, Sweden.

application. However, we do not deny that some court decisions and jurists may reflect the belief that the international humanitarian law of armed conflict cannot be applied in the case of the non-existence of armed conflict. This means that neither the provisions of Article 8 (2) (a) nor the provisions of Article 8 (2) (b) may be enforced without the establishment of a state of war. For instance, the decision of the Appeals Chamber in the Tadic case stated clearly that the humanitarian law of armed conflict may not be relevant in the absence of an absolute armed conflict.[183]

Despite the Appeals Chamber's statement, one may advocate that unlawful actions committed during the use of force by states may not only come under the provisions of Article 8 (2) (b) but may also be treated under the provisions of Article 8 (2) (a) because of the gravity or seriousness of actions committed by the armed forces. This interpretation may, of course, go against the ordinary purpose of Article 8 and the Elements of Crimes. This is because defining the concept of "intention" appears to be one of the decisive purposes of the Elements of Crimes, which requires the existence of the state of armed conflict.

More curiously, the provisions of Article (2) (a) and (b) do not apply to particular weapons that are not already enumerated in these provisions unless they are "subject to a comprehensive prohibition" or listed by states in the case of the amendment of the Statute. Unfortunately, this means that the Court may not, in any circumstances, have jurisdiction over states that have employed strong chemical or biological weapons unless the question is taken into the scope of crimes against humanity and serious attack against civilian population.[184] The most dangerous situation would be if a state engaged in the use of nuclear weapons without this being identified as a violation of the law of the Court. Obviously, the limitations of the provisions of Article 8, especially relating to the use of chemical, biological or nuclear weapons, may seriously endanger the maintenance of international peace, security, equality and justice. In other words, as long as the relevant provisions of the Statute are not amended, the Statute permits serious violations of the international humanitarian law of armed conflict in conditions of the use of force falling short of war.

---

[183] Prosecutor v. Tadic (Case No.IT-94-1-AR72), Decision on the Defence Motion for Interlocutory Appeal on Jurisdiction, para.67 (ICTY Appeals Chamber, Oct.2, 1995).

[184] A clear example is the situation of Syria and the use of chemical weapons against civilian population or combatantsin 2013.

6.4.3.4. Non-International Armed Conflict

Non-international armed conflict is dealt with by Article 8 (2) (c) of the Statute, the violation of which implies the commission of war crimes or, in other words, serious violations of article 3 common to the four Geneva Conventions of 1949.[185] This means the performance of certain prohibited acts against a person or persons taking no active part in the hostilities. This also includes members of armed forces who are no longer fighting and persons recognized as *hors de combat* on the basis of detention, sickness, wounds, or for any other reason. The provisions of paragraph (c) enumerate *inter alia* violence to life, murder of all kinds, torture, cruelty, humiliating and degrading treatment, mutilation, hostage taking and disregarding of all judicial guarantees which are recognised as indispensable.

One significant issue is that paragraph 8 (2) (c) is not applicable to certain situations which pertain to internal disturbances and tensions, including riots, isolated and sporadic acts of violence or any other act of the same nature. This is stated in Article 8 (d). It means that the prosecutor, judges and lawyers must be very cautious in the application of Article (c). The problem which may arise here is that the distinction between riots, insurgencies, civil war, internal conflicts and revolution is very difficult to assess. This is because their juridical and political definitions are very close to one another. The distance between all terms tends to be mostly hypothetical. Similarly, it will be very difficult for the Court to distinguish between various positions when one position may contribute to the other's terminology and the other, in its own terms, may be the result of another terminology. How can the Court separate the effect of insurgency in an internal armed conflict? A clear example is the French revolution, which was the development of riot and insurgency. It means that all terminologies and actions may be an integral part of the same conduct. "Elements of crimes" seems to be silent about this important matter. Moreover, the words of Article 8 (2) (f) clearly declare that paragraph 2 (e) applies to an armed conflict between governmental authorities and organised armed groups[186]

[185] Heike Spieker, The International Criminal Court and Non-International Armed Conflicts, 13 Leiden Journal of International Law 395 (2000). See also Lindsay Moir, Non-International Armed Conflict and Guerrilla Warfare, in International Criminal Law, VolI I (M. Cherif Bassiouni, ed. 2008) pp. 323-354.

[186] But Article 8 (2) (f) reads, "Paragraph 2 (e) applies to armed conflicts not of an international character and thus does not apply to situations of internal disturbances and tensions, such as riots, isolated and sporadic acts of violence or other acts of a similar nature. It applies to armed conflicts that take place in the

6.4.3.5. Intentional Position

Article 8(2) of the Statute of the ICC also concerns non-international armed conflict. It applies to other serious violations of the laws or customs of armed conflict which have long been established in international law. The purpose of the article is to bring to attention customary rules of armed conflict and recognises them under the provisions of conventional international law. Article 8 (2) (e) refers *inter alia* to intentionally directing attacks against the civilian population, medical units and transport units or vehicles involved in a humanitarian assistance or peacekeeping mission, civilian buildings dedicated to religion, education, art, science or charitable purposes. It also recognises as war crimes rape, sexual slavery, enforced prostitution, forced pregnancy, conscripting or enlisting children under the age of fifteen years into armed forces, killing or wounding treacherously a combatant adversary, physical mutilation, medical and scientific experimentation.

As demonstrated above, Articles 8 (2) (c) and 8 (2) (e) concern armed conflicts which are not of an international character. Their purpose is to enlarge the scope of applicability of the provisions of the Statute and recognise certain acts as constituting war crimes in the case of non-international armed conflict. The difference between Articles 8 (2) (c) and (e) is that the former takes into legislation the provisions of international conventional criminal law, whilst the latter provides the provisions of customary international criminal law. Both subparagraphs complement each other and are an integral part of Article 8 as a whole.

The provisions of Article 8 (2) (e) have been very controversial and the inclusion of them in Article 8 created a very long debate. Despite this, it must be stated that the criminalisation of acts in an international armed conflict is more specific than their criminalisation in internal armed conflicts. Thus, the borderlines of criminal acts in non-international armed conflicts are, unfortunately, limited.

In any event, the plea of unawareness by the perpetrator claiming that he/she did not know about the existence of the armed conflict does not reduce the scope of the applicability of offences.[187] In general, the

---

territory of a State when there is protracted armed conflict between governmental authorities and organized armed groups or between such groups."

[187] However, the international criminal tribunals have sometimes, for the purposes of reducing financial costs and bringing about a speedy outcome, engaged in plea bargaining which has consequently reduced punishment. That is why "the plea bargaining is a controversial practice." For instance, the prosecutor of the ICTY in the Todorovic case promised not to recommend a sentence over 5 to 12 years. Similarly, the prosecutor in the ICTR recommended the reduction of sentences for

existence of *nexus* between the armed conflict and the criminal actions during the conflict may be useful for the recognition of criminalisation, guilt and punishment.

The absence or the existence of armed conflict is solely a jurisdictional concept and does not relate to the material element of the crime. Otherwise, many groups under national systems might advocate that their actions do not necessarily fall under the humanitarian law of armed conflict although they actually are in armed conflicts against one another. They might commit torture, rape and other prohibited actions but easily flee from the proceedings of a national or international criminal court. This goes against the chief purposes and principles of the Statute.

6.5. Hierarchy among the Core Crimes

The Statute of the ICC divides crime into four categories. These are crimes against humanity, genocide, war crimes and aggression. At first glance, it seems that there is no difference between these four categories of crimes but a close examination of the Statute shows the contrary.

6.6. The Scope of Punishment

Generally speaking, the degree and gravity of the commission of a crime is the criterion for the application of penalties. When a crime is serious, the penalties will also be heavier. Other reasons, which may broaden the scope of penalties or make them heavier or lighter, are the degree of participation, assistance or involvement of the accused in the criminal actions. Thus, if the role of the accused in the commission of the crime is very small, this may, to a large extent, mitigate his/her punishment based on the criteria and the effect of his/her participation. That is why, in the proceedings of a criminal court, the evidence has a very significant function in determining the gravity of the punishment of the convicted person.

The question of punishment was one of the most serious issues in the procedures of the drafting of the Statute of the ICC. This was mostly based on the fact that the domestic systems of many states have different definitions of crimes and have also different measures and penalties for those crimes. The gravity of punishment varies according to the seriousness of the actions and this also depends on the method of

---

some of the criminals. See Nancy Amoury Combs, *Plea Bargains in International Criminal Prosecutions,* in International Criminal Law, Vol.III (M. Cherif Bassiouni, ed. 2008) pp. 561-579.

interpretation. In particular, it is possible that an action, which is considered a crime within the criminal law of a state, may not even be qualified as a minor crime in another state.[188] This means that the degree of punishment not only varies according to the nature of the crime, but also according to the social and cultural factors surrounding the concept of criminality in the given society. Therefore, the philosophy behind the punishment of the criminals was one of the serious conflicts between the representatives of different states during the drafting of the Statute.

In order to find a reasonable and appropriate clarification for punishment which would fit into all systems of the world, Article 77 of the Statute of the ICC specifies different types of punishment. It gives the judges of the Court free scope for the application of punishments in each individual case. The relevant article concerning the applicable penalties states that:

> 1. Subject to article 110, the Court may impose one of the following penalties on a person convicted of a crime referred to in article 5 of this Statute:
> (a) Imprisonment for a specified number of years, which may not exceed a maximum of 30 years; or
> (b) A term of life imprisonment when justified by the extreme gravity of the crime and the individual circumstances of the convicted person.
>
> 2. In addition to imprisonment, the Court may order:
> (a) A fine under the criteria provided for in the Rules of Procedure and Evidence;
> (b) A forfeiture of proceeds, property and assets derived directly or indirectly from that crime, without prejudice to the rights of bona fide third parties.

With the provisions of the above article, the Court is permitted to provide punishment in accordance with certain conditions. These are discussed in the sections below.

6.7. Specified Imprisonment

According to Article 77 of the Statute, the Court is allowed to decide imprisonment for the following crimes: crimes against humanity,

---

[188] For instance, sexual relations outside marriage are permitted in most states of Europe whilst it is considered a serious crime in the domestic systems of many other states. This can even be seen as a reason for stoning a person to death sometimes, which constitutes a form of penalty, as for example in Iran.

genocide, war crimes and aggression. This means that it is one of the duties of the Court to apply appropriate punishment for the crimes committed by different individuals of different states. It is nevertheless the case that the Court is not permitted to impose a penalty which exceeds its limitations. Therefore, imprisonment as a method of punishment of the criminal should not exceed, in any circumstances, a maximum of 30 years.

The rationale behind this restriction is to limit the power of the Court regarding the punishment of criminals and also to put an end to excessive punishment. This philosophy also coincides with the basic purposes of the documents of human rights law to prevent certain actions that are against the fundamental natural rights of man and his/her dignity. The problem is that no minimum sentences are drafted due to the provisions of the text and there are no specific sentences suggested for particular crimes. This means that the length of the particular sentence is at the discretion of the judges.

Whilst imprisonment for 30 years is written in the text of the Statute of the ICC, the expression "life imprisonment" seems to be unjustified and is recognised as going against the basic principles of human rights law. For this reason, the Statute has also foreseen situations that may reduce life imprisonment in order to mitigate its extreme harshness. Article 110 of the Statute has therefore, in particular situations, opened a window for the mitigation of the penalty that may seem necessary for the purpose of fair and impartial justice for the convicted person. Therefore, when the convicted person has been imprisoned for two thirds of the sentence, the ICC may reconsider the sentence in order to decide whether it should reduce it. The decision of the Court may be based on several factors such as the voluntary assistance of the person in the enforcement of judgments, continued willingness of the prisoner to cooperate with the Court in order to help the relevant investigative processes under the jurisdiction of the Court, or any other reason which may justify the reduction of sentences.

The Court is also empowered to review a case concerning life imprisonment when 25 years have been served by the convicted person. All these reviews may be started by the Court if it finds that one of the following factors is present. These are when the convicted person cooperates with the Court, assists in the enforcement of the judgements, or any other reason sufficient to justify the reduction of sentence.[189] Thus, it is at the discretion of the judges to see whether the evidence is strong enough for changing the terms of imprisonment or life imprisonment.

[189] Article 110 (4).

6.8. Life Imprisonment

Article 77 of the Statute also legitimates other provisions concerning punishment. The Court is permitted, according to the circumstance and the gravity of crimes, to provide a term of life imprisonment. This punishment is permitted when justified by the extreme gravity of the crime and the individual circumstances of the convicted person. Thus, it is one of the duties of the Court to investigate and evaluate the circumstances of the convicted person having in mind the gravity of the crime in order to give a proportionate and fair penalty.

It seems that the use of life imprisonment is not entirely in keeping with the function of the Court, but it is the way in which it may achieve appropriate justice and punishment. It may, therefore, in the best interests of the Court and international society, use the punishment not as a method of isolating the convicted person from the natural rights of man, but as a method of expressing the gravity of the crime in order to prevent its future occurrence. This is because imprisonment for life or a maximum of 30 years does not solve the problems of victims, but only creates a probable psychological defence for the future life of victims, especially in the case of grave violations of international criminal law such as genocide.

6.9. Fine

Article 77 of the Statute of the ICC has also given permission to the Court to apply certain other punishments in addition to imprisonment. Accordingly, the Court is allowed to impose a fine under the criteria provided for in the Rules of Procedure and Evidence. This means that imprisonment may be combined with a fine of a specific amount of money or objects of a similar value at the discretion of the Court.

6.10. Forfeiture

The Court is also, according to the provisions of Article 77, permitted to order forfeiture of proceeds, property and assets derived directly or indirectly from the relevant crime. This should, however, be without prejudice to the rights of bona fide third parties.[190] In this case, as in other situations concerning punishment, it is obvious that the Court has to follow the provisions of international human rights law and be cautious in the application of the relevant provisions of Article 77.

---

[190] Article 77(b).

6.11. Death Penalty

One of the most high-profile debates on the drafting of the Statute of the ICC relates to the death penalty.[191] Due to the variety of policies within the national systems of different states, this debate was not easy to resolve. Some states were of the view that the death penalty has to be implemented in particular situations and some were against this philosophy.[192] The debate was very heated and, finally, a particular expression was added to the text of the Statute of the ICC. According to Article 80 of the Statute, "Nothing in this Part affects the application by States of penalties prescribed by their national law, nor the law of States which do not provide for penalties prescribed in this Part."

The provisions above have ensured the protection of the national criminal systems of certain states that are interested in the implementation of their own penal systems, and no provision concerning the death penalty was inserted into the structure of the ICC.[193] Consequently, the death penalty is not permitted by the law of the Statute,[194] but it is permitted on the basis of national legal criminal systems.[195] This is a particular situation where the policy of the Court has taken two different measures concerning the application and abolition of the death penalty which depends heavily on the complementarity principle.[196] Accordingly, this principle permits the use and application of systems of justice that want to implement the death penalty in certain particular situations under national criminal laws. It is here that a double policy of jurisdiction is created in international criminal law.[197]

6.12. Double Policy

According to some states, the death penalty is not only permitted under national legal systems, but is also permitted under international criminal law as applied by the Nuremberg and Tokyo Tribunals. Thus, some drafters of the Court insisted on the direct formulation of the death penalty

---

[191] Rolf Einer Fife, *Penalties, in* The International Criminal Court: The Making of the Rome Statute 470 (Roy S. Lee, ed., 1999).
[192] Schabas William A., An Introduction to the International Criminal Court (2ed, 2004), at 162-166.
[193] *Id.*, at 165.
[194] *Id.*, at 165.
[195] Article 30 of the Statute.
[196] For this principle see *supera*.
[197] See section below.

in the Statute of the ICC and considered it an essential step in the development of the Court's jurisdiction. Despite this, there were many states that were against capital punishment and considered it an obsolete institution.

The double policy of the Statute concerning the death penalty has caused serious problems for the recognition of criminality and has led to the development of discrimination between persons. This is because the accused persons may try to choose a different jurisdiction among states parties. It may be a state which does not permit the death penalty in order to escape capital punishment. This is where the relevant punishment is already an abolished institution. Likewise, many European states may object to the surrendering of the accused to the jurisdiction of a state which exercises the death penalty.[198] In particular, states that are members of the Council of Europe are not permitted to apply the death penalty.[199] Although avoiding the use of capital punishment is one of the aims of the

---

[198] However, the practice of some states may be different. For instance see *infera* the Swedish practice.

[199] One significant European instrument of human rights law is the Protocol No. 13 to the Convention for the Protection of Human Rights and Fundamental Freedoms, concerning the abolition of the death penalty in all circumstances. The Protocol entered into force on 1 July 2003. According to the Protocol:
"The member States of the Council of Europe signatory hereto,
Convinced that everyone's right to life is a basic value in a democratic society and that the abolition of the death penalty is essential for the protection of this right and for the full recognition of the inherent dignity of all human beings;
Wishing to strengthen the protection of the right to life guaranteed by the Convention for the Protection of Human Rights and Fundamental Freedoms signed at Rome on 4 November 1950 (hereinafter referred to as "the Convention");
Noting that Protocol No. 6 to the Convention, concerning the Abolition of the Death Penalty, signed at Strasbourg on 28 April 1983, does not exclude the death penalty in respect of acts committed in time of war or of imminent threat of war;
Being resolved to take the final step in order to abolish the death penalty in all circumstances,
Have agreed as follows:
Article 1 – Abolition of the death penalty
The death penalty shall be abolished. No one shall be condemned to such penalty or executed.
Article 2 – Prohibition of derogations
No derogation from the provisions of this Protocol shall be made under Article 15 of the Convention.
Article 3 – Prohibition of reservations
No reservation may be made under Article 57 of the Convention in respect of the provisions of this Protocol."

relevant human rights instruments and the ICC, the policy of the ICC creates for politically powerful criminals more rights and possibilities than for politically weak criminals. The *abolition of capital punishment* under the jurisdiction of the states parties should have been one of the *strong conditions* for being a party to the Statute.

Again, although the abolition of the death penalty under the provisions of the Court is to be highly appreciated, this position may not be effective since the implementation of the principle of complementarity permits a state to ask the Court to relinquish a case when the relevant state wants to try it. This means that the implementation of the principles of international human rights law will be subverted because of different signals from the Statute of the Court.

Obviously, the death penalty has long been prohibited in the system of international criminal law and this may be proved from the practices of the ICTY and the ICTR.[200] Moreover, the imposition of the death penalty is certainly against the basic principles of justice and fairness.[201] The basic documents on international human rights law also imply this fact.[202] This means that the abolition of the death penalty constitutes today an integral part of international customary and conventional law and consequently an integral part of the international law of *jus cogens* that has to be respected and not violated in the practice of states.[203] Although this position is quite

---

[200] For a good analysis of the abolition of death penalty See William A Schabas, The Abolition of the Death Penalty in International Law (2002 and 2003). (3ed, 2002).

[201] *Id*., at 23, 24, 155 and 156.

[202] *Id*., 23, 45, 93, 155, 211, 259, 311 and 355.

[203] Unfortunately, the above writer argues that the abolition of the death penalty has not yet been achieved to the standard of *jus cogens* and accordingly such a norm may exist in the future. (*Id*., 3 and 19.) Contrary to this argumentation, the abolition of the death penalty exists in the system of international criminal law. This is based on the fact that what is meant with *jus cogens* is not necessarily the existence of a recognized rule of customary international criminal law but the existence of certain documents of human rights law that are already collectively recognized as the International Bill of Rights. These are the 1948 *Universal Declaration of Human Rights, the 1976 International Covenant on Civil and Political Rights, the 1976 International Covenant on Economic, Social and Cultural Rights, the 1976 Optional Protocol to the International Covenant on Civil and Political Rights* and *the 1989 Second Optional Protocol to the International Covenant on Civil and Political Rights Aiming at the Abolition of Death Penalty.* Additionally, the argument that the existing rule concerning the abolition of the death penalty is not yet a part of a universal norm or of customary law and neither is it qualified as a peremptory rule of *jus cogens* is indeed very narrow and creates doubt as to the real function of the International Bill of Rights for the protection of

clear, it demonstrates that there are certain conflicts between the international and national rules that should not be ignored.[204]

The promotion of justice must be one of the chief purposes of the ICC and the implementation of its Statute. Needless to say, the shortcomings of the ICC in both the definition of crimes, in particular aggression, and its complementarity policy, in order to satisfy national systems, have seriously reduced its international value.[205] In other words, the

---

mankind from any type of *atrocities* in the world. It may also create misinterpretation, misapplication and increase the rights of the state to the death penalty in certain situations. In addition, there are certain criteria for the recognition of a norm as peremptory. These are when it is essential for the maintenance of the international legal order of human rights; when the norm is embodied within the provisions of a multilateral agreement or customary international law prohibiting the derogation from the relevant norm; and when the practice of the international courts denotes the existence of a norm from which derogation is not permitted. All these conditions already exist in the case of the abolition of capital punishment. Examine Farhad Malekian Dcoument on the Principles of International Human Rrights (2007); see *also* Kha Q. Nguyen, Note, *In Defense of the Child: A* Jus Cogens *Approach to the Capital Punishment of Juveniles in the United States*, 28 The George Washington Journal of International Law and Economics. 401, 423 (1995).

[204] One serious problem is that although some states have ratified the Statute of the ICC and their national legislations also denote the abolition of death penalty, they may still violate these national and international legal systems. This is the position of Swedish governmental authorities who have taken several decisions concerning the returning or extradition of foreigners to countries notorious for the implementation of capital punishment. (See Swedish Utlänningslag 2005:716, Regeringsformen 1974:152). This means that the relevant authorities have not only gone against a) their own legislations, but also b) the basic documents on international Human Rights Law, c) the European Union's basic legislation, d) the Statute of the ICC, e) customary international law and f) *jus cogens* norms.

[205] One of the cheif policies of the United Nations organization, in particular the Security Council has been to prevent act of aggression. The Preamble of the Charter states its main principles. These are *inter alia* that "1. To maintain international peace and security, and to that end: to take effective collective measures for the prevention and removal of threats to the peace, and for the suppression of acts of aggression or other breaches of the peace, and to bring about by peaceful means, and in conformity with the principles of justice and international law, adjustment or settlement of international disputes or situations which might lead to a breach of the peace; 2. To develop friendly relations among nations based on respect for the principle of equal rights and self-determination of peoples, and to take other appropriate measures to *strengthen universal peace."* 3. To achieve international co-operation in solving international problems of an economic, social, cultural, or humanitarian character, and in promoting and

jurisdictional policy of the ICC is limited in order to have more states sign and ratify its Statute. This means that international justice is measured and drafted in response to the circumstances of national systems.

6.13. Aggression

See chapter eight.

encouraging respect for human rights and for fundamental freedoms for all without distinction as *to race, sex, language, or religion;* and 4. To be a centre for harmonizing the actions of nations in the attainment of these common ends."

CHAPTER FIVE

MAJOR CRIMINAL PROCEDURES IN THE TRIBUNALS AND THE COURTS

1. Introduction

An evaluation of the existing major criminal procedures of the tribunals and the courts must begin by placing emphasis on the inner structure of their systems. In this chapter we present and examine some of those procedures or provisions which have been effective in the development of the philosophy of the international criminal responsibility of individuals and the progressive consolidation of the system of international criminal justice. Obviously, the system of international criminal justice, such as it is, broadly depends for its efficacy on the Statutes of the international criminal tribunals and the courts. Consequently, all these courts, in one way or another, represent the same belief but in more or less creative ways. This chapter, therefore, will examine the major relevant provisions of the ICTY, the ICTR and the SCSL with particular emphasis on the framework of the ICC. Thus, we have, as far as possible, avoided repeating the presentation of the same subject matter.

2. The Legal Procedures in the Nuremberg Tribunal

2.1. The Trial Procedure

The trial of the accused from World War II was held before a panel of judges who were chosen by the Allies.[1] The judges had the right to bring the accused before the Tribunal's jurisdiction and to hear them for different reasons related to their crimes.[2] Article 17 of the Nuremberg Tribunal specified some of the powers and authorities of the Tribunal. Among many others, the Tribunal had the power:

---

[1] The judges were nominated from four different nations.

[2] The chair of the Tribunal was given to a British lawyer.

(a) to summon witnesses to the Trial and to require their attendance and testimony and to put questions to them,
(b) to interrogate any Defendant,
(c) to require the assembly of documents and other evidentiary material,
(d) to administer oaths to witnesses,
(e) to appoint officers for the carrying out of any task designated by the Tribunal including the power to have evidence taken on commission.[3]

The judgments of the Tribunal were mostly developed on the basis of evidence which was taken from German officers and men and members of the Nazi Party.[4] The decisions of the Tribunal were therefore based on the statements of the defendants themselves during the trial and in accordance with the evidence they had presented.

The Tribunal was consequently given a range of authorities concerning the prosecution of the accused persons. According to Article 18 of the Constitution of the Tribunal, it could:

(a) confine the Trial strictly to an expeditious hearing of the issues raised by the charges,
(b) take strict measures to prevent any action which will cause unreasonable delay, and rule out irrelevant issues and statements of any kind whatsoever,
(c) deal summarily with any contumacy, imposing appropriate punishment, including exclusion of any Defendant or his counsel from some or all further proceedings, but without prejudice to the determination of the charges.

As a whole, the Tribunal was not limited by technical rules of evidence. It could take a broad range of evidence into consideration and apply non-technical procedures.[5] It could even acknowledge any evidence deemed necessary, or supply proof or evidence under its jurisdiction.[6] The tribunal could also investigate the nature of any evidence that had been brought before its jurisdiction.[7] It did not, however, have any right to require proof of facts of common knowledge but could take judicial notice concerning the case. The Tribunal could "also take judicial notice of official governmental documents and reports of the United Nations,

[3] Article 17.
[4] See also M. Boot., Genocide, Crimes Against Humanity, War Crimes: v. 12: Nullum Crimen Sine Lege and the Subject Matter Jurisdiction of the International Criminal Court (2002), pp.188-189.
[5] Article 19.
[6] Article 19.
[7] Article 20.

including the acts and documents of the committees set up in the various Allied countries for the investigation of war crimes, and the records and findings of military or other Tribunals of any of the United Nations."[8] In addition, the proceedings at the trial had to be respected and enforce certain juridical principles. According to the Constitution of the Tribunal:

(a) The Indictment shall be read in court.
(b) The Tribunal shall ask each Defendant whether he pleads "guilty" or "not guilty."
(c) The Prosecution shall make an opening statement.
(d) The Tribunal shall ask the Prosecution and the Defence what evidence (if any) they wish to submit to the Tribunal, and the Tribunal shall rule upon the admissibility of any such evidence.
(e) The witnesses for the Prosecution shall be examined and after that the witnesses for the Defence. Thereafter such rebutting evidence as may be held by the Tribunal to be admissible shall be called by either the Prosecution or the Defence.
(f) The Tribunal may put any question to any witness and to any Defendant, at any time.
(g) The Prosecution and the Defence shall interrogate and may cross-examine any witnesses and any Defendant who gives testimony.
(h) The defence shall address the court.
(i) The Prosecution shall address the court.
(j) Each Defendant may make a statement to the Tribunal.
(k) The Tribunal shall deliver judgment and pronounce sentence.[9]

The judges of the Tribunal could also call witnesses who could illustrate certain evidence. This was especially arranged in the case of concentration camps. For instance, some officials from different nations such as France and the United States, who had been prisoners at Buchenwald, could testify. Evidence could also be taken from Nazi officers concerning how the crimes had been carried out against the Jews.

2.2. Judgment

The prevailing definition of judgment is the process of the investigation and hearing of the accused, victim(s), witnesses and the weighing up of evidence in order to come to a conclusion in accordance with the rules or the provisions of the constitution of a court. There are, in general, certain fundamental principles that must be respected and fulfilled in the judgment of criminal courts. This may, however, vary from one legal procedural

[8] Article 21.
[9] Article 24.

system to another. One of the generally accepted practices is that the judgment of a criminal court should be based on rules that are already recognised in its statute, constitution or charter. The following were some of the rules that were basically recognised as being important to respect in the judgment of the Nuremberg Tribunal.[10] These were:

The Tribunal was obliged to give the reasons as to the guilt or the innocence of any defendant;

The above reasons had to be the final reason and not subject to debate or more examination and analysis;

The tribunal had to attribute the concept of criminal responsibility to individuals and not entities;

The attribution of the concept of criminal responsibility could apply to all individuals without regard to their official positions;

The Tribunal had to make clear which type of punishment was applicable to the crime. The punishment could be more or less severe.

The rules above underlined the power of the Tribunal concerning the criminals and their criminal conduct. It made it clear that the judges of the Tribunal could not take any decision which might violate the elementary purposes of the Tribunal.[11] They had to formulate their judgments in accordance with the above principles and not violate the rights of the guilty by taking different measures concerning different cases brought under their jurisdiction.[12] But, in general, the Nuremberg Tribunal's standards for the proof of guilt applied not just to the provisions of the Charter of the Tribunal but also more widely to conventional and customary international law.[13]

---

[10] Consult also M. Boot., Genocide, Crimes Against Humanity, War Crimes: v. 12: Nullum Crimen Sine Lege and the Subject Matter Jurisdiction of the International Criminal Court (2002), pp.185-190.

[11] There was however some confusion concerning the scope of the definition of the crimes. This was based on the fact that the Russian text was rather different on this point. *Id.*

[12] *Id.*

[13] Therefore, the Tribunal eloquently stated that "Under written constitutions the ex post facto rule condemns statutes which defines as criminal, acts committed before the law passed, but the *ex post facto* rule cannot apply in the international field as it does under constitutional mandate in the domestic field … International law is not the product of statute for the simple reason that there is yet no world authority empowered to enact statutes of universal application. International law is the product of multipartite treaties, conventions, judicial decisions and customs which have received international acceptance or acquiescence. It would be sheer

2.2.1. The Right to Fair Trial

There are certain rules concerning interrogation, prosecution and punishment that should be respected during the procedures of an international criminal tribunal. As a general rule, the defendant should have the right to a fair and just trial. Some of the rules, which were entered into the Charter of the Nuremberg Tribunal, are the following:

i. The right to an indictment which specifies in detail the charges against the defendant,
ii. A copy of the indictment which is translated into the language of the defendant,
iii. The right to know about the indictment at a reasonable time before the trial,
iv. The right of the defendant to express himself concerning the charges,
v. The right of the defendant to express himself during any preliminary examination,
vi. The right of the defendant to express himself during the trial,
vii. The preliminary examination of the case should be in the language of the accused,
viii. The right of the defendant to confer with his or her own defence lawyer or counsel before the Tribunal or to have the assistance of the counsel,
ix. The right of the defendant to present evidence by himself or herself,
x. The right of the defendant to present evidence via his counsel,
xi. The right to cross-examine any witness presented by the prosecution.

As we shall see later within other sections of this book, the above rights have since then largely been retained and further developed and are considered an integral part of a just and fair trial. This development, in particular, may be examined within the instruments of international human

---

absurdity to suggest that the *ex post facto* rule, as known to no constitutional states, could be applied to a treaty, a custom, or a common law decision of an international tribunal, or to the international acquiescence which follows the events. To have attempted to apply *the ex post facto* principle to judicial decisions of common international law would have been to strangle that law at birth." Trial of War Criminals Before the Nuremberg Military Tribunal Under Control Council Law No.10, vol.III (Justice case), pp.974-975.

rights law, which have an important role in ensuring that the proceedings of international criminal justice are fair.

2.2.2. Punishment

The rules for punishment or sentencing under the authority of the Nuremberg Tribunal were regulated under Articles 27 to 29. Accordingly, the Tribunal was given permission to carry out its judgment. These rules are summarized in the following list:

a. The Tribunal was given the right to impose on the defendant capital punishment;
b. It was also permitted to take any other measures for punishment which could be considered as just punishment;
c. The Tribunal also had the right to deprive the convicted person of any stolen property and could order its delivery to the Control Council for Germany;[14]
d. The sentences could be carried out in accordance with the orders of the Control Council for Germany. It had the right to reduce or otherwise alter the sentences;
e. The Council was not permitted to increase the severity of the punishment;
f. The Council was permitted in the case of new evidence against the guilty person to submit the case to the Committee which could be established in accordance with the Charter. This led to a new charge against the guilty person.

After the lengthy prosecution of the perpetrators of World War II, the Nuremberg Tribunal delivered its judgment.[15] The judgment of the Tribunal gave different sentences to those who had been brought before its

---

[14] For the Control Council see *infra.*

[15] "The Allies presented their evidence which consisted almost entirely of the words and documents of the Nazis themselves. During the investigation that led up to the trial, the U.S. and British investigators had discovered literally tons of documents which proved the charges against the defendants. The decision was made, therefore, to rely on the words of the defendants themselves in the trial. Certain witnesses were presented to flesh out the evidence. This is especially true in the case against the concentration camps where witnesses ranging from a member of the French parliament -- who had been imprisoned as a slave labourer at Auschwitz – to an American army officer who had been imprisoned at Buchenwald testified. Several Nazi officers also testified about how the Holocaust occurred." www.holocaust-history.org/short-essays/nuremberg.shtml

jurisdiction.[16] The degree and level of the sentences varied slightly from each other depending on the function and the responsibility of members of the German authorities as leaders of the Nazi groups.[17] Strange as it may seem, for one reason or another, not all sentences were implemented.

2.2.3. Reasoning

The International Military Tribunal at Nuremberg functioned on the basis of provisions of the Charter. According to these provisions, the Tribunal had to establish the concept of the criminal responsibility of individuals for crimes against peace, war crimes, and crimes against humanity. The intention of the Tribunal was to establish a link between the criminal order and the accused. For instance, the statement of the chief prosecutor of the Nuremberg Tribunal concerning the punishment of defendants in his closing remarks clarifies the connection between the defendants and the head of state, Adolf Hitler. He stated that "I admit that Hitler was the chief villain. But for the defendants to put all the blame on him is neither manly nor true. We know that even the head of the state has the same limits to his senses and to the hours of his days, as do lesser men. He must rely on others to be his eyes and ears as to most of what goes on in a great empire. Other legs must run his errands; other hands must execute his plans. On whom did Hitler rely for such things more than upon these men in the dock?" This statement clarifies the chain of command and responsibility for atrocities, killings and destructions during the war. It makes it clear that the head of a state cannot alone be held responsible for committing international crimes. His orders must be completed and carried out by other men who are working under his power. In other words, the responsibility of a head of state or government cannot release other individuals from their own personal responsibility for their own criminal conduct. Here, the prosecutor has therefore identified the concept of the direct criminal responsibility of any commander or superior who worked under the auspices of the killing machinery of the German government.

---

[16] "The final phase of the trial was the defendants' cases. The defendants actually took more time in the court than the prosecutors. Although the defenses varied most either stated that they not involved in the Holocaust or did not know it was happening. All of the defendants testified at length and presented witnesses. One of the most important witnesses about the Holocaust, Rudolf Höß (or "Hoess"), the commandant of Auschwitz, was actually called as a witness for the defense."*Id.*

[17] The following were the sentences of the IMT in Nuremberg: *a)* death by hanging, *b)* imprisonment for life.

The trials of the German war criminals continued even after the closing date of the Nuremberg Tribunals, at which point the United States, Great Britain and France transferred the duty to carry out the trials to the German courts. The defendants were prosecuted as late as 1965 for violations of the law of war and for crimes against humanity. Unfortunately, none of the defendants of World War II were prosecuted for genocide because of the retroactivity of its provisions. But there is no doubt that they could have been punished for genocide if such a possibility had been granted to the IMT.[18]

3. The Legal Procedures in the Tokyo Tribunal

The rules of procedures for the International Military Tribunal were not drafted in its Constitution. Article 7 of it stated that "The Tribunal may draft and amend rules of procedure consistent with the fundamental provisions of this Charter." Thus, the Tribunal was free to decide about many legal matters. Furthermore, during the prosecution the defence did not need to demonstrate that the acts of superiors, officers, officials or government ministers were protected as acts of state. This was because there was no doubt for the Tribunal that the principles of universality and criminal responsibility were both consolidated within the customary and conventional provisions of international law and therefore did not require any further discussion.

During the trials, the Court refused to accept any discussion relating to the wartime conduct of the Allied powers. It simply stated that its power of jurisdiction only applied to the examination of the conduct of the Japanese officials and the existing evidence. However, the Charter and the trial insisted on the fair prosecution of the accused. For this reason, a fair trial was supposed to be guaranteed by the following provisions:

[18] Some writers on the history of international relations have argued that the holocaust did not occur during World War II. See, for instance, David Irving, Arthur Butz, Ernst Zündel, and Robert Faurisson. For instance consult Arthur R. Buts the Hoax of the Twentieth Century: A Case Against the Presumed Extermination of Europe Jewary (2003). According to Butz, the statistic concerning the loss of six million European Jews during World War II is not correct. He bases his argument *inter alia* on the fact that, for reasons of technical feasibility, the notorious extermination gas chambers did not have the capacity for killing several millions. According to him, it is possible that about a million Jews perished in the turmoil of deportation, including as a result of internment and the war.

(a) *Indictment.* The indictment shall consist of a plain, concise, and adequate statement of each offence charged. Each accused shall be furnished, in adequate time for defence, a copy of the indictment, including any amendment, and of this Charter, in a language understood by the accused.
(b) *Language.* The trial and related proceedings shall be conducted in English and in the language of the accused. Translations of documents and other papers shall be provided as needed and requested.
(c) *Counsel for Accused.* Each accused shall have the right to be represented by counsel of his own selection, subject to the disapproval of such counsel at any time by the Tribunal. The accused shall file with the General Secretary of the Tribunal the name of his counsel. If an accused is not represented by counsel and in open court requests the appointment of counsel, the Tribunal shall designate counsel for him. In the absence of such request the Tribunal may appoint counsel for an accused if in its judgment such appointment is necessary to provide for a fair trial.
(d) *Evidence for Defence.* An accused shall have the right, through himself or through his counsel (but not through both), to conduct his defence, including the right to examine any witness, subject to such reasonable restrictions as the Tribunal may determine.
(e) *Production of Evidence for the Defence.* An accused may apply in writing to the Tribunal for the production of witnesses or of documents. The application shall state where the witness or document is thought to be located. It shall also state the facts proposed to be proved by the witness or the document and the relevancy of such facts to the defence. If the Tribunal grants the application the Tribunal shall be given such aid in obtaining production of the evidence as the circumstances require.[19]

Although the above provisions were formulated into the Charter of the Tribunal, they did not work appropriately. The proceedings were conducted in a way detrimental to the accused, whose rights and future were seriously dependent on a defence panel. This is because the standards of the defence panel were very primitive regarding the provisions relevant to qualified international and even national advisors. The translators were not capable of performing the job properly. The understanding of language sometimes became very controversial. This became more serious when it came to the staff and other financial requirements necessary for the presentation of a good defence. All of these matters and the differing

[19] Article 9 of the Charter.

political opinions expressed at the trial made the presentation of evidence very difficult and problematic.[20]

4. The Legal Procedures in the ICTY

One of the most important aspects of the Statute of the ICTY is the special authority granted to the judges of the Tribunal. This is in order to adopt rules of procedures and evidence for the implementation of the provisions of the Statute. They are therefore responsible for taking the necessary measures to ensure that the rules of procedure and evidence govern the proceedings of the Tribunal. For this essential reason, the first rules of procedure and evidence were adopted between January and February 1994.[21]

The 1994 rules of procedure and evidence for the tribunal attempt to establish completely new principles for the development of international rules which are essential for the conduct of pre-trial proceedings, trials and appeals.[22] The rules are substantially a combination of two different legal

---

[20] Eleven states were involved in the court. Each state had one member in the prosecution. These states were in order Australia, Canada, Great Britain, India, and New Zealand. They came from the British Commonwealth and Empire. The other states were China, France, the Netherlands, Russia and the United States and its former Commonwealth of the Philippines.

[21] International Criminal Tribunal for the former Yugoslavia, Rules of Procedure and Evidence, U.N. Doc. IT/32/Rev.7 (1996) entered into force 14 March 1994, amendments adopted 8 January 1996.

[22] The rules have been criticised by one of the Prosecutors of the ICTY and the ICTR. Accordingly, "Le Règlement de procédureet preuveest largementinspiré du système de common law; le procèsmêmeconstituant la principale procédure d' établissement des faits, sur la base d'unepreuveessentiellementtestimoniale. Bien que la procédure internationale intègre aussi quelques éléments originaires de la procédure dite romano-germanique, on regrette que certains de ces traits, dont la participation des victimes aux procès, ou le procès par contumace, n'aientpas été retenus. Devant les Tribunaux ad hoc, conformément aux systèmes de common law, la victimeestreprésentée par le Procureur. La placeaccordée aux victimesest quasi-inexistantedans les Statuts et Règlements des Tribunaux, puisqu'elles ne sontconsidéréesquecomme des témoins. Ellesdoivent par exempleintenterune action civile, distincte de l'actionpénale, pour obtenirréparation. Nous soutenonsl'amendement de la procédure qui permettrait la constitution de partiecivile, notamments'agissant des affaires où les moyensfinanciers des accuséspermettraient de procédersoit à la restitution du bien aux victimes, soit à leursdédommagements. Nous saluonsdonc le fait que le Statut de la CPI remédie à ceproblème et accorde aux victimesune place dans le procès, en leurconférantcertainsdroits, à savoir celui de saisir le Procureur, de participer à la

systems. These are the common law and the civil law. The first is based on the development of case law and the second has evolved from legislative statutes which essentially emanate from continental Europe. The position is described as:

> International criminal procedure results from the gradual decanting of national criminal concepts and rules into the international receptacle. However, international criminal procedure does not originate from a uniform body of law. It substantially results from an amalgamation of two different legal systems, that obtaining in common-law countries and the system prevailing in countries of civil-law (although for historical reasons, there currently exists at the international level a clear imbalance in favour of the common-law approach). It is therefore only natural that international criminal proceedings do not uphold the philosophy behind one of the two national criminal systems to the exclusion of the other; nor do they result from the juxtaposition of elements of the two systems. Rather, they combine and fuse, in a fairly felicitous manner, the adversarial or accusatorial system (chiefly adopted in common-law countries) with a number of significant features of the inquisitorial approach (mostly taken in States of continental Europe and in other countries of civil-law tradition). This combination or amalgamation is unique and begets a legal logic that is qualitatively different from that of each of the two national criminal systems: the philosophy behind international trials is markedly at variance with that underpinning each of those national systems. Also the Statute and Rules of the International Tribunal, in outlining the criminal proceedings before the Trial and Appeals Chambers, do not refer to a specific national criminal approach, but originally take up the accusatorial (or adversarial) system and adapt it to international proceedings, while at the same time upholding some elements of the inquisitorial system.[23]

The rules of the ICTY have, however, been amended from time to time in order to be useful to the proceedings of the Tribunal. Thus, there have been a variety of reasons for the amendment of the rules of procedure, such as to protect and enhance the rights of the accused, to guarantee the

---

procédure et de demander des réparations. Uneautredéfaillance de la procédurepénaleinternationaleest, à nosyeux, l'absence d'un magistratinstructeur qui pourraitpréparer les dossiers, y intégrer les faitsjudiciairementétablis, ce qui auraitprobablementpermisdavantaged'efficacité et de clarté." Intervention de Carla Del Ponte, Procureur des Tribunauxpénauxinternationaux pour l'ex-Yougoslavie et le Rwanda, Ecolenationaled'administration, Paris, 6 juin 2003. www.ena.fr/ index.php?page=ressources/colloques/archives.

[23] Erdemovic (IT-96-22-A), Separate and Dissenting opinion of Judge Cassese, 7 October 1997, para.2.

protection of victims and witnesses,[24] to improve the consistency of the rules, to orient the rules with the will of the host country, to make the rules more flexible and enforceable and also to modify the rules with a view to making them more inclusive and functional.

4.1. Indictment

In contemporary international criminal law, the term "indictment" refers to a formal juridical accusation that a person has, in one way or another, been involved in the commission of an international crime. Although an indictment implies the accusation of a person, the defendant remains innocent unless and until proven guilty. An indictment may contain the name and the addresses of one or several persons and refer to some of the evidence as well as the relevant legislation. The Appeals Chamber of the ICTY has illustrated that the indictment:

> as the primary accusatory instrument, must plead with sufficient detail the essential aspect of the Prosecution case. If it fails to do so, it suffers from a material defect. A defective indictment, in and of itself, may, in certain circumstances cause the Appeals Chamber to reverse a conviction. The Appeals Chamber, however, does not exclude the possibility that, in some instances, a defective indictment can be cured if the Prosecution provides the accused with timely, clear and consistent information detailing the factual basis underpinning the charges against him or her.

According to the rules of procedures of the ICTY, an indictment has to respect certain provisions that are necessary for its legal validity. Thus, submission of a correct indictment is one of the duties of the prosecutor. In any event, when he/she has, based on his/her investigation, sufficient evidence to provide reasonable grounds for believing that a person has been involved in the commission of a crime, he/she may prepare an indictment. This must be forwarded together with supporting materials to the Registrar in order to be confirmed by a judge of the ICTY.[25] In addition:

> (B) The indictment shall set forth the name and particulars of the suspect, and a concise statement of the facts of the case and of the crime with which the suspect is charged.

---

[24] See also Å. Rydberg, *The Protection of the Interests of Witnesses – The ICTY in Comparison to the Future ICC*, 12 Leiden Journal of International Law 455 (1999).

[25] Rule 47 (A).

> (C) The Registrar shall forward the indictment and accompanying material to one of the Judges currently assigned under Rule 28, who will inform the Prosecutor of the date fixed for review of the indictment.
> (D) On reviewing the indictment, the Judge shall hear the Prosecutor, who may present additional material in support of any count. The Judge may confirm or dismiss each count or may adjourn the review.
> (E) The dismissal of a count in an indictment shall not preclude the Prosecutor from subsequently bringing a new indictment based on the acts underlying that count if supported by additional evidence.

It should be stated here that an indictment presented by the prosecutor does not need to be equal to an indictment under a domestic criminal jurisdiction. Consequently, the primary quality of an international indictment may be less than that of a national indictment, but the focus of accusation may be much more serious.In the *Miroslav Kvocka* case, the Trial Chamber stated that "as a general rule, the degree of particularity required in indictments before the International Tribunal is different from, and perhaps not as high as, the particularity required in domestic criminal law jurisdictions."[26] The Chamber went further and clarified the reasons for the above statement by saying that "The massive scale of the crimes with which the International Tribunal has to deal makes it impracticable to require a high degree of specificity in such matters as the identity of the victims and the dates for the commission of the crimes – at any rate, the degree of specificity may not be as high as that called for in domestic jurisdictions."[27] However, the Trial Chamber accepted that "there may be cases in which more specific information can be provided as to the time, the place, the identity of victims and the means by which the crime was perpetrated; in those cases, the Prosecution should be required to provide such information."[28]

Nevertheless, it is a fact that the indictment must have sufficient information in order to establish legal grounds for prosecution. This means that an indictment may be rejected or lose its validity because of the non-comprehensive presentation of the evidence. In other words, the concept of international criminal responsibility of individuals in the ICTY cannot be based on an unqualified indictment. The decisions of the Appeals Chamber of the ICTY vividly denote this point. For instance, in the *Mirjan Kupreskic* case, constituting one of the most interesting cases concerning

---

[26] Kovcka et al. (IT-98-30-PT), Decision on Defence Preliminary Motion on the Form of the Indictment, 12 April 1999, para.17.

[27] *Id.*

[28] *Id.*

the criticisms of an indictment, the Appeals Chamber demanded from the Prosecutor that:

> In the Appeals Chamber's view, the information given in the Prosecution Pre-Trial Brief is extremely general in nature and it is difficult to see how it could have assisted Zoran and Mirjan Kupreskic in the preparation of their defence. In the short section pertaining directly to Zoran and Mirjan Kupreskic it is stated that they "joined in the attack" on several houses, "participating in at least a half a dozen murders". There is no mention of which particular houses they attacked or whose murders they participated in. Similarly, the paragraph referring to "recently acquired evidence of individual acts of violence" does not establish whether those acts were additional to the attacks on the two houses and "the half a dozen murders". In light of the evidence actually presented at trial, it appears that they were not. During the opening statements, on the first day of the trial, the Prosecution stated that Zoran and Mirjan Kupreskic committed "specific crimes" during the attack on Ahmi}i on 16 April 1993. Although referring specifically to the attack on Witness KL's house in this connection, the Prosecution made no reference whatsoever to the attack on Suhret Ahmi}'s house or to Zoran and Mirjan Kupreskic's involvement in that event (Witness H's evidence). The Appeals Chamber emphasises that the vagueness of the Amended Indictment in the present case constitutes neither a minor defect nor a technical imperfection. It goes to the heart of the substantial safeguards that an indictment is intended to furnish to an accused, namely to inform him of the case he has to meet. If such a fundamental defect can indeed be held to be harmless in any circumstances, it would only be through demonstrating that Zoran and Mirjan Kupreskic's ability to prepare their defence was not materially impaired. In the absence of such a showing here, the conclusion must be that such a fundamental defect in the Amended Indictment did indeed cause injustice, since the Defendants' right to prepare their defence was seriously infringed. The trial against Zoran and Mirjan Kupreskic was, thereby, rendered unfair.[29]

A further criticism against the Prosecutor and the Trial Chamber concluded that:

> For the foregoing reasons, the Appeals Chamber holds that the Amended Indictment failed to plead the material facts of the Prosecution case against Zoran and MirjanKupreskic with the requisite detail. By returning convictions on count 1 (persecution) on the basis of such material facts, the Trial Chamber erred in law. The Appeals Chamber is unable to conclude that Zoran and Mirjan Kupreskic were, through the disclosed evidence, the

[29] *Kupreskic et al.* (IT-95-16-A), Appeal Judgement, 23 October 2001, para.117, 118 and 122.

> information conveyed in the Prosecution Pre-Trial Brief, and knowledge acquired during trial, sufficiently informed of the charges pertaining to the attack on Suhret Ahmic's house, his resulting murder as well as that of Meho Hrustanovic, the destruction of Suhret Ahmic's house, and the expulsion of the surviving members of the Suhret Ahmi} family. The right of Zoran and Mirjan Kupreskic to prepare their defence was thereby infringed and the trial against them rendered unfair. Accordingly, this ground of appeal by Zoran and Mirjan Kuprеškc is allowed.[30]

A summary of the above statement denotes the fact that the basis of conviction for an international crime should be sufficient and be included in the indictment,[31] in the process of pre-trial brief[32] or, according to the circumstances of the case, in the opening statement by the relevant Prosecutor.[33] Accordingly, an indictment has to offer the facts if not the evidence. However, a general indictment may be accepted by the ICTY. This was the case, in the *Milosevic* indictment regarding Bosnia. The indictment has referred to persons as "48 Bosnian Muslim and/or Bosnian Croat men, women and children." There are very notable examples of these general presentations in the relevant indictment. However, the Prosecutor must stipulate on which basis the accused is charged or has liability. This includes planning, instigation, ordering and so forth.[34] An

---

[30] *Id.*, 124.

[31] *Id.*, para.118.

[32] *Id.*

[33] *Id.*

[34] The *Krnojelac* case denotes this fact. According to the Judgment, "For the applicable law on the form of the indictment, the Appeals Chamber refers to the section of this Judgement on the issues of law raised by the parties. The Appeals Chamber reiterates that Article 18(4) of the Statute requires that the crime or crimes charged in the indictment and the alleged facts be set out concisely in the indictment. With respect to the nature of the liability incurred, the Appeals Chamber holds that it is vital for the indictment to specify at least on what legal basis of the Statute an individual is being charged (Article 7(1) and/or 7(3)). Since Article 7(1) allows for several forms of direct criminal responsibility, a failure to specify in the indictment which form or forms of liability the Prosecution is pleading gives rise to ambiguity. The Appeals Chamber considers that such ambiguity should be avoided and holds therefore that, where it arises, the Prosecution must identify precisely the form or forms of liability alleged for each count as soon as possible and, in any event, before the start of the trial. Likewise, when the Prosecution charges the "commission" of one of the crimes under the Statute within the meaning of Article 7(1), it must specify whether the term is to be understood as meaning physical commission by the accused or participation in a joint criminal enterprise, or both. The Appeals Chamber also considers that it is preferable for an indictment alleging the accused's responsibility as a participant in

indictment may however be withdrawn because of the circumstances surrounding the case. For instance, the *Kupreskic* case was withdrawn because of the absence of enough evidence for the proof of guilt.[35]

4.2. Sentence

A sentence is the final verdict of a court on the case that has been submitted to it by the prosecutor in a trial. The sentence is also, in other words, the punishment of a guilty person. The difference is that the word 'punishment' is a general term for criminal behaviour while the word 'sentence' is a term which is, most often, used in conjunction with the period of imprisonment or jail after conviction for an offence. A sentence will commonly sanction a decree of imprisonment or a probative sentence. The court may also decide if a fine, restitution and community service should be included in the sentence. However, it must not be forgotten that a probative sentence depends on the circumstances of the offence and is for those defendants who do not have any criminal record. A sentence may also contain other forms of punishment of the defendant convicted of an offence. However, we do not deny that the terms 'punishment', 'sentence', 'imprisonment', and even 'penalty' overlap each other in many respects and are used interchangeably. This means that they are all identical, and concern the final judgement of a Trial Chamber or Appeals Chamber.

4.2.1. Purpose of Sentence

The purpose of a sentence is one of the most significant questions in the science of criminal law including criminology and penology. A sentence is, in fact, the implementation of the provisions of criminal law. According to the ICTY, the purpose of a sentence is the practical implementation of the rule of law. The purpose of a sentence has been described by the tribunal "as a powerful means for the rule of law to prevail, as well as to deter the parties in the conflict in the former Yugoslavia from perpetrating further

---

a joint criminal enterprise also to refer to the particular form (basic or extended) of joint criminal enterprise envisaged. However, this does not, in principle, prevent the Prosecution from pleading elsewhere than in the indictment - for instance in a pre-trial brief - the legal theory which it believes best demonstrates that the crime or crimes alleged are imputable to the accused in law in the light of the facts alleged. This option is, however, limited by the need to guarantee the accused a fair trial."*Krnojelac* (IT-97-25-A), Judgement, 17 September 2003, para.138.

[35] *Kupreskic* (IT-95-16-PT), Decision on Motion by Prosecutor for Withdrawal of Indictment Against Marinko Katava, 19 December 1997.

crimes or to discourage them from committing further atrocities."[36] According to the ICTY, a sentence also has an educational intention. The tribunal explains that:

> One of the most important purposes of a sentence imposed by the International Tribunal is to make it abundantly clear that the international legal system is implemented and enforced. This sentencing purpose refers to the educational function of a sentence and aims at conveying the message that rules of humanitarian international law have to be obeyed under all circumstances. In doing so, the sentence seeks to internalise these rules and the moral demands they are based on in the minds of the public. The reprobation or stigmatisation associated with a sentence is closely related to the purpose of affirmative prevention. Similarly, putting an end to impunity for the commission of serious violations of international humanitarian law refers to affirmative prevention.[37]

Consequently, one of the purposes of the establishment of the ICTY is, according to the tribunal, the prevention of further violations. In the *Drazen Erdemovic* case, the tribunal goes further and states that the objectives of the ICTY "as seen by the Security Council - i.e. general prevention (or deterrence), reprobation, retribution (or 'just deserts'), as well as collective reconciliation - fit into the Security Council's broader aim of maintaining peace and security in the former Yugoslavia. These purposes and functions … may provide guidance in determining the punishment for a crime against humanity."[38] In other words, the ICTY makes it clear that deterrence[39] and retribution are two of the most

---

[36] *Erdemovic* (IT-96-22-T), Sentencing Judgement, 29 November 1996, para.58.
[37] *Kordić*and *Čerkez* (IT-95-14/2-A), 17 December 2004, paras.1080-1081.
[38] *Id.*
[39] "In the context of combating international crimes, deterrence refers to the attempt to integrate or to reintegrate those persons who believe themselves to be beyond the reach of international criminal law. Such persons must be warned that they have to respect the fundamental global norms of substantive criminal law or face not only prosecution but also sanctions imposed by international tribunals. In modern criminal law this approach to general deterrence is more accurately described as deterrence aiming at reintegrating potential perpetrators into the global society." *Stakic* (IT-97-24-T), Judgement, 31 July 2003, para.902. In another case, deterrence is defined by the Trial Chamber "to mean that deterrence is one of the principles underlying the determination of sentences, in that the penalties imposed by the International Tribunal must, in general, have sufficient deterrent value to ensure that those who would consider committing similar crimes will be dissuaded from doing so. Accordingly, while the Chamber recognises the importance of deterrence as a general consideration in sentencing, it will not treat

valuable objectives and tasks of the tribunal.[40] Of course, the term 'retribution' does not mean a desire for revenge but expresses the outrage of the international community as a whole at serious international crimes. In the *Stevan Todorovic* case, the Trial Chamber was of the view that the "principle of retribution, if it is to be applied at all in the context of sentencing, must be understood as reflecting a fair and balanced approach to the exaction of punishment for wrongdoing. This means that the penalty imposed must be proportionate to the wrongdoing; in other words, that the punishment be made to fit the crime."[41] The Trial Chamber of the ICTY has also underlined the significant function of the objectives of the tribunal. According to it, retribution should be regarded as "an objective, reasoned and measured determination of an appropriate punishment which properly reflects the culpability of the offender, having regard to the intentional risk-taking of the offender, the consequential harm caused by the offender, and the normative character of the offenders conduct. Furthermore, unlike vengeance, retribution incorporates a principle of restraint; retribution requires the imposition of a just and appropriate punishment, and nothing more."[42] Thus, one valuable task of the ICTY is to cultivate and promulgate justice alongside the implementation of punishment of the guilty person by means of its jurisdiction.

---

deterrence as a distinct factor in determining sentence in this case." *Stevan Todorovic* (IT-95-9/1-S), Judgement, 31 July 2001, para.30.

[40] *Id.*

[41] *Stevan Todorovic* (IT-95-9/1-S), Judgement, 31 July 2001, para.29. In the *Momir Nikolić* case, the Trial Chamber states further that the classical or traditional "retributive theory requires that the punishment be proportionate to the harm done. In light of the purposes of the Tribunal and international humanitarian law generally, retribution is better understood as the expression of condemnation and outrage of the international community at such grave violations of, and disregard for, fundamental human rights at a time that people may be at their most vulnerable, namely during armed conflict. It is also recognition of the harm and suffering caused to the victims." *Momir Nikolić* (IT-02-60/1-S), Sentencing Judgement, 2 December 2003, para.86. Moreover, "within the context of international criminal justice, retribution is understood as a clear statement by the international community that crimes will be punished and impunity will not prevail. Recourse to the gravity of the offence, with considerations for the role of the accused in the commission of the offence and the impact of the offence on victims, should help guide a trial chamber in its determination of what sentence is necessary to reflect the indignation and condemnation of the international community for the crimes committed."*Id.*, para.87.

[42] *Dragan Nikolic,* (IT-94-2-S), Sentencing Judgement, 18 December 2003, para.140.

4.2.2. Classification of Sentence

There are different categories of sentences. These are: *i)* a consecutive sentence, *ii)* a cumulative sentence, *iii)* a concurrent sentence, *iv)* an aggravated sentence, and *v)* a mitigated sentence.

The consecutive sentence implies imprisonment for a number of crimes committed by the convicted defendant. The defendant is imprisoned for the years of all the combined sentences.

In the cumulative sentence the defendant is convicted of several offences. The defendant may therefore be jailed for successive terms for each offence. It consists of the total sum of all the sentences. The consecutive sentence and the cumulative sentence are more or less similar to one another.

In contrast to the consecutive sentence, the concurrent sentence implies a sentence in which the lesser and the longer terms run simultaneously. Therefore, in a concurrent sentence, the longest sentence usually stipulates the length of the imprisonment.

With an aggravated sentence, a court may impose a longer imprisonment than the common limit, depending on the circumstances of a case.[43]

The mitigated sentence depends upon the circumstances of the case and whether there exist any reasons for mitigating the sentence. These are such as things as voluntary surrender, pleading guilty, assistance to the court, declaring remorse, forgiveness by victims, diminished mental responsibility, old age, intoxication and ill health.

4.2.3. Length of Sentence

The Statutes of the ICTY and the ICTR do not offer any particular indication regarding the length of an applicable sentence. It seems that the Trial Chamber of the ICTY has implemented all categories of sentences such as *i)* a consecutive sentence, *ii)* a cumulative sentence, *iii)* a concurrent sentence, *iv)* an aggravated sentence and *v)* a mitigated sentence. The application of all these categories is also permitted by the

---

[43] The reasons which may aggregate sentence vary from case to case. In the *Milomir Stakic* case, it was stated that the prosecution considers that "aggravation on the basis of 'white collar crime' is appropriate in this case. The crimes committed by the person at the top of the political or military hierarchy can have far more serious consequences on a larger scale than those committed by lower level perpetrators." *Milomir Stakic* (IT-97-24-A), Judgement, 22 March 2006, para.425.

provisions of the Statute. The Statute of the ICTY provides that the "penalty imposed by the Trial Chamber shall be limited to imprisonment. In determining the terms of imprisonment, the Trial Chambers shall have recourse to the general practice regarding prison sentences in the courts of the former Yugoslavia."[44] In other word, certain provisions of the criminal law of the former Yugoslavia are enforceable by the Trial Chamber or the Appeals Chamber. The ICTY should also "take into account such factors as the gravity of the offence and the individual circumstances of the convicted person."[45] These provisions probably denote a mitigated or consecutive sentence. The Statute of the ICTY has also made it the duty of the tribunal to "take into account the extent to which any penalty imposed by a national court on the same person for the same act has already been served."[46] Despite this, it must be asserted that the provisions of the Statute do not permit the imposition of other sanctions on the convicted defendant. These are things such as penal servitude or a fine.[47] Consequently, the length of a sentence varies upon the gravity of the crimes and the circumstances of the case brought before the ICTY.

4.2.4. Imprisonment

The terms of imprisonment decided by the ICTY have been based on different kinds of criteria used in the assessment of a case. One of the lowest terms has been three years. In the *Sikirica* case, the sentence imposed on *Kolundzija*[48] by the tribunal read that "a sentence of 3 years' imprisonment with credit for 2 years, 5 months and 6 days as of the date of this Sentencing Judgement, together with such additional time as he may

---

[44] Article 24 (1).

[45] Article 24 (2).

[46] Article 10 (3).

[47] This is confirmed in the practice of the ICTY and the ICTR. For instance, the latter has stated that "the only penalties the Tribunal can impose on an accused who pleads guilty or is convicted as such are prison terms up to and including life imprisonment, pursuant in particular to Rule 101 (A) of the Rules, whose provisions apply to all crimes which fall within the jurisdiction of the Tribunal, namely genocide, (Article 2 of the Statute), crimes against humanity (Article 3) and violations of Article 3 common to the Geneva Conventions and of Additional Protocol II thereto (Article 4). The Statute of the Tribunal excludes other forms of punishment such as the death sentence, penal servitude or a fine." *Jean Kambanda,* (ICTR 97-23-S), Judgement and Sentence, 4 September 1998, para.4.

[48] He was a commander at the Bosnian Serb-run Keraterm detention camp established in 1992.

serve pending the determination of any appeal."[49] The length of imprisonment terms imposed by the tribunal has often been much longer than the above. For instance, in the *Krstic* case, the tribunal imposed a maximum of forty-six years. The Trial Chamber in the disposition part of the sentencing judgement based on the facts and the legal findings presented in the procedure of the trial states that it finds *Radislav Krstic* guilty of committing *a)* genocide, *b)* persecution with the intention to commit murder, cruel and inhumane treatment, terrorising the civilian population, the destruction and the forcible transfer of the personal property of Bosnian Muslim civilians and, *c)* murder as a violation of the laws and customs of war. Therefore, the Trial Chamber sentenced *Radislav Krstic* to forty six years' imprisonment and stated that "the full amount of time spent in the custody of the Tribunal will be deducted from the time to be served."[50] This length of imprisonment was however later modified to thirty-five years by the Appeals Chamber.[51]

4.2.5. Life Imprisonment

The ICTY has also imposed life imprisonment. This has been permitted by the provisions of the Rules of Procedure and Evidence of the tribunal. The relevant provisions read that "a convicted person may be sentenced to imprisonment for a term up to and including the remainder of the convicted person's life."[52] The first life imprisonment term was given by the ICTY in 2003. Before this date, the Trial Chambers of the tribunal were rather hesitant to approve life imprisonment. However, their *raison d'être* has been based largely on the statement of the Appeals Chamber in the *Jelisic* case. This case developed the idea of the implementation of life imprisonment rather than capital punishment. The Appeals Chamber in the interpretation of life imprisonment has stated that:

> In this case the cross-appellant has alleged an error in the exercise of the Trial Chamber's discretion. It falls on the cross-appellant to show that the Trial Chamber has erred by imposing a sentence outside the discretionary framework provided by the Statute and the Rules. The Statute provides in Article 24 that penalties shall be limited to imprisonment. Rule 101(A) of the Rules provides that "[a] convicted person may be sentenced to

---

[49] Sikirica et al. (IT-95-8-S), Sentencing Judgement, 13 November 2001, para.245.

[50] *Krstic* (IT-98-33-T), Sentencing Judgement, 2 August 2001, para.726.

[51] *Krstic* (IT-98-33-T), Judgement, 19 April 2001, para.275.

[52] See Rule 101 (A). The International Criminal Tribunal for the former Yugoslavia, Rules of Procedure and Evidence, U.N. Doc. IT/32/Rev.7 (1996) entered into force 14 March 1994,amendments adopted 8 January 1996.

> imprisonment for a term up to and including the remainder of the convicted person's life". Thus, it falls within the Trial Chamber's discretion to impose life imprisonment. The Trial Chamber has a broad discretion as to which factors it may consider in sentencing and the weight to attribute to them.[53]

Nevertheless, it must not be forgotten that the concept of life imprisonment has been objected to because it conflicts with the provisions of the constitutions of some European states. The ICTY has defended the policy of life imprisonment or maximum sentence by asserting that the total abolition of the death penalty has been one of the aims of the United Nations and the Council of Europe.[54] In particular, the General Assembly has taken certain measures for this end. The Council of Europe has required that its membership should also be based on the abolition of the death penalty.[55] For these reasons the death penalty "can no longer be imposed in states of the former Yugoslavia and has been replaced by the maximum penalty of life imprisonment except where a lower maximum is specified."[56] With reference to the abolition of the death penalty, the Trial Chamber asserts that "where a penalty becomes more lenient, the more lenient version must be applied."[57] In practice, this means that if the provisions of the Criminal Code of the Socialist Federative Republic of Yugoslavia were implemented, the maximum sentence would be life imprisonment and not the death penalty.[58] Consequently, the Trial Chamber goes further and clarifies that the prosecution recognises that "the most appropriate sentence is life imprisonment. The Trial Chamber notes that in a number of countries the killing of only one person results in mandatory life sentence, whereas in others, life imprisonment is forbidden by constitution."[59] This means that there are different policies for the implementation of sentences. According to the Chamber, the provisions of the Statute reflect "the global policy of the United Nations aims at the abolition of the death penalty and favours life imprisonment as the maximum sanction to be imposed."[60] In other words, life imprisonment is employed in order to abolish the death penalty and promote the principles

---

[53] *Jelisic* (IT-95-10-A), Judgement, 5 July 2001, para.100.
[54] *Stakic* (IT-97-24-T), Judgement, 31 July 2003, para.890.
[55] *Id.*
[56] *Stakic* (IT-97-24-T), Judgement, 31 July 2003, para.890.
[57] *Id.*
[58] *Id.*
[59] *Id.*, para.932.
[60] *Id.*

of justice. The principle of the abolition of the death penalty is considered to have a global character and should be respected by all states.

4.2.6. Concurrent Sentencing

The decisions of the ICTY demonstrate that convictions have mostly been based on several offences. This is because the defendants were found guilty of several separate violations of the Statute of the tribunal or because a single violation has been dealt with under other provisions. Although distinct sentences have been imposed for categories of offences, sentences have been based on a concurrent sentencing principle.[61] The Rules of Procedure and Evidence of the tribunal have particularly stated that if the Trial Chamber "finds the accused guilty on one or more of the charges contained in the indictment, it shall impose a sentence in respect of each finding of guilt and indicate whether such sentences shall be served consecutively or concurrently, unless it decides to exercise its power to impose a single sentence reflecting the totality of the criminal conduct of the accused."[62]Despite all of these provisions and their inherent flexibility, the Appeals Chamber of the ICTY has emphasised the policy of the internationalisation of the principles of sentences and has made it clear that it is within the discretion of each Trial Chamber to decide about the terms of the implementation of sentences. Therefore, the Appeals Chamber explains that "the aggregate sentence reflects the totality of the criminal conduct. This can be achieved through either the imposition of one sentence in respect of all sentences, or several sentences ordered to run concurrently, consecutively or both."[63] Furthermore, the Appeals Chamber describes that:

> "sentencing in relation to more than one offence involves more than just an assessment of the appropriate period of imprisonment for each offence and the addition of all such periods so assessed as a simple mathematical exercise. The total single sentence, or the effective total sentence where several sentences are imposed, must reflect the totality of the offender's criminal conduct but it must not exceed that totality. Where several sentences are imposed, the result is that the individual sentences must

---

[61] See the above paragraphs.

[62] Rule 87 (c) of the ICTY.

[63] *Music* (IT-96-21-A*bis),* Judgement on Sentence Appeal, 8 April 2003,para.46.

> either be less than they would have been had they stood alone or they must be ordered to be served either concurrently or partly concurrently."[64]

The Trial Chamber has even explained that the Rules of Procedure and Evidence of the ICTY do not preclude the passing of a single sentence for several crimes. In certain circumstances, according to the Trial Chamber, it is possible that a single sentence be used instead of imposing multiple sentences. Clear examples of the employment of single sentences are the *Kambanda* and *Serushago* cases in which Trial Chamber I of the ICTR preferred to delete multiple sentences and impose single sentences on the convicted persons.[65] Similarly, a single sentence was passed even for multiple crimes by the International Military Tribunal in Nuremberg and Tokyo.[66] The Trial Chamber explains its judgement by asserting that:

> Here, the crimes ascribed to the accused have been characterised in several distinct ways but form part of a single set of crimes committed in a given geographic region during a relatively extended time-span, the very length of which served to ground their characterization as a crime against humanity, without its being possible to distinguish criminal intent from motive. The Trial Chamber further observes that crimes other than the crime of persecution brought against the accused rest fully on the same facts as those specified under the other crimes for which the accused is being prosecuted. In other words, it is impossible to identify which acts would relate to which of the various counts - other than those supporting the prosecution for and conviction of persecution under count 1 which, moreover, covers a longer period of time than any of the other counts. In light of this overall consistency, the Trial Chamber finds that there is reason to impose a single sentence for all the crimes of which the accused has been found guilty.[67]

---

[64] *Id.* Yet, according to the Appeals Chamber, "the cumulative convictions of themselves involve an additional punishment – not only by reason of the social stigmatization inherent in being convicted of that additional crime, but also the risk that, under the law of the State enforcing the sentence, the eligibility of a convicted person for early release will depend to some extent upon the number or nature of the convictions entered. The quashing of the cumulative convictions undoubtedly removed the punishment involved in the additional convictions themselves." *Id.*, para.25.

[65] *Blaskic* (IT-95-14-T), Judgement, 3 March 2000, para.807. It must not be forgotten that the Rules of Procedure and Evidence of both tribunals, namely the ICTY and the ICTR are almost equal.

[66] *Id.*, para.806.

[67] *Id.*, para.807.

However, it must be noted that sentences imposed by the ICTY have been of a different character depending on the nature of the offences and their gravity. According to a judgement of the tribunal the "sentence must reflect the gravity of the criminal conduct of the accused. This requires consideration of the underlying crimes as well as the form and degree of the participation of the individual accused".[68] Although the ICTY has mostly deferred to the general practice of the former Yugoslavia regarding prison sentences, this does not mean that it has mechanically applied the same law and obligations. The Trial Chamber clarifies that "because very important underlying differences often exist between national prosecutions and prosecutions in this jurisdiction, the nature, scope and the scale of the offences tried before the International Tribunal do not allow for an automatic application of the sentencing practices of the former Yugoslavia."[69] Consequently, any reference to the sentencing practice of the relevant state must be seen as an aid and guideline to the sentencing decisions of the ICTY and not as a decisive factor.[70]

4.2.7. Appropriate Sentence

One of the most significant aspects of the present Statute of the ICTY is that it does not allow the death penalty. However, this does not necessarily mean that the ICTY does not provide severe penalties. In the *Drazen Erdemovic* case, the Trial Chamber stated that "in international law, the States which included crimes against humanity in their national laws provided that the commission of such crimes would entail the imposition of the most severe penalties permitted in their respective systems."[71] According to the Trial Chamber, the relevant laws in the Criminal Code of the Socialist Federative Republic of Yugoslavia legalized "the harshest penalties for the commission of acts of genocide or war crimes against the civilian population."[72]

But what exactly the criteria of appropriate sentence or punishment are is also one of the questions of international criminal justice in the former Yugoslavia and the other *ad hoc* tribunals such as the ICTR and the Sierra Leone Court. This means that the ICTY should apply the principle of legality and should not violate its Statute or Rules of Procedure and

---

[68] *Stakic* (IT-97-24-T), Judgement, 31 July 2003, para.903.

[69] *Kunarac et al.* (IT-96-23-T and IT-96-23/1-T), Judgement, 22 February 2001, para.829.

[70] *Id.*

[71] *Drazen Erdemovic*, Sentencing and Judgement, 29 November 1996, para.30.

[72] *Id.*

Evidence. Naturally, in imposing sentence, the ICTY is not bound by any maximum term of imprisonment applied in the national criminal system of the former Yugoslavia.[73] Therefore, the following outlines the steps to be taken by the ICTY when assessing a sentence:

> The Trial and Appeals Chambers of the International Tribunal generally consider what is variously and often interchangeably referred to, for example, as sentencing "objectives", "purposes", "principles", "functions" or "policy" in the assessment of the term of actual imprisonment for convicted persons. These are considered in addition to the gravity of the offence and mitigating and aggravating circumstances. What appear to be justifications for imprisoning convicted persons, or theories of punishment, actually are treated as or resemble sentencing factors, in the sense that these considerations are consistently said to affect, usually in an unspecified manner, the length of imprisonment. In the present case, the Prosecutor submits that the Trial Chamber ought to consider the principles of retribution, incapacitation of the dangerous, deterrence, punishment and rehabilitation when determining the sentences to be imposed on each of the accused.[74]

According to the Appeals Chamber, the chief intention of the ICTY is therefore to apply an appropriate sentence and to create justice with due regard to the circumstances of each case. In the view of the Appeals Chamber, the "Trial Chambers are vested with a broad discretion in determining an appropriate sentence, due to their obligation to individualise the penalties to fit the circumstances of the accused and the gravity of the crime."[75] An appropriate sentence also encourages the principle of non-impunity and helps victims.[76] The policy of appropriate sentence has also been embraced by other *ad hoc* tribunals such as the ICTR and the Sierra Leone Court. This policy is also formulated among the provisions of the Statute of the ICC.[77]

---

[73] As was explained in the above.

[74] *Id.*, para.836

[75] *Stanislav Galic* (IT-98-29-A), Judgement, 30 November 2006, para.393.

[76] In the case, the Appeals, the "concrete gravity of the crime remains 'the litmus test' in the imposition of an appropriate sentence. The Trial Chamber's duty remains to tailor the penalty to fit the individual circumstances of the accused and the gravity of the crime. By doing so, Trial Chambers contribute to the promotion of and respect for the rule of law and respond to the call from the international community to end impunity 'while ensuring that the accused are punished solely on the basis of their wrongdoings and receive a fair trial'." *Milomir Stakic*(IT-97-24-A), Judgement, 22 March 2006, para.375.

[77] See chapter seven.

5. The Legal Procedures in the ICTR

Whilst the ICTR has its own Statute and its laws are applicable to those who have committed crimes in the territory of Rwanda and to Rwandan citizens responsible for genocide and other such violations committed in the territory of neighbouring States, the tribunal has, in many respects, followed similar provisions to the ICTY.[78] In other words, the structure of the Tribunal has essentially followed the structure of the ICTY.

6. The Legal Procedures in the SCSL

Worthy of note are the rules of procedure and evidence of the Special Court which are based on The Rules of Procedure and Evidence of the International Criminal Tribunal for Rwanda. These rules may however be amended by the Judges of the Special Court if required. In this case, the 1965 Criminal Procedure Act of Sierra Leone may guide the judges.[79] Therefore, the SCSL has approximately similar rules governing its procedures to the ICTY and the ICTR.

6.1. Rights of the Accused

The Statute of the Special Court has given, as have the other international tribunals, the utmost consideration to the rights of those who are accused of committing crimes within the provisions of Articles 2 to 5. In this case, the Statute tries to meet an international standard for the protection of the rights of the accused persons under the jurisdiction of the Court. According to the provisions of the Statute all the accused should enjoy these rights equally and, in the application of the rights, they should not be discriminated against because of their social or official positions. The rights of the accused persons establish also minimum guarantees for the accused concerning other legal matters of the proceedings. Actually, it is one of the rights of the accused to be informed of the cause of the charge against him/her and this should be in a language that the accused can

[78] Article 4 of the Statute of the ICTR concerning the competence of the tribunal reads that "The International Tribunal for Rwanda shall have the power to prosecute persons responsible for serious violations of international humanitarian law committed in the territory of Rwanda and Rwandan citizens responsible for such violations committed in the territory of neighbouring States between 1 January 1994 and 31 December 1994, in accordance with the provisions of the present Statute."

[79] Article 14.

understand adequately. In particular, the accused person should have the free assistance of an interpreter within the trial procedure if he/she does not understand or speak the language employed in the Court. In any case, he/she should also be given adequate time and facilities in order to prepare a defence and communicate with counsel.

More significant are the rights of the accused to be tried without undue delay and not to be tried in his/her absence. He/she should, in all these situations, have the right to legal assistance. If he/she does not have the financial capacity to afford counsel during the procedures, legal assistance may be assigned to him/her when the interests of justice require it. In addition, he/she has the legal right to examine the witnesses. Finally, the accused should not be forced to testify against himself/herself in order to confess guilt.

In all these procedures concerning the investigation of the crime and the presentation of evidence and witnesses, the Special Court should remain objective regarding the accused. Therefore, the accused has a legal right to a fair and public hearing with the reservation that the protection of victims and witnesses be respected during the procedure of the trial.[80] Obviously, the rights of the victims and witnesses should not be violated to meet the rights of the accused. In other words, there must be a balance between these rights in order for a fair and just trial to be carried out. Moreover, it is the responsibility of the Registrar to set up a Victims and Witnesses Unit within the Registry in order to take protective measures and to provide other appropriate assistance that may be useful to them.[81]

7. The Legal Procedures in the ICC

7.1. Application of the Law

Whilst the concept of various international crimes has been developed within the system of international criminal law, the procedural application of the law and its norms and provisions under a criminal court are very rare. Some reasons for the non-applicability of international criminal law in an international court are a result of political considerations and others are due to the fact that the consolidation of the system of international criminal law has been very slow. There have been only a few international criminal tribunals for the practical implementation of international criminal law, all of which have had an *ad hoc* character or a temporary jurisdictional power. As a consequence, the development of the procedural

[80] Article 17.
[81] Article 16.

aspects of international criminal law has been heavily based on the provisions of national criminal jurisdictions which vary from state to state. These together with argumentation presented by different lawyers have made the procedural aspects of the law very conservative.

It was only after the start of the war in the territories of the former Yugoslavia that the urgent need for the creation of a court was felt by the international legal community as a whole. The war in Yugoslavia became so serious and brutal in nature that the process for the adoption of an international criminal court was started among different political entities of the world. The adoption of certain procedural aspects for the implementation of international criminal law was therefore seen as a necessary condition to protect the fundamental rights of man enumerated within a considerable number of international human rights law instruments. Thus, the grave violations of the system of the international humanitarian law of armed conflict within the territory of the former Yugoslavia and the serious violations of the basic rights of man within the jurisdiction of different states, such as apartheid, slavery, torture, disappearance and, most seriously of all, genocide committed by dictatorial regimes, made the adoption of procedural rules for the application of international criminal law unavoidable.

To examine the background to the procedural development of international criminal law, one has to investigate the procedural provisions of the ICTY and the ICTR. The Statutes of both tribunals are complemented by the Rules of Procedure and evidence formulated and adopted by the judges of the tribunals. These were effective in influencing the procedural character of the Statute of the ICC. The Statute does not, however, adopt the policy of those tribunals and is certainly different from its predecessors. The negotiation of the Statute of the ICC was not easy. Many controversies had to be resolved and many provisions had to be formulated and reformulated before the law for the investigation and prosecution of international criminals could be adopted. The aim was to adopt unified procedural provisions that could be useful for the prevention of international crimes and that would not be criticised by the adherents of civil law or common law systems.

Finally, the procedural aspects of the Statute and its application were adopted by negotiating states. They achieved a combination of provisions that has taken into consideration the civil law and common law elements which are useful for the establishment of the Court and the application of the provisions of international criminal law. The provisions of the Statute governing its application are divided into different parts and sections. Some of the most relevant parts of the Statute are discussed below.

7.1.1. Investigation and Prosecution

Investigation and prosecution constitute an important aspect of criminal procedure in order to implement an effective criminal justice system. Part 5 of the Statute of the ICC concerns this matter and provides a large number of provisions that have to be applied by the Court.

7.1.1.1. Initiation of an Investigation

When the possibility of prosecuting a crime within the jurisdiction of the Court occurs, an investigation must be officially initiated in order to prosecute the accused. This task is normally given to a prosecutor who is authorized to initiate a case for the purpose of finding evidence, facts and proof in order to support his/her arguments before a court.

Article 53 of the Statute of the ICC authorizes a prosecutor to initiate an investigation based on the information made available to him/her. This information must, however, be authentic and should be based on facts proving its genuine nature. Thus, a prosecutor may not initiate a case upon evidence that is not complete and the real value of which is doubtful. There are therefore several conditions which must be fulfilled.

Firstly, there must be a reasonable basis for investigation. This means that the prosecutor must believe that a crime within the jurisdiction of the Court has been or is being committed. Secondly, the case must be admissible according to the conditions under Article 17 of the Statute. Thirdly, there must be a considerable number of reasons to believe that an investigation would serve the interests of justice. Whenever the prosecutor concludes that there is no reasonable basis for investigation, the Pre-Trial Chamber must be informed about this matter. This decision may be based on the fact that the prosecution of the case is not in the interests of justice due to circumstances like the insufficient gravity of the crime, the interests of the victims or the age of the accused or his/her infirmity. In any event, the Pre-Trial Chamber may decide not to continue a case or to inform the prosecutor that he should reconsider his/her decision regarding the prosecution of the case.

Article 54 of the Statute of the ICC relates to the duties and powers of the prosecutor concerning the investigation of a case. These duties are considered an integral part of his/her task and should continuously be respected by the prosecutor during his/her investigation. The article has, in fact, made the framework clear under which the prosecutor can use his/her authority in the interests of justice and, in particular that this should be done in conformity with the provisions of the Statute regarding the jurisdiction of the Court. The article stresses the significant position of the prosecutor in securing the fundamental principles of human rights law.

Furthermore, Article 54 provides several important principles governing the duties of a prosecutor. The prosecutor must take "appropriate measures to ensure the effective investigation and prosecution of crimes within the jurisdiction of the Court, and in doing so, respect the interests and personal circumstances of victims and witnesses, including age, gender as defined in article 7, paragraph 3, and health, and take into account the nature of the crime, in particular where it involves sexual violence, gender violence or violence against children"[82]. This means that he/she is responsible for respecting all rights of a person arising under the provisions of the Statute.[83]

Other important tasks of the prosecutor are to collect evidence, question persons being investigated, such as victims and witnesses, and to seek the cooperation of any state or intergovernmental organisation, in order to enter into agreements, which require the parties not to reveal, at any stage of the proceedings, documents or information that the prosecutor obtains on the condition of confidentiality.[84] He/she is therefore

---

[82] Article 54 (1) (b). One of the most significant provisions of this section is the consideration of acts which involve violence against children. This provision would have been more appreciated if it had been mentioned in a separate sub-section. This would help the interests of justice and the safeguarding of the basic principles governing the protection of children, such as those provided within the Geneva Declaration of the Rights of the Child, 1924, Declaration of the Rights of the Child, 1959, United Nations Standard Minimum Rules for the Administration of Juvenile Justice, 1985, Convention on the Rights of the Child, 1989, United Nations Guidelines for the Prevention of Juvenile Delinquency (The Riyadh Guidelines), 1990, Optional Protocol to the Convention on the Rights of the Child on the Sale of Children, Child Prostitution and Child Pornography, 2000, Optional Protocol to the Convention on the Rights of the Child on the Involvement of Children in Armed Conflict, 2000, Convention concerning the Prohibition and Immediate Action for the Elimination of the Worst Forms of Child Labour, 1999, European Convention on the Exercise of Children's Rights, 1996, African Charter on the Rights and Welfare of the Child, 1990.

[83] Article 54 (1) (c).

[84] Jeffrey L. Bleich, *Cooperation with National Systems,* 13 Nouvelles Études Pénales 245 (1997); 29 Denver Journal of International Law and Policy 293 (1997); V. Oosterveld and J. McManus, *The Cooperation of States with the International Criminal Court,* 25 Fordham International Law Journal 767 (2002). See also Patricia A. McKeon, *An International Criminal Court: Balancing the Principle of Sovereignty Against the Demands for International Justice,* 12 ST John's Journal of Legal Commentary 535 (1997); Betty Kaari Murungi, *Implementing the International Criminal Court Statute in Africa,* International Legal Practitioner 87 (2001); Florian Jessberg and Cathleen Powell, *Prosecuting Pinochets in South Africa – Implementing the Rome Statute of the International*

responsible for taking the measures necessary to ensure the confidentiality of the collected information and of any other relevant matter which has come under his/her authority on the proviso of confidentiality.[85] This is in order not to release information that may be used against the victims or the accused. In particular, arrangements that are agreed on between the prosecutor and other parties have to be respected.

One essential point here is that all of these actions should be based on the interests of justice and fairness and the initiation of the investigation of a case should not violate the interests of the victims or the accused or suspected person. That is why the Statute insists on the proper investigation of crimes that come within the jurisdiction of the Court. Furthermore, it is also important that the gravity of the crime be established and the prosecutor should not start a case which is not of extreme importance, the prosecution of which has no effective function in the implementation of the provisions of the Statute. In other words, the prosecutor's duties and powers are not unlimited and he/she cannot act contrary to the provisions of the Statute. In addition, the Pre-Trial Chamber is authorised in some situations to see whether the prosecutor performs his/her duties in conformity with the requirements of the Statute.

7.1.1.2. Guarantees for Rights of Persons

One of the chief principles for achieving international justice is not to violate the rights of persons who have, for one reason or another, come under investigation. These rights may be found within many instruments of international human rights law that call upon all states to respect certain rights of the accused. The respect of these rights is especially important in the case of criminal procedures and constitutes a guarantee of the personal integrity of the person under investigation. The tendency within the constitution of international criminal tribunals has therefore increasingly been to protect individuals from any unlawful measures. The predecessors of the ICC also tried not to violate the rights of persons before, during and after investigations.

The Statute of the ICC in Article 55 makes a serious consideration of the rights of persons who are the object of investigation for the crimes

---

Criminal Court, 14 South African Journal of Criminal Justice 344 (2001); Giuseppe Palmisano, *Co-operation by Non-States parties, in* The International Criminal Court: Commentson the Draft Statute (Flavia Lattanzi, ed. 1998) pp. 339-66; Helmut Satzger, *German Criminal Law and the Rome Statute – A Critical Analysis of the German Code of Crimes Against International Law,* 2 International Criminal law Review 261 (2002).

[85] Article 54 (2).

within the jurisdiction of the Court. Accordingly, during an investigation, a person:

> (a) Shall not be compelled to incriminate himself or herself or to confess guilt;
> (b) Shall not be subjected to any form of coercion, duress or threat, to torture or to any other form of cruel, inhuman or degrading treatment or punishment;
> (c) Shall, if questioned in a language other than a language the person fully understands and speaks, have, free of any cost, the assistance of a competent interpreter and such translations as are necessary to meet the requirements of fairness; and
> (d) Shall not be subjected to arbitrary arrest or detention, and shall not be deprived of his/her liberty except on such grounds and in accordance with such procedures as are established in this Statute.[86]

Obviously, the above provisions ensure the personal integrity of the person under suspicion and protect him or her from various types of physical or psychological violation, such as torture or cruel behaviour. Other provisions of Article 55 have also strengthened the rights listed above. These rights concern a person who may come before an inquiry under the provisions of the Statute. Accordingly, when there are reasons to believe that the person has committed one of the crimes within the jurisdiction of the Court, he/she has to be informed prior to being questioned by the prosecutor, of four basic rights, i.e., the right to know that he/she is under suspicion, the right to remain silent, the right to have legal assistance, and the right to be questioned in the presence of counsel.

7.1.2. Role of the Pre-Trial Chamber

7.1.2.1. Functions Governing Investigation

The Pre-Trial Chamber has different functions in the initiation and investigation of a case. These functions have three very significant aims. These are to protect the accused and victims and to ensure the implementation of the appropriate jurisdiction in order to achieve fair and equal justice.

For the fulfilment of the above functions, the Statute has foreseen several decisive techniques. Article 56 of the Statute provides one of the most important functions of the Pre-Trial Chamber. It makes it the duty of the prosecutor to consider all the possibilities in relation to each investigative opportunity. Consequently, it is the duty of the prosecutor to

[86] Article 55 (1).

inform the Pre-Trial Chamber when certain possibilities for the collection of evidence exist and access to them may not subsequently be possible for the purposes of a trial. The purpose is here to save and keep all relevant material under control so that it will not be tampered with or destroyed by the passing of time.[87] In that case, the Pre-Trial Chamber has a legal duty to take such necessary measures as may be important for the proceedings and for the protection of the rights of the defendant.[88]These include:

> (a) Making recommendations or orders regarding procedures to be followed;
> (b) Directing that a record be made of the proceedings;
> (c) Appointing an expert to assist;
> (d) Authorizing counsel for a person who has been arrested, or appeared before the Court in response to a summons, to participate, or where there has not yet been such an arrest or appearance or counsel has not been designated, appointing another counsel to attend and represent the interests of the defence;
> (e) Naming one of its members or, if necessary, another available judge of the Pre-Trial or Trial Division to observe and make recommendations or orders regarding the collection and preservation of evidence and the questioning of persons;
> (f) Taking such other action as may be necessary to collect or preserve evidence.[89]

It is also the prosecutor's duty to inform the person who has been arrested or summoned that she/he may be heard on the matter unless the Pre-Trial Chamber orders the contrary.[90] All these procedures are in connection with the investigation that may then be carried out according to the provisions of Article 56. The Pre-Trial Chamber is also responsible for judging when the prosecutor has failed in his/her duty concerning measures pursuant to Article 56. The Pre-Trial Chamber may, in that case,

---

[87] Article 56 (1) (a).

[88] *Id.*, (1) (b).Se further H. Friman, *Rights of Persons Suspected or Accused of a Crime, in* The International Criminal Court: The Making of the Rome Statute: Issues, Negotiations, and Results (Roy S. Lee, ed. 1999) pp. 247-62; Stuart Beresford and Lahiouel Hafida, *The Right to be Defended in Person or Through Legal Assistance and the International Criminal Court,* 13 Leiden Journal of International Law 949 (2000); L. M. Baum, *Pursuing Justice in a Climate of Moral Outrage: An Evaluation of the Rights of the Accused in the Rome Statute of the International Criminal Court,* 19 Wisconsin International Law Journal 197 (2001).

[89] Article 56 (2).

[90] Article 56 (1) (c).

take such measures on its own initiative.[91] The prosecutor has, however, the right to appeal. The appeal shall be heard on an expedited basis.[92]

In all the possible situations above, it is obvious that not only the prosecutor, but also the Pre-Trial Chamber has a great responsibility for the initiation of an investigation. The duty of the Pre-Trial Chamber is to see that the prosecutor has really taken all the necessary measures for the fulfilment of his/her duties, for the purpose of an effective examination, and in the recording of the evidence that may be important for the case. The problem is, however, that if both inter-organs of the Court, i.e., the Pre-trial Chamber and the Office of the Prosecutor, fail in the performance of their functions and duties, there is a risk that the evidence of criminality may be damaged.

7.1.2.2. Powers of the Pre-Trial Chamber

The Pre-Trial Chamber has to follow the provisions of the Statute governing its functions. Certain other functions that may be followed by the Pre-Trial Chamber may be provided for by the Rules of Procedure and Evidence. The Chamber may issue such orders and warrants as may be required for the purposes of an investigation. The Chamber may also, if it deems it necessary, provide measures necessary for the protection of victims and witnesses and their privacy. These may also include the preservation of evidence and the protection of persons who have been arrested or who have appeared in response to a summons.[93]

In the case of some problems within the juridical machinery of a state and its consequent failure to introduce an authorised person to cooperate with the prosecutor or Pre-Trial Chamber, the latter may authorise the prosecutor to take specific investigational steps within the territory of that state in order to prevent the destruction of the evidence. The purpose of the Pre-Trial Chamber may here be to compile all the information that may be necessary for the proceedings of the Court and for proof of guilt.[94] The Pre-Trial Chamber should also, with the cooperation of relevant states, take protective measures for the benefit of the victims.[95]

It is also one of the functions of the Pre-Trial Chamber to issue a warrant for arrest or a summons to appear.[96] This should be based on the

---

[91] Article 56 (3) (a).
[92] Article 56 (3) (b).
[93] Article 57 (3) (c).
[94] Article 57 (3) (d).
[95] Article 57 (3) (e).
[96] The example is the warrant of arrest for *Germain Katanaga*. The Pre-Trial wrote "HEREBY ISSUES A WARRANT OF ARREST for Germain KATANGA, whose

application of the prosecutor and on the existence of reasonable information and evidence for this purpose.[97] There must, however, be reason to believe that the person in question has committed a crime within the jurisdiction of the Court and that the arrest of that person is necessary in order "(i) To ensure the person's appearance at trial, (ii) To ensure that the person does not obstruct or endanger the investigation or the court proceedings, or (iii) Where applicable, to prevent the person from continuing with the commission of that crime or a related crime which is within the jurisdiction of the Court and which arises out of the same circumstances."[98]

One may also take other measures in order to ensure the safety of the evidence of the case, such as provisional arrest, amending the warrant of

---

photograph is attached, who is believed to be a national of the Democratic Republic of the Congo, born on 28 April 1978 in Mambasa, Mambasa Territory, Ituri District, who is believed to be of Ngiti ethnicity, married to Denise Katanga and father of two children, son of Jacob Nduru and Elizabeth Regine, alleged leader of the FRPI, who, according to available information, is detained at the *Centre Pénitentiaire et de Rééducation de Kinshasa* and is also known as "Simba"."*Germain Katanaga* (ICC-01/04-01/07), Situation in the Democratic Republic of Congo, 2 July 2007, p.7.

[97] Article 58 (1) and(2).

[98] Article 58 (1) (b). For instance, in the *Jean-Pierre Bemba* case, the Pre-Trial Chamber believes that "there are reasonable grounds to believe that Mr Jean-Pierre Bemba is criminally responsible, jointly with another person or through other persons, under article 25(3)(a) of the Statute, for: (i) rape as a crime against humanity, punishable under article 7(1)(g) of the Statute; (ii) rape as a war crime, punishable under article 8(2)(e)(vi) of the Statute; (iii) torture as a crime against humanity, punishable under article 7(1)(f) of the Statute; (iv) torture as a war crime, punishable under article 8(2)(c)(i) of the Statute; (v) committing outrages upon personal dignity, in particular humiliating and degrading treatment, as a war crime, punishable under article 8(2)(c)(ii) of the Statute; (vi) murder as a crime against humanity, punishable under article 7(1)(a) of the Statute; (vii) murder as a war crime, punishable under article 8(2)(c)(i) of the Statute; (viii) pillaging a town or place as a war crime, punishable under article 8(2)(e)(v) of the Statute. Lastly, the Chamber considers that there are reasonable grounds to believe that the arrest of Mr Jean-Pierre Bemba appears necessary at this stage in order to ensure, within the meaning of article 58(1)(b)(i) and (ii) of the Statute, that he appears before the Court and does not obstruct the investigation or court proceedings." *Jean-Pierre Bemb."* (ICC-01/05-01/08), Warrant of Arrest Replacing the one issued on 23 May 2008, 10 June 2008, paras.24-25.

arrest by modifying or adding to the crimes specified therein or issuing a summons for the person to appear.[99]

The function of the Pre-Trial Chamber is to guarantee a procedure based on a right and fair trial so that no one is brought before the Court without sufficient evidence of the commission of a crime within the jurisdiction of the Court. The Pre-Trial Chamber has thus, not only the function of the prevention of the destruction of any relevant evidence, but also ensures that the legal procedures concerning arrest, provisional arrest and issue of an arrest warrant are based on the right information.[100]

---

[99] Article 58 (4), (5), (6) and (7). For instance, the Pre-Trial Chamber decided to suspend the confirmation hearing in the case of *Jean-Pierre Bemba Gombo* on 3 March 2009. It also asked the Prosecutor to consider submitting to the Pre-Trial Chamber an amended document presenting the charges against Gombo, "taking into account that the legal characterization of the facts of the case may correspond to a mode of liability other than the individual responsibility relied on by the Prosecutor, namely criminal responsibility as a military commander or superior within the meaning of article 28 of the Statute."On 15 June 2009, as a consequence of this amendment, the Pre-Trial Chamber II decided that "there is sufficient evidence to establish substantial grounds to believe that Jean-Pierre Bemba is criminally responsible, for having effectively acted as a military commander within the meaning of article 28(a) of the Statute, for war crimes (murder, rape and pillaging) and crimes against humanity (murder and rape)." *Jean-Pierre Bemba Gombo* (ICC-01/05-01/08), Situation in the Central African Republic The Prosecutor, Case Information Sheet, 29 October 2009.

[100] For instance, in the *Mathieu Ngudjolo* case, the Pre-Trial Chamber, after examining the case, stated that: "for the foregoing reasons, there are reasonable grounds to believe that Mathieu Ngudjolo is criminally responsible under article 25(3)(a) or, in the alternative, under article 25(3)(b) of the Statute, for: i) murder as a crime against humanity, punishable under article 7(1)(a) of the Statute; ii) wilful killing as a war crime, punishable under article(2)(a)(i) or article 8(2)(c)(i) of the Statute; iii) inhumane acts as a crime against humanity, punishable under article 7(1)(k) of the Statute; iv) inhuman treatment as a war crime, punishable under article 8(2)(a)(ii) or cruel treatment as a war crime, punishable under article 8(2)(c)(i) of the Statute; v) the war crime of using children under the age of fifteen years to participate actively in hostilities, punishable under article 8(2)(b)(xxvi) or article 8(2)(e)(vii) of the Statute; vi) sexual slavery as a crime against humanity, punishable under article 7(1)(g) of the Statute; vii) sexual slavery as a war crime, punishable under article 8(2)(b)(xxii) or article 8(2)(e)(vi) of the Statute; viii) the war crime of intentionally directing attacks against the civilian population as such or against individual civilians not taking direct part in hostilities, punishable under article 8(2)(b)(i) or article 8(2)(e)(i) of the Statute; ix) pillaging a town or place, even when taken by assault as a war crime, punishable under article 8(2)(b)(xvi) or article 8(2)(e)(v) of the Statute." *Mathieu Nagudjolo (*ICC-01/04-02/07), Situation in the Democratic Republic of the Congo, 6 July 2007, p.6.

Furthermore, the Pre-Trial Chamber may even go further in taking other reasonable measures concerning the protection of the evidence relating to the case. This may be with the permission of the remaining authorities in a state where its system of jurisdiction no longer fully functions. This role of the Pre-Trial Chamber will help in the prevention of further crimes, protect victims and guarantee that the accused does not escape from future prosecution and punishment.

7.1.2.3. Arrest Proceedings in the Custodial State

The procedure for the arrest of a person should always be based on legal measures and should not violate the system of human rights law. This is because certain provisions of international human rights law apply to persons who are suspected or accused of committing national or international crimes. These rights should also be respected in the custodial state which has received a request for a provisional arrest.

By the provisions of Article 59, a state party to the Statute of the ICC has a conventional obligation to take the necessary measures to arrest a person suspected of committing crimes under the jurisdiction of the Court. The arrest must be in accordance with its laws and the Statute.[101] The arrested person should immediately be brought before the competent juridical authority in the custodial state which shall determine, in accordance with the law of that State, that "(a) The warrant applies to that person; (b)The person has been arrested in accordance with the proper process; and (c) The person's rights have been respected."[102]

Furthermore, it is an integral right of a person who has been arrested to apply to the competent authority in the custodial State for provisional release pending surrender.[103] This provisional or interim release depends on the decisions of the authority of the custodial state in considering the circumstances and the gravity of the alleged crimes and the possible submission of the person to the Court.[104] In any event, the Pre-Trial Chamber should be notified of any measures concerning any application for interim release and may make, to this effect, a recommendation to the competent authority of the custodial state. In addition, the relevant authority should pay attention to the recommendations of the Pre-Trial Chamber and ensure that the person does not escape prosecution and punishment because of the interim release.[105]

---

[101] Article 59 (1).
[102] Article 59 (2).
[103] Article 59 (3).
[104] Article 59 (4).
[105] Article 59 (5).

In cases where the custodial state grants interim release, the Pre-Trial Chamber may ask for periodic reports on the status of the interim release.[106] The person may also be surrendered to the Court. This should, as soon as possible, be carried out by the custodial state.[107]

As is evident above, the purpose of the legislator here is to guarantee the proper arrest of a suspected person and prevent his/her fleeing by resorting to interim release. Simultaneously, the legislator aims to provide the measures necessary for the prevention of more violations and to surrender the accused person to the Court should the custodial state not be able to prosecute the accused.

It would have been more advisable if Article 59 of the Statute of the ICC had contained one more clear sub-section governing the basic rights of the accused within all its provisions. This would not only promote the rights of the accused but also the rights of the victims and the proper application of justice.[108]

Although, we do not deny that some of the provisions of Article 60 concerning the initial proceedings before the Court ensure certain rights of the accused, the inclusion of such a sub-section would decrease any possible violations of the basic rights of the accused. It may be for this reason that Article 60 of the Statute refers to the rights of the arrested person under the Statute, such as interim release, interim release with and without condition, and that a person should not be detained for an unreasonable period of time prior to trial due to an inexcusable delay by the prosecutor. At the same time, the Pre-Trial Chamber may issue a warrant of arrest in order to secure the presence of a person who has been released. Obviously, the legislator here has taken both sides of the situation into account and has tried to strike a balance between the rights of the accused and the rights of the international society concerning the demand for custody, arrest or detention and the basic rights of a person before criminal procedures.

It must be stated that the arrest of a person must be legal and any arrest that is carried out with prejudice is subject to compensation. Similarly, the conviction of a person based upon mistakes of fact and evidence is also subject to compensation. Therefore, any unlawful arrest or detention creates the right for the arrested, detained or convicted person to submit an application for compensation. In particular, when a person has been convicted and suffered punishment as a result of that conviction which is, in fact, a miscarriage of justice, he has, according to the law, a right to

[106] Article 59 (6).

[107] Article 59 (79).

[108] See below section on the rights of the accused.

compensation. However, it must be proved that he/she has not, in one way or another, participated in the commission of those acts that resulted in his/her conviction.[109] Furthermore, if the Court finds conclusive facts demonstrating that justice has been seriously violated, it may at its discretion award compensation.[110]

7.1.2.4. Confirmation of the Charges before Trial

Confirmation of the charges before the trial is another stage for the continuation of the procedure against the person who has been arrested, has surrendered or has appeared voluntarily before the ICC. The Pre-Trial Chamber is responsible for holding a hearing to confirm charges against the accused person in which the prosecutor may continue the trial. In order for a hearing to be correct, it has to be carried out in the presence of the prosecutor, the person charged and his/her counsel.[111]

One difficulty of the provisions governing the confirmation of the charges before the trial is that the Pre-Trial Chamber, on its own initiative or upon that of the prosecutor, can hold a hearing in the absence of the person charged to confirm the charges of the crimes within the jurisdiction of the Court on account of which the prosecutor has decided to seek trial. This confirmation of the charges in the absence of the relevant person may take place under two conditions. These are: a) when he/she has waived his/her right to be present, and b) when he/she has fled and cannot be found. In this case, all reasonable measures should have been taken in order to secure his/her appearance before the Court to face the charges and hearing.[112] Still, the Pre-Trial Chamber may be held in cases when his/her counsel presents the person.[113]

Some other measures which should be taken before the trial are that the prosecutor must within a reasonable amount of time inform the person of the charges against him and a copy of these charges must be submitted to him. The prosecutor is also responsible for informing the person of the evidence to which the prosecutor has decided to refer at the hearing.[114] This means that if a person is absent and is not present to confirm the charges, a copy of the document relating to the charges must be submitted to his/her counsel.

---

[109] Article 85 (2).
[110] Article 85 (3).
[111] Article 61 (1).
[112] Article 61 (2).
[113] Article 61 (2) (b).
[114] Article 61 (3).

The prosecutor may also before a hearing continue his/her investigation and amend the charges. He may even withdraw charges against the person. Any amendment or withdrawal should be reported to the Pre-Trial Chamber and also to the person who has been charged.[115] It is the duty of the prosecutor at the hearing to provide sufficient evidence relating to each charge.[116] At the same time, it is the right of the accused to object to the charges and challenge evidence presented against him/her and also to present evidence contrary to the prosecutor's statement.[117]

The Pre-Trial Chamber after the hearing may take various measures concerning the evidence presented by the prosecutor or the person accused of committing crimes under the jurisdiction of the Statute. It may decide that the evidence was not sufficient or confirm charges which establish that the evidence was sufficient. This means that there is the possibility of complete acceptance or rejection and acceptance or rejection of part of the charges. The prosecutor may even be requested to present further evidence. The Pre-Trial Chamber may even amend the charge because the evidence may imply the commission of different crimes within the jurisdiction of the Court.[118] The Pre-Trial Chamber's rejection of the charge against a defendant does not necessarily mean that the prosecutor cannot subsequently support the charge with additional evidence.[119]

The prosecutor may amend the charges after their confirmation but only with the permission of the Pre-trial Chamber and after notice to the accused. If more serious charges are presented, a hearing must again be established to that effect. The prosecutor may also withdraw the charges after the beginning of the trial but only with the permission of the Pre-Trial Chamber.[120] Any warrant previously issued will lose its legal validity and cease to have effect concerning the charges that have been withdrawn or have not been confirmed.[121] When, however, the charges are confirmed in line with the provisions of the Statute, the presidency shall constitute a Trial Chamber which shall be responsible for the conduct of subsequent proceedings.[122]

---

[115] Article 61 (4).
[116] Article 61 (5).
[117] Article 61 (6).
[118] Article 61 (7).
[119] Article 61 (8).
[120] Article 61 (9).
[121] Article 61 (9) and (10).
[122] Article 61 (11).

7.1.2.5. The Trial of the Accused

7.1.2.5.1. Basis of the Trial

The trial of the accused is a judicial examination of the case which has been investigated and submitted to a criminal court consisting of various judges who deliver their judgment of whether the accused is or is not guilty of violations of the prevailing criminal law. A trial is normally open to the public but only under certain conditions in order that the judges, jury, victims, witnesses and accused(s) can be protected from any actions against them. During the trial, the prosecutor defends the rights of the society and a counsel protects the rights of the accused. A considerable number of measures are normally taken in order to maintain a fair and just trial of the case.

The Statute of the ICC also takes many measures regarding the fair and lawful treatment of a case brought before its jurisdiction for examination and judgment. When the Pre-Trial Chamber confirms the charges before trial, the presidency shall be made up of three judges of the Trial Chamber. The provisions governing the trial are formulated into part 6 of the Statute. These provisions are, more or less, a combination of common law and civil law traditions that open a new door for the implementation of the jurisdiction of the Court over the accused.

The place of the trial is ordinarily the seat of the Court but it may also be held in other places.[123] The accused shall be present during the trial procedures, but if his/her presence disturbs the Court, other measures may be taken. Examples of such measures are reminding him/her that he/she should observe the rules of the trial and removing the accused from the courtroom.[124] In that case the Court instructs counsel outside the courtroom. This may be carried out by using communications technology if it is considered necessary. An important aspect here is that the "Trial Chamber shall ensure that a trial is fair and expeditious and is conducted with full respect for the rights of the accused and due regard for the protection of the victims and witnesses."[125] This means that the Trial Chamber is responsible for ensuring a fair trial for all the parties involved in the procedures of its jurisdiction. Depending on the provisions of its Statute, the trial may be held in public. The Trial Chamber may, under special circumstances, require that certain proceedings be in closed session in order to protect confidential or sensitive information.[126]

---

[123] Article 62.
[124] Article 63.
[125] Article 64 (2).
[126] Article 64 (7).

The Trial Chamber will determine the language used at the trial.[127] This does not, however, disregard the language of the accused. It is the right of the accused to be informed of the charges in a language he/she is capable of understanding.[128] This right is one of the integral rights of the accused and cannot be ignored by the Trial Chamber.

7.1.2.5.2. False Testimony

Obviously, evidence that is given to the Trial Chamber of the ICC should be true and should not be based on false information. This will interrupt the proceedings of a fair trial and cause enormous difficulties for it. For the purpose of prevention of any attempt at deceiving the trial, the legislators have taken certain measures governing offences against the administration of justice. Therefore, the Court has jurisdiction over the following offences when they are committed intentionally:

> (a)Giving false testimony when under an obligation pursuant to article 69, paragraph 1, to tell the truth;
> (b)Presenting evidence that the party knows is false or forged;
> (c)Corruptly influencing a witness, obstructing or interfering with the attendance or testimony of a witness, retaliating against a witness for giving testimony or destroying, tampering with or interfering with the collection of evidence;
> (d)Impeding, intimidating or corruptly influencing an official of the Court for the purpose of forcing or persuading the official not to perform, or to perform improperly, his/her duties;
> (e)Retaliating against an official of the Court on account of duties performed by that or another official;
> (f) Soliciting or accepting a bribe as an official of the Court in connection with his/her official duties.[129]

Further provisions protect the application of the above provisions. In any event, the Court may impose a term of imprisonment not exceeding five years, or a fine.[130] The state parties to the Statute are also responsible for supporting the relevant provisions and penalising offences against the integrity of their own criminal jurisdiction.[131] The purpose is to minimize any possibility of presenting false or corrupt information which may bring the administration of justice into disrepute.

---

[127] Article 64(3) (b).
[128] Article 67 (1) (a).
[129] Article 70 (1).
[130] Article 70 (3).
[131] Article 70 (4).

7.1.2.5.3. Guilty Pleas

One of the problems faced by the Court is the question of guilty pleas. The issue is whether the Court can succeed in procuring a guilty plea from the defendant. This means that he/she willingly accepts the conviction. The result is that the proceedings will be less complicated. This means also that the accused accepts his/her criminal responsibility for the commission of certain crimes. However, the problem is often that guilty pleas are extracted from the accused by resorting to different types of coercive measures or acts amounting to torture. Thus, the value of such guilty pleas will be reduced dramatically which also creates difficulty for the Court. A clear example of this occurred in the case of the *Drazen Erdemovic* case relating to crimes against humanity. The Appeals Chamber rejected the plea of guilt[132] which had been accepted by the Trial Chamber.[133] In other words, if a guilty plea is going to be accepted by the Court, it must be based on the fact that an accused pleaded guilty voluntarily and was fully aware of the character and nature of the charges. This means that the statement of the accused and his/her cooperation with the jurisdiction and judgment of the Court has a decisive function in the implementation of a lawful and fair trial. By the same token, the accused may not be able to realise the difference between categories of international crimes before accepting a plea of guilty or not guilty. He may confuse the reality of the situation under moral or physical duress arising from the order of superiors or other circumstances. To accept a guilty plea may not therefore be as easy as it may seem.

Even though we accept that the defendant's admission of his/her guilt is important, it is not always clear that such an admission has any legal value and this may also prevent the Court from taking additional procedures regarding criminal acts for the purpose of appropriate investigation. The guilty pleas may be asserted by the defendant in order not to reveal his/her other criminal activities and receive more penalties. Furthermore, the civil law countries do not put any essential weight on pleading. This is, however, contrary to common law traditions. Arguably, it is sometimes not important to find out if an accused pleads guilty or not from the beginning. This is because, if he/she accepts the commission of the crime, he/she naturally accepts his/her guilt. Again, if he/she does not accept the guilt, it means that he/she is not guilty unless the Court proves otherwise. This is because admission of the commission of a crime under the jurisdiction of the Court does not necessarily mean the end of the hearing. On the contrary, the Court is under a recognized obligation, by its

---

[132] Prosecutor v. Erdemovic (Case No.IT-96-22-A).

[133] Prosecutor v. Erdemovic (Case No.IT-96-22-T).

Statute, to investigate the case appropriately to find the true nature of the criminal conducts.[134] It should examine evidence or confessions in order to state the proper penalty. This process also opens up the possibility of examining the reliability of the plea of guilt by the accused. Thus, in the case of the admission of guilt, the Trial Chamber shall determine whether:

> (a) The accused understands the nature and consequences of the admission of guilt;
> (b) The admission is voluntarily made by the accused after sufficient consultation with defence counsel; and
> (c) The admission of guilt is supported by the facts of the case that are contained in:
> (i) The charges brought by the Prosecutor and admitted by the accused;
> (ii) Any materials presented by the Prosecutor which supplement the charges and which the accused accepts; and
> (iii) Any other evidence, such as the testimony of witnesses, presented by the Prosecutor or the accused.[135]

The Trial Chamber of the ICC may state that the presentation of the facts is not sufficient and therefore other facts must be presented.[136] The purpose of this provision is to secure the interests of justice, in particular, in the case of victims. Consequently, the Chamber may ask the prosecutor to present additional evidence, including the testimony of witnesses. The Chamber may also order that the trial be continued under the ordinary conditions of a trial and the admission of guilt may be considered not to have been made. These measures are to protect the interests of justice where the Trial Chamber sees that it is necessary to question the admission of guilt. In the case of the conviction of the accused, the Trial Chamber decides on an appropriate sentence. The decision of the Chamber should be based on the evidence presented.[137] The Trial Chamber may also, before deciding on the sentence, hold a further hearing on its own initiative, or

---

[134] Article 65 clearly states that "2. Where the Trial Chamber is satisfied that the matters referred to in paragraph 1 are established, it shall consider the admission of guilt, together with any additional evidence presented, as establishing all the essential facts that are required to prove the crime to which the admission of guilt relates, and may convict the accused of that crime. 3. Where the Trial Chamber is not satisfied that the matters referred to in paragraph 1 are established, it shall consider the admission of guilt as not having been made, in which case it shall order that the trial be continued under the ordinary trial procedures provided by this Statute and may remit the case to another Trial Chamber."

[135] Article 65 (1).

[136] Article 65 (4).

[137] Article 76 (1).

that of the prosecutor or the accused.[138] The sentence is to be pronounced in public and also in the presence of the accused.[139]

7.1.2.5.4. Value of Evidence

Evidence is constituted by documents, records, statements of witnesses, victims, or any other objects which are legally presented at a criminal trial in order to prove the guilt or lack of guilt of the accused. The prosecutor or the counsel may present evidence. Evidence presented in a criminal court must be correct and based on authentic documentation. This is one of the basic principles for the implementation of fair and equal justice. The reason for this is that the evidence should be presented to persuade the Court that there are facts which may, positively or negatively, change the judgment of the court against or in favour of the accused.

There are different types of evidence. One is direct evidence such as eyewitness accounts and the other is indirect evidence such as records and facts regarding the case.[140] The evidence must be legally obtained; illegally obtained evidence does not create any legal obligations for a criminal court. Thus, a court must examine the level, degree and the way in which the evidence is obtained and evidence which is not sufficient as proof or cannot convince the minds of the judges for particular reasons, may therefore lose its juridical effect.

The Charter of the Nuremberg Tribunal, the Statute of the ICTY and the ICTR have also dealt with the question of evidence and aim to protect the accused, the victims and justice by specifying appropriate standards of evidence. However, the most illustrative and progressive provisions may be seen in the Statute of the ICC which focuses on different aspects of evidence in order to create correct and fair justice. Article 69 of the Statute of the ICC refers to this important matter.

The Court may, pursuant to this article, take all measures that may be necessary for examining the relevance or admissibility of any evidence. For this purpose, it may look at the probative value of the evidence which may be prejudicial to the legal rights of the accused and a fair trial.[141] The Court is therefore, before each witness testifies, responsible for examining

---

[138] Article 76 (2).

[139] Article 76 (4).

[140] Direct or indirect evidence can also be divided into several other categories. These are for example documentary evidence, proof beyond any reasonable doubt, best evidence, oral evidence, written evidence, direct eyewitness account and individual evidence by indirect hearing.

[141] Article 69 (4).

the reliability of the evidence. This should, however, be in conformity with the Rules of Procedures and Evidence.[142]

The Court may ask for the submission of all evidence that may be necessary in order to find out the truth.[143] It may also receive the testimony of a witness by different methods such as *viva voce* (oral) and record testimony of a witness by means of video or audio technology.[144]

Evidence may also be collected and submitted by a state. In this case, however, the Court is not obliged to fulfil the application of the national law of the relevant state. Evidence provided in such a way is subject only to the provisions of the Statute.[145] The Court may therefore decide about the legal validity and the role of the evidence regarding the investigation of a case. In any event, the Court may neither ignore nor accept evidence without the necessary examination of their nature with due reference to the provisions of its Statute.

One chief aspect of the provisions of Article 69 of the Statute of the ICC concerns respect of the internationally recognised human rights law. Accordingly, evidence that is against the provisions of the Statute or international human rights law has no legal value and cannot therefore be used as proof of guilt. Thus, a violation may create substantial doubt regarding the value of the evidence and it may therefore not be reliable. Moreover, the admission of the evidence may damage the integrity of the proceedings.[146]

It must be stated that judges may take judicial notice of facts of common knowledge[147] and may also base their decision on the evidence submitted to the Court during the proceedings of the Trial.[148] However, the Court does not need to require proof of facts of common knowledge. The decisions of the judges must be in conformity with the principles of justice and if they are based on different evidence, the quality of the evidence must be beyond reproach. Of greatest importance here is that evidence has an influence on the judgment and therefore the following general principles must always be taken into serious consideration. These are:

Direct or indirect character
Relevancy

---

142 Article 69 (1).
143 Article 69 (3).
144 Article 69 (2).
145 Article 69 (8).
146 Article 69 (7).
147 Article 69 (6).
148 Article 69 (2).

Right evidence
Correct information
Lawfulness
Truthfulness
Impartiality
Wrongfulness
Inviolability of international law
Inviolability of international human rights
Inviolability of the Statute of the ICC
Conformability with the Rules of Procedures and Evidence
Conflicts with the principles of justice
Conflicts with the rights of the accused
Conflicts with the rights of victims
Conflicts with the rights of witnesses
Effects during the trial
Effects on the final judgment
Effects on the degree of punishment
Effects after the trial
Authenticityin the future

7.1.3. Rights of the Accused

7.1.3.1. The Basis

Discussions regarding the rights of the accused before criminal jurisdictions are rather new within the system of international criminal law. Although the tribunals in Nuremberg and Tokyo gave some weight to the rights of the Major War Criminals of the Second World War, the subject has been developed more efficiently after the establishment of the United Nations and has led to the adoption of a number of international human rights treaties or instruments dealing, in one way or another, with the rights of the accused before national or international criminal courts.[149]

---

[149] Modern international law has largely developed according to the principles of the protection of human beings from unnecessary, inhuman or unjustified suffering. This also includes judicial guarantees for persons who are accused of having committed national and international crimes. Documents applicable in international human rights law have largely guaranteed the protection of individuals, although the practice of states differs from their general purposes. In addition, the protection of an accused person constitutes one of the imperative principles of the international law of *jus cogens*. It is therefore a duty of states to take appropriate measures in order to be sure that certain principles of international human rights law are not violated within the decisions of their national organs. This conclusion is based on the contents of many documents of human rights law

Among these are the 1955 Standard Minimums Rules for the Treatment of Prisoners, the 1966 International Covenant on Civil and Political Rights, the 1988 Body of Principles for the Protection of All Persons under Any Form of Detention or Imprisonment, the 1990 Basic Principles for the Treatment of Prisoners, and the 1990 United Nations Rules for the Protection of Juveniles Deprived of their Liberty.

It is important to mention some of the most generally accepted conditions for the application of justice in case of the accused here.[150] These are:

i) The right of the accused to be informed of the charges against him.
ii) The right of the accused to remain silent.
iii) Respect for the rights of the accused at pre-indictment stages.
iv) Accused persons shall not be kept with convicted persons and shall be subjected to separate treatment as appropriate to their status according to international criminal rules.
v) Accused persons should not be discriminated against on account of sex.
vi) The treatment of accused persons should not depend on their former positions.
vii) Accused persons should not be deprived of sleep or rest.
viii) Primary living conditions must be available to accused persons.
ix) Under necessary supervision, accused persons shall be allowed to have contact with their family and friends at regular intervals, both by correspondence and in person. Further, accused persons have the right to read books and newspapers.
x) Accused persons should not be kept in a place that is harmful to their health.
xi) The health conditions of accused persons should be respected at all times.
xii) Based on an official certificate from a legitimate doctor, an accused person has a legal right to medical treatment.
xiii) The right to food should not be ignored.

---

and international criminal law constituting an integral part of international legal order. A very early example is the Charter of the International Military Tribunal in Nuremberg which aimed at the protection of the rights of the accused before the Tribunal. These rights were limited solely to particular rights within the provisions of Article 16 of the Nuremberg Charter. Judicial guarantees can also be examined in the content of Article 14 of the International Covenant on Civil and Political Rights of 1966, Articles 6 and 7 of the European Convention on Human Rights of 1950, Articles 5 and 7 and of the American Convention on Human Rights of 1969, Article 7 of the African Charter on Human and People's Rights of 1981, Article 3 common to the four Geneva Conventions of 1949 and Articles 6 and 75 of the 1977 Additional Protocols to the Geneva Conventions of 1949.

[150] Farhad Malekian, *Emasculating the Philosophy of International Criminal Justice in the Iraqi Special Tribunal*, pp.711-713. Footnotes omitted.

xiv) All those who are dealing with the accused persons during a criminal tribunal should be wholly impartial toward the accused person's political, juridical, economic, social, cultural, religious, and theoretical beliefs.
xv) The rights of the accused should not be interrupted or disregarded during the proceedings due to certain judicial expediencies.
xvi) An accused person has a legal right to be informed immediately of the charges against him, and the grounds for such charges, in a language that he understands.
xvii) The accused person has a legal right to adequate facilities and time for the preparation of his defense.
xviii) The accused person has a legal right to the assistance of legal counsel.
xix) The accused person has a legal right not to testify during the proceedings.
xx) The accused person has a legal right to a fair proceeding and a public hearing within a reasonable period of time.
xxi) The accused person has a right to public hearings when brought before a criminal court.This right is granted by international norms governing the protection of human rights.The right is based on the theory that if a tribunal wants to ensure fairness, it has to hold primarily open and public hearings, including publicly pronounced judgments.
xxii) An accused person is presumed innocent until proven otherwise.
xxiii) The accused person has the right to be present when the trial begins.
xxiv) No political officials should overlook the rights of the accused during the proceedings of the tribunal.
xv) The accused person has a legal right to defend himself in person or through any other judicial assistance in accordance with his own choice.
xxvi) Since the understanding of certain international criminal law terms may be difficult, the accused person should have access to a free interpreter.
xxvii) The accused person has the right to examine witnesses. In certain extraordinary circumstances, the witness may be examined under oath prior to the tribunal hearings, upon authorization by the tribunal or judges of the tribunal.
xxviii) The accused should not be convicted for an act or omission that was not a crime at the time it was committed or omitted according to the provisions of national law or international criminal law.
xxix) Confessions obtained through coercion do not have legal or juridical validity in the proceeding of a criminal tribunal. This principle has an important place within conventional international criminal law.
xxx) The threat or use of degrading and humiliating treatment against accused persons or their families for the purpose of extracting evidence should not be admissible in a fair and just proceeding of a national or international criminal court.
xxxi) The accused person has a right to appeal. It is very doubtful in the case of the Iraqi Special Tribunal that this principle can be workable from a procedural point of view. In the international criminal tribunals, an appeal is heard by the Appeals Chamber of the tribunal.

xxxii) Capital punishment is prohibited. This principle has been established in customary international criminal law and has been utilized by the international criminal tribunals.

Provisions similar to those of the above may also be found within the growing body of international criminal law, since the creation of the ICTY, the ICTR and the ICC. The Statute of the ICC has therefore clearly stated that everyone is innocent until proved guilty before the Court. Thus, it is the responsibility of the prosecutor to prove the guilt of the accused before the Court. However, statements by the prosecutor concerning the criminality of the accused do not, by themselves, prove his/her culpability unless the Court is convinced of the guilt of the accused beyond reasonable doubt.[151] This means that the presumption of the innocence of the accused must, during the procedures of the prosecution, be regarded as a principle of fair justice. It is the judgment of the Court which determines the conviction of the accused and not the procedures. As long as the Court has not reached this conclusion, the accused must be presumed innocent. This is regardless of his/her social or economic position including his/her rank as a subordinate, superior or commander.

7.1.3.2. Minimum Guarantees

Article 67 of the Statute of the ICC governs the rights of the accused before the Court. According to it, the accused has a legal right to a fair and public hearing. The hearing must be conducted impartially. Some of the minimum guarantees set out by the article are the following:

(a) To be informed promptly and in detail of the nature, cause and content of the charge, in a language which the accused fully understands and speaks;
(b) To have adequate time and facilities for the preparation of the defence and to communicate freely with counsel of the accused's choosing in confidence;
(c) To be tried without undue delay;
(d) Subject to article 63, paragraph 2, to be present at the trial, to conduct the defence in person or through legal assistance of the accused's choosing, to be informed, if the accused does not have legal assistance, of this right and to have legal assistance assigned by the Court in any case where the interests of justice so require, and without payment if the accused lacks sufficient means to pay for it;
(e) To examine, or have examined, the witnesses against him or her and to obtain the attendance and examination of witnesses on his or her behalf under the same conditions as witnesses against him or her. The accused

[151] Article 66.

> shall also be entitled to raise defences and to present other evidence admissible under this Statute;
> (f) To have, free of any cost, the assistance of a competent interpreter and such translations as are necessary to meet the requirements of fairness, if any of the proceedings of or documents presented to the Court are not in a language which the accused fully understands and speaks;
> (g) Not to be compelled to testify or to confess guilt and to remain silent, without such silence being a consideration in the determination of guilt or innocence;
> (h) To make an unsworn oral or written statement in his or her defence; and
> (i) Not to have imposed on him or her any reversal of the burden of proof or any onus of rebuttal.

The prosecutor is also responsible, whenever it is deemed necessary, for informing the authorities about evidence which may prove the innocence of the defendant or mitigate the charges against him/her. Obviously, the prosecutor must not just base his/her application against the accused on information already submitted by him/her to the Court. This is because information may continuously come into his/her office and it may be so significant that it proves the complete innocence of the accused before the Court. According to the Statute, the new information must immediately be submitted to the Court so that it can decide about the matter.

In any event, it is obvious that the rights of the defendant must be respected by the Court and procedures should be in conformity with the principles of international human rights law.[152] Reference to and the

---

[152] In particular, Article 14 of the Covenant on Civil and Political Rights emphasises the importance of the rights of the accused before criminal jurisdictions. It reads that:

"1. All persons shall be equal before the courts and tribunals. In the determination of any criminal charge against him, or of his rights and obligations in a suit at law, everyone shall be entitled to a fair and public hearing by a competent, independent and impartial tribunal established by law. The press and the public may be excluded from all or part of a trial for reasons of morals, public order (ordre public) or national security in a democratic society, or when the interest of the private lives of the parties so requires, or to the extent strictly necessary in the opinion of the court in special circumstances where publicity would prejudice the interests of justice; but any judgement rendered in a criminal case or in a suit at law shall be made public except where the interest of juvenile persons otherwise requires or the proceedings concern matrimonial disputes or the guardianship of children.

2. Everyone charged with a criminal offence shall have the right to be presumed innocent until proved guilty according to law.

3. In the determination of any criminal charge against him, everyone shall be entitled to the following minimum guarantees, in full equality:

respect of human rights' principles and the dignity of man are clearly stated in the Statute.[153] This means that the application and interpretation of the Statute shall be in conformity with contemporary international law and without regard to distinctions of age, race, colour, language, religion or belief, political or other opinion, national, ethnic or social origin, wealth, birth or other status. The purpose of the legislator is to guarantee the equal application of rights and obligations and to create substantive justice based on the rules of law and international order.

7.1.3.3. Difficulty of Implementation

The legislator of the Statute of the ICC intends to protect the most fundamental rights of man at each stage of the investigations concerning the crime, accused, criminal, victim and witness. These protections should

---

(a) To be informed promptly and in detail in a language which he understands of the nature and cause of the charge against him;
(b) To have adequate time and facilities for the preparation of his defence and to communicate with counsel of his own choosing;
(c) To be tried without undue delay;
(d) To be tried in his presence, and to defend himself in person or through legal assistance of his own choosing; to be informed, if he does not have legal assistance, of this right; and to have legal assistance assigned to him, in any case where the interests of justice so require, and without payment by him in any such case if he does not have sufficient means to pay for it;
(e) To examine, or have examined, the witnesses against him and to obtain the attendance and examination of witnesses on his behalf under the same conditions as witnesses against him;
(f) To have the free assistance of an interpreter if he cannot understand or speak the language used in court;
(g) Not to be compelled to testify against himself or to confess guilt.
4. In the case of juvenile persons, the procedure shall be such as will take account of their age and the desirability of promoting their rehabilitation.
5. Everyone convicted of a crime shall have the right to his conviction and sentence being reviewed by a higher tribunal according to law.
6. When a person has by a final decision been convicted of a criminal offence and when subsequently his conviction has been reversed or he has been pardoned on the ground that a new or newly discovered fact shows conclusively that there has been a miscarriage of justice, the person who has suffered punishment as a result of such conviction shall be compensated according to law, unless it is proved that the non-disclosure of the unknown fact in time is wholly or partly attributable to him.
7. No one shall be liable to be tried or punished again for an offence for which he has already been finally convicted or acquitted in accordance with the law and penal procedure of each country."

[153] Article 21 (3).

not only be available before the start of the work of the Court but also during the trial. It is thus the right of the defendant or accused to challenge the jurisdiction of the Court or the admissibility of a case.[154] Consequently, according to the provisions of the Statute, the charges against the accused are not definite and may be questioned by the accused and his/her counsel, the final stage of which may free the accused from all accusations without any further investigation. This may even make the ICC responsible for incorrect charges against the integrity of the defendant.[155] However, it must be asserted that there is no specific provision or remedy protecting the accused's violated rights.

Whilst the Statute of the ICC has, in a considerable number of articles, protected the rights of the accused during the procedures of the Court, these rights may or may not be fundamental. This is because the power behind the implementation of the rights depends on the conditions and ability of the accused to use those rights. The rights listed in the Statute are not given as a gift to the defendant but as a right to be used. And, since the use of these rights may depend on the political and economic ability of the accused, the implementation of the rights may be difficult. In other words, finding a person guilty or not guilty is institutionalised under the provisions of the Statute, but receiving counsel is limited to the economic conditions of the accused.[156] Moreover, there is a difference between the ability of counsels to defend their clients. If the accused has a considerable number of politically or culturally influential friends in his home state(s) on account of his/her political situation, then well-known international lawyers supported by his home state, may easily be assigned to defend him. On the other hand, an accused, whose country has already lost juridical and political power, may, for various reasons, not be able to defend himself/herself.

One may therefore wonder why the legislators of the Statute have not established a "public defenders' office". Although the Office of Public Counsel has recently been established for the defence in order to ensure

---

[154] Article 19 (2) (a).

[155] This is found in Article 85 relating to compensation for an arrested or convicted person.

[156] Although we do not deny that the Court may give assistance to the accused if he/she is not capable of supporting the costs, the implementation of justice will here be very difficult since the accused may choose his counsel on certain recommendations depending on the economic conditions accessible to the Court. The scope of justice may here be limited to the conditions offered by the Court, rather than being determined by the condition and gravity of the crime and accusation.

"the equality of arms", the right to a fair trial and the rights of the defence, this is not yet a "public defenders' office." How then may human rights' norms be protected for all individuals accused of committing serious international crimes? International criminal justice has to guarantee the full application of international human rights law. This can, however, not be done as a set of rights to be used with regard to the political or economic conditions of the accused, but rather in accordance with the basic theory that all human beings possess the same integrity and should be respected as part of the obligations of international criminal justice. The value of the Court should be based on the respect of human beings without any regard for superficial values.

7.1.4. Protection of Victims and Witnesses

One of the most important achievements of the newly established international criminal courts is their strong commitment to protect victims and witnesses of international criminal violations. In fact, both predecessors of the ICC have certain rules governing the protection of the victims and witnesses of armed conflicts. These rules make it possible for the relevant tribunals to protect the victims or witnesses who may appear in the procedures of the tribunals in order to confirm or reject certain information. The aims of the relevant provisions protecting victims and witnesses therefore overlap one another. Firstly, they aim to protect the subject of jurisdiction. Secondly, the evidence should be confirmed or reconfirmed by eye witnesses. Thirdly, the aim is to create an equal implementation of the principles of international criminal law based on justice and respect. The work of the ICTY and the ICTR proves how important their roles are concerning the above matters. However, one cannot deny that the protection of the identity of the witnesses has been very difficult and problematic. It has been very expensive to create a safe locality and transporting and keeping the witnesses in a secure social position has been very complicated.

Despite the existence of certain practical problems for the protection of victims and witnesses, the Statute of the ICC has correctly put heavy weight on the protection of these valuable subjects of criminal proceedings. Article 68 deals with this matter. The Court is responsible for taking certain measures for the protection of the victims and witnesses. These measures may concern:

- safety
- physical and psychological well-being,
- dignity and privacy of victims and witnesses,

- factors like age, gender and health,
- the nature of the crime and risk for victims and witnesses,
- gender violence,
- crimes against children,
- security during investigation and prosecution,
- proceeding s*in camera* when necessary,
- presentation of evidence by electronic or other special means,
- victims of sexual violence,
- child victims or witnesses of sexual violence,
- expressing their views as long as this does not prejudice the rights of the accused and a fair trial,
- security arrangements based on the advice of the Victims and Witnesses Unit,
- counselling and assistance based on the advice of Victims and Witnesses Unit,
- protecting the victims and witnesses by a summary of the evidence when there is grave danger for the security of their lives and families. This should not be inconsistent with the rights of the accused to an impartial and fair trial,
- protection of servants or agents of the ICC in order to protect sensitive or confidential information.

The above list presents some of the most important measures, which must be taken by the Court to protect victims and witnesses against any antagonism or danger. Although the provisions above aim to protect the relevant subjects of criminal proceedings, it is still very difficult to guarantee that the life of victims and witnesses will not be endangered by the procedures of the Court. It has been proved that the protection of certain persons who are either victims or witnesses or both at the same time has been very difficult and problematic for the international courts.[157]

When a person appears as a victim or witness, there are always certain risks to his/her own and life and that of his/her family that cannot be avoided, even by the formulation and adoption of rules and provisions. In particular, the situation is more tangible and sensitive in the case of a person who appears as both a victim and a witness. He/she may not have the courage to appear in the Court and may also be humiliated and abused by the accused in the case of his/her participation. This occurred during the proceedings of the ICTY in the prosecution of the Serbian president Milosevic, despite the existence of a number of international instruments

[157] M. Cherif Bassiouni, International Recognition of Victims' Rights, 6(2) Human Rights Law Reviews (2006), 203-279; doi:10.1093/hrlr/ngl009.

for the protection of victims or witnesses.[158] It seems that, at the beginning of his trial, Ex-Bosnian Serb army head, Ratko Mladic, is following similar habits to Milosevic.[159]

The effect of the regulations of the Statute governing the protection of victims and witnesses will be seen in the near future when they are implemented in the proceedings of the ICC.

In any event, the Court has a duty to establish principles relating to the compensation of victims. These may include restitution, compensation and rehabilitation. The Court may also determine the scope and extent of any damage.[160] Furthermore, the rights of victims to damages may not be prejudiced under the provisions of the Statute. Naturally, the Court is responsible for violations of the victim's rights during the proceedings of the trial.

7.1.5. Requirements for the Decision

Decisions taken by the ICC must be correct and must be based on authentic information, evidence and rightful proceedings. A decision of the Court, which goes against the provisions of the Statute, does not have any legally-binding force. The Statute therefore has set out certain requirements so that the Court can make a just and right decision. These are dealt with under the provisions of Article 74.

7.1.5.1. Presence of Judges

One important requirement concerns the judges of the Trial Chamber.[161] All judges are obliged to be present at each stage of the trial. For this reason the presidency may, on a case-by-case basis, depending on the availability of the judges, designate a new member for the Trial if one of the earlier members is not able to attend one of the stages of the trial. Thus, the Trial Chamber cannot continue its work when one of its members is absent. This is because a decision of the Trial Chamber depends on its judges, and the absence of one of the judges of the Court decreases the value of the proceedings.

---

[158] Two of the most well-known of these instruments are the 1985 Declaration of Basic Principles of Justice for Victims of Crime and Abuse of Power and the 2006 Basic Principles and Guidelines on the Right to a Remedy and Reparation for Victims of Gross Violations of International Human Rights Law and Serious Violations of International Humanitarian Law.

[159] www.bbc.co.uk/news/world-europe-14012057.

[160] Article 75.

[161] Article 74 (1).

7.1.5.2. The Basis of Decisions

Another significant requirement of the decision of the Trial Chamber of the ICC is based, not only on the evaluation of evidence, but also, on the entire proceedings.[162] This means that the evidence presented during the proceedings of the Court has a very decisive function in the decision of the judges and, therefore, as we have stated elsewhere, must be correct and authentic. Furthermore, the Court decision has to be based on submitted evidence which has been discussed at the trial. It is considered a source for the final judgment.

However, a decision of the Court must examine the entire proceedings and not be based on an isolated proceeding. The reason for this is that the Court has to assess the effect of the whole proceedings and analyse these proceedings both separately and jointly in order to reach a correct judgement. Therefore, the decision of the Court must correspond to the facts and circumstances described in the charges and any amendment to them. The Court is thus obliged to examine even its own outcome and not to prejudice its judgement on any evidence or provision regarding the case which is not wholly clear. The decision of a court is supposed to be fair and just, especially when it deals with core international crimes. Legal validity, the origins of the decision, and values of its conclusions are crucial for the framework of international criminal justice.

7.1.5.3. Unanimity

Another important requirement is the principle of unanimity. This principle supports the judgment regarding the case, so that it is not divided into several opinions. Therefore, the Statute encourages the judges to achieve unanimity in their relevant decision, unless it is taken by a majority of the judges.[163] As an accepted principle of jurisdiction, the deliberation of a trial has to remain secret.[164] This principle has to be followed by the Trial Chamber of the ICC. The decision of the Trial Chamber must be in writing. It should contain full justifications and the statement of the Trial Chamber's findings on the evidence and conclusions. If a decision presents a majority opinion concerning the case, the minority opinion must also be presented. Finally, the decision or a summary of it may be expressed in open court.[165] Normally, anyone may attend an open court.

---

[162] Article 74 (2).
[163] Article 74 (3).
[164] Article 74 (4).
[165] Article 74 (4).

7.1.5.4. Imperative Pillars

The provisions presented in the above three sections demonstrate some imperative pillars of the Court's proceedings. These are: a) the presence of the judges, b) the pure value of evidence, c) the value of each proceeding, d) the integrated value of the entire proceedings, e) the limitation of a decision on the charges, f) the principle of unanimity, g) the reasons for the majority decision, h) the reasons for the minority decision(s), i) the principle of secret deliberation, and j) the delivering of the decision in an open court.

7.1.6. Appeal and Revision

The contemporary system of international criminal justice has opened up new possibilities for the proper enforcement of justice and the prohibition of any misuse of its machinery. This has been particularly developed since the establishment of several international criminal courts. They provide certain provisions containing rights for those who, for one reason or another, have come under the procedures of international criminal jurisdiction. Two of the most powerful rights that have been created under the constitution of the courts, are the right to appeal and the right to revision.

The right to appeal gives the accused or convicted person the possibility of protecting his/her integrity against humiliation or being forced to do what he/she never would have gone through had the proceedings of the jurisdiction been based on correct evidence. Consequently, if a case turns out to be different, the decisions also have to be modified and there must be a revision of judgment or sentence. This will definitely help to fulfil the principles of human rights law and to improve the efficiency of the international criminal justice system.

7.1.6.1. Appeal against Judgement

The right to appeal against the decision of a court constitutes, today, one of the cornerstones of jurisdiction, impartiality and justice. This right was not recognised in the earlier history of international criminal jurisdiction. It was explicitly rejected and was thus not included in the Charters of the Nuremberg and Tokyo Tribunals. Thus, the defendants of the tribunals did not have any right to appeal against the decisions taken by the tribunals or to ask for further examination of the judgments. The European Court of Justice has also ignored the right of appeal. However, the creation of the European Court of First Instance has modified the non-existence of this right in some cases.

The right to appeal has been explicitly written into the Statutes of the ICTY and the ICTR which have the character of *ad hoc* tribunals. The grounds for an appeal against the decision of a criminal court include cases where the court might have treated the case incorrectly and not been impartial in its final judgment. There may also be cases where an error in the trial proceedings emerges, which is of fundamental importance for the implementation of or revision of the judgement. Consequently, an appeal may sometimes succeed in proving that something went wrong.

The Statute of the ICC has also adopted several provisions concerning the right to appeal.[166] Part 8 of the Statute concerns the matters of appeal and revision. According to this part, the right to appeal should be in conformity with the Rules of Procedure and Evidence. Various persons may make an appeal. This is normally a written paper, although other forms of appeal may be considered as an introduction to the written appeal. This means that an appeal may be a signed statement by various persons having the right of appeal. In any event, an appeal must fulfil the requirements of the procedures of the Court.

The prosecutor is one of those who may make an appeal. The reasons may be i) procedural error, ii) error of fact, or iii) error of law.[167] Although, the use of the above alternatives may be seen as one of the principles for the implementation of fair justice, their use may also go against the rights of the accused in specific situations. Consequently, the prosecutor must be very cautious concerning the use of these rights in order not to violate the fundamental principles of human rights law. The use of these rights without strong justification may place the defendant in double jeopardy because of the proceedings of jurisdiction. Yet, it is true that appeals against acquittals are accepted under civil law systems.

The convicted person may alone or together with the prosecutor make an appeal based on the above three errors or any other reason that has affected fair proceedings or decisions.[168] This means that the Appeals Chamber has an effective function in the implementation of a fair and rightful jurisdiction. It also makes it clear that the Trial Chamber must be very careful when examining evidence and establishing its real value. In other words, one of the leading functions of the Appeals Chamber is to examine and hear the opinions of the parties concerning errors that have materially affected the outcome of the Court.

---

[166] The proceedings of appeal suggest that the Appeals Chamber should have all the powers of the Trial-Chamber. Article 83.

[167] Article 81 (1)

[168] Article 81 (1).

7.1.6.2. Appeal against Decision of Punishment

The Statute of the ICC has also foreseen a situation which may cause the revision of a sentence. Therefore, a sentence may be appealed by the prosecutor or convicted person.[169] The Court is responsible for examining the case and if it finds that there is sufficient evidence to believe that the crime has not been committed by the accused or convicted person, it may bring the case into its proceedings for the mitigation of the sentence or release of the convicted person. Thus, a sentence may be revised wholly because of the circumstances of evidence or because the punishment does not fit the nature of the crime. In such cases the Court may invite the prosecutor and the convicted person to submit grounds. Thenceforth, the Appeals Chamber has all the powers of the Trial Chamber.[170]

In the case of an acquittal, the accused may be released but only under certain conditions.[171] The execution of the decision or sentence has to be suspended if the time for appeal has not ended. Similarly, if an appeal is accepted, the sentence cannot be implemented during the time of appeal.[172] This provision of the Statute aims to guarantee the possibility of mitigation or release from imprisonment if the accused has not committed the given crime.

7.1.6.3. Appeal against Other Decisions

According to the Statute of the ICC, either party has the right to appeal against other decisions as necessary. This is in order to give an opportunity to every party to give his/her reasons and express his/her views before any additional procedure begins. Thus, either party may appeal against a decision with respect to jurisdiction or admissibility, granting or denying the release of the person being investigated or prosecuted.[173] According to the relevant provisions, either party may appeal by leave of the Court against a decision that involves "an issue that would significantly affect the fair and expeditious conduct of the proceedings or the outcome of the trial, and for which, in the opinion of the Pre-Trial or Trial Chamber, an immediate resolution by the Appeals Chamber may materially advance the proceedings."[174]

A state concerned or a prosecutor may appeal against a decision of the Pre-Trial Chamber due to Article 57 (3,d). Such an appeal has to be heard

---

[169] Article 81 (2).
[170] Article 82 (1).
[171] Article 81 (3) (c).
[172] Article 81 (4).
[173] Article 82(1) (a, b, c).
[174] Article 82 (1) (d).

on an expedited basis.[175] Yet, an appeal may also be made by the legal representatives of the victims, the convicted person or a bona fide owner of property affected by an order. This appeal may be for the purpose of compensation.[176]

Generally, different appeals may be made against a decision. Obviously, the appeals must correspond to the relevant provisions of the Statute and should demonstrate the existence of a sufficient amount of information giving rise to the question of appeal. This information must strongly suggest a serious question concerning the case that has either not previously been dealt with or not dealt with correctly. This means that the appeal should be based on fundamental reasons and it should provide sufficient grounds for the ICC to consider them in the light of its Statute.

7.1.6.4. Revision of Conviction or Sentence

Appeal before the Appeals Chamber of the ICC may partly or wholly change the sentence. This may occur because of certain circumstances and new items of evidence that are effective in the decision of the Appeals Chamber. Thus, the accused or convicted person or his/her relatives may bring a claim before the Appeals Chamber in order to change the sentence. Thus, a person who has been given written permission may bring a claim before the Appeals Chamber in order to have the judgment of conviction or sentence revised. The prosecutor may also receive certain permissions. An appeal may be based on the fact that new proof has been found which was not available at the time of the trial. The evidence must be sufficient to prove that it would have been likely to result in a different verdict. Furthermore, it may prove that important evidence previously heard was false or had been forgotten by the time the final decision of the Court was taken.[177]

In some circumstances, a sentence or conviction may be revised on the basis of an act of serious misconduct or a breach on the part of one or more judges. The actions of the judges must be so serious, that this may lead to their removal under the provisions of the Statute.[178]

In all the above circumstances, it is the Appeals Chamber which has the legal authority to decide regarding the matter and whether to pass a new trial.[179]

---

[175] Article 82 (2).
[176] Article 82 (4).
[177] Article 84 (1)
[178] Article 84 (1) (c).
[179] Article 84 (2).

7.1.7. Cooperation and Judicial Assistance

One of the more notable parts of the Statute of the ICC is Part 9 relating to international cooperation and judicial assistance between states parties. This part also constitutes one of the most complicated parts of the ICC. It aims to channel the law of different states into practical actions in order to implement the principles of the Statute over crimes committed under the jurisdiction of the Court. According to the introduction to this part, states are strongly encouraged to cooperate fully with the ICC for the prosecution and punishment of those individuals accused or convicted of serious violations of international criminal law.[180]

Generally speaking, Part 9 has two conditions for the implementation of the provisions of the Statute. These are to obtain sufficient cooperation from the states parties in order to arrest the suspected persons and to ensure states parties cooperate with the ICC in order to gather information and evidence relating to the crimes committed.

Thus, states parties are under conventional obligations for the arrest and surrender of a person. This means that if a state party receives a request for the arrest from the Court, it is responsible for handing over the relevant person to the Court.[181] The person may fall into one of the following juridical categories. These are a suspected, an accused or a convicted person. This obligation is binding only on a state party and therefore a non-party to the Statute is not under any obligation to respect such a request.[182]

In the case of a request for the arrest and surrender of a person, the Court may also askfor any material supporting the case to be delivered. According to the Statute, the states parties shall comply with requests for arrest and surrender.[183] However, this is based on the conditions of their national law systems which may make the proper application of Part 9 very difficult. This is because the term "procedure under their national law" which is included in the structure of the Statute may cause problems for its appropriate application.[184] Basing its argument on one reason or another, a state may refuse to help the authorities of the Court in this matter. Furthermore, the arrest of a person depends also on the gravity of

---

[180] Article 86.

[181] This is, however, only if the state does not want to prosecute the relevant person. Thus, all actions of the Court may be based on the principle of complementarity.

[182] Article 87.

[183] Article 89.

[184] Article 89 (1).

his/her crime and whether or not the parties are willing to submit that person to the jurisdiction of the Court. A party may not be ready to fulfil the request of the Court because of the circumstances at the time and because other persons, who may still be the leading authorities within the state, are involved in the criminal behaviour. The party may also not therefore submit all information to the Court. As a result, prosecution of the accused varies according to the decision of each individual state which is a member of the Court. The state may take the view that it is going to prosecute the accused in the very near future. This means that the complementarity principle does not function properly here either.

The cooperation and assistance of a state in other matters is also a significant aspect of Part 9. It encourages the states parties to collect and take into account all information relevant to the commission of the crime that may be helpful for proving guilt. This includes any document which may be relevant in the case requested by the Court. The Court may also transmit requests for cooperation through any regional organisation deemed appropriate. It may also be addressed to the International Criminal Police Organization.[185] The state is also under a conventional obligation to keep a request for cooperation confidential.[186]

The Court may take measures as demanded by the circumstances relating to the protection of information in order to ensure the safety or physical or psychological well-being of persons concerned in the case. This includes any victims, as well as potential witnesses and their families

---

[185] Article 87 (1). The Court may also ask other any organisation to cooperate with it. Article 87 (6).

[186] Article 87 (3). Although the purpose of the legislation is understandable here, this provision is also subject to debate. This is because the question of confidentiality varies from case to case depending on the policy of the administration of justice and the relationship of police authorities. In some states, the police authorities and the administration of justice are very corrupt and it may be extremely difficult to fulfil the requirements of the relevant article. Moreover, if the friends and the supporters of the accused work in the responsible departments, confidentiality may be difficult to achieve. In addition to this, it has been proved that it is almost impossible to be sure that the subordinates and superiors, who were active under the machinery of the accused, do not any longer work and cooperate with the accused. If the accused has lost his/her power, this may not necessarily mean that all his/her associates are without strong social positions. For instance, after almost thirty years, one may find a large number of persons who are still loyal to the last Iranian shah. The same position will be created when the present regime of Iran has lost its entire political and juridical power. Its administration is so corrupt that it may even function if the regime falls.

who, by one means or another, may be affected by the request of the Court.[187]

The Court may also make a temporary arrangement with a state which is not a party to the Statute in order to receive its assistance for the case.[188] The state that has temporarily entered into an arrangement with the Court has to comply with the provisions of the arrangement, *pacta sunt servanda*. Non-compliance with the provisions of the arrangement by the relevant state may be reported to the Assembly of States Parties. In situations when the investigation of a crime is referred by the Security Council to the Court, the Security Council may be informed about the failure of the relevant state to respect the arrangement.[189] Likewise, a state which is a permanent party to the Statute has, as specified above, a duty to comply with the Court.[190] This is regardless of whether the request is directly referred by the Court or to the Court by the Security Council.[191]

It must be emphasised that, in most situations relating to such a request, the Court has to take into account the Rules of Procedure and Evidence in order to obtain information and other relevant matters. It is

---

[187] Article 87 (4).

[188] Article 87 (5).

[189] Article 87 (5). It is extremely difficult to understand the policy of the Statute concerning the arrangement and the Security Council's function. This is because, by the provisions of the Charter, members of the United Nations are under conventional obligations to respect the important decisions of the Security Council regardless of their other conventional obligations. This means that any state, entity or organisation may report to the Security Council concerning the failure of the relevant state to fulfil its obligations concerning an arrangement. In other words, if the Council has already decided to force a state to fulfil its obligations under the Charter, the Security Council does not need to refer to any international arrangement. This means that, the duty to comply with the provisions of the Statute may be seen as an integral part of a state's duty under the provisions of the Charter due to certain conditions which may be necessary for maintaining international peace, security and justice. Any obligation under any statute, convention or arrangement may be interpreted as an integral part of breach of the peace, threat to peace and acts of aggression, if the permanent members of the Security Council are of that view. The Security Council may even order a state to arrest and surrender a person without regard to whether the state has or has not temporarily entered into any arrangement with the Court.

[190] Here it seems that the Security Council has great control over certain matters of the Court. This is regardless of the negative participation of the United States in the ratification of the Statute. In other words, the United States, because of its position in the Security Council, has certain opinions concerning the policy and interpretation of the Statute.

[191] Article 87 (7).

also a duty of a state party to the Statute to ensure that there are procedures available under their national legal systems for cooperation as set out by the requirements of Part 9 of the Statute.[192]

7.1.7.1. The Scope of Surrender

7.1.7.1.1. Terminology

Juridically, different means may be used in order to bring a suspected, accused or convicted person within the jurisdiction of the Court. These terms may be capture, yield, seizure, detention, arrest, surrender, expulsion, and extradition.[193] Each of these terms denote by one means or

---

[192] Article 88.

[193] Extradition means the surrender of a person accused or convicted of a crime by one state to another for the purpose of prosecution and punishment or to fulfil a criminal procedure in the requesting state. Extradition in international criminal law constitutes an important institution. The subject of extradition has developed mainly from the criminal proceedings of domestic criminal law and has played an important part in the prosecution of those who previously escaped punishment and also those who have not yet been brought before a criminal jurisdiction. It is on this basis that the extradition of convicted criminals and accused persons has been broadly treated by a number of conventions which deal exclusively with their legal or political status. Extradition of criminals is essentially based on conventional provisions and there are a large number of international conventions applicable to this important area of international criminal law. Although cooperation for extradition has been widely exercised between states, extradition has mostly been granted for the trial of ordinary criminals and the granting of political extradition is rare. This means that the institution of extradition has traditionally been based on the extradition of those who have no political position under international criminal law.

The most controversial part of the institution of extradition concerns the extradition of political criminals and mostly applies to persons accused of having committed transnational or international crimes but who have, for one reason or another, escaped prosecution and punishment under an appropriate criminal jurisdiction. This controversial part of the law of international extradition becomes more complicated when one examines the question of refugees who cannot be surrendered to the country of prosecution due to the provisions of the 1951 Convention on the Status of Refugees (189 UNTS 137). Although it is true that a state may request the extradition of a person on the basis that he has committed international crimes within its territory, the reasons for extradition and prosecution must be clear and should not violate the fundamental principles of international human rights law. This means that the prosecution of the accused in the requesting state must not be based on grounds of race, religion, membership of a particular nationality, political opinions, ethnic or social origin. In addition, the application of extradition must not be against a person who is a member of an organisation fighting against a dictatorial or occupying power when the legitimacy of the

another giving up or submitting a person to certain legal authorities which have made a request to the official authorities of a state. The terms have, in fact, some interrelation with one another and point to the same result. Simultaneously, each of the terms has its own legal definition. For this reason, it was absolutely essential to formulate the provisions of the Statute of the ICC in such a way that there would be no conflict with an issue of legal process.[194] For instance, although the terms arrest, surrender and extradition may have the same result of giving up a person to the legal authorities, a conflict may arise between the extradition of a person and their arrest or surrender.[195] Furthermore, the term "extradition" is, itself, subject to debate between two or several states. It may imply political or criminal extradition, or both. More significantly, a state may not wish to hand over its nationals to the Court in line with extradition procedures and, in certain situations, such an extradition may even be in conflict with its constitutional legislation. In addition, the question is not just a matter of terminology but involves the traditional models of cooperation and assistance between different sovereign states.[196]

In order to avoid the above conflicts between different national legislations and to solve the problem of definition between different

---

struggle is recognised by international legal standards; including the key principles of the Charter of the United Nations.

The practices and the interpretations of states greatly diverge upon the meaning and the legal scope of the term "prosecution". Prosecution of a person must be based on the principles of fair trial and must obviously be equivalent to the principles of international human rights law. This brings a legal harmony to the law of international extradition. The general tendency in the contemporary system of international criminal law is to bring all criminals before a competent jurisdiction and this tendency has also been formulated into many other international documents having the character of conventional, customary or soft regulations.

[194] Consult Göran Sluiter, *The Surrender of War Criminals to the International Criminal Court*, 25 Loyola of Los Angeles International and Comparative Law Review, 605-51 (2003), at 608.

[195] M. Cherif Bassiouni and Edward M. Wise,Aut Dedere, Aut Judicare: The Duty to Extradite or Prosecute in International Law (1995).

[196] *Id.*, at 608-9. See also M. Cherif Bassiouni, *The Modalities of International Cooperation in Penal Matters,* in International Criminal Law, Vol. II (M. Cherif Bassiouni, ed. 2008) pp. 3-34; M. Cherif Bassiouni, *The Duty to Prosecute and/or Extradite: Aut Dedere Aut Judicare, in* INTERNATIONAL CRIMINAL LAW, VOL II (M. Cherif Bassiouni, ed. 2008) pp. 35-45; Paul Gully-Hart, *The European Approach to Extradition, in* International Criminal Law, Vol. II (M. Cherif Bassiouni, ed. 2008) pp. 343-376; Demostenes Chryssikos, *Commentary on the United Nations Draft Model Law on Extradition, in* INTERNATIONAL CRIMINAL LAW, VOL II (M. Cherif Bassiouni, ed. 2008) pp. 377-382.

terminologies, the Statute uses the term "surrender", which seems to be the most impartial option.[197] According to the Statute, the term "surrender" is defined as the "delivering up of a person by one State to another as provided by treaty, convention or national legislation".[198] This means that the surrender of a person to another state is based on certain types of written document. The term "extradition" is defined as the "delivering up of a person by one State to another as provided by treaty, convention or national legislation".[199] As is evident, the terms "surrender" and "extradition" are defined at the same level and both mean delivering a person. However, in order to reduce any conflict, Part 9 uses the term "surrender", which is relatively neutral and does not create the difficulties that may arise if the term "extradition" is used.

---

[197] Practically, all factors are important in considering the matter of surrender or extradition. An alternative, to avoid the complications of extradition, is to invoke the principle of universality. Although this principle is useful in some cases for the prevention of certain international crimes and for the effective prosecution and punishment of criminals, the principle cannot easily be used for all international criminal issues and the application of the principle is indeed subject to debate. The universality principle has, however, been invoked for the prosecution and punishment of those who engage in piracy and in some cases for war crimes and crimes against humanity recognised in the Charter of the Nuremberg Tribunal. In order to employ the universality principle in the case of crimes against the peace and security of mankind, states must accept its application and in the present situation it is indeed very doubtful that states would accept its application concerning most international crimes. This is because the universality principle means that all states can arrest those accused of committing international crimes and claim to have jurisdiction over those accused. This means that they can easily avoid giving effect to a request for extradition by other states and run their own criminal jurisdictions with reference to the principle of universality.

Another problem of the universality principle is that the accused may be judged by his home state or other states which have also been effective in the commission of certain international crimes. Application of the universality principle can also create a conflict between states which seek to bring the accused under their own criminal jurisdiction. This is because there will always be competition between states for the arrest or detention of the accused and the application of their criminal jurisdictions. With these arguments we do not reject the value of the universality principle, but our purpose is to underline the problems in the application of the universality principle with respect to such international crimes, the prosecution and punishment of which are indeed necessary and essential for the maintenance of international peace and justice.

[198] Article 102 (a).

[199] Article 102 (b).

7.1.7.1.2. Surrender to the Court

The term "surrender" describes the act of submitting persons to the Court. In the term "surrender", the term "arrest of the person" is also integrated and this means that a request for the surrender of a person is also a request for the arrest of the relevant person. However, these terms are not interchangeable. This is because a request for the arrest of a person does not necessarily mean a request for the surrender of the relevant person. It may only mean an official investigation of the suspected or accused. It is probably for this reason that the Statute presents these two terms in this order in Part 9 with the words "the Court may transmit a request for the arrest and surrender of a person".[200] The use of the terms, "arrest" and "surrender" clears up any possible confusion which might otherwise arise if they are used. The words of the Statute make, at the same time, any state party responsible for complying with the request of the Court. This means that a state party has to cooperate for this end. Any state on the territory of which the requested person may be found, has a duty to cooperate in the arrest and surrender of the person by the provisions of its national law.[201]

However, when there is a challenge before a domestic court by the person sought for surrender based on the principle of *ne bis in idem*, the requested state may postpone the request of the Court if the admissibility ruling is pending. Thus, the state is not conventionally responsible for the execution of the request in the event of the non-stable situation of admissibility. However, if the case is admissible in the Court, the requested State has to fulfil the implementation of the request.[202]

Furthermore, a state party is responsible for cooperating in the surrender of a person by another state through its territory to the Court. All this should be carried out according to the provisions of procedural law. The transportation of a suspected or accused person may, however, not be possible through the state if this transit would impede or delay surrender. There is no need for authorisation if the person is transported by air and there will be no landing on the territory of the transit state unless there is an unscheduled landing.[203]

There is also a possibility that the requested state has already applied a sentence to the accused person under its own jurisdiction for certain other crimes. In this case, the requested state has the option of surrendering or not surrendering him/her to the Court.[204] This provision of the Statute,

[200] Article 89 (1).
[201] Article 89 (1).
[202] Article 89 (2).
[203] Article 89 (3).
[204] Article 89 (4).

together with other similar provisions as in Article 97, permits a state to reject a request for the surrender of a requested person. For instance, the relevant article permits a requested state to adopt a policy against the surrender of a person to the Court by reasoning that this would breach its treaties of extradition ratified by other states. This means that the Court has to consult all parties to the relevant treaties and the requested state on whether they agree to surrender the person to the jurisdiction of the Court. The conclusion may be that a state party may escape its obligations under the Statute because of its given obligations under other bilateral or multilateral conventions. There is therefore a gap between the purposes of the Statute for the prosecution and punishment of certain criminals and the provisions which may free states parties from listening to the requests of the Court. This may be seen in other provisions of the Statute which compete with the requests of the Court.

7.1.7.1.3. Competing Requests

A request for jurisdiction over a person by the Court may face other difficulties. This is when the same person is requested by another state to be extradited in order to come under its jurisdiction for the purpose of prosecution and punishment. The Statute of the ICC has foreseen two possible scenarios. These are requests that relate to the same conduct that outlines the basis of the crime for which the Court demands the person's surrender and requests for extradition for conduct other than that which constitutes the crime for which the Court asks the person's surrender.[205]

Concerning the first legal characterisation, one has to say that the requesting state may give priority to a request addressed by the Court. In this situation, the requested state does not need to surrender the relevant person to the Court unless the Court states that the case is admissible and the State requesting extradition is also one of the parties to the Statute.[206] Consequently, in a situation where the state requesting extradition is not a party to the Statute, the requested state is not under any legal obligation to arrest and surrender the person to the jurisdiction of the Court. The requested state may only consider all the relevant factors concerning the person's surrender to the jurisdiction of the Court or the state requesting extradition.[207]

Relating to the second legal characterisation, concerning requests for extradition for conduct other than that which constitutes the crime for which the Court requests the person's surrender, the requested state has to

---

[205] Article 90 (1) and (7).

[206] Article 90 (2).

[207] Article 90 (6).

give priority to the request addressed by the Court. This is only in cases where the requested state is not under any international obligation to extradite the person to the requesting state, unless there are certain international obligations to extradite the person to the requesting state.[208] In this case, a state should take account of the relevant factors in deciding to give priority to the request of the Court.[209] Urgency may also be a factor.[210]

Despite these various provisions of the Statute intended to bring a suspected, accused or convicted person within its jurisdiction, the provisions are not as strong as they may seem. Since the real territory of the Court is the territories of the states parties, it depends upon the juridical or political strength of each state party to challenge the will of the Court. Each party may hinder the implementation of the Statute. Even though we accept that the provisions of the Statute are powerful and wholly reliable for the states parties, the final decision depends on the humanitarian and practical application of the Statute. Of course, in certain situations when the government of a requested state is not particularly strong and is suffering from various political and juridical crises, the Court may easily ask for the surrender of a person accused of committing crimes to its jurisdiction. It will, however, not be so easy to ask for the arrest and surrender of a person to the Court from a state when the state may wish to defend the suspected person. This means that the Court has to be very cautious in its application of a request for arrest and surrender.

7.1.7.2. Other forms of Cooperation

The Statute of the ICC is formulated in order to create an effective procedure for the prevention, prosecution and punishment of international crimes.[211] The Statute has certain provisions intended to encourage

---

[208] Article 90 (7).

[209] In other words, the requested state has, generally speaking, two alternatives. One is to violate the law of the Court and the other is to ignore its obligations given under other international conventions. A priority may, however, be given to serious international crimes. This situation will often be very problematic for the requested state and its policy may provoke the authorities of the requesting state.

[210] In certain urgent cases, the Court may request the provisional arrest of the person sought. Article 92.

[211] See generally M. L. Smidt, *The International Criminal Court: An Effective Means of Deterrence?,* 167 Military Law Review 156 (2001); Leila Nadya Sadat and S. Richard Carden, *The New International Criminal Court: An Uneasy Revolution,* 88 Georgetown Law Journal 381 (2000;DaneshSarooshi, *The Statute of the International Criminal Court,* 48 International and Comparative Law Quarterly 387 (1999); G. Sluiter, *An International Criminal Court Is Hereby*

cooperation between states parties and the Court. Thus, parties to the Statute have accepted compliance with requests by the Court to assist with, whenever necessary, the processes of investigation and prosecution. Assistance to the Court may be given in different forms, including providing evidence, testimony under oath, expert opinions, identification of persons or the location of various items, any necessary report to the Court, provision of documents, facilitating the voluntary appearance of persons as witnesses or experts before the Court, the execution of searches and seizures, official records and documents, the freezing or seizure of proceeds, property, assets and instrumentalities of crimes and any other assistance that a state party may consider necessary for the proof of guilt.[212] In circumstances where a state may refuse assistance, that state should inform the Court or the prosecutor about its decision and the reasons underlying its refusal.[213]

States parties may give the Court the authority to offer an assurance to a witness or an expert appearing before the jurisdiction of the Court. This assurance will guarantee that he/she will not be detained and prosecuted. Neither will the witness or expert be subjected to any type of limitation on their personal freedom by the Court. The assurance is given in connection with any act or omission that could constitute a reason for the departure of the witness or expert from the requested state.[214] The purpose of the legislator is here to ensure some legal protection for certain subjects of the law in order to give them the courage to appear before the jurisdiction of the Court.

Established, 3 Netherlands Quarterly of Human Rights 413 (1998); Lyn L. Stevens, *Towards a Permanent International Criminal Court,* 6 European Journal of Crime, Criminal Law and Criminal Justice 236(1998); Robert W. Tucker, *The International Criminal Court Controversy,* 18 World Policy Journal 71 (2001); Minna Schrag, *Observations on the Rome Statute,* 1 International Law Forum34 (1999); Theo C. van Boven, *The European Union and the International Criminal Court,* 5 Maastricht Journal of European Comparative Law 325 (1998); H. Verweij, *The International Criminal Court: Alive, Still Kicking,* 25 Fordham International Law Journal 737 (2002); Jelena Pejic, *Creating a Permanent International Criminal Court: The Obstacles to Independence and Effectiveness,* 29 Columbia Human Rights Law Review 291 (1998); Diane Orentlicher, *Politics by Other Means: The Law of the International Criminal Court,* 32 Cornell International Law Journal 489 (1999); Roy S. Lee, *An Assessment of the ICC Statute,* 25 Fordham International Law Journal 650 (2002).

[212] Article 93.

[213] Article 93 (6).

[214] Article 93 (2).

The Court may also, if necessary, request the temporary transfer of a person in custody in order to identify them or to obtain testimony or other assistance from the relevant person.[215] Naturally, he/she should give his/her consent to the transfer. Concerning other matters such as the postponement of execution, waiver of immunity, and consultation with the Court, the requested state and the Court should decide on the enforcement of the relevant provisions of Part 9.[216]

7.1.7.3. Enforcement of Sentences

One of the essential parts of criminal justice is the enforcement of the sentences of convicted persons. When the ICC has delivered its judgment, its decisions must be enforced so that it can apply the sentences and enforce the relevant provisions of the Statute. The Court is empowered to issue different types of judgement depending on the gravity of the crimes committed and the level of participation of the convicted person in the planning, preparation and implementation of the criminal conduct. The judgment of the Court may also vary depending on its final decision of conviction or acquittal. The judgment may declare further proceedings inadmissible or find the accused guilty and pronounce sentence. It may decide on the terms of imprisonment and/or sentences imposing fines. In all these examples, states parties have a very significant role in the enforcement of sentences of imprisonment.

There may be a list of states that have shown their willingness to implement the judgment of the Court relating to the sentenced persons. If there is no designated state, a host state may take responsibility for the application of the imprisonment. The Court will recover the costs for this.[217] A state which has expressed its consent to implementing the decision of the Court may at the same time, declare its willingness to accept the sentenced persons and impose some conditions. This means that the Court must know about the relevant conditions and should not be informed of them after its decision.

Thus, a sentence may be enforced in a state chosen by the Court for the implementation of its final judgment. Yet, the state designated must also immediately inform the Court about whether it is prepared to carry out the decision of the Court.[218] The relevant state is also conventionally responsible for informing the Court of any circumstances which may materially affect the terms or extent of the imprisonment. For this reason,

[215] Article 93 (7).
[216] Articles 94-101.
[217] Article 103 (4).
[218] Article 103 (1).

the state has to give a time limit of not less than 45 days for the Court to consider the situation. During this time, the state has to be careful not to prejudice its obligation set out in the provisions of Article 110. This is because, according to this article, it is the Court that has the legal right concerning the modification of the sentence or any other matter relating to the sentenced persons. The state in which the enforcement is carried out has, therefore, no legal right to release the convicted person before the expiry of the sentence that has been decided by the Court.[219] This means that if certain conditions exist, the Court may, on its own initiative, mitigate the remaining sentence.[220] The following conditions may be grounds for the modification of the sentence:

> 3. When the person has served two thirds of the sentence, or 25 years in the case of life imprisonment, the Court shall review the sentence to determine whether it should be reduced. Such a review shall not be conducted before that time.
> 4. In its review under paragraph 3, the Court may reduce the sentence if it finds that one or more of the following factors are present:
> (a) The early and continuing willingness of the person to cooperate with the Court in its investigations and prosecutions;
> (b) The voluntary assistance of the person in enabling the enforcement of the judgements and orders of the Court in other cases, and in particular providing assistance in locating assets subject to orders of fine, forfeiture or reparation which may be used for the benefit of victims; or
> (c) Other factors establishing a clear and significant change of circumstances sufficient to justify the reduction of sentence, as provided in the Rules of Procedure and Evidence.[221]

A further significant matter is that the Court has a basic duty, in the case of the designation of a state for the implementation of the sentence, to take some other important matters into consideration. These include, for example, ensuring that the designated state has understood its international responsibility under the provisions of international treaties. The state has to share responsibility for the enforcing of sentences of imprisonment in accordance with the Rules of Procedure and Evidence. The Court has also, when exercising its discretion to make a designation, to take into consideration the nationality and the views of the sentenced person, the application of the basic principles of international conventions concerning

[219] Article 110 (1).
[220] See also Article 105.
[221] Article 110. The Court is also empowered to reduce the sentence under the Rules of Procedure and Evidence, if it does not seem appropriate to reduce it under the provisions of Article 110.

the treatment of prisoners and any other factors relevant to the circumstances of the crime and the sentenced person.[222] Thus, it is a duty of the Court to consider the internal standards of the state designated or the host state concerning the period of imprisonment of the sentenced person. Such a person should not be humiliated or treated in a manner which is against the provisions of international standards regarding the treatment of prisoners.[223] In other words, in no case shall the conditions of the treatment of the sentenced person be less favourable than those available to prisoners convicted of similar offences in the host state or state designated by the Court.[224]

Furthermore, the implementation of the imprisonment in a state designated by the Court may be modified whenever the Court deems it necessary. This means that the Court may, in view of the circumstances and if appropriate, transfer the sentenced person to another state. The sentenced person also has a right to apply to the Court for reconsideration of the place of imprisonment.[225]

In certain circumstances when a sentenced person escapes his/her imprisonment, the Court may be consulted by the state responsible for enforcement in order to return him/her to its territory to serve the sentence. He/she may also be sent to another state designated by the Court.[226]

---

[222] Article 103 (3). See also Article 106 governing the supervision of the enforcement of sentences and conditions of imprisonment.

[223] These provisions can be found within a number of international human rights conventions, See Malekian Documents on Principles of International Human Rights.

[224] Article 106

[225] Article 104.

[226] Article 111.

CHAPTER SIX

CRIMINAL RESPONSIBILITY IN THE INTERNATIONAL CRIMINAL TRIBUNALS AND THE COURTS

1. International Criminal Responsibility in the Nuremberg Tribunal

1.1. The Origin

Among the major developments in the history of international jurisprudence owed to the Nuremberg Tribunal is the consolidation of the concept of the international criminal responsibility of individuals.[1] The Constitution of the International Military Tribunal under the section regarding jurisdiction and general principles made it clear that crimes coming within the jurisdiction of the Tribunal, namely crimes against peace, war crimes, and crimes against humanity, create the concept of individual criminal responsibility.[2] In addition, all the three categories of crimes were identified as equal and a person could be convicted of all three categories of crimes. The two following articles went even further and created the concept of international criminal responsibility in international criminal law for a person who engaged in conduct which was recognised as being a crime under the jurisdiction of the Tribunal. This responsibility was imputable to the person without any due regard to his/her position. The articles declared that:

---

[1] The Tribunal based the concept of the criminal responsibility of individuals on violations of customary or conventional law. According to the judgment of the IMT, provisions of a considerable number of treaties were violated during the war. For instance, according to the IMT, the individuals of the German government violated a number of the provisions of the Versailles Treaty.

[2] Article 6 of the Constitution.

Article 7
The official position of defendants, whether as Heads of State or responsible officials in Government Departments, shall not be considered as freeing them from responsibility or mitigating punishment.

Article 8
The fact that the Defendant acted pursuant to order of his Government or of a superior shall not free him from responsibility, but may be considered in mitigation of punishment if the Tribunal determines that justice so requires.

The Judgment of the Tribunal made it clear that there is no possibility of escaping international criminal responsibility by resorting to the concepts of superior order or national independence and sovereignty. Accordingly, "that a soldier was ordered to kill or torture in violation of the international law of war has never been recognised as a defense to such acts of brutality, though, as the Charter here provides, the order may be urged in mitigation of the punishment. The true test, which is found in varying degrees in the criminal law of most nations, is not the existence of the order, but whether a moral choice was in fact possible."[3] Therefore, the IMT declared that "Crimes against International law are committed by men not by abstract entities, and only by punishing individuals who commit such crimes can the provisions of International Law be enforced."[4] Whilst one cannot deny that the argument of the IMT was essentially based on the decision of the United States Supreme Court in *Ex Parte Quirin,*[5] the idea was eventually

[3] Nuremberg Trial.Judgment, *Crnd.*No 6964. at12.
[4] 22 Trial of the Major War Criminals Before the International Military Tribunal, Nuremberg 447(1950); See also 1 Trial of the Major War Criminals Before the International Military Tribunal 223 (1947).
[5] In 1942, the court emphasised the criminal responsibility of several German individuals for violations of the laws of war. It stated that "By universal agreement and practice the law of war draws a distinction between the armed forces and the peaceful populations of belligerent nations and also between (317 U.S. 1, 31) those who are lawful and unlawful combatants. Lawful combatants are subject to capture and detention as prisoners of war by opposing military forces. Unlawful combatants are likewise subject to capture and detention, but in addition they are subject to trial and punishment by military tribunals for acts which render their belligerency unlawful. The spy who secretly and without uniform passes the military lines of a belligerent in time of war, seeking to gather military information and communicate it to the enemy, or an enemy combatant who without uniform comes secretly through the lines for the purpose of waging war by the destruction of life or property, are familiar examples of belligerents who are generally deemed not to be entitled to the status of prisoners of war, but to be offenders against the

developed in the system of international criminal law and settled in international issues. This means that, in reality, the domestic analogy was accepted by the IMT and also became a basis for subsequent developments. Thus, the lack of a solid basis for advocating the principle of individual criminal responsibility in international law by the IMT did not prevent its development under the procedures of the Tribunal and other international criminal courts.

1.2. The principle of *actus reus*

The idea of the concept of the international criminal responsibility of individuals which was adopted by the IMT was also conveyed by other Tribunals which had no international character.[6] There was one clear policy for the adoption of the concept of international criminal responsibility by all these tribunals. The fact was that this policy was based on the principle of *actus reus* which denotes the objective element of a crime giving rise to the concept of international criminal responsibility. The principle should also be understood in connection with the principle of *mens rea* dealing with the guilty mind of perpetrators.

Most obviously, the IMT based its judgment on the principle of *actus reus:* the IMT argued that acts were committed which were not justified by the rules of international armed conflicts and which were criminal in nature. In other words, the concept of *actus reus* requires the existence of an act which is committed voluntarily or involuntarily. The act may consist of omission, possession and commission. This was the only way for the IMT to announce the criminal responsibility of the perpetrators. The IMT made it clear that the acts of certain Nazi criminals were not accepted within the legal system of international law, although they were not previously recognised within the system. This meant that the IMT

---

law of war subject to trial and punishment by military tribunals." Consult Winthrop, Military Law, 2d Ed., pp. 1196-1197, 1219-1221; Instructions for the Government of Armies of the United States in the Field, approved by the President, General Order No. 100, April 24, 1863, sections IV and V. laws.findlaw.com/us/317/1.html. The Court continued that "By a long course of practical administrative construction by its military authorities, our Government has likewise recognised that those who during time of war pass surreptitiously from enemy territory into our own, discarding their uniforms upon entry, for the commission of hostile acts involving the destruction of life or property, have the status of unlawful combatants, punishable as such by military commission. This precept of the law of war has been so recognised in practice both here and abroad, and has so generally been accepted as valid by authorities on international law." *Id.*

[6] See the following section.

searched for a practical solution of the problem of the imputation of the concept of international criminal responsibility and did not put much weight on the legal concept. The IMT wanted to put the weight mostly on *reason*.[7]

The intention of the IMT was not necessarily to take any account of the legal phenomena but rather to get to the heart of the internationally criminal wrongful acts of perpetrators. Thus, many of the legal rules could not be applied, since the rules of the international humanitarian law of armed conflicts formulated in the Hague Conventions of 1907 were not applicable to the Second World War. This was based on the fact that several of the belligerent states had not ratified the relevant conventions.[8] However, the IMT announced simply that the relevant provisions of the Hague Conventions were an integral part of customary international law and consequently, their violations gave rise to the concept of the international criminal responsibility of individuals.[9]

1.3. Participation

The IMT also did not distinguish between perpetrators for the purpose of the imputation of the concept of international criminal responsibility, but it clearly stated that any form of participation in criminal conduct gives rise to the concept of individual criminal responsibility. Obviously, the intention behind this type of attribution of the concept of criminal responsibility was to bring under its jurisdiction any person who had, by one means or another, co-operated with, administrated or had knowledge

---

[7] As Jackson stated in the IMT, "The wrongs which we seek to condemn and punish have been so calculated, so malignant, and so devastating, that civilization cannot tolerate their being ignored, because it cannot survive their being repeated. That four great nations, flushed with victory and stung with injury, stay the hand of vengeance and voluntarily submit their captive enemies to the judgment of the law is one of the most significant tributes that Power has ever paid to reason." 2 Trial of the Major War Criminals Before the International Military Tribunal, Nuremberg 98-99 (1947).

[8] http://www.yale.edu/lawweb/avalon/imt/proc/judlawch.htm. Visited 2009-09-02.

[9] However, it must be stated here that the provisions of The Hague Convention of 1907 did not establish the concept of international criminal responsibility or punishment of the perpetrators of war crimes, crimes against humanity or crimes against peace. They aimed, at least officially, to establish the concept of compensation by the violating state.

of criminal plans.[10] For the IMT, this meant criminal participation in the crimes planned under the authority of the German government.[11]

Thus any form of participation in committing the categorised crimes was recognised by the IMT to be sufficient on its own to constitute the commission of crimes and to lead to the recognition of the concept of criminal responsibility of the individuals concerned. The IMT had eventually two methods for the conclusion of the concept of individual responsibility. One method was predicated on a violation of international law under the state's international legal personality. This meant that the proof of state responsibility also gave rise to the concept of individual responsibility. The second method relied on the principles of natural law emphasising that certain rules of the "law of nations" were certainly applicable to the conduct of individuals and not necessarily states only. This meant that the IMT did not need to prove that the relevant state had violated international law. On the contrary, the disputation of the Nuremberg Tribunals relating to the direct or indirect participation of individuals was based on the fact that they were actively planning, preparing or committing crimes in various ways.[12]

1.4. The Control Council Law

The Control Council Law No.10 was created by the four Allied powers. It was a law which created another opportunity for the international legal community to bring the violators of the law of war before criminal courts for prosecution and punishment.[13] It permitted the trial of both German military and civilian personnel. It entered into force on December 1945.

The chief difference between the functions of the Nuremberg Tribunal and the Control Council Law was the degree and the gravity of the crimes

---

[10] As Robert Jackson has argued "I shall not dissent from this consensus, nor do I deny that all these dead and missing men shared the guilt. In crimes so reprehensible that degrees of guilt have lost their significance they may have played the most evil parts. But their guilt cannot exculpate the defendants. Hitler did not carry all responsibility to the grave with him. All the guilt is not wrapped in Himmler's shroud. It was these dead men whom these living chose to be their *partners in this great conspiratorial brotherhood*, and the crimes that they did together they must pay for one by one." Emphasis added. www.derechos.org/nizkor/nurem berg/jackson2.html.Visited on 2009-08-22.

[11] *Id.*

[12] See also section on Joint Criminal Enterprise in chapter three.

[13] See also Accountability for Human Rights Atrocities in International Law: Beyond the Nuremberg Legacy (Steven R. Ratner and Jason S. Abrams, eds., 2001), pp.51-52.

committed by the perpetrators. The Nuremberg Tribunal's function was to bring the Major War Criminals before its jurisdiction for prosecution and punishment but the Control Council Law was applicable only to those individuals who were not considered to be major war criminals. Since the Control Council Law was applicable within the territory of the Allied powers, it used definite definitions of crimes and made use of the Charter of the Nuremberg Tribunal. These crimes were slightly different from the definitions of the crimes under the Charter. They included crimes against peace, war crimes and crimes against humanity. The Council did not specify particular penalties for each crime but it listed penalties that could apply to any person who had been convicted of committing the crime.[14]

---

[14] The following crimes created the concept of international criminal responsibility for the convicted persons. These were stated in Article II. The article provided that: "1. Each of the following acts is recognized as a crime: (a) Crimes against Peace. Initiation of invasions of other countries and wars of aggression in violation of international laws and treaties, including but not limited to planning, preparation, initiation or waging a war of aggression, or a war of violation of international treaties, agreements or assurances, or participation in a common plan or conspiracy for the accomplishment of any of the foregoing. (b) War Crimes. Atrocities or offenses against persons or property constituting violations of the laws or customs of war, including but not limited to, murder, ill treatment or deportation to slave labour or for any other purpose, of civilian population from occupied territory, murder or ill treatment of prisoners of war or persons on the seas, killing of hostages, plunder of public or private property, wanton destruction of cities, towns or villages, or devastation not justified by military necessity. (c) Crimes against Humanity. Atrocities and offenses, including but not limited to murder, extermination, enslavement, deportation, imprisonment, torture, rape, or other inhumane acts committed against any civilian population, or persecutions on political, racial or religious grounds whether or not in violation of the domestic laws of the country where perpetrated. (d) Membership in categories of a criminal group or organization declared criminal by the International Military Tribunal. 2. Any person without regard to nationality or the capacity in which he acted, is deemed to have committed a crime as defined in paragraph 1 of this Article, if he was (a) a principal or (b) was an accessory to the commission of any such crime or ordered or abetted the same or (c) took a consenting part therein or (d) was connected with plans or enterprises involving its commission or (e) was a member of any organization or group connected with the commission of any such crime or (f) with reference to paragraph 1 (a) if he held a high political, civil or military (including General Staff) position in Germany or in one of its Allies, co-belligerents or satellites or held high position in the financial, industrial or economic life of any such country. 3. Any persons found guilty of any of the crimes above mentioned may upon conviction be punished as shall be determined by the tribunal to be just. Such punishment may consist of one or more of the following:

2. International Criminal Responsibility in the Tokyo Tribunal

The concept of the international criminal responsibility of individuals violating the system of international law was also recognised in the Constitution of the Tokyo Tribunal. This concept of responsibility was also a model taken from the Charter of the Nuremberg Tribunal. The Constitution of the Tokyo Tribunal did not accept the defence of superior order and rejected it entirely. It stated that:

> *Responsibility of Accused.* Neither the official position, at any time, of an accused, nor the fact that an accused acted pursuant to order of his government or of a superior shall, of itself, be sufficient to free such accused from responsibility for any crime with which he is charged, but such circumstances may be considered in mitigation of punishment if the Tribunal determines that justice so requires.[15]

The Tokyo Tribunal could not, however, bring all those accused of committing international crimes before its jurisdiction.

The defendants who were selected for the first trials of the Tokyo Tribunal were not recognised as the only major war criminals that had to face prosecution and punishment for the alleged violations of the system of international law. Many accused were held in custody with the purpose of bringing them before the jurisdiction of the Tribunal, but, because of political reasons and financial reasons, this never occurred. Most of those

---

(a) Death.
(b) Imprisonment for life or a term of years, with or without hard labour.
(c) Fine, and imprisonment with or without hard labour, in lieu thereof.
(d) Forfeiture of property.
(e) Restitution of property wrongfully acquired.
(f) Deprivation of some or all civil rights.
Any property declared to be forfeited or the restitution of which is ordered by the Tribunal shall be delivered to the Control Council for Germany, which shall decide on its disposal. 4. (a) The official position of any person, whether as Head of State or as a responsible official in a Government Department, does not free him from responsibility for a crime or entitle him to mitigation of punishment. (b) The fact that any person acted pursuant to the order of his Government or of a superior does not free him from responsibility for a crime, but may be considered in mitigation. 5. In any trial or prosecution for a crime herein referred to, the accused shall not be entitled to the benefits of any statute of limitation in respect to the period from 30 January 1933 to 1 July 1945, nor shall any immunity, pardon or amnesty granted under the Nazi regime be admitted as a bar to trial or punishment."

[15] Article 6 of the International Military Tribunal for Far East.

accused and even those convicted were released without any further prosecution or enforcement of penalties.

3. International Criminal Responsibility in the ICTY

The chief function of the ICTY is to find out the proper subjects of accountability by imposing the concept of international criminal responsibility for the purpose of appropriate prosecution and punishment. This is the same principle upon which the Nuremberg Tribunal was created for the prosecution of responsible individuals. The concept of criminal responsibility is to secure the implementation of the law and prevent, as far as it is possible, systematic violations of the provisions of criminal law. In fact, international criminal law without reference to the concept of international criminal responsibility becomes meaningless and its legal validity falls to the ground. This means that the system of international criminal law should have, especially in the case of jurisdiction over international criminals, a method of proceeding, prosecuting and punishing the accused persons. That is why there are normally certain rules of procedure in order to implement the provisions of the law.

The concept of international criminal responsibility has been entered into Article 7 of the Statute of the ICTY. The content of the article is the first official international legal document to have been formulated and adopted for the practical application of the system of international criminal law with the exception of the Nuremberg Tribunal. Although we do not deny that the provisions of the article are borrowed from different instruments of international criminal law governing the concept of the international criminal responsibility of natural persons, such as the Draft Code of Crimes Against the Peace and Security of Mankind in 1976, it is a unique contribution to criminal justice.

The article has divided the concept of the criminal responsibility of individuals into several categories. This is in order to prevent criminals from fleeing from appropriate prosecution and punishment. The judgments of the Tribunal have implemented this principle in practice.[16] Accordingly, the ICTY is not only permitted to bring ordinary individuals under its jurisdiction, but it has also received the authority to prosecute persons who enjoy certain national immunities under constitutional provisions, such as

---

[16] ICTY *Deliac case,* IT- 96-21-A, Appeals Chamber Judgment, 20.02.2001, paras.195-197.

heads of state or government.[17] The Tribunal therefore has jurisdiction over the following natural persons:

> 1. A person who planned, instigated, ordered, committed or otherwise aided and abetted in the planning, preparation or execution of a crime referred to in articles 2 to 5 of the present Statute, shall be individually responsible for the crime.
> 2. The official position of any accused person, whether as Head of State or Government or as a responsible Government official, shall not relieve such person of criminal responsibility nor mitigate punishment.
> 3. The fact that any of the acts referred to in articles 2 to 5 of the present Statute was committed by a subordinate does not relieve his superior of criminal responsibility if he knew or had reason to know that the subordinate was about to commit such acts or had done so and the superior failed to take the necessary and reasonable measures to prevent such acts or to punish the perpetrators thereof.
> 4. The fact that an accused person acted pursuant to an order of a Government or of a superior shall not relieve him of criminal responsibility, but may be considered in mitigation of punishment if the International Tribunal determines that justice so requires.[18]

As a matter of principle, international criminal accountability may involve several categories of rank under the jurisdiction of the Tribunal. These are subordinate, superior, heads of state and government.[19] One of the chief principles of the Nuremberg Tribunal concerning the direct responsibility of the superior can be seen replicated in the provisions of Article 7.

---

[17] "In determining questions of responsibility it is necessary to look to effective exercise of power or control and not to formal titles ... The Appeals Chambers considers that the ability to exercise effective control is necessary for the establishment of *de facto* command or superior responsibility and thus agrees with the Trial Chamber that the absence of formal appointment is not fatal to a finding or criminal responsibility." ICTY *Deliac case,* IT- 96-21-A, Appeals Chamber Judgment, 20.02.2001, para.197. The ICTY has in fact concurrent jurisdiction. This can be seen in the provisions of its Article 9. The article reads that "1. The International Tribunal and national courts shall have concurrent jurisdiction to prosecute persons for serious violations of international humanitarian law committed in the territory of the former Yugoslavia since 1 January 1991. 2. The International Tribunal shall have primacy over national courts. At any stage of the procedure, the International Tribunal may formally request national courts to defer to the competence of the International Tribunal in accordance with the present Statute and the Rules of Procedure and Evidence of the International Tribunal."

[18] Article 7 of the Statute of the ICTY.

[19] Consult Mark J. Osiel, *Modes of Participation in Mass Atrocity*, 38:3 Cornell International Law Journal 791-822 (2005).

Moreover, the mitigation of international criminal responsibility is only acceptable where the question of the implementation of fair and reasonable justice so requires it for the maintenance of the true and just application of international criminal norms. Therefore, the tribunal's jurisdiction is not limited and has been empowered accordingly to determine the criminal responsibility of those who have, by one means or another, engaged in the preparation of crimes such as war crimes, crimes against humanity and genocide.[20] Therefore, the concept of criminal responsibility has been applied in most cases before the jurisdiction of ICTY.[21]

---

[20] But for a critical view of the problems of ICTY see *id.*, at 798.

[21] For instance, in *Krstic* case, the Chamber stated that "600. The Prosecution alleges that General Krsti is criminally responsible for his participation in the crimes charged in the indictment, pursuant to Article 7(1) of the Statute…601. The Trial Chambers of the ICTY and the ICTR and the Appeals Chamber of the ICTY have identified the elements of the various heads of individual criminal responsibility in Article 7(1) of the Statute. The essential findings in the jurisprudence may be briefly summarised as follows:
- "Planning" means that one or more persons design the commission of a crime at both the preparatory and execution phases;
- "Instigating" means prompting another to commit an offence;
- "Ordering" entails a person in a position of authority using that position to convince another to commit an offence;
- "Committing" covers physically perpetrating a crime or engendering a culpable omission in violation of criminal law;
- "Aiding and abetting" means rendering a substantial contribution to the commission of a crime; and
- "Joint criminal enterprise" liability is a form of criminal responsibility which the Appeals Chamber found to be implicitly included in Article 7(1) of the Statute. It entails individual responsibility for participation in a joint criminal enterprise to commit a crime;
602. Since the Prosecution has not charged any specific head of criminal responsibility under Article 7(1) of the Statute, it is within the discretion of the Trial Chamber to convict the Accused under the appropriate head within the limits of the Indictment and fair notice of the charges and insofar as the evidence permits. As to joint criminal enterprise liability, in its Final Trial Brief the Defence contends that it is not open to the Trial Chamber to apply this doctrine because it has not been pleaded in the Indictment. The Trial Chamber rejects this submission. The Prosecutor's Pre-trial Brief discussed this form of liability, specifically in the context of ethnic cleansing; the Defence acknowledged this pleading in its Pre-trial Brief and did not object to the concept itself but only to some details of the legal submissions on the matter.1350 Moreover, the Trial Chamber finds that the "nature and cause of the charge against the accused" pleaded in the indictment contains sufficient references to his responsibility for the alleged crimes committed in concert with others."*Krstic* (IT-98-33-T), Judgment, 2 August 2001.

3.1. Core Principles

The judgements of the ICTY have based the international criminal responsibility of individuals on two significant principles. The first principle is the *mens rea* and *actus reus* principle which are translated into English as "the mental and material elements", or as the so-called "objective and subjective elements". The judgements also refer to the principle by the terms "*mens rea*" and "a*ctus reus*". Taken as a whole, the principle denotes the guilty mind and the guilty act. The attribution of the concept of international criminal responsibility is sometimes achieved by the employment of the term "*dolus specialis*" referring to specific intent. This implies a very high level of intent to commit, for example, genocide.[22] Yet, according to these judgements, the requirement of intent is not always an absolute condition for the attribution of the concept of international criminal responsibility.[23] The intent may be inferred from the actions.[24]

---

[22] *Kunarac, Kovac, &Vukovic*, (IT-96-23-T & IT-96-23/1-T), Judgment, 22 February 2001.

[23] *Id.*

[24] "Because the distinction in the judgement between references to the views of the ICRC and expression of the Trial Chamber's own understanding of the *mens rea* requirement is not always easy to identify, the precise scope of the relevant *mens rea* for the crime of outrages upon personal dignity is left somewhat open. It is apparent from the Appeals Chamber's judgement that it did not regard the mental element of the offence as involving any *specific intent* to humiliate, ridicule or degrade the victims. It noted particularly that it did not interpret the ICRC Commentaries' statement that the term "outrages upon personal dignity" refers to acts "aimed at humiliating and ridiculing" the victim as suggesting a requirement of a *specific intent* to humiliate, ridicule or degrade, but as seeking "simply to describe the conduct which the provision seeks to prevent". The Appeals Chamber did not comment on the alternative indication in the Trial Chamber's judgement that, as well as deliberately committing the relevant act or omission, the perpetrator must have "been able to perceive" that the humiliation or degradation of the victim was a foreseeable and reasonable consequence of his actions. In its discussion of the facts of the case, the Appeals Chamber stated that it was "satisfied that the Trial Chamber found that the Appellant deliberately participated in or accepted the acts which gave rise to his liability under Articles 7(1) and 7(3) of the Statute for outrages upon personal dignity and was therefore guilty of those offences", which leaves open the question of whether there is any requirement of knowledge of the foreseeable consequences. In the discussion of the offence of inhuman treatment in the judgement of the Trial Chamber in the *Delalic* case, reference to the mental element is limited to the requirement that the relevant act or omission be intentional: [...] inhuman treatment is *an intentional act or omission, that is an act*

The second principle of international criminal responsibility is based on criminal participation.[25] This refers to committing, planning, instigating, ordering, aiding and abetting the preparation or execution of a crime. All these involve the concept of individual criminal responsibility. The term "committing" implies the physical or direct participation of the guilty person in the actual acts which constitute a crime. The ICTY defines the term "committing" "as meaning that the accused participated, physically or otherwise directly or indirectly, in the material elements of the crime charged through positive acts or, based on a duty to act, omissions, whether individually or jointly with others. The accused himself need not have participated in all aspects of the alleged criminal conduct."[26]

The word "planning" refers to the accused's role in designing or preparing the commission of an offence. The act of planning may either be at the preparatory stage or in the act's execution. The Trial Chamber of the ICTY, referring to "the established jurisprudence", has stated that "planning implies that one or several persons contemplate designing the commission of a crime at both the preparatory and execution phases. The Trial Chamber agrees that where an accused is found guilty of having committed a crime, he cannot be convicted of having planned the same crime, even though his involvement in the planning may be considered an aggravating factor."[27]

"Instigating" a crime refers to the act of promoting or encouraging another person to commit an offence. According to the ICTY, "instigating" refers also to the concept of the criminal responsibility of the instigator.[28] In the *Tadic* case, the Trial Chamber stated that "When an accused is present and participates in the beating of one person and remains with the group when it moves on to beat another person, his presence would have an encouraging effect, even if he does not physically take part in this second beating, and he should be viewed as participating in this second beating as well. This is assuming that the accused has not actively

---

which, judged objectively, is deliberate and not accidental, which causes serious mental or physical suffering or injury or constitutes a serious attack on human dignity." *Kunarac, Kovac, & Vukovic*, (IT-96-23-T & IT-96-23/1-T), Judgment, 22 February 2001, Paras.509-511.

[25] See Article 7 (I) above.

[26] *Stakic* (IT-97-24-T), Judgement, 31 July 2003, para.439.

[27] *Stakic* (IT-97-24-T), Judgement, 31 July 2003, para.443.

[28] *Tadic* (IT-94-1-T), opinion and Judgement, 7 May 1997, paras.659-690.

withdrawn from the group or spoken out against the conduct of the group."[29]

"Ordering" denotes the act of convincing a person to commit an offence. Ordering also involves the concept of the criminal responsibility of the person who used his/her position to give the order.[30] The Chamber of the ICTY explains in detail the position and clarifies that "This form of liability requires that at the time of the offence, an accused possessed the authority to issue binding orders to the alleged perpetrator. A formal superior-subordinate relationship between the person giving the order and the one executing it is not a requirement in itself, nor need the order be given in writing, or in any one particular form, or directly to the individual executing it. The existence of an order may be proven through direct or circumstantial evidence."[31] The concept of an order to commit an offence is also assimilated to instigation. According to the ICTY, the *mens rea* of the accused does not necessarily need to be clearly substantiated; it can also be understood from the circumstances of the case.[32]

Finally, the two terms "aiding" and "abetting" are similar to one another with the difference that "aiding" refers to practical assistance and "abetting" to encouraging psychologically a person to commit an offence. The term "abetting" is also, more or less, synonymous to "inciting", planning the direct or public incitement to commit genocide and ordering the preparation or execution of an offence. In the *Strugar* case, the judgement of the Trial Chamber defines the terms with the following

---

[29] *Id.*, para.690.

[30] *Krstic* (IT-98-33-T), Judgement, 2 August 2001, para.601.

[31] *Strugar* (It-01-42-T) Judgement 31 January 2005, para.331.

[32] The Chamber of the ICTY goes further and states that "As this form of liability is closely associated with "instigating," subject to the additional requirement that the person ordering the commission of a crime have authority over the person physically perpetrating the offence, a causal link between the act of ordering and the physical perpetration of a crime, analogous to that which is required for "instigating", also needs to be demonstrated as part of the *actus reus* of ordering. The Chamber further accepts that, similar to instigating, this link need not be such as to show that the offence would not have been perpetrated in the absence of the order. With regard to the requisite *mens rea*, it must be established that the accused in issuing the order intended to bring about the commission of the crime, or was aware of the substantial likelihood that it would be committed in the execution of the order. The *mens rea* of the accused need not be explicit, it may be inferred from the circumstances. Indeed, as *mens rea* is a state of mind, its proof is typically a matter of inference. The standard of proof dictates, of course, that it be the only reasonable inference from the evidence."*Strugar* (It-01-42-T) Judgement 31 January 2005, paras.332-333.

words "aiding and abetting has been defined in the case-law of the Tribunal as the act of rendering practical assistance, encouragement or moral support, which has a substantial effect on the perpetration of a crime, before, during or after the commission of the crime, and irrespective of whether these acts took place at a location other than that of the principal crime."[33] It must be emphasised that aiding and abetting imply a form of complicity in the commission of an offence. The proof of the *mens rea* concerning aiding and abetting depends on the character and circumstances of the offence. Furthermore, both crimes may be carried out either by omission or active participation and neither of them requires the physical presence of the person accused of aiding and abetting when the crime is completed.

The judgements of the ICTY have dealt with all of the above concepts of participation. However, it must be noted that the criminal responsibility of individuals has, sometimes, arisen from the result of collective criminality, performed by groups of individuals who were acting in pursuance of a common criminal design.[34]

---

[33] *Id*., para.249. The Chamber of the ICTY continues that "It is not necessary to establish a cause-effect relationship between the conduct of the aider and abettor and the commission of the crime, or that such conduct served as a *conditio sine qua non* to the commission of the crime. However, the acts of the aider and abettor must have "a direct and substantial effect on the commission of the illegal act." The *Bla{ki}* Appeals Judgement left open the possibility that in the circumstances of a given case an omission may constitute the *actus reus* of aiding and abetting.1043 Trial Chambers have held that this is the case, for example, if a person with superior authority is present at the crime scene, provided that his presence had a significant encouraging effect on the principal offender, or if there was an explicit duty to act. Regarding the requisite *mens rea*, it must be established that the aider and abettor was aware that his acts were assisting in the commission of the crime by the principal. This awareness need not have been explicitly expressed, but it may be inferred from all relevant circumstances. While the aider and abettor need not share the *mens rea* of the principal, he must be aware of the essential elements of the crime ultimately committed by the principal. It is not necessary that the aider and abettor know the precise crime that was intended or actually committed, as long as he was aware that one or a number of crimes would probably be committed, and one of these crimes was in fact committed." *Id*., paras.249-250.

[34] See the following sections.

3.2. Superior Responsibility

Superior responsibility is dealt with in Article 7 of the Statute of the ICTY. The fact that any act within the provisions of the Statute "was committed by a subordinate does not relieve his superior of criminal responsibility if he knew or had reason to know that the subordinate was about to commit such acts or had done so and the superior failed to take the necessary and reasonable measures to prevent such acts or to punish the perpetrators thereof."[35] In the light of international criminal justice, the *raison d'être* for the concept of the criminal responsibility of the superior is based on three specific elements. These are *a)* he/she knew or had reason to know that the subordinate had committed or was about to commit the crime; *b)* he/she failed to prevent the commission of the crime or to prosecute and punish the perpetrators by the procedures of legislation; *c)* there was a clear connection between the superior and subordinate in the criminal conduct carried out. This is also called the superior-subordinate relationship which implies the obvious knowledge of the superior concerning the intention of the subordinate to commit the crime. All three of these elements incorporate the concept of the participation of the superior in the process of the preparation and commission of the crime. This position is illustrated in connection with the international crime of genocide by the Trial Chamber of the ICTY in the following judgement:

> As a matter of statutory interpretation, there is in the Trial Chamber's view no inherent reason why, having verified that it applies to genocide, Article 7(3) should apply differently to the crime of genocide than to any other crime in the Statute.[36]The Appeals Chamber has observed that superior criminal responsibility requires the Prosecution to establish that a superior knew or had reason to know of the criminality of subordinates. In the case of genocide, this implies that the superior must have known or had reason to know of his or her subordinate's specific intent, with all the evidentiary difficulties that follow. The Appeals Chamber has held that superior

---

[35] Article 7 (3).

[36] All that the *Secretary-General's Report* states to this effect is that: "A person in a position of superior authority should, therefore, be held individually responsible for giving the unlawful order to commit a crime under the present statute. But he should also be held responsible for the failure to prevent a crime or to deter the unlawful behaviour of his subordinates. This imputed responsibility or criminal negligence is engaged if the person in superior authority knew or had reason to know that his subordinates were about to commit or had committed crimes and yet failed to take the necessary and reasonable steps to prevent or repress the commission of such crimes or to punish those who had committed them": *Secretary-General's Report*, para.56.

> criminal responsibility is a form of criminal liability that does not require proof of intent to commit a crime on the part of a superior before criminal liability can attach. It is therefore necessary to distinguish between the *mens rea* required for the crimes perpetrated by the subordinates and that required for the superior. The Appeals Chamber has warned against the danger of "conflating the mens rea requirement of the crime of genocide with the mental requirement of the mode of liability by which criminal responsibility is alleged to attach to the accused". If the elements dictated by Article 7(3) are fulfilled, there is no reason why superiors should not be convicted pursuant to Article 7(3) for genocide; genocide is, after all, the crime with which the superiors associated themselves with, through the deliberate failure to carry out their duty to exercise control. Thus, the Trial Chamber is satisfied that the *mens rea* required for superiors to be held responsible for genocide pursuant to Article 7(3) is that the superiors knew or had reason to know that their subordinates (1) were about to commit or had committed genocide and (2) that the subordinates possessed the requisite specific intent.[37]

The statement of the Trial Chamber indicates the fact that the criminal responsibility of the subordinate does not relieve the superior of his/her criminal responsibility where the perpetrator has acted under his/her orders. Since the concept of the criminal responsibility of the superior is one of the most difficult questions of international criminal justice, contemporary theories have tended to favour the principle of joint criminal enterprise.[38]

3.3. Responsibility of Heads of State

The Statute of the ICTY gives serious recognition to the concept of the criminal responsibility of heads of state. It reads that: "The official position of any accused person, whether as Head of State or Government or as a responsible Government official, shall not relieve such person of criminal responsibility nor mitigate punishment."[39] The purpose of the above provisions is to emphasise that heads of state cannot escape international criminal responsibility by resorting to constitutional immunities. This was because a considerable number of heads of state of the conflicting parties had committed serious international crimes. Their decisions were not only against the principles of the Statute, but also the customary norms of international criminal law. For instance, there were

---

[37] Brdanin (IT-99-36-T), Judgement, 1 September 2004, paras.720-721.

[38] See the relevant section below.

[39] Article 7 (4).

very serious indictments by the Prosecutor against Slobodan Milosevic,[40] Milan Milutinovic,[41] Nikola Sainovic,[42]Dragoljub Ojdanic[43] and Vlajko Stojiljkovic.[44] The indictment indicated that they had, by one means or another, participated in serious violations of international criminal law and employed the *de jure* as well as *de facto* powers available to them. The indictment clarified that:

> Each of the accused is individually responsible for the crimes alleged against him in this indictment under Articles 3, 5 and 7(1) of the Statute of the Tribunal. The accused planned, instigated, ordered, committed, or otherwise aided and abetted in the planning, preparation, or execution of these crimes. By using the word "committed" in this indictment, the Prosecutor does not intend to suggest that any of the accused physically perpetrated any of the crimes charged, personally. "Committing" in this indictment refers to participation in a joint criminal enterprise as a co-perpetrator. The purpose of this joint criminal enterprise was, *inter alia,* the expulsion of a substantial portion of the Kosovo Albanian population from the territory of the province of Kosovo in an effort to ensure continued Serbian control over the province. To fulfil this criminal purpose, each of the accused, acting individually or in concert with each other and with others known and unknown, significantly contributed to the joint criminal enterprise using the *de jure* and *de facto* powers available to him.[45]

However, it must be asserted that the prosecution of heads of state has not been an easy task. For instance, Milosevic rejected the juridical authority of the ICTY.[46] This has also been difficult in the case of other participants

---

[40] He was born in 1941. He graduated in law and began his political career in 1983 and became the official president of Serbia in 1990. He was also re-elected in 1992.

[41] He was born in 1942. He graduated in law and became the president of Serbia in 1997.

[42] He was born in 1948. He graduated as a chemical engineer. He had several positions within the government and became Prime Minister of Serbia in 1993 and he has subsequently had many other positions.

[43] He was born in 1941. He graduated from the School of Army General Staff and of National Defence with a degree in Military Science. He has had several military positions since 1992. He was, *inter alia*, the Commander of the First Army between 1994 and 1996.

[44] He was born in 1937 and graduated in law. He became Deputy Prime Minister of the Serbian Government and Minister of Internal Affairs of Serbia in 1997 and the Minister of Internal Affairs of Serbia in 1998.

[45] Milosevic et al. (IT-99-37-PT), Indictment, 22 May 1999, para.17.

[46] Milosevic (IT-02-54-PT), Decision on Preliminary Motions, 8 November 2001, paras.26-34.

who have had high positions within the Serbian government or army.[47] The ICTY is still dealing with their cases.[48] One of the chief purposes of the ICTY is to abolish the impunity of heads of state based on constitutional immunity.[49] Another purpose is to bring the perpetrators of heinous international crimes under international criminal jurisdiction and therefore reduce any possibility of partial justice under national criminal courts.

3.4. Joint Criminal Enterprise

3.4.1. Theory

In contemporary international criminal law, participation in different manners and forms is called joint criminal enterprise. This means the contribution of two or more persons to conspiring to commit or committing a crime or criminal conduct. It also means that the participators had a common aim and plan in carrying out the criminal conduct. Consequently, it does not necessarily need to be proved to what extent a person committed the crimes since his/her various contributions imply the commission of the act under their authority by different means. This theory was originally developed in the aftermath of the Nuremberg Tribunal and draws upon its methods of attribution of the concept of international criminal responsibility to individuals who had participated in the commission of crimes against the innocent Jews. However, officially, the concept of joint criminal enterprise was incorporated into the body of international criminal law by the ICTY.[50]

---

[47] For instance see Prosecutor V. Millan Milutinovicet. al., Case (IT-05-87-A), Decision on Motions for Extension of Time to file notices of Appeal, 23, March 2009.

[48] Nikola Sainovic, Dragolub Ojdanic, Nebojsa Pavkovic, Vladimir Lanzarevic, Sreten Lukic, (IT-05-87-A), Decision on Nikola Sainovic, Dragolub Ojdanic Ojdanic's Joint Motion for Extension of Wolrd Limit, 11 September 2009.

[49] Strange as it may seem, the International Court of Justice delivered a contrary decision on the Case Concerning the Arrest Warrant of 11 April 2000 (Democratic Republic of the Congo v Belgium) in 2002. According to it, the circulated arrest warrant by the Belgian court against the Foreign Minister of the Congo for war crimes and crimes against humanity did not meet the international criteria and was therefore illegal and went against the immunity of relevant minister.

[50] In *Stakic*, an ICTY Trial Chamber explains the position using the following words: "For co-perpetration it suffices that there was an explicit agreement or silent consent to reach a common goal by coordinated co-operation and joint control over the criminal conduct. For this kind of co-perpetration it is typical, but

This concept is not formulated within the provisions of the Statute of the ICTY, but it has practically been used to recognise individuals participating in the criminal conduct of groups responsible for the consequences of criminal behaviour. The concept of joint criminal enterprise is, however, recognised by the ICTY Appeals Chamber.[51] According to it, the spirit and purposes and objects of the Statute denote implicitly and explicitly the condemnation of such criminal acts. The relevant statement of the Appeals Chamber affirms that "all those who have engaged in serious violations of international humanitarian law, whatever the manner in which they may have been perpetrated, or participated in the perpetration of those violations, must be brought to justice."[52] In the *Tadic* case, the Appeals Chamber underlined that common design and collective criminality create the legal obligations of all

---

not mandatory, that one perpetrator possesses skills or authority which the other perpetrator does not. These can be described as shared acts which when brought together achieve the shared goal based on the same degree of control over the execution of the common acts. In the words of *Roxin*: "The coperpetrator can achieve nothing on his own…The plan only 'works' if the accomplice works with the other person." Both perpetrators are thus in the same position. As *Roxin* explains, "they can only realise their plan insofar as they act together, but each individually can ruin the whole plan if he does not carry out his part. To this extent he is in control of the act." *Roxin* goes on to say, "[t]his type of 'key position' of each co-perpetrator describes precisely the structure of joint control over the act." Finally, he provides the following very typical example: If two people govern a country together - are joint rulers in the literal sense of the word - the usual consequence is that the acts of each depend on the co-perpetration of the other. The reverse side of this is, inevitably, the fact that by refusing to participate, each person individually can frustrate the action. The Trial Chamber is aware that the end result of its definition of co-perpetration approaches that of the aforementioned joint criminal enterprise and even overlaps in part. However, the Trial Chamber opines that this definition is closer to what most legal systems understand as "committing" and avoids the misleading impression that a new crime not foreseen in the Statute of this Tribunal has been introduced through the backdoor." *Stakic* (IT-97-24-T), Judgement, 31 July 2003, paras.440-441.

[51] For instance, Dragoljub Ojdanic was "charged both as a superior pursuant to Article 7 (3) of the Statute and for planning, instigating, ordering, committing and otherwise aiding and abetting in the planning, preparation or execution of those crimes, pursuant to Article 7(1). The indictment alleges that his liability pursuant to Article 7(1) stems, *inter alia*, from his part in a joint criminal enterprise to commit those crimes."Prosecutor v. Milutinovic et al., *Decision on Dragoljub Ojdanie's Motion Challenging Jurisdiction-Joint Criminal Enterprise*, Appeals Chamber, case No. IT-99-37-AR72 (May 21, 2003).

[52] Prosecutor v. *Tadic, Judgement, Appeals Chamber*, case No. IT-94-1-A para.190 (15 July 1999).

defendants to answer charges in a court. These charges in the indictments may ultimately give rise to the attribution of criminal responsibility to the defendants.[53] According to the Appeals Chamber, different categories of cases, such as "concentration camp" and "common design", involve the concept of the accountability of a person.[54] These may create criminal responsibility:

> where one of the perpetrators commits an act which, while outside the common design, was nevertheless a natural and foreseeable consequence of the effecting of that common purpose. An example of this would be a common, shared intention on the part of a group to forcibly remove members of one ethnicity from their town, village or region (to effect "ethnic cleansing") with the consequence that, in the course of doing so, one or more of the victims is shot and killed. While murder may not have been explicitly acknowledged to be part of the common design, it was nevertheless foreseeable that the forcible removal of civilians at gunpoint might well result in the deaths of one or more of those civilians. Criminal responsibility may be imputed to all participants within the common enterprise where the risk of death occurring was both a predictable consequence of the execution of the common design and the accused was either reckless or indifferent to that risk. Another example is that of a common plan to forcibly evict civilians belonging to a particular ethnic group by burning their houses; if some of the participants in the plan, in carrying out this plan, kill civilians by setting their houses on fire, all the other participants in the plan are criminally responsible for the killing if these deaths were predictable.[55]

The concept of joint criminal enterprise essentially requires a prosecutor to have sufficient evidence denoting the fact that a group of individuals have together had a common design, plan or purpose to commit a crime. Thus, the prosecutor does not need to prove one by one the purpose of each individual working and acting in the group. The direct or indirect participation of the individual in the plans of the group involves his/her criminal responsibility regardless of the level or degree of his/her participation.[56] This means that the defendant participated in one way or

[53] *Tadic* (IT-94-1-A), Judgement, 15 July 1999.
[54] *Id.*, para.202.
[55] *Tadic* (IT-94-1-A), Judgement, 15 July 1999, para.204.
[56] For instance, the ICTY in one of its judgements stated that "The Trial Chamber takes account of the fact that most of the crimes were committed within the context of participating in a joint criminal enterprise. Several aspects of this case were critical to our decision that the five defendants did participate significantly and unlawfully in a persecutory system against non-Serb detainees, and these aspects

another in the common plan or he/she had intended the object of the common plan.[57] The following statement clarifies this position:

> Each of the accused is individually responsible for the crime alleged against him in this indictment under Article 3, 5 and 7(1) of the Statute of the Tribunal. The accused planned, instigated, ordered, committed or otherwise aided and abetted in the planning, preparation or execution of these crimes. By using the world "committed" in this indictment, the Prosecutor does not intend to suggest that any of the accused physically perpetrated any of the crimes charged personally. 'Committing in this indictment refers to participation in a joint criminal enterprise as a co-perpetrator. The purpose of this joint criminal enterprise was, *inter alia*, the expulsion of a substantial portion of the Kosovo Albanian population from the territory of the province of Kosovo in an effort to ensure continued Serbian control over the province. To fulfil this criminal purpose, each of the accused, acting individually or in concert with each other and with others known and unknown, significantly contributed to the joint criminal enterprise using the *de jure* and *de facto* powers available to him.[58]

Yet, according to the statement of the prosecutor, the concept of joint criminal enterprise is not based only on the provisions of the Statute of ICTY but also emanates from the provisions of customary international criminal law.[59] As a whole, in order for an individual be tried under the

---

deserve recalling, even though they will not be considered as aggravating circumstances. The first aspect is the pervasive and intense nature of the cruelties and deprivations, recounted in detail in Parts II and IV. Omarska was not a place where occasional random acts of cruelty against inmates occurred or where living conditions were simply hard. This was a hellish environment in which men and women were deprived of the most basic needs for their survival and of their humanity: food of edible quality; the opportunity to freely perform basic bodily functions; a place to sleep; water to drink and use for washing; and access to friends or family. Omarska was a place where beatings occurred daily and with devilish instruments of torture. No one could mistake Omarska for merely a badly run prison; it was *a criminal enterprise designed to operate in a way that destroyed the mind, body, and spirit of its prisoners*." Kvocka et al. (IT-98-30/1-T), Judgement, 2 November 2001, para.706. Emphasis added.

[57] Prosecutor v. Milutinovic et al., *Decision on Dragoljub Ojdanie's Motion Challenging Jurisdiction-Joint Criminal Enterprise*, Appeals Chamber, case No. IT-99-37-AR72 (May 21, 2003).

[58] *Id.* It further stated that "This joint criminal enterprise came into existence no later than October 1998 and continued throughout the time period when the crimes alleged in counts 1 to 5 of this indictment occurred: beginning on or about 1 January 1999 and continuing until 20 June 1999."

[59] *Id.*

concept of joint criminal enterprise, it does not necessarily require the existence of clear norms applying to the concept.[60] This is because the concept does not rest on the existence of direct norms but the criminal purpose within which the criminal conduct has been carried out.[61] It is on this basis that the ICTY argues strongly for the application of the concept of joint criminal enterprise under Article 7 of the Statute.[62] Article 7 (1) provides that "A person who planned, instigated, ordered, committed or otherwise aided and abetted in the planning, preparation or execution of a crime referred to in articles 2 to 5 of the present Statute, shall be individually responsible for the crime." Faithful to the spirit of the above provisions, the Appeals Chamber concludes that "On the basis, under Article 7 (1) of the Statute, each of the accused and other participants in the joint criminal enterprise bear individual criminal responsibility for the crimes alleged in counts 1 to 5."[63]

3.4.2. Active Participation

The Appeals Chambers for *Tadic* and *Slobodan Milosevic* also based their judgment on the concept of joint criminal enterprise and established the criminal responsibility of the accused persons.[64] Both cases proved that the relevant individuals had actively participated in criminal conduct.[65]

---

[60] *Id.*

[61] *Id.*

[62] *Id.*

[63] *Id.* In addition, there are certain differences between the various concepts of criminal responsibility. In the words of the prosecutor "joint criminal liability is different from both 'conspiracy' and membership in a criminal organization and, contrary to both of them, is a punishable mode of participation in the actual commission crimes. Conspiracy… is a mere agreement or understanding between two or more persons to commit a crime, whilst membership in a criminal organization implies the existence of a stable organizational structure directed at the commission of crimes, irrespective of the actual commission of any such crime. The prosecution submits further that, individual liability for participation in a joint criminal enterprise arises from a 'significant contribution to the execution of a common plan that either entails the commission of a crime, or leads to the commission of a crime, as its natural and foreseeable consequence.'"

[64] See above paragraphs.

[65] According to the indictment: "This joint criminal enterprise came into existence no later than October 1998 and continued throughout the time period when the crimes alleged in counts 1 to 5 of this indictment occurred: beginning on or about 1 January 1999 and continuing until 20 June 1999. A number of individuals participated in this joint criminal enterprise during the entire duration of its existence, or, alternatively, at different times during the duration of its existence,

Although both accused persons denied the concept of joint enterprise within the Statute of ICTY, the chambers did not accept their statements, rejecting them based on the fact that the system of international criminal law does not arise exclusively from the provisions of the statute but from the body of a large number of international agreements, customary norms and international judicial decisions.

Whilst the concept of joint criminal enterprise has been raised and stated within several discussions and statements of the appeals chambers, one should be very cautious in the case of its employment and application. This is because the concept may imperil several principles of criminal law such as *nullum crimen sine lege* and *de lege lata* and create controversy regarding the interpretation of the criminal justice system and the power of the prosecutor as a whole. It may partly increase the prosecutor's authority at the expense of the power of judges and consequently bring justice into disrepute. However, one cannot deny that the principle of joint criminal enterprise has to be used in the case of serious international crimes such as genocide, crimes against humanity and war crimes. This is because it will otherwise be impossible to reach the heart of justice for the prosecution and punishment of those who have committed criminal acts against generations of mankind.[66]

---

including the accused Slobodan MILOSEVIC, Milan MILUTINOVIC, Nikola SAINOVIC, Dragoljub OJDANIC, Vlajko STOJILJKOVIC and others known and unknown. The crimes enumerated in Counts 1 to 5 of this Indictment were within the object of the joint criminal enterprise. Alternatively, the crimes enumerated in Counts 3 to 5 were natural and foreseeable consequences of the joint criminal enterprise and the accused were aware that such crimes were the likely outcome of the joint criminal enterprise. Despite their awareness of the foreseeable consequences, Slobodan MILOSEVIC, Milan MILUTINOVIC, Nikola SAINOVIC, Dragoljub OJDANIC, Vlajko STOJILJKOVIC and others known and unknown, knowingly and wilfully participated in the joint criminal enterprise. Each of the accused and other participants in the joint criminal enterprise shared the intent and state of mind required for the commission of each of the crimes charged in counts 1 to 5. On this basis, under Article 7(1) of the Statute, each of the accused and other participants in the joint criminal enterprise bear individual criminal responsibility for the crimes alleged in counts 1 to 5." Milosevic et al. (IT-99-37-PT), Indictment, 22 May 1999, paras.17-18. Generally, the counts were: Count 1. Deportation, count 2.other inhuman acts or forcible transfer, counts 3-4 murder, count 5. Persecutions. Each one of these counts consisted of a number of criminal conducts.

[66] See also the Separate opinion of judge David Hunt on Challenge by Ojdanic to Jurisdiction Joint Criminal Enterprise, Prosecutor v. Milutinovic et al., Decision on Dragoljub Ojdanie's Motion Challenging Jurisdiction-Joint Criminal Enterprise,

3.5. *Ne Bis in Idem*

One of the most important principles of criminal jurisdiction is to avoid punishing again a person who has already been prosecuted and punished for the same crime.This is called the principle of *ne bis in idem*. This principle constitutes one of the most important principles of international criminal justice today and is also entered into the structure of the Statute of ICTY. Thus, no national court may prosecute a person who has been punished under the jurisdiction of the ICTY. However, the Tribunal is permitted to try a person who has already been punished according to the proceedings of a national court under certain conditions. These are when the act of the accused was treated by the court as an ordinary crime and not in accordance with the provisions of Articles 2 to 5 of the Statute and when the court's proceedings were not impartial in the application of international criminal responsibility as formulated in the Statute. In any event, the Tribunal is responsible for taking the punishment that has already been inflicted on the guilty party into effective recognition. The relevant article of the Statute of the ICTY reads that:

> 1. No person shall be tried before a national court for acts constituting serious violations of international humanitarian law under the present Statute, for which he or she has already been tried by the International Tribunal.
> 2. A person who has been tried by a national court for acts constituting serious violations of international humanitarian law may be subsequently tried by the International Tribunal only if:
> (a) the act for which he or she was tried was characterized as an ordinary crime; or
> (b) the national court proceedings were not impartial or independent, were designed to shield the accused from international criminal responsibility, or the case was not diligently prosecuted.
> 3. In considering the penalty to be imposed on a person convicted of a crime under the present Statute, the International Tribunal shall take into account the extent to which any penalty imposed by a national court on the same person for the same act has already been served.[67]

Appeals Chamber, case No. IT-99-37-AR72 (May 21, 2003). See *also* www.un.org/icty/milutinovic/appeal/decision-e/030521.pdf.

[67] Article 10 of the Statute.

3.6. Defences

The term "defence" applies to the way in which a criminal charge is responded to by a defendant. There are several words which have a more or less similar meaning such as "excuse", "justification" and "apology". All of these words are employed in criminal jurisdiction to justify the commission of an offence, to reject the accusation of its commission, or to call for the mitigation of a sentence or release from criminal responsibility. The Statute of the ICTY, contrary to the Statute of the ICC, is generally silent about the various modes of defence, but, this does not mean that accused persons are not permitted to invoke them. In fact, equality of arms is the basic foundation of the Statute.[68] However, one cannot deny that the provisions of the Statute of the ICTY governing war crimes speak, to some extent, of the defence of 'military necessity' concerning violations of the laws or customs of war and specific grave breaches.

In addition, the Rules of Procedure and Evidence of the ICTY admit also 'special defence'. Accordingly, the accused is asked to notify the prosecutor of his/her intention to plead a special defence. The Rules of Procedure also do not provide the list of defences which may be invoked. Nevertheless, they clarify that "any special defence, including that of diminished or lack of mental responsibility; in which case the notification shall specify the names and addresses of witnesses, and any other evidence upon which the accused intends to rely to establish the special defence."[69] This means that the Tribunal, without this being stated openly, admits to scrutinising various forms of practical justification brought by the accused to the court.

---

[68] According to the ICTY "(U)nder the Statute of the International Tribunal the principle of equality of arms must be given a more liberal interpretation than that normally upheld with regard to proceedings before domestic courts. This principle means that the Prosecution and the Defence must be equal before the Trial Chamber. It follows that the Chamber shall provide every practicable facility it is capable of granting under the Rules and Statute when faced with a request by a party for assistance in presenting its case. The Trial Chambers are mindful of the difficulties encountered by the parties in tracing and gaining access to evidence in the territory of the former Yugoslavia where some States have not been forthcoming in complying with their legal obligation to cooperate with the Tribunal. Provisions under the Statute and the Rules exist to alleviate the difficulties faced by the parties so that each side may have equal access to witnesses." *Tadic* (IT-94-1-A), Judgement, 15 July 1999, para.52.

[69] Rule 67 (b). See also appendix.

3.6.1. Intoxication

It is worth mentioning here that although the ICTY has not dealt with a specific case concerning intoxication, it has, nevertheless, in one of its judgments analysed the state of intoxication of the defendant. According to it, intoxication, voluntary or otherwise, is not a defence and does not mitigate the criminal responsibility of the accused. An ICTY Trial Chamber in the Kvocka case stated that:

> The Zigic's Defense submits that committing a crime under the influence of drugs or alcohol serves as a mitigating factor because the defendant's mental capacity is diminished. In this regard, the Trial Chamber acknowledges that mental impairment is considered relevant in mitigation of sentences in many countries. However, when mental capacity is diminished due to use of alcohol or drugs, account must be taken of whether the person subjected himself voluntarily or consciously to such a diminished mental state. While a state of intoxication could constitute a mitigating circumstance if it is forced or coerced, the Trial Chamber cannot accept Zigic's contention that an intentionally procured diminished mental state could result in a mitigated sentence. Indeed, the Trial Chamber considers that, particularly in contexts where violence is the norm and weapons are carried, intentionally consuming drugs or alcohol constitutes an aggravating rather than a mitigating factor.[70]

The defence of intoxication is also refused in other similar cases by the ICTY. This means that the general policy of the Tribunal is that evidence of alcohol abuse cannot be the *raison d'être* for mitigating penalties.[71] Neither can it create the right to a judicial determination of sentence.[72]

---

[70] Kvocka et al. (IT-98-30/1-T), Judgement, 2 November 2001, para.706.

[71] Todorovic (IT-95-9/1-S), Sentencing Judgment, 31 July 2001, para.93.

[72] In another case, the Trial Chamber says that "Following the Defence's notice of its intent to raise the question of diminished responsibility (in mitigation of sentence only) and its request for a medical examination of Stevan Todorovic, the Trial Chamber ordered such an examination to be performed by two experts. The conclusion of Dr. Soyka's examination of Stevan Todorovic was that there was no evidence of a major mental disorder or any other psychiatric disorder for the relevant period and that there was no evidence of diminished capacity or responsibility. The conclusion of Dr. Lecic-Tosevski's examination was that Stevan Todorovic has no personality disorder as such, but that he had a post-traumatic stress disorder and abused alcohol during the war. During her testimony at the Sentencing Hearing, Dr. Lecic-Tosevski said that in her opinion the onset of the post-traumatic stress disorder occurred in April 1992, but that Stevan Todorovic manifested acute stress reaction before that period, due to the heavy bombardment of the area, witnessing killings and the deaths of relatives and friends. The Trial

Undoubtedly, the evaluation of the defence of intoxication must also depend on the circumstances of each case and whether the relevant individual had sufficient knowledge and adequate intent for the commission of the relevant crime.

3.6.2. Diminished Mental Responsibility

"Diminished mental responsibility" is a term which has been employed by the ICTY. It refers to the position of an individual who cannot distinguish between the lawfulness and unlawfulness of his/her conduct. The policy of the ICTY is based on the assumption of the sanity of the person accused of committing the relevant offence. In the *Mitar Vasiljevic* case, for instance, the Tribunal stated that:

> As was established in the *Delalic* Appeal Judgment, and conceded by the defence at the trial, the issue of diminished mental responsibility is relevant only to the sentence to be imposed. It is not a defence that if established would lead to the acquittal of the Accused. The Accused bears the onus of establishing this defence on the balance of probabilities. In the *Delalic* Appeal Judgment the Appeals Chamber stated that: 'As a defendant bears the onus of establishing matters in mitigation of sentence, where he relies upon diminished mental responsibility in mitigation, he must establish that condition on the balance of probabilities – that more probably than not such a condition existed at the relevant time.' The Trial Chamber is satisfied that an accused suffers from a diminished mental responsibility where there is an impairment to his capacity to appreciate the unlawfulness of or the nature of his conduct or to control his conduct so as to conform to the requirements of the law.[73]

The Trial Chamber of the ICTY went even further and rejected the evidence that the accused was, at the time of the commission of the offence, suffering from an involuntary psychiatric problem. It illustrates the *Mitar Vasiljevic* case, by the following words:

Chamber observes that, while both experts concluded that Stevan Todorovic was not suffering from a personality disorder during the relevant period, they differed in their conclusions with respect to the post-traumatic stress disorder. In the Trial Chamber's opinion, Stevan Todorovic's condition at the time the crimes were committed was not one which would give rise to mitigation of sentence. Accordingly, this consideration will not be taken into account in mitigation of sentence."*Todorovic* (IT,95-9/1-S), Sentencing Judgment, 31 July 2001, paras.94-95.

[73] *Vasiljevic* (IT-98-32-T), Judgement, 29 November 2002, paras.282-283.

> The Trial Chamber accepts the evidence of Dr Folnegovic-Smalc (who was called by the Prosecution) that, if Dr Vasiljevic had diagnosed the Accused as suffering from a reactive psychoneurosis, the mandatory course of action for a doctor diagnosing such a condition would be to ensure hospitalisation of the patient. This action is necessary because, by definition, a psychotic patient is one who is not able to take care of themselves or to control his or her actions. Furthermore, she said that it is very unlikely that a patient in such a condition would be released without some follow-up, or that a reasonable doctor would have made such a recommendation. Accordingly, the Trial Chamber rejects the evidence of Dr Vasiljevic that the Accused was suffering from such a disorder at the relevant time.[74]

As is evident, the Appeals Chamber of the ICTY has explicitly stated that diminished mental capacity or insanity may only be relevant to sentencing. According to the Chamber, it has no value concerning a defence.[75] This statement of the ICTY seems to be in contradiction with the rule of the Tribunal which states that the defence shall notify the Prosecutor of its intent to offer "any special defence, including that of diminished or lack of mental responsibility; in which case the notification shall specify the names and addresses of witnesses and any other evidence upon which the accused intends to rely to establish the special defence."[76] Although the ICTY has adopted a certain policy in the case of diminished mental responsibility or capacity, mental disorder should have a very significant role in its judgement based on appropriate factors. The Statute of the ICC also confirms acquittal where insanity is obvious.

3.6.3. *Tu quoque*

The ICTY has rejected the plea of *tu quoque*. This is a plea by which one may make similar argumentation in law. In other words, a *tu quoque* argument aims to demonstrate that a legal criticism or a juridical objection also concerns the party making it. This argument was made by some of the accused persons in the ICTY in order to justify their own atrocities. In fact, in one of the cases before the ICTY, the defence argued that the attack on civilians in Ahmici was justified because Muslim military forces had attacked Croat civilians in other areas. Although the Trial Chamber accepted that attacks by Muslims had probably been carried out, it rejected

---

[74] *Vasiljevic (*IT-98—32-T), Judgement, 29 November 2002, paras.285.

[75] Delalic et al. (IT-96-21-A), Judgement, 20 February 2001, para.590.*Vasiljevic* (IT-98—32-T), Judgement, 29 November 2002, para.282.

[76] Rule 67 (a) (ii) (b). See also appendix.

the argument that international law permits a defence of *tu quoque.* According to it, the plea of *tu quoque* is against the body of international humanitarian law of armed conflicts. This simply means that a conflicting party cannot excuse its own act by referring to similar acts by other conflicting parties in an armed conflict. Therefore, the Trial Chamber of the ICTY has described:

> the *tu quoque* defence as absolutely *fallacious and inapplicable*. The *tu quoque* defence can be defined as an argument based on the alleged reciprocal nature of the obligations under international humanitarian law which would entitle a party to violate its obligations under such law if they are being committed by the enemy… there existed no international precedent supporting this defence and that, in any case, such an argument misconstrued the nature of the rules of international humanitarian law. This body of law cannot be conceived as an aggregate of bilateral obligations, namely, as an exchange of rights and obligations. "Instead, the bulk of this body of law lays down absolute obligations, namely obligations that are unconditional or in other words not based on reciprocity." The Trial Chamber found that this is evidence of the progressive trend towards the so-called "humanisation" of international legal obligations. Humanitarian rules were designed primarily to benefit individuals *qua* human beings, not to protect State interests. They thus constitute obligations erga omnes, obligations towards the international community as a whole, not merely obligations of States vis-à-vis one another. In addition, most norms of international humanitarian law have attained the status of *jus cogens*, i.e. non-derogable and overriding rules.[77]

The statement of the Chamber is therefore very simple. The *tu quoque* principle may not be applied to the provisions of the international humanitarian law of armed conflicts. In other words, humanitarian law does not lay down reciprocal obligations, but obligations *erga omnes* which imply the duties of individuals or states "designed to safeguard fundamental human values and therefore must be complied with regardless of the conduct of the other party or parties."[78] Thus, the ICTY rejected the character of *synallagmatic* obligations or reciprocal obligations regarding humanitarian law and gave high legal value to obligations *erga omnes*

---

[77] secnet069.un.org/x/file/Legal%20Library/jud...e/kupreskic.htm.

[78] Zoran Kupreskic, Mirjan Kupreskic, Vlatko Kupreskic, Drago Josiprovic, Dragan Papoc, Vladimir Santic, also known as "VLADO", Decision on Evidence of the Good Character of the Accused and the Defence of Tu Quoque, 17 February 1999. The statement was made by the Chamber in its *Decision On Defence Motion to Summon Witness* of 3 February 1999.

contractantes or *erga omnes partes*. These are treaty based obligations in which all contracting parties have a similar legal interest.[79]

3.6.4. *Alibi*

The word "alibi" means "elsewhere". In legal proceedings, it refers to a judicial form of defence by which an accused attempts to prove that he/she was in another place when the offence in question was committed. The rationale behind alibi is, as a whole, to prove that the defendant is innocent and has not committed the crime. Rule 67 of the ICTY deals with 'defence of alibi'. This means that this type of judicial mode of defence is accepted by the ICTY. The relevant provisions state that the defence shall notify the Prosecutor of its intent to offer: "the defence of alibi; in which case the notification shall specify the place or places at which the accused claims to have been present at the time of the alleged crime and the names and addresses of witnesses and any other evidence upon which the accused intends to rely to establish the alibi."[80]

The defence of alibi may or may not be accepted by the ICTY. In the *Vasiljevic* case, an ICTY Trial Chamber concluded that:

> In response to the Prosecution's allegations that the Accused personally participated in the looting, the transfer of the group to the Omeragi house, and the setting on fire of that house, the Accused raised a "defence" of alibi. He claimed that, at the time of these events, he was either on his way to, or present in, the General Hospital in Užice ("the Užice Hospital"). The Trial Chamber does not accept all of the evidence of the Accused in relation to the alibi. However, the Trial Chamber is not satisfied that the evidence of Prosecution witnesses who claimed to have seen the Accused

---

[79] The position is described by the following words: "The defence of *tu quoque* concerns the allegation that the opposing party to the conflict committed similar atrocities and, in the case in point, also included the allegation that that party was responsible for the commencement of the said conflict. Following its *Decision on Defence Motion to Summon Witness* of 3 February 1999 and its ruling at the hearing of 15 February 1999, the Trial Chamber held that evidence to prove such a defence is inadmissible because it does not tend to (dis)prove any of the allegations against the accused. In its Decision of 3 February 1999, the Trial Chamber had ruled that the principle of *tu quoque* does not apply to international humanitarian law since that body of law creates obligations erga omnes *(contractantes)* and not obligations based on reciprocity." Kupreskic et al. (IT-95-16-T), Decision on Evidence of the Good Character of the Accused and the Defence of TuQuoque, 17 Febraury 1999.Cited in secnet069.un.org/x/file/Legal%20Library/jud.../supp2-e/kup.htm.

[80] Rule 67 (i) (a). See the appendix.

> participating in the different stages of the Pionirska Street incident establishes beyond reasonable doubt that the Accused was not on the way to, or present in, the U`ice Hospital at the relevant time, when that evidence was considered in light of the alibi raised by the Accused.[81]

Although, reference to alibi is acceptable under the provisions of the Tribunal, it must be correct and appropriate. The use of a false or misleading alibi must be proved beyond reasonable doubt by the Prosecutor. According to the ICTY:

> The Trial Chamber is satisfied that sufficient doubt is cast upon the evidence which suggests that the Accused was present in Pionirska Street during the transfer of the group to the Omeragic house, and the fire, by the evidence which suggests that the Accused was either in or on the way to the U`ice Hospital at that time. It is the alibi evidence which ultimately leads the Trial Chamber to reject the Prosecution case that he was in Pionirska Street at the relevant times…The Trial Chamber is satisfied that the evidence of Prosecution witnesses who claimed to have seen the Accused after 14 June 1992 cannot establish, beyond reasonable doubt, the falsity of the alibi raised by the Accused.[82]

However, it must be asserted that the Appeals Chamber of the ICTY has not accepted resort to alibi as constituting a defence. Accordingly, "it is a common misuse of the word to describe an alibi as a 'defence'."[83] This statement of the Appeals Chamber seems to be in contrast to the language of Rule 67 of the ICTY. In any event, the proof of an alibi or otherwise does not reveal the non-participation of the defendant in the commission of the offence.

3.6.5. Duress

With a defence of duress, the accused argues that he/she should not be held responsible because his/her conduct was the result of coercion. Duress is also considered as a defence under the practice of the ICTY, but it is not considered as a complete defence. In the words of the Appeals Chamber majority "international law … cannot admit duress in cases which involve the slaughter of innocent human beings on a large scale."[84] It continued further that "Duress cannot afford a complete defence to a soldier charged

---

[81] *Vasiljevic* (IT-98—32-T), Judgement, 29 November 2002, para.129.
[82] *Vasiljevic* (IT-98—32-T), Judgement, 29 November 2002, paras.152-156.
[83] *Delalic et al.* (IT-96-21-A), Judgement, 20 February 2001, para.581.
[84] Erdemovic (IT-96-22-A), 7 October, 1997, Joint Separate Opinion of Judge McDonald and Judge Vohrah, para.55, 66, 72, 75, 88.

with crimes against humanity or war crimes in international law involving the taking of innocent lives. We do so having regard to our mandated obligation under the Statute to ensure that international humanitarian law, which is concerned with the protection of humankind, is not in any way undermined."[85] This nuanced treatment of duress as an element of defence before the ICTY has opened intensive discussions.[86] Despite the above view, the ICC recognises the defence of duress.

3.6.6. Self-Defence

The term 'self-defence' is one of the most recognised terms of international criminal law and it has been entered into a number of international conventions including the Statute of the United Nations Organization. Accordingly, the resort to self-defence is permitted to all states, but under certain conditions. Similarly, most sources of international law, including customary and general principles of law, permit the resort to self-defence. In addition, certain resolutions of the General Assembly recognise the rights of individuals, groups and states to struggle for the inalienable right of independence. In fact, the right to resort to self-defence arises where there is an actual danger or a serious threat which cannot be avoided. However, it has to be stated that various concepts of self-defence are based on the principle of proportionality and this principle has to be respected where the resort to self-defence against certain acts is inevitable.

Self-defence may also be invoked as an admissible defence by the accused in the procedures of the ICTY. The Tribunal has therefore dealt with the questions of self-defence and the claims brought by defendants. The Appeals Chamber of the ICTY incorporates the defence of self-defence when there are issues of motive. According to it:

> … reference to 'factors' ought not obscure the distinction between *mens rea* and motive. *Mens rea* is the mental state or degree of fault which the accused held at the relevant time. Motive is generally considered as that which causes a person to act. The Appeals Chamber has held that, as far as criminal responsibility is concerned, motive is generally irrelevant in international criminal law, but it "becomes relevant at the sentencing stage in mitigation or aggravation of the sentence". Motive is also to be considered in two further circumstances: first, where it is a required element in crimes such as specific intent crimes, which by their nature

---

[85] *Id.*

[86] See Illan Rua Wall, Duress, International Criminal Law and Literature (2006), pp. 724-744.

> require a particular motive; and second, where it may constitute a form of defence, such as self-defence.[87]

In most cases relevant to the defence of self-defence, the character of self-defence has been cumulative in order to justify the use of force and the atrocities resulting from it. However, the ICTY has clearly stated that the defence of self-defence cannot be pleaded in excuse of a serious offence which is an integral part of customary law. The Trial Chamber with reference to Article 31 of the ICC goes further and says that "The principle of self-defence enshrined in this provision reflects provisions found in most national criminal codes and may be regarded as constituting a rule of customary international law."[88] The Trial Chamber has however refused to admit the plea of self-defence in the case of serious violations of the international humanitarian law of armed conflicts. Therefore, it concludes that:

> Article 31(1)(c) of the ICC Statute sets forth two conditions which must be met in order for self-defence to be accepted as a ground for excluding criminal liability: (a) the act must be in response to "an imminent and unlawful use of force" against an attack on a "protected" person or property; (b) the act of defence must be "proportionate to the degree of danger". In relation to the specific circumstances of war crimes, the provision takes into account the principle of military necessity. ... Of particular relevance to this case is the last sentence of the above provision to the effect that the involvement of a person in a "defensive operation" does not "in itself" constitute a ground for excluding criminal responsibility. It is therefore clear that any argument raising self-defence must be assessed on its own facts and in the specific circumstances relating to each charge. The Trial Chamber will have regard to this condition when deciding whether the defence of self-defence applies to any of the charges. The Trial Chamber, however, would emphasise that military operations in self-defence do not provide a justification for serious violations of international humanitarian law.[89]

3.6.7. Military Necessity

The plea of military necessity is another mode of defence to a criminal charge. The Statute of ICTY has, in Article 3 (b), stated that "wanton destruction of cities, towns or villages, or devastation not justified by

---

[87] Blaskic (IT-95-14-A), Judgement, 29 July 2004, para.694.

[88] Kordic and Cerkez et al (IT-95-14/2-T), Judgement, 26 February 2001, paras.451.

[89] *Id.*, paras.451-452.

military necessity" constitute violations of the laws or customs of war. In Article 2 (d), the same Statute clarifies that "extensive destruction and appropriation of property, not justified by military necessity and carried out unlawfully and wantonly" constitute grave breaches. Here, the Statute asserts that certain acts are not permitted during armed conflicts. Ironically, this means that the destruction of cities and towns may be permitted when there is a requirement of military necessity and as a result the concept of international criminal responsibility may not be applied. But the conditions amounting to military necessity are subject to various interpretations. There are no specific consolidated rules concerning this matter in international law. In the *Blaskic* case, the Trial Chamber explained that:

> The parties to the conflict are obliged to attempt to distinguish between military targets and civilian persons or property. Targeting civilians or civilian property is an offence when not justified by military necessity. Civilians within the meaning of Article 3 are persons who are not, or no longer, members of the armed forces. Civilian property covers any property that could not be legitimately considered a military objective. Such an attack must have been conducted intentionally in the knowledge, or when it was impossible not to know, that civilians or civilian property were being targeted not through military necessity.[90]

Thus, according to the statement of ICTY, the defence of military necessity did not exist in the above case.[91] For instance, "it was impossible to ascertain any strategic or military reasons for the 16 April 1993 attack on Vitez and Stari Vitez. In the event that there had been, the devastation visited upon the town was out of all proportion with military necessity. On the contrary, the attack was designed to implement an expulsion plan, if necessary by killing Muslim civilians and destroying their possessions."[92] The Trial Chamber further asserted that "these events amount to devastation without any military necessity and forcible transfers of civilians."[93] According to the Chamber, the Bosnian Croats intentionally burned Muslim houses and acts of looting were carried out in order to dissuade Muslims from returning to their home. Those acts were not justified by military necessity.[94] The Trial Chamber concluded that "By

---

[90] *Blaskic* (IT-95-14-T), Judgement, 3 March 2000, para.180.

[91] See *id*., paras.12, 73, 148, 157, 159, 180, 183, 234, 510, 544, 550, 553, 559 and 651.

[92] *Id*., para.510.

[93] *Id*., para.550.

[94] *Id*., para.559.

advocating the vigorous use of heavy weapons to seize villages inhabited mainly by civilians, General Bla{ki} gave orders which had consequences out of all proportion to military necessity and knew that many civilians would inevitably be killed and their homes destroyed."[95]

There have been different interpretations concerning the scope of military necessity within the judgements of the ICTY. Some controversies have therefore arisen. The basic assumption has been that civilians and their property are protected by international humanitarian law. For instance, the Appeals Chamber in the *Blaskic* case objected to the view of the Trial Chamber.[96] The statement of the Appeals Chamber was even stronger in response to the *Kordic* and *Cerkez* case. It stated that the Appeals Chamber is of the view that "the prohibition against attacking civilians and civilian objects would not be a crime when justified by military necessity. The prohibition against attacking civilians stems from a fundamental principle of the international humanitarian law, the principle of distinction, which obliges warring parties to distinguish *at all times* between the civilian population and combatants, between civilian objects and military objectives and accordingly to direct military operations only against military objectives."[97]

The above statement of the Appeals Chamber was strengthened by Article 48 of Additional Protocol I stipulating the significant function of the 'principle of distinction' as constituting one of the basic rules of armed conflict.[98] In addition, the Appeals Chamber, with reference to the International Court of Justice view regarding the Advisory Opinion on the Legality of Nuclear Weapons, emphasises the value of Article 48.[99] According to this, the description of the Court is highly important when it points out that the 'principle of distinction', along with the principle of the protection of the civilian population, are "the cardinal principles contained in the texts constituting the fabric of humanitarian law" and further clarifies that "States must never make civilians the object of attack." The Appeals Chamber goes even further and quotes the International Court of

---

[95] *Id*., para.651.

[96] The Appeals Chamber stated that "Before determining the scope of the term "civilian population," the Appeals Chamber deems it necessary to rectify the Trial Chamber's statement, contained in paragraph 180 of the Trial Judgement, according to which "[t]argeting civilians or civilian property is an offence when not justified by military necessity." The Appeals Chamber underscores that there is an absolute prohibition on the targeting of civilians in customary international law." *Blaskic* (IT-95-14-A), Judgement, 29 July 2004, para.109.

[97] *Kordic et al.* (IT-95-14/2-A), Judgement, 17 December 2004, para.54.

[98] *Id.*

[99] *Id.*

Justice statement with the following words: "These fundamental rules are to be observed by all States whether or not they have ratified the conventions that contain them, because they constitute intransgressible principles of international customary law".[100]

The defence of military necessity may also be invoked against a charge of crimes against humanity. It has, in certain circumstances, been accepted by the ICTY.[101] This means that the concept of international criminal responsibility may be mitigated because of the conditions of a case.

4. International Criminal Responsibility in the ICTR

One of the significant functions of international criminal law is to attribute the concept of international criminal responsibility to the perpetrators of international crimes. The international legal community seeks, in fact, to impose international punishment for core international crimes on inferiors, superiors and heads of states or governments. According to the contemporary development of international criminal law and justice, the core crimes include war crimes, crimes against humanity, genocide and aggression. The *ad hoc* tribunals established under the auspices of the United Nations do not deal with the international crime of aggression, although they should have done so. One of the most challenging crimes to come before the jurisdiction of the ICTR is genocide. This is a crime which is recognised as an integral part of the international law of *jus cogens.* Therefore, the purpose of the Trial and Appeals Chambers of the ICTR is to put an end to impunity for the perpetrators of heinous crimes, in particular, genocide. According to the ICTR, it is one of the most serious tasks of the international legal community to find persons responsible for the commission of genocide in Rwanda. This includes either planning or aiding and abetting in the planning, preparation or execution of genocide, crimes against humanity and other violations.

---

[100] Legality of the Threat or Use of Nuclear Weapons, requested by the United Nations General Assembly for an Advisory Opinion, 1996, ICJ Reports, 226, 78. The International Court of Justice further asserted that "these fundamental rules are to be observed by all States whether or not they have ratified the conventions that contain them, because they constitute intransgressible principles of international customary law".

[101] *Blagojevic*(IT-02-60-T), Judgement, 17 January 2005.

4.1. Criminal Responsibility of Individuals

The concept of the criminal responsibility of individuals is also well developed within the Statute of the ICTR. The Tribunal's aim is to bring accused persons under its jurisdiction for crimes against humanity, genocide or serious violations of the international humanitarian law of armed conflicts. For this reason, a person may be recognised as being criminally responsible if he/she planned, instigated, ordered, committed or otherwise aided and abetted in the planning, preparation or execution of a crime.[102] More importantly, the concept of international criminal responsibility is applied to any individual regardless of his/her position, including heads of state and any responsible government officials.[103] Thus, the Statute of the ICTR clearly states that a superior cannot escape from his/her criminal responsibility by invoking a subordinate's responsibility.[104] In other words, the criminal responsibility of a subordinate does not relieve the criminal responsibility of commanders if there are sufficient reasons to prove that they knew or had reason to know that the subordinate was about to commit one of the listed crimes in the Statute.[105] The ICTR has, in one of its judgements, clarified the concept of the criminal responsibility of superiors and subordinates in a political entity which engages, in one way or another, in the commission of criminal activities. According to the Trial Chamber:

> The Chamber notes that in *Musema*, the Tribunal found that superior responsibility extended to non-military settings, in that case to the owner of a tea factory. The Chamber has considered the extent to which Barayagwiza, as leader of the CDR, a political party, can be held responsible pursuant to Article 6(3) of its Statute for acts committed by CDR party members and *Impuzamugambi*. The Chamber recognises that a political party and its leadership cannot be held accountable for all acts committed by party members or others affiliated to the party. A political party is unlike a government, military or corporate structure in that its members are not bound through professional affiliation or in an employment capacity to be governed by the decision making body of the party. Nevertheless, the Chamber considers that to the extent that members of a political party act in accordance with the dictates of that party, or otherwise under its instruction, those issuing such dictates or instruction can and should be held accountable for their implementation. In this case,

---

102 Article 6 (1).

103 Artcle 6 (2).

104 Mark J. Osiel, *Modes of Participation in Mass Atrocity*, 38:3 Cornell International Law Journal 791-822 (2005).

105 Article 6 (3).

> CDR party members and *Impuzamugambi* were following the lead of the party, and of Barayagwiza himself, who was at meetings, at demonstrations, and at roadblocks, where CDR members and *Impuzamugambi* were marshaled into action by party officials, including Barayagwiza or under his authority as leader of the party. In these circumstances, the Chamber holds that Barayagwiza was responsible for the activities of CDR members and *Impuzamugambi*, to the extent that such activities were initiated by or undertaken in accordance with his direction as leader of the CDR party. The Chamber finds that Barayagwiza had superior responsibility over members of the CDR and its militia, the *Impuzamugambi*, as President of CDR at Gisenyi Prefecture and from February 1994 as President of CDR at the national level. He promoted the policy of CDR for the extermination of the Tutsi population and supervised his subordinates, the CDR members and *Impuzamug ambi* militia, in carrying out the killing sand other violent acts. For his active engagement in CDR, and his failure to take necessary and reasonable measures to prevent the killing of Tutsi civilians by CDR members and *Impuzamugambi*, the Chamber finds Barayagwiza guilty of genocide pursuant to Article 6(3) of its Statute.[106]

The attribution of criminal responsibility may be mitigated by the fact that an accused person acted pursuant to an order from a government. The concept of criminal responsibility may also be mitigated by the fact that one has acted following the order of a superior. In any event, it is the ICTR

---

[106] *Nahimana* et al. (ICTR-99-52-T), Judgement and Sentence, 3 December 2003, para.976-977. The Trial Chamber has explained the leadership of Barayagwiza with using the following words: "Jean Bosco Barayagwiza was one of the principal founders of CDR and played a leading role in its formation and development. He was a decision-maker for the party. The CDR had a youth wing, called the *Impuzamugambi*, which undertook acts of violence, often together with the *Interahamwe*, the MRND youth wing, against the Tutsi population. The killing of Tutsi civilians was promoted by the CDR, as evidenced by the chanting of "*tubatsembatsembe*" or "let's exterminate them" by Barayagwiza himself and by CDR members in his presence at public meetings and demonstrations. The reference to "them" was understood to mean the Tutsi population. Barayagwiza supervised roadblocks manned by the *Impuzamugambi,* established to stop and kill Tutsi. The Chamber notes the direct involvement of Barayagwiza in the expression of genocidal intent and in genocidal acts undertaken by members of the CDR and its *Impuzamugambi*. Barayagwiza was at the organizational helm. He was also on site at the meetings, demonstrations and roadblocks that created an infrastructure for and caused the killing of Tutsi civilians. For this reason, the Chamber finds Jean-Bosco Barayagwiza guilty of instigating acts of genocide committed by CDR members and *Impuzamugambi*, pursuant to Article 6(1) of its Statute." *Id.*, para.975. See *also* paras.276, 301, 339-341.

which determines and evaluates the circumstances of each case as justice requires.[107]

4.2. Criminal Responsibility of Heads of States

The ICTR has greatly contributed to the consolidation of certain principles of the international humanitarian law of armed conflicts and in the development of international criminal law. This can be seen within the decisions of the Tribunal concerning certain questions of customary and conventional international criminal law. The most notable of these contributions deals with the integrity of individuals, in particular women, during armed conflicts. The Tribunal has made it clear that rape is an international crime and may constitute genocide when it is carried out systematically and is widespread. The Tribunal has therefore convicted those responsible for sexual crimes and outrages against the dignity of man.[108] For example, in the Akayesu case, the Tribunal found him guilty of committing genocide.[109]

In particular, the ICTR has successively tried and condemned heads of state. An illustrative example is the sentencing of former Prime Minister Jean Kambanda. He was found guilty on four counts of genocide and two counts of crimes against humanity simultaneously.[110] His case has without

---

[107] Article 6 (4).

[108] ICTR, Akayesu, verdict of 2.9.1998, §478.

[109] The Tribunal stated that "specific intention of the crime of genocide does not have to be clearly expressed. (…) It can be inferred from a certain number of elements, such as the general doctrine of the political project (…) or the repetition of discriminatory destructive acts (or) the perpetration of acts undermining the foundation of the group." E. David, *Legal Principles of Armed Conflict*, Brussels, Bruylant, 1999, p. 661. In addition "This intention can be deduced from a certain number of elements, concerning genocide, of the crime against humanity and war crimes, by example of their massive and/or systematic character or of their atrocity (…)" ICTR, Akayesu, verdict of 2.9.1998, § 478.

[110] According to the Judgement: "In light of the admissions made by Jean Kambanda in amplification of his plea of guilty, the Trial Chamber, on 1st May 1998, accepted his plea and found him guilty on the following counts:

(1) By his acts or omissions described in paragraphs 3.12 to 3.15, and 3.17 to 3.19 of the indictment, Jean Kambanda is responsible for the killing of and the causing of serious bodily or mental harm to members of the Tutsi population with intent to destroy, in whole or in part, an ethnic or racial group, as such, and has thereby committed GENOCIDE, stipulated in Article 2(3)(a) of the Statute as a crime, and attributed to him by virtue of Article 6(1) and 6(3), and punishable in reference to Articles 22 and 23 of the Statute of the Tribunal.

doubt opened a new chapter in the history of jurisdiction and international criminal law. The trial of the former Prime Minister also proved that heads of state or government might not escape prosecution and punishment for committing international crimes. In other words, impunity is not permitted. Moreover, the work of the Tribunal consolidates *the principle of*

---

(2) By his acts or omissions described in paragraphs 3.8, 3.9, 3.13 to 3.15 and 3.19 of the indictment, Jean Kambanda did conspire with others, including Ministers of his Government, such as Pauline Nyiramasuhuko, Andre Ntagerura, Eliezer Niyitegeka and Edouard Karemera, to kill and to cause serious bodily or mental harm to members of the Tutsi population, with intent to destroy in whole or in part, an ethnic or racial group as such, and has thereby committed CONSPIRACY TO COMMIT GENOCIDE, stipulated in Articles 2(3)(b) of the Statute as a crime, and attributed to him by virtue of Article 6(1) and punishable in reference to Articles 22 and 23 of the Statute of the Tribunal.
(3) By his acts or omissions described in paragraphs 3.12 to 3.14 and 3.19 of the indictment, Jean Kambanda did directly and publicly incite to kill and to cause serious bodily or mental harm to members of the Tutsi population, with intent to destroy, in whole or in part, an ethnic group as such, and has thereby committed DIRECT AND PUBLIC INCITEMENT TO COMMIT GENOCIDE, stipulated in Article 2(3)(c) of the Statute as a crime, and attributed to him by virtue of Article 6(1) and 6(3), which is punishable in reference to Articles 22 and 23 of the Statute of the Tribunal.
(4) By his acts or omissions described in paragraphs 3.10, 3.12 to 3.15 and 3.17 to 3.19 of the indictment, which do not constitute the same acts relied on for counts 1,2 and 3, Jean Kambanda was complicit in the killing and the causing of serious bodily or mental harm to members of the Tutsi population, and thereby committed COMPLICITY IN GENOCIDE stipulated in Article 2(3)(e) of the Statute as a crime, and attributed to him by virtue of Article 6(1) and 6(3), which is punishable in reference to Articles 22 and 23 of the Statute of the Tribunal.
(5) By his acts or omissions described in paragraphs 3.12 to 3.15 and 3.17 to 3.19 of the indictment, Jean Kambanda is responsible for the murder of civilians, as part of a widespread or systematic attack against a civilian population on ethnic or racial grounds, and has thereby committed a CRIME AGAINST HUMANITY, stipulated in Article 3(a) of the Statute as a crime, and attributed to him by virtue of Article 6(1) and 6(3), which is punishable in reference to Articles 22 and 23 of the Statute of the Tribunal.
(6) By his acts or omissions described in paragraphs 3.12 to 3.15, and 3.17 to 3.19 of the indictment, Jean Kambanda is responsible for the extermination of civilians, as part of a widespread or systematic attack against a civilian population on ethnic or racial grounds, and has thereby committed a CRIME AGAINST HUMANITY, stipulated in Article 3(b) of the Statute as a crime, and attributed to him by virtue of Article 6(1) and 6(3), which is punishable in reference to Articles 22 and 23 of the Statute of the Tribunal."*Jean Kambanda* (ICTR 97-23-S), Judgment, 4 September 1998, para.40.

international tribunality of jurisdiction for international crimes and the punishment of heads of states in international criminal courts.[111] It makes it clear that international criminal responsibility may be attributed to any individual regardless of his or her social position within the political and juridical systems of states. The judgment of the Tribunal has also strengthened the theory of the international criminal responsibility of individuals which was strongly supported in the Nuremberg Judgment and evolved within the provisions of other international documents. The judgment of the Tribunal concerning the Prime Minister of the government of Rwanda - *Jean Kambanda* - proved various forms of conspiracy and assistance given by him in order to carry out atrocities and genocide.[112]

4.3. *Ne Bis in Idem*

The Statute of the ICTR, as in many other international criminal courts, tries to guarantee the principle of the protection of criminals who have already been punished for the same crimes by another court. Thus, the Tribunal cannot prosecute or punish those individuals who have already been prosecuted or punished for the same crime in Rwanda or other places. But this does not mean that the criminals can escape their criminal responsibility by referring to punishments previously enforced by other courts.[113] This is because the Tribunal is entitled to bring any person under its jurisdiction who has not been punished for the crimes listed in the Statute.[114] Thus, the situation is subject to the position of a case, and to whether or not acts or omissions, which have been carried out by an accused, have all been properly handled and prosecuted by the prior court.

The ICTR may prosecute a person who has been tried by a national court if the crime of that person was characterised as an ordinary crime.[115] It may also have jurisdiction over a person when it considers that the

[111] Consult Farhad Malekian, *Emasculating the Philosophy of International Criminal Justice in the Iraqi Special Tribunal*, 38:3 Cornell International Law Journal 673-723 (2005).

[112] *Jean Kambanda* (ICTR 97-23-S). Later after the delivery of judgment, Jean Kambanda rejected his confession for the admission of criminal acts asserting that he was forced to make it. On 19th October 2000, TPIR House of Appeal did not accept his statement and confirmed the prior judgment. He is now serving his sentence in Mali, at the Central House of Arrest of Bamako.

[113] For some discussions on punishment see J.D. van der Vyver, *Prosecution and Punishment of the Crime of Genocide*', 23 Fordham International Law Journal (1999), p. 286.

[114] Consult *Id.*

[115] Article 9 (2) (a).

relevant national court has not been impartial or competent or where prosecution has not been proper.[116] A person should not be tried simultaneously before a national court for acts constituting serious violations of international humanitarian law for which that person is already being tried by the ICTR.[117] The Tribunal has a duty to consider the penalty imposed on a person by another court and should be very careful in the application of a further penalty.[118]

In general, it is the responsibility of the Tribunal to take a decision concerning the different matters of proceedings and prosecutions. In other words, if the domestic courts do not meet the necessary requisite standards of independence or impartiality, or if they do not apply the necessary penalties to the person found criminal, the ICTR is empowered to investigate the case of the relevant person and, if it seems necessary, to transfer him or her under the jurisdiction of the Tribunal. The jurisdiction of the Tribunal is exhaustive in nature and cannot be changed by other authorities or national courts.

Obviously, the Tribunal's policy is based on cooperation between different states in transferring and submitting the accused to the jurisdiction of the Tribunal. This task has been very difficult and since there have been a large number of individuals accused of committing crimes against humanity, genocide and serious violations of humanitarian law of armed conflicts, the Tribunal's work is still going on.

4.4. Effective Enforcement of Responsibility

The ICTR is one of the most important tribunals to have been established under the United Nations authority. The Tribunal rejects the classical positions of international criminal law regarding the impunity of heads of state with its direct attribution of the concept of international criminal responsibility. This is especially notable concerning the prosecution and punishment of the most responsible persons in governments. In several cases, the Tribunal has proved that international crimes are not just a matter of the formulation of certain provisions but are rather capable of the recognition of genocide and crimes against humanity. In order to

---

[116] Article 9 (2) (b).

[117] Article 9 (1).

[118] For a critical analysis of the policy of punishment of the ICTR consult Orna Ben-Naftali and Miri Sharon, *What the ICJ Did not Say About the Duty to Punish Genocide: The Missing Pieces in a Puzzle,* Journal of International Criminal Justice (2007).

summarise the effects of the structure and the jurisdiction of the Tribunal, the following may be useful:

- The Tribunal has consolidated the principle of individual criminal responsibility.
- The criminal responsibility of heads of state or government has clearly been proved in the Tribunal.
- It has obviously brought to an end the classical idea of the protection of kings, presidents and prime ministers by resorting to the plea of constitutional immunity.
- The 1948 Convention on Genocide was for the second time applied in an international criminal court.
- Rape was recognised as being a crime against human dignity and constituting genocide and therefore contributes to the concept of the international criminal responsibility of the perpetrators.
- The protection of victims and witnesses has been one of the most important functions of the ICTR. This is carried out according to special rules.
- The Tribunal has made a great contribution to restorative justice and the maintenance of international peace, equality, security and the fundamental principles of human rights. It demonstrates that individuals should bear criminal responsibility for their grave violations of the system of international criminal law.

5. International Criminal Responsibility in the SCSR

The concept of the international criminal responsibility of individuals, which is one of the basic principles of the system of international criminal law, has also been entered into the structure of the Statute of the Special Court.[119] Thus, Article 6 of the Statute deals with different notions of criminal responsibility. According to it, those who have been responsible for atrocities against civilians and the destruction of their installations have to be brought before the jurisdiction of the Special Court for prosecution and punishment.[120] According to the provisions of the article, the concept of criminal responsibility is attributable to any individual without regard to his/her position.[121]

---

[119] Consult Geoffrey Robertson, *Ending Immunity: How International Criminal Law Can Put Tyrants on Trial,* 38:3 Cornell International Law Journal 649-671 (2005), 665.

[120] *Id.*, at 664.

[121] *Id.*, at 664-665.

5.1. Division of Criminal Responsibility

The provisions of Article 6 of the Statute of the SCSL are divided into five sub-paragraphs, which are integral to each other and should not be read in isolation. According to the provisions of paragraph 1, a person may bear individual criminal responsibility for his/her conduct if he/she has planned, aided, abetted, instigated, ordered, prepared or committed the criminal conduct which is described within articles 2, 3 and 4. The provisions of paragraph 2 clarify that the official position of the accused person does not have any effect on the concept of the international criminal responsibility of the accused. Consequently, a head of state or government or a responsible government official may not be absolved of his/her criminal responsibility because of his/her official or constitutional position.[122] Thus, his/her position cannot be a justification for avoiding prosecution and punishment.[123]

The provisions of sub-paragraph 3 relate to the concept of the criminal responsibility of superiors where acts listed and described within Articles 2, 3 and 4 are committed. According to the content of this sub-paragraph, the commission of criminal acts mentioned in the Statute by a subordinate does not relieve his/her superior of criminal responsibility "if he or she knew or had reason to know that the subordinate was about to commit such acts or had done so and the superior had failed to take the necessary and reasonable measures to prevent such acts or to punish the perpetrators thereof".

Sub-paragraph 4 takes into recognition certain situations that may mitigate the criminal responsibility of the accused. It emphasises that acting pursuant to an order of a superior or government may not relieve an accused person from his/her criminal responsibility, but may mitigate the attribution of criminal responsibility if the Special Court, in the interests of justice, determines its mitigation.

Finally, sub-paragraph 5 of Article 6 clarifies that the concept of criminal responsibility for the crimes listed in Article 5 of the Statute is accomplished within the provisions of the relevant laws of Sierra Leone.

A significant fact here is that the provisions of Article 6 are, in most respects, similar to the provisions of the system of international criminal law, which have been undertaken by other international criminal tribunals. The only difference is the provisions of sub-paragraph 5, which refer to the concept of criminal responsibility under a defined domestic system.

---

[122] *Id.*

[123] *Id.* 665.

This is also limited to the crimes that are recognised under Article 5 of the Statute in accordance with Sierra Leonean law.

5.2. Criminal Responsibility for the Recruitment of Children

One of the most significant principles dealt with by the Statute of the Special Court is the recognition of the recruitment of child soldiers as a serious crime under the structure of the international humanitarian law of armed conflict.[124] According to the Statute, individuals may have criminal responsibility for the use of children during war. Article 4 (c) of the Statute has particularly stated that "Conscripting or enlisting children under the age of 15 into armed forces or groups or using them to participate actively in hostilities" constitutes a violation of international humanitarian law.[125]

There were several reasons for the formulation of Article 4 (c) within the provisions of the Statute.[126] One essential reason relies on the fact that during the civil war in Sierra Leone, children were influenced or kidnapped and forced to take part in the armed conflicts.[127] This military

---

[124] Consult Alison Smith, *Child Recruitment and the Special Court for Sierra Leone*, 2 Journal of International Criminal Justice 1141-1153 (2004).

[125] For the examination of the views of the Special Court consult *id.*

[126] See www.crin.org/law/Instrument.asp?InstID=1263 - 21k. Visited on 2009-01-20.

[127] According to the Prosecutor of the Special Court for Sierra Leone, the politician Samuel Hinga Norman had criminal responsibility for the use of children under the age of 15. He stressed "The crime of child recruitment was part of customary international law at the relevant time. The Geneva Conventions established the protection of children under 15 as an undisputed norm of humanitarian law. The number of states that made the practice of child recruitment illegal under their domestic law and the subsequent international conventions addressing child recruitment demonstrate the existence of this customary international norm." Moreover, a considerable number of other international instruments establish the prohibition of child recruitment such as the ICC Statute, which represents the codification of the rules of customary international law. The *Tadic case* is another example proving the existence of customary rules for the prohibition of child recruitment. According to the prosecutor, the president of the Security Council has also declared the condemnation of child recruitment in the body of the international humanitarian law of armed conflicts on 29 June 1998. The concept of the prohibition of child recruitment has in fact entered into the declaration on the Prevention of Children into Armed Forces and Demobilization and Social Reintegration of Child Soldiers in Africa which clearly states that "those responsible for illegally recruiting children should be brought to justice." [Cape Town Principles and Best Practices on the Recruitment of Children in to the Armed Forces and on Demobilization and Social Reintegration of Child Soldiers in Africa,

strategy was not only against the Convention on the Rights of Child, but was also against a considerable number of international documents supporting the rights of children in peace and wartime.[128] An examination of different cases brought before the Special Court indicates the widespread misuse of children less than 15 years of age.

Symposium of the NGO working on the Convention of the Rights of the Child and UNICEF, 30 April 1997, para 4.]
In addition to the above discussion, "The principle of *nullum crimen sine lege* should not be rigidly applied to an act universally regarded as abhorrent. The question is whether it was foreseeable and accessible to a possible perpetrator that the conduct was punishable." According to the prosecutor, the system of international law has no governmental machinery for the legislation of its rules and emphasizing which rules are and are not integral parts of customary international criminal law. International criminal responsibility is the culmination of a considerable number of factors, which must be examined in conjunction to one another and not in isolation. Furthermore, it is the dictates of public conscience, which specifies which acts are criminal and not necessarily the "specific definition of the offence." For the above statements see more closely http://www.sc-sl.org/Documents/CDF/SCSL-04-14-AR72(E)-131-7383.pdf. Visited on 2009-06-18. The Appeals Chamber found that the prohibition of child recruitment was as an integral part of international criminal law and therefore a prosecutable and punishable crime. According to it "a norm need not be expressly stated in an international convention for it to crystallize as a crime under customary international law." (Norman died because of sickness in 2007.) But for dissenting opinion stated by justice Robertson see http://www.sc-sl.org/Documents/CDF/SCSL-04-14-AR72(E)-131-7413.pdf. He goes obviously against most statements of the Court. See further http://www.sc-sl.org/Documents/CDF/SCSL-04-14-AR72(E)-131-7430.pdf. Although, the dissenting opinion contains some useful argumentation, it has obviously lost sight of the value of family integrity, which was violated by force in order to take children into war zones. Even the voluntary contribution of children in armed conflict entails the superior's responsibility based on the fact that their use is against the spirit of Article 3 of the Geneva Convention and the normal definition of soldiers in armed fields. Consult Farhad Malekian., *Prohibition Governing Child Soldiers Constituting an Integral Part of Jus Cogens and Obligatio Erga Omnes,* XVII World Congress of the International Association of Youth and Family Judges and Magistrates, Belfast, Northern Ireland, 27 August – 2 September, 2006. http://www.youthandfamily 2006.com/welcome.htm. Published also by the Institute of International Criminal Law, Uppsala, Sweden 2006.

[128] Consult http://www.sc-sl.org/Documents/CDF/SCSL-04-14-AR72(E)-131-7398.pdf. Visited on 2009-04-22.

5.3. *Ne Bis in Idem*

The Statute of the Special Court contains different principles for the proper implementation and application of justice. One of the most notable principles is the principle of *ne bis in idem*,[129] which emphasises the juridical validity of the decision of the Special Court. Accordingly, a person who has already been tried by the Special Court should not be brought before other national courts of Sierra Leone. This jurisdictional immunity has also been conditionally granted to a person who has been tried by a national court. This means that the Special Court does not have jurisdiction over a person who has already been tried by a national court. But the Special Court may subsequently try such a person if "(a) The act for which he or she was tried was characterized as an ordinary crime; or (b) The national court proceedings were not impartial or independent, were designed to shield the accused from international criminal responsibility or the case was not diligently prosecuted."[130]

In any event, the Special Court in the case of the application of a penalty should take into consideration the extent to which any penalty imposed by a national court has served as sufficient punishment for the criminal person.[131] Yet, the Statute emphasises that, with regard to the crimes listed in articles 2, 3 and 4, an amnesty previously granted to any person coming under the jurisdiction of the Special Court may not be a bar to prosecution.[132]

---

[129] This principle is also called *non bis in idem*.
[130] Articles 9, 1 and 2.
[131] Articles 9 and 3.
[132] Article 10.

6. International Criminal Responsibility in the ICC

The rapid development of the system of international criminal law has undoubtedly established as predominant the concept of the international criminal responsibility of individuals.[133] This concept has been

[133] The concept of international criminal law, since the early twentieth century, has been developed through the concept of international criminal responsibility of individuals. However, individual responsibility has also been objected to in various international conflicts. The concept of individual responsibility in international criminal law was mostly documented after the First World War and has since been consolidated by the events of the Second World War and the establishment of the United Nations Organization. The concept of individual criminal responsibility has constantly been developing within a number of international criminal instruments including international conventions on international crimes and is based upon the general assumption that individuals have criminal responsibility for violations of the system of international criminal law. This responsibility is regardless of whether or not the criminal activities committed by the individual are pursuant to an order of a superior authority. Two of the most recognized conventions on international criminal law dealing with the concept of individual criminal responsibility are the 1948 Genocide Convention and the 1973 Convention on the Prevention and Punishment of Apartheid. Both conventions call strictly on the criminal responsibility of individuals who have seriously violated their provisions.
It must also be added that the concept of the criminal responsibility of individuals has been discussed in the works of a number of jurists and the general assumption is that individuals bear criminal responsibility for violations of the principles of international criminal law. The criminal responsibility of individuals does, however, differ from state criminal responsibility. Although both concepts may overlap, they contain two different criminal characterisations. One of the strongest objections to the concept of the criminal responsibility of states being that legal entities do not have physical bodies for punishment and it is therefore impossible to bring states before an international criminal court for prosecution and punishment. This is one of the strongest reasons for the profound controversy regarding these two types of international criminal responsibility. Nevertheless, it is believed that alongside the international criminal responsibility of individuals, there also exists the concept of the international criminal responsibility of states. Although no legal conclusion has been achieved, the theory of the international criminal responsibility of states occupies an important place in the system of international criminal law. Therefore, it may be useful here to refer to the commentary of Article 3 of the 1996 Draft Code of Crimes Against the Security of Mankind. Accordingly "Paragraph 1 deals specifically with the responsibility of the perpetrators of the crime and limits criminal responsibility and the resulting punishment to individuals, to the exclusion of States. It is true that the act for which an individual is responsible might also be attributable to a State if the individual acted as an "agent of the State", "on behalf of the State", "in the name

consolidated especially since the creation of several international criminal tribunals for the prosecution and punishment of those who violated the law of armed conflict. In fact, the first international recognition of the concept of the international criminal responsibility of individuals was created by the two military tribunals in Nuremberg and Tokyo and enlarged more specifically under the authority of the United Nations in the ICTY and the ICTR.[134]

The chief purpose of the recognition of the concept of criminal responsibility of individuals is to find the proper subject of responsibility for the wrongful conduct. This means to attribute criminal responsibility to those who have been primary agents in violations of international criminal law. It is also a fact that the concept of individual responsibility was originally based on three main international crimes. These were crimes against peace, war crimes and crimes against humanity. The development of the concept of the criminal responsibility of individuals since that time has also been affected by the acknowledgement of other international crimes such as genocide, torture and rape. The constitutions of the ICTY, the ICTR, the Special Court for Sierra Leone and the ICC implicitly confirm this development.

One significant reason for the development of the concept of the criminal responsibility of individuals is the recognition of the concept of criminal responsibility of those who are the primary agents of violations of the law by subordinate individuals who carry out official orders. That is why, since World War II, the international legal community has aimed at consolidating the concept of the criminal responsibility of all the

---

of the State" or as a de facto agent, without any legal power. Draft article 3 clearly establishes the criminal responsibility of the individual and is without prejudice to the international responsibility of the State. In this connection and during the discussion of the draft Code in plenary, some members of the Commission supported the proposition that not only an individual but also a State could be held criminally responsible. At its thirty-sixth session, the Commission nevertheless decided that the draft Code should be limited at the current stage to the criminal responsibility of individuals, without prejudice to subsequent consideration of the possible application to States of the notion of international criminal responsibility, in the light of the opinions expressed by Governments. It should be pointed out that assuming that the criminal responsibility of the State can be codified, the rules applicable to it cannot be the same as regards investigation, appearance in court and punishment. The two regimes of criminal responsibility would be different." (Report of the International Law Commission on the Work of Its forty-third session, 29 April - 19 July 1991, General Assembly Official Records: Forty-Sixth Session, Supplement No.10 (A/46/10), p.251.)

[134] For all these tribunals see the relevant chapters.

individuals of a state without regard to their claims of constitutional immunity.[135] This has, however, not been an easy task and confrontation has been unavoidable between the opponents of the concept of criminal responsibility of individuals and those who were against its implementation.

In any event, the Statutes of the ICTY, ICTR and ICC are built upon the principle of the criminal responsibility of individuals for violations of the humanitarian law of armed conflicts, war crimes, crimes against humanity and genocide. Each of these crimes has also been divided into several concepts of violation that have given rise to the concept of individual criminal responsibility.[136] Concerning the question of responsibility, the Statute of the ICC is the most progressive of these regulations and the general principles of criminal responsibility have therefore been drafted.[137]

---

[135] Rosanne van Alebeek, *From Rome to the Hague: Recent Developments on Immunity Issues in the ICC Statute*, 13 Leiden Journal of International Law 485 (2000).

[136] The fact is that the 1996 Draft Code of Crimes Against the Peace and Security of Mankind has also adopted an article dealing with the concept of the international criminal responsibility of individuals. The problem of the Draft is that it basically combines the question of the criminal responsibility of individuals with that of *mens rea, actus reus* and punishment. See Article 2 of the Code.

[137] The theory of criminal responsibility invokes the theory of punishment. The application of the theory of international responsibility and conditions under which a person can be recognised as being responsible can also be found under the relevant provisions of the 1996 Draft Code of Crimes against the Peace and Security of Mankind. Although the provisions of the ICC governing the criminal responsibility of individuals are rather new, some of its basic elements can be seen under the provisions of other international documents. For instance, Article 2 of the Code contains several important principles governing the international criminal responsibility of individuals violating both the fundamental principles of the draft code and the principles of international criminal law. The article also divides the criminal responsibility of individuals under the Code into two different categories. This is under paragraph 2 and 3 of the Code. Clearly, the Code has a special policy for the consideration and attribution of the international criminal responsibility of individuals who violate the provisions of the Code governing the international crime of aggression[137] and the provisions which are employed in connection with the violation of other international crimes, namely, genocide, crimes against humanity, crimes against the United Nations and associated personnel, and war crimes. But this does not mean that the relevant provisions of the ICC concerning criminal responsibility will not apply to the international crime of aggression once the definition of that crime has been adopted under the Rome Statute. The reason for the use of two different policies in the Code governing international crimes

6.1. The Dimension of Criminal Responsibility

The Statute of the ICC exclusively focuses on the concept of the international criminal responsibility of individuals. This is one of the most basic purposes of the Statute. Article 25 of the Statute deals with this concept and regulates rules under which a person may be recognized as criminally responsible for the violations of crimes listed in the Statute.

6.1.1. Natural Person

Article 25 of the Statute makes it quite clear that the ICC has sole jurisdiction over a natural person with regard to its provisions. This means that the ICC has no legal power to bring a case before the Court against a juridical person or state for the violations of the system of international criminal law regulated in the Statute. Any such concept has to be dealt with by other future courts or the Statute of the ICC has to be modified. Thus, in this case, the authority of the ICC to investigate a case is solely based on the traditional concepts of the international criminal responsibility of individuals and any other interpretation concerning the authority of the Court to define the notion of the international criminal responsibility of states is groundless.[138]

Obviously, by a "natural person" the ICC means any individual who is, according to the provisions of the Statute, considered capable of committing crimes against humanity, genocide, war crimes and aggression.[139] The Statute does not distinguish between individuals and consequently all individuals in the world are explicitly and implicitly the direct *subjects* of the Court and may be recognised as being criminally responsible for the violations of the ICC Statute.[140] This means that the

---

against the peace and security of mankind is the prolonged controversy and conflict which has hindered the drafting of a definition of the crime of aggression. The conflict was not resolved and the question is now under particular examination by the states members to the Statute of the ICC. The Assembly of States Parties Inter-Sessional Meeting on the Crime of Aggression, chaired by Prince Zeid Ra'ad Zeid Al-Husscin of Jordan, was assembled from 8 to 10 June in New York. The Assembly of States Parties also prepared a conference in Kampala in 2010 in order to review the 1998 Rome Statute. The purpose is to consider any amendments to it submitted by States Parties. www.icc-cpi.int/Menus/ASP/Crime+of+Aggression. The 2010 Review Conference has now adopted a definition on the crime of aggression. See *infera* section on The Review Conference in Kampala.

[138] See Article 25 (1).

[139] See Article 25 (2).

[140] This is with reservation to mentally ill persons.

ICC recognises the personal responsibility of individuals who commit a crime within the jurisdiction of the Court.[141] In other words, the concept of "individually responsible" makes it clear that the violators of the Statute of the ICC cannot escape from the concept of international criminal responsibility with the plea of superior orders or by referring to the acts of a state organ.[142] International criminal punishment should apply to any person who violates its rules.[143]

6.1.2. Condition for Individual Responsibility

The Statute of the ICC enumerates a number of provisions for the concept of the international criminal responsibility of a person.[144] Consequently, a person shall be criminally responsible and liable for punishment for a crime according to the provisions of Articles 6, 7 and 8 if one of the reasons below exists.[145] These reasons, as will be shown, create various degrees of criminal responsibility under the provisions of the Statute. By

---

[141] Antonio Cassese, *The Statute of the International Criminal Court: Some Preliminary Reflections*, 10 European Journal of International Law 144-171 (1999).

[142] *Id.*, 156.

[143] Any person committing a crime within the jurisdiction of the Court is solely responsible for their criminal conduct and liable for punishment. *Id.* Considering this important matter, the concept of punishment is attributed to the natural person who has been recognized as being guilty of committing international crimes. The advantage of this provision of the Statute is to clarify that individuals are the only subjects of the attribution of punishment and the appropriate penalty must be carried out. See Article 25.

[144] "It is well known that the current rules of international law on individual criminal responsibility make up a body of law that is still rudimentary and fairly unsophisticated. These rules, among other things, suffer from a major defect. Unlike national law, where the principle of specificity of criminal law (Bestimmtheitsgrundsatz, tassativitadelle more penali, nullum crimen sine legestricta) is prevalent, international criminal law includes many provisions that do not determine the essential elements of the crime in detail. To this extent, international criminal law departs from the fundamental principle of specificity, which requires that a criminal rule be detailed and indicate in clear terms the various elements of the crime.. This principle constitutes a fundamental guarantee for the potential accused and any indicated person, because it lays down in well-defined terms the confines of the prohibited conduct, thus giving him notice of what he stands accused. By the same token, that principle greatly restricts the courts' latitude (arbitriumjudicis)." Antonio Cassese, *The Statute of the International Criminal Court: Some Preliminary Reflections*, at 148.

[145] See *also id.*, at 148-152.

comparison, some of the above provisions overlap with the provisions of other previous instruments in international criminal law.[146]

6.1.2.1. Irrelevance of Completion

The Statute of the ICC is essentially built on individuals.[147] According to the provisions of the Statute a person may be recognised as criminally responsible and therefore liable for punishment without regard to the fact that that person has committed a crime as an individual of his own accord or jointly in connection with another person. A person may also have criminal responsibility when he has committed a crime through another person. This is regardless of the fact that the other person is also held

---

[146] While international crimes may be committed by individuals, it is also true that all individuals may not have the same degree of responsibility in the commission of an international crime. This is also one of the most recognised principles of domestic criminal law. Different concepts of participation in the commission of international crimes have also been formulated in the Draft Code of Crimes against the Peace and Security of Mankind. The chief reason for this is that no individual should be able to escape criminal responsibility and punishment by invoking his/her position in the commission of international crimes. Article 2 (3) of the Draft Code discusses this matter. It reads that: "An individual shall be responsible for a crime set out in article 17, 18, 19 or 20 if that individual: (a) intentionally commits such a crime; (b) orders the commission of such a crime which in fact occurs or is attempted; (c) fails to prevent or repress the commission of such a crime in the circumstances set out in article 6; (d) knowingly aids, abets or otherwise assists, directly and substantially, in the commission of such a crime, including providing the means for its commission; (e) directly participates in planning or conspiring to commit such a crime which in fact occurs; (f) directly and publicly incites another individual to commit such a crime which in fact occurs; (g) attempts to commit such a crime by taking action commencing the execution of a crime which does not in fact occur because of circumstances independent of his intentions." The provisions of Article 2(3) are obviously a development of the provisions of national criminal law and international criminal law implemented in the Nuremberg Tribunal and have also developed within the provisions of other instruments of international criminal law since the end of the Second World War. The paragraph above criminalizes several acts and recognizes them as punishable crimes. According to the Draft Code these acts are of a different nature and are enumerated in the Code with different legal terms. Their purpose is to identify all types of acts which may, in way or another, lead to the commitment of acts against the peace and security of mankind."

[147] See Lamia Mekhemar, *The Status of the Individual in the Statute of the International Criminal Court, in* The Rome Statute of the International Criminal Court: a Challenge to Impunity (Mauro Politi and Guiseppe Nesi, eds. 2001), pp. 123-30.

criminally responsible for the crime before the jurisdiction of the ICC.[148] In fact, different modalities of individuals' criminal responsibility are distinguished by the Statute, some of which have been adopted in their entirety from the norms of customary international criminal law.[149] They imply various forms of participation and the irrelevance of completion.[150]

Here, the purpose of the legislator is to emphasise that every natural person bears his/her own responsibility for violations of the provisions of the Statute. It makes no difference to the concept of criminal responsibility whether that person has committed the crime in complicity or in the company of another person. The legislator calls upon every person's criminal responsibility with reference to the responsibility of the others who are equally responsible for the criminal conduct.[151]

---

[148] Article 23.

[149] Gerhard Werle, Principles of International Criminal Law (2005), at 119.

[150] *Id.*

[151] Complicity in the commission of criminal acts is one of the most recognised concepts within criminal law. Complicity may be defined as participation in guilt. In other words complicity in international criminal law may be defined as an action or inaction helping, assisting or promoting, in one way or another, the commission of an act which is recognised as a crime in international criminal law. Complicity in the commission of an international crime therefore brings a person, as in national criminal law, under international criminal jurisdiction for prosecution and punishment. The word "complicity" may, however, coincide with other subjects of criminal law. For example, in some situations it is indeed very difficult to distinguish between the legal status of complicity and conspiracy. This is because the legal differences between these two are very minor and caution must therefore be exercised in the recognition of these two different subjects of criminal law. The same is consequently true in the system of international criminal law which borrows many of its practical definitions from domestic concepts of criminal law. The confusion between complicity and other areas of criminal law was also raised in the drafting of the Code of Crimes against the Peace and Security of Mankind. Accordingly, "Complicity, as a form of participation in the crime, was already provided for by Principle VII of the Nürnberg Principles, by article 2, paragraph 13 (iii), of the 1954 draft Code and by article III (e) of the 1948 Genocide Convention. Most members agreed that any aiding, abetting or means provided prior to the perpetration of the crime or during its commission constituted obvious cases of complicity. On the other hand, opinions were divided on how to deal with aiding, abetting or means provided *ex post facto*, in other words, after the commission of the crime, for example, when the perpetrator was helped to get away or to eliminate the instruments or the proceeds of the crime, and so on. A conclusion seemed to be reached that complicity should be regarded as aiding, abetting or means provided *ex post facto*, if they had been agreed on prior to the perpetration of the crime. However, opinions were divided as to aiding, abetting or means provided *ex post facto* without any prior agreement. In the view of some

6.1.2.2. Active Participation

Under the provisions of the Statute of the ICC, the concept of the international criminal responsibility of a person does not solely rest on the direct commission of a criminal act. The criminal responsibility of a person may also occur when such a person has, in one way or another, been active in the commission of the crime. This may be carried out in various ways.

A person may therefore be recognized as bearing criminal responsibility if he/she has ordered, solicited or induced the commission of the relevant acts which constitute crimes under the framework of the Statute. This criminal responsibility of the person is regardless of the fact that the crime has been committed or attempted by a third person. The essential reason for the criminality of a person is not here necessarily the commission of the crime but simply actively ordering, soliciting or inducing the commission of the crime.

6.1.2.3. Facilitating the Commission

The legislator has foreseen other situations in which a person may be involved in the commission of the crime under the jurisdiction of the ICC and be recognised as criminally responsible and liable for punishment.[152] This is when for the purpose of facilitating the commission of a crime a person contributes to its performance. These may include, for example,

---

members who represented certain legal systems, that was also complicity and the accomplice would be known under those legal systems as "an accessory after the fact". For other members, that was an offence of a different kind, known as "harbouring a criminal". They did not see how, for example, a person who gave shelter to the perpetrator of genocide could be compared to that perpetrator as a participant in a crime against the peace and security of mankind. That person did, of course, commit a crime, but he did not take part in the perpetration of a crime against the peace and security of mankind." Report of the International Law Commission on the Work of Its forty-third session, 29 April - 19 July 1991, General Assembly Official Records: Forty-Sixth Session, Supplement No.10 (A/46/10), at 252-3. The difference between conspiracy, complicity, assistance, abetting and aiding is very negligible indeed and creates a substantial amount of confusion. Conspiracy and complicity are distinct in the criminal law of most states and both imply a type of knowing participation in the commission of international crimes. Both terms also imply the accomplishment of act(s) which are legally wrong and criminal. This means that the distinction between them is first jurisdictional and than substantial. In international criminal law there is no elaborated distinction between these two terms as in national criminal law so that the criteria for such a distinction are very difficult to define and, for this reason, they may depend on the discretion of the criminal court.

[152] Article 25 (3) (c).

aiding, abetting or otherwise assisting in the commission of the crime. Any attempt at the commission of the crime, including providing any means for its commission, also implies the criminal responsibility of the person who has aided, abetted or assisted in the crime.

6.1.2.4. Contribution

The words of the Statute are also clear concerning situations in which a person may bear criminal responsibility for his/her contribution to the commission or attempted commission of a crime under the jurisdiction of the Court. Such a crime may be committed by a group of persons acting with a common purpose. Accordingly, the contribution has to be intentional and "Be made with the aim of furthering the criminal activity or criminal purpose of the group, where such activity or purpose involves the commission of a crime within the jurisdiction of the Court."With the above provisions, the legislator has foreseen the situation where the contributor intentionally aims, by one means or another, at furthering the criminal activities of a group. Such a contribution may also "Be made in the knowledge of the intention of the group to commit the crime." Both positions above give rise to the concept of the criminal responsibility of the contributor. The purpose of the legislator is here to prevent any possibility of the contributor escaping criminal liability by referring to other reasons.

6.1.2.5. Genocide

In the case of the crime of genocide, a personmay also, in accordance with the Statute of the ICC, be recognised as being criminally responsible for the crimes under the jurisdiction of the Court. He/she may directly and publicly incite others to commit genocide.[153] In other words, the concept

---

[153] The term "incitement" in international criminal law has since the Second World War been explicitly recognised in the codification of international criminal provisions. This term was explicitly recognised in the Charter of the International Military Tribunal in Nuremberg in Article 6. This recognition was soon developed in the International Convention on Genocide in its Article III and extended in the Statutes of the ICTY in Article 7, and of the ICTR in Article 6. The term has also been entered into the provisions of the Code of Crimes Against the Peace and Security of Mankind. According to the Code, incitement to commit a criminal act gives rise to the criminal responsibility of the relevant individual. The Code states that a person may have criminal responsibility before rules of international law if that person "directly and publicly incites another individual to commit such a crime which in fact occurs." Accordingly, incitement gives rise to the criminal responsibility of a person who publicly encourages another individual to commit a

of the criminal responsibility of a person for genocide does not consist only of the actual commission of the crime. This is because a single individual alone cannot commit genocide; it is a group decision and needs many contributions, which directly or indirectly permit the commission of the crime by natural persons.[154] Due to the position of the crime and the mass killing of persons and destruction of groups, any form of incitement has to give rise to the concept of criminal responsibility.[155]

6.1.2.6. Attempt

According to Article 25, attempts to commit crimes within the jurisdiction of the Court also give rise to criminal responsibility. A person is thus responsible when attempts are made to commit one of the crimes in the Statute by taking an effective measure or "a substantial step"[156] intended to

---

crime set out in articles 17 to 20 of the Code. This criminal responsibility occurs only when the other individual actually commits the crimes mentioned in the Code. It must be emphasised that the rapid development of communication by various means can be used by an individual to encourage another individual to commit a crime set out in Articles 17 to 20 of the Code. Thus, a person may incite other persons to commit a criminal act by different means, including a meeting in a public place, or by encouraging other persons to commit one of the crimes listed in the Code. The term "incitement" has not, however, been seriously taken into consideration within the provisions of the Statute of the ICC. It has only been used in connection with the crime of genocide. This implies the fact that incitement of individuals by the leaders of a country may be considered a crime if the incitement causes serious suffering for its object. Gerhard Werle, Principles of International Criminal Law (2005), at 119.

[154] One or several individuals might be found to bear more responsibility than others.

[155] Criminal responsibility for genocide has long been established within the documents of international criminal law. The 1948 Convention on Genocide also refers to this fact.

[156] Article 25 (3) (f). However, the term "a substantial step" is not defined under the provisions of the article and the Statute is silent about the term. This is because a substantial step can be interpreted differently and there is not a clear definition of the term. This means that the judges of the ICC may define the legal scope of the term as being "a substantial step" and clarify to what extent the action can be considered an effective step for the preparation, encouragement, completion and commission of the crime. Furthermore, it will be very difficult for the Court to choose the right decision concerning what does and does not constitute a substantial step in committing the criminal action. At the same time, it will again be very difficult for the Court to refer to the constitution of different states concerning the scope of the definition of "a substantial step". This is especially important in the case of the countries which have already, to a certain extent, developed the concept of substantial step as for example the United States (the

lead to the implementation of the illegal act, but where for one reason or another, the crime does not occur because of circumstances which do not depend on his/her intentions.

The concept of criminal responsibility does not, under the Statute, apply to a person who abandons or prevents the commission of the crime. This lack of responsibility under the Statute depends on the condition that the attempted person completely and voluntarily gave up their criminal purpose. Although one may understand the purpose of the legislator, proving that a person has by all means available prevented the criminal action is not easy. An act which causes the initiation of a crime may be so effective and decisive that abandonment or prevention of the crime by that person may not have any constructive effect. This is especially to be considered in the case of an attempt to commit genocide or crimes against humanity. The legislative force of a technical development may cause the crime to be quickly implemented although the person who made the attempt may regret this attempt and try to abandon the criminal actions. What then will the function of the Court be?

6.2. Criminal Responsibility for Legal Age

It is one of the consolidated principles of law and international criminal law that all persons that are brought before the jurisdiction of a court should have attained legal age. Thus, a court may not have jurisdiction over persons who have not reached the legal age which is accepted by the relevant laws. This is a general rule in jurisprudence and has been accepted by most nations of the world. The United Nations Convention on the Rights of the Child also refers to the significant function of the legal age concerning various questions of the law.[157]

The Statute of the ICC also emphasises the importance of respecting the principle of legal age. It cannot therefore exercise jurisdiction over a

---

U.S. Model Penal Code, Explanatory, 1985) and those which do not yet have clear lines for identifying the crime. Any reference of the judges of the ICC to the criminal law of any state may discriminate between various understandings of the term among civilisations. Obviously, the Court may also take into account the general principles of law concerning the given case.

[157] Article 1 of the Convention provides that "For the purposes of the present Convention, a child means every human being below the age of eighteen years unless under the law applicable to the child, majority is attained earlier." The Convention on the Rights of the Child, adopted and opened for signature, ratification and accession by General Assembly resolution 44/25 of 20 November 1989, entered *into force* on 2 September 1990, in accordance with article 49.

person who is less than 18 years old. The jurisdiction of the Court is thus limited to persons who have reached the age of 18 at the time of the commission of the alleged offences.[158]

One of the most serious problems concerning the age of the persons accused of committing one of the crimes under the jurisdiction of the ICC is that some countries do not yet have a functioning registration office or their registration system is not very accurate when it comes to the precise registration of their inhabitants. This is especially the case when the birth of a person is recorded after a time which may be effective for the recognition of their criminality. In some societies a family may even give the identity paper of an older child to their next child if the first child has, for one reason or another, died. This means that a person may have the identity of another person who is older than himself/herself.[159] The result is that in the case of the commission of a crime of a very serious nature that person will be charged for the crime when he/she was, at the time of the commission of the crime, younger than his/her identity papers suggest.[160]

6.3. Responsibility of States

It must be stated that, in the system of international law, the concept of the criminal responsibility of individuals is basically different from the concept of the responsibility of states. The latter arises from an internationally wrongful conduct committed independently of any one individual's responsibility. This means that when we speak about the concept of the criminal responsibility of individuals, we do not necessarily speak about the international responsibility of their states. For example, the commission of the crime of genocide does not only give rise to the concept of the criminal responsibility of individuals who have, by one means or another, carried out the criminal conduct, but it also gives rise to

[158] Article 26.

[159] Although we do not deny that, according to international regulations, every child must be registered, this is not yet wholly implemented by states. The Convention on the Rights of the Child states that "1. The child shall be registered immediately after birth and shall have the right from birth to a name, the right to acquire a nationality and, as far as possible, the right to know and be cared for by his/her parents. 2. States parties shall ensure the implementation of these rights in accordance with their national law and their obligations under the relevant international instruments in this field, in particular where the child would otherwise be stateless." Article 7.

[160] In particular, the problem is more serious when one looks at the identity of children who do not have a clear background or an identified mother or father.

the concept of the responsibility of the state under the international legal personality of which the criminal conduct has been motivated, planned and committed in another territory. This means that a state may be considered responsible for the criminal conduct of its nationals or of those who have been employed under its authority to carry out criminal actions.

The international responsibility of states is not attributed under the provisions of the Statute. This is because the function of the ICC is exclusively to investigate the international criminal responsibility of individuals.[161] Thus, the attribution of criminal responsibility to individuals does not in any way affect the responsibility of states in accordance with the principles of international law.

6.4. Official Capacity

Whilst most concepts of serious crimes under the system of international criminal law are collective, this does not mitigate the concept of the international criminal responsibility of individuals in international law. The fact is that due to the rapid development of international criminal law, the irrelevance of official capacity for attributing the concept of criminal responsibility is considered to be one of the basic principles of the law.

Historically, the irrelevance of official capacity was not accepted by states.[162] But the position was changed by the outbreak of World Wars I and II. The treaties, which were signed after the wars, established the concept of criminal responsibility for all persons who have violated the system of international criminal law. This includes not only ordinary individuals but also superiors, members of government and any head of state. This evolution may be seen especially clearly in the provisions of the Charter of the Nuremberg Tribunal and of the ICTY, ICTR and ICC. These tribunals and the Court have dealt with the concept of the criminal responsibility of all individuals without regard to their national ranks.

---

[161] Article 25 (4).

[162] One of the strongest arguments concerning the immunity of heads of state before criminal jurisdiction was based on the concept of sovereign independence and the immunity of heads of state before their national courts. Consequently, a head of state had juridical immunity and he could never be brought before a criminal court. Similarly, certain individuals could reject the concept of their criminal responsibility through reference to superior orders. And the latter could also deny criminal responsibility through reference to state power and personality in order to wage war or to act in self-defence without due regard to the principle of proportionality.

One of the most recognised constitutions of these tribunals is that of the ICTY which establishes the concept of the criminal responsibility of heads of state without regard to their official position.[163] It was as a result of these provisions that the Serbian head of state, Milosevic was brought before the ICTY for the prosecution and punishment of crimes committed during his presidency by the Serbian soldiers under his authority. Whilst it is true that he could not be punished and his prosecution was never finished because of his ill health, he was the first head of state to be officially brought before an international criminal tribunal under the authority of the United Nations. The Tribunal had many meetings concerning his prosecution and a large number of questions were included in the procedures of his prosecution. The principle of immunity of heads of state before criminal jurisdiction proved to have no legal value and his refusal to acknowledge that the Tribunal had the authority to charge him for crimes against humanity, war crimes and genocide received no particular recognition.[164]

There was, however, some serious criticism directed against the law of the ICTY and this was mainly based on the fact that the authority of the Tribunal was retroactive and did not exist at the time of the commission of the crimes.[165] The ICTY was also criticised because it was created at the order of the leading political powers of the world. It was for this and many other reasons that the international legal community opened the door for the creation of a permanent international criminal court which could prosecute and punish individuals of all states without regard to their governmental position.

It would be impossible for the world to accept that a subordinate might face criminal prosecution and punishment but his chief officials who ordered the commission of serious crimes could go without sufficient punishment. It is on account of this that Article 27 of the Statute clearly addresses the concept of the criminal responsibility of heads of state and the irrelevance of their official capacity to attempts to exempt them from prosecution and punishment.

---

[163] See the relevant chapter *supera*.

[164] Consult Geoffrey Robertson, *Ending Immunity: How International Criminal Law Can Put Tyrants on Trial* 38:3 Cornell International Law Journal, 649-671 (2005).

[165] See the relevant chapter *supera*.

6.4.1. High Officials

As was noted in the section above, the Statute of the ICC has included in its legal body, the principle of irrelevance of official capacity. In particular, the Statute aims at the definite abolition of any national concept for the protection of heads of state and members of governments. It clearly points out that:

> This Statute shall apply equally to all persons without any distinction based on official capacity. In particular, official capacity as a Head of State or Government, a member of a Government or parliament, an elected representative or a government official shall in no case exempt a person from criminal responsibility under this Statute, nor shall it, in and of itself, constitute a ground for reduction of sentence.[166]

The above provisions have especially referred to the consolidation of some vital principles governing the position of heads of state. These are a) the Statute applies equally to all persons in the world, b) their official capacity has no legal validity within the law of the Court, c) the officials of government bear responsibility for the violation of the law of the ICC; d) heads of state, such as presidents, also bear responsibility for their criminal decisions, e) no one may be exempt from criminal responsibility and f) official capacity does not mitigate punishment. Today, the above six principles constitute some of the most basic principles of the law of international criminal responsibility and are obviously an integral part of the international law of *jus cogens.*

6.4.2. Dismissal of Immunities

The second part of Article 27 of the Statute of the ICC re-emphasises the importance of the concept of the international criminal responsibility of all individuals regardless of their position under the law of their own state. It is on this basis that it rejects any immunity or procedural rules which protect, in one way or another, the position of heads of state or government. This means that the Court cannot be prevented by the provisions of national or international law from initiating a jurisdiction over a head of state because of his/her position.

With these clarifications, the Statute of the ICC guarantees the application of equal law and the principle of the *non-immunity* of heads of

---

[166] Article 27 (1).

state and government.[167] Its purpose is to achieve equal international criminal justice in the case of all individuals without regard to various legislations protecting and supporting the high officials of states.[168]

Although, the Statute of the ICC dismisses the immunities of certain persons within their constitutions, it is hard to believe that it could be successful in bringing all individuals or heads of state and members of government to appropriate international criminal justice when they have severely violated the provisions of international criminal law. The law of the ICC may be applied fully when it comes to the prosecution of the leaders of nations or states which are weak and cannot properly support their political leaders. It would, however, be very problematic to bring the heads of powerful nations, who have strong political, economic and military support, before the jurisdiction of the ICC when the Court basically depends on their power.

The position is therefore very simple. The law of the Court concerning the irrelevance of official capacity will be used against nations that are not militarily strong and cannot juridically argue against the interests of the Court. While the position of the Court regarding the imposition of the international criminal responsibility of individuals of any category is appreciated, it will remain to be seen to what extent the law of the Court will be useful for the prevention of corporate and white collar criminality.[169]

Therefore, a considerable amount of caution must be exercised in the interpretation of Article 27 (2). This is because provisions of Article 98 limit the authority of the Court. The article has simply strengthened the position of states which are requested by the ICC to surrender the accused to the jurisdiction of the Court. It reads that "The Court may not proceed with a request for surrender or assistance which would require the requested State to act inconsistently with its obligations under international law with respect to the State or diplomatic immunity of a person or property of a third State, unless the Court can first obtain the cooperation of that third State for the waiver of the immunity."[170] The

[167] Consult Geoffrey Robertson, *Ending Immunity: How International Criminal Law Can Put Tyrants on Trial,* note 445, at 649-671.

[168] *Id.,* at 668-671.

[169] Today, it has been proven that the Court is powerless regarding this matter.

[170] Article 98 (1).

above provisions in practice hamper the Court when the state in question wishes to surrender the relevant person to the Court.[171]

It also means that the provisions of Article 27 (2) contradict the provisions of Article 98 (1). The result is that the Court and its respected judges are obliged to accept the conditions of the requested state for surrendering or not surrendering the accused person. If the waiver of immunity is not granted, the Court cannot take any measure to the contrary effect. Consequently, the Court may have some individuals under its jurisdiction while others, who are accused of committing the same crime with the same persons, may not be tried because of their immunities. The judgment of the Court may finally be very complicated and not easy to deliver. In fact, the provisions of Article 98 were intentionally written into the Statute in the hope that the United States government would be a party to the Statute.[172] In the same way, the article will hinder the ICC from exercising appropriate jurisdiction over crimes which are recognised in its Statute. This means that the principle of irrelevance of official capacity will not properly be implemented unless the accused is voluntarily brought into the jurisdiction of the Court by the relevant parties.

The fact is that the United States has worked for the strengthening of the above principle by supporting the provisions of the article.[173] This has also been proved in its foreign policy agreements concluded with other

---

[171] For an examination of the position of third states with the ICC see Gennady M. Danilenko, *The Statute of the International Criminal Court and Third States,* 21 Michigan Journal of International Law 445 (2000).

[172] In fact, Article 98 of the Court was included in the provisions of the Statute of the ICC due to the interests of the United States government. The United States insisted that if the article was not included in the Statute, it would not sign the treaty. It was upon this request that the article was accepted as an integral part of the Statute in the hope that the United States government would ratify the treaty. It was, however, later demonstrated that the article was used in order to strengthen the position of individuals of the United States in the hope that they will not be brought before the jurisdiction of the Court. With this ambition, the United States government entered into a number of bilateral international treaties with other parties to the ICC. The contents of these treaties provide immunities for the individuals of the United States so that they are not prosecuted or punished by the Court. The parties to the relevant treaties are under an obligation not to surrender American nationals to the Court but to send them to the United States for further investigation under the jurisdiction of the United States criminal courts.

[173] Scott W. Andreasen, "*The International Criminal Court: Does the Constitution Preclude Its Ratification By the United States?*", 85 Iowa Law Review 697 (January 2000, no. 2).

states.[174] However, its argumentation has been rejected by the European Union.[175]

6.4.3. Responsibility of Commanders and Other Superiors

6.4.3.1. Preceding Tribunals

One of the most serious questions of criminal responsibility concerns the responsibility of commanders and other superiors who have, for one reason or another, been involved in the commission of certain crimes by their subordinates.[176] The criminal responsibility of commanders and superiors has broadly been discussed in the system of international criminal law.[177] Different views have been expressed and opinions vary between writers depending upon from which angle they interpret the concept of responsibility of commanders and superiors. The most serious discussion concerning the responsibility of different ranks started at the outbreak of the Second World War and resulted in the formulation of the Charter of the International Military Tribunal for Nuremberg.[178]

---

[174] Consult the above note.

[175] "The European Union restates its belief that the anxieties expressed by the United States with regard to the future activities of the ICC are unfounded and that the Rome Statute provides all necessary safeguards against the misuse of the Court for politically motivated purposes. It is confident that this will become self-evident when the Court begins its work. The European Union is disappointed that the United States has felt obliged to act as it has without the benefit of actual experience of the Court's activities. It believes that such experience will show that the United States can associate itself fully with the Court." Statement of the European Union on the position of the United States of America towards the International Criminal Court, adopted on May 20, 2002, PCNICC/2002/INF/7.

[176] William J. Fenrick, *Responsibility of commanders and other superiors, in* (Commentary on the Rome Statute of the International Criminal Court Otto Triffterer, ed., 1999);

[177] See Otto Triffterer, *Causality, a Separate Element of the Doctrine of Superior Responsibility as Expressed in Article 28 of the Rome Statute*, 15 Leiden Journal of International Law 179 (2002); Charles Garraway, *Superior Orders and the International Criminal Court: Justice Delivered or Justice Denied*, 836 International Review of the Red Cross 785 (1999); Paola Gaeta, *The Defence of Superior Orders: The Statute of the International Criminal Court Versus Customary International Law*, 10 European Journal of International Law 172 (1999).

[178] The judgment of the Nuremberg Tribunal rejected any concept of the irresponsibility of commanders. See United States v. von Leeb (High Command case), Trials of War Criminals before the Nuremberg Military Tribunals under Control Council Law No. 10, vol. 11 (Trials), 1950, p. 1462; Government

The Charter is one of the most well-known international documents dealing with the very significant questions of international criminal law. In the earlier discussions of the formulation of the Charter, there was a serious conflict regarding the adoption of an article which referred to the criminal responsibility of commanders and superiors. These were, however, finally formulated into an article which recognizes the international criminal responsibility of those who have engaged in or ordered the commission of atrocities during the war. Two very well-known articles of the Constitution of the International Military Tribunal concerning the jurisdiction and general principles rejected the concept of the lack of responsibility of commanders, superiors, subordinates and heads of states. These stated that:

> Article 7: The official position of defendants, whether as Heads of State or responsible officials in Government Departments, shall not be considered as freeing them from responsibility or mitigating punishment.
>
> Article 8: The fact that the Defendant acted pursuant to order of his Government or of a superior shall not free him from responsibility, but may be considered in mitigation of punishment if the Tribunal determines that justice so requires.[179]

The provisions of the articles above were later strengthened by the United Nations in its document on the Principles of International Law Recognized in the Charter of the Nuremberg Tribunal and in the Judgment of the Tribunal.[180]Articles 7 and 8 of the Charter were slightly modified in the following way:

> Principle III
> The fact that a person who committed an act which constitutes a crime under international law acted as Head of State or responsible Government official does not relieve him from responsibility under international law.
>
> Principle IV
> The fact that a person acted pursuant to order of his Government or of a superior does not relieve him from responsibility under international law, provided a moral choice was in fact possible to him.

Commissioner of the General Tribunal of the Military Government for the French Zone of Occupation in Germany v. Roechling (Roechling case), vol. 14 (Trials), 1950, p. 1097.

[179] See *supera* the Constitution of the International Military Tribunal.

[180] The International Law Commission of the United Nations adopted this in 1950.

A close examination of Articles 7 or 8 and principles III and IV proves that some changes were made in the articles so that they would be accepted as the principles of international law. Article 7 disallows the avoidance of responsibility or mitigation of the punishment of heads of state or officials in government departments whilst principle III speaks of their responsibility under international law. The former is more specific and the latter is broad and very controversial. The problem with the latter is that it bases the source of responsibility on international law which is very broad and it is not clear on which part of the law it is based. It may mean that any violation of the law of armed conflict gives rise to the concept of the international criminal responsibility of heads of state.

Similarly, Article 8 speaks of responsibility in connection with the mitigation of punishment if the Nuremberg Tribunal determines that justice so requires it, whilst principle IV talks about responsibility in connection with moral choice. The latter principle emphasises that every person is responsible for his/her acts and the plea of one who has acted pursuant to the orders of superiors does not release that person from responsibility.

This movement towards the consolidation of the criminal responsibility of commanders and other superiors was later legislated in the provisions of the ICTY and the ICTR. These Tribunals like the earlier tribunals rejected any concept of the irresponsibility of commanders or superiors for grave violations of the provisions of international criminal law. The Statute of the ICTY has partially combined some of the provisions of the Nuremberg Tribunal with those of the Principles of the Charter recognized in the United Nations. It has especially emphasised that "A person who planned, instigated, ordered, committed or otherwise aided and abetted in the planning, preparation or execution of a crime referred to in articles 2 to 5 of the present Statute, shall be individually responsible for the crime."[181]

Other provisions focusing on the responsibility of superiors and commanders complete the above provisions. Thus, the Statute of the ICTY specifies that when a crime within its provisions "was committed by a subordinate does not relieve his superior of criminal responsibility if he knew or had reason to know that the subordinate was about to commit such acts or had done so and the superior failed to take the necessary and reasonable measures to prevent such acts or to punish the perpetrators thereof."[182] Similar provisions to the above may also be examined within the Statute of the ICTR.

---

[181] Article 7 (1).

[182] Article 7 (3).

The most recent provisions are those of the Statute of the ICC which assert the responsibility of commanders and superiors for the acts of their subordinates. This responsibility is, however, applied under certain jurisdictional conditions, even where they do not directly order the commission of the crimes. These are considered in the sections below.

6.4.3.2. ICC

The legal provisions of the Statute of the ICC concerning the responsibility of commanders are formulated under Article 28. The content of this article is in fact the main resource for the protection of the fundamental natural and positive rights of man from antagonists, atrocities and genocide ordered and committed directly or indirectly under the authority of commanders. The provisions of the article were thus accepted in order to put an end to disagreement among delegates over whether the omissions of certain acts by commanders or only the actual acts could lead to their criminal liability. The Statute has taken rather a neutral position concerning the commanders' responsibility.

The question of a commander's responsibility may be treated from different aspects depending on the conditions under which a crime has been committed. The Statute of the ICC clearly states that criminal responsibility may be attributed to a military commander or a person acting in the position of a military commander for crimes which are enumerated within the jurisdiction of the Court. According to the Statute, the commander therefore bears criminal responsibility for atrocities committed by military forces under his/her effective command and control.[183] This criminal responsibility is, however, subject to the condition that the criminal acts must, whatever the case may be, be the consequence of his/her failure to exercise control properly over such forces. Therefore, certain conditions have to be met in order to find a military commander responsible for the criminal conduct. These are when:

> (i) That military commander or person either knew or, owing to the circumstances at the time, should have known that the forces were committing or about to commit such crimes; and
> (ii) That military commander or person failed to take all necessary and reasonable measures within his/her power to prevent or repress their commission or to submit the matter to the competent authorities for investigation and prosecution.

---

[183] For a discussion on command responsibility consult Mark J. Osiel., *Modes of Participation in Mass Atrocity*, 38:3 Cornell International Law Journal 791-822 (2005).

In the above provisions, the commander's responsibility varies according to whether he knew or should have known. He may have failed to take all necessary measures for the prevention and repression of the crimes. He may also have omitted to submit the case to the competent authorities, although he had the relevant information concerning the violation of the law of armed conflicts or international human rights law. All these imply that the commander must have had some knowledge concerning the commission of the crimes in order to be appropriately treated under the jurisdiction of the Statute. It also means that the Court is responsible for proving that the commander in question has, by one means or another, permitted the crimes to be committed by his/her subordinates.

6.4.3.3. Criticism

Although the provisions of Article 28 are to be appreciated for their consolidation and recognition of the international criminal responsibility of the commanders, they place the Court in a very weak position regarding the engagement of commanders in the commission of certain crimes by their subordinates. It is, in certain situations, very difficult and problematic for the Court to prove that the commander knew about the criminal activities or had ordered them or had control over them. On the other hand, it is not difficult for commanders to prove that they did not have any knowledge of criminal conduct.

The paragraphs of Article 28 open a window for the commanders to escape prosecution and punishment where proof of guilt is very difficult in the Court. However, we do not necessarily suggest here that the concept of vicarious responsibility should have been applied. This is because the acceptance of this concept would mean that many states would not have access to the Statute. The doctrine of vicarious responsibility or liability recognises the commanders' and superiors' criminal liability for the crimes of their subordinates without the need to prove their prior knowledge and without requiring the subsequent prosecution and punishment of subordinates based on the report of their commanders or superiors.[184]

---

[184] In any event, it may not be similar to the Yamashita (a Japanese General) case that was prosecuted by the United States Supreme Court. His prosecution was very controversial. He was charged for war crimes which consisted of permitting and not controlling the members of his command in order to stop atrocities. According to the Supreme Court, a commander could be held responsible for the operation of armed forces, even though he had not ordered or controlled the forces. This was based on the fact that he was officially the commander of the forces and should have known and thought about the disregard of armed regulations by his forces. The charges were therefore based on the concept of omission.

Although this doctrine has been presented in the ICTY,[185] it may be difficult to present it in the Court if the judges of the Court have a different interpretation of Article 28 concerning the liability of the commanders.

However, it is very surprising that command responsibility has not been considered within Article 28 dealing with the violations of the fundamental principles of human rights law.[186] A commander, who has authority over his armed forces, should know that they might, in any situation, break the law and violate the basic principles of human rights law.[187] Under the jurisdiction of the Court, it may not always be necessary or essential to prove that the commander did not have sufficient knowledge of crimes committed by his/her forces.[188] The general concept of human rights law is based on the fact that every individual, especially the authoritative organs of a state, must have sufficient knowledge of their duties to protect the fundamental rights of man. In fact, transmitting this knowledge is a part of their duties and these duties are an integral part of armed activities without regard to operational or administrative control by the commander. What is wrong here is not just the misunderstanding of duties but also the misuse of those duties. The United States Army Captain, Ernest Medina's case is a clear example of violations of the duty to protect human rights in his official capacity. He was prosecuted for the My Lai Massacre during the Vietnam War. It was noted that a commander, who has a duty to know about human rights violations or war crimes, bears criminal liability for the criminal conduct of his armed forces.[189]

Another point is that the word "commander" is sometimes used instead of the word "superior", both of which may overlap with each other and make not only the problem of terminology, but also the juridical understanding of the position of superior and commander very difficult for the Court. Therefore, it may be argued that the provisions of Article 28 concerning the liability of commanders are rather vague. It creates

---

[185] ICTY, Prosecutor v. Delalic and Others (*Celebici* case).

[186] For further examination see Kim Carter, *Command Responsibility and Superior Orders in the Rome Statute, in* The Changing Face of International Criminal Law: Selected Papers (Vancouver: International Centre for Criminal Law Reform and Criminal Justice Policy, 2002) pp. 169-81; Greg Vetter, *Command Responsibility of Non-Military Superiors in the International Criminal Court (ICC),* 25 Yale Journal of International Law 89 (2000).

[187] Consult Jamie A. Williamson, '*Command Responsibility in the Case Law of the International Criminal Tribunal for Rwanda',* in 13 (3) Criminal Law Forum, Official Journal of the Society for the Reform of Criminal Law, 2002, pp. 365-384.

[188] *Id.*

[189] Surprisingly, Ernest Medina was released and acquitted of all charges against him.

criminal responsibility for the commanders only to a certain extent as accused commanders may escape prosecution and punishment because of the shortcomings of the article concerning precise and definite responsibility. The language of the article should have been more carefully written in the case of certain crimes where command liability is impossible to deny or acquit. Clear examples of these are genocide and crimes against humanity that are impossible to carry out or commit without the definite involvement of the highest ranking military officers.

The question is also what the difference between the criminal responsibility of individuals and the criminal responsibility of commanders and superiors is.[190] The fact is that there is indeed no difference between the responsibility of individuals and the responsibility of commanders. Generally speaking, all individuals who have committed serious international crimes have responsibility for their actions. This is regardless of their position as a subordinate, a commander or a superior. Thus, the purpose of the legislator here has not been to give a different idea of criminal responsibility for the crimes under the jurisdiction of the Court, but, as Article 28 emphasises, its function is to create additional grounds for criminal responsibility under the Statute with respect to the crimes within the jurisdiction of the Court. Thus, the legislator has strengthened the concept of the responsibility of individuals, in particular the responsibility of commanders. This means that the commander, as a matter *of de facto* or *de jure,* has a duty to control armed forces acting under his command and cannot solely refer to his ordinary responsibility. In other words, with the definition of the responsibility of commanders, we approach the question of responsibility more strongly and effectively in order to duplicate the order of the legislator to the commanders and emphasise that a commander cannot easily escape from his/her criminal responsibility by resorting to other justifications.

6.4.4. Responsibility of Superiors

6.4.4.1. Military Rank

The question of individual responsibility can be tackled from different points of view depending on the position of the individual who has committed crimes within the jurisdiction of the Court. The responsibility of superiors is therefore another concept of responsibility in the system of international criminal law. Within the military ranks one may find different

[190] For an examination of individual criminal responsibility consult Sliedregt Elies van, The Criminal Responsibility of Individuals for Violations of International Humanitarian Law (2003).

categories of superiors who may have subordinates under their order or control. Thus, when one speaks of the responsibility of superiors one may refer to the relationship between superiors and subordinates.

Article 28 of the Statute of the ICC refers to the above fact and concerns the relationships between at least two military categories. For this reason, it makes it clear that the legislator recognises special responsibility for the superiors when a crime under the provisions of the Statute has been committed and this responsibility is without regard to the responsibility of subordinates. This means that the criminal responsibility of subordinates does not release superiors from their criminal liability under international criminal law. Article 28 reads that "a superior shall be criminally responsible for crimes within the jurisdiction of the Court committed by subordinates under his/her effective authority and control, as a result of his/her failure to exercise control properly over such subordinates."

In the above version, the article refers to the term "failure to exercise" which is the condition for the recognition of the criminal liability of a superior. This implies the fact that, in the proceedings of the Court, it must be proved that the accused had failed to exercise control over the subordinate, which is the key reason for the attribution of the concept of criminal responsibility. Thus, if the Court is not able to prove his/her failure to exercise control, the accused may be released from prosecution and will not consequently be charged for the subordinate's conduct.

6.4.4.2. Conditions for Responsibility

In order to recognise the criminal liability of a superior and his/her failure to exercise proper control over the subordinate, the legislator has provided three conditions for the recognition of liability. These conditions build a bridge between the actions of the subordinate and the superior for the commission of the crimes under the jurisdiction of the Court.

Firstly, in order for the superior not to be released from criminal liability, it must be proved that he/she either knew about the criminal conduct of the subordinate or deliberately disregarded information concerning the criminal conduct.[191] The information must also clearly indicate that the subordinates were committing or were about to commit the crimes under the Statute. This means that a superior must have had clear information about the criminal conduct and must, for one reason or another, have chosen to ignore the relevant information.

The legislator does not, however, give any definition of the word "information". Thus, the degree and the level of the information may

---

[191] Article 28 (b), (i).

depend on the proper value of its content with due regard to the fact that the superior is supposed always to have control over the information. However, the information may not be correct and may intentionally be incorrect. It is easy for a superior to be informed by one of his/her subordinates that the subordinates are doing what they are supposed to do, but the information may be incorrect and misleading. Here, it is up to the superior to see that the given information is not corrupted. But if he/she does not consider the information incorrect, he may argue in the Court that he did not know about the quality of the information and therefore he should not be charged for the wrong information and should not have criminal liability for the criminal conduct of subordinates. This interpretation of the article may, although correct, surely be dangerous for the security of international criminal justice.

Therefore Article 28 concerning the criminal liability of superiors is also very controversial and may open a door for impunity. Furthermore, the definition of failure to exercise control properly over subordinates makes the application of criminal liability very complicated. Reasonably, superiors are responsible for any criminal acts of their subordinates and this is based on the fact that by virtue of their functions they are answerable before any court and this must clearly be applied where the questions of crimes against humanity or genocide are involved. This is especially important when one examines the next sub-section of the relevant paragraph.[192]

Secondly, according to the legislator, the crimes within the jurisdiction of the Court should concern activities that were within the effective responsibility and control of the superior. This means that the type of activities of the subordinate may be a reason to find or not to find that the superior has failed to exercise his duties concerning the given matters. In other words, the concept of responsibility is subject to the characterisation of the act and whether it falls within the effective responsibility and control of the relevant superior. Here, again, it may be difficult for the Court to specify which activities are under the effective responsibility or control of the superior and which are not. The Court cannot obtain a definite list concerning this matter. This is also based on the fact that every superior may have different functions depending on his/her responsibility and these functions may also be different from state to state depending on their administrative regulations. Special attention must be given to the fact that certain information or responsibilities of certain military organisations are so top secret that they may not be available to the Court and may not be released for several decades. This means that the Court has to build its

[192] Article 28 (a), (ii).

judgment on information that is not complete and this may be a reason why a superior escapes from prosecution and punishment.

Thirdly, the superior may be recognised to have criminal liability when he/she has failed to take all the necessary and reasonable measures within his/her power in order to prevent or repress the commission of crimes within the jurisdiction of the Court. He/she may also fail to submit a matter concerning the criminal conducts of the subordinates to the competent authorities for investigation and prosecution. This is because the superior is responsible for reporting all illegal actions of subordinates to the relevant authorities and any shortcomings of the superior may be interpreted as his/her positive reaction to the criminal conducts. This is particularly important when it comes to crimes against humanity, war crimes and genocide.

The above provisions are similar to the provisions concerning the responsibility of a commander. They indicate that a superior cannot directly be recognised as bearing criminal liability for acts of subordinates. To prove their guilt, the prosecutor in the Court has to prove that he/she has not taken all the necessary and reasonable measures under their control to prevent the criminal conduct. In other words, if a superior proves that he/she has taken all the necessary and reasonable measures for the prevention of the crime within the jurisdiction of the Court, he/she will not have criminal liability for the criminal conduct of the subordinate. This means that both parties to the Court, i.e., the prosecutor and the accused, have to prove the contrary to the other's view. The effect is that they may have a different definition for the term "all necessary and reasonable measures" which may restrict or broaden the application of the term. Whatever definition may be used, it is clear that all necessary and reasonable measures must fall under a juridical definition in order to avoid impunity. In addition, the prosecutor must have the burden of proof in accordance with the principle that the accused is treated as not guilty unless the contrary is proved.

6.4.4.3. Non-Applicability of Statute of Limitations

One of the problems of criminal law is that if the criminals have not received proper prosecution and punishment, they may easily escape prosecution and punishment based on the principle of statutory limitation for the given crime.[193] Consequently, a criminal may walk away despite

---

[193] One of the most recognised problems of national criminal law is that there are often statutory limitations for crimes committed by the accused, the criminal or the convicted person. Juridically, statutory limitations mean that no criminal charge can be made against a person who is accused of having committed a crime. The

position taken on statutory limitations varies from country to country and depends essentially on the system of criminal law and on the seriousness of the relevant crimes. The time period of statutory limitations may also vary from one state to another. Some states may not even apply statutory limitations while others may only apply them to ordinary crimes and not crimes committed against the security of a state, the commission of which has been recognised as dangerous to national security. The events of the Second World War and especially both the prosecution and non-prosecution of criminals gave rise to many serious questions concerning the extradition and punishment of criminals. Questions were raised in particular regarding the punishment of persons who had committed crimes against peace, war crimes and crimes against humanity but could escape from prosecution and punishment. It was for this reason that the United Nations Convention on the Non-applicability of Statutory Limitations to War Crimes and Crimes against Humanity was adopted on 26 November 1968. Another instrument is the 1974 European Convention on the Non-applicability of Statutory Limitation to Crimes Against Humanity and War Crimes. A similar position has been taken in the codification of the 1996 Code of Crimes against the Peace and Security of Mankind in Article 7. (See Year Book of International Law Commission, Vol.II, Part II, pp.15-16.) It is useful to mention Article 1 of the European Convention here. It reads that "Each Contracting State undertakes to adopt any necessary measures to secure that statutory limitation shall not apply to the prosecution of the following offences, or to the enforcement of the sentences imposed for such offences, in so far as they are punishable under its domestic law:

1. the crimes against humanity specified in the Convention on the Prevention and Punishment of the Crime of Genocide adopted on 9 December 1948 by the General Assembly of the United Nations;

2 a. the violations specified in Article 50 of the 1949 Geneva Convention for the Amelioration of the Condition of the Wounded and Sick in Armed Forces in the Field, Article 51 of the 1949 Geneva Convention for the Amelioration of the Condition of Wounded, Sick and Shipwrecked Members of Armed Forces at Sea, Article 130 of the 1949 Geneva Convention relative to the Treatment of Prisoners of War and Article 147 of the 1949 Geneva Convention relative to the Protection of Civilian Persons in Time of War,

b. any comparable violations of the laws of war having effect at the time when this Convention enters into force and of customs of war existing at that time, which are not already provided for in the above-mentioned provisions of the Geneva Conventions,

when the specific violation under consideration is of a particularly grave character by reason either of its factual and intentional elements or of the extent of its foreseeable consequences;

3. any other violation of a rule or custom of international law which may hereafter be established and which the Contracting State concerned considers according to a declaration under Article 6 as being of a comparable nature to those referred to in paragraphs 1 or 2 of this article." The European Convention (Strasbourg, 25.I.1974).

his/her criminal conduct and not necessarily be involved in the proceedings of a criminal court. This problem of criminal law was generally accepted by most national criminal legislations before the establishment of the Nuremberg Tribunal. They recognised that because of the circumstances of the crimes and the passing of a certain amount of time, a criminal may be free from prosecution and punishment. Of course, this should not be interpreted as implying that national criminal laws accepted criminal conduct but as the result of a society's desire to move forward with its policy and public interests.[194] This means sometimes putting an end to the legal process and litigation of the criminal court. Consequently, criminal law permitted the defendants to return to society after a period of time depending on legal provisions which could vary from country to country. This was a move towards reintegration. It also meant impunity from criminal conduct by the rules of the law in line with domestic social policy. However, contrary views have been argued concerning certain international crimes, the gravity of which harms international society as a whole.

Article 29 of the Statute of the ICC aims to put an end to impunity and therefore provides explicitly that crimes within the jurisdiction of the ICC shall not be subject to any statute of limitations.[195] Other provisions similar to these provisions may be examined in the Control Council Law No. 10 concerning the Punishment of Persons Guilty of War Crimes, Crimes against Peace and Crimes against Humanity. It states that for the crimes referred to in the above, the accused shall not be entitled to the benefits of any statute of limitation. The significant function of the non-application of the statute of limitation makes the prosecution and punishment of criminals more effective and creates the idea of the prevention of categories of crimes in their primary stages.

---

[194] For further examination of subject see the above footnote.

[195] For the examination of crimes dealt with by the court see Lyal S. Sunga, *The Crimes Within the Jurisdiction of the International Criminal Court (Part II, Articles 5-10),* 6 European Jounral of Crime and Criminal Justice 61 (1998). See also Milan Tepavac, *Establishment of a Permanent International Criminal Court,* 49 Review of International Affairs 25 (1998).

6.5. Mental Elements

The mental element of the crime refers to the *mens rea* of a criminal offence or behaviour.[196] The term "mens rea" implies the guilty mind of a person who carries out a wrongful purpose.[197] It implies, therefore, criminal intent and knowledge of the conduct which is already recognised as wrong.[198]

The predecessors of the ICC such as the ICTY and the ICTR do not have any discussion concerning mental elements as in the Statute itself.[199] The Statute of the ICC in its Article 30 deals with the mental element as constituting one of the chief elements of criminal law. In fact, this element constitutes the main element for the proof of guilt.[200] It is a guarantee for the prevention of unjustified prosecution and punishment.[201] It recognises that there must be a clear identification of intent to commit a crime within the jurisdiction of the Court.[202] Accordingly "a person shall be criminally responsible and liable for punishment for a crime within the jurisdiction of the Court only if the material elements are committed with intent and knowledge."[203] Here the article underlines that the *mens rea*, or intent and knowledge, is in particular essential for the recognition of the criminal conduct. In other words, if a person did not know they were committing a crime, they cannot be recognized as having criminal responsibility for their acts. The principle of mental element applies to all individuals regardless of their positions or ranks within the machinery of a state. Thus, an ordinary individual, commander or superior cannot have criminal liability for acts that have not been predicted before the commission of the crime.

---

[196] Antonio Cassese, *The Statute of the International Criminal Court: Some Preliminary Reflections*, 10 European Journal of International Law 144-171 (1999), at 153.

[197] *Id.*, at 153-154.

[198] *Id.*

[199] Mohamed Elewa Badar, *The Mental Element in the Rome Statute of the International Criminal Court: A Commentary from A Comparative Criminal Law Perspective*, 19 Criminal Law Forum, DOI 10.1007/s10609-008-9085-6, 1-46 (2008).

[200] *Id.*, at 2

[201] Roger S. Clark, *The Mental Element in International Criminal Law: The Rome Statute of the International Criminal Court and the Elements of Offences*, 12 Criminal Law Forum 291 (2001).

[202] Consult also Kittichaisaree Kriangsak, International Criminal Law (2005 (2005), at 264.

[203] Article 30 (1).

Article 30 goes further and defines certain legal terminologies for the clarification of its provisions. It states that "(a)In relation to conduct, that person means to engage in the conduct; (b)In relation to a consequence, that person means to cause that consequence or is aware that it will occur in the ordinary course of events."[204]

The above provisions refer to some important key terms for the recognition of the criminality of an accused person. These are i) conduct, ii) engaging in conduct, iii) consequence, iv) awareness that it will occur, v) ordinary course of events. These words demonstrate a chain of ideas between what may be specified as a crime and how it may be carried out with the intent of the individual, commander or superior.

The Statute has also defined the term "knowledge".[205] It reads that the term "'knowledge' means "awareness that a circumstance exists or a consequence will occur in the ordinary course of events. 'Know' and 'knowingly' shall be construed accordingly." The forgoing provisions imply that the Statute may refer to the questions around culpability meaning that the accused person's criminal culpability requires demonstrating that he acted knowingly or negligently. In other words, this must be proved for each material element of the offences.

The word knowledge may here also refer to intent. This is because these two terminologies are integrated and an intensive definition of both may result from the same definition.[206] It is, however, the case that the legislators of the Statute have formulated both terminologies into two separate paragraphs. The purpose of this may be to underline that both terminologies have their own perspective for defining engagement in the commission of crimes within the jurisdiction of the Court.

The provisions concerning mental elements, especially in the case of "intent" and "knowledge" refer to serious crimes defined in the Statute and may open the question of moral blame or serious moral culpability. This assumes the involvement of the accused in the violation of a legal duty or the commission of the fault. This is because the accused may have committed an error or mistake concerning their understanding of the information. Still further criteria may also be effective for defining the reasonable measures that should have been taken in order to prevent or repress the criminal conduct such as the geographical location of the act and geographical location of the superior or commander in relation to communications and troops.

---

[204] Article 30 (2).
[205] Article 30 (3).
[206] *Id.*, at 2.

6.6. Basis for Excluding Criminal Responsibility

There are certain provisions within criminal law which may be a reason for the mitigation of criminal responsibility and sometimes for excluding criminal responsibility for the crimes under the given code. The mental element of a person may become an issue in a criminal court in two ways. Firstly, the Court has to consider whether the accused is physically or mentally capable of standing trial. Secondly, when a person has been prosecuted and found guilty, he can be held criminally responsible for the offence. This is the practical aspect.

These provisions are also established in the structure of the system of international criminal law and constitute an important step for the safeguarding of the fundamental principles of international human rights law. Like the criminal law of many nations, the Statute of the ICC deals with certain provisions which may be a reason for excluding criminal responsibility in the Court.

Article 31 of the Statute takes into consideration some of the most significant elements that may be considered to remove the criminal responsibility of the accused or the person that has committed the crimes within the jurisdiction of the Statute. The provisions of the article were not easily accepted by the representatives of the states participating in the formulation of the Statute. As the article expresses, its provisions are in addition to other provisions which may also give rise to the concept of excluding criminal responsibility within the Statute. The article provides several reasons for excluding criminal responsibility. These are briefly studied below.

6.6.1. Mental Disease or Defect

It must be asserted that mental disease and defects which are established in the Statute of the ICC are traditionally well-acknowledged within the criminal legislation of most states being parties to the Statute and are obviously not innovations. They are also recognised as mental disorders.[207] The practice has been that such persons should not face the provisions of criminal law but should be brought into other social channels.

According to Article 31 a person cannot be held criminally responsible if, at the time of the commission of the crime, that person suffered from a

[207] In order to see if a person has a mental disorder, a psychiatric assessment of the mental condition of the accused person can be asked for by the relevant court. This is in order to know whether to exempt him/her from criminal responsibility and to establish what measures should be taken against him/her.

mental disease or defect. The condition for this is that the mental disease should effectively destroy the capacity of the person to appreciate the nature or unlawfulness of the conduct as a violation of the system of international criminal law. In addition, he/she may not have the capacity to control his/her actions in order to conform to the requirements of the given law.[208]

6.6.2. State of Intoxication

The state of intoxication is a position in which one is monopolised by himself, herself, others, spiritual feelings or materials so that the person is not in a state of normal awareness. Accepting the state of intoxication was controversial in the process of drafting the Statute. This was because intoxication should not be used as a means to flee prosecution and punishment.

According to Article 31 of the Statute of the ICC, a person may be free from responsibility if that person is in a state of intoxication that destroys that person's capacity to understand the nature or unlawfulness of the conduct carried out by him or her. He/she may also not have the capacity to control the conduct in question in order to obey the provisions of the relevant law. However, when a person has voluntarily intoxicated himself/herself in spite of previous knowledge, or has in one way or another disregarded the risk of committing the criminal conduct in the state of intoxication, he/she cannot be freed from criminal responsibility. This is because such a person knew that he/she might engage in conduct constituting a crime in accordance with the provisions of the Statute.

6.6.3. Categories of Self-Defence

As a fundamental rule of social integration and as a principle of law, resorting to self-defence constitutes one of the basic rights integrated into different legal systems.[209] The right appears to be an established institution within different systems of criminal law. This right is also integrated into the system of international criminal law and provides the right of self-protection under certain conditions when it seems necessary. The right of self-defence is similarly entered into the constitutions of different

---

[208] In any case, as a general rule of criminal procedures, there must be a medical investigation in order to prove the mental disease or defect of the accused.

[209] Antonio Cassese, *The Statute of the International Criminal Court: Some Preliminary Reflections*, 10 European Journal of International Law144-171 (1999).

international criminal courts, the most significant of which is the Statute of the ICC.

The Statute of the ICC recognises different categories of self-defence. These are when "the person acts reasonably to defend himself or herself or another person or, in the case of war crimes, property which is essential for the survival of the person or another person or property which is essential for accomplishing a military mission, against an imminent and unlawful use of force in a manner proportionate to the degree of danger to the person or the other person or property protected".[210]

The above section provides the following grounds: a) to defend himself/herself, b) to protect another person, c) to defend property d) to defend a property which is necessary for the accomplishment of a military mission. All four categories may be a reason for the Court to accept that the person in question had no choice and had to defend the relevant subject or object. However, the legislator makes it clear that the above factors should not be a reason for escaping prosecution and punishment.

Although the provisions of Article 31 relating to different categories of defence are aimed at the protection of the rights of individuals to defend themselves or others in certain special circumstances, a considerable degree of caution must be exercised when referring to the doctrines of self-defence.[211] This is because self-defence means, as a whole, defending a person or property against a particular attack. However, the question always arises as to what types of attack can constitute self-defence when they lead to the deaths of other persons.Nevertheless, the purpose of the article relating to the protection of property has been strongly criticised.[212] It has been argued that the extension of the definition of self-defence in order to protect property falls outside the *lex lata*.[213]

---

[210] Article 31 (c).

[211] Massimo Scaliotti, *Defences Before the International Criminal Court: Substantive Grounds for Excluding Criminal Responsibility – Part 1,* 1 International Criminal Law Review 111 (2001); Massimo Scaliotti, *Defences Before the International Criminal Court: Substantive Grounds for Excluding Criminal Responsibility – Part 2,* 2 International Criminal Law Review 1 (2002);

[212] Antonio Cassese, *The Statute of the International Criminal Court: Some Preliminary Reflections*, 10 European Journal of International Law 144-171 (1999), at 154-155.

[213] *Id.*, at 154. This is because "Firstly, via international criminal law a norm of international humanitarian law has been created whereby a serviceman may now lawfully commit an international crime for the purpose of defending any 'property essential for accomplishing a military mission' against an imminent and unlawful attack or use of force. So far such unlawful use of force against the 'property' at issue has not entitled the military to commit war crimes. They could only react by

The relevant paragraph of the article also does not clarify the degree or level of defence appropriate. Neither does it describe what measures should be taken or be seen as the condition for resorting to the right of self-defence. This means that one has to be very careful in the interpretation and application of the relevant paragraph of the article. An attack for defence must not violate the principle of proportionality and it must be recognised that an attack is different from an attempt to attack or an imminent attack. A person taking measures of self-defence for the protection of himself/herself and others has to be neutral about the activities carried out by his group, nation or government against another group. If another group is defending itself from criminal attacks and a person is participating in the criminal conduct of his/her own group, this may not, due to the conditions relating to the right of self-defence, be recognised as defence. It is just a reason for fleeing from prosecution and punishment. As the paragraph emphasises, the involvement of a person in a defensive operation, which was conducted by armed forces, cannot by itself constitute a ground for excluding criminal responsibility under the provisions of the paragraph.[214]

One of the essential conditions for resorting to the right of self-defence is that there was not any possibility to escape peril and one had reasonable grounds to believe that there was immediate danger to his/her life or that of one of family members or an immediate danger to property. In other words, any injury by the defendant must be carried out in justifiable self-defence and not as a matter of aggression. There must be a balance between the means and the end. An attack for the purpose of defence must be against the imminent use of unlawful force and use of force must be based on a reasonable amount of force and not become a violation. In addition, it must be clear that the operation of force is necessary to avoid the danger.

Article 31 has not taken the positions above under any consideration and the legislators have left the situation to the opinion of the judges. The only position of the article concerns "The fact that the person was involved in a defensive operation conducted by forces shall not in itself constitute a ground for excluding criminal responsibility under this subparagraph."[215]

---

using lawful means or methods of combat or, ex post facto, by resorting to lawful reprisals against enemy belligerents. Secondly, the notion of 'property essential for accomplishing a military mission' is very lose and may be difficult to interpret." *Id.*, at 154-155.

[214] Consult also Kittichaisaree Kriangsak, International Criminal Law (2005 (2005), at 258-260.

[215] Article 31(c).

This means that many positions are unclear and the Court has to elaborate when and how to accept a conduct as a legitimate action by the defendant.

However, there may not be any difference between various rules for excluding criminal responsibility. This means that any excuse the accused may have in order to be freed from criminal responsibility before the jurisdiction of the Court depends on the decisions of the Court itself. Since the policy of the Court is the prosecution and punishment of crimes that are of high gravity and endanger the safeguarding of the fundamental rights of man, it has to take measures that are appropriate for the purpose of the Statute and it may not easily free individuals, superiors or commanders from their criminal responsibility.

6.6.4. Other Reasons

There are other reasons for excluding criminal responsibility before the jurisdiction of the Court. The Statute of the ICC in Article 31 refers to these reasons. Thus, a conduct which is recognized as a crime in accordance with the provisions of the Statute may, because it occurred under duress, free a person from criminal responsibility. This is when the duress has been the result of several actions such as a) a threat of imminent death, b) of continuing or imminent serious bodily harm against that person and c) imminent serious harm to another person. In this situation, a person must have acted necessarily and reasonably in order to avoid this threat. The Court may, however, not accept a threat as an excuse to escape culpability if there is no evidence. It should, however, prove that the person who is threatened does not mean to cause a greater harm than the one to be avoided. In this case, such a threat may either be carried out by other persons or occur in circumstances beyond the control of the threatened person.

In all of these situations, it is up to the Court to determine the applicability of the grounds in order to exclude criminal responsibilities which are enumerated in the Statute.[216] The Court is also authorised to consider grounds other than those referred to in Article 31 as an excuse for excluding criminal responsibility.[217]

---

[216] Article 31 (2).

[217] Article 31 (3).

6.6.5. Mistake of Fact and Law

Another reason, which may exclude criminal responsibility under the provisions of the Statute of the ICC, is the mistake of fact or law.[218] As a whole, a mistake of fact and law constitutes a type of confusion between facts and laws but is in no case based on intention.[219] This may also be found within other national systems of criminal law that may exclude or mitigate the attribution of criminal responsibility to the suspected person.

In general, a mistake constitutes some unintentional act or omission that has not been planned.[220] It may arise from ignorance or some reasons which cause forgetfulness. Mistake may also be divided into two categories. One is the mistake of fact which does not arise from neglect of legal duty but from particular circumstances arising from unconscious ignorance. "The mistake of fact must be honestly, and reasonably, made on the basis of the conditions prevailing at the time of the commission of the unlawful act."[221] This means that the accused person seeking to avoid criminal responsibility may allege a mistake of fact as an excuse only under definite conditions. In general, a mistake of fact must be born of obvious forgetfulness or unconscious ignorance which is logical and acceptable within the jurisprudence of justice and cannot be merely an excuse for avoiding legal duties.

The other is mistake of law.[222] This is when one comes to a wrong conclusion regarding the law although one had full knowledge of the facts. Thus, a mistake of law implies the incorrect conclusion as to the legal effect of facts. This is a result of inaccurate interpretation, understanding or assumption. As a general rule, a mistake of law does not free a person from criminal responsibility.[223] This is based on the fact that he/she should have known because of his/her awareness of the law. A mistake of law is

---

[218] Article 32. See also Otto Triffterer, *Mistake of Fact or Mistake of Law, in* Commentary on the Rome Statute of the International Criminal Court 515 (Otto Triffterer, ed., 1999).

[219] Antonio Cassese, *The Statute of the International Criminal Court: Some Preliminary Reflections*, 10 European Journal of International Law144-171 (1999), at 155-156.

[220] *Id.*, at 155.

[221] Kittichaisaree Kriangsak, International Criminal Law (2005), at 264.

[222] Mohamed Elewa Badar, Nora Karsten., *Current Development at the International Criminal Tribunals*, 8 International Criminal Law Review (2008), 353-380.

[223] Kittichaisaree Kriangsak, International Criminal Law (2005).

also called*ignorantia iuris non excusat*, *ignorantia iuris neminem excusat* or *ignorantia iurisnocet.*[224]

Article 32 of the Statute of the ICC recognizes a mistake as grounds for excluding criminal responsibility. This is only when it negates the mental element required for the crime within the jurisdiction of the Court. At first glance, it seems that the provisions of Article 32 are self-evident. However, as a general rule of legal procedure in a court, the prosecutor must prove the mental element. Additionally, the provisions of Article 32 (2) "may constitute a disincentive to the dissemination and implementation of international humanitarian law."[225] In other words, the prosecutor's duty is to prove the mental element of the crime in each case. Thus, the relevant provisions of the article create some confusion between the power of the prosecutor and the position of the suspected person. One of the reasons for serious confusion is a consequence of the fact that it is not clear whether or not an error or ignorance should be considered reasonable grounds to exclude criminal responsibility.[226]

Furthermore, it is not easy to know the scope of the definition of the word "reasonable". The borderline of proof may vary according to several factors. The common law system did not accept reference to the claim of reasonableness and considered it irrelevant for certain intended crimes. However, its position when it came to crimes which have less intent was based on the fact that a mistake had to be reasonable and not hypothetical. With this in mind, intent and knowledge appear to be the most fundamental elements for the proof of criminality under the provisions of the Statute. Here, it will be very difficult to accept the argument from the defendant that his attack, for example, on a hospital, was based on mistake of facts and the misuse of the hospital flag by the victims.

The second paragraph of Article 32 refers to a mistake of law and emphasises that "A mistake of law as to whether a particular type of conduct is a crime within the jurisdiction of the Court shall not be a ground for excluding criminal responsibility."[227] According to the provisions of Article 32, these provisions may be a reason for excluding criminal responsibility "if it negates the mental element required by such a crime".[228] Here, the Statute again recognises the concept of the non-responsibility of a person, who, for one reason or another, lacks the mental element for the commission of one of the crimes within the jurisdiction of

---

[224] *Id.*, at 265.
[225] *Id.*, at 156.
[226] *Id.*
[227] Article 32 (2).
[228] *Id.*

the Statute. This means that if intent and knowledge are absent, the accused person may be freed from prosecution and punishment. According to the provisions of the Statute, intent means that the person has knowingly engaged in criminal conduct or he/she was, in one way or another, aware of the consequences of the criminal behaviour.[229]

Thus, a mistake of fact and law may relieve a person of criminal responsibility according to the provisions of the Statute but certain conditions must exist. The Statute, as a whole, does not accept ignorance of its provisions as an excuse to escape criminal culpability. One serious problem of a mistake of fact and law is that it does not take into consideration the principles of international human rights law. In other words, mistake of facts and laws should not prevent the enforcement of the principles of human rights law as the latter always gets priority over any other reasons. A person cannot claim that he/she committed serious crimes such as war crimes, crimes against humanity and genocide, just on the basis of a mistake of fact and law. Even though a mistake of fact existed, one has to evaluate whether such an attack against, for instance, a school building, is logical and humane from the point of view of an armed attack. In particular, one has to consider the provisions of international human rights law over all aspects of other laws when morality, humanity and laws are in contradiction with one another.

6.6.6. Superior Order and Prescription of Law

Since the establishment of the Nuremberg Tribunal and the new development of the system of international criminal law, many old theories of territorial or constitutional protections have gone through various changes in favour of justice and the maintenance of certain principles of international human rights law.[230] One of these changes may be examined

[229] Article 30.

[230] Certain legal arguments and legal decisions on criminal law are normally combined with the question of the legal effect of a superior order in the commission of certain crimes. Cases based on these types of arguments are indeed numerous in the domestic systems of states and the question is more problematic within systems, the constitutions of which do not specify the level and degree of responsibility of individuals for commission of certain acts. Obedience and disobedience to a superior in order to carry out certain acts have also occupied an important place in the system of international criminal law. The legal effect of the order of a government or a superior in international criminal law has mostly been examined in relation to armed conflicts. Although no direct agreement has been reached on the subject, it is a consolidated principle of international criminal law that obedience to an order of a government or a superior does not relieve a person

within the theory of the accountability before national or international criminal courts of all individuals who have committed international crimes.

In particular, it is today one of the consolidated principles of international criminal law that subordinates cannot escape from their criminal responsibility by referring to superior orders. This is because, due to the new development of the philosophy of international criminal law, subordinates have criminal responsibility for the commission of atrocities and this responsibility cannot be hidden behind the commander's, or superiors' orders. In other words, prosecution and punishment of those persons should be carried out without regard to the *sine qua non* or *conditio sine qua non* or an effective disciplinary military unity.[231] Thus, any argument which concerns maintaining military unity or preserving national unity is very controversial and may not be grounds for fleeing criminal responsibility. Article 32 of the Statute of the ICC vividly states that "The fact that a crime within the jurisdiction of the Court has been committed by a person pursuant to an order of a Government or of a superior, whether military or civilian, shall not relieve that person of criminal responsibility." This means that if the defendant knew or should have known that an order was unlawful and should not have been carried out, he/she is criminally responsible for the acts and cannot escape prosecution and punishment.

Despite the above developments, certain conditions may, in certain circumstances, be considered as excluding the criminal responsibility of a person before the jurisdiction of the ICC. Therefore, Article 33 of the

---

of his/her legal responsibility before the law. This view was developed especially after the outbreak of the First and Second World Wars. The International Military Tribunals rejected the plea of superior order in order to escape from prosecution and punishment. The Tribunal in Nuremberg based its judgment on its Charter and emphasised the international criminal responsibility of individuals regardless of their position and status under domestic law. (See chapter six) While the provisions of the Nuremberg Tribunal were controversial at the time of their adoption and implementation, they are considered an integral part of international criminal law today. This is for several reasons, *inter alia*, the implementation of the system of international criminal law cannot be guaranteed without the existence of the criminal responsibility of all individuals within the system. The provisions above can be found within the provisions of a number of international conventions applicable to international crimes, such as the 1948 Convention on the Prevention and Punishment of the Crime of Genocide and the 1973 International Convention on the Suppression and Punishment of the Crime of Apartheid, the Statutes of the ICTY, ICTR and SCSL.

[231] This means "but for" or "without which it could not be".

Statute clarifies the conditions under which a person may be relieved of his/her criminal responsibility.

(a) The person was under a legal obligation to obey orders of the Government or the superior in question;
(b) The person did not know that the order was unlawful; and
(c) The order was not manifestly unlawful.

The three sub-sections above are very controversial and make it possible for strong military powers to escape criminal responsibility and punishment. This means that a soldier may, with reference to one of the above alternatives, argue that he should be free from criminal responsibility under the provisions of the Statute. This is especially possible when one reads another paragraph of Article 32.[232] It emphasises that, for the purposes of the article, orders to commit crimes against humanity or genocide are manifestly unlawful. A close examination of this paragraph and the whole article means that the three above reasons can allow escape from prosecution for war crimes and aggression when the latter has come within the jurisdiction of the Court.

Of particular importance is the fact that the three channels argue for the lack of responsibility of subordinates and may therefore be used in certain military confrontations to commit crimes within the jurisdiction of the Court. A person may always claim that he/she was under a military legal obligation to obey the order of superiors or commanders. This is based on the fact that soldiers who are engaged in the battle and fighting against the enemy have not got enough time to calculate the legal validity of an order. In particular, when one is in combat, he/she will be so close to the questions of life and death and exposed to psychological pressure that will prevent him/her from different evaluations of orders. He/she may fight for the continuation of life and may always claim that he/she was defending himself/herself or acting upon the government's orders and had no right to question them. In addition, a subordinate may also claim that other soldiers were fighting and did not question the order. He/she was also obliged to fight without questioning the legal value of the order. When a subordinate is put in a situation which is dangerous and where he/she may be killed, he/she may commit war crimes because of the circumstances of the order. All these arguments imply the fact that the article creates a gap between the commission of crimes and impunity.

The provisions of Article 33 obviously open the door to violations of the international humanitarian law of armed conflict as a whole and go

[232] Article 32 (2).

against the provisions of the four 1949 Geneva Conventions and their two Protocols. The reason for this is that the frameworks of these instruments protect civilians and victims from unlawful military orders. One may wonder how their provisions can be effective when, in an international criminal court, especially one like the ICC, the Statute indirectly protects subordinates under its own laws. The ICC even permits states to adopt provisions that protect their subordinates. This is especially possible when one looks at the effect of the principle of complementarity. A national criminal court may have priority of jurisdiction when this is necessary. The three channels for excluding criminal responsibility under Article 33 may therefore often be interpreted in favour of an internal law system and allow the perpetrator to be found not guilty.

CHAPTER SEVEN

THE ELEMENTS OF JURISDICTION IN THE ICC

1. The Basic Elements

The permanent International Criminal Court has been created to establish justice. This justice is intended by the states parties to be the prescription of the international community's jurisdiction over certain international crimes that are recognised to be especially dangerous for the fundamental principles of international human rights law. For this reason, the purpose of the Court is not only to apply the appropriate prosecution and punishment but also to implement certain general elements of national jurisdictions that are accepted as the highest standard of international regulation for the implementation of justice.[1]

1.1. Jurisdiction *ratione temporis*

According to the Statute of the ICC, the jurisdiction of the Court is restricted to crimes committed after it has come into force.[2] This means that the Court has no jurisdiction over crimes which are committed before its establishment. The founders of the ICC did not want to create a retroactive implementation of the legislations of the Court. It was also practically impossible to establish a Court which might have jurisdiction over crimes committed before its establishment. This was because hardly any of the states parties would have signed and ratified a treaty which would create jurisdiction over their previous acts.[3] Similarly, if a state ratifies the Statute after its entry into force and becomes a party, the Court

---

[1] There have been long discussions concerning the method or methods of the jurisdiction of the court. Consult Eve La Haye, *The Jurisdiction of the International Criminal Court: Controversies over the Preconditions for Exercising Its Jurisdiction*, 46 Netherlands International Law Review 1-25 (No. 1, 1999).

[2] Article 11(1).

[3] This means that the jurisdiction of the Court is limited to crimes committed after the coming into force of the Statute and therefore we cannot transmit the cases from the ICTY and the ICTR to the Court.

may have jurisdiction over crimes committed after the entry into force of the Statute regarding that State. However, the new party may make a declaration accepting the jurisdiction of the Court for the earlier events.[4]

In general, the scope of the jurisdiction of the Court varies from case to case depending on the circumstances under which the case has been submitted to the Court. That is why the exercise of the jurisdiction of the Court is categorized under three main headings.[5] Therefore, the geographic position of the jurisdiction of the Court's *ratione loci* may vary considerably from one case to another, depending on which authority, state or organisation has brought the case before the jurisdiction of the Court. For instance, if the investigation of a case is suggested by the Security Council of the United Nations, the jurisdiction of the Court is extended to the territorial independence of every state without regard to their membership or non-membership under the provisions of the Charter of the United Nations. This is because under Chapter VII of the United Nations, the Security Council has the right to take authoritative decisions concerning the actions or omissions of those states that are considered to have brought about breaches of the peace, threats to peace or acts of aggression.[6]

There are, however, certain restrictions as to the scope of the jurisdiction of the Court if a case is initiated by the prosecutor or referred by a state party. Furthermore, it is obvious that when crimes are referred to the prosecutor by the Security Council, they are different from the crimes referred by a state party. The jurisdiction of the Court concerning a case referred by a state may be extended to the territorial jurisdiction of a non-party state if the latter permits it and gives its free consent. In such a case the accused must be a national of the consenting state or the criminal conduct must have been carried out within the territorial jurisdiction of the non-party state. In any event, the exercising of the jurisdiction of the Court in the territory of a state not party to the Statute should be based on special agreement.[7]

Another possibility is when a prosecutor starts an investigation *propriomotu* regarding the evidence of crimes committed and recognised under the provisions of the Statute. Thus, she or he must have sufficient information about the crime. In this case, the Court is entitled to exercise its jurisdiction when it comes to a crime referred to by the prosecutor.[8]

---

[4] Article 11(2).
[5] Article 13.
[6] Article 13(b).
[7] Article4(2). See *also* Article 12(2).
[8] Article 13(c).

Here again, if the state is a non-party state, the relevant state must give its permission.

Thus, as may be seen, the Court may exercise jurisdiction over a crime on the basis of three different applications submitted by the Security Council or a state party to the prosecutor. The prosecutor may also himself/herself initiate such an investigation. In all these situations, the statute offers jurisdiction *ratione personae* over individuals or natural persons. This means that claims cannot be brought to the Court for jurisdiction over states or organisations. The Court is not empowered to exercise jurisdiction over crimes which are committed under the juridical or political characterisation of a state or organisation. In other words, the Statute of the ICC unfortunately does not recognize the international criminal responsibility of organisations or states. Although, there is no doubt that the most dangerous international crimes are committed by states and organisations, the authority of the Court is limited to natural persons only; states, organisations or entities are therefore excluded.[9]

1.2. Age of Criminal Responsibility

Among the most important questions governing jurisdiction over a natural person is the age of criminal responsibility. Different legal aspects of this have been discussed and there are different provisions concerning the age of criminal responsibility within the criminal legislations of different states. This important question has also been taken into serious consideration within the provisions of international treaties including the ICC.

According to the provisions of the Rome Statute, the jurisdiction of the Court is limited to persons who have reached the age of eighteen. The Court does not have jurisdiction over persons under that age. This means that a person who committed the crimes listed in the Statute must, at the time they were committed, be at least eighteen years old. Thereby, the jurisdiction of the Court is limited to persons who have, at the time the crime was committed, already reached that age.[10]

The relevant provisions of the Statute concerning the age of criminal responsibility are somewhat ambiguous. This is because the Statute prefers a neutral policy concerning the age of criminal responsibility. In other

---

[9] However, the idea of state culpability was discussed in the earlier works of the International Law Commission but was rejected by some of the delegations. Consult Leila Sadat Wexler, *The Proposed Permanent International Criminal Court: An Appraisal*, 29 Cornell International Law Journal 665, no 75 (1996).

[10] Article 26.

words, it does not specify whether the age of eighteen is the age for the recognition of criminal responsibility. As a result of this policy, contradiction may be avoided between the various ages of criminal responsibility within national systems of different states.[11] Hence, the Statute does not provide any provision concerning the appropriate age of criminal responsibility. Similarly, this matter is not discussed in the International Law Commission draft.[12]

The problem of the provisions of the Statute governing the age of criminality is that a state party which recognises a limit under eighteen years old, as an appropriate age of criminal responsibility, may apply the provisions of international criminal law regardless of the provisions of the Statute. This means that there may be different policies for the implementation of the system of international criminal law since the different legislative systems of states do not necessarily have similar conclusions. Thus, crimes committed by minors may be treated differently by different states. This may also disregard the provisions of the Convention on the Rights of the Child which clarifies that a "child" means a person less than eighteen years of age.[13] This problem should have been avoided.

1.3. Jurisdiction *ratione materiae*

The scope of the jurisdiction of the ICC is limited to the crimes that are enumerated in the Statute. This means that the Court cannot, as long as the Statute is not modified, function in a different way. The Rome Statute declares that crimes within the jurisdiction of the Court are war crimes, crimes against humanity, genocide and aggression.[14] These crimes are, in accordance with the Statute, the most serious crimes concerning the international community as a whole. Naturally, the jurisdiction of the Court, when it comes to the crime of aggression, depends on the

---

[11] Consult Vincenzo, Militello.,*The Personal Nature of Individual Criminal Responsibility and the ICC Statute,* 5 Journal of International Criminal Justice (2007), Number 4, pp. 941-952. Published online.

[12] Yet the problem is very controversial in the case of those states which have no appropriate registration system concerning their populations. Moreover, states in some situations may decrease or increase the age of the accused depending on the political situation.

[13] Article 1 of the Convention on the Rights of the Child, adopted and opened for signature, ratification and accession by General Assembly resolution 44/25 of 20 November 1989, *came into force* on 2 September 1990, in accordance with article 49.

[14] Article 5 of the Statute of the ICC.

consideration of the definition of the crime stated by the Security Council and the provisions of articles 121 and 123 of the Statute.[15] This will remain the case for as long as the new modifications in the 2010 Review Conference are not accepted by the states parties.[16]

As we will see, the jurisdiction of the Court over the crimes enumerated in the Statute is subject to the consent of states parties and the complementarity principle.[17] There are however two exceptions. Firstly, the Court has no jurisdiction over the crime of aggression because the definition of the crime is subject to the will of the Security Council. Secondly, a state may, for a period of seven years after the Statute has come into force, choose not to accept the jurisdiction of the Court regarding war crimes when it concerns its nationals or crimes committed within its territorial jurisdiction.[18]

Furthermore, the Court is not permitted to exercise jurisdiction over the treaty crimes that were discussed under the procedure of the adoption of the Rome Statute.[19] By treaty crimes, we mean those crimes that have been defined under certain international conventions such as terrorism, illicit trafficking in drugs and crimes against United Nations personnel.[20] Some states were against the inclusion of those crimes within the Statute of the ICC. It was stated that the Court should have jurisdiction over only the most substantive crimes and should not therefore be overburdened by

---

[15] Article 5(2).

[16] See *infera* chapter on The Review Conference in Kampala.

[17] John T. Holmes, *The Principle of Complementarity, in* The International Criminal Court: The Making of the Rome Statute 470 (Roy S. Lee, ed., 1999); Jeffrey L. Bleich, *The International Criminal Court: Report of the ILA Working Group on Complementarity,* 25 Denver Journal of International Law and Policy 281 (1997); Jeffrey L. Bleich, *Complementarity,* 13 Nouvelles Etude Penales 231 (1997); Bartram S. Brown, *Primacy or Complementarity: Reconciling the Jurisdiction of National Courts and International Criminal Tribunals,* 23 Yale Journal of International Law 383 (1998); B. Jr. Concannon, *Beyond Complementarity: The International Criminal Court and National Prosecutions, A View from Haiti,* 32 Columbia Human Rights Law Review 201 (2000); Michael A. Newton, *Comparative Complementarity: Domestic Jurisdiction Consistent with the Rome Statute of the International Criminal Court,* 167Military Law Review 20 (2001).

[18] Article 124.

[19] Consult Neil Boister, *The Exclusion of Treaty Crimes from the Jurisdiction of the Proposed International Criminal Court: Law, Pragmatism, Politics*, 3Journal of Armed Conflict Law 27-43 (No.1, June 1998).

[20] *Id.*

other international crimes.[21] Nevertheless, it is not yet clear to this writer how the Court is going to deal adequately with crimes against humanity, war crimes and genocide when they, in certain situations, overlap with treaty crimes.[22] This means that the Court may, in certain situations, deal indirectly with treaty crimes, even though it has not, according to its Statute, permission to enlarge the scope of its jurisdiction.[23]

2. Types of Jurisdiction

The framework of the ICC is a combination of different theories, systems, legislations and politics. This means that the jurisdiction of the Court is very broad and adaptable in order to fulfil the requirements of the time. The Court has in fact opted for various different jurisdictional mechanisms for the implementation of its Statute.

2.1. The Complementarity Principle

The jurisdiction of the Court is based on several important principles. One of the most recognised of these principles is the complementarity principle.[24] Simply explained, this means that the Court is entitled to jurisdiction over certain enumerated crimes when states parties' proceedings fail to deal with those crimes.[25] The Rome Statute has clearly expressed this principle regarding the jurisdiction of the Court.[26] Whilst the complementarity principle is not defined within the articles of the

---

[21] See Grant M. Dawson, *Defining Substantive Crimes within the Subject Matter Jurisdiction of the International Criminal Court: What Is the Crime of Aggression?,* 19 New York Law School Journal of International and Comparative Law 413-452 (2000).

[22] The inclusion of treaty crimes was taken into examination at a Review Conference. See Resolution E adopted by the Diplomatic Conference in its Final Act, Annex 1.

[23] It will also be very difficult in the case of a state party which no longer wants to be a party to the Statute of the ICC and ends its signature and ratification. The question will always be what will be the role of the Statute concerning the state in question. The individuals of the state may release themselves from criminal investigation.

[24] See William A. Schabas., *Complementarity in Practice: Creative Solutions or a Trap for the Court* in The Rome Statute of the International Criminal Court: a Challenge to Impunity (Mauro Politi and Federica Gioia, editors, 2001), 25-48, at 31.

[25] *Id.*, at 25.

[26] *Id.*

Statute, its preamble reads that the International Criminal Court shall be complementary to national criminal jurisdictions.[27] This principle in the preamble is also strengthened within other parts of the Statute.[28] The first Review Conference on the Rome Statute of the ICC, which met in Kampala, Uganda from 31 May to 11 June 2010, discussed also the very significant role of the complementarity principle.

However, the definition of the principle of complementarity, and what it really is, is subject to debate since there is no universally-accepted definition of the principle. The definition of the principle may vary from occasion to occasion depending on whether the crime committed is acknowledged or not acknowledged by the states parties. Thus, the complementarity principle has double functions when it comes to the implementation of the provisions of the Statute. This means that wherever a state party is not willing to implement certain provisions, the Court is responsible for its implementation. It is on account of this that the issue of the admissibility of a case falls within the jurisdiction of the Court. The Court may therefore exercise jurisdiction over a case when i) the case is not investigated or prosecuted by a state within a reasonable time;[29] ii) a domestic jurisdiction is, in practice, unable or unwilling to prosecute a crime;[30] iii) the accused has not been tried for the conduct which is the reason for the complaint;[31] iv) the crime which has been committed is of sufficient gravity.[32]

In order to determine the unwillingness of states to investigate or prosecute a criminal case, the Court may take into consideration several important factors recognised by international law. These are when the proceedings which were or are being undertaken by the authorities of a state to protect a person from criminal responsibility, indicate impunity;[33] when there has been a delay in the proceedings for the recognition of criminal responsibility and this is not justified due to the circumstances;[34] when in the implementation of the proceedings, the principle of impartiality is not respected and when there is no intent to bring the

---

[27] Consult also *id*, at 26-28.

[28] For instance, see Article 1 of the Statute.

[29] Article 17(1) (a).

[30] Article 17(1) (b).

[31] Article 17(1) (c).

[32] Article 17(1) (d).

[33] Article 17(2) (a). See also *Impunity and Human Rights in International Law and Practice* (Naomi Roth-Arriaza, ed., 1995); M. Cherif Bassiouni, *Combating Impunity for International Crimes,* 71 University of Colorado Law Review 409 (2000);

[34] Article 17(2) (b).

accused under criminal procedures.[35] According to the Statute, the acts of a state relating to the committed crimes may be proof of its inability. The word "inability" implies the situation in which the state in question is unable to arrest the accused or provide sufficient evidence for investigation or prosecution under its national criminal jurisdiction.[36]

However, all of these situations depend on the independent will of the state party which has to decide about the submission of a case to the Court. In other words, it is not the merit of the rules of the system of international criminal law which brings a case for hearing before the Court's jurisdiction but the political decisions which have to be taken for the practical implementation of the system within an international criminal court.

Here the complementarity principle supplies a special mechanism for both, i.e. investigation and prosecution within the Court's jurisdiction and imposes responsibilities on states not to avoid their duties.[37] This means that the complementarity principle has a dual function; preventing the Court jurisdiction from going beyond its Statute and dealing with cases that have, for one reason or another, been put aside by states.[38] The legal characterisation of the complementarity principle is thus based on a policy of investigation, prosecution and the assessment of the jurisdiction by national criminal courts. Therefore, a complementarity regime creates for states parties the primary right to begin proceedings concerning cases which could otherwise meet the requirements of the ICC. This means that the basic policy of investigation of the ICC is in contradiction with the legal notion of the ICTY and the ICTR which have superiority over any national criminal proceedings. The ICC cannot claim jurisdiction over a case that has not met the conditions of complementarity. The Court has to respect all national jurisdictions and any action contrary to this effect may violate the Statute of the ICC. It should, however, not ignore the fact that the complementarity principle also has a policing function when it comes to the prosecution and punishment of criminals. This is because it forces states to take effective measures against criminals and not ignore their criminal conduct. Simultaneously, it is also true that the principle of complementarity limits the jurisdictional authority of the Court with regard to prosecution and punishment.

[35] Article 17(2) (c).
[36] Article 17(3).
[37] Ada Y. Sheng, *Analyzing the International Criminal Court Complementarity Principle Through a Federal Courts Lens*, *Bepress Legal Series* (2006), paper 1249, 30.
[38] *Id.*

2.2. Prescriptive Character

The Rome Statute, as we have stated elsewhere, basically has a legal mechanism which is based on different concepts of jurisdictions. Whilst one cannot deny the novelty of its conditional competence, secondary character and its conduct as the extension of national criminal law, the jurisdiction of the Court is principally built on prescriptive crimes. This means that the Court formulates its motivations and judgments on crimes, the nature, concept and definition of which are defined in its constitution.

These crimes, because of their particular nature, not only fall within the national jurisdiction of all states, but also come within the jurisdiction of the ICC. In reality, the crimes that are enumerated in the Statute are some of the most consolidated crimes in the system of international criminal law. These are war crimes, crimes against humanity, genocide and aggression. All of these crimes are also recognized by a considerable number of international lawyers as *jus cogens* crimes.[39] The Court therefore has a foundation for its jurisdiction based on the prescribed definitions of substantive crimes.[40]

Some writers may believe that it is the incapability of the national criminal court which creates rights of jurisdiction for the ICC. Although this argument may be partly true, it must be emphasized that the jurisdiction of the Court arises also from the norms of *jus cogens*.[41] These norms encourage all states, including the international community as a whole, to pay special attention to certain values of human civilisations. These are security, peace and the respect of certain fundamental principles of international human rights law. Hence, not only national criminal jurisdictions, but also international criminal jurisdictions have responsibility for the attribution of crimes which are recognised as substantive crimes. This means that the jurisdiction of the Court is not only based on its Statute, but also on the universal condemnation of those

---

[39] The scopes of these crimes are also defined in the Statute with reference to the crime of aggression.

[40] Consult Grant M. Dawson, *Defining Substantive Crimes within the Subject Matter Jurisdiction of the International Criminal Court: What Is the Crime of Aggression?,* 19 New York Law School Journal of International and Comparative Law 413-452 (2000).

[41] Examine A.J.J. de Hoogh, *The Relationship between jus Cogens, Obligations* Erga Omnes *and International Crimes: Peremptory Norms in Perspective,* 42 Austrian Journal of Public International Law 183 (1991).

crimes, violators of which are recognised as enemies of all human beings.[42]

The definite character of these four international crimes within the jurisdiction of the Court and the competence of the court are also important when it comes to the implementation of international criminal law. The violators of the crimes are liable to prosecution and punishment. Thus, if the defendant, because of his/her conduct is pursued by a State, the Court is obliged to hand over the jurisdiction to the relevant state on the grounds of its primacy of jurisdiction. The obligation of the Court is a necessary condition, even though the Court might seem to have more ability to investigate and prosecute the crime. This means that the prosecution as well as punishment of international crimes may be postponed because of the conditions surrounding the case. The Court is thus not permitted to adjudicate the case. Here neither the prescribed conduct nor the principle of universality of jurisdiction over war crimes, crimes against humanity, genocide and aggression can be powerful and decisive. The conditional complementarity principle, which is the only key principle of the Court, causes the functions of the ICC to be very complicated, and the old abolished principle of impunity may be enforced by the decision of the state in question. The jurisdiction of the Court may always be a serious problem because of the ownership claims of states parties in each case. Much more serious is the situation when the Court has to get permission from powerful states in order to be able to prosecute their individuals. The scope of international criminal justice may thus vary from case to case depending on the willingness or non-willingness of the parties.

2.3. The Principles of Jurisdiction

The Rome Statute offers different principles of jurisdiction for the purpose of implementing its Statute. This depends on the conditions under which the crime has been committed. In general, the crimes prescribed under the Statute of the Court fall under the following principles of jurisdiction.

[42] See also N. Strapatsas, *Universal Jurisdiction and the International Criminal Court,* 29 Manitoba Law Journal 1 (2002); M. Cherif Bassiouni, *Universal Jurisdiction for International Crimes: Historical Perspectives and Contemporary Practice, in* International Criminal Law, Vol ii (M. Cherif Bassiouni, ed. 2008) pp. 153-199; Christopher L. Blakesley, *Extraterritorial Jurisdiction, in* International Criminal Law, Vol II (M. Cherif Bassiouni, ed. 2008) pp. 85-152; Leila Nadya Sadat, *Competing and Overlapping Jurisdictions, in* International Criminal Law, vol ii (M. Cherif Bassiouni, ed. 2008) pp. 201-229.

These are: i) territoriality principle, ii) nationality principle, iii) flag principle, iv) cooperative principle and finally v) internationality principle.[43]

The difference between the application of these principles by the ICC and a national court rests on the fact that a national court may apply all the above principles, but the ICC may only resort to the cooperative principle or internationality principle. This is because the Court by itself cannot initiate a case in the territory of states parties or non-parties without their legal permission. This means that the ICC is supposed to cooperate with states parties for the implementation of its provisions. At the same time, the principle of cooperation is an integral part of the principle of internationality.[44] This is because the jurisdiction of the ICC has an international character. In other words, the ICC bases its theory of jurisdiction on two principles at the same time. These are the cooperative principle and the internationality principle.

It may even be argued that the jurisdiction of the ICC is also based on the territoriality principle. Although the classical definition of the principle implies the relation between states, the accused, the territory or the commission of the crime within the territorial boundaries of a state, the notion that each territory is also the territory of the ICC may not be an exaggeration. This is due to the fact that, once a state has admitted the jurisdiction of the Court, it has simultaneously accepted the exercise of the jurisdiction of the ICC over its territory in order for the Court to initiate investigation and proceedings for the prosecution and punishment of the guilty person. Therefore, the state in question permits the Court to have jurisdiction over its territories. In other words, the territoriality principle or other principles do not present any extraordinary power for the state but concern the legal personality of the state. If the Court does not have any temporary territorial right to exercise the territoriality principle, the question is then what type of action the Court takes when it enters into the jurisdiction of a state through its prosecutors.

One of the most important legal arguments for the limitation of the jurisdiction of the ICC is that the jurisdiction of the Court cannot compete with the jurisdiction of national courts. This is based on the fact that national courts have more access to evidence, can arrest accused persons more easily, can gather the necessary information, conduct an investigation, find the victims and witnesses and implement the

---

[43] See Farhad Malekian, *Emasculating the Philosophy of International Criminal Justice in the Iraqi Special Tribunal*, 38:3 Cornell International Law Journal 673-723 (2005), at 698-705.

[44] *Id.*

proceedings of a case without any need for other subjective materials, such as understanding the race, cultural attitudes, religion and language.

2.4. Jurisdiction over Non-Parties

Whilst the law of the Statute clearly applies to states parties, its provisions may in certain situations be used against any other state which is not party to the Statute. This is because the scope of the definition of aggression is not clear and depends on the interpretation of the Security Council of the United Nations. In practice, it means that the crimes within the Statute can be attributed by the Security Council to any state or organ which includes also any of its permanent members. While we do not deny that the attribution of the concept of international criminal responsibility to the permanent members of the Security Council is very controversial, this does not mean that a resolution of the Council has prohibited it in finding any member or a permanent member guilty of committing crimes within the Statute of the ICC.

Needless to say, the provisions of the Statute may apply to any state once the Security Council has decided to submit a case to the Court on the basis of its unlimited geographical authority. Again, although the scope of crimes within the jurisdiction of the Court is defined, the committing of genocide, crimes against humanity or war crimes may be recognised as a violation of the provisions of Chapter VII of the Charter on the basis of breaches of the peace or threats to peace. The reason for this is that the scope of the definition of aggression is still controversial.[45] This is regardless of the existence of the resolution governing the definition of aggression.[46] Moreover, the definitions of the four categories of

---

[45] M. Cherif Bassiouni and Benjamin B. Ferencz, *The Crime Against Peace and Aggression: From Its Origins to the ICC, in* International Criminal Law, vol i (M. cherif Bassiouni, ed. 2008) pp. 207-242; M. Cherif Bassiouni, *Introduction to International Humanitarian Law, in* INTERNATIONAL CRIMINAL LAW, VOL I (M. Cherif Bassiouni, ed. 2008) pp. 269-292; Roger S. Clark, *The Crime of Aggression and the International Criminal Court, in* International Criminal Law, Vol, I (M. Cherif Bassiouni, ed. 2008) pp. 243-265.

[46] Unfortunately, the United Nations General Assembly Resolution 3314 (XXIX) - 14 December 1974 has not been recognised. A main reason for this is that its content is simply based on a resolution and not a treaty. The resolution has defined the term aggression in the following way: "Aggression is the use of armed force by a State against the sovereignty, territorial integrity or political independence of another State, or in any other manner inconsistent with the Charter of the United Nations, as set out in this Definition." (Article 1) Article 2 of the same resolution completes the above definition. It reads that "The First use of armed force by a

international crime may in certain situations overlap one another. It means that it will be very difficult to avoid recognising that the crime of aggression does not simultaneously constitute genocide or a crime against humanity. The primacy of jurisdiction of a state over a substantive crime becomes, therefore, in certain situations, ineffective because of the Security Council's legal power. Consequently, to speak about the principle of primacy of jurisdiction may be acceptable in the case of a state and the ICC, but not in the case of the Security Council, the state and the ICC.

As a consequence of the content of a resolution of the Security Council, a state may be forced to submit its individuals to the jurisdiction of a court. The state may also be occupied *inter alia* for this purpose, as in the case of Iraq.[47] The question is thus what the function of the

---

State in contravention of the Charter shall constitute prima facie evidence of an act of aggression although the Security Council may, in conformity with the Charter, conclude that a determination that an act of aggression has been committed would not be justified in the light of other relevant circumstances, including the fact that the acts concerned or their consequences are not of sufficient gravity." See also Ahmed M. Rifatt, International Aggression: A Study of the Legal Concept: Its Development and Definition in International Law (1979).

[47] The United States even created a monopolised court for the prosecution of the heads of states in Iraq. See M. Wladimiroff, *Former Heads of State on Trial*, 38 (3) Cornell International Law Journal (2005), pp. 949-971; M. Kelly, *The Tricky Nature of Proving Genocide Against Saddam Hussein before the Iraqi Special Tribunal*, 38 (3) Cornell international law journal (2005), pp. 983-1012; M. Newton, *The Iraqi Special Tribunal: A Human rights Perspective*, 38 (3) Cornell international law journal (2005), pp. 863-897; G. Robertson, *Ending impunity: How International Criminal Law Can Put Tyrants on Trial*, 38 (3) Cornell international law journal (2005), pp. 649-671. See also R. Teitel, *The law and Politics of Contemporary Transitional Justice*, 38 (3) Cornell International Law Journal (2005), pp. 837-862. The Iraqi Special Tribunal which tried Saddam Hussein has been strongly criticised and rejected in the international legal and political community. Some of the reasons are the following "1) The Tribunal's statute was not drafted by a group of international lawyers chosen under the authority and supervisions of the United Nations, but rather exclusively by lawyers chosen by the United States government. 2) Given that the newly formed Iraqi government has no independent political or legal character, especially governing certain serious questions of law, politics, and economics, the juridical effect of the tribunal diminishes automatically. 3) The Statute of the IST does not coincide with the United Nations Charter. 4) Unlike international tribunals such as the ICTY, the Tribunal cannot function as an independent national or international criminal court having freedom of action regarding different judicial, historical, and political questions. (5) The Tribunal's ability to employ certain principles of justice is limited by procedure. 6) The proceedings of the Tribunal are at all times subject to the will of the occupying power. 7) Since Saddam Hussein is the most important

complementarity principle will be.[48] The only explanation is that the application of the principle of internationality by the Court takes priority over any other principle.[49] The internationality principle means, therefore, the protection of the fundamental rights of human beings in order to achieve the equal application of international norms.[50] As a result the primacy of jurisdiction can no longer function properly and falls to the ground.[51]

We do not, however, deny that bringing a non-party under the provisions of the Statute is not a simple matter and may face many serious difficulties when it comes to the prosecution of the heads of states or governments. On the one hand, the new government of a non-party state

---

subject of the tribunal, and since the Tribunal is mostly established to exercise its jurisdiction over him, the function and the significance of the Tribunal reduces its juridical effect. 8) The judges of the Tribunal are not elected in accordance with international norms, as is done in the ICTY, but rather by the occupying power. 9) The judges of the Tribunal have far less experience, as compared to the ICTY or ICTR judges, regarding criminal cases involving serious human rights violations. 10) Since the judges of the Tribunal are chosen by the Iraqi Governing Council, which lacks power to pass legislation, the power of all judges remains a question of politics and policies of the occupying power and authority within the territorial jurisdiction of another state. 11) Given that the Tribunal judges have been trained in London by the occupying power, they are likely to have difficulty being impartial. 12) Since the former Iraqi government is known to have seized power with the political assistance of the United States, the Tribunal cannot open any discussions that could divulge secret international political facts that may harm the position of the occupying power. 13) The cases that will come before the Tribunal are selective and not exhaustive. 14) The limitations on the presentations of different cases because of political concerns will affect the Hussein case and that of others accused of international crimes. 15) Because of bias, the Tribunal will be unable to consider those evidentiary rules that are supposed to control decisions of the court. 16) The judges and the Tribunal as a whole cannot, in any way, guarantee the just outcome of the monopolized court. 17) The principles of international human rights cannot appropriately be respected in a Tribunal that exclusively follows the rules of the victorious state. 18) The rights of the accused recognized by general principles of law are not free from political ties and therefore cannot function under the proceedings of the forum. 19) The Tribunal prosecutors are not free from monopolization by the victorious states, especially the United States." Footnotes omitted. Farhad Malekian, *Emasculating the Philosophy of International Criminal Justice in the Iraqi Special Tribunal*, pp.720-721.

[48] *Id*., pp.703-706.

[49] For the principle of internationality of the Court see *Id.,* 698

[50] *Id.* 704-705.

[51] *Id.* 699-706.

may refuse to submit its nationals to the ICC on account of the initiation of the office of prosecutor. On the other hand, it may be obliged to accept the jurisdiction of the Court on the basis of the Security Council's power or certain political considerations arising from a resolution of the Security Council.[52] The Statute cannot limit the Security Council's power over a case and this means that the Court has to follow a resolution of the Security Council when dealing with the case.

3. Jurisdictions and Admissibility

3.1. Permission to Admissibility

In general, when it comes to the admissibility of a case before the ICC, there are two essential principles that must be evaluated when deciding on the question of admissibility. One is the criterion of the principle of complementarity. This means that one is not willing to consider the case under certain provisions of the Statute within the national jurisdiction and the Security Council does not ask the Court for investigation of the case. The other is whether the gravity threshold for the Court jurisdiction has already been achieved. These two principles are in fact an integral part of one another and cannot be treated in isolation. This is because both principles are used by the ICC to determine the criteria for the recognition of perpetrators of crimes.

With the Rome Statute, procedural methods for jurisdiction and admissibility have been created which are rather dependent. According to the Statute, if the prosecutor is investigating *proprio motu*,[53] challenges to jurisdiction and admissibility are permitted. This means that admissibility may occur in any proceedings until trial. Thus, all parties related to a case, including the Court, are entitled during most stages of proceedings to a right of challenge. The Court may after examination of a case declare the application to be inadmissible.[54]

The problem of admissibility is that it allows all states, including non-parties to the Statute of the International Criminal Court, to challenge the investigations of the prosecutor or deputy prosecutor, at an early stage in the development of the case. This means that the work of the prosecutor

[52] If the Court does not have jurisdiction over non-parties, the international legal and political community is then obliged to establish a new *ad hoc* international criminal tribunal for the individuals of the states in question. This will not be ideal.
[53] Article 15(4).
[54] Article 17(1).

will be hampered by those parties to the case that do not, for one reason or another, agree with the proceedings of the case.[55]

3.2. The Criteria for Admissibility

At first glance, the Court is entitled to see whether it has the right of jurisdiction regarding the case.[56] Hence, the case should not violate the provisions of the complementarity principle and must be of sufficient gravity.[57] According to Pre-Trial Chamber I, by the word "gravity" one intends "to ensure that the Court initiates cases only against the most senior leaders suspected of being the most responsible for the crimes within the jurisdiction of the Court allegedly committed in any given situation under investigation."[58]

According to the Pre-Trial Chamber, when examining criteria for gravity, the following key questions must be taken into serious consideration:

> Is the conduct which is the object of a case systematic or large-scale (due consideration should also be given to the social alarm caused to the international community by the relevant type of conduct)?
> - Considering the position of the relevant person in the State entity, organization or armed group to which he belongs, can it be considered that such a person falls within the category of the most senior leaders of the situation under investigation?; and
> - Does the relevant person fall within the category of the most senior leaders suspected of being most responsible, considering (1) the role played by the relevant person through acts or omissions when the State entities, organizations or armed groups to which he belongs commit systematic or large-scale crimes within the jurisdiction of the Court, and (2) the role played by such State entities, organizations or armed groups in the overall commission of crimes within the jurisdiction of the Court in the relevant situation?[59]

---

[55] This is clear in the Case of Omar al-Bashir who was the president of Sudan. The ICC wants to start an investigation concerning the crime in Darfur but there have been increasing objections by Arab states concerning his trial in 2009.

[56] Article 17 and 19(1).

[57] See supera.

[58] *Thomas Lubanga Dyilo*, ICC, (ICC-01/04-01/06), Decision on the Prosecutor's Application for a warrant of arrest, Article 58, February 24, 2006, http://www.icc-cpi.int/library/cases/ICC-01-04-01-06-8-US-Corr_English.pdf, para.50.

[59] *Id.*, para.63.

For the above reasons, the Court must satisfy itself that it has jurisdiction in any case which has been brought under its authority. This will be in conformity with Article 17 of the Statute.[60] Thus, the Court must decide on the admissibility of a case under its jurisdiction on its own initiative, but should not, in any situation, ignore the requirements for admissibility.[61] In fact, in the recent Lubanga case,[62] Pre-Trial Chamber I

---

[60] See *supera*.

[61] See section on complementarity principle.

[62] *Prosecutor v. Thomas Lubanga Dyilo*, International Criminal Court (ICC), Case No. ICC-01/04-01/06, Warrant of Arrest, February 10, 2006, http://www.icc-cpi.int/library/cases/ICC-01-04-01-06-2_English.pdf. Quite recently (on 10 February, 2006), the ICC issued an arrest warrant for Lubanga. Thomas Lubanga Dyilo was arrested in the Democratic Republic of the Congo in March 2006. This happened in connection with the killing of nine Bangladeshi peacekeepers in the Ituri region which is rich in gold. The armed forces of Lubanga's Union of Congolese Patriots were involved in the killings of the peacekeepers of the Mission de l'Organisation des Nations Unies en République démocratique du Congo (MONUC) or Mission of the United Nations Organisation in the Democratic Republic of the Congo in 2005. The members of the armed force are largely people of the Hema ethnic group. The relevant armed group constitutes one of several military groups in Africa's Great Lakes region and was created by Lubanga in 2000. The Hema ethnic group is historically recognised as the enemies of the Lendu group. Both these groups live in the far Northeast region of the Democratic Republic of the Congo, opposite the territories of Sudan and Uganda. In fact, Lubanga is the first suspect to face charges against him at the permanent International Criminal Court. He is accused of serious violations of the system of international criminal law and particularly the use of children as soldiers. This is the result of the atrocities in the Democratic Republic of the Congo during 2004. Lubanga was brought to the first public pre-trial hearing of the ICC on 20 March 2006. The Court enumerates, among other acts of atrocities "enlisting and conscripting children under the age of fifteen and using them to participate actively in hostilities". The Trial of Lubanga was supposed to start on 23 June 2008 but it was prevented by the Pre-Trial Chamber on 13 June. This was based on the fact that the prosecutor had not properly respected the rights of the accused person. Consequently, his trial was suspended due to the circumstances of the case. He was released by the Court's orders on 2 July 2008. Pre-Trial Chamber I stated, "the detention of the accused cannot be justified in order to ensure his appearance at trial or to safeguard the investigation, because the trial (which was the result of the investigation) has been stayed. Furthermore, in the absence of the prospect of a trial, the accused cannot be held in custody or subjected to provisional release as purely preventative measures to deter him from committing further crimes." It further asserted, "Notwithstanding the grant of leave to appeal the Decision, the inevitable result is that the Chamber must order the immediate release of the accused. Although the prosecution has indicated that it intends to apply to the

has asserted that "it is *a conditio sine qua non* for a case arising from the investigation of a situation to be inadmissible that national proceedings encompass both the person and the conduct which is the subject of the case before the Court."[63]

The prosecutor to the Court also has the duty of notifying states parties and even those states which may have jurisdiction over certain crimes that are the subject of investigation. The relevant states should therefore in a limited time express their interests in the investigation and prosecution of a case. The time limit is accordingly one month.[64] A state may inform the Court within this time limit whether it is investigating or has already investigated accusers who are within its jurisdiction.[65] At the request of the state which is investigating the crime, the prosecutor must defer the case unless the Pre-Trial Chamber takes the case into its own consideration and authorizes the investigation.[66] A state, which has challenged a ruling of the Pre-Trial Chamber, may again confront the admissibility of a case if there is further evidence or a major change in the situation.[67]

3.3. Challenges to Jurisdiction

According to the Rome Statute several parties in addition to the prosecutor and the Court are permitted to bring challenges. The challenges to the jurisdiction of the Court or the admissibility of a case may be brought by: i) a person or accused for whom a warrant of arrest or a summons to come

---

Chamber to lift the stay, the outcome of any application of that kind is wholly uncertain and the Chamber will address any submissions that may be advanced in the future, on their own facts. As regards the effect of the grant of leave to appeal, given the order for release is the direct consequence of the Decision for which leave has been granted, it is for the Appeals Chamber and not, as has been submitted, for the Trial Chamber to determine any application for suspensive effect." See Situation in the Democratic Republic of the Congo in the case of the Prosecutor v. Thomas Lubanga Dyilo, Public Decision on the release of Thomas Lubanga Dyilo (ICC-01/04-01/06 1/17), 2 July 2008. On 18 November, the Court lifted the suspension. He was brought before the jurisdiction of the ICC in January 2009.

[63] *Prosecutor v. Thomas Lubanga Dyilo*, ICC, Case No. ICC-01/04-01/06, Decision on the Prosecutor's Application for a warrant of arrest, Article 58, February 24, 2006, http://www.icc-cpi.int/library/cases/ICC-01-04-01-06-8-US-Corr_English.pdf, para.31.

[64] Article 18(2).

[65] Article 18(2).

[66] Article 18(2).

[67] Article 18(7).

into the Court has been sent;[68] ii) a State which has, in one way or another, jurisdiction over a case;[69] iii) a state from which approval of jurisdiction is asked on account of the provisions of article 12.[70]

Parties or a person should challenge the jurisdiction of the Court only once, except by leave of the Court in particular circumstances.[71] States parties should submit challenges prior to the commencement of the trial. Challenges which are, at the beginning of a trial, brought by states parties to the Court should concern the admissibility of a case and should be based on certain important motives such as *ne bis in idem.*[72] Challenges to the admissibility of a case or jurisdiction of the Court should be referred to the Pre-Trial Chamber. This should be prior to the confirmation of charges but after confirmation is submitted to the Trial Chamber.[73] A challenge brought by a state based on its own investigation or prosecution of the case may be a reason for the prosecutor to suspend the investigation unless the Court determines that a case is admissible or inadmissible.[74] Yet, a prosecutor may seek authority to be granted by the Court the right to investigate certain necessary steps.[75]

Obviously, challenges may be brought to the Court in different ways and the prosecutor may have a broad range of functions for the appropriate treatment of the case.[76] In any case, it must be stated that bringing a challenge must not affect the legal validity of any act which is carried out by the prosecutor.[77]

One problem of the Statute is that it does not clarify whether challenges to the admissibility and jurisdiction of the Court should be brought together or separately. Although, a challenge to the jurisdiction of the Court is entirely different from a challenge to admissibility, it seems that the Statute permits the making of challenges by different means depending on the circumstances. In any event, the ICC must try to avoid taking political decisions concerning admissibility or inadmissibility. This must be one of the most significant purposes of the Court. There is no

---

[68] Article 19(2)(a).
[69] Article 19(2)(b).
[70] See also Y. S. Kim, *The Preconditions to the Exercise of the Jurisdiction of the International Criminal Court: With Focus on Article 12 of the Rome Statute*, 8 Journal of International Law and Practice 47 (1999).
[71] Article 19(4).
[72] Article 19(4).
[73] Article 19(6).
[74] Article19(7).
[75] Article 19(8).
[76] Article 19 (10) and (11).
[77] Article 19(9).

doubt that the future work of the Court will openly demonstrate the policy of the ICC regarding its true impartiality and the fulfilment of the principles of international criminal justice. Although the admissibility and inadmissibility of a case are two juridical terms regarding the procedures of the case, they may be used to develop or hamper the situation concerning the criminal investigation.

4. The Basic Principles for the Jurisdiction of the Court

The ICC bases its judgment on the principles of national and international criminal law which means that its structure is fixed and is interpreted according to the general principles that are formulated into its Statute.[78] This structure was developed on the basis that the former international tribunals, such as the Nuremberg and Tokyo Tribunals, had many difficulties and received criticism concerning their charters. These two tribunals were established after World War II and therefore their rules

[78] Daniel D. Ntanda Nsereko, The International Criminal Court: Jurisdictional and Related Issues, 10 Criminal Law Forum 87 (1999); Timothy L. H. McCormark and Sue Robertson, *Jurisdictional Aspects of the Rome Statute for the International Criminal Court* 23 Melbourne University Law Review 635 (1999); M. K. Marler, *The International Criminal Court: Assessing the Jurisdictional Loopholes in the Rome Statute*, 49 Duke Law Journal 825 (1999); Paul D. Marquardt, *Law Without Borders: The Constitutionality of an International Court*, 33 Columbia Journal of Transnational Law 73 (1995); Hans-Peter Kaul, *The International Criminal Court: Jurisdiction, Trigger Mechanism and Relationship to National Jurisdiction,* in The Rome Statute of the International Criminal Court: A Challenge to Impunity (Mauro Politi and Giuseppe Nesi, eds. 2001) pp. 59-64; Hans-Peter Kaul and Claus Kress, *Jurisdiction and Cooperation in the Statute of the International Criminal Court: Principles and Compromises*, 2 Yearbook of International Humanitarian Law 143 (1999); Eve La Haye, *The Jurisdiction of the International Criminal Court: Controversies over the Preconditions for Exercising its Jurisdiction,* 46 Netherlands International Law Review 1 (1999); Hans-Peter Kaul, *Special Note: The Struggle for the International Criminal Court's Jurisdiction,* 6 European Journal of Crime, Criminal Law and Criminal Justice 48 (1998); Sandra L. Jamison, *A Permanent International Court: A Proposal that Overcomes Past Objections*, 23 Denver Journal of International Law and Policy 419 (1995); Michael D. Greenberg, *Creating an International Criminal Court*, 10 Boston University International Law Journal 119 (1992); Leila Sadat Wexler, *A First Look at the 1998 Rome Statute for a Permanent International Criminal Court: Jurisdiction, Definition of Crimes, Structure and Referrals to the Court*, in International Criminal Law, Vol. III (M. Cherif Bassiouni, ed. 1999) pp. 655-91; David Stoelting, *Status Report on the International Criminal Court,* 3 Hofstra Law and Policy Symposium 233 (1999).

relied heavily on the retroactive aspects of the law. Although one cannot deny that the philosophy behind the punishments of the criminals of the war were ethically and naturally correct, the problem was, nonetheless, that their rules were not entirely based on positive aspects of international criminal law. Therefore, one serious criticism of the tribunals was that their laws were the law of the victorious states and consequently monopolised by the strong political parties in the world.

In order to avoid the above misunderstanding and misinterpretation of the law, the international legal community has continuously endeavoured to solve the problem of justice especially concerning the system of international criminal law. It was on this basis that the drafters of the ICC tried to give certain precise definitions to certain international crimes which fall under the jurisdiction of the Court. The machinery of the Court is based on the norms that are its framework and with which it may charge potential defendants. One cannot however deny that the crimes that are defined under the Statute are the models that will be used by the Court itself and therefore the scope of those crimes may consequently vary when they are treated by national courts for various reasons.

In general, the Court's jurisdiction is based on the principle of legality due to the progressive development of international criminal law and also on the principle of complementarity which offers jurisdiction if different national criminal courts are unable to carry out a prosecution. This means that where a state wishes to investigate a case under its jurisdiction, the Court is constitutionally required to relinquish the case to the requested state. At the same time the state in question has to respect the fundamental principles of international criminal law governing the law applicable to the relevant case. Thus, the state in question should not violate these principles because of its own criminal legislation.

4.1. Applicable Sources of Law

Various legal systems are based on sources of the law. It is upon these sources that the law is interpreted and applied. That is why the ICC puts great emphasis on the concept of the sources of the law and their application to certain given cases. Accordingly, the Statute of the ICC in Article 21 lists and recognises certain sources as its tool for the implementation of the law. These sources are examined in the following sub-sections.

4.1.1. The Priority of Statute

The Court is, according to Article 21 of the Statute, responsible for applying, in the first stage, the law of the Statute, Elements of Crimes and its Rules of Procedure and Evidence.[79] This means that the Court should fully respect its constitutional provisions and should not violate them in the application of the law. Simultaneously, the article emphasises that in the event of conflict between several sources, the Statute prevails and the Court should not disregard it. In addition, the Court should bear in mind that "The Elements of Crimes and amendments thereto shall be consistent with this Statute."[80] This version proves a further argument that the law of the Statute gets priority over the elements of crimes.

Deeper examination of the serious function of the Statute may be seen in the following provisions. Thus, "In the event of conflict between the Statute and the Rules of Procedure and Evidence, the Statute shall prevail."[81] This version and the version in the above paragraph have obviously a similar aim and result, and clarify the important value of the Statute. Thus, if there is any doubt about the interpretation and application of the provisions of the Elements of Crimes and Rules of Procedure and Evidence, the Court is, due to the statement of its Statute, obliged to apply its provisions. One essential reason for this is to emphasise that the Elements of Crimes have to be modified after the constitution of the Court and not the contrary. Another reason is to prevent judges from undermining the rules of the Statute by giving priority to other provisions.

---

[79] For some consideration of the rules of procedure see Daniel Mac Sweeney, *International Standards of Fairness, Criminal Procedure and the International Criminal Court,* 68 Revue Internationale de Driot Pénal 233 (1997); Vladimir Tochilovsky, *Rules of Procedure for the International Criminal Court: Problems to Address in Light of the Experience of the Ad Hoc Tribunals,* 46 Netherlands International Law Review 343 (1999); L. Watters, *Convergence and the Procedures of the International Criminal Court: An International and Comparative Perspective,* 25 Fordham International Law Journal 419 (2002); S. M. Yengejeh, *Rules of Procedure of the Assembly of States parties to the Rome Statute of the International Criminal Court,* 25 Fordham International Law Journal 674 (2002); Malcolm N. Shaw, *The International Criminal Court – Some Procedural and Evidential Issues,* 3 Journal of Armed Conflict Law 65 (1998).

[80] Article 9 (3).

[81] Article 51(5).

4.1.2. Principles of International Law

The Court is also empowered in accordance with Article 21(b) to apply, where necessary, the rules and principles of international law that are recognised by states. According to the article, these are law-making treaties and the principles and rules of international law, including the established principles of international law of armed conflict. With the term "principles and rules of international law", the article refers to the general sources of public international law that are listed in Article 38 of the Statute of International Court of Justice. This article refers to treaties, customary law, general principles of law, decisions of international courts and commonly qualified international works. Another interpretation of Article 38 is that certain resolutions of the General Assembly are also a part of the principles and rules of international law and they may therefore be applied as secondary sources in the procedure of the Court. Whilst the value of the above principles cannot be overestimated, it is obvious that the Court is responsible for taking into serious consideration the scope of its own Statute "in the first place".

Article 21 (b) has also empowered the Court to apply the established principles of the international law of armed conflict. This means that the Court is permitted to resort to the provisions of the relevant law wherever it seems necessary in the procedures of its jurisdiction. One may, nevertheless, argue that the phrase "established principles of the international law of armed conflict" is rather uncertain and may cause controversy over the jurisdiction of the Court. This is because it is very difficult to decide which rules constitute principles of the international law of armed conflict and which do not. One may, however, argue that the rules of the four Geneva Conventions and their Protocols constitute an integral part of the established principles of the international law of armed conflict. While this is surely true, there are other international instruments applicable in the time of armed conflicts, the value of which cannot be denied. In fact, a list of these conventions and their humanitarian purposes proves their important function.

Another issue, which may be raised, is that the established principles of the international law of armed conflicts are not solely conventional. There are also customary principles that may have several characterisations, namely, conventional, customary and jus cogens principles. These principles may have similar values within all three legal disciplines. Therefore, it seems that the vocabulary of the phrase is rather wide and may create different arguments within the procedures of the Court. Obviously, "the established principles of the international armed conflict" have to be used in favour of all parties, the accused, victims, convicted and the witnesses, if the terms "justice" or "equal justice" are to be respected in the procedures of the Court. This means that the judges of the Court have to be very careful in the consideration of the language of Article 21 (b). The controversy, which may arise in the application of the established principles of international armed conflict and the absolute rules of the Statute, is indeed very problematic. The latter is restricted to its provisions while the former extends beyond the circumstances of the time. There is not yet a clear fragment in international law which can be referred to as the manifestation of customary legal principles established for international armed conflict.

4.1.3. National Law

The Court is also, if necessary in certain situations, permitted to apply other sources of the law. Article 21 (c) emphasises in particular that general principles of law, which are also considered a source of international law within Article 38 of the International Court of Justice, may be applied by the Court. Furthermore, the Statute recognises that the status of national law, if appropriate, may also be regarded as a source in the procedure of the Court. However, the Court is under an obligation to examine the value of any rule to ensure that it is consistent with international law and internationally recognised norms and standards. In particular, this permission concerns the national laws of those states which would "normally exercise jurisdiction over the crime".

With the above phrase, Article 21 (c) makes it clear that the Court is not entirely free to refer to the national provisions of all states, but only to the laws of those states which may legally deal with the crime and have, by one means or another, been involved in the procedures. The paragraph has clearly rejected any inconsistency with the law of the Statute, international recognised norms and standards. In other words, the use of a rule of national law must be useful to the interpretation or application of the law of the ICC and at the same time it should provide additional support in the recognition of the crime.

Here, the purpose of the legislator is to protect the law of the Court and to underline the importance of ensuring that the rules of the national legislations of states are consistent with the generally accepted rules and principles of international law. The impression is that the provisions of Article 21 (c) are a compromise between two different ideologies. The first is those states which want to bind the framework of the Court to national legislations. The second is those states which see the whole Court as a separate international entity having an international legal personality of its own. Obviously, the Court will have a greater problem when it refers to the provisions of Article 21 (c) when the states parties, which would normally exercise jurisdiction over the crime, have two different principles concerning the case. Therefore, there may be a contradiction between three systems of laws, including the ICC, and the result may not be satisfactory.

As a whole, the use of national rules is permitted because the ICC operates in a normative forum and takes into consideration the general principles of criminal law of different states that have already achieved international recognition.

4.1.4. Application of Other Judgments

Another provision of Article 21 permits the ICC to apply principles and rules of law interpreted in its other judgments. This means that the authority of the ICC is not limited and it may even use its own decisions as a source of the law. In other words, case law is accepted within the jurisdiction of the Court. In practice, this develops the future sources of the law and slowly modifies the attitude of the Statute regarding the application of its judgments.

The ICC has, however, on account of its own constitution received this vital power which will be useful for the development of its own decisions and more effective settlement of disputes concerning international crimes and criminality.[82] This power of the Court will also surely help in the development of customary international criminal law concerning the recognition of certain international crimes, as well as impositions of its rules and punishments. Thus, the question of being a non-party which concerns the decisions of the International Court of Justice does not arise here and the law which is developed in one case may with due regard to the circumstances be used by the judges in other cases.

4.1.5. Human Rights

The final provisions of Article 21 (3) concerning the applicable law aim at protecting the fundamental principles of international human rights law when the ICC uses other provisions of the article. The Court is thus under a recognised obligation to see whether the sources, rules and principles which are going to be applied by the Court are consistent with the basic principles of human rights law.[83]

---

[82] National courts may use the decisions of the ICC in their own proceedings.

[83] For some aspects of human rights in the court see Fausto Pocar, *The Rome Statute of the International Criminal Court and Human Rights, in* The Rome

In other words, the Court is not permitted to use the rules of one state which would normally exercise jurisdiction over the crime and ignore the rules of other states in similar situations. This means that the impartiality of the Court must be maintained and justice must be carried out without any adverse distinction on grounds such as gender as defined in Article 7 (3) of the Statute. It also includes race, colour, age, religion, belief, political opinion, language, ethnic, national or social origin, wealth, birth or other status.The provisions of Article 21 (3) certainly aim at the progressive development of international criminal law and the consolidation of the principle of non-discrimination. This is also one of the conditions for achieving equal international criminal justice.

4.2. The Legality Principle

The principle of legality is one of the most consolidated principles of criminal law and international criminal law. The respect of this principle is so crucial and essential that no part of international criminal law can function properly without to some extent examining this principle. The imperative function of the principle of legality was largely developed after

---

Statute of the International Criminal Court: a Challenge to Impunity (Mauro Politi and Guiseppe Nesi, eds. 2004), pp. 67-74; Jelena Pejic, *The International Criminal Court and the Human Rights Revolution,* 34 International Lawyer 65 (2000); Vesselin Popovski, *The International Criminal Court: A Necessary Step Towards Global Justice,* 31 Security Dialogue 405 (2000); S.B. Shah, *The Oversight of the Last Great International Institution of the Twentieth Century: The International Criminal Court's Definition of Genocide,* 16 Emory International Law Review 351 (2002); Jelena Pejic, *The Tribunal and the ICC: Do Precedents Matter,* 60 Albany Law Review 841 (1997); Toni Pfanner, *The Establishment of a Permanent International Criminal Court: ICRC Expectations of the Rome Diplomatic Conference,* 322 International Review of the Red Cross 21 (1998); P. K. Rakate, *An International Criminal Court for a New Millennium – The Rome Conference,* 23 South Africa Yearbook of International Law 217 (1998); J. Schense, Necessary Steps for the Creation of the International Criminal Court, 25 Fordham International Law Journal 717 (2002). See further George E. Edwards, *International Human Rights Law Challenges to the New International Criminal Court: The Search and Seizure Right to Privacy,* 26 Yale Journal of International Law 343 (2001); Lucius Caflisch, *The Rome Statute and the European Convention on Human Rights,* 23 Human Rights Law Journal 1 (2002); Nicole Eva Erb, *Gender-Based Crimes under the Draft Statute for the Permanent International Criminal Court,* 29 Columbia Human Rights Law Review 401 (1998); Dorean M. Koenig and Kelly D. Askin, *International Criminal Law and the International Criminal Court Statute: Crimes Against Women, in* Women and International Human Rights Law (Kelly D. Askin and Doreen M. Koenig, eds. 1999) pp. 3-29.

the outbreak of World War II and the various subsequent criticisms of the constitutions of international criminal tribunals. It was emphasised that the principle of legality was one of the chief elements of national criminal law and that this concept also has to be protected under the procedures of international tribunals. Therefore, it was established long ago that the *maxim nullum crimen nulla poena sine lege* is the cornerstone of any international criminal jurisdiction.[84] This means that one cannot be punished for a crime that has not been defined.[85] In other words, punishment is based upon the existence of the definition of the crime. If a conduct is not identified as a crime or is not recognised as a criminal violation of the existing law, one cannot be prosecuted for acts that are not criminal acts on account of the existing literature of international criminal law.

The principle of legality should denote respect for the principle of fair justice in accordance with the principles of human rights. By "human rights justice", we mean that all procedures of a tribunal concerning the prosecution of an accused respect the provisions of the system of international human rights law and are not in any way against the fundamental principles of this law. In particular, the principle of legality is strongly protected by the provisions of the Universal Declaration of Human Rights which constitute an integral part of the international law of *jus cogens*.[86] A similar policy is integrated into the provisions of the International Covenant on Civil and Political Rights.[87]

However, one of the chief differences between the principles of legality in the system of international criminal law and that of national criminal law is that, within the status of the former, the principle relies on several sources. These are, essentially, treaties and customary international criminal law. Customary law makes the precise definition of an international crime very difficult and controversial. This is because the scope of customary international criminal law is sometimes subject to debate and what does and does not constitute an international crime may be examined according to the circumstances of a case and political considerations. For this reason, the definition of crimes under the system

[84] See Bruce Broomhall, *Article 22, Nullum crimen sine lege, in* Commentary on the Rome Statute of the International Crimnal Court 447 (Otto Triffterer, ed., 1999); Machteld Boot, Genocide, Crimes Against Humanity, War Crimes: Nullum Crimen Sine Lege and the Subject Matter Jurisdiction of the International Criminal Court(2002).

[85] *Id.*

[86] See Article 11 (2).

[87] See Article 15.

of international criminal law may differ slightly from that of the national criminal systems which are based on legislation.

It was because of the above issues that the Statute of the ICC was drafted with the full ambition of giving a clear definition of crimes and of avoiding any future difficulty in facing different definitions of crimes under several national criminal systems. Thus, under the provisions of the Statute, the judges of the Court should not be affected by their own national legal system's criminal definitions. The principle of legality should solely be based on the definitions of crimes within the framework of the Statute.[88]

The principle of legality is in fact a legal guarantee for the accused protecting him/her from any external interference by different legal systems and preventing inconsistent judgements by different judges. Therefore, the principle of legality not only protects the accused person, but also, some of the conditions for equal international justice. Some of the most central articles of the Statute stipulating the principle of legality are Articles 22, 23 and 24. The articles present a significant framework for the implementation of the principle of legality in the Court.

4.2.1. *Nullum Crimes sine lege*

One of the central articles of the Statute of the ICC emphasising the significant function of the principle of legality is Article 22.[89] It affirms that no one shall be criminally responsible according to the provisions of the Statute, unless the conduct in question constitutes a crime within the jurisdiction of the Court, at the time it takes place.[90] This means that a person cannot be held criminally responsible for what is not defined as a crime and does not have legislative recognition. In other words, the executive and judicial powers of the Court are obliged to respect the provisions of the legislative part of the Statute.

---

[88] Otherwise, any other policy would make the implementation of the provisions of the Court very difficult and different argumentations would be presented for the principle of legality and the implementation of different criminal legislations. In particular, this would be more tangible in the case of the conduct of accused persons which falls within the national definitions of two or several states.

[89] Jordan J. Paust, *Nullem Crimen and Related Claims, in* The International Criminal Court: Observations and Issues Before the 1997-98 Preparatory Committee; and Adminstrative and Finanacial Impelications, 13*ter* Nouvelles Etudes Penales 275 (1997).

[90] Article 22 (1).

The above principle is also strengthened by another principle of similar character. Accordingly the "definition of a crime shall be strictly construed and shall not be extended by analogy. In the case of ambiguity, the definition shall be interpreted in favour of the person being investigated, prosecuted or convicted."[91] This means that the principle of legality in the case of the definition of international crimes should, under no circumstances, be violated and compared with other definitions of national criminal law.[92] In any event, the Statute guarantees the full application of the principle of legality in favour of the accused and his/her rights when he/she is being questioned on account of the provisions of the Statute.[93]

The provisions of Article 22 have also underlined that the framework of the Statute should not in any way affect the characterisation of any conduct that has already been recognized as criminal conduct under the system of international criminal law. Consequently, the provisions of the Statute do not limit the progressive development of international criminal law from the recognition and consolidation of other conducts as being criminal, independently of the Statute. This concerns *de lege lata* and also *de lege ferenda,* both of which are considered essential for the construction of international criminal law.

4.2.2. *Nulla Poena Sine Lege*

Another chief aspect of the Statute of the ICC concerns the principle of *nulla poena sine lege*.[94] This principle was consolidated long ago within different systems of criminal law and also implies the importance of the principle of legality. The principle of *nulla poena sine lege* ensures the application of the punishment that is already pre-set by the Statute. Accordingly, the judges of the Court cannot provide a punishment that is against the framework of the Statute or violates its limitations. The legislator has therefore circumscribed the possible punishment that may be decided by the Court according to the circumstances and to the gravity of the crime. The decision of the Court should therefore represent the applicable provisions of the legislation of the Statute and much more

---

[91] Article 22 (2).

[92] The provisions of Article 22 (2) are not comparable to the provisions of Islamic criminal law which permits analogy in certain cases.

[93] The provisions of Article 22(2) are also in conflict with the common law systems which permit analogy and allow that the principle of legality can be developed due to the development of case law.

[94] Article 23.

significantly, the principles of international human rights law concerning the attribution of punishment.

4.2.3. *Non-retroactivity Ratione Personae*

One of the very well-known principles of law is the principle of non-retroactivity. This principle implies the fact that a law should not be applied for an act that was not recognised as wrong at the time of the commission of the act. Therefore, the principle prevents the application of *ex post facto* law.[95]

The principle of non-retroactivity has different aims: to protect the system of legislation, to prevent accusation or conviction and to prevent severe punishment. The use of the principle has therefore been seen as going against the basic elements of the Statute of the ICC and the basic human rights of the accused in the procedures of the Court. The judges are not thereby permitted to hold a person responsible for their conduct prior to the adoption of the Statute.[96]

The legislators of the ICC have also foreseen the situation in which the law may be modified due to the conditions of the time. Accordingly, a change in the law which was applicable prior to a final judgement may be a reason for the law to be used in the interest of the person under investigation, prosecution, conviction or punishment. Thus, if the new law applies a lighter punishment to the given conduct, this should be a reason to mitigate punishment. The changes must, however, be prior to the final judgment.[97]

With all these provisions within the Statute of the ICC, the legislator has tried to avoid the problematic situations that have arisen with the establishment of several international criminal tribunals before 1998. All these international criminal tribunals had one common problem based on the fact that they were created after the commission of the crimes.[98] The legislators of the ICC were consequently very careful to avoid such situations.

---

[95] This principle was discussed in the beginning of the book.

[96] Article 24 (1).

[97] Article 24 (2)

[98] These were, for example, the Nuremberg and Tokyo tribunals, the ICTY and the ICTR.

4.2.4. The Principle of *Ne bis in idem*

4.2.4.1. Prohibition

The protection of the principle of *ne bis in idem* is one of the most recent progressive developments in the recognition of the principles of international criminal law.[99] The principle protects those who have already been punished from further punishment for the same crime. Although the term "*ne bis in idem*" is rather new in the system of international criminal law, the principle has largely been supported by the basic instruments of international human rights law. The principle was explicitly entered into the structure of the 1966 International Covenant on Civil and Political Rights which clearly states that "No one shall be liable to be tried or punished again for an offence for which he has already been finally convicted or acquitted in accordance with the law and penal procedure of each country."[100] The relevant provisions of the Covenant are reconfirmed in the Statute of the ICC with much more specific clarifications.

---

[99] However, the principle of *ne bis in idem* is one of the oldest and most accepted principles in national criminal law. This principle guarantees the application of a fair and just jurisdiction and prevents the double application of the machinery of criminal justice to the same crime. The principle is also integrated into some regional agreements and some states have also contributed to its development in the international system. The principle has correctly been formulated into the 1996 Code of Crimes against the Peace and Security of Mankind and it can be asserted that it constitutes one of the core principles for the accurate implementation of the Code. The provisions of the relevant article of the Statute of the ICC are more or less taken from the relevant article of the Code. It is useful to examine Article 22 of the Code on *ne bis in idem* here. The article reads that "1.No one shall be tried for a crime against the peace and security of mankind which he has already been finally convicted or acquitted by an international criminal court. 2.An individual may not be tried again for a crime which he has been finally convicted or acquitted for by a national court except in the following cases: (a) by an international criminal court, if: (i) the act which was the subject of the judgment in the national court was characterized by that court as an ordinary crime and not as a crime against the peace and security of mankind; or (ii) the national court proceedings were not impartial or independent or were designed to shield the accused from international criminal responsibility or the case was not diligently prosecuted; (b) by a national court of another State, if: (i) the act which was the subject of the previous judgment took place in the territory of that State; or (ii) that State was the main victim of the crime. 3. In the case of a subsequent conviction under the present Code, the court, in the passing sentence, shall take into account the extent to which any penalty imposed by a national court on the same person for the same act has already been served."

[100] Article 14 (7).

4.2.4.2. Ground for Inadmissibility

Article 20 of the Statute relates to the matter of double jeopardy. Accordingly, if the question of *ne bis in idem* is proved, this will be a ground for inadmissibility.[101] This means that the Court is not permitted to initiate a case to which this principle applies. The article says that "no person shall be tried before the Court with respect to conduct which formed the basis of crimes for which the person has been convicted or acquitted by the Court."[102] These provisions clearly guarantee the fundamental rights of a person to protest at procedures that are against the basic principles of criminal law.

There are also other basic conditions for the application of the principle of *ne bis in idem*. Accordingly, no person shall be tried by another court for a crime listed in Article 5 of the Statute for which he/she has already been convicted or found not guilty by the Court.[103] This provision provides a juridical guarantee for a person who has been tried already by the ICC. The purpose is to prevent people from being tried twice for the same offence.[104]

---

[101] According to one writer, "Ne-bis-in-idem (double jeopardy) is not truly a ground to refuse surrender to the court. Whether or not the arrested person has already been diligently tried by another court for conduct within the jurisdiction of the ICC, which is the basis for the arrest warrant and surrender request, is a matter best left to the court pursuant to Article 20 of the Statute." Göran Sluiter, *The Surrender of War Criminals to the International Criminal Court*, 25 Loyola of Los Angeles International & Comparative Law Journal 605-51 (2003), at 633; see also S. N. M. Young, *Surrendering the Accused to the International Criminal Court,* 71 British Yearbook of International Law 317 (2000).

[102] Article 20 (1).

[103] Article 20 (2).

[104] Whilst the value of the rule of *ne bis in idem* is highly important in criminal proceedings, the possibility of rejecting the application of this principle may occur when moving between several criminal jurisdictions. This is because the conviction and punishment of a person for a crime by a domestic court may not be accepted by other domestic systems and there may be profound objections to a court's decision. It is for this reason that in drafting international criminal conventions, there is normally a prolonged disagreement concerning which state has the competence to have jurisdiction over the accused and which state has jurisdictionally legal priority. For this reason many principles of international criminal law, including the territoriality principle, the nationality principle, the passive personality principle, the protective principle and the principle of flag, have been invoked in order for a state to take priority over other states in the application of its criminal jurisdiction. These principles are also intended to prevent the punishment of a person twice for the same criminal behaviour.

4.2.4.3. Fatal Circumstances

The provisions regarding the inadmissibility of a case on the basis of double jeopardy are limited in certain fatal circumstances. Thus, inadmissibility may be admissible by the further provisions of Article 20.[105] Accordingly, the ICC with respect to the same conduct, shall not try a person who has already been tried by any other court for genocide, crimes against humanity and war crimes unless the proceedings in the other court were biased in favour of the accused in order to mitigate the concept of criminality or release the guilty person from punishment. This means that a national court may have shielded the person from the attribution of the concept of criminal responsibility in order to release that person from their obligation to appear within the jurisdiction of the ICC.

A person may also be brought before the jurisdiction of the ICC when it can be proved that a national court has not upheld the principle of neutrality set out in the norms of international law. Nevertheless, a person may be brought into the jurisdiction of the ICC if it can be proved that the circumstances were inconsistent with the appropriate intent to prosecute or punish such a person.

Thus, the principle of *ne bis in idem* cannot be effective where a national court has knowingly helped the accused to escape from appropriate prosecution and the application of international criminal responsibility. In other words, the ICC's function is not solely limited to prosecution and judgment, but also involves ensuring that other courts have treated a case brought into their jurisdiction properly and assessing whether the system of international criminal justice has been applied properly. The philosophy behind the principle of *ne bis in idem* is the implementation of fair justice and it cannot be the basis for avoiding or mitigating prosecution and punishment under the provisions of the ICC.

It was upon these criteria that the question arose concerning the prohibition of double jeopardy.[106] The main controversy was whether the principle of *ne bis in idem* was to prevent two similar prosecutions for the

---

[105] Article 20 (3).

[106] To avoid dual prosecution and to maintain the priority of international criminal law over the provisions of internal criminal law, the criminal court must, before any action against the accused, examine all the records, documents, evidence, the result of prosecution and if the accused has been found guilty by a domestic criminal court, the level and the degree of punishment must be examined appropriately. When this has been achieved by the court, it must be sure that the prosecution of the accused under the internal criminal system does not coincide with the provisions of international criminal law. This means that the court must not violate the principle of justice or the rights of the condemned persons before any complementary degree of prosecution has taken place.

same crime or two prosecutions for the same criminal conduct. The provisions of Article 20 in two separate paragraphs use two different terminologies. One states that "no person shall be tried by another court for a crime referred to in article 5"[107] and the other says that "no person who has been tried by another court for conduct also prescribed under article 6, 7 or 8 shall be tried by the Court with respect to the same conduct."[108] The legislator must have some reasons for using the different words "crime" and "conduct." The essential difference between these two expressions within the two paragraphs may only oblige states to follow rules concerning the offences listed in the Statute. This may, therefore, allow a person who has been convicted for a crime by the Court to be tried by the provisions of national criminal law for the same conduct but primarily for different crime(s). However, the word "conduct" within two other paragraphs of Article 20, is intended to increase the boundaries of legislation in order to give more authoritative power to the ICC to deal with a suspected case. The article clearly states the grounds upon which the ICC is permitted to examine the case again.[109]

4.2.4.4. Impunity

Although the provisions of the principle of *ne bis in idem* are to be highly appreciated, the expectation that they may not be used as a channel for escaping punishment is perhaps too optimistic. This is because they all depend on particular circumstances and whether or not the political and

[107] Article 20 (2).

[108] Article 20 (3).

[109] For instance, when the criminal acts under the ICC are not criminalised within the system of internal criminal law. In this situation one cannot resort to the principle of *ne bis in idem* since the perpetrators of criminal acts can only be prosecuted and punished under the provisions of international criminal law. Therefore, the involvement of the principle seems irrelevant in this situation. Another situation is when the act constituting an international crime under the provisions of international criminal law is also recognized as a crime under the relevant national criminal law. It is here that the principle of *ne bis in idem* may be invoked against the approval of international prosecution and the punishment of perpetrators of international crimes which has been requested by an international criminal court. This situation is a form of conflict between the provisions of international criminal law and the provisions of the relevant national criminal law. The situation is, however, more complex than this and all that can be said is that a person who has been prosecuted and punished in accordance with an internal criminal law cannot *simply* be brought before an international criminal court for prosecution and punishment for the same crime. A considerable degree of caution must, nevertheless, be exercised in such situations.

legal authorities within a state wish to investigate a case properly. The historical background of the development of the law of the ICC has proved that many states were not interested in the creation of the Court. In fact, after the formulation of the Statute of the ICC, a considerable number of conflicts have arisen around its signature and ratification. The United States government has, since the adoption of the Statute, refused to ratify it. It has even undertaken a number of treaties with other states in order to reduce the juridical effect of the Statute. The value of one of the most central treaties of worldcivilisation has become unstable because of the ratification of a number of treaties with a contrary effect. Thus, the potential value of the principle of *ne bis in idem* for the protection of the fundamental rights of man may become a way of escaping criminality.[110]

[110] The ICC may find that either the internal prosecution or punishment has been disregarded or that they have already been discharged by the internal legal authorities. In any event, the punishment inflicted by a domestic court must not only be taken into account but must also be a criterion for further punishment and/or for declaring culpability without passing any sentence. Therefore, if a person is punished for an act which is recognised as a crime under internal law and a similar act is also recognized as a crime under the ICC but with a different characterisation, the difference(s) in characterisation and criminal procedures cannot be a reason for punishment to be repeated. Clearly, such punishment does not in any way affect the rights of an international criminal court to bring the perpetrators of the relevant international crimes under its prosecution. The court must not, however, inflict further punishment, if the earlier punishment is considered by the court to be sufficient. The situation is better clarified in a commentary to Article 1 (2) of the Code of Crimes Against Peace and Security of Mankind. It says that "the characterization, or the absence of characterization, of a particular type of behaviour as criminal under national law has no effect on the characterization of that type of behaviour as criminal under international law. It is conceivable that a particular type of behaviour characterized as a crime against the peace and security of mankind ... might not be prohibited or might even be imposed by national law. It is also conceivable that such behaviour might be characterized merely as a crime under national law, other than as a crime against the peace and security of mankind under international law. The distinction between characterization as a crime under national law and characterization as a crime under international law is significant since the corresponding legal regimes differ. This distinction has important implications with respect to the *non bis in idem* principle." (International Law Commission Report, 1996, para 10.) It is obvious that conflicts between domestic criminal law and the system of international criminal law must not be resolved in isolation from their actual purposes. Furthermore, it must be admitted that certain provisions of international criminal law have in all situations priority over national criminal provisions and the respect of the principle of *ne bis in idem* must not be used as a plea not to prosecute and punish the perpetrators of international crimes under the jurisdiction of an

Although one cannot deny that the ICC is surely aware of this problem and is working against any misuse of the principle, it has no extraordinary power within the jurisdiction of states. Its right is solely to inquire into a particular case, but even here it is limited to certain conditions. Consequently, the principle of *ne bis in idem* may be used opportunistically in order to avoid criminalisation at an international level. Impunity may be increased and many individuals, claiming that they have already been prosecuted and punished for the same crime or conduct in accordance with their national criminal courts, may escape prosecution and punishment based on the fact that the ICC cannot bring them under its jurisdiction. The principle of complementarity may consequently be hampered by the principle of *ne bis in idem*.

---

international criminal court. The reason for this is that scarcely any national criminal jurisdiction has been in favour of the prosecution and punishment of its high-ranking officials for the commission of certain international crimes. According to Bassiouni, proscriptions and applications of the present state of international criminal law "are not dependent upon the characterization of a given act as constituting a crime under domestic law. Nor can national law justify or exclude the commission of international crimes. This postulate derives from the Nuremberg principles which correctly provide that international criminal law supersedes domestic criminal law. But while the principle of accountability under international criminal law irrespective of national law is certainly valid, there is some question as to whether the same principle applies without qualification to punishability. There is surely a corollary between criminal accountability and punishability but there are also obvious distinctions. There is no recognized international policy on punishment and penalties in international criminal law. Furthermore, questions relating to the general part of international criminal law are not yet codified. Thus it is difficult to ascertain the principles and contents of criminal responsibility and punishability except by reference to general principles of international law, which in this respect are most difficult to ascertain by reference to national law, because of the wide divergence in national criminal laws." M Cherif Bassiouni, 'Commentary on the International Law Commission's 1991 Draft Code of Crimes against the Peace and Security of Mankind' 11 Nouvelles Études Pénales (1993), p.107.

CHAPTER EIGHT

FINAL TREATY PROVISIONS WITHIN THE LAW OF THE ICC

1. Necessary Requirements

The Statute of the ICC is based on the law of international treaties. According to this law, each international treaty should be formulated in view of the requirements of the Vienna Convention on the Law of Treaties. The Vienna Convention was formulated in 1969 and came into force in 1980. Its provisions are considered an integral part of customary international law and are also a significant part of the international law of *jus cogens*. Consequently, the provisions of the Statute of the ICC have been strictly based on the Vienna Convention and its rules regarding the final provisions within an international treaty. The relevant provisions of the Statute are briefly presented below.

2. Languages

As has been stated elsewhere, the Statute of the ICC is based on six languages, but the working languages of the Court are English and French. The Court may designate another language on a case-by-case basis depending on the needs of the accused, victims, witnesses and condemned persons.[1] This means that the judges, the prosecutor, the registrar and their deputies, including the defence counsel, should know at least English or French. The issues before the Court have to be published in Arabic, Chinese, English, French, Russian and Spanish.[2] Publishing the judgment of the Court in six languages may, however, create some difficulties for the administration of the Court, particularly, when a case extends over several hundred pages.

---

[1] Article 50 (2).

[2] Rules of Procedure and Evidence, Rules 40 and 43.

3. Financing

The ICC is an independent international organisation. This means that it has its own international legal personality which creates the capacity for it to enter, in response to the requirements of the time, into a variety of international treaties. It also means that it is not an organ of the United Nations and therefore has to be financed on its own initiative by various means of collecting money.[3] Consequently, the Statute permits the Court to finance its operations through the contributions of states parties. According to the relevant part of the Statute "The contributions of States parties shall be assessed in accordance with an agreed scale of assessment, based on the scale adopted by the United Nations for its regular budget and adjusted in accordance with the principles on which that scale is based."[4] In addition to this, the Court may be given financial assistance by the United Nations because of the cases brought by the Security Council to the Court. Thus, there are two basic sources of income for the Court, the Assembly of the States parties and the United Nations, but these are subject to the approval of the General Assembly.[5]

There is also the possibility of a third source of income for the Court. This is when funds are donated voluntarily by governments, international organisations, groups or individuals, corporations or any other national, regional or international entities.[6] However, any such financial contributions are subject to the approval of the Assembly of the States Parties.[7] This model of financial contribution has been taken from the system of other international organisations such as the United Nations and the Red Cross. In addition, some of the most significant functions of

---

[3] S. Rama Rao, *Financing of the Court, Assembly of States parties and the Preparatory Commission,* in The International Criminal Court: Making of the Rome Statute 470 (Roy S. Lee, ed., 1999); Frank Jarasch, *Establishment, Organization and Financing of the International Criminal Court (Parts I, IV, XI-XIII),* 6 European Journal of Crime, Criminal Law and Criminal Justice 9 (1998); Thomas S. Warrick, *Organization of the International Criminal Court: Administrative and Financial Issues,* 25 Denver Journal of International Law and Policy 333 (1997); The International Criminal Court: Observations and Issues before the 1997-98 Preparatory Committee and the Administrative and Financial Implications, 13 Nouvelles Études Pénales (1997).

[4] Article 117

[5] Article 115.

[6] Article 116.

[7] See G. Witschel, *Financial Regulations and Rules of the Court,* 25 Fordham International Law Journal 665 (2002).

the ICTY and the ICTR have been established through voluntary contributions.

Although a resolution of the Assembly of States Parties underlines that "voluntary contributions ... are not intended to affect the independence of the Court,"[8] there may be some influence exerted by economically strong states in the administration of justice. For this reason, the Court and the Assembly of States Parties must be very cautious when accepting any funds and of the risk that they may affect the rulings of the Court. Therefore, it has been stated that a contribution should "not affect the independence of the Court", and should "fulfil any criteria the Assembly of States parties may establish".[9] The largest part of the funding of the Court comes from the Assembly. The Assembly adopted a budget of £30 million at its first session in September 2002. The funds of the Court are used to pay the expenses of the Court, the Assembly of States Parties, its Bureau and any other subsidiary bodies.[10]

4. Settlement of Disputes

The Statute of the ICC is based on an international convention. Therefore, it is based on the provisions and rules of treaties. Generally speaking, procedures for the formulation and adoption of international treaties are also based on the 1969 Vienna Convention known as the "root" for law-making treaties. Thus, it is recommended that disputes concerning the interpretation of treaties may be resolved or reduced by respecting the relevant provisions in the Vienna Convention.

Since the Statute is a multilateral treaty, there may be some problems in its application and interpretation. Disputes concerning the judicial functions of the Court have to be settled by the decision of the Court. The Statute calls upon the states parties to refer any other dispute between them to the Assembly of States Parties or, if this is not possible, to the International Court of Justice.[11]

5. Reservation

"Reservation" means the way in which one may understand the provisions of a treaty and the scope of their applicability. The Vienna Treaty defines

---

[8] ASP/1/Res.11.

[9] *Id.*

[10] Article 114.

[11] Article 119.

"reservation" as "a unilateral statement, however phrased or named, made by a State, when signing, ratifying, accepting, approving or acceding to a treaty, whereby it purports to exclude or to modify the legal effect of certain provisions of the treaty in their application to that State."[12]

Reservation to an international treaty may or may not be permitted depending on the general content of the treaty. One obvious matter concerning reservation is that a reservation is not permitted against the purpose or the object of the treaty and such a reservation is invalid. Thus, if the purpose of the treaty is the prohibition of the international crime of slavery, a reservation to the contrary effect is not permitted as it violates the chief purpose of the treaty.

The Statute of the ICC clearly states that "no reservations may be made to this Statute."[13] It means that any reservation to the Statute is invalid. However, this has not been respected fully and some states, without necessarily approaching directly the question of reservation, have made interpretative declarations at the time of the ratification of the Statute. Clear examples of this are the reservations expressed by France,[14] Argentina, Austria[15], Belgium,[16] Egypt and New Zealand.[17]

---

[12] Article 2 (d), the Vienna Convention on the Law of Treaties, 23 May, 1969.

[13] Article 120.

[14] The interpretative declaration of France states that "1. The provisions of the Statute of the International Criminal Court do not preclude France from exercising its inherent right of self-defence in conformity with Article 51 of the Charter. 2. The provisions of article 8 of the Statute, in particular paragraph 2 (b) thereof, relate solely to conventional weapons and can neither regulate nor prohibit the possible use of nuclear weapons nor impair the other rules of international law applicable to other weapons necessary to the exercise by France of its inherent right of self-defence, unless nuclear weapons or the other weapons referred to herein become subject in the future to a comprehensive ban and are specified in an annex to the Statute by means of an amendment adopted in accordance with the provisions of articles 121 and 123. 3. The Government of the French Republic considers that the term 'armed conflict' in article 8, paragraphs 2 (b) and (c), in and of itself and in its context, refers to a situation of a kind which does not include the commission of ordinary crimes, including acts of terrorism, whether collective or isolated. 4. The situation referred to in article 8, paragraph 2 (b) (xxiii), of the Statute does not preclude France from directing attacks against objectives considered as military objectives under international humanitarian law." www.icrc.org/ihl.nsf/NORM/6D97C3E21CCF24E2412566BB002F5C1A?Open Document - 6k.

[15] The Australian declaration reads that "The Government of Australia, having considered the Statute, now hereby ratifies the same, for and on behalf of Australia, with the following declaration, the terms of which have full effect in Australian law, and which is not a reservation: Australia notes that a case will be inadmissible

before the International Criminal Court (the Court) where it is being investigated or prosecuted by a State. Australia reaffirms the primacy of its criminal jurisdiction in relation to crimes within the jurisdiction of the Court. To enable Australia to exercise its jurisdiction effectively, and fully adhering to its obligations under the Statute of the Court, no person will be surrendered to the Court by Australia until it has had the full opportunity to investigate or prosecute any alleged crimes. For this purpose, the procedure under Australian law implementing the Statute of the Court provides that no person can be surrendered to the Court unless the Australian Attorney-General issues a certificate allowing surrender. Australian law also provides that no person can be arrested pursuant to an arrest warrant issued by the Court without a certificate from the Attorney-General. Australia further declares its understanding that the offences in Article 6, 7 and 8 will be interpreted and applied in a way that accords with the way they are implemented in Australian domestic law." www.icrc.org/ihl.nsf/NORM/A255319F58A44982412566E100540E5E?Open Document - 4k.

[16] The Belgian ratification was companied by a declaration reading that: "Declaration concerning article 31, paragraph 1 (c) "Pursuant to article 21, paragraph 1 (b) of the Statute and having regard to the rules of international humanitarian law which may not be derogated from, the Belgian Government considers that article 31, paragraph 1 (c), of the Statute can be applied and interpreted only in conformity with those rules." www.icrc.org/ihl.nsf/NORM/3CCF98210412237641256 6BA0056FF54?OpenDocument - 3k -.

[17] The declaration announced by the government of New Zealand reads that "1. The Government of New Zealand notes that the majority of the war crimes specified in article 8 of the Rome Statute, in particular those in article 8 (2) (b) (i)-(v) and 8 (2) (e) (i)-(iv) (which relate to various kinds of attacks on civilian targets), make no reference to the type of the weapons employed to commit the particular crime. The Government of New Zealand recalls that the fundamental principle that underpins international humanitarian law is to mitigate and circumscribe the cruelty of war for humanitarian reasons and that, rather than being limited to weaponry of an earlier time, this branch of law has evolved, and continues to evolve, to meet contemporary circumstances. Accordingly, it is the view of the Government of New Zealand that it would be inconsistent with principles of international humanitarian law to purport to limit the scope of article 8, in particular article 8(2) (b), to events that involve conventional weapons only. 2. The Government of New Zealand finds support for its view in the Advisory Opinion of the International Court of Justice on the Legality of the Threat or Use of Nuclear Weapons (1996) and draws attention to paragraph 86, in particular, where the Court stated that the conclusion that humanitarian law did not apply to such weapons "would be incompatible with the intrinsically humanitarian character of the legal principles in question which permeates the entire law of armed conflict and applies to all forms of warfare and to all kinds of weapons, those of the past, those of the present and those of the future. 3. The Government of New Zealand further notes that international humanitarian law applies equally to aggressor and defender states and its application in a particular context is not

It is thus very doubtful whether the reservations mentioned above and others could change the effect of the Statute. A limited interpretation may be that they create at the same time positive and negative effects on the scope of the Statute and its application. The Statute itself permits some sort of reservation to Article 8 on war crimes. A state may declare that, for a period of seven years after the coming into force of the Statute, it does not accept the jurisdiction of the Court with respect to crimes in Article 8 when a crime is known to be committed by its nationals or on its territory.[18] This means that a reservation is applied for a definite time after which the provisions of the Statute governing war crimes are also applicable to the state in question.

6. Amendment

"Amendment" in treaty laws refers to the revision, reformulation, modification, alteration, improvement, adjustment, editing, increasing or decreasing of provisions or even the correction of certain provisions; changes which may be necessary for the continuation of the treaty. The Statute of the ICC like that of many other international conventions provides certain provisions for its amendment. It makes clear, however, that after the expiry of the seven years from the coming into force of the Statute, any state party has the right to suggest an amendment of the Statute. The Secretary-General of the United Nations shall receive the proposal and shall circulate it to all states parties. This may lead to a significant amendment of the Statute. The reason is that any minor changes may be decided by the Assembly of States Parties and do not need therefore to be submitted to the Secretary-General of the United Nations. Consequently, minor changes may be made at any time through the alteration of the Elements and the Rules.

---

dependent on a determination of whether or not a state is acting in self-defence. In this respect it refers to paragraphs 40-42 of the Advisory Opinion in the Nuclear Weapons Case." www.icrc.org/ihl.nsf/NORM/6FEC50D1DC1A7371412566BB0 03AB0E1?Opendocument - 5k -

[18] Article 124. In particular, Article 19 of the Vienna Convention states that "A State may, when signing, ratifying, accepting, approving or acceding to a treaty, formulate a reservation unless:(a) the reservation is prohibited by the treaty;(b) the treaty provides that only specified reservations, which do not include the reservation in question, may be made; or (c) in cases not falling under sub-paragraphs (a) and (b), the reservation is incompatible with the object and purpose of the treaty."

Whilst any state party has the right to submit a proposal for amendment, the Assembly of States Parties should deal with such proposals. A decision for the consideration of the proposal in a Review Conference has to be taken by at least a majority of states present in the Assembly. The amendment is enforceable upon those states which have accepted the amendment but not upon those which have not accepted it. This means that the Court cannot exercise its jurisdiction over crimes that have been covered by the amendment when committed by the nationals or within the territories of states which have not accepted the amendment.[19] But this limitation concerns only the amended part and not the earlier provisions.

Amendments of the Statute that are of an institutional nature such as the conditions of service, qualifications, nomination and election of judges may be proposed at any time by any state party. Such proposals may be submitted to the Secretary-General of the United Nations and the Assembly of States Parties. Amendments of an institutional nature are applicable to all states parties to the Statute.[20]

The Secretary-General of the United Nations may, after seven years or at any time thereafter, convene a review of the Statute. This may include also the list of crimes under the jurisdiction of the Court.[21] It means that the Review conferences may take into examination the inclusion of other international crimes that are already regulated within certain international treaties, such as drug trafficking and crimes against the natural environment. They may hopefully also include sex-trafficking and the prohibition of the possession of nuclear weapons by any state. The first Review Conference took into consideration the questions of the crime of aggression in 2010.[22] In any event, any amendment to Articles 5, 6, 7 and 8 of the Statute which govern the core crimes under the jurisdiction of the Court, may come into force for those states parties which have accepted the amendment. This will be enforced one year after the deposit of the instruments of ratification by those states parties.

---

[19] Article 121.
[20] Article 122.
[21] Article 123.
[22] See Chapter Nine.

7. Signature, Ratification, Acceptance, Approval and Accession

Signature, ratification, acceptance, approval and accession are the terms by which a state expresses its consent to reach certain effects of a treaty. They are also supported by the provisions of the Vienna Convention on the law of treaties. Above all, the ratification of a treaty is the most important event in the enforcement of the treaty. The Statute of the ICC deals with signature, ratification, acceptance, approval and accession. As it may be understood from the provisions of the Statute, a signature does not necessarily create obligations for the signatory states and the enforcement of the Statute also requires the deposit of the instruments of ratification, acceptance or approval. This is the only way that a state becomes a party to the Statute of the ICC.[23]

The Statute was open for signatures until 31 December, 2000. Its policy concerning the entry into force of its provisions depended on the deposit of the 60th instrument of ratification, acceptance, approval or accession.[24] A state party may withdraw from the Statute by written notification submitted to the Secretary-General of the United Nations.[25] This notification cannot affect its financial obligations and cooperation with the Court if there are any such requirements. Furthermore, a state cannot escape from any other obligations prior to the date on which its withdrawal becomes effective.[26] In any event, notification for withdrawal by a state takes effect one year after its submission to the Secretary-General of the United Nations. The state may even give a later date for its withdrawal. This means that the limit of one year is the minimum time in order for a notification of withdrawal to become effective. During this time, the state is still considered a party to the Statute and is responsible before the Court.

---

[23] Article 125.

[24] Article 126.

[25] For further analysis see Roy S. Lee, W. K. Lietzau, G. P. Fletcher, R. Dicker and P.R. Dubinsky, *The International Criminal Court: Contemporary Perspectives and Prospects for Ratification,* 19 New York School Journal of International and Comparative Law 505 (2000); Monroe Leigh, *The United States and the Statute of Rome,* 95 American Journal of International Law 124 (2001); D. A. Blumenthal, *The Politics of Justice: Why Israel Signed the International Criminal Court Statute and What the Signature Means,* 30 Georgia Journal of International and Comparative Law 593 (2002); The United States and the International Criminal Court: National Security and International Law, (Sarah B. Sewall and Carl Kaysen, eds., 2000).

[26] Article 127.

However, there is a possibility that a state may, with a notification to the Secretary-General of the United Nations, declare its intention not to be bound by the Statute and even depart from any effects of its signature. This was clearly stated in a letter by John R. Bolton, who was Under Secretary of State for Arms Control and International Security of the United States, to the United Nations Secretary-General Kofi Annan. The letter specifies that "This is to inform you, in connection with the Rome Statute of the International Criminal Court adopted on July 17, 1998, that the United States does not intend to become a party to the treaty. Accordingly, the United States has no legal obligations arising from its signature on December 31, 2000. The United States requests that its intention not to become a party, as expressed in this letter, be reflected in the depositary's status list relating to this treaty."[27] However, the jurisdictional effect of this letter is very doubtful for the future. It is possible that certain achievements will be made under customary international criminal law or international criminal law of *jus cogens* that will create legal obligations for all states regardless of their signature or ratification.

8. Authentic Texts

The important role of the authentic texts of treaties cannot be denied in the law of treaties. Texts have a significant role in determing both the future interpretation of a treaty's purposes and its achievements. Any error or use of wrong vocabulary and terminology may create serious conflicts between the contracting parties.

The Statute is written in six languages: Arabic, Chinese, English, French, Russian and Spanish. All of these texts are equally authentic and have the same interpretative effect. The duty of achieving consistency and reliability was given to the drafting committee which worked intensively with the texts. All texts were adopted on 17 July 1998.[28] However, it was later discovered that there were some errors in versions of the text. In response to this problem, corrections were given to all participants in the Conference for their approval. That is why the official text is somewhat different from the first original text which was the object of the voting at the conclusion of the international conference in Rome.

---

[27] Press Statement Richard Boucher, Spokesman Washington, DC, May 6, 2002.

[28] Article 128.

CHAPTER NINE

DEVELOPMENTS OF THE STATUTE OF THE ICC IN KAMPALA

1. The Review Conference in Kampala

The need for a more robust and practical internationalisation of the Statute of the ICC was already foreseen in 1998. The development and increase of the strength of the law of the ICC could not, however, occur before 2010. The Review Conference on the Rome Statute of the International Criminal Court (ICC) in Kampala, Uganda from 31 May to 11 June 2010 is the result of this significant global movement toward the internationalisation of the rule of law within the law of different states. The general debate of the Review Conference was concluded in its first days. The Conference consisted of 84 states of which 67 were states parties and the rest observers. Palestinian representatives and many international organisations also participated in the Conference.

At the Review Conference 112 pledges were made by 37 states parties with the intention of empowering the system of the Rome Statute. This intention was also strengthened by the United States and the European Union. Moreover, the Review Conference adopted several valuable instruments such as the Kampala Declaration which reaffirms the obligations of states regarding the Statute of the ICC, including its full implementation within their laws. The Declaration also encourages the confirmation of the universality and integrity of the Statute. Other significant adoptions are a resolution on strengthening the enforcement of sentences and a resolution on the definition of the crime of aggression. Based on the consequences of the first resolution, the ICC signed three agreements on the enforcement of sentences with Belgium, Denmark and Finland. The second resolution on the definition of aggression will amend the Statute of the ICC.[1] Other requisite amendments were the extension of the concept of the use of certain weapons as constituting war crimes in non-international armed conflicts and the agreement of states parties not to

[1] See the relevant section below.

delete Article 124 based on an optional protocol which permits states parties not to subject their nationals to the prosecutions of the Court or investigations over war crimes for a seven year period.

The Review Conference strongly encouraged the universal ratification of the Statute of the ICC and cooperation between states in order to deter impunity.[2] The value of the complementarity policy of the Statute of the ICC was also emphasized during the Conference. In the following sections, some of the most significant purposes of the Review Conference are briefly studied.

2. The Kampala Declaration

The Kampala Declaration demonstrates the approval by the international legal and political community of the creation of the Statute and the establishment of the International Criminal Court (ICC). As such, the Declaration aims to encourage, as effectively as possible the implementation of the provisions of the Statute, the prevention of crimes and the deterrence of impunity. It has consequently aimed at developing the rule of law on an international level and at minimising serious violations of international human rights law through the institution of justice, peace, equality and reciprocity.

The Kampala Declaration also reminds us of the value of multilateral cooperation between states parties and the Court, as well as realising the aims and purposes of the Statute and the mission of the Court. In order to protect human dignity and prevent the humiliation of mankind, in particular women and children, the declaring states emphasise the universality as well as the legal integrity of the Statute. They announce the acceptance of their obligations for the implementation of a fair trial and the prevention of crimes that threaten international peace, security and the well-being of the world. The States Parties also declare their efforts to promote victims' rights under the Rome Statute. In addition, they endeavour to enhance the capacity of national jurisdictions to prosecute the perpetrators of the most serious crimes in a fair trial, pursuant to the principle of complementarity. Among other matters encouraged by states parties, are the uses of diplomatic measures for the intensification of the Statute and the commemoration of the 17th of July, the day of the adoption of the Statute in 1998, as the Day of International Criminal Justice.

---

[2] On August 18, 2010, Saint Lucia deposited the instrument of ratification of the Rome Statute. The number of states parties to the Statute of the ICC is therefore raised to 113.

3. Declaration on Cooperation

One of the major achievements at the 2010 Review Conference was the Declaration on Cooperation.[3] Adoption of the Declaration is intended to strengthen the important parts of the Statute of the ICC governing the questions of cooperation between states parties and the Court. The Declaration, if it is respected, is likely to be considered a milestone in the appropriate enforcement of the provisions of the Statute and the deterrence of impunity. This is because it calls on the responsibility of states to enforce their obligations under the provisions of the Statute. It also aims to stress the responsibility of all states which have not hitherto genuinely assisted the Court in the implementation of the Statute. Clear examples of the latter are the governments of those states which have avoided giving effect to the provisions of the Statute for the arrest of President Omar Hassan Ahmad al-Bashir to bring him before their national criminal courts. They have also avoided any cooperation with the ICC for the purpose of the implementation of the principle of complementarity. Even so, states parties to the Statute have not taken any measures for his arrest.[4]

The Declaration also calls on states to take certain necessary measures concerning different matters of cooperation with the ICC under their national legislations. In particular, the Declaration has stated the importance of cooperation between states parties for the implementation of arrest warrants. It stipulates "the crucial role that the execution of arrest warrants plays in ensuring the effectiveness of the Court's jurisdiction and further *emphasizes* the primary obligation of States parties, and other States under an obligation to cooperate with the Court, to assist the Court in the swift enforcement of its pending arrest warrants." The Declaration has, in addition, encouraged all other states to cooperate with the Court through various arrangements. These measures are intended, among other things, to strengthen the understanding of issues relevant to the Court and to enhance public information, as well as promoting the operation of the Court.

4. Principle of Complementarity

The principle of complementarity was one of the hot issues in the 2010 Review Conference. The purpose of this principle is to combat impunity for the most serious crimes or the core crimes recognised by the

---

[3] Declaration RC/Decl.2, *Adopted at the 9th plenary meeting, on 8 June 2010, by consensus.*

[4] For example, Kenya did not arrest al-Bashir when he visited the country.

international legal community as a whole. The first function of the principle of complementarity is to see whether states parties have taken the necessary measures for the implementation of the provisions of the Statute of the ICC and prosecution of those who are accused of committing crimes against humanity, war crimes, genocide or aggression. The second function of the principle is to ensure that impunity is not developed and permitted by states parties. It aims to bring the perpetrators of core crimes under the jurisdiction of the ICC. Therefore, the Conference dealt with the matter of complementarity and adopted a resolution regarding this matter. The resolution strongly encourages states parties to comply with the aims of the Statute and asks the parties to cooperate effectively for that end.[5]

Although the seriousness of the core crimes and the requirements of the Statute of the ICC make the implementation of the principle of complementarity seem necessary, it is sometimes subject to the will of states parties. This is based on the fact that the principle of complementarity cannot be effective and workable as long as a state does not cooperate with the ICC's prosecutor. Moreover, the Prosecutor of the ICC is not guided exclusively by the legal machinery of the Statute. He/she must weigh up the political expediency of doing so with a vision to fulfilling the 'interests of justice'. Still, the state in question should take into examination the general purposes of the Court, the goal of establishing the most proper jurisdiction for trying the accused, the reasons for the implementation of the principle of complementarity and the general interests of justice if the state wishes the Court to suspend proceedings. Naturally, the investigative process and the gathering of evidence are in the hands of the state in question which also makes enforcement of the principle of complementarity rather difficult for the Court. In addition, certain provisions of the ICC regarding the Security Council's power make the question of the enforcement of the principle of complementarity more political than legal. That is why the adoption of the resolution concerning complementarity seemed to be necessary in the Kampala Conference.

5. Victims and Affected Communities

One of the most serious questions raised in the 2010 Review Conference concerned the position of victims. This question was taken up for examination and discussion and the participating states found that the protection of victims was one of the primary principles of the Statute of

[5] See Resolution RC/Res.1, a*dopted at the 9th plenary meeting, on 8 June 2010, by consensus.*

the ICC. After many discussions and commitments by the representatives of states the resolution concerning the Impact of the Rome Statute System on Victims and Affected Communities was adopted in the Conference by consensus.[6] The resolution refers to the chief purposes of the Statute and its function in the prevention of core crimes. It reaffirms "the importance of the Rome Statute to the victims and affected communities in its determination to put an end to impunity for the perpetrators of the crime of genocide, crimes against humanity and war crimes, thus contributing to their prevention." With the intention of strengthening the position of victims and their legal rights as well as protection under the system of international criminal justice, international human rights and the humanitarian law of armed conflicts, the resolution calls on the legality of several instruments. These are, for example, the 1985 United Nations General Assembly Resolution 40/34 Declaration of Basic Principles of Justice for Victims of Crime and Abuse of Power, and the 2005 United Nations General Assembly Resolution 60/147 Basic Principles and Guidelines on the Right to a Remedy and Reparation for Victims of Gross Violations of International Human Rights Law and Serious Violations of International Humanitarian Law.

Due to many reasons which have, in one way or another, hindered the development of the victim's rights to equal justice and their protection from various intrigues, the resolution suggests several practical ways in which to improve the recognition of victim's rights and integrity in the machinery of justice. It asks states parties to take the following measures for the protection of victims and affected communities. These are, *inter alia*,encouraging states parties to implement the relevant provisions of the Statute; supporting the Court to improve the way in which it addresses the concerns of victims and affected communities; paying special attention to the needs of women and children; underlining the rights of victims to participate in judicial proceedings and claims for reparations; and *encouraging* governments and other organisations to play an active role in making communities aware of the rights of victims according to the provisions of the Statute. In particular, the resolution aims at upholding the rights of victims of sexual violence and improving their social integration. It stresses the importance of an on-going dialogue between the Secretariat of the Trust Fund for Victims and the Court and States Parties on different aspects of the rights of victims.

---

[6] Resolution RC/Res.2, *Adopted at the 9th plenary meeting, on 8 June 2010, by consensus.*

6. Enforcement of Sentences

The experience of other international criminal courts, such as the ICTY, the ICTR and the SCSL, has proved that the enforcement of sentences of imprisonment has been one of the most difficult tasks of the tribunals. This is because of the fact that states have to be prepared to accept the period of enforcement of sentences within their territorial jurisdiction. For this reason, the 2010 Review Conference aimed at strengthening the enforcement of sentences basing its arguments on the Rome Statute and the key role of states in the enforcement of the Court's sentences of imprisonment. Therefore, the Conference adopted a resolution regarding this matter in which it asked states parties to cooperate with the Court for the purpose of the appropriate implementation of the Court's decisions.[7] For the purpose of strengthening the Court's policy on the enforcement of sentences, the Court requires states to participate in the empowering of the following measures: to indicate to the Court their willingness to accept sentenced persons in accordance with the Statute and to confirm that "a sentence of imprisonment may be served in a prison facility made available in the designated State through an international or regional organization, mechanism or agency." The resolution also advises states parties and states that have demonstrated their willingness to accept sentenced persons to encourage effective cooperation at all levels, in particular, at regional or sub regional levels. It asks, as well, that the Secretary General of the United Nations be cognizant of this matter.

7. Article 124 in the Review Conference

One of the tasks of the 2010 review Conference was related to the provisions of Article 124 governing transitional provision. The relevant provision of the article gives the possibility to a state party to declare that, for a period of seven years after the entry into force of the Statute for the State concerned, it does not accept the jurisdiction of the ICC in connection with the category of crimes listed in Article 8 of the Statute. This is when there is a possibility that a crime has been committed by individuals of the state or on its territory. According to the article, the declaring state also has the legal right to withdraw its declaration at any time. The Review Conference decided to retain Article 124 in its current

[7] Resolution RC/Res.3, *Adopted at the 9th plenary meeting, on 8 June 2010, by consensus.*

form.[8] This policy of the Statute is to encourage states which are not parties to become a party to the Statute. But, at the same time it also causes problems as it encourages impunity by providing measures which subvert the purpose of the Court. It is in contradiction with the intention of the Court to bring the perpetrators of core crimes under prosecution and punishment. This means that the provisions of the article handicap the application of national criminal law and the complementarity principle as a whole. In addition, because of the provisions of the article, states may discriminate between three or four different core crimes. More clearly, the article permits states to decide not to bring their nationals under the jurisdiction of the Court over war crimes for a seven year period after ratification. In general, it has been almost universally asserted that states should not make use of Article 124.[9]

8. Amendment to Article 8

There has been much serious criticism of the content of Article 8 concerning its shortcomings on war crimes. Much of this criticism was finally taken into examination in the 2010 Review Conference in Kampala.[10] The participating states were of the view that the provisions of Article 8 did not deal with all the aspects of armed conflicts of a non-international character completely. This was based on the fact that the provisions of the article concern many serious violations of the laws and customs applicable in armed conflicts not of an international character, but it apparently omitted certain other acts which are also recognised as being war crimes when committed during an international armed conflict, such as the use of poisonous weapons or gases. This meant that the article went against its own policy and its own definition of "established framework of international law."

The participants of the Review Conference took advantage of their meeting to work with some of the misunderstandings or shortcomings of Article 8. They added into the law of the Statute some of the limitations which were already accepted by states within customary and conventional international criminal law. According to the amendment, three more

---

[8] Article 24, Resolution RC/Res.4, *Adopted at the 11th plenary meeting, on 10 June 2010, by consensus.*

[9] See the statements of Coalition for the International Criminal Court.

[10] The 2010 Review Conference, Annex I, Amendment to article 8 Add to article 8, paragraph 2 (e). Resolution RC/Res.5, *Adopted at the 12th plenary meeting, on 10 June 2010, by consensus.*

chapeaus are added to Article (2)(e).[11] These are (xiii) employing poison weapons or poisoned weapons;[12] (xiv) employing or using asphyxiating, poisonous or other gases, and all analogous liquids, materials or devices which are inherently indiscriminate in violation of the international law of armed conflict;[13] and (xv) employing bullets which expand or flatten easily in the human body with the intention of causing additional injury, such as bullets with a hard envelope which do not cover the core entirely or which are pierced with incisions.[14] It is hoped that the amendment of Article 8, paragraph 2 (e) of the Statute and of the Elements of Crimes,

---

[11] The amendment to Article 8(2) (e) also led to the amendment of elements of crimes. The 2010 Review Conference, Annex II, Resolution RC/Res.5, *Adopted at the 12th plenary meeting, on 10 June 2010, by consensus.*

[12] The elements of crimes of the Statute is amended on Article 8 (2) (e) (xiii), relating to the war crime of employing poison or poisoned weapons. The amendment added the following to the elements of crimes. These are "1.The perpetrator employed a substance or a weapon that releases a substance as a result of its employment. 2. The substance was such that it causes death or serious damage to health in the ordinary course of events, through its toxic properties. 3. The conduct took place in the context of and was associated with an armed conflict not of an international character. 4. The perpetrator was aware of factual circumstances that established the existence of an armed conflict." Annex II, Resolution RC/Res.5.

[13] The element of crimes of the Statute is amended on Article 8 (2) (e) (xiv), relating to the war crime of employing prohibited gases, liquids, materials or devices. The amendment added the following to the elements of crimes. These are "1. The perpetrator employed a gas or other analogous substance or device. 2. The gas, substance or device was such that it causes death or serious damage to health in the ordinary course of events, through its asphyxiating or toxic properties. (Nothing in this element shall be interpreted as limiting or prejudicing in any way existing or developing rules of international law with respect to the development, production, stockpiling and use of chemical weapons.) 3. The conduct took place in the context of and was associated with an armed conflict not of an international character. 4. The perpetrator was aware of factual circumstances that established the existence of an armed conflict." Annex II, Resolution RC/Res.5.

[14] The element of crimes of the Statute is amended on Article 8 (2) (e) (xv), relating to the war crime of employing prohibited bullets. The amendment added the following to the elements of crimes. These are "1. The perpetrator employed certain bullets. 2. The bullets were such that their use violates the international law of armed conflict because they expand or flatten easily in the human body. 3. The perpetrator was aware that the nature of the bullets was such that their employment would uselessly aggravate suffering or the wounding effect. 4. The conduct took place in the context of and was associated with an armed conflict not of an international character. 5. The perpetrator was aware of factual circumstances that established the existence of an armed conflict."Annex II, Resolution RC/Res.5.

will prevent conflicting parties from using certain weapons and simultaneously be helpful in the interpretation of the provisions of the article under the jurisdiction of the Court. It is to be stated that the amendment to the article is subject to ratification or acceptance and enters into force in accordance with article 121, paragraph 5, of the Statute.

8.1. Aggression

The shortcomings of the Statute of the ICC regarding the inclusion and definition of the crime of aggression were taken into serious consideration in the Review Conference on the Rome Statute of the International Criminal Court (ICC) in Kampala, Uganda from 31 May to 11 June 2010. Among some of the significant work done by the Review Conference are the resolution on the definition of aggression and the Kampala Declaration, which deals essentially with the reaffirmation of the commitment of states to the Rome Statute. The Declaration also encourages the full implementation of the Statute in its full aspect of universality and integrity. This will also include the crime of aggression once it is ratified by states parties.[15]

The legal value of the resolution is one of the most serious questions of international criminal justice at the present time. This is based on the fact that the resolution is not enforceable and does not therefore have the character of the principle of *de lege lata*. In other words, the character of the resolution is, roughly speaking, *de lege ferenda* which means a law for the future conduct of the state. Although the relevant representatives of states parties were aware of the position of the resolution, the legal expectation is that the definition of aggression will be ratified by states parties and will be a legal source for the recognition of aggressors.

8.2. Adoption

One valuable achievement of the Review Conference was the amendment of the Statute of the ICC and the integration of the international crime of aggression into its framework. The question relating to the crime of aggression was not easy. In particular, the United States government was against the inclusion of a definition of the crime of aggression within the provisions of the Statute. These legal and political confrontations took place despite the fact that the United States government is not a party to

[15] Up until today only fifteen states have ratified the new amendment on crime of aggression.

the Statute and only had the position of observer in the Review Conference. This position practically means that the United States had no power to block the addition of the crime of aggression to the Statute and to oppose the relevant resolution on aggression.

Despite all these divergences, the resolution was adopted by states parties with a consensus. The adoption of the crime of aggression within the provisions of the Statute is a clear signal for the identification of international crimes, implementation of international criminal justice and the prevention of impunity. The resolution not only defines the crime of aggression but also provides the mechanisms for triggering an investigation. This demonstrates that the international legal community wants to ensure that the perpetrators of aggressive conduct are brought into the machinery of justice for the purpose of the imputation of criminal responsibility and the implementation of punishment.

8.3. Coming into Force

It is an unfortunate fact that the resolution of the 2010 Review Conference, although it has modified certain articles of the Statute of the ICC, will not be enforceable until 2017. Still, the position of the Statute and the resolution depends on the positive decision of the Assembly of States Parties. Thus, the activation of the jurisdiction of the ICC relating to the crime of aggression is not only subject to the decision of member states, but also to the ratification or acceptance of the present amendments by 30 states. The Court cannot *exercise* jurisdiction over the crime before the above condition is fulfilled. Another condition is that a decision has to be taken by two-thirds of the Assembly of States Parties in order to enforce the jurisdiction at any time after 1 January 2017. The amendment may then come into force, one year after the deposit of the last instrument of ratification. Still, the resolution gives the opportunity to states not to tie themselves to its provisions. They may exclude themselves from its jurisdiction over aggression by making a declaration. Equally, a state party which does not take any action concerning the provisions of the resolution on the definition of aggression is bound by the amendment of the Statute of the ICC.

8.4. Obstacles

The amendment of the Statute of the ICC, if it occurs due to the ratification of states, does not mean that the ICC can, automatically, investigate the commission of the crime of aggression. On the contrary, there are certain conditions that have to be respected before the Court is authorised to start its jurisdiction over the criminal act. These are when *a)* there is, for one reason or another, an obvious inability to deal with the crime on a national level and *b)* the Security Council of the United Nations, which has the main responsibility for determining if an act of aggression has been committed, takes the decision. This is a very controversial issue regarding the crime of aggression, the recognition of which is essentially the monopoly of the permanent members of the UN.[16] The reason for this is that the jurisdiction of the Court is based on the principle of complementarity and the Court cannot, therefore, pre-empt the jurisdiction of a national court. The Court also has no jurisdiction over non-member states and this makes its work very difficult and problematic. Thus far, the ICC has not been successful in bringing all the accused persons under its jurisdiction for other core international crimes, such as war crimes, crimes against humanity and genocide. It has initiated jurisdiction over incidents in the Central African Republic, Darfur, the Democratic Republic of Congo, Northern Uganda and Kenya, but has yet to work with the relevant cases. Furthermore, establishing jurisdiction over the crime of aggression is also hindered by other legal matters. For instance, jurisdiction over the crime depends on whether the situation was referred to it by the Security Council of the United Nations, or whether it came before the ICC through a State referral or upon the initiative of the Prosecutor of the ICC.

8.5. Definition

The international crime of aggression has finally been added to the Statute of the ICC. This means that the Court will have, after the amendment comes into force, the authority to deal with all four core crimes. These are war crimes, crimes against humanity, genocide and also, in the near future, the crime of aggression. But, it is true that this addition does not change the position of the Court at present. This is because in the negotiations during the 2010 Review Conference, the Court remained unable to exercise jurisdiction over the crime at least for several years. The Court will not consequently be able to examine the crime until after 1 January 2017. This also depends on the decision of states parties at that time. Nevertheless, one cannot deny that the crime of aggression constitutes one of the core crimes under the jurisdiction of the Court today and the

[16] Farhad Malekian, The Monopolization of International Criminal Law in the United Nations, A Jurisprudential Approach (1st ed., 1993), 2nd ed. (1995).

position of Article 5 of the Statute has been conditionally modified for the purpose of the implementation of the crime of aggression.

Article 8 *(bis)* adopted in the Review Conference of Kampala describes the crime of aggression which may be committed by an individual. It states that 'For the purpose of this Statute, "crime of aggression" means the planning, preparation, initiation or execution, by a person in a position effectively to exercise control over or to direct the political or military action of a State, of an act of aggression which, by its character, gravity and scale, constitutes a manifest violation of the Charter of the United Nations.'[17] Significantly, it affirms that one of the most elementary requirements for the recognition of the crime is that the act of aggression must constitute a manifest violation of the Charter of the United Nations. This may imply the fact that an act cannot be recognised as aggression if it does not, according to the decision of the members of the Security Council, manifestly violate the Charter. The reason is that the words of the article are clear. The fact is that a manifest violation of the Charter may also include the provisions of Chapter VII, and this obviously depends on the description of the Security Council. In other words, the condition for the recognition of an act of aggression is practically left to the interpretation of the permanent members of the United Nations. Although, we do not deny the fact that the Court is also authorised to make such a decision, there may always be a conflict between the decision of the members of the Security Council and the ICC. The question is more critical when the accused persons are the nationals of one of the permanent members or their close political allies. This is particularly evident when the important position of a permanent member is decisive in the recognition of an act of aggression. The conflict may occur when the Court decides that an act constitutes aggression and the Security Council decides that the same act does not constitute aggression; a confrontation between decisions may be raised automatically. Even so, the Court may conclude its judgment and assert a sentence of imprisonment, which can be very problematic if there is a decision taken by the Security Council contrary to the judgment of the Court.

According to the resolution of the Review Conference an act of aggression is defined as the use of armed force. The relevant definition reads that '"act of aggression" means the use of armed force by a State against the sovereignty, territorial integrity or the political independence of another State, or in any other manner inconsistent with the Charter of the United Nations."[18] The definition also provides a detailed seven

[17] Article 8 *bis,* para.1.

[18] Article 8 *bis*, para.2.

paragraphs listing acts that qualify as an act of aggression such as an invasion by armed forces, bombardment and blockade. All these are clearly affected by the UN General Assembly Resolution 3314 (XXIX) of 14 December 1974. They are as follows:

> a) The invasion or attack by the armed forces of a State of the territory of another State, or any military occupation, however temporary, resulting from such invasion or attack, or any annexation by the use of force of the territory of another State or part thereof;
> b) Bombardment by the armed forces of a State against the territory of another State or the use of any weapons by a State against the territory of another State;
> c) The blockade of the ports or coasts of a State by the armed forces of another State;
> d) An attack by the armed forces of a State on the land, sea or air forces, or marine and air fleets of another State;
> e) The use of armed forces of one State which are within the territory of another State with the agreement of the receiving State, in contravention of the conditions provided for in the agreement or any extension of their presence in such territory beyond the termination of the agreement;
> f) The action of a State in allowing its territory, which it has placed at the disposal of another State, to be used by that other State for perpetrating an act of aggression against a third State;
> g) The sending by or on behalf of a State of armed bands, groups, irregulars or mercenaries, which carry out acts of armed force against another State of such gravity as to amount to the acts listed above, or its substantial involvement therein.

The seven chapeaus are the result of the reintegration of the chapeaus of Resolution 3314 (XXIX) of 14 December 1974 within the new definition. As we have discussed earlier, their formulation has been very controversial with the historical background of international criminal justice. This includes the International Law Commission meetings, the Draft Code of Crimes against the Peace and Security of Mankind and also during the adoption of the 1974 Resolution on aggression in the General Assembly. States were divided into several groups regarding the words of the paragraphs. The most well-known confrontation was caused by the United States government and the Soviet Union both holding different understandings regarding an armed attack and the use of force as a whole. The hope is that the integration of the wording of the 1974 resolution will bring about justice and put an end to impunity. It should also be added that although the 1974 resolution does not have the binding effect of the international treaties, its provisions are entirely an integral part of the international law of *jus cogens* that because of their integration into the system of international criminal law cannot be denied.

8.6. Exercise of Jurisdiction

The provisions of Article 15 *bis* and 15 *ter* provide the conditions under which the Court may exercise jurisdiction over the crime of aggression. This article creates an exceptional juridical system whereby the Prosecutor of the ICC can initiate an investigation into the concept of the crime of aggression. The Article adopts several policies to indicate the way for the jurisdiction of the Court. The reason for this is that the legislator does not want to limit the concept of initiation for the proof of the crime of aggression. The provisions of Article 15 *ter* state that where a 'situation' is referred to the Prosecutor of the ICC by the Security Council of the United Nations, the jurisdiction of the Court applies as to the other crimes in the Statute. This means that the prosecutor of the ICC is permitted to proceed with an investigation into the crime of aggression. Nevertheless, according to the provisions of Article 15 *bis*, the Prosecutor of the ICC may proceed with his/her own motion for an investigation or an investigation based on a State referral. This investigation may be carried out *a)* after first ascertaining whether the Security Council of the United Nations has recognised the commission of an act of aggression according to the provisions of Chapter VII of the Charter and within six months after the date of notification; *b)* where the Prosecutor of the ICC considers that an act of aggression has been committed between States Parties; *c)* when according to the provisions of Article 15, the Pre-Trial Division of the Court has permitted the beginning of the investigation in respect of the crime of aggression. This is where the Security Council has not yet decided according to the provisions of Article 16. In any event, both paragraphs in Article 15 *bis* and 15 *ter* make it clear that the recognition of an act of aggression by an organ outside the Court realm should be treated without prejudice to the Court's own identification of an act of aggression.

CHAPTER TEN

CASES BEFORE INTERNATIONAL CRIMINAL JUSTICE

1. Introduction

The case law of the tribunals and the courts is very extensive and significant. This includes the Nuremberg Tribunal, the Tokyo Tribunal, the ICTY, the ICTR, the SCSL and the permanent international criminal court, the ICC. In general, the case law emphasises the importance of the sources of international criminal law for the proof of the guilt of the accused. The case law persistently invokes the concept of the international criminal responsibility of individuals under customary and conventional law. There are therefore a large number of relevant cases which have been treated before the international criminal tribunals and the courts. Two of the most notorious cases are the *Tadic* case and *Furundzija* case. The first consisted of grave breaches of the 1949 Geneva Conventions and crimes against humanity.[1] The second included torture and serious sexual assaults as well as rape.[2] Throughout the chapters of the book, we have analysed a considerable number of cases which have been relevant to the special subject matter under discussion. This chapter examines a limited number of cases brought before the jurisdiction of international criminal courts since a thorough examination of all relevant cases would not be possible due to limitations of space.

1.1. Process of Identification

There arc six procedures followed by the International Criminal Court for the identification and settlement of guilt.

---

[1] Trial Chamber II, 7 May 1997.

[2] Trial Chamber II, 10 December 1998.

1) A warrant and indictment may be issued if there are "reasonable grounds" to believe that the person has committed crimes against humanity or war crimes.
2) If the accused is before the court, there must be a confirmation of charges hearing where the accused should participate and challenge the evidence presented against him.
3) The Court after hearing the evidence must prove that there are "substantial grounds" to believe that the person is guilty of the crimes charged.
4) After a successful procedure concerning 1 to 3, a trial may be held against the accused where the prosecutor is responsible for proving the case beyond reasonable doubt.
5) The accused is declared guilty beyond any reasonable doubt or cleared of all charges against him.
6) The condemned person is sentenced to imprisonment.

2. International Court of Justice

2.1. Claim before the Court

A very interesting case dealing with the concept of international crimes and criminal responsibility is the 2001 case brought before the International Court of Justice, in which the Congo claimed that the Belgian authorities breached the provisions of diplomatic protection in international law by issuing an arrest warrant for a Congolese Foreign Minister for Grave Breaches of the 1949 Geneva Conventions and for crimes against humanity allegedly perpetrated before he came into office. The Congo particularly emphasised the breach of equal rights of sovereignty granted under customary law and the United Nations Charter for all states of the world.

2.2. Impact on Sovereignty

The concept of state sovereignty and its legal personality has long been recognised in the system of international law. This concept was, however, to a great extent modified by the creation of the Nuremberg Tribunal and also with the establishment of the *ad hoc* tribunals under the auspices of the United Nations Organization. This means that the creation of the concept of the international criminal responsibility of individuals regardless of their position under the state's legal personality has reduced to a great degree the concept of state sovereignty. It proved that the supreme power of the sovereign state is an almost outdated concept. In other words, the legal personality of sovereignty is extinguished or reduced when a state fails to meet its international duties. The limitation on state sovereignty, because of the crimes of its individuals, is a fact that cannot be denied under the customary rules of international law which was particularly developed after the creation of the International Military Tribunal in Nuremberg and other tribunals or courts under the United Nations Charter.

2.3. The Judgment of the Court

Many believe that the concept of state sovereignty provides legal immunity for certain individuals, such as diplomats, foreign ministers and heads of state. This is also called the inviolability of diplomatic privileges. The question of immunity is particularly serious when it comes to the immunity of heads of state and government ministers from criminal jurisdiction. The question relates to the wrongful conduct of those persons during their periods of office and those crimes which have the character of international crimes of *jus cogens,* such as crimes against humanity, war crimes, genocide, torture, rape or apartheid. The position was dealt with in the Judgment of the International Court, namely the *Arrest Warrant*, case relating to the Congo.[3] The International Court, with reference to the status of an incumbent Minister for Foreign Affairs, came to the following conclusions:

> 53. In customary international law, the immunities accorded to Ministers for Foreign Affairs are not granted for their personal benefit, but to ensure the effective performance of their functions on behalf of their respective States. In order to determine the extent of these immunities, the Court must therefore first consider the nature of the functions exercised by a Minister for Foreign Affairs. He or she is in charge of his or her Government's diplomatic activities and generally acts as its representative in international negotiations and intergovernmental meetings. Ambassadors and other diplomatic agents carry out their duties under his or her authority. His or her acts may bind the State represented, and there is a presumption that a Minister for Foreign Affairs, simply by virtue of that office, has full powers to act on behalf of the State (see, e.g., Art. 7, para. 2 *(a)*, of the 1969 Vienna Convention on the Law of Treaties). In the performance of these functions, he or she is frequently required to travel internationally, and thus must be in a position freely to do so whenever the need should arise. He or she must also be in constant communication with the

[3] Democratic Republic of Congo v. Belguim.

> Government, and with its diplomatic missions around the world, and be capable at any time of communicating with representatives of other States. The Court further observes that a Minister for Foreign Affairs, responsible for the conduct of his or her State's relations with all other States, occupies a position such that, like the Head of State or the Head of Government, he or she is recognized under international law as representative of the State solely by virtue of his or her office. He or she does not have to present letters of credence: to the contrary, it is generally the Minister who determines the authority to be conferred upon diplomatic agents and countersigns their letters of credence. Finally, it is to the Minister for Foreign Affairs that *chargés d'affaires* are accredited.
>
> 54. The Court accordingly concludes that the functions of a Minister for Foreign Affairs are such that, throughout the duration of his or her office, he or she when abroad enjoys full immunity from criminal jurisdiction and inviolability. That immunity and that inviolability protect the individual concerned against any act of authority of another State which would hinder him or her in the performance of his or her duties.[4]

It was on the basis of the above judgment that the International Court of Justice finally concluded that:

> the issue against Mr. Abdulaye Yerodia Ndombasi of the arrest warrant of 11 April 2000, and its international circulation, constituted violations of a legal obligation of the Kingdom of Belgium towards the Democratic Republic of the Congo, in that they failed to respect the immunity from criminal jurisdiction and the inviolability which the incumbent Minister for Foreign Affairs of the Democratic Republic of the Congo enjoyed under international law.

2.4. The Problem of Judgment

Unfortunately, the decision of the International Court denoted the protection of such immunity even in the case of the alleged commission of war crimes and crimes against humanity. In addition, the European Court of Human Rights has also sought to secure the principle of diplomatic immunity in the provisions of the European Convention.[5] However, the statement of the International Court and the position of the European Court of Human Rights are without doubt against the legal system of

[4] Arrest Warrant of 11 April 2000, (Democratic Republic of the Congo v. Belgium), Judgment of 14 February 2002, pp.21-22.

[5] *Fogarty v. United Kingdom* (21 Nov. 2001); *Al-Adsani v. United Kingdom* (21 No.2001) and *McElhinney v. United kingdom* (21 No. 2001).

international criminal law and justice. This is because, the provisions of the system are not limited to particular persons but to all human beings as a whole. Obviously, the Court wrongly distinguished between the two terms "in a private capacity" and "official acts".[6]

Diplomatic immunity does not mean permission to violate the provisions of international criminal law because of periods of office. Many cases before national criminal courts refer to the fact that state authorities do not enjoy immunity for their international crimes. In addition, such crimes are not permitted to be committed under private or other capacities. It is forbidden for any person in whatever position to commit international crimes, in particular those of a *jus cogens* nature. Examples of those cases before national criminal courts are Barbie in France, Kappler and Priebke in Italy, Rauter, Albrecht and Bouterse in the Netherlands, Pinochet in the UK, Yamashita in the US, Pinochet and Scilingo in Spain.[7] Although all these relate to military officials, this does not necessarily mean that there are different provisions in customary or conventional international criminal law for the proof of the criminal responsibility of individuals. All persons are equal and treated with the same provisions.[8] This is particularly important in the case of international crimes, the legal characterisations of which come under the *jus cogens* framework. In other words, the standard of what constitutes an international crime is set by the system of international criminal law and not by national criminal provisions.[9] This means that crimes against peace, war crimes, genocide, torture, apartheid or rape cannot constitute acts carried out in the performance of the official duties of a foreign minister or a head of state. Furthermore, the concept of diplomatic immunity *ratione personae* or immunity *ratione materiae* only covers the acts of diplomats completed in the course of their official duties to promote the interests of their states. This means that a diplomat is solely immune on a restrictive basis for acts characterised as official duties and does not have immunity for violations of the system of international criminal law. Any provision of the 1961 Vienna Convention on Diplomatic Relations or any other international treaty whose intention is to preclude or prevent the provisions of international criminal law governing *jus cogens* law is thus absolutely null and void. The number of ratifications of the relevant international

---

[6] Antonio Cassese, When My Senior State Officials be Tried for International Crimes? Some Commands on the Congo v. Belgium Case, EJIL (2002), Vol.13, No.4, p.867.

[7] *Id.*, pp.870-1.

[8] *Id.*

[9] Ian Brownlie, Principles of Public International Law (6th ed., 2003), pp.573-5.

convention does not have any effective function for the application of *jus cogens* law. In 1992, the Federal Appeals Court in the United States concluded that neither Ferdinand Marcos, the dictator of the Philippines, nor his daughter could claim any form of immunity for the crimes committed in their country. This was based on the fact that torture and arbitrary killing were contrary to the principles of international criminal law and were also not a part of an official function.[10] The Court stated that a ruler loses diplomatic immunity for conducts violating *jus cogens* law.[11] In other words, such violations do not constitute sovereign acts. The dissenting opinion of the judge is worth mentioning here. He concludes that:

> The effective combating of grave crimes has arguably assumed a *jus cogens* character reflecting recognition by the international community of the vital community interests and values it seeks to protect and enhance. Therefore when this hierarchically higher norm comes into conflict with the rules on immunity, it should prevail. Even if we are to speak in terms of reconciliation of the two sets of rules, this would suggest to me a much more restrictive interpretation of the immunities of high-ranking officials than the Judgment portrays. Incidentally, such a restrictive approach would be much more in consonance with the now firmly established move towards a restrictive concept of State immunity, a move that has removed the bar regarding the submission of States to jurisdiction of other States often expressed in the maxim *pur* in *purern rzon Iiuhrt inzperiurn.* It is difficult to see why States would accept that their conduct with regard to important areas of their development be open to foreign judicial proceedings but not the criminal conduct of their officials. ... While, admittedly, the readiness of States and municipal courts to admit of exceptions is still at a very nebulous stage of development, the situation is much more fluid than the Judgment suggests. I believe that the move towards greater persona1accountability represents a higher norm than the rules on immunity and should prevail over the latter.[12]

3. *Srebrenica Genocide* Case

The Srebrenica genocide was committed against the Muslim population of the former Yugoslavia in Bosnia and Herzegovina during the Balkan Wars. The genocide was carried out through the military activities and financial

---

[10] *In re. Estate of Ferdinand E. Marcos,* US Court of Appeals 9th Circuit (21 October 1992).

[11] *Estate of Ferdinand E. Marcos* (1994), 25 F3d I467 (9th Circuit).

[12] Dissenting Opinion of Judge Al-Khasawneh, Arrest Warrant of 11 April 2000 (Democratic Republic of the Congo *v.* Belgium), p.99.

investment of both the Bosnian Serb and Serbian authorities. At least 8,000 Muslim men, women and children were killed and many others were tortured, gang-raped, humiliated and otherwise seriously harmed and mistreated when the area was under the United Nations' protection. The unanimous ruling of the Appeals Chamber Judgement in the case the *Prosecutor v. Radislav Krstic* clearly testifies to the scandal of a genocide allowed to take place in modern Europe. The Appeal Chamber's statement explaining the qualification of this pre-mediated intended genocide in 1995 declares that:

> Among the grievous crimes this Tribunal has the duty to punish, the crime of genocide is singled out for special condemnation and opprobrium. The crime is horrific in its scope; its perpetrators identify entire human groups for extinction. Those who devise and implement genocide seek to deprive humanity of the manifold richness its nationalities, races, ethnicities and religions provide. This is a crime against all of humankind, its harm being felt not only by the group targeted for destruction, but by all of humanity.
>
> The gravity of genocide is reflected in the stringent requirements which must be satisfied before this conviction is imposed. These requirements – the demanding proof of specific intent and the showing that the group was targeted for destruction in its entirety or in substantial part – guard against a danger that convictions for this crime will be imposed lightly. Where these requirements are satisfied, however, the law must not shy away from referring to the crime committed by its proper name. By seeking to eliminate a part of the Bosnian Muslims, the Bosnian Serb forces committed genocide. They targeted for extinction the forty thousand Bosnian Muslims living in Srebrenica, a group which was emblematic of the Bosnian Muslims in general. They stripped all the male Muslim prisoners, military and civilian, elderly and young, of their personal belongings and identification, and deliberately and methodically killed them solely on the basis of their identity. The Bosnian Serb forces were aware, when they embarked on this genocidal venture, that the harm they caused would continue to plague the Bosnian Muslims. The Appeals Chamber states unequivocally that the law condemns, in appropriate terms, the deep and lasting injury inflicted, and calls the massacre at Srebrenica by its proper name: genocide. Those responsible will bear this stigma, and it will serve as a warning to those who may in future contemplate the commission of such a heinous act.[13]

However, in *the Bosnia Genocide Case*, the International Court of Justice expresses a different view concerning the commission of genocide

[13] Appeals Chamber Judgement in the Case the Prosecutor v. Radislav Krstic.The Hague, 19 April 2004, CC/P.I.S./839e); http://www.icty.org/sid/8434.

by the Serbian authorities against the Muslim population. According to it, although the atrocities committed in Srebrenica constituted genocide, war crimes and crimes against humanity, the Court believed that the Government of Serbia neither committed genocide, nor conspired to, nor incited the commission of genocide. The Court therefore irrationally states that it:

> Finds that Serbia has not committed genocide, through its organs or persons whose acts engage its responsibility under customary international law, in violation of its obligations under the Convention on the Prevention and Punishment of the Crime of Genocide; … Finds that Serbia has not conspired to commit genocide, nor incited the commission of genocide, in violation of its obligations under the Convention on the Prevention and Punishment of the Crime of Genocide; … Finds that Serbia has not been complicit in genocide, in violation of its obligations under the Convention on the Prevention and Punishment of the Crime of Genocide.[14]

This opinion of the ICJ, expressed by its President, Rosalyn Higgins, is one of the most unsatisfactory decisions to have been delivered in its history. The opinion of the Court here not only violates the principles of international justice, international human rights law, but also the basic principles of international criminal law and, in particular, the provisions of the genocide convention. The legal value of the opinion has been questioned by many international lawyers and the conclusion is that the opinion has compromised international trust in the practical reliability of the Court's decision, particularly because it overlooks the destruction of evidence by the Serbs. According to the Vice-President of the ICJ, Mr.AL-Khasawneh:

> Serbia's involvement, as a principal actor or accomplice, in the genocide that took place in Srebrenica is supported by massive and compelling evidence — Disagreement with the Court's methodology for appreciating the facts and drawing inferences there from — The Court should have required the Respondent to provide unedited copies of its Supreme Defence Council documents, failing which, the Court should have allowed a more liberal recourse to inference —The "effective control" test for attribution established in the Nicaragua case is not suitable to questions of State responsibility for international crimes committed with a common

[14] Application for Revision of the Judgment of 11 July 1996 in the Case concerning *Application of the Convention on the Prevention and Punishment of the Crime of Genocide (Bosnia and Herzegovina v. Yugoslavia), Preliminary Objections* (Yugoslavia *v.* Bosnia and Herzegovina). http://www.icj-cij.org/docket/index.php?sum=667&code=bhy&p1=3&p2=2&case=91&k=f4&p3=5.

> purpose — The "overall control" test for attribution established in the Tadic′ case is more appropriate when the commission of international crimes is the common objective of the controlling State and the non- State actors — The Court's refusal to infer genocidal intent from a consistent pattern of conduct in Bosnia and Herzegovina is inconsistent with the established jurisprudence of the ICTY — The FRY's knowledge of the genocide set to unfold in Srebrenica is clearly established — The Court should have treated the Scorpions as a de jure organ of the FRY — The statement by the Serbian Council of Ministers in response to the massacre of Muslim men by the Scorpions amounted to an admission of responsibility — The Court failed to appreciate the definitional complexity of the crime of genocide and to assess the facts before it accordingly … I feel that I should explain the nature of my dissent before explaining the reasons for it. I am not in total disagreement with the majority: regarding jurisdiction, I come to the same conclusion contained in paragraph 1 of the disposed if that the Court's jurisdiction is established, although I have serious doubts whether, in terms of the proper administration of justice, the already settled question of jurisdiction should have been re-examined in the Judgment.[15]

According to another legal expert there are three main reasons why the decision of the Court was a conservative expression:

> First, as far as the jurisdictional part of the decision goes, the court has been severely criticized for unjustifiably over-stretching the concept of *res judicata* to decisions on jurisdiction rendered at an earlier stage of the same proceedings; for over-relying on legal conclusions that were decided at earlier stages without serious consideration; and for narrowly construing its powers of revision. Indeed, seven out of the fifteen judges on the bench expressed varying degrees of unease with this particular outcome.
>
> Second, as for the actual findings on the commission of genocide, some writers have criticized the court for refusing to look at the 'bigger picture' of the events in Bosnia – a picture that seems to suggest that the various atrocious crimes meted out by the Bosnian Serbs were all part of the same 'master-plan' of creating an ethnically homogeneous Serbian state. Others have questioned the court's readiness to rely on the absence of individual convictions in genocide by the ICTY (except with relation to the massacre in Srebrenica), without properly considering the difference between standards of liability under criminal law and state responsibility or fully appreciating the limited probative value of reduced charges as the result of plea bargains.

---

[15] Dissenting Opinion of Vice-President Al.Khasawneh http://www.icj-cij.org/docket/files/91/13689.pdf, pp.202-203.

> Third, with respect to the question of Serbian responsibility, the court's legal analysis of attribution standards, the reluctance to find Serbia to be an accomplice to genocide, and the decision to refrain from ordering reparations, have all been criticized as excessively conservative. At the same time, the court's expansive reading of Article 1 of the Genocide Convention as potentially imposing on all states a duty to prevent genocide, even if committed outside their territory, has been noted for its remarkable boldness. Still, some writers have criticized the court for not clarifying whether Article 1 can provide an independent basis for exercising of universal jurisdiction against individual perpetrators of genocide. So, arguably, the court construed broadly the duty to prevent genocide while narrowly construing the duty to punish its perpetrators.[16]

The former prosecutor in the trial of Slobodan Milosevic is also of the opinion that the international crime of genocide was without doubt committed by the relevant authorities of the Serbs. According to him:

> … it is important to note that Serbia did not hand over to the Prosecution (OTP) the complete collection of SDC records. For example, for the year 1995 the OTP received recordings for only about half of all the sessions held by SDC. Further, some ofthe SDC records were not handed over in their full stenografically recorded form but were produced as extended minutes. That means that they were shorter than steno-notes but longer than the regular minutes. The dates of the missing meetings or the meetings where this lesser form of record was provided, as I recall, were significant – namely dates leading up to, surrounding and in the aftermath of the Srebrenica massacre.The full records of those meetings need yet to be provided.At the same time, these documents, significant as they are, do not constitute a single body of evidence that will explain once and for all what happened and who was culpable.They do provide a much fuller context and provide some very valuable testimonials of things that were said by Milosevic and others.In their un-redacted form they would point all who are interested (not just governments and lawyers) to other documents that have never been provided and that might well be more candid than the words of those at the SD Council meetings who knew they were being recorded by a stenographer. Second, it should also be remembered that there are other protected document collections and individual documents which were, and still are, protected by direct agreements between Belgrade and the former OTP Prosecutor, i.e. they were not protected by the Trial Chamber.These documents are difficult now to identify but if and when Bosnia-Herzegovina decides to reopen the ICJ case it will be essential to

[16] The International Association of Jewish Lawyers and Jurists (Justice No. 45, Spring 2008. Pages 21–26) http://www.infolink.co.il/intjewishlawyers/docenter/frames.asp?id=16867.

> require Serbia and/or the ICTY to produce all those documents for the ICJ.[17]

The first president of the ICTY, Antonio Cassese argues that the judgement of the ICJ has set unrealistically high conditions for the recognition of the Srebrenica genocide as such. He explains that the opinion of the Court undermines the principles of the system of international criminal law relating to genocide and that it may provide grounds for the release of criminals. Furthermore, the judgment nullifies the involvement of the Serbian authorities in the massacre of Bosnian Muslims at Srebrenica in 1995. According to him, although the court ruled that the crime of genocide had been committed, it incorrectly concluded that Serbia was not responsible in international law for the suffering of victims. Thus, the Court's statement was a facile judgment amounting to running with the hare and hunting with the hounds.[18] He further says that:

> More importantly, the ICJ's decision that Serbia is responsible for not having prevented a genocide in which it was not complicit makes little sense. According to the court, Serbia was aware of the very high risk of acts of genocide and did nothing. But Serbia was not complicit, the court argued, because "it has not been proven" that the intention of committing

---

[17] KBSA 2000, Interview with Sir Geofrey Nice, "The Victims of Srebrenica, Living and Dead, Deserve Truth". http://www.kbsa2000kbs.org/index.php?option=com_content&view=article&id=256:sir-geoffrey-nice-rtve-srebrenice-ivi-i-mrtvi-zasluuju-istinu&catid=45:intervju&Itemid=107.

[18] "According to the court, the Bosnian Serb generals who were guilty of this genocide, the various Mladics and Kristics, were neither acting as Serbia's agents nor receiving specific instructions from Belgrade. The genocide could not therefore be imputed to Serbia, even if the Serbian government was paying salaries to Mladic and his colleagues, as well as providing them with financial and military assistance. Nor was Serbia guilty of complicity, because, though it exercised considerable influence over Mladic and his people, it did not know, at the moment when the genocide was taking place, that such a crime was being committed. The court's decision thus attempts to run with the hare and hunt with the hounds. To decide whether Mladic acted on Serbia's account when he was planning and ordering the Srebrenica massacre, the court demanded proof that Serbian officials sent him specific "instructions" to commit this act of genocide. Obviously, such instructions would never be found. Why was it not enough to prove that the Bosnian Serb military leadership was financed and paid by Serbia and that it was tightly connected to Serbia's political and military leadership?." Antonio Cassese, A judicial massacre, The international court has set an unrealistically high standard of proof for finding Serbia complicit in genocide, guardian.co.uk, Tuesday 27 February 2007 19.50 GMT, http://www.guardian.co.uk/commentisfree/2007/feb/27/thejudicialmassacreofsrebr.

> the acts of genocide at Srebrenica "had been brought to Belgrade's attention". This is a puzzling statement at best. The massacre was prepared in detail and took place over the course of six days (between July 13 and 19). Is it plausible that the Serbian authorities remained in the dark while the killing was in progress and reported in the press all over the world? It seems far more reasonable to believe that Serbia's leaders were informed about what was going on, and that, despite this, Serbia's military, financial, and political assistance to Mladic was never interrupted. The fundamental problem with the ICJ's decision is its unrealistically high standard of proof for finding Serbia to have been legally complicit in genocide. After all, one can also be guilty of complicity in a crime by not stopping it while having both the duty and the power to do so, and when, through one's inaction, one decisively contributes to the creation of conditions that enable the crime to take place.[19]

The criticism of the Court judgment by Antonio Cassese is most significant when he draws the correct conclusion concerning the survivors of Srebrenica who received no damages for the commission of genocide against them because of the illogical judgment of the ICJ. According to him, if the late *Slobodan Milosevic* was alive, he would have been absolved of the charge of genocide.[20]

4. *Mladic* Case

The *Ratko Mladic Case* is one of the most notorious cases to have been brought before the jurisdiction of the ICTY. Serbia and the United States offered €5million for any information which may lead to his capture and the sum was later increased by Serbia to €10million. Mladic or, known as 'the Butcher of Bosnia', was a Bosnian Serb former military leader born in the municipality of *Kalinovik* in 1942. He is notorious for his alleged role in the worst massacre in Europe since the end of World War II. He became a high-ranking officer of the Yugoslav People's Army and thereafter the Chief of Staff of the Army of the Republika Srpska, or Bosnian Serb Army, in the Bosnian War from 1992 to 1995. He has been accused of

---

[19] Ibid.

[20] Ibid. Slobodan Milosevic was a Serbian and Yugoslavian politician. He was the President of the Socialist Republic of Serbia (1989 to 1997) and President of the Federal Republic of Yugoslavia (1997 to 2000). He resigned the presidency in 2000 and was arrested by the Yugoslav Federal authorities and brought before the ICTY in 2001. Milosevic conducted his own defence from the beginning of the trial up until his death due to a heart attack in 2006. He was accused of committing crimes against humanity, war crimes and genocide during the 1990 Balkan wars, mostly in connection with the murder of Bosnian Muslims.

committing war crimes, crimes against humanity and genocide in Srebrenica by the ICTY since 1995. Long after the warrant for his arrest was issued by the ICTY in 1996, Mladic was finally arrested in Lazarevo, Serbia and submitted to the jurisdiction of the ICTY in 2011. His arrest was preceded by the arrest in 2008 of his close friend Radovan Karadzic, the notorious former President of Republika Srpska. Both persons are accused of committing many of the same crimes together against the Bosnian Muslims and Bosnian Croats.

Under the system of international criminal law, the concept of superior criminal responsibility has been applied to Mladic since 1996. The ICTY has accused him of international crimes committed in the Siege of Sarajevo between 1992 to 1996 and during the Srebrenica massacre. His prosecution for war crimes, crimes against humanity and genocide was begun in The Hague in May 2012. The ICTY has charged him with two counts of genocide. The first count relates to rape, torture and other acts committed by Bosnian Serb forces against Bosnian Muslims and Croats after the initiation of the war in 1992 and the second relates to the mass killing of at least 7,000 Bosnian Muslims in the Bosnian town of Srebrenica in 1995. The prosecution of Mladic continues in the ICTY.

Hearings of the trial started on 16 May 2012. Many witnesses have testified to the ICTY. On 10 April 2013 a witness testified about the massacre of almost 8,000 men and boys at Srebrenica in July 1995. The testimony of witnesses may take several further months due to the gravity and seriousness of the crimes committed under the authority of Mladic. He has pleaded not guilty to all the charges against him and declines responsibility therefore for all of the crimes he stands accused of committing.

5. The *Charles Ghankay Taylor* Case in the SCSL

Since the creation of the Nuremberg Tribunal, the Charles Taylor case is one of the most significant cases to have been brought before the jurisdiction of international criminal courts. It is the first time in the history of international criminal law and documents that a head of state has been successfully prosecuted by international criminal tribunals/courts. Other attempted prosecutions of former heads of state have not been possible for various fundamental reasons. These include political, constitutional, juridical and health reasons. For instance, during the prosecution of the former head of state of Serbia, Slobodan Milosevic, the accused dismissed the legitimacy of the procedures of justice. He succeeded in prolonging the procedures for his prosecution and finally died because of a heart attack.

Charles Taylor, the President of the Republic of Liberia, was born in Arthington, Liberia on 28 February 1948 into a family which descended from slaves in the United States. He was educated in economics at Bentley College in Waltham, Massachusetts in the United States. In the 1970s because of a threat to occupy the Liberian diplomatic mission in New York, Taylor was arrested in 1979. He later returned to Liberia, where he was accused of embezzling almost $1 million by the president of Liberia. In 1983, he fled from Liberia and was detained in the United States on account of a Liberian arrest warrant, but succeeded in escaping from a jail in Massachusetts in 1985. Meanwhile, he established a rebel group named the National Patriotic Front of Liberia claiming rights in Liberia from the late 1980s. Taylor was fighting against his earlier colleague, Samuel Kanyon Doe, a dictator who was killed by a military figure, Prince Y. Johnson in 1990. Thereafter, Taylor engaged in armed conflicts against the Liberian government forces and on 2 August 1997 was elected President of Liberia.

As a result of a series of atrocities during the civil war, including the killing of a large number of civilians, rape, sexual slavery, and the employment of child soldiers in the Republic of Sierra Leone (the neighbouring country to Liberia), the Special Court called for Taylor's prosecution on 3 March 2003. After that, Charles Taylor resigned and accepted the invitation of the Nigerian government to take asylum in Nigeria on 11 August 2003. This went against the request of the Special Court to charge him for war crimes and crimes against humanity in Sierra Leone. In March 2006, as a result of international movements against the criminal activities of Taylor, he disappeared in the territory of Nigeria. Subsequently, the newly elected president of Liberia, Ellen Johanson Sirleaf, made a request to Nigeria to hand over Taylor to the Special Court in accordance with the provisions of the agreement which was signed between the Nigerian government and the Special Court. On 29 March he was arrested by Nigerian police officers when he was trying to escape from Nigeria to Cameroon. Thereafter, he was transported to Liberia and was taken into the custody of the United Nations. He was then handed over to the Special Court in Freetown in Sierra Leone.

For security reasons, the President of the Special Court asked the United Nations to hold Charles Taylor's trial at The Hague. However, the Netherlands imposed several conditions for the Special Court to continue the charges against him at The Hague. These included among other things, the provision of facilities by another country to incarcerate Taylor in the event of his guilt being proven and a resolution by the Security Council concerning his relocation. On June 15, 2006, at the request of the United Nations, the British government agreed to jail Taylor after his conviction, on the condition that the Dutch government agreed to cooperate in his prosecution in the building of the ICC.

Thereafter, for security reasons and in order not to allow Taylor to escape again, he was sent to the United Nations detention block at The Hague. His trial started in the Netherlands on 4 June 2007. Taylor boycotted the trial in various ways and rejected his attorney. He sometimes argued that he did not have enough money for the defence and sometimes that he wanted to defend himself personally. The Court has, also, instead of hearing the witnesses, been forced to take decisions on whether Taylor had the right to refuse to appear, reject his lawyer or defend himself. The proceedings of the trial have therefore been hampered on several occasions. Since Taylor has pleaded "not guilty" on all accounts, this has created a lot of difficulty for the Special Court in the ICC.

According to the indictment presented by Stephen Rapp, the prosecutor of the Special Court, Taylor helped, in various ways, the Revolutionary United Front (RUF) led by Foday Snakohs and the Armed Forces Revolutionary Council (AFRC) in the preparation of armed activities and civil war in Sierra Leone. This was mainly intended to control Sierra Leone's diamond wealth. He sold the diamonds and bought weapons for these armed groups who used them to attack civilians. The attacks occurred in the districts of Bo, Kono, Kenema, Bombali and Kailahun and in Freetown. These attacks were mainly against the civilian population and their services, as well as humanitarian assistance projects and United Nations peacekeepers. For instance, 500 United Nations peacekeepers were taken hostage by the RUF. The attacks aimed at terrorising the civilian population and punishing them for not helping the RUF and AFRC. To this end they committed acts of mutilation and perpetrated the rape of women, children and men.[21] In addition, they engaged in the abduction of civilians, especially children, using them as sexual slaves, soldiers and forced labour. According to the witnesses, militias allegedly authorised by Charles Taylor, abducted and seriously terrorized children in different ways. They trained children in Small Girls Units and Small Boys

[21] For the examination of rape and sexual violence as a serious international crime, consult David. S Mitchell, *The Prohibition of Rape in International Humanitarian Law as a Norm of Jus Cogens: Clarifying the Doctrine*, 15 Duke Journal of Comparative & International Law 219 (2005).

Units and sent them to the villages and cities in order to kill and mutilate people, and if possible, even their own families.[22]

Brenda Hollis, the former US military attorney was the Prosecutor of the case. Taylor was first charged on 17 counts, but the indictment was modified to 11 counts in March 2006. According to the new indictment, Taylor would be charged with the following: crimes against humanity, violations of Article 3 Common to the Geneva Conventions and of Additional Protocol II, and other serious violations of international humanitarian law. Accordingly, these include:

- Terrorizing the civilian population and collective punishment which comes under "acts of terrorism" (count 1). They constitute the violation of Article 3 Common to the Geneva Conventions and of Additional Protocol II. This is also called war crimes.
- Count 2, "murder" deals with unlawful killings and it falls under the category of crimes against humanity.
- Violence to life, health and physical or mental well-being of persons, in particular murder, constitutes count 3 and is in violation

[22] "Sexual violence peaked during the rebels' military operations, which occurred countrywide as the rebels sought to capture more territory. After capturing a town or a village, the combatants rewarded themselves by looting and by raping women and girls, many of whom they later abducted. Human Rights Watch has documented crimes of sexual violence committed during and following military operations, such as 'Operation No Living Thing' and 'Operation Pay Yourself' that took place in 1998.Human Rights Watch has also extensively documented the January 1999 invasion of Freetown by the RUF/AFRC, during which sexual violence was systematically committed against women and girls on a massive scale. The sexual violence committed during January 1999 serves as an illustration of the widespread nature of sexual violence committed by the rebel forces. Among the perpetrators were child combatants, and many of the victims were also children. Members of the Small Boys Units (SBUs) within the rebel forces were known to be particularly cruel and committed egregious human rights abuses. Although there are no exact figures for the number of women and girls subjected to sexual violence during the January 1999 invasion, Médecins Sans Frontières (MSF) and the Sierra Leone chapter of the Forum for African Women Educationalists (FAWE Sierra Leone), a nongovernmental organization that has been treating survivors of sexual violence since 1999, provided medical treatment and counselling to 1,862 female survivors of sexual violence who had been raped and/or abducted during the invasion. According to MSF, 55 percent of these survivors reported having been gang raped and 200 had become pregnant." Sexual Violence in the Sierra Leone Conflict, 15 Human Rights Watch (Africa Division) 1(A) (Jan. 2003), at 6-8, 28-63, 76-7, available at http://www.hrw.org/reports/2003/ sierral eone/ Visited on 11/11/2008.

of the provisions of Article 3 Common to the Geneva Conventions and Additional Protocol II. This means unlawful killings denoting war crimes.

- Count 4 of the indictment refers to the systematic use of sexual violence, such as rape, constituting a crime against humanity.
- Count 5, states that sexual slavery and any other form of sexual violence constitute a crime against humanity.
- Count 6 refers to outrages against personal dignity constituting violations of Article 3 Common to the Geneva Conventions and of Additional Protocol II and falling under the category of war crimes.
- Count 7 states that violence to life, health and the physical or mental well-being of persons, in particular cruel treatment, constitute violations of Article 3 Common to the Geneva Conventions and of Additional Protocol II.
- Count 8 states that other inhumane acts, such as physical violence, may come under the category of crimes against humanity.
- According to the statement of count 9, conscripting or enlisting children under the age of 15 into armed forces or groups, or using them to participate actively in hostilities constitute serious violations of the international humanitarian law of armed conflict.
- Enslavement is the focus of count 10. It states that abductions and forced labour constitute crimes against humanity.
- Count 11 concerns looting, stating that pillage constitutes a violation of Article 3 Common to the Geneva Conventions and of Additional Protocol II dealing broadly with war crimes.

Charles Taylor rejected all eleven of the above counts. Up until recently, the Special Court's prosecutor was not able to succeed in the case. Although there were several victims and witnesses for the confirmation of the events, the result was not satisfactory. The defence lawyer objected to the evidence of twenty-two witnesses.[23] He called upon the responsibility of the prosecutor to use the financial resources of the Special Court to bring many witnesses from West Africa to The Hague for testimony in the relevant trial. But, according to the prosecutor, the defence lawyer for Charles Taylor created difficulties for victim witnesses by asking for the presence of the witnesses in the Special Court when their evidence was not in dispute.[24] Nevertheless, the Trial Chamber was of the view that the defence lawyer could require the witnesses' presence in the Special Court

[23] www.sc-sl.org/ - 12k. Visited on 20 November 2008.
[24] *Id.*

if it seemed necessary.[25] Twenty further witnesses were then asked to come to The Hague in order to give their testimony. It was calculated that the testimony of witnesses might not end before the Special Court's judicial recess began on 12 December 2008.[26] The trial was eventually continued in July, August, October, and November 2009. This caused the judgment of the Special Court to be delayed and it was delivered in 2012.[27] Furthermore, if more evidence or facts are presented after the Trial Chamber's judgment, the judgment of the Appeals Chamber would require more time.[28]

The testimony of witnesses amounted to more than 50,000 pages. Charles Taylor is the first head of state to be prosecuted and punished for several crimes, including war crimes and crimes against humanity, after the conclusion of the Nuremberg Tribunal for the prosecution and punishment of Major War Criminals of the Second World War.[29] Although one cannot deny that Charles Taylor was not found guilty of directly commanding crimes against humanity or war crimes, the judges of the SCSL were of the view that he had supplied soldiers and weapons to the Revolutionary United Front. Therefore the Court concluded that Taylor was guilty of abetting and aiding war crimes during the relevant armed conflict. According to the Court, Charles Taylor had obtained clear knowledge that the Revolutionary United Front (RUF) was conducting atrocities against the general civilian population, such as recruiting child soldiers, the sexual exploitation of children, as well as mutilating victims.

Finally, Taylor was convicted on 12 April 2012 and sentenced to 50 years imprisonment on 30 May of the same year. The SCSL has however delivered other lengthier sentences after Taylor's sentence, such as that

---

[25] *Id.*

[26] *Id.*

[27] In the SCSL in The Hague, Taylor has recently stated that Olusegun Obasanjo, who was the President of Nigeria when he was arrested, told him lies that led to his arrest. (2009-11-10). Olusegun Obasanjo is currently a United Nations peace envoy.

[28] Interestingly, the Domestic Security Section of the United States Department of Justice for torture has simultaneously prosecuted Taylor's son Charles Taylor, Jr. (Chuckie) in 2008. "Taylor Jr. to stand trial on charges of torture abroad", *CNN*. http://www.cnn.com/2008/CRIME/09/27/taylor.torture.trial/index.html?section=cnn_latest. Retrieved on 2008-09-28.

[29] Of course one can also refer to the prosecution of Alberto Fujimori from Peru who was condemned to 25 years imprisonment because of the killings and kidnappings that occurred during his Presidency and Saddam Hussein's execution in Iraq.

delivered to Issa Sesay who was commander in the RUF and was condemned to 52 years of imprisonment.[30]

6. Dimensions of Cases in ICC

6.1. Introduction

Studying cases of international criminal justice is not easy. One has to understand both the nature and the reasons for the formulation of a particular decision. The same is true for any national system of criminal justice. Thus, a decision of the ICJ, the ICTY, the ICTR, the SCSL, the ICC, the European Court of Justice and any other human rights courts is the manifestation of the power of the court to deliver a decision with due regard to the existing regulations and circumstances of a case. The conclusion of a court may go against or for the accused. In addition, the decision of a court may not be authorised and enforced because of the rights of the condemned or the victim to bring complaints to a higher court. This may be carried out when the victim/counsel or the accused are not satisfied with the content of the decision. Further, the decision of a higher court or the appeal court may be rejected by the defendant or the victim and complaints will then be submitted to a supreme court.

The decision of a court must be reliable and should be based on proper and correct evidence. Some of the most significant reasons why the decision must keep its impartiality and not violate the integrity of the machinery of judgement are the following: *i)* A decision may interpret certain ambiguities of the law, *ii)* A decision may open the door for the understating of customary international law, *iii)* A decision may create a new norm for international law, *iv)* A decision may help in the discovery of certain norms of the law, *v)* A decision may find a person guilty or not guilty, *vi)* A decision may demand the application of a different punishment, *vii)* A decision may strongly affect the circumstances of a victim, *viii)* A decision may be effective in the prevention of certain crimes. Many other reasons could also be listed which are vital considered by a court or the ICC when delivering a judgment.

Bringing the violators of the law of the ICC before the Court is not easy because of the existence of the principle of complementarity and political realities. There have only been a few cases before the jurisdiction of the Court since the ICC came into force in 2001, and the ICC has not,

---

[30] Issa Sesay was convicted by the SCSL in Freetown on 25 February 2009. He was found guilty of 16 out of 18 charges against him including crimes against humanity, sexual violence and the use of child soldiers.

for one reason or another, tried to bring other cases put forward by governmental or non-governmental bodies before its jurisdiction. Sometimes, the prosecutor has also been silent or very cautious about the initiation of a case. Illustrative examples are the Gaza Strip case against the Israeli authorities, the criminal activities committed by the Bush administration in Iraq and the criminal activities of the Iranian regime against its own population.

The Pre-Trial Chambers of the ICC, based on the investigations and the request of the Prosecutor, have issued arrest warrants for ten persons up until today. Of these ten cases, four have successfully been brought before the jurisdiction of the Court. All ten cases deal with one or several of the crimes under the Statute of the Court; these are, namely, war crimes, crimes against humanity and genocide. One of the most specific arrest warrants is the warrant for the head of state of Sudan which has opened up serious discussions in the international legal and political community concerning the criminal liability of heads of state. However, the Court is entirely incapable of the implementation of the law in the relevant case.

6.2. *Thomas Lubanga Dyilo* Case

6.2.1. Position

The Thomas Lubanga Dyilo case concerns the alleged crimes committed in the Democratic Republic of the Congo.[31]There are allegations that Lubanga was the former President of a political group, namely, Union des Patriotes Congolais (UPC), since its establishment in September 2000. He is also suspected of having been Commander-in-Chief of its military wing, the Forces Patriotiques pour la Libération du Congo (FPLC). With Ugandan assistance, the UPC was formed during the Ituri conflict.[32] After the deaths of nine members of the United Nations Peacekeeping Force in the Democratic Republic of the Congo in 2005, Lubanga was, alongside other leaders of the conflicting party, arrested by Congolese authorities and imprisoned in Kinshasa. He was than later arrested by the ICC in 2006.

---

[31] *Thomas Lubanga Dyilo*, (ICC-01/04-01/06),Warrant of Arrest, 10 February 2006.

[32] It should be stated here that the Ituri region is rich in natural resources including gold, oil, timber, coltan, and also diamonds. There have therefore been many conflicts in order to gain power over the region by different persons.

6.2.2. Arrest Warrant

In 2006, based on an investigation by the Prosecutor of the ICC and his request of an arrest warrant, the Pre-Trial Chamber I of the Court granted Thomas Lubanga Dyilo's arrest.[33] Thereafter he was arrested and brought before trial in The Hague.[34] Shortly afterwards, in March 2006, he made his initial appearance before the Chamber. The charges against him were confirmed in January 2007 and the case was transferred to the Trial Chamber. On June 2008, the trial was suspended because the Prosecution was, due to confidentiality restrictions, incapable of revealing a large amount of material. This was because the provisions of the Statute have to be respected by the Prosecutor. These provisions were related to Article 54 (3) (e) relating to the powers of the Prosecutor with respect to investigations. It reads that the Prosecutor may "agree not to disclose, at any stage of the proceedings, documents or information that the Prosecutor obtains on the condition of confidentiality and solely for the purpose of generating new evidence, unless the provider of the information consents." Finally, in October 2008, the Prosecution announced that it had concluded positive agreements. Subsequently, the trial could proceed after a confirmation by the judges of the Chamber who reviewed the material. The trial began and many victims have been granted the right to participate in the trial.

6.2.3. Charges and Admissibility

There are many charges against Thomas Lubanga Dyilo. He is charged with criminal responsibility as a co-perpetrator, jointly with other active members of two different groups. The Prosecution has alleged that Thomas Lubanga Dyilore recruited children under the age of fifteen years. He subjected them to many forms of military training. After the training, he forced them to participate in various military hostilities. The children were also used as bodyguards for military officers. For the Prosecutor, there was no doubt that the accused effectively exercised authority within the Union des Patriotes Congolais and the Forces Patriotiques pour la Libération du Congo. The intention was to have full control over their power and policies. Lubanga is represented by lead counsel Maître Catherine Mabille and co-counsel Jean-Marie Biju-Duval.

---

[33] His request was submitted to the Pre-Trial Chamber on 12 January 2006 and was approved by the Chamber I, on 10 February.

[34] Lubanga was arrested by the ICC on 17 March 2006.

Contrary to the presentation of evidence by the Prosecutor, which related to the national armed conflict in the Democratic Republic of the Congo, the Pre-Trial Chamber stated the charges in the context of both international and non-international armed conflict. According to the statement of Pre-Trial Chamber I, there are sufficient reasons to believe that Thomas Lubanga Dyilo is responsible as a co-perpetrator under the Statute of the ICC. He has enlisted children under the age of fifteen years into military activities, including combat. Therefore, he has violated the provisions of Article 8 (xxvi) relating to war crimes. The relevant sub-paragraph reads that "Conscripting or enlisting children under the age of fifteen years into the national armed forces or using them to participate actively in hostilities." His criminal responsibility is based on the provisions of Article 25(3)(a) of the Statute which reads that "In accordance with this Statute, a person shall be criminally responsible and liable for punishment for a crime within the jurisdiction of the Court if that person: (a)Commits such a crime, whether as an individual, jointly with another or through another person, regardless of whether that other person is criminally responsible."

The charges presented by the Pre-Trial Chamber are the following:

> Charges arising in the context of "Non-international armed conflict":
> Count 1: CONSCRIPTING CHILDREN INTO ARMED GROUPS, a WAR CRIME, punishable under Articles 8(2)(e)(vii) and 25(3)(a) of the Rome Statute.
> Count 2: ENLISTING CHILDREN INTO ARMED GROUPS, a WAR CRIME, punishable under Articles 8(2)(e)(vii) and 25(3)(a) of the Rome Statute.
> Count 3: USING CHILDREN TO PARTICIPATE ACTIVELY IN HOSTILITIES, a WAR CRIME, punishable under Articles 8(2)(e)(vii) and 25(3)(a) of the Rome Statute.
> Charges arising in the context of "International armed conflict":
> Count 4: CONSCRIPTING CHILDREN INTO NATIONAL ARMED FORCES, a WAR CRIME, punishable under Articles 8(2)(b)(xxvi) and 25(3)(a) of the Rome Statute.
> Count 5: ENLISTING CHILDREN INTO NATIONAL ARMED FORCES, a WAR CRIME, punishable under Articles 8(2)(b)(xxvi) and 25(3)(a) of the Rome Statute.
> Count 6; USING CHILDREN TO PARTICIPATE ACTIVELY IN HOSTILITIES, a WAR CRIME, punishable under Articles 8(2)(b)(xxvi) and 25(3)(a) of the Rome Statute.

The legal position of the Thomas Lubanga trial is still not clear as witnesses have continued to be heard up until recently. The hearing and the cross-examination of witness by the defence attorney continued up until

May 2010. Two intermediaries and an investigator from the Office of The Prosecutor at the ICC have also testified in the case. Based on the preparation of the case and the circumstances of the accused, the trial of the accused was postponed. The suspension of the case was due to the failure of the prosecution to correctly complete the orders of the trial chamber to disclose the identity of an intermediary whose assistance was useful for the facilitation of the investigations.[35] On 15 July 2010, the Trial Chamber I ordered the release of the accused. According to the Court, an accused could not be held in preventative custody on a provisional basis. The speculation that his alleged crimes might be proven later, would not be enough to require his custody. The order for the release was however based on the argument that the prosecutors had refused to hand all the information to the defence. However, the Trial Chamber again questioned the prosecution's late disclosure on 5 November 2010. According to the prosecution, the material submitted was solely a work paper and not subject to disclosure based on the ICC Rules.

On December 2010, the trial heard allegations from the defence of abuse of process by the prosecution. This was based on the fact that one of the witnesses had withdrawn and had also accused prosecution intermediaries of corrupting him financially and instructing him to provide incorrect testimony. At the continuation of the case in January 2011, the Chamber reached a negative assessment of this prosecution witness's credibility in the case. After a series of events, on 14 March 2012, Thomas Lubanga was convicted by the verdict of Trail Chamber I as a participant in war crimes consisting of:

> Enlisting and conscripting of children under the age of 15 years into the Force patriotique pour la libération du Congo [Patriotic Force for the Liberation of Congo] (FPLC) and using them to participate actively in hostilities in the context of an armed conflict not of an international character from 1 September 2002 to 13 August 2003 (punishable under article 8(2)(e)(vii) of the Rome Statute).

Thomas Lubanga was sentenced by Trail Chamber I to 14 years imprisonment on 10 July 2012. The sentence was based on his violation of two very crucial principles. These are the principles outlawing the recruitment of children in armed conflict and prohibiting the use of children as soldiers in actual fighting. Thomas had violated both principles between 2002 and 2003. According to the judgment, approximately 60,000

---

[35] ICC: Appeals Chamber Says Lubanga Case Should Resume, www.iccnow.org/?mod=drctimeline Lubanga.

were killed in the conflict between ethnic groups in Ituri in the north-eastern DR Congo.

6.3. *Germain Katanga* and *Mathieu Ngudjolo Chui* Cases

6.3.1. Positions

Germain Katanga who is also known as "Simba" or "lion" is the youngest accused to face the ICC. He is considered to be the former leader of the Front des Nationalistes et Intégrationistes (FNI), a militia group of primarily Lendu ethnicity which was fighting in the region of Ituri in the Democratic Republic of Congo. The group was formed in November 2002. One of the chief intentions of the group was to fight against Hema militias and also to stop the exploitation of non-Hema civilians during the forgoing Ituri conflict. The accused was appointed by the President of Congo as Brigadier-General in the regular armed forces of the Republic in 2004. After the death of nine members of the Peacekeepers in the Democratic Republic of the Congo in 2005, he was arrested together with several other militia leaders and was thereafter detained in Kinshasa.

The second accused is Mathieu Ngudjolo Chu, who is alleged to be the former leader of the FNI, a militia group of primarily Lendu ethnicity which had been mobilized to operate against the opposite party in the region of Ituri in the Democratic Republic of Congo. The group was formed in November 2002. The accused had its leadership in 2003. The intention of the group was primarily to fight against Hema militias and also to stop the exploitation of non-Hema civilians under the Ituri conflict. Meanwhile, it is also alleged that Mathieu Ngudjolo Chu was one of the founding members of the Mouvement Révolutionnaire Congolais which organised the activities of other armed groups.

Based on his position and engagements, Mathieu Ngudjolo Chu signed a peace agreement with the Government of the Democratic Republic of Congo in August 2006. Thereafter, he declared that he and his friends had been granted amnesty. The agreement promoted his position and he received the rank of Colonel in the regular armed forces of the country.

6.3.2. Arrest Warrants

In response to the repeated commission of crimes in the Democratic Republic of Congo since 1 July 2002, an investigation into the alleged crimes was seen to be necessary by the Prosecutor. Therefore, the second and third arrest warrants which were taken into serious examination by the ICC were also related to the Democratic Republic of Congo. In fact, the arrest warrants against Germain Katanga and Mathieu Ngudjolo Chui were launched one year after the first arrest warrant by the ICC concerning the Thomas Lubanga case in 2007. At the request of the Prosecutor in June, the Pre-Trial Chamber I approved arrest warrants in July. Germain Katanga was surrendered to the ICC on 18 October 2007. He submitted his initial appearance before the Court in October of the same year.

The second arrest warrant concerned Mathieu Ngudjolo Chui. Pre-Trial Chamber I issued a warrant of arrest for Mathieu Ngudjolo Chui on 6 July 2007. He was arrested on 6 July 2008 and transferred to the ICC on 7 July. The difference between the former and the latter arrest warrant is that Germain Katanga was already taken into custody in Congo in 2005, after the allegations about the killing of nine peacekeepers, but Mathieu Ngudjolo Chui was not detained by national authorities. In other words, the proceedings against Katanga in the Congo Republic were ended on 17 October 2007. This was in order to facilitate the proceedings for the application of the complementarity principle. Mathieu Ngudjolo Chui had escaped from his personal liability by the provisions of the peace agreement signed between him and the government. Therefore, his arrest and surrender were based on a request by the ICC. This is also based on the fact that because of his position the national authorities of the Congo could not, apparently, for one reason or another, charge him for the commission of serious crimes such as crimes against humanity or war crimes. His initial appearance was submitted to the Court in February 2008.

6.3.3. Accusations

Germain Katanga and *Mathieu Ngudjolo Chui* have both been accused of ordering attacks on the inhabitants of a village in which over 200 people were killed. The village is in the province of Ituri and is called Bogoro. Both accused were two of the three leading commanders in their groups. Therefore, they had a leading role in the enforcement of the common plan and joint control of the situation. The arrest warrant concerning Germain Katanga contains the following accusations:

> there are reasonable grounds to believe that there was a common plan between Germain Katanga and other senior FNI and FRPI military commanders to carry out an indiscriminate attack on the village of Bogoro on or around 24 February 2003; that criminal acts committed during, and in the aftermath of, the attack, namely i) the murder of 200 civilians, ii) causing serious bodily harm to civilians, iii) arresting, threatening with weapons and imprisoning civilians in a room filled with corpses, iv)

> pillaging,v) the sexual enslavement of several women and girls, and vi) the active participation of children under the age of fifteen years in hostilities, were part of a common plan or, were, at the very last, a probable and accepted consequence of implementation of the said common plan.[36]

Similar words to those of the arrest warrant for *Germain Katanga* can be found in the arrest warrant for *Mathieu Ngudjolo Chui*. The warrant points to a considerable number of activities which were carried out under the orders of *Mathieu Ngudjolo Chui*. For instance, it alleges that:

> there are reasonable grounds to believe that between January 2003 and at least March 2003, the FNI and FRPI carried out an attack directed against the civilian population of certain parts of the territory of Ituri, primarily of Hema ethnicity; that the attack was a systematic or widespread nature; and that during such as a systematic or widespread attack, on or around 24 February 2003, during, and in the aftermath of, the attack on the village of Bogoro, the following crimes were committed: the murder of about 200 civilians, causing serious bodily harm to civilians and sexual enslavement of several women or girls.[37]

Both suspected persons are accused of committing war crimes and crimes against humanity, thereby violating the provisions of the Statute of the ICC. According to the arrest warrants, Germain Katanga and Mathieu Ngudjolo Chui are answerable for those violations and bear criminal responsibility under the law of the ICC. The warrants have therefore presented many other pieces of evidence proving the engagement of both sides in the criminal activities in the village of Bogoro.

6.3.4. Charges and Admissibility

The Germain Katanga and Mathieu Ngudjolo Chui cases are clear indications of the application of the principle of complementarity. This is because the legal authorities in the Congo Republic were not, for one reason or another, able to bring the accused persons under their national criminal jurisdiction. That is why in April 2004, the President of Congo referred the situation to the ICC pursuant to the content of Article 14 of the Statute.[38] Based on the provisions of this article, the Office of Prosecutor

---

[36] No.ICC-01/04-01/07. The arrest warrant was issued on 2 July 2007.

[37] No: ICC-01/04-02/07. The arrest warrantwas issued on 6 July 2007.

[38] Article 14 reads that "1.A State Party may refer to the Prosecutor a situation in which one or more crimes within the jurisdiction of the Court appear to have been committed requesting the Prosecutor to investigate the situation for the purpose of determining whether one or more specific persons should be charged with the

started its investigations and finally brought the accused persons into the province of the Court. The Trial-Chamber II confirmed the charges by the Prosecutor against Germain Katanga and Mathieu Ngudjolo Chui in 28 October 2009. Thereafter, the Appeals Chamber of the ICC confirmed the admissibility of the case against Germain Katanga on 25 September 2009, and decided the start date for his joint trial with Mathieu Ngudjolo Chui on 24 November 2009. Accordingly, both accused persons, Germain Katanga and Mathieu Ngudjolo Chui, are charged with crimes against humanity and war crimes. This means the provisions of Articles 7 and 8 of the Statute of the ICC are applicable to both cases. It is alleged that Katanga, acting jointly with Ngudjolo, committed the offences of sexual slavery, murder, rape, using children under 15 years to take active part in hostilities and targeting the civilian population with different unlawful acts. However, it should be noted that Katanga has challenged the admissibility of his case due to the provisions of Article 17 of the Statute. This Statute concerning the issues of admissibility provides that a case is inadmissible where:

> (a) The case is being investigated or prosecuted by a State which has jurisdiction over it, unless the State is unwilling or unable genuinely to carry out the investigation or prosecution;
> (b) The case has been investigated by a State which has jurisdiction over it and the State has decided not to prosecute the person concerned, unless the decision resulted from the unwillingness or inability of the State genuinely to prosecute;
> (c) The person concerned has already been tried for conduct which is the subject of the complaint, and a trial by the Court is not permitted under article 20, paragraph 3;
> (d) The case is not of sufficient gravity to justify further action by the Court.
>
> 2. In order to determine unwillingness in a particular case, the Court shall consider, having regard to the principles of due process recognized by international law, whether one or more of the following exist, as applicable:
> (a) The proceedings were or are being undertaken or the national decision was made for the purpose of shielding the person concerned from criminal responsibility for crimes within the jurisdiction of the Court referred to in article 5;

---

commission of such crimes. 2. As far as possible, a referral shall specify the relevant circumstances and be accompanied by such supporting documentation as is available to the State referring the situation."

> (b) There has been an unjustified delay in the proceedings which in the circumstances is inconsistent with an intent to bring the person concerned to justice;
> (c) The proceedings were not or are not being conducted independently or impartially, and they were or are being conducted in a manner which, in the circumstances, is inconsistent with an intent to bring the person concerned to justice.

Essentially, two major challenges have been expressed by Katanga to the admissibility of his case in the Court. He has stated that the 'same conduct' test developed and applied by the Pre-Trial Chamber I in order to justify its preliminary review of the case is an invalid test.[39] He argues that the clarification by the Pre-Trial Chamber I did not have juridical foundation, even though the practice of other *ad hoc* tribunals such as the ICTR was taken into examination. Therefore, according to the Defence:

> As submitted earlier, even if the 'same conduct test' is applied the result remains the same- the case is not admissible. Form the evidence submitted in support of this motion it appears that Mr. Katanga was charged in DRC with the participation in the attack in Bogoro, as a crime against humanity. The charges confirmed by the Pr-Trial Chamber are identical. They do not differ sufficiently to justify admissibility of the case at the ICC....If this evidence was not in the possession of both the Prosecutor and the Pre-Trial Chamber, the question arises as to what degree they have properly investigated and compared the DRC investigations and the ICC Prosecutor's intended charges. It might be argued that the procedure concerning the application of arrest warrant is not the appropriate moment for a full scale investigation and that the decision is without prejudice to the later admissibility challenges, but this is hardly convincing.[40]

The defence goes further and, with reference to the Appeals Chamber ruling in the Ntaganda case, states that "the *propriomotu* review of admissibility in the framework of the application for an arrest warrant is at the discretion of the Pre-Trial Chamber." It therefore maintains that:

> *propriomotu* review of admissibility in the context of Article 58-proceedings should not take place where (a) admissibility is not raised by the prosecutor in his application, (b) the review was ex parte without participation of suspect, victims and entities concerted, and (c) no ostensible cause or self-evident factor was manifest impelling the exercise

[39] Prosecutor v Germain Katanga and Mathieu Ngudjolo Chui, Motion Challenging the Admissibility of the Case by the Defence of Germain Katanga (Public Redacted Version), ICC-01/04-01/07 (2009), para.39.
[40] *Id.*, paras.53-54.

> of propriomotu review. The defence submits, however, that the arrest warrant application is a vital stage of the proceedings with serious consequences when no admissibility analysis is conducted or where such analysis is flawed. … The most obvious and the most serious consequence of absent or defective admissibility analysis is that, in the present case, it has resulted in the arrest and transfer of Mr. Katanga to the ICC. His fate has thereby become the full responsibility of the Court. While the Defence appreciates the Appeals Chamber concern that the suspect has not participated in these arrest warrant proceedings and that this requires caution, the consequences of absence of or flawed admissibility-analysis are far more damaging to the suspect. The Defence raises concerns with the Appeals Chamber analysis whereby impediment of the interests of the suspect in the initial admissibility determination are not outweighed by its benefits.[41]

The second challenge by Katanga concerns the interpretation of two relatively similar terms in Article 17 (1) (a) in the Statute. These are the terms 'unwilling' or 'unable'. According to the Defence the Pre-Trial Chamber did not consider the matter at all. The Defence claimed that there was no indication of unwillingness or inability in the Katanga case from the Congo when the decision of an arrest warrant was issued by the Pre-Trial Chamber. Thus, a tacit acceptance does not imply a definite unwillingness.[42] In short, the outcome of the Appeals Chamber decision has also been asserted to conflict with the provisions of the Statute and to violate the intent of the ICC to act as a court of last resort. In other words, the case has enlarged the legal scope of the ICC's complementarity principle and permits it to initiate prosecution against a person, even where a state has already initiated prosecution against that person for the same crimes. However, this is as long as the state wants to close the prosecution at the request of the Prosecutor of the ICC. It has therefore been suggested that where the ICC deems it necessary to take prosecution of a case under its own jurisdiction, despite legal activity by a national system, the ICC should clearly list the reasons that are the motive for its decision.[43] However, all these arguments have been rejected by the Trial Chamber II[44]

---

[41] *Id.*, paras.54-55.

[42] *Id.*, para.58.

[43] Susana Sacouto and Katherine Cleary, The Katanga Complementarity Decisions: Sound Law but Flawed policy, 23 Leiden Journal of International Law (2010), pp.363-374.

[44] Prosecutor v Germain Katanga and Mathieu Ngudjolo Chui, Reasons for the Oral Decision on the Motion Challenging the Admissibility of the Case, ICC-01/04-01/07, the Trial-Chamber II, 16 June 2009, paras.77, 90-95.

and the Appeals Chamber.[45] The latter has clearly stated that the case against the accused is admissible and dismisses the grounds of Appeal.[46] None of the articulations by the accused were accepted as a reasonable basis for the inadmissibility of the case. Accordingly, a state may for a variety of reasons not wish to exercise criminal jurisdiction over certain individuals and therefore refer the case to the jurisdiction of the ICC. According to the ICC, this constitutes the acceptance of the jurisdiction of the Court or the application of the principle of complementarity. Finally, in its decision the Appeal Chamber, like the Pre-trial Chamber and Trial Chamber, completely rejected any claim that the Katanga case was inadmissible.[47] Similarly, the Appeals Chamber of the International Criminal Court relating to the appeal of Mr Germain Katanga against the decision of Trial Chamber II entitled "Decision on the Modalities of Victim Participation at Trial" of 22 January 2010, rejected the appeal. The Decision of the Modalities was therefore confirmed.[48]

On 20 April 2012, Trial Chamber II of the International Criminal Court (ICC) issued an order on procedures for the presentation of closing statements concerning *The Prosecutor v. Germain Katanga and Mathieu Ngudjolo Chui* case. It was decided that the closing statements would take place from 15 to 23 May 2012. The Trial proper concluded on May 23.

---

[45] Prosecutor v Germain Katanga and Mathieu Ngudjolo Chui, ICC-01/04-01/07 OA8, 31 July 2009.

[46] *Id.*, para.92.

[47] Prosecutor v Mr Germain Katanga and Mathieu Ngudjolo Chui, Judgment on the Appeal of Germain Katanga against the Oral Decision of Trial Chamber II of 12 June 2009 on the Admissibility of the Case, Case No: ICC-01/04-01/07 OA 8 (2009), Appeals Chamber 25 September 2009,(Admissibility Appeal Decision).

[48] See The Appeals Chamber, No. ICC-01/04-01/07 OA 11, on 16 July 2010. The Appeals Chamber concluded that "In sum, the Appeals Chamber finds that the possibility for the Victims to testify on matters including the role of the accused in the crimes charged against them, grounded on the Trial Chamber's authority to request evidence necessary for the determination of the truth, is not per se inconsistent with the rights of the accused and the concept of a fair trial. However, and as the Appeals Chamber held previously in the Lubanga case, the Trial Chamber must ensure, on a case-by-case basis, that the right of the accused to a fair trial is respected. Therefore, whether a victim will be requested to testify on matters relating to the conduct of the accused will depend on the Trial Chamber's assessment of whether such testimony: (i) affects the victim's personal interests; (ii) is relevant to the issues of the case; (iii) contributes to the determination of the truth; and (iv) whether the testimony would be consistent with the rights of the accused, and in particular the right to have adequate time and facilities to prepare his defence (article 67 (1) (b) of the Statute), and a fair and impartial trial." para.114.

The judgment was expected before the end of 2012. Meanwhile, the defence teams for Germain Katanga and Mathieu Ngudjolo Chui have filed motions with Trial Chamber II asking for an examination of a Registry decision that halts their legal aid while they wait for delivery of the trial judgment. They argued that the prevention is a violation of the right of the accused to a fair trial, including the facilities to prepare a defence, the right to adequate time and the right to legal assistance. Thus, according to the decision, only lead lawyers would receive payment which is unfair compared with the case of Thomas Lubanga, who was allowed to keep his defence team during this period in his trial. Trial Chamber II has not however accepted the defence team's statement.

The joint trial of *Germain Katanga and Mathieu Ngudjolo Chui* for directing the Bogoro attack was finally separated on 21 November 2012. On 18 December 2012 Mathieu Ngudjolo Chui was found not guilty by the ICC Trial Chamber II. The decision of the Chamber was unanimous. Ngudjolo was acquitted of the charges of war crimes and crimes against humanity. According to the Court's verdict, the prosecutors had:

> "not proved beyond reasonable doubt [that] Ngudjolo was responsible" for war crimes, and evidence presented had been "too contradictory and too hazy".

The verdict against Katanga was issued later and based on separate charges. His trial is still a controversial case in the chambers of the ICC. Katanga is allegedly responsible for committing crimes against humanity and war crimes. The crimes were thought to have been committed jointly with other military officials. On 27 March 2013 the Appeals Chamber of the International Criminal Court dismissed an appeal by Katanga against the decision of the Trial Chamber which had sought to modify the legal characterization of the case. On 20 November 2013, the Trial Chamber II of the International Criminal Court scheduled a hearing which delivere the judgement concerning The Prosecutor v. Germain Katanga on 7 February 2014. He will most probably be found guilty of alleged war crimes and crimes against humanity by the Court.

6.4. *Bosco Ntaganda* Case

6.4.1. Position

The fourth person who has been the subject of an arrest warrant by the Office of Prosecutor of the ICC is Bosco Ntaganda also known as "the terminator".[49] He was one of the former deputy chiefs of the General Staff for Military Operations of the *Forces Patriotiques pour la libération du Congo (*FPLC) or the Patriotic Forces for the Liberation of Congo prior to 8 December 2003, and Chief of Staff for the FPLC from the above-mentioned date. Bosco Ntaganda also had other positions in Rwanda and Congo aiming at the liberation of those countries. In fact, he first became known for his role in the Rwandan Patriotic Army and for putting an end to the Rwandan genocide from 1990 to 1994. He is alleged to be one of the commanders of the Mouvement Revolutionnaire du Congo (MRC). This is a militia group which has been operating in and around the district of Ituri since the beginning of 2005. One year later he joined Laurent Nkunda's National Congress for the Defence of the People (CNDP). It is also alleged that he has worked as the CNDP chief of staff since 2008. After some conflicts and negotiations, the CNDP has been incorporated into the United Nations Mission in the Democratic Republic of Congo (MONUC). Bosco Ntaganda functions as a General in the MONUC.[50]

6.4.2. Arrest Warrant

Since there had been the possibility of the impunity of the accused, Bosco Ntaganda, the arrest warrant was originally issued by the Pre-Trial Chamber I under seal on 22 August 2006.[51] Some of the main reasons were the strong position of the accused and the gravity of his activities violating the framework of the Statute of the ICC. The situation was therefore foreseen as being very difficult by the Prosecutor of the ICC, Luis Moreno-Ocampo. According to him, there had been a considerable number of facts that proved the commission of serious crimes in North Kivu. These included the forced displacement of populations, murders, attacks against the civilian population, rapes, looting and pillaging. According to the Prosecutor's statement, the ICC therefore had the right to investigation and jurisdiction over the crimes. He was convinced that since July 2002, several core crimes were committed by the perpetrators of the conflict. The crimes included war crimes, crimes against humanity and genocide, the victims of which were both in North and South Kivu. With this intention, he brought the case into the Pre-Trial Chamber in order to issue an arrest warrant against Bosco Ntaganda. Consequently, the Pre-

[49] Case The Prosecutor v. BoscoNtaganda, ICC-01/04-02/06-2.

[50] http://www.guardian.co.uk/world/2010/feb/05/congo-child-soldiers-ntaganda-monuc.

[51] The Prosecution's application for warrant of arrest was made on 12 January 2006.

Trial Chamber of the ICC, after an examination of the case, found that there were reasonable grounds to believe that Ntaganda should be brought before the jurisdiction of the Court, for the commission of crimes by the Forces patriotiques Pour la Libération du Congo/Patriotic Forces for the Liberation of Congo (FPLC) between July 2002 and December 2003. Therefore, the Chamber issued a warrant for his arrest. On 28 April 2008, the Court unsealed the arrest warrant on the basis of changes of circumstances suggesting that there was no longer the possibility of the accused escaping.

6.4.3. Charges and Admissibility

The arrest warrant concerning Bosco Ntaganda clearly referred to war crimes and states that enlisting and conscripting children under the age of fifteen and using them to participate actively in hostilities are serious violations of the Statute of the ICC and give rise to the criminal responsibility of the perpetrator. Therefore, he is charged with the following crimes "the war crime of enlistment of children under the age of fifteen punishable under Article 8 (2)(b)(xxvi), or Article 8 (2)(e)(vii), of the Statute; the war crime of conscription of children under the age of fifteen punishable under Article 8 (2)(b)(xxvi) or Article 8(2)(e)(vii), of the Statute; and the war crime of using children under the age of fifteen to participate actively in hostilities punishable under Article 8(2)(b)(xxvi), or article 8(2)(e)(vii) of the Statute."[52]

Despite the accusations or charges against *Bosco Ntaganda*, he has worked officially under the auspices of the United Nations peacekeeping mission known as MONUC. The fact that the United Nations mission has continued to work with *Ntaganda* and has made use of his combat experience demonstrates that the implementation of the provisions of the Statute of the ICC can be far from easy at times. Although *Bosco Ntaganda* had been asked to appear before the jurisdiction of the ICC for violations of the system of international criminal law, it was not clear when the content of his active arrest warrant was practically going to be implemented. This was because the ICC was not successful in producing any more evidence against him up until recently. However, on 18 March 2013 *Bosco Ntaganda* came to the United States Embassy in Rwanda and thereafter was transferred to the ICC in The Hague. He appeared before the Court on 26 March and pleaded not guilty.

---

[52] The Prosecutor v. BoscoNtaganda, ICC-01/04-02/06 (22 August 2006).

6.5. *Jean-Pierre Bemba Gombo* Case

6.5.1. Position

The *Jean-Pierre Bemba Gombo case* concerns the Central African Republic while the other four above-mentioned cases are related to the situation in the Democratic Republic of Congo. However, all five cases deal with the question of war crimes or crimes against humanity in the Congo. Bemba Gombo was originally from Bokada which is in the province of Equateur, the Democratic Republic of the Congo. Bemba Gombo was educated in both his country and in Belgium. He went into exile in 1997 because of the Seizure of power by Laurent–Desire Kabila's forces. He was one of those who established the Movement for the Liberation of Congo/Mouvement de Libération du Congo (MLC) which was connected to an armed force called the Liberation Army of Congo in 1998. It is also alleged that Bemba Gombo was the president and commander-in-chief of the MLC. Between 1998 and 2003, the MLC was involved in the civil war in the DRC. It also took part, between October 2002 and March 2003, in the conflict in the Central African Republic. The conflict was between the armed forces of President Ange-Felic Patasse and the rebels led by Francois Bozize.[53] Bemba Gombo became the vice-president of the Democratic Republic of Congo in 2006 and a Senator in Parliament in 2007.

6.5.2 Arrest Warrant

The prosecutor's application for a warrant for arrest, which was based on some of the important evidence, was issued on 9 May 2008. In response, Pre-Trial Chamber III issued an arrest warrant concerning the Central African Republic on 23 May 2008. The warrant calls for the immediate arrest of Jean-Pierre Bemba Gombo. According to the warrant of arrest, the Chamber is of the view that there was an armed conflict between different parties between 25 October 2002 and 15 March 2003. The armed conflict was of both a non-international character and an international character.

According to the arrest warrant, the combatants committed war crimes, such as attacks on the civilian population, rape and torture. They also carried out activities constituting crimes against humanity. All these criminal activities were, according to the statement of the Chamber, in

[53] He is now the president of Central African Republic.

violation of the law of the Statute and were carried out on the basis of Bemba Gombo's, de facto or de jure authority. For many other reasons, the Chamber finally concluded that the arrest of the suspect was necessary.

The Democratic Republic of Congo issued an arrest warrant against Bemba Gombo for high Treason in June 2007. The sealed arrest warrant delivered by the IIC was unsealed on 24 May 2008.[54] This was because the ICC had already made a request to Belgium for his provisional arrest on 23 May. Thereafter, the suspect was arrested by the authorities in Brussels, Belgium after the lifting of the condition, on the same day. On 10 June 2008, the Chamber issued a warrant for arrest replacing the warrant for arrest of 23 May. This was based on the emergence of further evidence and additional charges brought against the suspect.[55] On 10 June, the Court also made a request for the arrest and surrender of the accused and, on 3 July 2008, he was transferred and surrendered to the ICC detention centre in The Hague.

6.5.3. Charges and Admissibility

The Jean-Pierre Bemba Gombo case emanates from the investigation of the Prosecutor into the situation in the Central African Republic. According to the Prosecution, Bemba Gombo has international criminal responsibility according to the provisions of Article 25(3)(a) of the Statute of the ICC. The Prosecution alleges that during an armed conflict from 25th October 2002 and 15th March 2003, many serious crimes were committed in the Central African Republic. Bema Gombo is charged with three counts of crimes against humanity. These are *i)* rape under Article 7(1)(g); *ii)* torture under Article 7(1)(f); and *iii)* murder under Article 7(1)(a). He is also charged with five counts of war crimes. These are *i)* rape under Article 8(2)(e)(vi); *ii)* torture under Article 8(2)(c)(i); *iii)* committing outrages against personal dignity, in particular, humiliating and degrading treatment, under Article 8(2)(c)(ii)); *iv)* pillaging a town or place under Article 8(2)(e)(v); and *v)* murder under Article 8(2)(c)(i). The conclusion is that Bemba Gombo is charged, not only with war crimes, but also with crimes against humanity. Two of the main reasons for the charges have been the role of the accused as the president as well as the commander-in-chief of the Mouvement de Libération du Congo. These positions were essential to the implementation of the common plan between Bemba Gombo and the President Ange-Felic Patasse. In particular, as a result of a decision between the above two persons, the

[54] ICC-01/05-01/08-1.
[55] ICC-01/05-01/08-15.

Mouvement de Libération du Congo sent combatants coming from different interested groups to the Central African Republic to provide an effective contribution to Patasse. The accused should have known that this joint decision would lead to the commission of crimes against humanity and war crimes.

Bemba Gombo has, however, objected to the charges against him. He made his first appearance on 4 July 2008, precisely one day after he was surrendered to the jurisdiction of the ICC by the Belgian authorities. According to the Defence, it was the responsibility of President Patasse to stop the crimes. In particular, it emphasized that the Mouvement de Libération du Congo armed forces were, during the commission of the crimes, under the order of Patasse and not Bemba Gombo. The date for the confirmation of charges hearing by the Chamber has, however, been postponed on several occasions and was only finally carried out on 12 to 15 January 2009. The intention of the hearing was for the Judges of the ICC to decide whether the charges issued by the Prosecutor against the accused should be confirmed in order to send the case to trial. This meant that the confirmation of charges hearing by the Chambers of the ICC functioned as a re-examination of the case to determine whether it should proceed to a trial or be terminated.

In the circumstances, the Office of the Prosecutor submitted an amended document containing the charges including a statement of the international criminal responsibility of the superior.[56] This was pursuant to the provisions of Article 28 of the Statute of the ICC. On 15 June 2009, Pre-Trial Chamber II delivered its decision and accordingly sent the case to trial. The Chamber of the ICC confirmed the charges of rape and murder constituting two counts of crimes against humanity and rape, murder and pillaging constituting three counts of war crimes. The international criminal responsibility of the accused was based on the provisions of Article 28 (a) of the Statute and not Article 25. Article 28 articulates the concept of criminal responsibility of the superior and commander while Article 25 relates to the concept of individual criminal responsibility. The Trial of Bemba Gombo was planned to take place on 5 July 2010,[57] but this date was changed due to administrative reasons as well as the likely change in the composition of the Bench, and also to facilitate the necessary preparation for the commencement of the trial. In

---

[56] Prosecution's Submission of Amended Document Containing the Charges, Amended List of evidence and Amended In-Depth Analysis Chart of Incriminatory Evidence, ICC-01/05-01/08-395; ICC-01/05-01/08-395-Anx3; ICC-01/05-01/08-395-Anx4; ICC-01/05-01/08-395-Anx5.

[57] The interim release of the accused was not granted by the Pre-Trial Chamber II.

October 2010, although Bemba Gombo was charged with three counts of crimes against humanity and five counts of war crimes, the Chamber reduced the charges against him to two counts of crimes against humanity and three counts of war crimes. Furthermore, in November, upon the appeal of Bemba Gombo against the decision of the Trial Chamber III of 28 July 2010 entitled "Decision on the review of the detention of Mr Jean-Pierre Bemba Gombo pursuant to Rule 118(2) of the Rules of Procedure and Evidence", according to which Bemba's detention was continued, the Court delivered the conclusion that:

> 1. The "Decision on the review of the detention of Mr Jean-Pierre Bemba Gombo pursuant to Rule 118(2) of the Rules of Procedure and Evidence" is reversed.
>
> 2. Trial Chamber III is directed to carry out a new review under article 60 (3) of the Statute as to whether Mr Jean Pierre Bemba Gombo should remain in detention or whether he should be released, with or without conditions, in light of paragraphs 40 to 56 of the present judgment. Until, and subject to, that review, Mr Jean-Pierre Bemba Gombo shall remain in detention.[58]

It must be noted that the Bemba Gombo trial has not yet succeeded in proving the accusations. Although the Courts found that there was considerable evidence to believe that a non-international armed conflict had been conducted during the period under review, this finding has not been effective for proving the criminal responsibility of the accused. Nevertheless, the Court has insisted that there is a lack of evidence to suggest that another state had sent military forces to fight against the Central African Republic government.

The Bemba trial effectively began in 2012. According to two experts who testified in defence of Jean-Pierre Bemba Gombo, he should not be held responsible for acts of violence which were conducted under Central African military command. They therefore deny all charges against him. The Bemba trial is still in progress at the ICC in 2013 and the Court has not yet completed the case.[59]

---

[58] The Appeals Chamber, No. ICC-01/05-01/08 OA 4, 19 November 2010.

[59] Also it is relevant to note that Judge Cuno Tarfusser issued a warrant of arrest for Jean-Pierre Bemba Gombo, his lead Counsel Aimé Kilolo Musamba, Jean-Jacques Mangenda Kabongo (a member of Mr Bemba's Defence team and case manager), Fidèle Babala Wandu (a member of the DRC Parliament and Deputy Secretary General of the Mouvement pour la Libération du Congo), and Narcisse Arido (a Defence witness) on 20 November 2013. The warrant of arrest was for offences

6.6. *Bahr Idriss Abu Garda* Case

6.6.1. Position

The Bahr Idriss Abu Garda case concerns the notorious international crimes which were committed in Darfur in Sudan.[60] Abu Garda was the former commander of the Justice and Equality Movement. This was a rebel group which was involved in the Darfur conflict. He is also the leader of the United Resistance Front. This is a rebel group which has long fought against the Sudanese government in the region of Darfur.

The Abu Garda case has a special merit of its own since it does not necessarily concern the Darfur crimes which were committed under the supervision of Al-Bashir. The charges against Abu Garda relate to the 2007 attack in which twelve African Union Peacekeepers who were serving under the auspices of the United Nations were killed. Consequently, Abu Garda was charged by the ICC with war crimes.

6.6.2. Summons

The *Bahr Idriss Abu Garda Case* concerning the commission of war crimes against the peacekeepers of the United Nations missions was presented by Luis Moreno-Ocampo who is the Prosecutor of the International Criminal Court in the ICC.[61] According to the evidence submitted by the Prosecutor in 2007, the attack on the peacekeepers occurred when approximately a thousand rebels surrounded a camp belonging to the African Union peacekeepers in Haskanita in Darfur in Sudan. The attack was carried out with anti-aircraft guns, artillery guns and rocket-propelled grenade launchers. According to the evidence presented by the Prosecutor, a Pre-Trial Chamber found that there were reasonable grounds to believe that Abu Garda, the leader of the United Resistance Front, had the international criminal responsibility for the murder of the twelve soldiers of the African Union peacekeepers.[62] The Pre-Trial Chamber based its findings on three counts of war crimes. These were murder, pillage and intentionally directing attacks against African

---

against the administration of justice allegedly occurred in relation to the case of The Prosecutor v. Jean-Pierre Bemba Gombo.

[60] He born in 1963 in Nanda situated in the North Darfur in Sudan. He is a member of the Zaghawa tribe.

[61] The allegation to the Court was submitted by the Prosecutor on 20 November 2008.

[62] The finding of the Pre-Trial Chamber was on 7 May 2007.

Union installations, material, units or vehicles, and the personnel of the African Union peacekeepers involved in Darfur in Sudan.

One of the most interesting aspects of this case is that the Prosecutor had submitted that there was no need for issuing an arrest warrant concerning Abu Garda. This was based on the fact that the accused had already expressed his willingness to appear before the ICC. Consequently, the Court issued a summons according to which the accused had to be present before the Court on 18 May 2009. In response to the summons, Abu Garda came to The Hague one day before the appearing date. His voluntarily appearance was appreciated by the Court.

6.6.3. Charges and Admissibility

Abu Garda was charged with crimes committed against the African Union peacekeepers. According to the Pre-Trial Chamber, he was accused of three counts of war crimes. These are murder, pillaging and intentionally directing attacks against the installations of peacekeepers. Pre-Trial Chamber I was of the view that there were reasonable grounds to believe that Abu Garda was criminally responsible as a co-perpetrator or as an indirect co-perpetrator under article 25(3)(a) of the Rome Statute. The Pre-Trial Chamber statement read that:

> violence to life in the form of murder, whether committed or attempted, within the meaning of article 8(2)(c)(i) of the Statute;
> intentionally directing attacks against personnel, installations, material, units or vehicles involved in a peacekeeping mission within the meaning of article 8(2)(e)(iii) of the Statute; and
> pillaging within the meaning of article 8(2)(e)(v) of the Statute.[63]

Abu Garda, however, rejected all of the above charges, basing his argument on the claim that he was the victim of a dispute between the United Resistance Front, and Justice and Equality Movement. After his appearance, he left the Court in The Hague. He remained at liberty pending the trial. The next hearing to confirm the charges against Abu Garda was dated 12 October 2009. This date also extended to 8 February 2010. However, because of the examination of the case, the charges against Abu Garda were not confirmed by Pre-Trial Chamber I. Subsequently, the Chamber issued a decision in which it refused the application of the Prosecutor to appeal the decision, declining to confirm the charges. The decision of the Pre-Trial Chamber was taken on 23 April,

[63] The Prosecutor v. Bahr Idriss Abu Garda, ICC-02/05-02/09.

2010. Juridically, the decision of the Chamber is not absolute if new additional evidence is presented implying the guilt of the accused.

6.7. *Callixte Mbarushimana* Case

6.7.1. Position

One of the most recent cases dealt with by the ICC is the *Callixte Mbarushimana case. Callixte,* an ethnic Hutu was born in Northern Rwanda in 1963. He was educated as a technology specialist. *Callixte Mbarushimana* was not only politically active in the Democratic Republic of the Congo, but worked also in the service of the United Nations. This was on a contract with the United Nations Development Programme until 2001. This is the year when he was dismissed from United Nations service. However, he later won a court case in 2004 against his dismissal by the United Nations. Mbarushimana is also alleged to have functioned as the Executive Secretary of the *Forces Démocratiques pour la Libération du Rwanda* since July 2007. *Callixte* is accused of having participated in the murder of 32 persons. He is also accused of having committed crimes against the employees of the United Nations during the Rwandan Genocide.

6.7.2. Arrest Warrant

It is alleged that *Callixte Mbarushimana,* during his services to the United Nations, handed over supplies and vehicles from the organization to the Rwandan militias and, that, at the same time, he was directly involved in murdering people, including the director of personnel at the United Nations Development Programme office. On 11 October 2010, *Callixte Mbarushimana* was arrested by the French authorities on a sealed warrant arrest from the International Criminal Court issued by the Pre-Trial Chamber I on 28 September 2010.

6.7.3. Charges

The charges against *Callixte Mbarushimana* are for crimes against humanity and war crimes which were allegedly committed in Kivus, situated in the Democratic Republic of the Congo. The warrant for arrest addresses the widespread attacks committed by the troops of the Democratic Forces for the Liberation of Rwanda against the population in North and South Kivu. The warrant for arrest emphasises the criminal responsibility of *Callixte* according to the provisions of Article 25 (3)(d) of the Statute of the ICC. This indicates that he is responsible for the following counts of crimes against humanity:

> iv) acts of murder, constituting crimes against humanity under article 7(1)(a) of the Statute;
> vi) acts of torture, constituting crimes against humanity under article 7(1)(f) of the Statute;
> viii) acts of rape, constituting crimes against humanity under article 7(1)(g) of the Statute;
> ix) inhumane acts, constituting crimes against humanity under article 7(1)(k) of the Statute;
> xi) acts of persecution, constituting crimes against humanity under article 7(1)(h) of the Statute.

The warrant for arrest also listed six counts of war crimes. These are:

> i) attacks against the civilian population, constituting war crimes under article 8(2)(b)(i) or 8(2)(e)(i) of the Statute;
> ii) acts of destruction of property, constituting war crimes under article 8(2)(a)(iv) or 8(2)(e)(xii) of the Statute;
> iii) acts of murder, constituting war crimes under article 8(2)(a)(i) or 8(2)(c)(i) of the Statute;
> v) acts of torture, constituting war crimes under article 8(2)(a)(ii) or 8(2)(c)(i) of the Statute;
> vii) acts of rape, constituting war crimes under article 8(2)(b)(xxii) or 8(2)(e)(vi) of the Statute;
> x) acts of inhuman treatment, constituting war crimes under article 8(2)(a)(ii) of the Statute;

All these crimes were, according to the Court, carried out in connection with an armed conflict which was conducted in the Kivu Provinces of the Democratic Republic of the Congo. These crimes were committed between the *Forces Démocratiques pour la Libération du Rwanda - Forces Combattantes Abacunguzi* (FDLR) and the *Forces Armées de la République Démocratique du Congo* (FARDC) together with the Rwandan Defence Forces from 20 January to 25 February 2009. They were also committed between the FDLR and the FARDC from 2 March to 31 December 2009. This is when the United Nations Peacekeeping forces were in Congo.

According to Chamber I, there are reasonable grounds to believe that the *Forces Démocratiques pour la Libération du Rwanda* offensively attacked the population of a considerable number of villages and committed various serious crimes such as rape, torture, murder and the destruction of property.[64] His intention was to ultimately obtain political concessions through different methods including the use of international and local media channels.

6.7.4. Trial

Pre-Trial Chamber I of the International Criminal Court met on 28 January 2011. It decided on the date of the confirmation of charges hearing concerning the *Callixte Mbarushimana case.* The prosecution began its case on 4 July 2011. Callixte *Mbarushimana* was informed of the charges brought against him by the Prosecutor of the ICC and of his rights under the provisions of the Statute of the ICC. The Pre-Trial Chamber examined whether there existed satisfactory evidence to establish substantial grounds to believe that the accused had committed the alleged crimes in North and South Kivu. However, the Pre-Trial Chamber declined to confirm the charge against the accused and stated that there was not sufficient evidence to establish substantial grounds to believe that he had ordered the commission of genocide or rape. In addition, on 30 May 2012, the Appeal Chamber of the ICC rejected the appeal of the Prosecutor against the decision not to prosecute *Mbarushimana*.

6.8. Other Cases

There are several other persons who are the subject of arrest warrants issued by the ICC. However, their cases have been suspended because of legal or political hindrances to their arrest and surrender to the Court. One of the cases relates to the situation in Uganda and the commission of war crimes and crimes against humanity in that region. The names of four persons are consequently on the list of the arrest warrant of the Court. These are Joseph Kony, Vincent Otti, Okot Odhiambo and Dominic Ongwen.[65] Their arrest warrant was issued under seal on 8 July 2005 and unsealed on 13 October. None of the above suspected persons appeared in the Court.

---

[64] These were of Busheke in Kalehe territory, South Kivu; Kipopo in Masisi territory, North Kivu; Mianga in Waloa-Loanda *groupement*, Walikale territory, North Kivu; Luofu and Kasiki in Lubero territory, North Kivu; Busurungi in Walikale territory, North Kivu; Manje in Masisi territory, North Kivu; and Malembe in Waloa-Loanda *groupement*, Walikale territory, and North Kivu.

[65] Case the Prosecutor, v. Joseph Kony, Vincent Otti, Okot Odhiambo and Dominic Ongwen, ICC-02/04-01/05.

The second and third cases refer to the situation in Darfur, Sudan, and the murders or genocide of a large number of the population of the region. The second suspended case is the arrest warrant issued for Ahmad Muhammad Harun and Ali Muhammad Ali Abd-Al-Rahman on 2 May 2007.[66] The Third concerns the President of Sudan namely Omar Hassan Ahmad Al Bashir who is one of the most wanted persons for serious violations of the Statute of the ICC. His arrest warrant was issued by the Pre-Trial Chamber I on 4 March 2009. Al Bashir has refused to accept his case and has worked continuously for the withdrawal of the warrant for his arrest.[67]

The arrest warrant for Al Bashir has listed seven counts concerning his individual criminal responsibility under Article 25(3)(a) of the Statute as an indirect (co-)perpetrator. This includes five counts of crimes against humanity: murder - Article 7(1)(a); extermination - Article 7(1)(b); forcible transfer - Article 7(1)(d); torture – Article 7(1)(f); and rape - Article 7(1)(g). There are also two counts of war crimes. These include intentionally directing attacks against a civilian population as such or against individual civilians not taking part in hostilities -Article 8(2)(e)(i); and pillaging - Article 8(2)(e)(v).[68] The ICC's hope is that the Al Bashir case will be dealt with according to the complementarity power of the Court and the victims may see that criminal justice has been achieved. Nevertheless, the president of Sudan has refused to accept the demands of the Prosecutor of the ICC and has not yielded himself to the Court. Similarly, most of the other states in the region have supported Al-Bashir and have therefore refused to cooperate with the ICC for his arrest.

6.9. Future Enhancement of the ICC

The cases which have been brought before the jurisdiction of the ICC demonstrate that the principle of complementarity and the principle of internationality may be strong enough to deal with the criminal responsibility of the suspected persons. The cases also support the thesis that the system of international criminal law cannot always be applied by national criminal courts. This is based on the fact that national criminal courts may not be able to accomplish their roles, and even that in many situations they may not bar impunity. Therefore access to the accused, criminal and suspected persons may be difficult and violations may be

[66] Case The Prosecutor v. Ahmad Muhammad Harun ("Ahmad Harun") and Ali Muhammad Ali Abd-Al-Rahman ("Ali Kushayb"), ICC-02/05-01/07.
[67] The Prosecutor V. Omar Hassan Ahmad Al Bashir, ICC-02/05-01/09.
[68] See also other sections.

continued without any progrees on the part of the international legal and political community in the interest of the victims.

These cases also imply the fact that the principles of complementarity and internationality are not workable when there is a strong tendency in certain states not to submit the accused before the jurisdiction of the Court. A clear example is the Omar Hassan Ahmad al-Bashir case concerning the notorious international crimes committed in Darfur under his presidency in Sudan. He has not yet been brought before the Court and has established good relations with the neighbouring states. Consequently, his case has been suspended before the jurisdiction of the Court without any further effective measures being taken against him.

The al-Bashir case also points to the existence of a double morality in the international criminal system and its shortcomings in other similar situations. A clear example is the Gaza Strip crimes which were committed under the authority of the Israeli government.[69] Other examples are the commission of serious international crimes in Iraq under the supervision of Tony Blair and George W. Bush or grave violations of the international humanitarian law of armed conflicts, war crimes, crimes against humanity, genocide and aggression under the administration of Barack Hussein Obama. None of the above-mentioned persons or members of governments have been brought before the Court. Similarly, the crimes committed against the Iranian population under the presidency of Mahmoud Ahmadinejad have not been treated by the Court either. A comparable conclusion can be reached regarding Muammar Muhammad al-Gaddafi, the Libyan leader who was killed before an investigation was opened in an international criminal court.

Consequently, the system of international criminal justice which has been established under the Statute of the Court is very weak and needs particular attention under the supervision of the Assembly of States Parties. In other words, the member states must realise that the system of international criminal law should be applied not only to those who are easily arrested by the police authorities and are no longer serious criminals, but should also be applied to all those who have finished or not finished their term of office and are protected by the policy of their home states.

---

[69] Farhad Malekian, 'Judging International Criminal Justice in the Occupied Territories', 12 *International Criminal Law Review* (2012) 827–869.

CHAPTER ELEVEN

NON-TRIAL JUSTICE

1. Overview

The principles of international criminal justice may be fulfilled by different means. The chief purpose of international criminal justice is principally to deter international violations and bring the perpetrators of crimes under the proceedings of jurisdiction for prosecution and punishment.[1] Meanwhile, international criminal justice attempts to create international peace, security, equality before the law and to put an end to impunity.[2]

The purposes of the system of international criminal justice can be achieved by national, regional or international criminal courts. However, it is possible that in certain situations, states may not, for one reason or another, wish to implement the principles of international criminal law against the perpetrators of international crimes. These may generally depend on the juridical or political conditions of the time. Thus, criminals can fully or partly be exempted from prosecution and punishment without any need to appear in the proceedings of a criminal court.

The above situation can occur when a large number of people have been involved, have participated or abetted in the preparation of the criminal acts and when the relevant society is willing, for one reason or another, to forgive but not forget the crimes committed under a particular government. For this, or other similar reasons, they may create a truth or conciliation commission, which is empowered to investigate the cases and hear the victims of the offences. In some situations, the criminals may be granted amnesty for their criminally wrongful conduct because it is impossible to prosecute them. The society may also want to move forward and mitigate the probability of future conflicts between different national groups. This means that it has to deal with prior criminal actions with a

---

[1] Broomhall Bruce, International Justice and the International Criminal Court: Between Sovereignty and the Rule of Law (2003).

[2] *Id.*

policy that creates less conflict and which, at the same time, leaves the victims satisfied by the decision.

The philosophy behind the amnesty or truth commissions is very sophisticated and controversial. This situation may lead to impunity and in many cases the violation of the social rights of the community and the theory of international criminal justice. This is because criminal justice must be fulfilled and applied in accordance with the principle of proportionality and should not be limited. In other words, international criminal justice should not, in principle, discriminate between its subjects through the application or non-application of its basic principles. In this chapter, we focus, therefore, on some of these non-trial courts and the questions of the accountability of minor or high officials, including heads of state, before certain national courts.

2. Grounds for Non-Trial Courts

In the event of serious violations of international treaties and the repeated commission of crimes by certain governments, the aim of the international community has been to criminalize the internationally wrongful conduct of states or governments including those who are acting as the official authorities of the relevant states or their agents. But it has most often been impossible to bring the perpetrators of crimes under an appropriate criminal jurisdiction for prosecution and punishment. The reasons for this impunity and non-punishment of criminals may vary from one nation to another or from one government to the other. These may be:

- Political reasons,
- Religious reasons,
- Impossibility of implementation,
- Non-existence of sufficient evidence,
- Threat of more violence,
- Violations of human rights principles,
- To strengthen the violated integrity of victims in order to protect their families,
- Protection of females,
- Protection of children,
- Development of a common understanding of one another,
- Decreasing social problems,
- Increasing educational norms,
- Economic costs,
- Cultural factors,

- International political factors,
- International juridical factors,
- The impossibility of punishing a large proportion of the population of a county,
- The granting of asylum by different countries,
- The risk of armed conflicts,
- The non-existence of an appropriate national criminal jurisdiction,
- A political agreement between the victors and oppressors,
- Non-trial as a condition for relinquishing power,
- The sole way to end tyranny, and
- The strong will of a nation to move away from past history.

It is in situations such as the above that the truth commission may be established or amnesty given in order to forgive and to mitigate the punishment.

3. Truth Commission

A truth commission is a body which is established under the authority of a government with the task of discovering the past crimes of the former government/regime with the purpose of exempting the criminals, in one way or another, from prosecution and punishment. A truth commission may also be named a reconciliation commission, as it has been authorised in a special emergency situation. Here the purpose is not the non-application of criminal sanction, but the resolving of the situation in an elaborate manner that may result in the fulfilment of certain primary conditions in favour of the victims.

The purpose of the truth commission is thus to collect proof of the acts of government authorities which have been engaged in the commission of serious national or international crimes and grave abuses of the principles of international human rights law. One of the most well-known truth commissions was assembled in South Africa by the new government in order to investigate and provide evidence of the commission of apartheid by the authorities of the previous government. The victims of apartheid were asked to come to this non-trial court which was intended for the reconciliation of the victims. However, the task of South Africa's Truth and Reconciliation Commission was not easy. The negotiations were started in 1990.[3] It endeavoured to forge a compromise between two

[3] www.info.gov.za/otherdocs/2003/trc/ - 21k. Visited on 2008-03-19.

particular groups that had different opinions concerning forgiveness.[4] As a whole, an Amnesty Committee was established and amnesty applications were submitted to the Committee in order to get full amnesty or amnesty in part from the application of criminal sanctions.[5] As a general rule, the Committee took a political decision, but based it on the theological and ethical understanding of the situation.

Some of the most well-known truth commissions, which have been created after the commission of serious international crimes and violations of the fundamental principles of international human rights law, are the following:

The National Commission on the Disappearances of persons, Argentina, 1983.[6]

The United Nations Truth Commission in El Salvador, 1992/3.[7]

---

[4] According to the Promotion of National Unity and Reconciliation Act of 1995, the following Act was declared: "To provide for the investigation and the establishment of as complete a picture as possible of the nature, causes and extent of gross violations of human rights committed during the period from 1 March 1960 to the cut-off date contemplated in the Constitution, within or outside the Republic, emanating from the conflicts of the past, and the fate or whereabouts of the victims of such violations; the granting of amnesty to persons who make full disclosure of all the relevant facts relating to acts associated with a political objective committed in the course of the conflicts of the past during the said period; affording victims an opportunity to relate the violations they suffered; the taking of measures aimed at the granting of reparation to, and the rehabilitation and the restoration of the human and civil dignity of, victims of violations of human rights; reporting to the Nation about such violations and victims; the making of recommendations aimed at the prevention of the commission of gross violations of human rights; and for the said purposes to provide for the establishment of a Truth and Reconciliation Commission, a Committee on Human Rights Violations, a Committee on Amnesty and a Committee on Reparation and Rehabilitation; and to confer certain powers on, assign certain functions to and impose certain duties upon that Commission and those Committees; and to provide for matters connected therewith."

[5] Consult also www.info.gov.za/otherdocs/2003/trc/ - 21k. Visited on 2011-03-19.

[6] The Commission was an Argentinean organisation created by President Raul Alfonsin in order to properly investigate the human rights law violations in Argentina.

[7] The duty of this Commission was to investigate crimes against humanity which were committed from 1980 to 1991. The Commission was in fact the result of a peace agreement. The Commission had to work with "the exceptional importance that may be attached to the acts to be investigated, their characteristics and impact, and the social unrest to which they gave rise." The United Nations, Mexico Agreements, 27 April 1991, Commission on the Truth, "Functions" section, para.2 (a). Document A/46/553-S/23130, p. 16.

The Historical Clarification Commission, Guatemala, 1994.[8]
The Truth and Reconciliation Commission, Chile, 1994.[9]
Haiti's Truth and Justice Commission, 1994.
The Truth and Reconciliation Commission, Sierra Leone, 1999.
The Truth Commission, Panama, 2001.
The Truth and Reconciliation Commission, Peru, 2001.
The National Reconciliation Commission, Ghana, 2002.
The Truth and Reconciliation Commission (Liberia), agreed upon in 2003 and established in accordance with 2005 legislation.
The Moroccan Equity and Reconciliation Commission, 2004.
The National Commission on Political Imprisonment and Torture, Chile, 2004/5.
The Reconciliation and Unity Commission, Fiji, 2005.
The Truth and Reconciliation Commission, Republic of Korea, South Korea, 2005.
The Commission for Reception, Truth and Reconciliation in East Timor, 2002.[10]
Greensboro Truth and Reconciliation Commission, United States, 2001.

---

[8] The Commission was created on the basis of an agreement between the Guatemalan government and the National Guatemalan Revolutionary Unit. Its task was to investigate violations of international human rights law during the 36-year armed conflict in Guatemala.

[9] Some of the purposes of the Commission were "to establish as complete a picture as possible of human rights violations under the Pinochet regime; to gather evidence to allow for victims to be identified; to recommend reparations; and to recommend legal and administrative measures to prevent a repetition of past abuses."
www.beyondintractability.org/case_studies/Chilean_Truth_Commission.jsp?nid=5221 - 34k -. Visited on 2008-10-29.

[10] The United Nations has strongly condemned amnesty for human rights violators and war criminals. But see Suzannah Linton, *Indonesia and Accountability for Serious Crimes in East Timor, in* International Criminal Law, vol iii (M. cherif Bassiouni, ed. 2008) pp. 399-406; Suzannah Linton, *East Timor and Accountability for Serious Crimes, in* International Criminal Law, vol iii (M. cherif Bassiouni, ed. 2008) pp. 257-282.

4. Amnesty

4.1. Substance

The term "amnesty" implies forgiveness of the crimes which have been committed during a particular time under the supervision of the authorities of a government. Thus, amnesty is a general pardon given to the perpetrators. Amnesty is mostly granted in the case of mass criminality with the purpose of allowing the continuation of the political, juridical or economic life of the society.

The granting of amnesty has been practiced since 403 BC in Athens and has also been granted at other times during the civilisation of mankind. For instance, Abraham Lincoln granted amnesty and entire oblivion for the past by the Proclamation of Amnesty and Reconstruction to all those who had committed crimes during the rebellion in the United States. It was also supposed to be granted after 1945 to war criminals, but was not accepted by the United States. However, the United States selected and later pardoned war criminals in its custody on the condition that they helped the United States during the Cold War.[11]

In general, the scope of amnesty and truth commissions is sometimes similar and it is very difficult to underline the differences between them here. Both may be described as giving forgiveness to certain criminals and their frameworks for pardon, reconciliation, indemnity and understanding of the situation are almost identical. However, one cannot deny that the principle of amnesty has, more often, been used in order to ignore or reduce punishment for grave violations of the fundamental principles of human rights law, which have been committed by a dictatorial or fanatical regime in a country.[12]

---

[11] Peter Krapp, *Amnesty: Between an Ethics of Forgiveness and the Politics of Forgetting,* 6 German Law Journal (2005). For the cold war period see Michael C. Davis, Wolfgang Dietrich, Bettina Scholdan, Dieter Sepp, International Intervention in the Post-Cold War World: Moral Responsibility and Power Politics (2003).

[12] For instance, the present Iranian regime gave amnesty to those who were serving under the SAVAK organization, being one of the most notorious organs working under the direct order of the last Iranian Shah. The duties of the members of the organization were to report different political activities inside and outside Iranian territories in order to arrest Iranians and if necessary to kill them and hinder any political gathering. Many members of the SAVAK staff were later accepted to work under the secret police security system of the Islamic regime or are working with other governments in the world. Ironically, some of them have also occupied professorial chairs of *international law/human rights* law in Europe or other parts

4.2. Categories of Amnesties

Generally speaking, there are two different categories of amnesty. These are limited and blanket amnesty. Limited amnesty implies the granting of amnesty to a limited number of criminals, whilst blanket amnesty implies the granting of amnesty to almost all perpetrators of criminal conduct.

The granting of a blanket amnesty may seriously violate the foundation of international criminal justice. Therefore, there have been different arguments concerning the permitting or not permitting of the use of amnesty. Some arguments are based on the provisions of Article 6 (5) of Protocol II relating to the Protection of Victims of Non-International Armed Conflict.[13] According to the article: "At the end of hostilities, the authorities in power shall endeavour to grant the broadest possible amnesty to persons who have participated in the armed conflict, or those deprived of their liberty for reasons related to the armed conflict, whether they are interned or detained."[14] The afore-mentioned provisions, it is argued, cover those combating the State and not those acting as its agents. Moreover, there is, in certain special situations, a strong tendency in the system of international criminal justice to grant amnesty solely to minor perpetrators and not to superiors or heads of states. In particular, relating to certain core crimes, the concept of amnesty is strongly rejected.[15]

---

of the world. They are simultaneously working in the universities of the Islamic Republic of Iran where they teach, *inter alia*, human rights, United Nations law, sea laws or sovereign independence. According to the definite policy of the last Iranian Shah, it was almost impossible for a person to work in his foreign departments/embassies if he/she had not given an oath and had not accepted to work, assist, cooperate and share in SAVAK's criminal activities. Similarly, oaths are taken from all workers in foreign embassies by the present dictatorial regime of Iran.

[13] Consult International Committee of the Red Cross. *Commentary on the Additional Protocols of 8 June 1977 to the Geneva Conventions of 12 August 1949.* Geneva: International Committee of the Red Cross, 1987.

[14] Protocol Additional to the Geneva Conventions of 12 August 1949, and Relating to the Protection of Victims of Non-International Armed Conflicts, June 8, 1977, Article 6 (5), 1125 UNTS.609, 614.

[15] According to the Report of the Secretary-General on the Establishment of a Special Court for Sierra Leone, the questions of amnesty were also tackled. The Secretary General rejected any concept of amnesty relating to certain serious international crimes. He explained in the report that "(w)hile recognizing that amnesty is an accepted legal concept and a gesture of peace and reconciliation at the end of a civil war or an internal armed conflict, the United Nations has consistently maintained the position that amnesty cannot be granted in respect of international crimes, such as genocide, crimes against humanity or other serious

4.3. Defects of Forgiveness

As a whole, neither truth commissions nor amnesties may be recommended under the principles of international criminal justice. This is because their aims and purposes may strongly diminish the effect of the application of appropriate international criminal justice. In fact, the result may be that different political groups, depending on the consequences of their criminal actions, may bargain away the application of the system of international criminal justice. Amnesty or truth commissions may affect the proceedings for the finding of certain historical facts and eventually encourage criminal behaviour between different political parties or terrorism based on the fact that crimes may be given pardon by the newly established political powers. Consequently, as a consolidated principle of international criminal justice and human rights law, amnesty should not be granted when it concerns certain crimes such as genocide, serious violations of international humanitarian law and crimes against humanity, including torture, apartheid and rape. The reason for this is that these crimes are the concern of the international community and their prosecution and punishment aim at the safeguarding of the fundamental principles of humanity, which should not be pardoned by acts of amnesty or reconciliation committees.

---

violations of international humanitarian law. At the time of the signature of the Lomé Peace Agreement, the Special Representative of the Secretary-General for Sierra Leone was instructed to append to his signature on behalf of the United Nations a disclaimer to the effect that the amnesty provision contained in article IX of the Agreement ("absolute and free pardon") shall not apply to international crimes of genocide, crimes against humanity, war crimes and other serious violations of international humanitarian law. This reservation is recalled by the Security Council in a preambular paragraph of resolution 1315 (2000). In the negotiations on the Statute of the Special Court, the Government of Sierra Leone concurred with the position of the United Nations and agreed to the inclusion of an amnesty clause which would read as follows: "An amnesty granted to any person falling within the jurisdiction of the Special Court in respect of the crimes referred to in articles 2 to 4 of the present Statute shall not be a bar to prosecution."With the denial of legal effect to the amnesty granted at Lomé, to the extent of its illegality under international law, the obstacle to the determination of a beginning date of the temporal jurisdiction of the Court within the pre-Lomé period has been removed." Report of the Secretary-General on the Establishment of a Special Court for Sierra Leone, UN Doc. S/2000/915, paras.22-24.

CHAPTER TWELVE

THE POSITION OF INTERNATIONAL CRIMINAL JUSTICE IN *JUS COGENS* LAW

1. Characterisation

The rapid evolution of the system of international criminal law in the literature of the discipline of jurisprudence and the strong consolidation of certain norms of this law in the international legal community for the purpose of the effective protection of the fundamental rights of man from different types of violations is unavoidable.[1] This evolution has given recognition to norms of international criminal law that cannot be denied in state practice. These norms are included in the framework of *jus cogens*. Thus, *jus cogens* norms refer to norms, the respect of which is fundamentally essential for the safeguarding of the principles of natural and positive law and the maintenance of international equality, justice and peace.

The ideas behind the recognition of certain norms constituting *jus cogens* norms are indeed numerous and cannot be discussed here. As a whole, the purpose of identifying certain norms of international criminal law under *jus cogens* norms is to emphasise the significant character of the norms from which no derogation is permitted. Some of these norms are

---

[1] The norms are not only developed from the history of international criminal law, but also from the law of the Nuremberg Tribunal, Tokyo Tribunal, ICTY, ICTR and ICC. Even some of the functions of the ICTY and ICTR will be continued after completion of their works by the Mechanism for International Criminal Tribunals (MICT) created by the Security Council in 2010. The MICT is supposed for Completion Strategies of the two Tribunals. In fact, the MICT takes over the task of the "jurisdiction, rights and obligations and essential functions" of the previous tribunals. Even many believe that the recognition of specific norms of international criminal justice is not an invention of the 20th century. "Rather, the roots of this development may, apparently, be traced to the threshold of the 16th century." Albin Eser, "Towards an International Criminal Court: Genesis and Main Feature of the Rome Statute", *Vol.20, n.1 University of Tasmania Law Review (2001),* pp.-28, at 3.

rules prohibiting torture, crimes against humanity, genocide, aggression, slavery, apartheid and war crimes. Thus, with the term *jus cogens* we do not necessarily mean only the prohibition but also the prevention of the commission of certain international crimes. This is because *jus cogens* norms have several characteristics which are an integral part of their nature and cannot therefore be separated from their existing forms. These are, for example, prohibitions, preventions, exterminations, prosecutions and punishments of the acts of genocide which are an integral part of the response to this international crime and have to be respected and followed by all means. This means that by identifying certain provisions as constituting genocide and also identifying *jus cogens* norms, the aim is to eliminate the occurrence of genocide, not only by establishing provisions, but also in changing the practice of nations, large or small.

Similarly, the purpose of the recognition of apartheid as an integral part of *jus cogens* laws is to emphasise the prohibition of this crime on an international level. It is supposed to prevent the crime by an international standard and with international force. This is because, when we speak of a crime as an international crime having the international character of *jus cogens*, we simultaneously want to prohibit the act by all means available without regard to the territory in which the act is committed. The reason for this interpretation is based on the fact that the effect of certain international crimes is so serious and hazardous that they violate the integrity of mankind and this cannot be ignored on the basis of the territoriality effect of such international crimes. Thus, with the term *jus cogens*, the aim is to protect the integrity of mankind from any unlawful and inhuman action that is not permitted by law or morality. Consequently, the term *"jus cogens"* does not only mean internationalisation of the effect of the crime but also the globalisation of prosecution and punishment for the purpose of the prevention of the crime in the future. The *Bosco Ntaganda Case* highlights why the Statute of the ICC provides a variety of means for the punishment of those who commit international crimes. States parties which are, for one reason or another, incapable of punishing the perpetrators of international crimes, may seek assistance from the ICC. A number of states, such as the Central African Republic, the Democratic Republic of the Congo, Mali and Uganda, have requested the assistance of the Court. In addition, the Security Council has asked the Court to initiate appropriate investigations for the purpose of the prosecution and punishment of those who have committed international crimes in Darfur, Sudan and Libya. Neither of these states is a state party.[2] More recently,

[2] However, both cases denote the monopolization of international criminal justice by the Security Council and the political instrumentality of the Court. See Farhad

Rios Montt the former chief of military intelligence in Guatemala has been found guilty of genocide and will face punishment.[3]

2. Permission

Without doubt the crimes, which are listed under the Statute of the ICC, have a *jus cogens* character and are prosecutable and punishable accordingly. This is based on the fact that crimes against humanity, war crimes, genocide and aggression have long been recognised as crimes, the consequence of which reaches the heart of every human being. This means that because of the nature of the crimes, every nation in the world may prosecute and punish the perpetrators of the crimes by all means permitted by national or international rules. In fact, the ICC has an important function in the identification, recognition, prosecution and punishment of the crimes within its jurisdiction. In other words, its international legal personality permits it to have jurisdiction over *jus cogens* crimes, the prosecution and punishment of which are necessary for the safeguarding of the fundamental rights of man and for the restoration of equality, justice and peace. By all this, however, we do not mean that the basic principles of international human rights law may have to be violated for the purpose of the prevention, prosecution and punishment of *jus cogens* crimes. On the contrary, we mean that international human rights law, in particular of the type represented by the ICC, has to be respected by all means in all possible situations.

Therefore, the position is very simple. If the crimes under the Statute of the ICC constitute *jus cogens* crimes and the ICC has the power to prosecute these crimes, its jurisdiction must also have a *jus cogens* character. In other words, whenever a court is authorised to act over certain *jus cogens* crimes, it has also received the international community's recognition of its power over certain crimes. *Jus cogens* crimes are enforceable over all nations, and individuals of any nation, big or small, may be found guilty of committing *jus cogens* crimes. Consequently, they are answerable before national courts or international tribunals, and accordingly the Court has, in certain cases, the capacity to

---

Malekian, *The Monopolization of International Criminal Law in the United Nations* (1995).

[3] Between 100, 000 and 200,000 Guatemalans were killed in the 1960 to 1996 civil war. A vast number of international human rights law violations such as murder, torture, rape and illegal imprisonment were carried out, mostly against the indigenous Maya peoples. Rios Montt ordered the genocide of 1,771 people of the Lxil Maya ethnic group.

implement rules from which no derogation is permitted. These are *jus cogens* norms. As a result, the ICC only deals with *jus cogens* crimes and since *jus cogens* norms must be respected by all states without regard to their signature or ratification, the ICC rules of procedures, prosecutions and punishments may, sooner or later, be considered as an integral part of *jus cogens* legislation from which no disobedience is permitted by any state.

The question is, however, what measures the ICC may take concerning crimes against humanity, war crimes, genocide and aggression when one or several of them have been committed by the individuals of a state which is not a party to the Statute. A state may even claim the immunity of certain individuals from a criminal process in the light of national criminal provisions. However, the principles of the ICC denote quite the contrary. This means that the concept of the immunity of heads of state to criminal prosecution is without any support in international criminal law. The Statute of the Court reads that "official capacity as a Head of State or Government, a member of a Government or parliament, an elected representative or a government official shall in no case exempt a person from criminal responsibility under this Statute." In the *Abdoulaye Yerodia Ndombasi* case,[4]the International Court of Justice clearly stated that although it is true that a head of state could not be prosecuted under the criminal jurisdiction in Belgium based on his national immunities,[5] she/he

[4] He was one of the four vice-presidents of Congo under the transitional government in 2003.

[5] The authorities in Belgium had based their argumentation on universal jurisdiction which was rejected by the International Court of Justice. The Court went further and stated that "The Court found that the issue and international circulation by Belgium of the arrest warrant of 11 April 2000 against Abdulaye Yerodia Ndombasi failed to respect the immunity from criminal jurisdiction and the inviolability which the incumbent Minister for Foreign Affairs of the Congo enjoyed under international law; and that Belgium must cancel the arrest warrant. In its Judgment, which is final, without appeal and binding for the Parties, the Court found, by 13 votes to 3, "that the issue against Mr. Abdulaye Yerodia Ndombasi of the arrest warrant of 11 April 2000, and its international circulation, constituted violations of a legal obligation of the Kingdom of Belgium towards the Democratic Republic of the Congo, in that they failed to respect the immunity from criminal jurisdiction and the inviolability which the incumbent Minister for Foreign Affairs of the Democratic Republic of the Congo enjoyed under international law"; and, by 10 votes to 6, "that the Kingdom of Belgium must, by means of its own choosing, cancel the arrest warrant of 11 April 2000 and so inform the authorities to whom that warrant was circulated". The Court reached these findings after having found, by 15 votes to 1, that it had jurisdiction, that the Application of the Democratic Republic of the Congo ("the Congo") was not

was subject to prosecution according to the provisions of international criminal courts.[6] Therefore, the Court has stated that:

> An incumbent or former Minister for Foreign Affairs may be subject to criminal proceedings before certain international criminal courts, where they have jurisdiction. Examples include the International Criminal Tribunal for the former Yugoslavia, and the International Criminal Tribunal for Rwanda, established pursuant to Security Council resolutions under Chapter VII of the United Nations Charter, and the future International Criminal Court created by the 1998 Rome Convention. The latter's Statute expressly provides, in Article 27, paragraph 2, that 'immunities or special procedural rules which may attach to the official capacity of a person, whether under national or international law, shall not bar the Court from exercising its jurisdiction over such a person.[7]

At first glance, it would seem difficult to apply the provisions of the Statute to the individuals of a state which is not a party. This is because the Statute applies to states which have signed and ratified it in accordance with its provisions. A state that has not ratified the Statute may reject the jurisdiction of the Court over its nationals and may legally reject any claim concerning this matter. At the same time, it is very difficult and problematic to accept that crimes against humanity, war crimes and genocide, which have achieved the position of *jus cogens* norms, may only be prosecuted and punished within those states who are parties to the Statute. In other words, the provisions of the Statute cannot by themselves limit the scope of *jus cogens* crimes and their attribution.

More clearly, the crime of genocide, because of its very inhuman nature, is punishable by any state and a state cannot claim that since it has not ratified the convention on genocide, it may commit genocide. The provisions of *jus cogens* oblige any nation to respect the convention on

---

without object (and the case accordingly not moot) and that the Application was admissible, thus rejecting the objections which the Kingdom of Belgium ("Belgium") had raised on those questions." The conclusion is that the prosecution of a head of state has to be exercised by international criminal courts which means that heads of state cannot escape their criminal responsibility before international criminal courts. This principle is, at present, exercised by many *ad hoc* international criminal tribunals. ICJ rejects Belgian arrest warrant for foreign ministers of Democratic Republic of Congo, United Nations Information Service. Copy of The International Court of Justice, Press Release 2002/042002 issued on 14 February 2002.

[6] *Arrest Warrant 11 April 2000 (Democratic Republic of Congo v. Belgium),* Judgment, 14 February 2002, para.61.

[7] *Id.*

genocide and avoid any act which is assimilated to genocide. *Jus cogens* crimes are not recognised based on the ratification of treaties but on their grave infringement of the integrity of mankind. These crimes are also more obviously an integral part of customary international criminal law. Thus, those who commit genocide are enemies of mankind and may be arrested and brought before a court for prosecution and punishment regardless of whether their governments have ratified the convention. It is also the same in the case of war crimes, involvement in slavery, crimes against humanity and torture.

3. International Personality

One may argue that it is the international legal personality of states which gives them the authority to act against international crimes and bring perpetrators of crimes under their own jurisdiction for prosecution and punishment. Therefore, the identification of certain actions as constituting international crimes and the recognition of certain crimes under the *jus cogens* norms as well as the international legal personality of states create the power of jurisdiction over the perpetrators. This means that individuals by themselves are not permitted to bring the perpetrators of international crimes under prosecution and punishment. No individual may by himself/herself act against the violators of international crimes under his/her own capacity. It is solely under the international legal personality of states or entities acting as international criminal tribunals that the perpetrators of international crimes may be prosecuted and punished.

Alongside the above facts and arguments, one may also state that since the ICC has, in accordance with its constitution, received an international legal personality, it has the power of jurisdiction over all perpetrators of the relevant crimes regardless of whether or not their countries have ratified the Statute of the ICC. This authority may also be exercised in accordance with the principle of universality concerning certain international crimes.[8] In other words, the limitation within its Statute on

---

[8] The principle of universality permits a state or the ICC to bring a person under its jurisdiction for prosecution and punishment. See also Marc Henzelin, Le principe de l'universalité en droit pénal international (2000); Kenneth C. Randell, *Universal Jurisdiction Under International Law,* 66 Texas Law Review 785 (1988); Leila Nadya Sadat, *Universal Jurisdiction and National Amnesties, Truth Commissions and Other Alternatives to Prosecution: Giving Justice a Chance,* Princeton Project on Universal Jurisdiction (2001). See *also* Albin Eser, "For Universal Jurisdiction: Against Fletcher's Antagonism", Vol.39, no.4 *Tulsa Law Review* (2004), pp.955-978.

the prosecution of those individuals whose governments are not parties is solely conventional and its jurisdiction is not restricted concerning *jus cogens* norms.

Even though the international legal personality of the ICC is limited to the crimes listed in its Statute, it is not limited in the case of *jus cogens* crimes. And since the crimes within the Statute are also *jus cogens* crimes, the ICC has the power of jurisdiction over all states regardless of their ratification. With analogy to the provisions of the United Nations, this also suggests that the obligations of the members under the Charter, in the event of a conflict, do not prevail over *jus cogens* norms. In other words, the provisions of Article 103 of the Charter cannot be read as permitting deviations from the norms from which no derogation is possible.[9]*Jus cogens* is the basis for the ICC's jurisdiction over all states of the world and also a limitation of the power of the United Nations Security Council to prevent the establishment of the ICC's primacy of jurisdiction over *jus cogens* crimes.

4. Obligations *Erga Omnes*

The intention for the development of the system of international criminal justice is not only to bring the perpetrators of international crimes before an international criminal jurisdiction for the application of appropriate punishment, but also to strengthen the policy of prevention and implementation regarding *jus cogens* crimes. These are those crimes that have the character of creating obligations *erga omnes*. This means obligations which all states have a legal interest in upholding. In fact, due to the universal character of obligations *erga omnes* all states of the world have duties to maintain their legal nature. These duties of states are undeniable and are recognised as duties towards the international human community as a whole. Clear examples of obligations *erga omens* are crimes against humanity, war crimes, torture, genocide, slavery and apartheid, racial discrimination or prohibition of sexual exploitation of children in any form and by any means. Consequently, any state in the world regardless of whether it is a member of the United Nations or not, has a right to bring a complaint before international courts and ask for its resolution according to legal measures.

---

[9] Article 3 of the United Nations Charter reads that "In the event of a conflict between the obligations of the Members of the United Nations under the present Charter and their obligations under any other international agreement, their obligations under the present Charter shall prevail."

The concept of obligations *erga omens* was recognised in the decision of the International Court of Justice concerning the *Barcelona Traction* case. The Court stated that:

> …an essential distinction should be drawn between the obligations of a State towards the international community as a whole, and those arising vis-à-vis another State in the field of diplomatic protection. By their very nature, the former are the concern of all States. In view of the importance of the rights involved, all States can be held to have a legal interest in their protection; they are obligations erga omnes. [at 34] Such obligations derive, for example, in contemporary international law, from the outlawing of acts of aggression, and of genocide, as also from the principles and rules concerning the basic rights of the human person, including protection from slavery and racial discrimination. Some of the corresponding rights of protection have entered into the body of general international law … others are conferred by international instruments of a universal or quasi-universal character.[10]

Obligations *erga omnes* in international criminal law are those obligations of international criminal law which are beyond any doubt an integral part of customary or conventional international criminal law, irrespective of their acceptance or ratification by all states of the world. This is also true regardless of whether a state or states have, according to the provisions of the international law of treaties, adhered to those obligations of *erga omnes* and duly incorporated the provisions of customary or conventional international criminal law into their national criminal law. The International Court of Justice, in its judgment concerning the *Genocide* case, *Bosnia and Herzegovina v. Yugoslavia*, clearly stated that the statute of territorial provisions does not embrace rights and obligations which have the character of obligations *erga omens*. Therefore, the Court after various investigations of the case stated that:

> … as to the territorial problems linked to the application of the Convention, the Court would point out that the only provision relevant to this, Article VI, merely provides for persons accused of one of the acts prohibited by the Convention to "be tried by a competent tribunal of the State in the territory of which the act was committed …" It would also recall its understanding of the object and purpose of the Convention, as set out in its Opinion of 28 May 1951, cited above:
>
> The origins of the Convention show that it was the intention of the United Nations to condemn and punish genocide as "a crime under international

[10] ICJ Rep 1970 3 at paragraphs 33-34.

law" involving a denial of the right of existence of entire human groups, a denial which shocks the conscience of mankind and results in great losses to humanity, and which is contrary to moral law and to the spirit and aims of the United Nations (Resolution 96 (I) of the General Assembly, December 11th 1946). The first consequence arising from this conception is that the principles underlying the Convention are principles which are recognized by civilized nations as binding on States, even without any conventional obligation. A second consequence is the universal character both of the condemnation of genocide and of the co-operation required "in order to liberate mankind from such an odious scourge" (Preamble to the Convention). (I.C.J. Reports 1951, p. 23.)

It follows that the rights and obligations enshrined by the Convention are rights and obligations erga omnes. The Court notes that the obligation each State thus has to prevent and to punish the crime of genocide is not territorially limited by the Convention.[11]

In a related context, the Judgment of the Trial Chamber of the ICTY in the *Furundzija* case[12] affirmed the legal character of the prohibition of the crime of torture and the importance of the compulsory obligations for states to respect the legal character of the obligations *erga omnes* which apply to the legal status of *jus cogens* norms.[13] The Judgment clarified that the prohibition imposes obligations *erga omnes.* It asserted that:

151. Furthermore, the prohibition of torture imposes upon States obligations *erga omnes*, that is, obligations owed towards all the other members of the international community, each of which then has a correlative right. In addition, the violation of such an obligation simultaneously constitutes a breach of the correlative right of all members of the international community and gives rise to a claim for compliance accruing to each and every member, which then has the right to insist on fulfilment of the obligation or in any case to call for the breach to be discontinued.

152. Where there exist international bodies charged with impartially monitoring compliance with treaty provisions on torture, these bodies enjoy priority over individual States in establishing whether a certain State has taken all the necessary measures to prevent and punish torture and, if they have not, in calling upon that State to fulfil its international obligations. The existence of such international mechanisms makes it

---

[11] ICJ Reports (1996), 615-16.

[12] Anto *Furundzija* was a citizen of Bosnia and Herzegovina and was born in 1969.

[13] See also Chapter6 section 3.6.3.

> possible for compliance with international law to be ensured in a neutral and impartial manner.

The ICTY justified its Judgement by asserting that the prohibition has acquired the status of *jus cogens*. It affirmed that:

> 153. While the *erga omnes* nature just mentioned appertains to the area of international enforcement (*latosensu*), the other major feature of the principle proscribing torture relates to the hierarchy of rules in the international normative order. Because of the importance of the values it protects, this principle has evolved into a peremptory norm or *jus cogens*, that is, a norm that enjoys a higher rank in the international hierarchy than treaty law and even "ordinary" customary rules. The most conspicuous consequence of this higher rank is that the principle at issue cannot be derogated from by States through international treaties or local or special customs or even general customary rules not endowed with the same normative force.
>
> 154. Clearly, the *jus cogens* nature of the prohibition against torture articulates the notion that the prohibition has now become one of the most fundamental standards of the international community. Furthermore, this prohibition is designed to produce a deterrent effect, in that it signals to all members of the international community and the individuals over whom they wield authority that the prohibition of torture is an absolute value from which nobody must deviate.
>
> 155. The fact that torture is prohibited by a peremptory norm of international law has other effects at the inter-state and individual levels. At the inter-state level, it serves to internationally de-legitimise any legislative, administrative or judicial act authorising torture. It would be senseless to argue, on the one hand, that on account of the *jus cogens* value of the prohibition against torture, treaties or customary rules providing for torture would be null and void *ab initio*, and then be unmindful of a State say, taking national measures authorising or condoning torture or absolving its perpetrators through an amnesty law. If such a situation where to arise, the national measures, violating the general principle and any relevant treaty provision, would produce the legal effects discussed above and in addition would not be accorded international legal recognition. Proceedings could be initiated by potential victims if they had *locus standi* before a competent international or national judicial body with a view to asking it to hold the national measure to be internationally unlawful; or the victim could bring a civil suit for damage in a foreign court, which would therefore be asked *inter alia* to disregard the legal value of the national authorising act. What is even more important is that perpetrators of torture acting upon or benefiting from those national measures may nevertheless be held criminally responsible for torture, whether in a foreign State, or in

their own State under a subsequent regime. In short, in spite of possible national authorisation by legislative or judicial bodies to violate the principle banning torture, individuals remain bound to comply with that principle. As the International Military Tribunal at Nuremberg put it: "individuals have international duties which transcend the national obligations of obedience imposed by the individual State".

156. Furthermore, at the individual level, that is, that of criminal liability, it would seem that one of the consequences of the *jus cogens* character bestowed by the international community upon the prohibition of torture is that every State is entitled to investigate, prosecute and punish or extradite individuals accused of torture, who are present in a territory under its jurisdiction. Indeed, it would be inconsistent on the one hand to prohibit torture to such an extent as to restrict the normally unfettered treaty making power of sovereign States, and on the other hand bar States from prosecuting and punishing those torturers who have engaged in this odious practice abroad. This legal basis for States' universal jurisdiction over torture bears out and strengthens the legal foundation for such jurisdiction found by other courts in the inherently universal character of the crime. It has been held that international crimes being universally condemned wherever they occur, every State has the right to prosecute and punish the authors of such crimes. As stated in general terms by the Supreme Court of Israel in *Eichmann*, and echoed by a USA court in *Demjanjuk*, "it is the universal character of the crimes in question [*i.e.* international crimes] which vests in every State the authority to try and punish those who participated in their commission".

157. It would seem that other consequences include the fact that torture may not be covered by a statute of limitations, and must not be excluded from extradition under any political offence exemption.[14]

5. Transmission of State Power

As we have discussed above, no conventional provisions may limit the exercise of jurisdiction over *jus cogens* crimes. This means that states which are not parties to the Statute of the ICC are, according to the merit of the *jus cogens* decree, responsible for surrendering their individuals to the Court or prosecuting and punishing them under their own

[14] The Trial Chamber of the International Tribunal for the Prosecution of Persons Responsible for Serious Violations of International Humanitarian Law Committed in the Territory of the Former Yugoslavia since 1991 (ICTY), Judgement IT-95-17/1-T, 10 December 1998.

jurisdiction.[15] Yet, any other state that has arrested them may submit them to the jurisdiction of the ICC based on the fact that *jus cogens* crimes are prosecutable by any state and no state may properly claim it has jurisdiction over those accused persons on the basis of their nationality. They are like pirates who are enemies of mankind and may be punished by the capturing state. More significantly, a state which does not have the capacity to prosecute those who have committed crimes against humanity, war crimes and genocide but has captured them, may submit the arrested persons to the jurisdiction of the Court in order to exercise the state's right of jurisdiction over the enemies of mankind. This is a temporary transmission of a certain relevant state power regarding the relevant case under international law.

Whilst one cannot deny that the ICC does not have the power to extend its authority over the perpetrators of international crimes whose governments are not parties to the Statute, the problem which is more controversial is that the crimes within the Statute are within the realm of *jus cogens* crimes and are therefore prosecutable and punishable by any state or organisation that has the power of jurisdiction over crimes against humanity, war crimes and genocide. The question is how can we limit the prosecution and punishment of *jus cogens* crimes.

If an international crime is identified under *jus cogens* crimes, the scope of its prosecution and punishment cannot be limited and shall not be bound by various constitutional or conventional limitations. One of the most important principles of *jus cogens* crimes is the unlimited scope of their jurisdiction over all types of regulations that create a limitation for their prosecution and punishment. This key principle may lead the Statute of the ICC into conflict with the principles of *jus cogens* concerning its broad juridical attribution over all perpetrators of international crimes of a *jus cogens* character. Furthermore, it is very doubtful whether one should accept that the ICC, which has the capacity as an international legal person with regard to its given function, is incapable of exercising jurisdiction over all perpetrators of crimes listed under its Statute. The function of the ICC is based, quite simply, on the principle of complementarity. The

[15] The Court has been invited by four States Parties to investigate the commission of international crimes on their territories. These are Uganda, the Democratic Republic of the Congo, the Central African Republic and Mali. The Court has also opened investigation in several other cases submitted by the Security Council of the United Nations. These are Darfur in Sudan and Libya, both non-States Parties. Other countries under investigations are Kenya and Côte d'Ivoire. The prosecution has opened investigations *proprio motu* granted by Pre-Trial Chamber I and II on both countries on 31 March 2010 and on 3 October 2011.

principle gives the Court the right of prosecution and punishment where the state cannot, in one way or another, exercise its jurisdiction over certain international crimes. If a state which is not a party to the Statute gives its right of jurisdiction over certain international criminals to the Court; the Court is, according to the principle of complementarity, responsible for their prosecution. The Court may therefore, if it does not accept the case, violate the framework of the Statute and also the *jus cogens* norms.

One may also argue that the ICC has a limited international legal personality according to the will of the signatory states and therefore its Statute does not conflict with the basic principles of law such as *jus cogens* norms. It may even be stated that the Court's jurisdiction is directed towards the prosecution rather than the prevention of certain international crimes against certain parties. Its function is not, therefore, the exhaustive prosecution and punishment of all international criminals. According to this argument, the drafters of the Statute had in mind a theory of a permanent international criminal court which could be accepted by the majority of states which participated in the Rome conferences and therefore did not put heavy weight on the complete enforcement of *jus cogens* norms. One of the problems of this argument is that it will create great difficulty in the fulfilment of *jus cogens* principles and may interfere in the implementation of international criminal law.

The question will always remain as to how the international legal community can create an international legal person which can deal with the most dangerous and harmful international crimes but cannot, for one reason or another, prosecute individuals of all states committing the same crimes. If there is to be an effective international criminal justice system in the world and its purpose is to protect the fundamental rights of man against antagonism and inhuman actions, it must also be authorised to bring under prosecution and punishment individuals of all states of the world and not discriminate between some criminals and others. In order that the system of international criminal justice to be correct and comprehensive, it must be applicable to all without any discrimination on grounds of race, language, nationality or religion, neither must it pay regard to cultural, political or economic strength. International criminal justice may not properly be applied without the reciprocal understanding and application of its basic principles and phenomena. How can the system of international criminal justice distinguish between individuals for their accountability regarding *jus cogens* crimes?

APPENDIX A

ROME STATUTE OF THE INTERNATIONAL CRIMINAL COURT[1]

PREAMBLE

The States Parties to this Statute,

Conscious that all peoples are united by common bonds, their cultures pieced together in a shared heritage, and concerned that this delicate mosaic may be shattered at any time,

Mindful that during this century millions of children, women and men have been victims of unimaginable atrocities that deeply shock the conscience of humanity,

Recognizing that such grave crimes threaten the peace, security and well-being of the world,

Affirming that the most serious crimes of concern to the international community as a whole must not go unpunished and that their effective prosecution must be ensured by taking measures at the national level and by enhancing international cooperation,

Determined to put an end to impunity for the perpetrators of these crimes and thus to contribute to the prevention of such crimes,

Recalling that it is the duty of every State to exercise its criminal jurisdiction over those responsible for international crimes,

Reaffirming the Purposes and Principles of the Charter of the United Nations, and in particular that all States shall refrain from the threat or use of force against the territorial integrity or political independence of any State, or in any other manner inconsistent with the Purposes of the United Nations,

---

[1] Text of the Rome Statute circulated as document A/CONF.183/9 of 17 July 1998 and corrected by procès-verbaux of 10 November 1998, 12 July 1999, 30 November 1999, 8 May 2000, 17 January 2001 and 16 January 2002. The Statute entered into force on 1 July 2002.

Emphasizing in this connection that nothing in this Statute shall be taken as authorizing any State Party to intervene in an armed conflict or in the internal affairs of any State,

Determined to these ends and for the sake of present and future generations, to establish an independent permanent International Criminal Court in relationship with the United Nations system, with jurisdiction over the most serious crimes of concern to the international community as a whole,

Emphasizing that the International Criminal Court established under this Statute shall be complementary to national criminal jurisdictions,

Resolved to guarantee lasting respect for and the enforcement of international justice,

Have agreed as follows:

PART 1. ESTABLISHMENT OF THE COURT

Article 1
The Court

An International Criminal Court ("the Court") is hereby established. It shall be a permanent institution and shall have the power to exercise its jurisdiction over persons for the most serious crimes of international concern, as referred to in this Statute, and shall be complementary to national criminal jurisdictions. The jurisdiction and functioning of the Court shall be governed by the provisions of this Statute.

Article 2
Relationship of the Court with the United Nations

The Court shall be brought into relationship with the United Nations through an agreement to be approved by the Assembly of States Parties to this Statute and thereafter concluded by the President of the Court on its behalf.

Article 3
Seat of the Court

1. The seat of the Court shall be established at The Hague in the Netherlands ("the host State").

2. The Court shall enter into a headquarters agreement with the host State, to be approved by the Assembly of States Parties and thereafter concluded by the President of the Court on its behalf.

3. The Court may sit elsewhere, whenever it considers it desirable, as provided in this Statute.

Article 4
Legal status and powers of the Court

1. The Court shall have international legal personality. It shall also have such legal capacity as may be necessary for the exercise of its functions and the fulfilment of its purposes.

2. The Court may exercise its functions and powers, as provided in this Statute, on the territory of any State Party and, by special agreement, on the territory of any other State.

PART 2. JURISDICTION, ADMISSIBILITY AND APPLICABLE LAW

Article 5
Crimes within the jurisdiction of the Court

1. The jurisdiction of the Court shall be limited to the most serious crimes of concern to the international community as a whole. The Court has jurisdiction in accordance with this Statute with respect to the following crimes:

(a) The crime of genocide;

(b) Crimes against humanity;

(c) War crimes;

(d) The crime of aggression.

2. The Court shall exercise jurisdiction over the crime of aggression once a provision is adopted in accordance with articles 121 and 123 defining the crime and setting out the conditions under which the Court shall exercise jurisdiction with respect to this crime. Such a provision shall be consistent with the relevant provisions of the Charter of the United Nations.

Article 6
Genocide

For the purpose of this Statute, "genocide" means any of the following acts committed with intent to destroy, in whole or in part, a national, ethnical, racial or religious group, as such:

(a) Killing members of the group;

(b) Causing serious bodily or mental harm to members of the group;

(c) Deliberately inflicting on the group conditions of life calculated to bring about its physical destruction in whole or in part;

(d) Imposing measures intended to prevent births within the group;

(e) Forcibly transferring children of the group to another group.

Article 7
Crimes against humanity

1. For the purpose of this Statute, "crime against humanity" means any of the following acts when committed as part of a widespread or systematic attack directed against any civilian population, with knowledge of the attack:

(a) Murder;

(b) Extermination;

(c) Enslavement;

(d) Deportation or forcible transfer of population;

(e) Imprisonment or other severe deprivation of physical liberty in violation of fundamental rules of international law;

(f) Torture;

(g) Rape, sexual slavery, enforced prostitution, forced pregnancy, enforced sterilization, or any other form of sexual violence of comparable gravity;

(h) Persecution against any identifiable group or collectivity on political, racial, national, ethnic, cultural, religious, gender as defined in paragraph 3, or other grounds that are universally recognized as impermissible under international law, in connection with any act referred to in this paragraph or any crime within the jurisdiction of the Court;

(i) Enforced disappearance of persons;

(j) The crime of apartheid;

(k) Other inhumane acts of a similar character intentionally causing great suffering, or serious injury to body or to mental or physical health.

2. For the purpose of paragraph 1:

(a) "Attack directed against any civilian population" means a course of conduct involving the multiple commission of acts referred to in paragraph 1 against any civilian population, pursuant to or in furtherance of a State or organizational policy to commit such attack;

(b) "Extermination" includes the intentional infliction of conditions of life, inter alia the deprivation of access to food and medicine, calculated to bring about the destruction of part of a population;

(c) "Enslavement" means the exercise of any or all of the powers attaching to the right of ownership over a person and includes the exercise of such power in the course of trafficking in persons, in particular women and children;

(d) "Deportation or forcible transfer of population" means forced displacement of the persons concerned by expulsion or other coercive acts from the area in which they are lawfully present, without grounds permitted under international law;

(e) "Torture" means the intentional infliction of severe pain or suffering, whether physical or mental, upon a person in the custody or under the control of the accused; except that torture shall not include pain or suffering arising only from, inherent in or incidental to, lawful sanctions;

(f) "Forced pregnancy" means the unlawful confinement of a woman forcibly made pregnant, with the intent of affecting the ethnic composition of any population or carrying out other grave violations of international law. This definition shall not in any way be interpreted as affecting national laws relating to pregnancy;

(g) "Persecution" means the intentional and severe deprivation of fundamental rights contrary to international law by reason of the identity of the group or collectivity;

(h) "The crime of apartheid" means inhumane acts of a character similar to those referred to in paragraph 1, committed in the context of an institutionalized regime of systematic oppression and domination by one racial group over any other racial group or groups and committed with the intention of maintaining that regime;

(i) "Enforced disappearance of persons" means the arrest, detention or abduction of persons by, or with the authorization, support or acquiescence of, a State or a political organization, followed by a refusal to acknowledge that deprivation of freedom or to give information on the fate or whereabouts of those persons, with the intention of removing them from the protection of the law for a prolonged period of time.

3. For the purpose of this Statute, it is understood that the term "gender" refers to the two sexes, male and female, within the context of society. The term "gender" does not indicate any meaning different from the above.

Article 8
War crimes

1. The Court shall have jurisdiction in respect of war crimes in particular when committed as part of a plan or policy or as part of a large-scale commission of such crimes.

2. For the purpose of this Statute, "war crimes" means:

(a) Grave breaches of the Geneva Conventions of 12 August 1949, namely, any of the following acts against persons or property protected under the provisions of the relevant Geneva Convention:

(i) Wilful killing;

(ii) Torture or inhuman treatment, including biological experiments;

(iii) Wilfully causing great suffering, or serious injury to body or health;

(iv) Extensive destruction and appropriation of property, not justified by military necessity and carried out unlawfully and wantonly;

(v) Compelling a prisoner of war or other protected person to serve in the forces of a hostile Power;

(vi) Wilfully depriving a prisoner of war or other protected person of the rights of fair and regular trial;

(vii) Unlawful deportation or transfer or unlawful confinement;

(viii) Taking of hostages.

(b) Other serious violations of the laws and customs applicable in international armed conflict, within the established framework of international law, namely, any of the following acts:

(i) Intentionally directing attacks against the civilian population as such or against individual civilians not taking direct part in hostilities;

(ii) Intentionally directing attacks against civilian objects, that is, objects which are not military objectives;

(iii) Intentionally directing attacks against personnel, installations, material, units or vehicles involved in a humanitarian assistance or peacekeeping mission in accordance with the Charter of the United Nations, as long as they are entitled to the protection given to civilians or civilian objects under the international law of armed conflict;

(iv) Intentionally launching an attack in the knowledge that such attack will cause incidental loss of life or injury to civilians or damage to civilian objects or widespread, long-term and severe damage to the natural environment which would be clearly excessive in relation to the concrete and direct overall military advantage anticipated;

(v) Attacking or bombarding, by whatever means, towns, villages, dwellings or buildings which are undefended and which are not military objectives;

(vi) Killing or wounding a combatant who, having laid down his arms or having no longer means of defence, has surrendered at discretion;

(vii) Making improper use of a flag of truce, of the flag or of the military insignia and uniform of the enemy or of the United Nations, as well as of the distinctive emblems of the Geneva Conventions, resulting in death or serious personal injury;

(viii) The transfer, directly or indirectly, by the Occupying Power of parts of its own civilian population into the territory it occupies, or the deportation or transfer of all or parts of the population of the occupied territory within or outside this territory;

(ix) Intentionally directing attacks against buildings dedicated to religion, education, art, science or charitable purposes, historic monuments, hospitals and places where the sick and wounded are collected, provided they are not military objectives;

(x) Subjecting persons who are in the power of an adverse party to physical mutilation or to medical or scientific experiments of any kind which are neither justified by the medical, dental or hospital treatment of the person concerned nor carried out in his or her interest, and which cause death to or seriously endanger the health of such person or persons;

(xi) Killing or wounding treacherously individuals belonging to the hostile nation or army;

(xii) Declaring that no quarter will be given;

(xiii) Destroying or seizing the enemy's property unless such destruction or seizure be imperatively demanded by the necessities of war;

(xiv) Declaring abolished, suspended or inadmissible in a court of law the rights and actions of the nationals of the hostile party;

(xv) Compelling the nationals of the hostile party to take part in the operations of war directed against their own country, even if they were in the belligerent's service before the commencement of the war;

(xvi) Pillaging a town or place, even when taken by assault;

(xvii) Employing poison or poisoned weapons;

(xviii) Employing asphyxiating, poisonous or other gases, and all analogous liquids, materials or devices;

(xix) Employing bullets which expand or flatten easily in the human body, such as bullets with a hard envelope which does not entirely cover the core or is pierced with incisions;

(xx) Employing weapons, projectiles and material and methods of warfare which are of a nature to cause superfluous injury or unnecessary suffering or which are inherently indiscriminate in violation of the international law of armed conflict, provided that such weapons, projectiles and material and methods of warfare are the subject of a comprehensive prohibition and are included in an annex to this Statute, by an amendment in accordance with the relevant provisions set forth in articles 121 and 123;

(xxi) Committing outrages upon personal dignity, in particular humiliating and degrading treatment;

(xxii) Committing rape, sexual slavery, enforced prostitution, forced pregnancy, as defined in article 7, paragraph 2 (f), enforced sterilization, or any other form of sexual violence also constituting a grave breach of the Geneva Conventions;

(xxiii) Utilizing the presence of a civilian or other protected person to render certain points, areas or military forces immune from military operations;

(xxiv) Intentionally directing attacks against buildings, material, medical units and transport, and personnel using the distinctive emblems of the Geneva Conventions in conformity with international law;

(xxv) Intentionally using starvation of civilians as a method of warfare by depriving them of objects indispensable to their survival, including wilfully impeding relief supplies as provided for under the Geneva Conventions;

(xxvi) Conscripting or enlisting children under the age of fifteen years into the national armed forces or using them to participate actively in hostilities.

(c) In the case of an armed conflict not of an international character, serious violations of article 3 common to the four Geneva Conventions of 12 August 1949, namely, any of the following acts committed against persons taking no active part in the hostilities, including members of armed forces who have laid down their arms and those placed hors de combat by sickness, wounds, detention or any other cause:

(i) Violence to life and person, in particular murder of all kinds, mutilation, cruel treatment and torture;

(ii) Committing outrages upon personal dignity, in particular humiliating and degrading treatment;

(iii) Taking of hostages;

(iv) The passing of sentences and the carrying out of executions without previous judgement pronounced by a regularly constituted court, affording all judicial guarantees which are generally recognized as indispensable.

(d) Paragraph 2 (c) applies to armed conflicts not of an international character and thus does not apply to situations of internal disturbances and tensions, such as riots, isolated and sporadic acts of violence or other acts of a similar nature.

(e) Other serious violations of the laws and customs applicable in armed conflicts not of an international character, within the established framework of international law, namely, any of the following acts:

(i) Intentionally directing attacks against the civilian population as such or against individual civilians not taking direct part in hostilities;

(ii) Intentionally directing attacks against buildings, material, medical units and transport, and personnel using the distinctive emblems of the Geneva Conventions in conformity with international law;

(iii) Intentionally directing attacks against personnel, installations, material, units or vehicles involved in a humanitarian assistance or peacekeeping mission in accordance with the Charter of the United Nations, as long as they are entitled to the protection given to civilians or civilian objects under the international law of armed conflict;

(iv) Intentionally directing attacks against buildings dedicated to religion, education, art, science or charitable purposes, historic monuments, hospitals and places where the sick and wounded are collected, provided they are not military objectives;

(v) Pillaging a town or place, even when taken by assault;

(vi) Committing rape, sexual slavery, enforced prostitution, forced pregnancy, as defined in article 7, paragraph 2 (f), enforced sterilization, and any other form of sexual violence also constituting a serious violation of article 3 common to the four Geneva Conventions;

(vii) Conscripting or enlisting children under the age of fifteen years into armed forces or groups or using them to participate actively in hostilities;

(viii) Ordering the displacement of the civilian population for reasons related to the conflict, unless the security of the civilians involved or imperative military reasons so demand;

(ix) Killing or wounding treacherously a combatant adversary;

(x) Declaring that no quarter will be given;

(xi) Subjecting persons who are in the power of another party to the conflict to physical mutilation or to medical or scientific experiments of any kind which are neither justified by the medical, dental or hospital treatment of the person concerned nor carried out in his or her interest, and which cause death to or seriously endanger the health of such person or persons;

(xii) Destroying or seizing the property of an adversary unless such destruction or seizure be imperatively demanded by the necessities of the conflict;

(f) Paragraph 2 (e) applies to armed conflicts not of an international character and thus does not apply to situations of internal disturbances and tensions, such as riots, isolated and sporadic acts of violence or other acts of a similar nature. It applies to armed conflicts that take place in the territory of a State when there is protracted armed conflict between governmental authorities and organized armed groups or between such groups.

3. Nothing in paragraph 2 (c) and (e) shall affect the responsibility of a Government to maintain or re-establish law and order in the State or to defend the unity and territorial integrity of the State, by all legitimate means.

Article 9
Elements of Crimes

1. Elements of Crimes shall assist the Court in the interpretation and application of articles 6, 7 and 8. They shall be adopted by a two-thirds majority of the members of the Assembly of States Parties.

2. Amendments to the Elements of Crimes may be proposed by:

(a) Any State Party;

(b) The judges acting by an absolute majority;

(c) The Prosecutor.

Such amendments shall be adopted by a two-thirds majority of the members of the Assembly of States Parties.

3. The Elements of Crimes and amendments thereto shall be consistent with this Statute.

Article 10

Nothing in this Part shall be interpreted as limiting or prejudicing in any way existing or developing rules of international law for purposes other than this Statute.

Article 11
Jurisdiction ratione temporis

1. The Court has jurisdiction only with respect to crimes committed after the entry into force of this Statute.

2. If a State becomes a Party to this Statute after its entry into force, the Court may exercise its jurisdiction only with respect to crimes committed after the entry into force of this Statute for that State, unless that State has made a declaration under article 12, paragraph 3.

Article 12
Preconditions to the exercise of jurisdiction

1. A State which becomes a Party to this Statute thereby accepts the jurisdiction of the Court with respect to the crimes referred to in article 5.

2. In the case of article 13, paragraph (a) or (c), the Court may exercise its jurisdiction if one or more of the following States are Parties to this Statute or have accepted the jurisdiction of the Court in accordance with paragraph 3:

(a) The State on the territory of which the conduct in question occurred or, if the crime was committed on board a vessel or aircraft, the State of registration of that vessel or aircraft;

(b) The State of which the person accused of the crime is a national.

3. If the acceptance of a State which is not a Party to this Statute is required under paragraph 2, that State may, by declaration lodged with the Registrar, accept the exercise of jurisdiction by the Court with respect to the crime in question. The accepting State shall cooperate with the Court without any delay or exception in accordance with Part 9.

Article 13
Exercise of jurisdiction

The Court may exercise its jurisdiction with respect to a crime referred to in article 5 in accordance with the provisions of this Statute if:

(a) A situation in which one or more of such crimes appears to have been committed is referred to the Prosecutor by a State Party in accordance with article 14;

(b) A situation in which one or more of such crimes appears to have been committed is referred to the Prosecutor by the Security Council acting under Chapter VII of the Charter of the United Nations; or

(c) The Prosecutor has initiated an investigation in respect of such a crime in accordance with article 15.

Article 14
Referral of a situation by a State Party

1. A State Party may refer to the Prosecutor a situation in which one or more crimes within the jurisdiction of the Court appear to have been committed requesting the Prosecutor to investigate the situation for the purpose of determining whether one or more specific persons should be charged with the commission of such crimes.

2. As far as possible, a referral shall specify the relevant circumstances and be accompanied by such supporting documentation as is available to the State referring the situation.

Article 15
Prosecutor

1. The Prosecutor may initiate investigations proprio motu on the basis of information on crimes within the jurisdiction of the Court.

2. The Prosecutor shall analyse the seriousness of the information received. For this purpose, he or she may seek additional information from States, organs of the United Nations, intergovernmental or non-governmental organizations, or other reliable sources that he or she deems appropriate, and may receive written or oral testimony at the seat of the Court.

3. If the Prosecutor concludes that there is a reasonable basis to proceed with an investigation, he or she shall submit to the Pre-Trial Chamber a request for authorization of an investigation, together with any supporting material collected. Victims may make representations to the Pre-Trial Chamber, in accordance with the Rules of Procedure and Evidence.

4. If the Pre-Trial Chamber, upon examination of the request and the supporting material, considers that there is a reasonable basis to proceed with an investigation, and that the case appears to fall within the jurisdiction of the Court, it shall authorize the commencement of the investigation, without prejudice to subsequent determinations by the Court with regard to the jurisdiction and admissibility of a case.

5. The refusal of the Pre-Trial Chamber to authorize the investigation shall not preclude the presentation of a subsequent request by the Prosecutor based on new facts or evidence regarding the same situation.

6. If, after the preliminary examination referred to in paragraphs 1 and 2, the Prosecutor concludes that the information provided does not constitute a reasonable basis for an investigation, he or she shall inform those who provided the information. This shall not preclude the Prosecutor from considering further information submitted to him or her regarding the same situation in the light of new facts or evidence.

Article 16
Deferral of investigation or prosecution

No investigation or prosecution may be commenced or proceeded with under this Statute for a period of 12 months after the Security Council, in a resolution adopted under Chapter VII of the Charter of the United Nations, has requested the Court to that effect; that request may be renewed by the Council under the same conditions.

Article 17
Issues of admissibility

1. Having regard to paragraph 10 of the Preamble and article 1, the Court shall determine that a case is inadmissible where:

(a) The case is being investigated or prosecuted by a State which has jurisdiction over it, unless the State is unwilling or unable genuinely to carry out the investigation or prosecution;

(b) The case has been investigated by a State which has jurisdiction over it and the State has decided not to prosecute the person concerned, unless the decision resulted from the unwillingness or inability of the State genuinely to prosecute;

(c) The person concerned has already been tried for conduct which is the subject of the complaint, and a trial by the Court is not permitted under article 20, paragraph 3;

(d) The case is not of sufficient gravity to justify further action by the Court.

2. In order to determine unwillingness in a particular case, the Court shall consider, having regard to the principles of due process recognized by international law, whether one or more of the following exist, as applicable:

(a) The proceedings were or are being undertaken or the national decision was made for the purpose of shielding the person concerned from criminal responsibility for crimes within the jurisdiction of the Court referred to in article 5;

(b) There has been an unjustified delay in the proceedings which in the circumstances is inconsistent with an intent to bring the person concerned to justice;

(c) The proceedings were not or are not being conducted independently or impartially, and they were or are being conducted in a manner which, in the circumstances, is inconsistent with an intent to bring the person concerned to justice.

3. In order to determine inability in a particular case, the Court shall consider whether, due to a total or substantial collapse or unavailability of its national judicial system, the State is unable to obtain the accused or the necessary evidence and testimony or otherwise unable to carry out its proceedings.

Article 18
Preliminary rulings regarding admissibility

1. When a situation has been referred to the Court pursuant to article 13 (a) and the Prosecutor has determined that there would be a reasonable basis to commence an investigation, or the Prosecutor initiates an investigation pursuant to articles 13 (c) and 15, the Prosecutor shall notify all States Parties and those States which, taking into account the information available, would normally exercise jurisdiction over the crimes concerned. The Prosecutor may notify such States on a confidential basis and, where the Prosecutor believes it necessary to protect persons, prevent destruction of evidence or prevent the absconding of persons, may limit the scope of the information provided to States.

2. Within one month of receipt of that notification, a State may inform the Court that it is investigating or has investigated its nationals or others within its jurisdiction with respect to criminal acts which may constitute crimes referred to in article 5 and which relate to the information provided in the notification to States. At the request of that State, the Prosecutor shall defer to the State's investigation of those persons unless the Pre-Trial Chamber, on the application of the Prosecutor, decides to authorize the investigation.

3. The Prosecutor's deferral to a State's investigation shall be open to review by the Prosecutor six months after the date of deferral or at any time when there has been a significant change of circumstances based on the State's unwillingness or inability genuinely to carry out the investigation.

4. The State concerned or the Prosecutor may appeal to the Appeals Chamber against a ruling of the Pre-Trial Chamber, in accordance with article 82. The appeal may be heard on an expedited basis.

5. When the Prosecutor has deferred an investigation in accordance with paragraph 2, the Prosecutor may request that the State concerned periodically inform the Prosecutor of the progress of its investigations and any subsequent prosecutions. States Parties shall respond to such requests without undue delay.

6. Pending a ruling by the Pre-Trial Chamber, or at any time when the Prosecutor has deferred an investigation under this article, the Prosecutor may, on an exceptional basis, seek authority from the Pre-Trial Chamber to pursue necessary investigative steps for the purpose of preserving evidence where there is a unique opportunity to obtain important evidence or there is a significant risk that such evidence may not be subsequently available.

7. A State which has challenged a ruling of the Pre-Trial Chamber under this article may challenge the admissibility of a case under article 19 on the grounds of additional significant facts or significant change of circumstances.

Article 19
Challenges to the jurisdiction of the Court or the admissibility of a case

1. The Court shall satisfy itself that it has jurisdiction in any case brought before it. The Court may, on its own motion, determine the admissibility of a case in accordance with article 17.

2. Challenges to the admissibility of a case on the grounds referred to in article 17 or challenges to the jurisdiction of the Court may be made by:

(a) An accused or a person for whom a warrant of arrest or a summons to appear has been issued under article 58;

(b) A State which has jurisdiction over a case, on the ground that it is investigating or prosecuting the case or has investigated or prosecuted; or

(c) A State from which acceptance of jurisdiction is required under article 12.

3. The Prosecutor may seek a ruling from the Court regarding a question of jurisdiction or admissibility. In proceedings with respect to jurisdiction or admissibility, those who have referred the situation under article 13, as well as victims, may also submit observations to the Court.

4. The admissibility of a case or the jurisdiction of the Court may be challenged only once by any person or State referred to in paragraph 2.

The challenge shall take place prior to or at the commencement of the trial. In exceptional circumstances, the Court may grant leave for a challenge to be brought more than once or at a time later than the commencement of the trial. Challenges to the admissibility of a case, at the commencement of a trial, or subsequently with the leave of the Court, may be based only on article 17, paragraph 1 (c).

5. A State referred to in paragraph 2 (b) and (c) shall make a challenge at the earliest opportunity.

6. Prior to the confirmation of the charges, challenges to the admissibility of a case or challenges to the jurisdiction of the Court shall be referred to the Pre-Trial Chamber. After confirmation of the charges, they shall be referred to the Trial Chamber. Decisions with respect to jurisdiction or admissibility may be appealed to the Appeals Chamber in accordance with article 82.

7. If a challenge is made by a State referred to in paragraph 2 (b) or (c), the Prosecutor shall suspend the investigation until such time as the Court makes a determination in accordance with article 17.

8. Pending a ruling by the Court, the Prosecutor may seek authority from the Court:

(a) To pursue necessary investigative steps of the kind referred to in article 18, paragraph 6;

(b) To take a statement or testimony from a witness or complete the collection and examination of evidence which had begun prior to the making of the challenge; and

(c) In cooperation with the relevant States, to prevent the absconding of persons in respect of whom the Prosecutor has already requested a warrant of arrest under article 58.

9. The making of a challenge shall not affect the validity of any act performed by the Prosecutor or any order or warrant issued by the Court prior to the making of the challenge.

10. If the Court has decided that a case is inadmissible under article 17, the Prosecutor may submit a request for a review of the decision when he or she is fully satisfied that new facts have arisen which negate the basis on which the case had previously been found inadmissible under article 17.

11. If the Prosecutor, having regard to the matters referred to in article 17, defers an investigation, the Prosecutor may request that the relevant State make available to the Prosecutor information on the proceedings. That information shall, at the request of the State concerned, be confidential. If the Prosecutor thereafter decides to proceed with an

investigation, he or she shall notify the State to which deferral of the proceedings has taken place.

Article 20
Ne bis in idem

1. Except as provided in this Statute, no person shall be tried before the Court with respect to conduct which formed the basis of crimes for which the person has been convicted or acquitted by the Court.

2. No person shall be tried by another court for a crime referred to in article 5 for which that person has already been convicted or acquitted by the Court.

3. No person who has been tried by another court for conduct also proscribed under article 6, 7 or 8 shall be tried by the Court with respect to the same conduct unless the proceedings in the other court:

(a) Were for the purpose of shielding the person concerned from criminal responsibility for crimes within the jurisdiction of the Court; or

(b) Otherwise were not conducted independently or impartially in accordance with the norms of due process recognized by international law and were conducted in a manner which, in the circumstances, was inconsistent with an intent to bring the person concerned to justice.

Article 21
Applicable law

1. The Court shall apply:

(a) In the first place, this Statute, Elements of Crimes and its Rules of Procedure and Evidence;

(b) In the second place, where appropriate, applicable treaties and the principles and rules of international law, including the established principles of the international law of armed conflict;

(c) Failing that, general principles of law derived by the Court from national laws of legal systems of the world including, as appropriate, the national laws of States that would normally exercise jurisdiction over the crime, provided that those principles are not inconsistent with this Statute and with international law and internationally recognized norms and standards.

2. The Court may apply principles and rules of law as interpreted in its previous decisions.

3. The application and interpretation of law pursuant to this article must be consistent with internationally recognized human rights, and be

without any adverse distinction founded on grounds such as gender as defined in article 7, paragraph 3, age, race, colour, language, religion or belief, political or other opinion, national, ethnic or social origin, wealth, birth or other status.

PART 3. GENERAL PRINCIPLES OF CRIMINAL LAW

Article 22
Nullum crimen sine lege

1. A person shall not be criminally responsible under this Statute unless the conduct in question constitutes, at the time it takes place, a crime within the jurisdiction of the Court.

2. The definition of a crime shall be strictly construed and shall not be extended by analogy. In case of ambiguity, the definition shall be interpreted in favour of the person being investigated, prosecuted or convicted.

3. This article shall not affect the characterization of any conduct as criminal under international law independently of this Statute.

Article 23
Nulla poena sine lege

A person convicted by the Court may be punished only in accordance with this Statute.

Article 24
Non-retroactivity ratione personae

1. No person shall be criminally responsible under this Statute for conduct prior to the entry into force of the Statute.

2. In the event of a change in the law applicable to a given case prior to a final judgement, the law more favourable to the person being investigated, prosecuted or convicted shall apply.

Article 25
Individual criminal responsibility

1. The Court shall have jurisdiction over natural persons pursuant to this Statute.

2. A person who commits a crime within the jurisdiction of the Court shall be individually responsible and liable for punishment in accordance with this Statute.

3. In accordance with this Statute, a person shall be criminally responsible and liable for punishment for a crime within the jurisdiction of the Court if that person:

(a) Commits such a crime, whether as an individual, jointly with another or through another person, regardless of whether that other person is criminally responsible;

(b) Orders, solicits or induces the commission of such a crime which in fact occurs or is attempted;

(c) For the purpose of facilitating the commission of such a crime, aids, abets or otherwise assists in its commission or its attempted commission, including providing the means for its commission;

(d) In any other way contributes to the commission or attempted commission of such a crime by a group of persons acting with a common purpose. Such contribution shall be intentional and shall either:

(i) Be made with the aim of furthering the criminal activity or criminal purpose of the group, where such activity or purpose involves the commission of a crime within the jurisdiction of the Court; or

(ii) Be made in the knowledge of the intention of the group to commit the crime;

(e) In respect of the crime of genocide, directly and publicly incites others to commit genocide;

(f) Attempts to commit such a crime by taking action that commences its execution by means of a substantial step, but the crime does not occur because of circumstances independent of the person's intentions. However, a person who abandons the effort to commit the crime or otherwise prevents the completion of the crime shall not be liable for punishment under this Statute for the attempt to commit that crime if that person completely and voluntarily gave up the criminal purpose.

4. No provision in this Statute relating to individual criminal responsibility shall affect the responsibility of States under international law.

Article 26
Exclusion of jurisdiction over persons under eighteen

The Court shall have no jurisdiction over any person who was under the age of 18 at the time of the alleged commission of a crime.

Article 27
Irrelevance of official capacity

1. This Statute shall apply equally to all persons without any distinction based on official capacity. In particular, official capacity as a Head of State or Government, a member of a Government or parliament, an elected representative or a government official shall in no case exempt a person from criminal responsibility under this Statute, nor shall it, in and of itself, constitute a ground for reduction of sentence.

2. Immunities or special procedural rules which may attach to the official capacity of a person, whether under national or international law, shall not bar the Court from exercising its jurisdiction over such a person.

Article 28
Responsibility of commanders and other superiors

In addition to other grounds of criminal responsibility under this Statute for crimes within the jurisdiction of the Court:

(a) A military commander or person effectively acting as a military commander shall be criminally responsible for crimes within the jurisdiction of the Court committed by forces under his or her effective command and control, or effective authority and control as the case may be, as a result of his or her failure to exercise control properly over such forces, where:

(i) That military commander or person either knew or, owing to the circumstances at the time, should have known that the forces were committing or about to commit such crimes; and

(ii) That military commander or person failed to take all necessary and reasonable measures within his or her power to prevent or repress their commission or to submit the matter to the competent authorities for investigation and prosecution.

(b) With respect to superior and subordinate relationships not described in paragraph (a), a superior shall be criminally responsible for crimes within the jurisdiction of the Court committed by subordinates under his or her effective authority and control, as a result of his or her failure to exercise control properly over such subordinates, where:

(i) The superior either knew, or consciously disregarded information which clearly indicated, that the subordinates were committing or about to commit such crimes;

(ii) The crimes concerned activities that were within the effective responsibility and control of the superior; and

(iii) The superior failed to take all necessary and reasonable measures within his or her power to prevent or repress their commission or to submit the matter to the competent authorities for investigation and prosecution.

Article 29
Non-applicability of statute of limitations

The crimes within the jurisdiction of the Court shall not be subject to any statute of limitations.

Article 30
Mental element

1. Unless otherwise provided, a person shall be criminally responsible and liable for punishment for a crime within the jurisdiction of the Court only if the material elements are committed with intent and knowledge.

2. For the purposes of this article, a person has intent where:

(a) In relation to conduct, that person means to engage in the conduct;

(b) In relation to a consequence, that person means to cause that consequence or is aware that it will occur in the ordinary course of events.

3. For the purposes of this article, "knowledge" means awareness that a circumstance exists or a consequence will occur in the ordinary course of events. "Know" and "knowingly" shall be construed accordingly.

Article 31
Grounds for excluding criminal responsibility

1. In addition to other grounds for excluding criminal responsibility provided for in this Statute, a person shall not be criminally responsible if, at the time of that person's conduct:

(a) The person suffers from a mental disease or defect that destroys that person's capacity to appreciate the unlawfulness or nature of his or her conduct, or capacity to control his or her conduct to conform to the requirements of law;

(b) The person is in a state of intoxication that destroys that person's capacity to appreciate the unlawfulness or nature of his or her conduct, or capacity to control his or her conduct to conform to the requirements of law, unless the person has become voluntarily intoxicated under such circumstances that the person knew, or disregarded the risk, that, as a result of the intoxication, he or she was likely to engage in conduct constituting a crime within the jurisdiction of the Court;

(c) The person acts reasonably to defend himself or herself or another person or, in the case of war crimes, property which is essential for the survival of the person or another person or property which is essential for accomplishing a military mission, against an imminent and unlawful use of force in a manner proportionate to the degree of danger to the person or the other person or property protected. The fact that the person was involved in a defensive operation conducted by forces shall not in itself constitute a ground for excluding criminal responsibility under this subparagraph;

(d) The conduct which is alleged to constitute a crime within the jurisdiction of the Court has been caused by duress resulting from a threat of imminent death or of continuing or imminent serious bodily harm against that person or another person, and the person acts necessarily and reasonably to avoid this threat, provided that the person does not intend to cause a greater harm than the one sought to be avoided. Such a threat may either be:

(i) Made by other persons; or

(ii) Constituted by other circumstances beyond that person's control.

2. The Court shall determine the applicability of the grounds for excluding criminal responsibility provided for in this Statute to the case before it.

3. At trial, the Court may consider a ground for excluding criminal responsibility other than those referred to in paragraph 1 where such a ground is derived from applicable law as set forth in article 21. The procedures relating to the consideration of such a ground shall be provided for in the Rules of Procedure and Evidence.

Article 32
Mistake of fact or mistake of law

1. A mistake of fact shall be a ground for excluding criminal responsibility only if it negates the mental element required by the crime.

2. A mistake of law as to whether a particular type of conduct is a crime within the jurisdiction of the Court shall not be a ground for

excluding criminal responsibility. A mistake of law may, however, be a ground for excluding criminal responsibility if it negates the mental element required by such a crime, or as provided for in article 33.

Article 33
Superior orders and prescription of law

1. The fact that a crime within the jurisdiction of the Court has been committed by a person pursuant to an order of a Government or of a superior, whether military or civilian, shall not relieve that person of criminal responsibility unless:

(a) The person was under a legal obligation to obey orders of the Government or the superior in question;

(b) The person did not know that the order was unlawful; and

(c) The order was not manifestly unlawful.

2. For the purposes of this article, orders to commit genocide or crimes against humanity are manifestly unlawful.

PART 4. COMPOSITION AND ADMINISTRATION OF THE COURT

Article 34
Organs of the Court

The Court shall be composed of the following organs:

(a) The Presidency;

(b) An Appeals Division, a Trial Division and a Pre-Trial Division;

(c) The Office of the Prosecutor;

(d) The Registry.

Article 35
Service of judges

1. All judges shall be elected as full-time members of the Court and shall be available to serve on that basis from the commencement of their terms of office.

2. The judges composing the Presidency shall serve on a full-time basis as soon as they are elected.

3. The Presidency may, on the basis of the workload of the Court and in consultation with its members, decide from time to time to what extent

the remaining judges shall be required to serve on a full-time basis. Any such arrangement shall be without prejudice to the provisions of article 40.

4. The financial arrangements for judges not required to serve on a full-time basis shall be made in accordance with article 49.

Article 36
Qualifications, nomination and election of judges

1. Subject to the provisions of paragraph 2, there shall be 18 judges of the Court.

2. (a) The Presidency, acting on behalf of the Court, may propose an increase in the number of judges specified in paragraph 1, indicating the reasons why this is considered necessary and appropriate. The Registrar shall promptly circulate any such proposal to all States Parties.

(b) Any such proposal shall then be considered at a meeting of the Assembly of States Parties to be convened in accordance with article 112. The proposal shall be considered adopted if

approved at the meeting by a vote of two thirds of the members of the Assembly of States Parties and shall enter into force at such time as decided by the Assembly of States Parties.

(c) (i) Once a proposal for an increase in the number of judges has been adopted under subparagraph (b), the election of the additional judges shall take place at the next session of the Assembly of States Parties in accordance with paragraphs 3 to 8, and article 37, paragraph 2;

(ii) Once a proposal for an increase in the number of judges has been adopted and brought into effect under subparagraphs (b) and (c) (i), it shall be open to the Presidency at any time thereafter, if the workload of the Court justifies it, to propose a reduction in the number of judges, provided that the number of judges shall not be reduced below that specified in paragraph 1. The proposal shall be dealt with in accordance with the procedure laid down in subparagraphs (a) and (b). In the event that the proposal is adopted, the number of judges shall be progressively decreased as the terms of office of serving judges expire, until the necessary number has been reached.

3. (a) The judges shall be chosen from among persons of high moral character, impartiality and integrity who possess the qualifications required in their respective States for appointment to the highest judicial offices.

(b) Every candidate for election to the Court shall:

(i) Have established competence in criminal law and procedure, and the necessary relevant experience, whether as judge, prosecutor, advocate or in other similar capacity, in criminal proceedings; or

(ii) Have established competence in relevant areas of international law such as international humanitarian law and the law of human rights, and extensive experience in a professional legal capacity which is of relevance to the judicial work of the Court;

(c) Every candidate for election to the Court shall have an excellent knowledge of and be fluent in at least one of the working languages of the Court.

4. (a) Nominations of candidates for election to the Court may be made by any State Party to this Statute, and shall be made either:

(i) By the procedure for the nomination of candidates for appointment to the highest judicial offices in the State in question; or

(ii) By the procedure provided for the nomination of candidates for the International Court of Justice in the Statute of that Court.

Nominations shall be accompanied by a statement in the necessary detail specifying how the candidate fulfils the requirements of paragraph 3.

(b) Each State Party may put forward one candidate for any given election who need not necessarily be a national of that State Party but shall in any case be a national of a State Party.

(c) The Assembly of States Parties may decide to establish, if appropriate, an Advisory Committee on nominations. In that event, the Committee's composition and mandate shall be established by the Assembly of States Parties.

5. For the purposes of the election, there shall be two lists of candidates:

List A containing the names of candidates with the qualifications specified in paragraph 3 (b) (i); and

List B containing the names of candidates with the qualifications specified in paragraph 3 (b) (ii).

A candidate with sufficient qualifications for both lists may choose on which list to appear. At the first election to the Court, at least nine judges shall be elected from list A and at least five judges from list B. Subsequent elections shall be so organized as to maintain the equivalent proportion on the Court of judges qualified on the two lists.

6. (a) The judges shall be elected by secret ballot at a meeting of the Assembly of States Parties convened for that purpose under article 112. Subject to paragraph 7, the persons elected to the Court shall be the 18

candidates who obtain the highest number of votes and a two-thirds majority of the States Parties present and voting.

(b) In the event that a sufficient number of judges is not elected on the first ballot, successive ballots shall be held in accordance with the procedures laid down in subparagraph (a) until the remaining places have been filled.

7. No two judges may be nationals of the same State. A person who, for the purposes of membership of the Court, could be regarded as a national of more than one State shall be deemed to be a national of the State in which that person ordinarily exercises civil and political rights.

8. (a) The States Parties shall, in the selection of judges, take into account the need, within the membership of the Court, for:

(i) The representation of the principal legal systems of the world;

(ii) Equitable geographical representation; and

(iii) A fair representation of female and male judges.

(b) States Parties shall also take into account the need to include judges with legal expertise on specific issues, including, but not limited to, violence against women or children.

9. (a) Subject to subparagraph (b), judges shall hold office for a term of nine years and, subject to subparagraph (c) and to article 37, paragraph 2, shall not be eligible for re-election.

(b) At the first election, one third of the judges elected shall be selected by lot to serve for a term of three years; one third of the judges elected shall be selected by lot to serve for a term of six years; and the remainder shall serve for a term of nine years.

(c) A judge who is selected to serve for a term of three years under subparagraph (b) shall be eligible for re-election for a full term.

10. Notwithstanding paragraph 9, a judge assigned to a Trial or Appeals Chamber in accordance with article 39 shall continue in office to complete any trial or appeal the hearing of which has already commenced before that Chamber.

Article 37
Judicial vacancies

1. In the event of a vacancy, an election shall be held in accordance with article 36 to fill the vacancy.

2. A judge elected to fill a vacancy shall serve for the remainder of the predecessor's term and, if that period is three years or less, shall be eligible for re-election for a full term under article 36.

Article 38
The Presidency

1. The President and the First and Second Vice-Presidents shall be elected by an absolute majority of the judges. They shall each serve for a term of three years or until the end of their respective terms of office as judges, whichever expires earlier. They shall be eligible for re-election once.

2. The First Vice-President shall act in place of the President in the event that the President is unavailable or disqualified. The Second Vice-President shall act in place of the President in the event that both the President and the First Vice-President are unavailable or disqualified.

3. The President, together with the First and Second Vice-Presidents, shall constitute the Presidency, which shall be responsible for:

(a) The proper administration of the Court, with the exception of the Office of the Prosecutor; and

(b) The other functions conferred upon it in accordance with this Statute.

4. In discharging its responsibility under paragraph 3 (a), the Presidency shall coordinate with and seek the concurrence of the Prosecutor on all matters of mutual concern.

Article 39
Chambers

1. As soon as possible after the election of the judges, the Court shall organize itself into the divisions specified in article 34, paragraph (b). The Appeals Division shall be composed of the President and four other judges, the Trial Division of not less than six judges and the Pre-Trial Division of not less than six judges. The assignment of judges to divisions shall be based on the nature of the functions to be performed by each division and the qualifications and experience of the judges elected to the Court, in such a way that each division shall contain an appropriate combination of expertise in criminal law and procedure and in international law. The Trial and Pre-Trial Divisions shall be composed predominantly of judges with criminal trial experience.

2. (a) The judicial functions of the Court shall be carried out in each division by Chambers.

(b) (i) The Appeals Chamber shall be composed of all the judges of the Appeals Division;

(ii) The functions of the Trial Chamber shall be carried out by three judges of the Trial Division;

(iii) The functions of the Pre-Trial Chamber shall be carried out either by three judges of the Pre-Trial Division or by a single judge of that division in accordance with this Statute and the Rules of Procedure and Evidence;

(c) Nothing in this paragraph shall preclude the simultaneous constitution of more than one Trial Chamber or Pre-Trial Chamber when the efficient management of the Court's workload so requires.

3. (a) Judges assigned to the Trial and Pre-Trial Divisions shall serve in those divisions for a period of three years, and thereafter until the completion of any case the hearing of which has already commenced in the division concerned.

(b) Judges assigned to the Appeals Division shall serve in that division for their entire term of office.

4. Judges assigned to the Appeals Division shall serve only in that division. Nothing in this article shall, however, preclude the temporary attachment of judges from the Trial Division to the Pre-Trial Division or vice versa, if the Presidency considers that the efficient management of the Court's workload so requires, provided that under no circumstances shall a judge who has participated in the pre-trial phase of a case be eligible to sit on the Trial Chamber hearing that case.

Article 40
Independence of the judges

1. The judges shall be independent in the performance of their functions.

2. Judges shall not engage in any activity which is likely to interfere with their judicial functions or to affect confidence in their independence.

3. Judges required to serve on a full-time basis at the seat of the Court shall not engage in any other occupation of a professional nature.

4. Any question regarding the application of paragraphs 2 and 3 shall be decided by an absolute majority of the judges. Where any such question concerns an individual judge, that judge shall not take part in the decision.

Article 41
Excusing and disqualification of judges

1. The Presidency may, at the request of a judge, excuse that judge from the exercise of a function under this Statute, in accordance with the Rules of Procedure and Evidence.

2. (a) A judge shall not participate in any case in which his or her impartiality might reasonably be doubted on any ground. A judge shall be disqualified from a case in accordance with this paragraph if, inter alia, that judge has previously been involved in any capacity in that case before the Court or in a related criminal case at the national level involving the person being investigated or prosecuted. A judge shall also be disqualified on such other grounds as may be provided for in the Rules of Procedure and Evidence.

(b) The Prosecutor or the person being investigated or prosecuted may request the disqualification of a judge under this paragraph.

(c) Any question as to the disqualification of a judge shall be decided by an absolute majority of the judges. The challenged judge shall be entitled to present his or her comments on the matter, but shall not take part in the decision.

Article 42
The Office of the Prosecutor

1. The Office of the Prosecutor shall act independently as a separate organ of the Court. It shall be responsible for receiving referrals and any substantiated information on crimes within the jurisdiction of the Court, for examining them and for conducting investigations and prosecutions before the Court. A member of the Office shall not seek or act on instructions from any external source.

2. The Office shall be headed by the Prosecutor. The Prosecutor shall have full authority over the management and administration of the Office, including the staff, facilities and other resources thereof. The Prosecutor shall be assisted by one or more Deputy Prosecutors, who shall be entitled to carry out any of the acts required of the Prosecutor under this Statute. The Prosecutor and the Deputy Prosecutors shall be of different nationalities. They shall serve on a full-time basis.

3. The Prosecutor and the Deputy Prosecutors shall be persons of high moral character, be highly competent in and have extensive practical experience in the prosecution or trial of criminal cases. They shall have an

excellent knowledge of and be fluent in at least one of the working languages of the Court.

4. The Prosecutor shall be elected by secret ballot by an absolute majority of the members of the Assembly of States Parties. The Deputy Prosecutors shall be elected in the same way from a list of candidates provided by the Prosecutor. The Prosecutor shall nominate three candidates for each position of Deputy Prosecutor to be filled. Unless a shorter term is decided upon at the time of their election, the Prosecutor and the Deputy Prosecutors shall hold office for a term of nine years and shall not be eligible for re-election.

5. Neither the Prosecutor nor a Deputy Prosecutor shall engage in any activity which is likely to interfere with his or her prosecutorial functions or to affect confidence in his or her independence. They shall not engage in any other occupation of a professional nature.

6. The Presidency may excuse the Prosecutor or a Deputy Prosecutor, at his or her request, from acting in a particular case.

7. Neither the Prosecutor nor a Deputy Prosecutor shall participate in any matter in which their impartiality might reasonably be doubted on any ground. They shall be disqualified from a case in accordance with this paragraph if, inter alia, they have previously been involved in any capacity in that case before the Court or in a related criminal case at the national level involving the person being investigated or prosecuted.

8. Any question as to the disqualification of the Prosecutor or a Deputy Prosecutor shall be decided by the Appeals Chamber.

(a) The person being investigated or prosecuted may at any time request the disqualification of the Prosecutor or a Deputy Prosecutor on the grounds set out in this article;

(b) The Prosecutor or the Deputy Prosecutor, as appropriate, shall be entitled to present his or her comments on the matter;

9. The Prosecutor shall appoint advisers with legal expertise on specific issues, including, but not limited to, sexual and gender violence and violence against children.

Article 43
The Registry

1. The Registry shall be responsible for the non-judicial aspects of the administration and servicing of the Court, without prejudice to the functions and powers of the Prosecutor in accordance with article 42.

2. The Registry shall be headed by the Registrar, who shall be the principal administrative officer of the Court. The Registrar shall exercise his or her functions under the authority of the President of the Court.

3. The Registrar and the Deputy Registrar shall be persons of high moral character, be highly competent and have an excellent knowledge of and be fluent in at least one of the working languages of the Court.

4. The judges shall elect the Registrar by an absolute majority by secret ballot, taking into account any recommendation by the Assembly of States Parties. If the need arises and upon the recommendation of the Registrar, the judges shall elect, in the same manner, a Deputy Registrar.

5. The Registrar shall hold office for a term of five years, shall be eligible for re-election once and shall serve on a full-time basis. The Deputy Registrar shall hold office for a term of five years or such shorter term as may be decided upon by an absolute majority of the judges, and may be elected on the basis that the Deputy Registrar shall be called upon to serve as required.

6. The Registrar shall set up a Victims and Witnesses Unit within the Registry. This Unit shall provide, in consultation with the Office of the Prosecutor, protective measures and security arrangements, counselling and other appropriate assistance for witnesses, victims who appear before the Court, and others who are at risk on account of testimony given by such witnesses. The Unit shall include staff with expertise in trauma, including trauma related to crimes of sexual violence.

Article 44
Staff

1. The Prosecutor and the Registrar shall appoint such qualified staff as may be required to their respective offices. In the case of the Prosecutor, this shall include the appointment of investigators.

2. In the employment of staff, the Prosecutor and the Registrar shall ensure the highest standards of efficiency, competency and integrity, and shall have regard, mutatis mutandis, to the criteria set forth in article 36, paragraph 8.

3. The Registrar, with the agreement of the Presidency and the Prosecutor, shall propose Staff Regulations which include the terms and conditions upon which the staff of the Court shall be appointed, remunerated and dismissed. The Staff Regulations shall be approved by the Assembly of States Parties.

4. The Court may, in exceptional circumstances, employ the expertise of gratis personnel offered by States Parties, intergovernmental

organizations or non-governmental organizations to assist with the work of any of the organs of the Court. The Prosecutor may accept any such offer on behalf of the Office of the Prosecutor. Such gratis personnel shall be employed in accordance with guidelines to be established by the Assembly of States Parties.

Article 45
Solemn undertaking

Before taking up their respective duties under this Statute, the judges, the Prosecutor, the Deputy Prosecutors, the Registrar and the Deputy Registrar shall each make a solemn undertaking in open court to exercise his or her respective functions impartially and conscientiously.

Article 46
Removal from office

1. A judge, the Prosecutor, a Deputy Prosecutor, the Registrar or the Deputy Registrar shall be removed from office if a decision to this effect is made in accordance with paragraph 2, in cases where that person:

(a) Is found to have committed serious misconduct or a serious breach of his or her duties under this Statute, as provided for in the Rules of Procedure and Evidence; or

(b) Is unable to exercise the functions required by this Statute.

2. A decision as to the removal from office of a judge, the Prosecutor or a Deputy Prosecutor under paragraph 1 shall be made by the Assembly of States Parties, by secret ballot:

(a) In the case of a judge, by a two-thirds majority of the States Parties upon a recommendation adopted by a two-thirds majority of the other judges;

(b) In the case of the Prosecutor, by an absolute majority of the States Parties;

(c) In the case of a Deputy Prosecutor, by an absolute majority of the States Parties upon the recommendation of the Prosecutor.

3. A decision as to the removal from office of the Registrar or Deputy Registrar shall be made by an absolute majority of the judges.

4. A judge, Prosecutor, Deputy Prosecutor, Registrar or Deputy Registrar whose conduct or ability to exercise the functions of the office as required by this Statute is challenged under this article shall have full opportunity to present and receive evidence and to make submissions in

accordance with the Rules of Procedure and Evidence. The person in question shall not otherwise participate in the consideration of the matter.

Article 47
Disciplinary measures

A judge, Prosecutor, Deputy Prosecutor, Registrar or Deputy Registrar who has committed misconduct of a less serious nature than that set out in article 46, paragraph 1, shall be subject to disciplinary measures, in accordance with the Rules of Procedure and Evidence.

Article 48
Privileges and immunities

1. The Court shall enjoy in the territory of each State Party such privileges and immunities as are necessary for the fulfilment of its purposes.

2. The judges, the Prosecutor, the Deputy Prosecutors and the Registrar shall, when engaged on or with respect to the business of the Court, enjoy the same privileges and immunities as are accorded to heads of diplomatic missions and shall, after the expiry of their terms of office, continue to be accorded immunity from legal process of every kind in respect of words spoken or written and acts performed by them in their official capacity.

3. The Deputy Registrar, the staff of the Office of the Prosecutor and the staff of the Registry shall enjoy the privileges and immunities and facilities necessary for the performance of their functions, in accordance with the agreement on the privileges and immunities of the Court.

4. Counsel, experts, witnesses or any other person required to be present at the seat of the Court shall be accorded such treatment as is necessary for the proper functioning of the Court, in accordance with the agreement on the privileges and immunities of the Court.

5. The privileges and immunities of:

(a) A judge or the Prosecutor may be waived by an absolute majority of the judges;

(b) The Registrar may be waived by the Presidency;

(c) The Deputy Prosecutors and staff of the Office of the Prosecutor may be waived by the Prosecutor;

(d) The Deputy Registrar and staff of the Registry may be waived by the Registrar.

Article 49
Salaries, allowances and expenses

The judges, the Prosecutor, the Deputy Prosecutors, the Registrar and the Deputy Registrar shall receive such salaries, allowances and expenses as may be decided upon by the Assembly of States Parties. These salaries and allowances shall not be reduced during their terms of office.

Article 50
Official and working languages

1. The official languages of the Court shall be Arabic, Chinese, English, French, Russian and Spanish. The judgements of the Court, as well as other decisions resolving fundamental issues before the Court, shall be published in the official languages. The Presidency shall, in accordance with the criteria established by the Rules of Procedure and Evidence, determine which decisions may be considered as resolving fundamental issues for the purposes of this paragraph.

2. The working languages of the Court shall be English and French. The Rules of Procedure and Evidence shall determine the cases in which other official languages may be used as working languages.

3. At the request of any party to a proceeding or a State allowed to intervene in a proceeding, the Court shall authorize a language other than English or French to be used by such a party or State, provided that the Court considers such authorization to be adequately justified.

Article 51
Rules of Procedure and Evidence

1. The Rules of Procedure and Evidence shall enter into force upon adoption by a two-thirds majority of the members of the Assembly of States Parties.

2. Amendments to the Rules of Procedure and Evidence may be proposed by:

(a) Any State Party;

(b) The judges acting by an absolute majority; or

(c) The Prosecutor.

Such amendments shall enter into force upon adoption by a two-thirds majority of the members of the Assembly of States Parties.

3. After the adoption of the Rules of Procedure and Evidence, in urgent cases where the Rules do not provide for a specific situation before the

Court, the judges may, by a two-thirds majority, draw up provisional Rules to be applied until adopted, amended or rejected at the next ordinary or special session of the Assembly of States Parties.

4. The Rules of Procedure and Evidence, amendments thereto and any provisional Rule shall be consistent with this Statute. Amendments to the Rules of Procedure and Evidence as well as provisional Rules shall not be applied retroactively to the detriment of the person who is being investigated or prosecuted or who has been convicted.

5. In the event of conflict between the Statute and the Rules of Procedure and Evidence, the Statute shall prevail.

Article 52
Regulations of the Court

1. The judges shall, in accordance with this Statute and the Rules of Procedure and Evidence, adopt, by an absolute majority, the Regulations of the Court necessary for its routine functioning.

2. The Prosecutor and the Registrar shall be consulted in the elaboration of the Regulations and any amendments thereto.

3. The Regulations and any amendments thereto shall take effect upon adoption unless otherwise decided by the judges. Immediately upon adoption, they shall be circulated to States Parties for comments. If within six months there are no objections from a majority of States Parties, they shall remain in force.

PART 5. INVESTIGATION AND PROSECUTION

Article 53
Initiation of an investigation

1. The Prosecutor shall, having evaluated the information made available to him or her, initiate an investigation unless he or she determines that there is no reasonable basis to proceed under this Statute. In deciding whether to initiate an investigation, the Prosecutor shall consider whether:

(a) The information available to the Prosecutor provides a reasonable basis to believe that a crime within the jurisdiction of the Court has been or is being committed;

(b) The case is or would be admissible under article 17; and

(c) Taking into account the gravity of the crime and the interests of victims, there are nonetheless substantial reasons to believe that an investigation would not serve the interests of justice.

If the Prosecutor determines that there is no reasonable basis to proceed and his or her determination is based solely on subparagraph (c) above, he or she shall inform the Pre-Trial Chamber.

2. If, upon investigation, the Prosecutor concludes that there is not a sufficient basis for a prosecution because:

(a) There is not a sufficient legal or factual basis to seek a warrant or summons under article 58;

(b) The case is inadmissible under article 17; or

(c) A prosecution is not in the interests of justice, taking into account all the circumstances, including the gravity of the crime, the interests of victims and the age or infirmity of the alleged perpetrator, and his or her role in the alleged crime;

the Prosecutor shall inform the Pre-Trial Chamber and the State making a referral under article 14 or the Security Council in a case under article 13, paragraph (b), of his or her conclusion and the reasons for the conclusion.

3. (a) At the request of the State making a referral under article 14 or the Security Council under article 13, paragraph (b), the Pre-Trial Chamber may review a decision of the Prosecutor under paragraph 1 or 2 not to proceed and may request the Prosecutor to reconsider that decision.

(b) In addition, the Pre-Trial Chamber may, on its own initiative, review a decision of the Prosecutor not to proceed if it is based solely on paragraph 1 (c) or 2 (c). In such a case, the decision of the Prosecutor shall be effective only if confirmed by the Pre-Trial Chamber.

4. The Prosecutor may, at any time, reconsider a decision whether to initiate an investigation or prosecution based on new facts or information.

Article 54
Duties and powers of the Prosecutor with respect to investigations

1. The Prosecutor shall:

(a) In order to establish the truth, extend the investigation to cover all facts and evidence relevant to an assessment of whether there is criminal responsibility under this Statute, and, in doing so, investigate incriminating and exonerating circumstances equally;

(b) Take appropriate measures to ensure the effective investigation and prosecution of crimes within the jurisdiction of the Court, and in doing so, respect the interests and personal circumstances of victims and witnesses, including age, gender as defined in article 7, paragraph 3, and health, and take into account the nature of the crime, in particular where it involves sexual violence, gender violence or violence against children; and

(c) Fully respect the rights of persons arising under this Statute.

2. The Prosecutor may conduct investigations on the territory of a State:

(a) In accordance with the provisions of Part 9; or

(b) As authorized by the Pre-Trial Chamber under article 57, paragraph 3 (d).

3. The Prosecutor may:

(a) Collect and examine evidence;

(b) Request the presence of and question persons being investigated, victims and witnesses;

(c) Seek the cooperation of any State or intergovernmental organization or arrangement in accordance with its respective competence and/or mandate;

(d) Enter into such arrangements or agreements, not inconsistent with this Statute, as may be necessary to facilitate the cooperation of a State, intergovernmental organization or person;

(e) Agree not to disclose, at any stage of the proceedings, documents or information that the Prosecutor obtains on the condition of confidentiality and solely for the purpose of generating new evidence, unless the provider of the information consents; and

(f) Take necessary measures, or request that necessary measures be taken, to ensure the confidentiality of information, the protection of any person or the preservation of evidence.

Article 55
Rights of persons during an investigation

1. In respect of an investigation under this Statute, a person:

(a) Shall not be compelled to incriminate himself or herself or to confess guilt;

(b) Shall not be subjected to any form of coercion, duress or threat, to torture or to any other form of cruel, inhuman or degrading treatment or punishment;

(c) Shall, if questioned in a language other than a language the person fully understands and speaks, have, free of any cost, the assistance of a competent interpreter and such translations as are necessary to meet the requirements of fairness; and

(d) Shall not be subjected to arbitrary arrest or detention, and shall not be deprived of his or her liberty except on such grounds and in accordance with such procedures as are established in this Statute.

2. Where there are grounds to believe that a person has committed a crime within the jurisdiction of the Court and that person is about to be questioned either by the Prosecutor, or by national authorities pursuant to a request made under Part 9, that person shall also have the following rights of which he or she shall be informed prior to being questioned:

(a) To be informed, prior to being questioned, that there are grounds to believe that he or she has committed a crime within the jurisdiction of the Court;

(b) To remain silent, without such silence being a consideration in the determination of guilt or innocence;

(c) To have legal assistance of the person's choosing, or, if the person does not have legal assistance, to have legal assistance assigned to him or her, in any case where the interests of justice so require, and without payment by the person in any such case if the person does not have sufficient means to pay for it; and

(d) To be questioned in the presence of counsel unless the person has voluntarily waived his or her right to counsel.

Article 56
Role of the Pre-Trial Chamber in relation to a unique investigative opportunity

1. (a) Where the Prosecutor considers an investigation to present a unique opportunity to take testimony or a statement from a witness or to examine, collect or test evidence, which may not be available subsequently for the purposes of a trial, the Prosecutor shall so inform the Pre-Trial Chamber.

(b) In that case, the Pre-Trial Chamber may, upon request of the Prosecutor, take such measures as may be necessary to ensure the efficiency and integrity of the proceedings and, in particular, to protect the rights of the defence.

(c) Unless the Pre-Trial Chamber orders otherwise, the Prosecutor shall provide the relevant information to the person who has been arrested or appeared in response to a summons in connection with the investigation referred to in subparagraph (a), in order that he or she may be heard on the matter.

2. The measures referred to in paragraph 1 (b) may include:

(a) Making recommendations or orders regarding procedures to be followed;

(b) Directing that a record be made of the proceedings;

(c) Appointing an expert to assist;

(d) Authorizing counsel for a person who has been arrested, or appeared before the Court in response to a summons, to participate, or where there has not yet been such an arrest or appearance or counsel has not been designated, appointing another counsel to attend and represent the interests of the defence;

(e) Naming one of its members or, if necessary, another available judge of the Pre-Trial or Trial Division to observe and make recommendations or orders regarding the collection and preservation of evidence and the questioning of persons;

(f) Taking such other action as may be necessary to collect or preserve evidence.

3. (a) Where the Prosecutor has not sought measures pursuant to this article but the Pre-Trial Chamber considers that such measures are required to preserve evidence that it deems would be essential for the defence at trial, it shall consult with the Prosecutor as to whether there is good reason for the Prosecutor's failure to request the measures. If upon consultation, the Pre-Trial Chamber concludes that the Prosecutor's failure to request such measures is unjustified, the Pre-Trial Chamber may take such measures on its own initiative.

(b) A decision of the Pre-Trial Chamber to act on its own initiative under this paragraph may be appealed by the Prosecutor. The appeal shall be heard on an expedited basis.

4. The admissibility of evidence preserved or collected for trial pursuant to this article, or the record thereof, shall be governed at trial by article 69, and given such weight as determined by the Trial Chamber.

Article 57
Functions and powers of the Pre-Trial Chamber

1. Unless otherwise provided in this Statute, the Pre-Trial Chamber shall exercise its functions in accordance with the provisions of this article.

2. (a) Orders or rulings of the Pre-Trial Chamber issued under articles 15, 18, 19, 54, paragraph 2, 61, paragraph 7, and 72 must be concurred in by a majority of its judges.

(b) In all other cases, a single judge of the Pre-Trial Chamber may exercise the functions provided for in this Statute, unless otherwise provided for in the Rules of Procedure and Evidence or by a majority of the Pre-Trial Chamber.

3. In addition to its other functions under this Statute, the Pre-Trial Chamber may:

(a) At the request of the Prosecutor, issue such orders and warrants as may be required for the purposes of an investigation;

(b) Upon the request of a person who has been arrested or has appeared pursuant to a summons under article 58, issue such orders, including measures such as those described in article 56, or seek such cooperation pursuant to Part 9 as may be necessary to assist the person in the preparation of his or her defence;

(c) Where necessary, provide for the protection and privacy of victims and witnesses, the preservation of evidence, the protection of persons who have been arrested or appeared in response to a summons, and the protection of national security information;

(d) Authorize the Prosecutor to take specific investigative steps within the territory of a State Party without having secured the cooperation of that State under Part 9 if, whenever possible having regard to the views of the State concerned, the Pre-Trial Chamber has determined in that case that the State is clearly unable to execute a request for cooperation due to the unavailability of any authority or any component of its judicial system competent to execute the request for cooperation under Part 9.

(e) Where a warrant of arrest or a summons has been issued under article 58, and having due regard to the strength of the evidence and the rights of the parties concerned, as provided for in this Statute and the Rules of Procedure and Evidence, seek the cooperation of States pursuant to article 93, paragraph 1 (k), to take protective measures for the purpose of forfeiture, in particular for the ultimate benefit of victims.

Article 58
Issuance by the Pre-Trial Chamber of a warrant of arrest or a summons to appear

1. At any time after the initiation of an investigation, the Pre-Trial Chamber shall, on the application of the Prosecutor, issue a warrant of arrest of a person if, having examined the application and the evidence or other information submitted by the Prosecutor, it is satisfied that:

(a) There are reasonable grounds to believe that the person has committed a crime within the jurisdiction of the Court; and

(b) The arrest of the person appears necessary:

(i) To ensure the person's appearance at trial,

(ii) To ensure that the person does not obstruct or endanger the investigation or the court proceedings, or

(iii) Where applicable, to prevent the person from continuing with the commission of that crime or a related crime which is within the jurisdiction of the Court and which arises out of the same circumstances.

2. The application of the Prosecutor shall contain:

(a) The name of the person and any other relevant identifying information;

(b) A specific reference to the crimes within the jurisdiction of the Court which the person is alleged to have committed;

(c) A concise statement of the facts which are alleged to constitute those crimes;

(d) A summary of the evidence and any other information which establish reasonable grounds to believe that the person committed those crimes; and

(e) The reason why the Prosecutor believes that the arrest of the person is necessary.

3. The warrant of arrest shall contain:

(a) The name of the person and any other relevant identifying information;

(b) A specific reference to the crimes within the jurisdiction of the Court for which the person's arrest is sought; and

(c) A concise statement of the facts which are alleged to constitute those crimes.

4. The warrant of arrest shall remain in effect until otherwise ordered by the Court.

5. On the basis of the warrant of arrest, the Court may request the provisional arrest or the arrest and surrender of the person under Part 9.

6. The Prosecutor may request the Pre-Trial Chamber to amend the warrant of arrest by modifying or adding to the crimes specified therein. The Pre-Trial Chamber shall so amend the warrant if it is satisfied that there are reasonable grounds to believe that the person committed the modified or additional crimes.

7. As an alternative to seeking a warrant of arrest, the Prosecutor may submit an application requesting that the Pre-Trial Chamber issue a summons for the person to appear. If the Pre-Trial Chamber is satisfied that there are reasonable grounds to believe that the person committed the crime alleged and that a summons is sufficient to ensure the person's appearance, it shall issue the summons, with or without conditions restricting liberty (other than detention) if provided for by national law, for the person to appear. The summons shall contain:

(a) The name of the person and any other relevant identifying information;

(b) The specified date on which the person is to appear;

(c) A specific reference to the crimes within the jurisdiction of the Court which the person is alleged to have committed; and

(d) A concise statement of the facts which are alleged to constitute the crime.

The summons shall be served on the person.

Article 59
Arrest proceedings in the custodial State

1. A State Party which has received a request for provisional arrest or for arrest and surrender shall immediately take steps to arrest the person in question in accordance with its laws and the provisions of Part 9.

2. A person arrested shall be brought promptly before the competent judicial authority in the custodial State which shall determine, in accordance with the law of that State, that:

(a) The warrant applies to that person;

(b) The person has been arrested in accordance with the proper process; and

(c) The person's rights have been respected.

3. The person arrested shall have the right to apply to the competent authority in the custodial State for interim release pending surrender.

4. In reaching a decision on any such application, the competent authority in the custodial State shall consider whether, given the gravity of the alleged crimes, there are urgent and exceptional circumstances to justify interim release and whether necessary safeguards exist to ensure that the custodial State can fulfil its duty to surrender the person to the Court. It shall not be open to the competent authority of the custodial State to consider whether the warrant of arrest was properly issued in accordance with article 58, paragraph 1 (a) and (b).

5. The Pre-Trial Chamber shall be notified of any request for interim release and shall make recommendations to the competent authority in the custodial State. The competent authority in the custodial State shall give full consideration to such recommendations, including any recommendations on measures to prevent the escape of the person, before rendering its decision.

6. If the person is granted interim release, the Pre-Trial Chamber may request periodic reports on the status of the interim release.

7. Once ordered to be surrendered by the custodial State, the person shall be delivered to the Court as soon as possible.

Article 60
Initial proceedings before the Court

1. Upon the surrender of the person to the Court, or the person's appearance before the Court voluntarily or pursuant to a summons, the Pre-Trial Chamber shall satisfy itself that the person has been informed of the crimes which he or she is alleged to have committed, and of his or her rights under this Statute, including the right to apply for interim release pending trial.

2. A person subject to a warrant of arrest may apply for interim release pending trial. If the Pre-Trial Chamber is satisfied that the conditions set forth in article 58, paragraph 1, are met, the person shall continue to be detained. If it is not so satisfied, the Pre-Trial Chamber shall release the person, with or without conditions.

3. The Pre-Trial Chamber shall periodically review its ruling on the release or detention of the person, and may do so at any time on the request of the Prosecutor or the person. Upon such review, it may modify its ruling as to detention, release or conditions of release, if it is satisfied that changed circumstances so require.

4. The Pre-Trial Chamber shall ensure that a person is not detained for an unreasonable period prior to trial due to inexcusable delay by the Prosecutor. If such delay occurs, the Court shall consider releasing the person, with or without conditions.

5. If necessary, the Pre-Trial Chamber may issue a warrant of arrest to secure the presence of a person who has been released.

Article 61
Confirmation of the charges before trial

1. Subject to the provisions of paragraph 2, within a reasonable time after the person's surrender or voluntary appearance before the Court, the Pre-Trial Chamber shall hold a hearing to confirm the charges on which the Prosecutor intends to seek trial. The hearing shall be held in the presence of the Prosecutor and the person charged, as well as his or her counsel.

2. The Pre-Trial Chamber may, upon request of the Prosecutor or on its own motion, hold a hearing in the absence of the person charged to

confirm the charges on which the Prosecutor intends to seek trial when the person has:

(a) Waived his or her right to be present; or

(b) Fled or cannot be found and all reasonable steps have been taken to secure his or her appearance before the Court and to inform the person of the charges and that a hearing to confirm those charges will be held.

In that case, the person shall be represented by counsel where the Pre-Trial Chamber determines that it is in the interests of justice.

3. Within a reasonable time before the hearing, the person shall:

(a) Be provided with a copy of the document containing the charges on which the Prosecutor intends to bring the person to trial; and

(b) Be informed of the evidence on which the Prosecutor intends to rely at the hearing.

The Pre-Trial Chamber may issue orders regarding the disclosure of information for the purposes of the hearing.

4. Before the hearing, the Prosecutor may continue the investigation and may amend or withdraw any charges. The person shall be given reasonable notice before the hearing of any amendment to or withdrawal of charges. In case of a withdrawal of charges, the Prosecutor shall notify the Pre-Trial Chamber of the reasons for the withdrawal.

5. At the hearing, the Prosecutor shall support each charge with sufficient evidence to establish substantial grounds to believe that the person committed the crime charged. The Prosecutor may rely on documentary or summary evidence and need not call the witnesses expected to testify at the trial.

6. At the hearing, the person may:

(a) Object to the charges;

(b) Challenge the evidence presented by the Prosecutor; and

(c) Present evidence.

7. The Pre-Trial Chamber shall, on the basis of the hearing, determine whether there is sufficient evidence to establish substantial grounds to believe that the person committed each of the crimes charged. Based on its determination, the Pre-Trial Chamber shall:

(a) Confirm those charges in relation to which it has determined that there is sufficient evidence, and commit the person to a Trial Chamber for trial on the charges as confirmed;

(b) Decline to confirm those charges in relation to which it has determined that there is insufficient evidence;

(c) Adjourn the hearing and request the Prosecutor to consider:

(i) Providing further evidence or conducting further investigation with respect to a particular charge; or

(ii) Amending a charge because the evidence submitted appears to establish a different crime within the jurisdiction of the Court.

8. Where the Pre-Trial Chamber declines to confirm a charge, the Prosecutor shall not be precluded from subsequently requesting its confirmation if the request is supported by additional evidence.

9. After the charges are confirmed and before the trial has begun, the Prosecutor may, with the permission of the Pre-Trial Chamber and after notice to the accused, amend the charges. If the Prosecutor seeks to add additional charges or to substitute more serious charges, a hearing under this article to confirm those charges must be held. After commencement of the trial, the Prosecutor may, with the permission of the Trial Chamber, withdraw the charges.

10. Any warrant previously issued shall cease to have effect with respect to any charges which have not been confirmed by the Pre-Trial Chamber or which have been withdrawn by the Prosecutor.

11. Once the charges have been confirmed in accordance with this article, the Presidency shall constitute a Trial Chamber which, subject to paragraph 9 and to article 64, paragraph 4, shall be responsible for the conduct of subsequent proceedings and may exercise any function of the Pre-Trial Chamber that is relevant and capable of application in those proceedings.

PART 6. THE TRIAL

Article 62
Place of trial

Unless otherwise decided, the place of the trial shall be the seat of the Court.

Article 63
Trial in the presence of the accused

1. The accused shall be present during the trial.

2. If the accused, being present before the Court, continues to disrupt the trial, the Trial Chamber may remove the accused and shall make provision for him or her to observe the trial and instruct counsel from outside the courtroom, through the use of communications technology, if required. Such measures shall be taken only in exceptional circumstances after other reasonable alternatives have proved inadequate, and only for such duration as is strictly required.

Article 64
Functions and powers of the Trial Chamber

1. The functions and powers of the Trial Chamber set out in this article shall be exercised in accordance with this Statute and the Rules of Procedure and Evidence.

2. The Trial Chamber shall ensure that a trial is fair and expeditious and is conducted with full respect for the rights of the accused and due regard for the protection of victims and witnesses.

3. Upon assignment of a case for trial in accordance with this Statute, the Trial Chamber assigned to deal with the case shall:

(a) Confer with the parties and adopt such procedures as are necessary to facilitate the fair and expeditious conduct of the proceedings;

(b) Determine the language or languages to be used at trial; and

(c) Subject to any other relevant provisions of this Statute, provide for disclosure of documents or information not previously disclosed, sufficiently in advance of the commencement of the trial to enable adequate preparation for trial.

4. The Trial Chamber may, if necessary for its effective and fair functioning, refer preliminary issues to the Pre-Trial Chamber or, if necessary, to another available judge of the Pre-Trial Division.

5. Upon notice to the parties, the Trial Chamber may, as appropriate, direct that there be joinder or severance in respect of charges against more than one accused.

6. In performing its functions prior to trial or during the course of a trial, the Trial Chamber may, as necessary:

(a) Exercise any functions of the Pre-Trial Chamber referred to in article 61, paragraph 11;

(b) Require the attendance and testimony of witnesses and production of documents and other evidence by obtaining, if necessary, the assistance of States as provided in this Statute;

(c) Provide for the protection of confidential information;

(d) Order the production of evidence in addition to that already collected prior to the trial or presented during the trial by the parties;

(e) Provide for the protection of the accused, witnesses and victims; and

(f) Rule on any other relevant matters.

7. The trial shall be held in public. The Trial Chamber may, however, determine that special circumstances require that certain proceedings be in closed session for the purposes set forth in article 68, or to protect confidential or sensitive information to be given in evidence.

8. (a) At the commencement of the trial, the Trial Chamber shall have read to the accused the charges previously confirmed by the Pre-Trial Chamber. The Trial Chamber shall satisfy itself that the accused understands the nature of the charges. It shall afford him or her the opportunity to make an admission of guilt in accordance with article 65 or to plead not guilty.

(b) At the trial, the presiding judge may give directions for the conduct of proceedings, including to ensure that they are conducted in a fair and impartial manner. Subject to any directions of the presiding judge, the parties may submit evidence in accordance with the provisions of this Statute.

9. The Trial Chamber shall have, inter alia, the power on application of a party or on its own motion to:

(a) Rule on the admissibility or relevance of evidence; and

(b) Take all necessary steps to maintain order in the course of a hearing.

10. The Trial Chamber shall ensure that a complete record of the trial, which accurately reflects the proceedings, is made and that it is maintained and preserved by the Registrar.

Article 65
Proceedings on an admission of guilt

1. Where the accused makes an admission of guilt pursuant to article 64, paragraph 8 (a), the Trial Chamber shall determine whether:

(a) The accused understands the nature and consequences of the admission of guilt;

(b) The admission is voluntarily made by the accused after sufficient consultation with defence counsel; and

(c) The admission of guilt is supported by the facts of the case that are contained in:

(i) The charges brought by the Prosecutor and admitted by the accused;

(ii) Any materials presented by the Prosecutor which supplement the charges and which the accused accepts; and

(iii) Any other evidence, such as the testimony of witnesses, presented by the Prosecutor or the accused.

2. Where the Trial Chamber is satisfied that the matters referred to in paragraph 1 are established, it shall consider the admission of guilt, together with any additional evidence presented, as establishing all the essential facts that are required to prove the crime to which the admission of guilt relates, and may convict the accused of that crime.

3. Where the Trial Chamber is not satisfied that the matters referred to in paragraph 1 are established, it shall consider the admission of guilt as not having been made, in which case it shall order that the trial be continued under the ordinary trial procedures provided by this Statute and may remit the case to another Trial Chamber.

4. Where the Trial Chamber is of the opinion that a more complete presentation of the facts of the case is required in the interests of justice, in particular the interests of the victims, the Trial Chamber may:

(a) Request the Prosecutor to present additional evidence, including the testimony of witnesses; or

(b) Order that the trial be continued under the ordinary trial procedures provided by this Statute, in which case it shall consider the admission of guilt as not having been made and may remit the case to another Trial Chamber.

5. Any discussions between the Prosecutor and the defence regarding modification of the charges, the admission of guilt or the penalty to be imposed shall not be binding on the Court.

Article 66
Presumption of innocence

1. Everyone shall be presumed innocent until proved guilty before the Court in accordance with the applicable law.

2. The onus is on the Prosecutor to prove the guilt of the accused.

3. In order to convict the accused, the Court must be convinced of the guilt of the accused beyond reasonable doubt.

Article 67
Rights of the accused

1. In the determination of any charge, the accused shall be entitled to a public hearing, having regard to the provisions of this Statute, to a fair hearing conducted impartially, and to the following minimum guarantees, in full equality:

(a) To be informed promptly and in detail of the nature, cause and content of the charge, in a language which the accused fully understands and speaks;

(b) To have adequate time and facilities for the preparation of the defence and to communicate freely with counsel of the accused's choosing in confidence;

(c) To be tried without undue delay;

(d) Subject to article 63, paragraph 2, to be present at the trial, to conduct the defence in person or through legal assistance of the accused's choosing, to be informed, if the accused does not have legal assistance, of this right and to have legal assistance assigned by the Court in any case where the interests of justice so require, and without payment if the accused lacks sufficient means to pay for it;

(e) To examine, or have examined, the witnesses against him or her and to obtain the attendance and examination of witnesses on his or her behalf under the same conditions as witnesses against him or her. The accused shall also be entitled to raise defences and to present other evidence admissible under this Statute;

(f) To have, free of any cost, the assistance of a competent interpreter and such translations as are necessary to meet the requirements of fairness, if any of the proceedings of or documents presented to the Court are not in a language which the accused fully understands and speaks;

(g) Not to be compelled to testify or to confess guilt and to remain silent, without such silence being a consideration in the determination of guilt or innocence;

(h) To make an unsworn oral or written statement in his or her defence; and

(i) Not to have imposed on him or her any reversal of the burden of proof or any onus of rebuttal.

2. In addition to any other disclosure provided for in this Statute, the Prosecutor shall, as soon as practicable, disclose to the defence evidence in the Prosecutor's possession or control which he or she believes shows or tends to show the innocence of the accused, or to mitigate the guilt of the accused, or which may affect the credibility of prosecution evidence. In case of doubt as to the application of this paragraph, the Court shall decide.

Article 68
Protection of the victims and witnesses and their participation in the proceedings

1. The Court shall take appropriate measures to protect the safety, physical and psychological well-being, dignity and privacy of victims and witnesses. In so doing, the Court shall have regard to all relevant factors, including age, gender as defined in article 7, paragraph 3, and health, and the nature of the crime, in particular, but not limited to, where the crime involves sexual or gender violence or violence against children. The Prosecutor shall take such measures particularly during the investigation

and prosecution of such crimes. These measures shall not be prejudicial to or inconsistent with the rights of the accused and a fair and impartial trial.

2. As an exception to the principle of public hearings provided for in article 67, the Chambers of the Court may, to protect victims and witnesses or an accused, conduct any part of the proceedings in camera or allow the presentation of evidence by electronic or other special means. In particular, such measures shall be implemented in the case of a victim of sexual violence or a child who is a victim or a witness, unless otherwise ordered by the Court, having regard to all the circumstances, particularly the views of the victim or witness.

3. Where the personal interests of the victims are affected, the Court shall permit their views and concerns to be presented and considered at stages of the proceedings determined to be appropriate by the Court and in a manner which is not prejudicial to or inconsistent with the rights of the accused and a fair and impartial trial. Such views and concerns may be presented by the legal representatives of the victims where the Court considers it appropriate, in accordance with the Rules of Procedure and Evidence.

4. The Victims and Witnesses Unit may advise the Prosecutor and the Court on appropriate protective measures, security arrangements, counselling and assistance as referred to in article 43, paragraph 6.

5. Where the disclosure of evidence or information pursuant to this Statute may lead to the grave endangerment of the security of a witness or his or her family, the Prosecutor may, for the purposes of any proceedings conducted prior to the commencement of the trial, withhold such evidence or information and instead submit a summary thereof. Such measures shall be exercised in a manner which is not prejudicial to or inconsistent with the rights of the accused and a fair and impartial trial.

6. A State may make an application for necessary measures to be taken in respect of the protection of its servants or agents and the protection of confidential or sensitive information.

Article 69
Evidence

1. Before testifying, each witness shall, in accordance with the Rules of Procedure and Evidence, give an undertaking as to the truthfulness of the evidence to be given by that witness.

2. The testimony of a witness at trial shall be given in person, except to the extent provided by the measures set forth in article 68 or in the Rules of Procedure and Evidence. The Court may also permit the giving of viva

voce (oral) or recorded testimony of a witness by means of video or audio technology, as well as the introduction of documents or written transcripts, subject to this Statute and in accordance with the Rules of Procedure and Evidence. These measures shall not be prejudicial to or inconsistent with the rights of the accused.

3. The parties may submit evidence relevant to the case, in accordance with article 64. The Court shall have the authority to request the submission of all evidence that it considers necessary for the determination of the truth.

4. The Court may rule on the relevance or admissibility of any evidence, taking into account, inter alia, the probative value of the evidence and any prejudice that such evidence may cause to a fair trial or to a fair evaluation of the testimony of a witness, in accordance with the Rules of Procedure and Evidence.

5. The Court shall respect and observe privileges on confidentiality as provided for in the Rules of Procedure and Evidence.

6. The Court shall not require proof of facts of common knowledge but may take judicial notice of them.

7. Evidence obtained by means of a violation of this Statute or internationally recognized human rights shall not be admissible if:

(a) The violation casts substantial doubt on the reliability of the evidence; or

(b) The admission of the evidence would be antithetical to and would seriously damage the integrity of the proceedings.

8. When deciding on the relevance or admissibility of evidence collected by a State, the Court shall not rule on the application of the State's national law.

Article 70
Offences against the administration of justice

1. The Court shall have jurisdiction over the following offences against its administration of justice when committed intentionally:

(a) Giving false testimony when under an obligation pursuant to article 69, paragraph 1, to tell the truth;

(b) Presenting evidence that the party knows is false or forged;

(c) Corruptly influencing a witness, obstructing or interfering with the attendance or testimony of a witness, retaliating against a witness for giving testimony or destroying, tampering with or interfering with the collection of evidence;

(d) Impeding, intimidating or corruptly influencing an official of the Court for the purpose of forcing or persuading the official not to perform, or to perform improperly, his or her duties;

(e) Retaliating against an official of the Court on account of duties performed by that or another official;

(f) Soliciting or accepting a bribe as an official of the Court in connection with his or her official duties.

2. The principles and procedures governing the Court's exercise of jurisdiction over offences under this article shall be those provided for in the Rules of Procedure and Evidence. The conditions for providing international cooperation to the Court with respect to its proceedings under this article shall be governed by the domestic laws of the requested State.

3. In the event of conviction, the Court may impose a term of imprisonment not exceeding five years, or a fine in accordance with the Rules of Procedure and Evidence, or both.

4. (a) Each State Party shall extend its criminal laws penalizing offences against the integrity of its own investigative or judicial process to offences against the administration of justice referred to in this article, committed on its territory, or by one of its nationals;

(b) Upon request by the Court, whenever it deems it proper, the State Party shall submit the case to its competent authorities for the purpose of prosecution. Those authorities shall treat such cases with diligence and devote sufficient resources to enable them to be conducted effectively.

Article 71
Sanctions for misconduct before the Court

1. The Court may sanction persons present before it who commit misconduct, including disruption of its proceedings or deliberate refusal to comply with its directions, by administrative measures other than imprisonment, such as temporary or permanent removal from the courtroom, a fine or other similar measures provided for in the Rules of Procedure and Evidence.

2. The procedures governing the imposition of the measures set forth in paragraph 1 shall be those provided for in the Rules of Procedure and Evidence.

Article 72
Protection of national security information

1. This article applies in any case where the disclosure of the information or documents of a State would, in the opinion of that State, prejudice its national security interests. Such cases include those falling within the scope of article 56, paragraphs 2 and 3, article 61, paragraph 3, article 64, paragraph 3, article 67, paragraph 2, article 68, paragraph 6, article 87, paragraph 6 and article 93, as well as cases arising at any other stage of the proceedings where such disclosure may be at issue.

2. This article shall also apply when a person who has been requested to give information or evidence has refused to do so or has referred the matter to the State on the ground that disclosure would prejudice the national security interests of a State and the State concerned confirms that it is of the opinion that disclosure would prejudice its national security interests.

3. Nothing in this article shall prejudice the requirements of confidentiality applicable under article 54, paragraph 3 (e) and (f), or the application of article 73.

4. If a State learns that information or documents of the State are being, or are likely to be, disclosed at any stage of the proceedings, and it is of the opinion that disclosure would prejudice its national security interests, that State shall have the right to intervene in order to obtain resolution of the issue in accordance with this article.

5. If, in the opinion of a State, disclosure of information would prejudice its national security interests, all reasonable steps will be taken by the State, acting in conjunction with the Prosecutor, the defence or the Pre-Trial Chamber or Trial Chamber, as the case may be, to seek to resolve the matter by cooperative means. Such steps may include:

(a) Modification or clarification of the request;

(b) A determination by the Court regarding the relevance of the information or evidence sought, or a determination as to whether the evidence, though relevant, could be or has been obtained from a source other than the requested State;

(c) Obtaining the information or evidence from a different source or in a different form; or

(d) Agreement on conditions under which the assistance could be provided including, among other things, providing summaries or redactions, limitations on disclosure, use of in camera or ex parte proceedings, or other protective measures permissible under the Statute and the Rules of Procedure and Evidence.

6. Once all reasonable steps have been taken to resolve the matter through cooperative means, and if the State considers that there are no means or conditions under which the information or documents could be provided or disclosed without prejudice to its national security interests, it shall so notify the Prosecutor or the Court of the specific reasons for its decision, unless a specific description of the reasons would itself necessarily result in such prejudice to the State's national security interests.

7. Thereafter, if the Court determines that the evidence is relevant and necessary for the establishment of the guilt or innocence of the accused, the Court may undertake the following actions:

(a) Where disclosure of the information or document is sought pursuant to a request for cooperation under Part 9 or the circumstances described in paragraph 2, and the State has invoked the ground for refusal referred to in article 93, paragraph 4:

(i) The Court may, before making any conclusion referred to in subparagraph 7 (a) (ii), request further consultations for the purpose of considering the State's representations, which may include, as appropriate, hearings in camera and ex parte;

(ii) If the Court concludes that, by invoking the ground for refusal under article 93, paragraph 4, in the circumstances of the case, the requested State is not acting in accordance with its obligations under this Statute, the Court may refer the matter in accordance with article 87, paragraph 7, specifying the reasons for its conclusion; and

(iii) The Court may make such inference in the trial of the accused as to the existence or non-existence of a fact, as may be appropriate in the circumstances; or

(b) In all other circumstances:

(i) Order disclosure; or

(ii) To the extent it does not order disclosure, make such inference in the trial of the accused as to the existence or non-existence of a fact, as may be appropriate in the circumstances.

Article 73
Third-party information or documents

If a State Party is requested by the Court to provide a document or information in its custody, possession or control, which was disclosed to it in confidence by a State, intergovernmental organization or international organization, it shall seek the consent of the originator to disclose that document or information. If the originator is a State Party, it shall either consent to disclosure of the information or document or undertake to resolve the issue of disclosure with the Court, subject to the provisions of article 72. If the originator is not a State Party and refuses to consent to disclosure, the requested State shall inform the Court that it is unable to provide the document or information because of a pre-existing obligation of confidentiality to the originator.

Article 74
Requirements for the decision

1. All the judges of the Trial Chamber shall be present at each stage of the trial and throughout their deliberations. The Presidency may, on a case-by-case basis, designate, as available, one or more alternate judges to be present at each stage of the trial and to replace a member of the Trial Chamber if that member is unable to continue attending.

2. The Trial Chamber's decision shall be based on its evaluation of the evidence and the entire proceedings. The decision shall not exceed the facts and circumstances described in the charges and any amendments to the charges. The Court may base its decision only on evidence submitted and discussed before it at the trial.

3. The judges shall attempt to achieve unanimity in their decision, failing which the decision shall be taken by a majority of the judges.

4. The deliberations of the Trial Chamber shall remain secret.

5. The decision shall be in writing and shall contain a full and reasoned statement of the Trial Chamber's findings on the evidence and conclusions. The Trial Chamber shall issue one decision. When there is no unanimity, the Trial Chamber's decision shall contain the views of the majority and the minority. The decision or a summary thereof shall be delivered in open court.

Article 75
Reparations to victims

1. The Court shall establish principles relating to reparations to, or in respect of, victims, including restitution, compensation and rehabilitation. On this basis, in its decision the Court may, either upon request or on its own motion in exceptional circumstances, determine the scope and extent of any damage, loss and injury to, or in respect of, victims and will state the principles on which it is acting.

2. The Court may make an order directly against a convicted person specifying appropriate reparations to, or in respect of, victims, including restitution, compensation and rehabilitation.

Where appropriate, the Court may order that the award for reparations be made through the Trust Fund provided for in article 79.

3. Before making an order under this article, the Court may invite and shall take account of representations from or on behalf of the convicted person, victims, other interested persons or interested States.

4. In exercising its power under this article, the Court may, after a person is convicted of a crime within the jurisdiction of the Court, determine whether, in order to give effect to an order which it may make under this article, it is necessary to seek measures under article 93, paragraph 1.

5. A State Party shall give effect to a decision under this article as if the provisions of article 109 were applicable to this article.

6. Nothing in this article shall be interpreted as prejudicing the rights of victims under national or international law.

Article 76
Sentencing

1. In the event of a conviction, the Trial Chamber shall consider the appropriate sentence to be imposed and shall take into account the evidence presented and submissions made during the trial that are relevant to the sentence.

2. Except where article 65 applies and before the completion of the trial, the Trial Chamber may on its own motion and shall, at the request of the Prosecutor or the accused, hold a further hearing to hear any additional evidence or submissions relevant to the sentence, in accordance with the Rules of Procedure and Evidence.

3. Where paragraph 2 applies, any representations under article 75 shall be heard during the further hearing referred to in paragraph 2 and, if necessary, during any additional hearing.

4. The sentence shall be pronounced in public and, wherever possible, in the presence of the accused.

PART 7. PENALTIES

Article 77
Applicable penalties

1. Subject to article 110, the Court may impose one of the following penalties on a person convicted of a crime referred to in article 5 of this Statute:

(a) Imprisonment for a specified number of years, which may not exceed a maximum of 30 years; or

(b) A term of life imprisonment when justified by the extreme gravity of the crime and the individual circumstances of the convicted person.

2. In addition to imprisonment, the Court may order:

(a) A fine under the criteria provided for in the Rules of Procedure and Evidence;

(b) A forfeiture of proceeds, property and assets derived directly or indirectly from that crime, without prejudice to the rights of bona fide third parties.

Article 78
Determination of the sentence

1. In determining the sentence, the Court shall, in accordance with the Rules of Procedure and Evidence, take into account such factors as the gravity of the crime and the individual circumstances of the convicted person.

2. In imposing a sentence of imprisonment, the Court shall deduct the time, if any, previously spent in detention in accordance with an order of the Court. The Court may deduct any time otherwise spent in detention in connection with conduct underlying the crime.

3. When a person has been convicted of more than one crime, the Court shall pronounce a sentence for each crime and a joint sentence specifying the total period of imprisonment. This period shall be no less than the highest individual sentence pronounced and shall not exceed 30 years imprisonment or a sentence of life imprisonment in conformity with article 77, paragraph 1 (b).

Article 79
Trust Fund

1. A Trust Fund shall be established by decision of the Assembly of States Parties for the benefit of victims of crimes within the jurisdiction of the Court, and of the families of such victims.

2. The Court may order money and other property collected through fines or forfeiture to be transferred, by order of the Court, to the Trust Fund.

3. The Trust Fund shall be managed according to criteria to be determined by the Assembly of States Parties.

Article 80
Non-prejudice to national application of penalties and national laws

Nothing in this Part affects the application by States of penalties prescribed by their national law, nor the law of States which do not provide for penalties prescribed in this Part.

PART 8. APPEAL AND REVISION

Article 81
Appeal against decision of acquittal or conviction or against sentence

1. A decision under article 74 may be appealed in accordance with the Rules of Procedure and Evidence as follows:

(a) The Prosecutor may make an appeal on any of the following grounds:

(i) Procedural error,

(ii) Error of fact, or

(iii) Error of law;

(b) The convicted person, or the Prosecutor on that person's behalf, may make an appeal on any of the following grounds:

(i) Procedural error,

(ii) Error of fact,

(iii) Error of law, or

(iv) Any other ground that affects the fairness or reliability of the proceedings or decision.

2. (a) A sentence may be appealed, in accordance with the Rules of Procedure and Evidence, by the Prosecutor or the convicted person on the ground of disproportion between the crime and the sentence;

(b) If on an appeal against sentence the Court considers that there are grounds on which the conviction might be set aside, wholly or in part, it may invite the Prosecutor and the convicted person to submit grounds under article 81, paragraph 1 (a) or (b), and may render a decision on conviction in accordance with article 83;

(c) The same procedure applies when the Court, on an appeal against conviction only, considers that there are grounds to reduce the sentence under paragraph 2 (a).

3. (a) Unless the Trial Chamber orders otherwise, a convicted person shall remain in custody pending an appeal;

(b) When a convicted person's time in custody exceeds the sentence of imprisonment imposed, that person shall be released, except that if the Prosecutor is also appealing, the release may be subject to the conditions under subparagraph (c) below;

(c) In case of an acquittal, the accused shall be released immediately, subject to the following:

(i) Under exceptional circumstances, and having regard, inter alia, to the concrete risk of flight, the seriousness of the offence charged and the probability of success on appeal, the Trial Chamber, at the request of the Prosecutor, may maintain the detention of the person pending appeal;

(ii) A decision by the Trial Chamber under subparagraph (c) (i) may be appealed in accordance with the Rules of Procedure and Evidence.

4. Subject to the provisions of paragraph 3 (a) and (b), execution of the decision or sentence shall be suspended during the period allowed for appeal and for the duration of the appeal proceedings.

Article 82
Appeal against other decisions

1. Either party may appeal any of the following decisions in accordance with the Rules of Procedure and Evidence:

(a) A decision with respect to jurisdiction or admissibility;

(b) A decision granting or denying release of the person being investigated or prosecuted;

(c) A decision of the Pre-Trial Chamber to act on its own initiative under article 56, paragraph 3;

(d) A decision that involves an issue that would significantly affect the fair and expeditious conduct of the proceedings or the outcome of the trial, and for which, in the opinion of the Pre-Trial or Trial Chamber, an immediate resolution by the Appeals Chamber may materially advance the proceedings.

2. A decision of the Pre-Trial Chamber under article 57, paragraph 3 (d), may be appealed against by the State concerned or by the Prosecutor, with the leave of the Pre-Trial Chamber. The appeal shall be heard on an expedited basis.

3. An appeal shall not of itself have suspensive effect unless the Appeals Chamber so orders, upon request, in accordance with the Rules of Procedure and Evidence.

4. A legal representative of the victims, the convicted person or a bona fide owner of property adversely affected by an order under article 75 may appeal against the order for reparations, as provided in the Rules of Procedure and Evidence.

Article 83
Proceedings on appeal

1. For the purposes of proceedings under article 81 and this article, the Appeals Chamber shall have all the powers of the Trial Chamber.

2. If the Appeals Chamber finds that the proceedings appealed from were unfair in a way that affected the reliability of the decision or sentence, or that the decision or sentence appealed from was materially affected by error of fact or law or procedural error, it may:

(a) Reverse or amend the decision or sentence; or

(b) Order a new trial before a different Trial Chamber.

For these purposes, the Appeals Chamber may remand a factual issue to the original Trial Chamber for it to determine the issue and to report back accordingly, or may itself call evidence to determine the issue. When the decision or sentence has been appealed only by the person convicted, or the Prosecutor on that person's behalf, it cannot be amended to his or her detriment.

3. If in an appeal against sentence the Appeals Chamber finds that the sentence is disproportionate to the crime, it may vary the sentence in accordance with Part 7.

4. The judgement of the Appeals Chamber shall be taken by a majority of the judges and shall be delivered in open court. The judgement shall state the reasons on which it is based. When there is no unanimity, the judgement of the Appeals Chamber shall contain the views of the majority and the minority, but a judge may deliver a separate or dissenting opinion on a question of law.

5. The Appeals Chamber may deliver its judgement in the absence of the person acquitted or convicted.

Article 84
Revision of conviction or sentence

1. The convicted person or, after death, spouses, children, parents or one person alive at the time of the accused's death who has been given express written instructions from the accused to bring such a claim, or the Prosecutor on the person's behalf, may apply to the Appeals Chamber to revise the final judgement of conviction or sentence on the grounds that:

(a) New evidence has been discovered that:

(i) Was not available at the time of trial, and such unavailability was not wholly or partially attributable to the party making application; and

(ii) Is sufficiently important that had it been proved at trial it would have been likely to have resulted in a different verdict;

(b) It has been newly discovered that decisive evidence, taken into account at trial and upon which the conviction depends, was false, forged or falsified;

(c) One or more of the judges who participated in conviction or confirmation of the charges has committed, in that case, an act of serious misconduct or serious breach of duty of sufficient gravity to justify the removal of that judge or those judges from office under article 46.

2. The Appeals Chamber shall reject the application if it considers it to be unfounded. If it determines that the application is meritorious, it may, as appropriate:

(a) Reconvene the original Trial Chamber;

(b) Constitute a new Trial Chamber; or

(c) Retain jurisdiction over the matter, with a view to, after hearing the parties in the manner set forth in the Rules of Procedure and Evidence, arriving at a determination on whether the judgement should be revised.

Article 85
Compensation to an arrested or convicted person

1. Anyone who has been the victim of unlawful arrest or detention shall have an enforceable right to compensation.

2. When a person has by a final decision been convicted of a criminal offence, and when subsequently his or her conviction has been reversed on the ground that a new or newly discovered fact shows conclusively that there has been a miscarriage of justice, the person who has suffered

punishment as a result of such conviction shall be compensated according to law, unless it is proved that the non-disclosure of the unknown fact in time is wholly or partly attributable to him or her.

3. In exceptional circumstances, where the Court finds conclusive facts showing that there has been a grave and manifest miscarriage of justice, it may in its discretion award compensation, according to the criteria provided in the Rules of Procedure and Evidence, to a person who has been released from detention following a final decision of acquittal or a termination of the proceedings for that reason.

PART 9. INTERNATIONAL COOPERATION AND JUDICIAL ASSISTANCE

Article 86
General obligation to cooperate

States Parties shall, in accordance with the provisions of this Statute, cooperate fully with the Court in its investigation and prosecution of crimes within the jurisdiction of the Court.

Article 87
Requests for cooperation: general provisions

1. (a) The Court shall have the authority to make requests to States Parties for cooperation. The requests shall be transmitted through the diplomatic channel or any other appropriate channel as may be designated by each State Party upon ratification, acceptance, approval or accession.

Subsequent changes to the designation shall be made by each State Party in accordance with the Rules of Procedure and Evidence.

(b) When appropriate, without prejudice to the provisions of subparagraph (a), requests may also be transmitted through the International Criminal Police Organization or any appropriate regional organization.

2. Requests for cooperation and any documents supporting the request shall either be in or be accompanied by a translation into an official language of the requested State or one of the working languages of the Court, in accordance with the choice made by that State upon ratification, acceptance, approval or accession.

Subsequent changes to this choice shall be made in accordance with the Rules of Procedure and Evidence.

3. The requested State shall keep confidential a request for cooperation and any documents supporting the request, except to the extent that the disclosure is necessary for execution of the request.

4. In relation to any request for assistance presented under this Part, the Court may take such measures, including measures related to the protection of information, as may be necessary to ensure the safety or physical or psychological well-being of any victims, potential witnesses and their families. The Court may request that any information that is made available under this Part shall be provided and handled in a manner that protects the safety and physical or psychological well-being of any victims, potential witnesses and their families.

5. (a) The Court may invite any State not party to this Statute to provide assistance under this Part on the basis of an ad hoc arrangement, an agreement with such State or any other appropriate basis.

(b) Where a State not party to this Statute, which has entered into an ad hoc arrangement or an agreement with the Court, fails to cooperate with requests pursuant to any such arrangement or agreement, the Court may so inform the Assembly of States Parties or, where the Security Council referred the matter to the Court, the Security Council.

6. The Court may ask any intergovernmental organization to provide information or documents. The Court may also ask for other forms of cooperation and assistance which may be agreed upon with such an organization and which are in accordance with its competence or mandate.

7. Where a State Party fails to comply with a request to cooperate by the Court contrary to the provisions of this Statute, thereby preventing the Court from exercising its functions and powers under this Statute, the Court may make a finding to that effect and refer the matter to the Assembly of States Parties or, where the Security Council referred the matter to the Court, to the Security Council.

Article 88
Availability of procedures under national law

States Parties shall ensure that there are procedures available under their national law for all of the forms of cooperation which are specified under this Part.

Article 89
Surrender of persons to the Court

1. The Court may transmit a request for the arrest and surrender of a person, together with the material supporting the request outlined in article 91, to any State on the territory of which that person may be found and shall request the cooperation of that State in the arrest and surrender of such a person. States Parties shall, in accordance with the provisions of this Part and the procedure under their national law, comply with requests for arrest and surrender.

2. Where the person sought for surrender brings a challenge before a national court on the basis of the principle of ne bis in idem as provided in article 20, the requested State shall immediately consult with the Court to determine if there has been a relevant ruling on admissibility. If the case is admissible, the requested State shall proceed with the execution of the request. If an admissibility ruling is pending, the requested State may postpone the execution of the request for surrender of the person until the Court makes a determination on admissibility.

3. (a) A State Party shall authorize, in accordance with its national procedural law, transportation through its territory of a person being surrendered to the Court by another State, except where transit through that State would impede or delay the surrender.

(b) A request by the Court for transit shall be transmitted in accordance with article 87. The request for transit shall contain:

(i) A description of the person being transported;

(ii) A brief statement of the facts of the case and their legal characterization; and

(iii) The warrant for arrest and surrender;

(c) A person being transported shall be detained in custody during the period of transit;

(d) No authorization is required if the person is transported by air and no landing is scheduled on the territory of the transit State;

(e) If an unscheduled landing occurs on the territory of the transit State, that State may require a request for transit from the Court as provided for in subparagraph (b). The transit State shall detain the person being transported until the request for transit is received and the transit is effected, provided that detention for purposes of this subparagraph may not be extended beyond 96 hours from the unscheduled landing unless the request is received within that time.

4. If the person sought is being proceeded against or is serving a sentence in the requested State for a crime different from that for which

surrender to the Court is sought, the requested State, after making its decision to grant the request, shall consult with the Court.

Article 90
Competing requests

1. A State Party which receives a request from the Court for the surrender of a person under article 89 shall, if it also receives a request from any other State for the extradition of the same person for the same conduct which forms the basis of the crime for which the Court seeks the person's surrender, notify the Court and the requesting State of that fact.

2. Where the requesting State is a State Party, the requested State shall give priority to the request from the Court if:

(a) The Court has, pursuant to article 18 or 19, made a determination that the case in respect of which surrender is sought is admissible and that determination takes into account the investigation or prosecution conducted by the requesting State in respect of its request for extradition; or

(b) The Court makes the determination described in subparagraph (a) pursuant to the requested State's notification under paragraph 1.

3. Where a determination under paragraph 2 (a) has not been made, the requested State may, at its discretion, pending the determination of the Court under paragraph 2 (b), proceed to deal with the request for extradition from the requesting State but shall not extradite the person until the Court has determined that the case is inadmissible. The Court's determination shall be made on an expedited basis.

4. If the requesting State is a State not Party to this Statute the requested State, if it is not under an international obligation to extradite the person to the requesting State, shall give priority to the request for surrender from the Court, if the Court has determined that the case is admissible.

5. Where a case under paragraph 4 has not been determined to be admissible by the Curt, the requested State may, at its discretion, proceed to deal with the request for extradition from the requesting State.

6. In cases where paragraph 4 applies except that the requested State is under an existing international obligation to extradite the person to the requesting State not Party to this Statute, the requested State shall determine whether to surrender the person to the Court or extradite the person to the requesting State. In making its decision, the requested State shall consider all the relevant factors, including but not limited to:

(a) The respective dates of the requests;

(b) The interests of the requesting State including, where relevant, whether the crime was committed in its territory and the nationality of the victims and of the person sought; and

(c) The possibility of subsequent surrender between the Court and the requesting State.

7. Where a State Party which receives a request from the Court for the surrender of a person also receives a request from any State for the extradition of the same person for conduct other than that which constitutes the crime for which the Court seeks the person's surrender:

(a) The requested State shall, if it is not under an existing international obligation to extradite the person to the requesting State, give priority to the request from the Court;

(b) The requested State shall, if it is under an existing international obligation to extradite the person to the requesting State, determine whether to surrender the person to the Court or to extradite the person to the requesting State. In making its decision, the requested State shall consider all the relevant factors, including but not limited to those set out in paragraph 6, but shall give special consideration to the relative nature and gravity of the conduct in question.

8. Where pursuant to a notification under this article, the Court has determined a case to be inadmissible, and subsequently extradition to the requesting State is refused, the requested State shall notify the Court of this decision.

Article 91
Contents of request for arrest and surrender

1. A request for arrest and surrender shall be made in writing. In urgent cases, a request may be made by any medium capable of delivering a written record, provided that the request shall be confirmed through the channel provided for in article 87, paragraph 1 (a).

2. In the case of a request for the arrest and surrender of a person for whom a warrant of arrest has been issued by the Pre-Trial Chamber under article 58, the request shall contain or be supported by:

(a) Information describing the person sought, sufficient to identify the person, and information as to that person's probable location;

(b) A copy of the warrant of arrest; and

(c) Such documents, statements or information as may be necessary to meet the requirements for the surrender process in the requested State, except that those requirements should not be more burdensome than those applicable to requests for extradition pursuant to treaties or arrangements between the requested State and other States and should, if possible, be less burdensome, taking into account the distinct nature of the Court.

3. In the case of a request for the arrest and surrender of a person already convicted, the request shall contain or be supported by:

(a) A copy of any warrant of arrest for that person;

(b) A copy of the judgement of conviction;

(c) Information to demonstrate that the person sought is the one referred to in the judgement of conviction; and

(d) If the person sought has been sentenced, a copy of the sentence imposed and, in the case of a sentence for imprisonment, a statement of any time already served and the time remaining to be served.

4. Upon the request of the Court, a State Party shall consult with the Court, either generally or with respect to a specific matter, regarding any requirements under its national law that may apply under paragraph 2 (c). During the consultations, the State Party shall advise the Court of the specific requirements of its national law.

Article 92
Provisional arrest

1. In urgent cases, the Court may request the provisional arrest of the person sought, pending presentation of the request for surrender and the documents supporting the request as specified in article 91.

2. The request for provisional arrest shall be made by any medium capable of delivering a written record and shall contain:

(a) Information describing the person sought, sufficient to identify the person, and information as to that person's probable location;

(b) A concise statement of the crimes for which the person's arrest is sought and of the facts which are alleged to constitute those crimes, including, where possible, the date and location of the crime;

(c) A statement of the existence of a warrant of arrest or a judgement of conviction against the person sought; and

(d) A statement that a request for surrender of the person sought will follow.

3. A person who is provisionally arrested may be released from custody if the requested State has not received the request for surrender and the documents supporting the request as specified in article 91 within the time limits specified in the Rules of Procedure and Evidence. However, the person may consent to surrender before the expiration of this period if permitted by the law of the requested State. In such a case, the requested

State shall proceed to surrender the person to the Court as soon as possible.

4. The fact that the person sought has been released from custody pursuant to paragraph 3 shall not prejudice the subsequent arrest and surrender of that person if the request for surrender and the documents supporting the request are delivered at a later date.

Article 93
Other forms of cooperation

1. States Parties shall, in accordance with the provisions of this Part and under procedures of national law, comply with requests by the Court to provide the following assistance in relation to investigations or prosecutions:

(a) The identification and whereabouts of persons or the location of items;

(b) The taking of evidence, including testimony under oath, and the production of evidence, including expert opinions and reports necessary to the Court;

(c) The questioning of any person being investigated or prosecuted;

(d) The service of documents, including judicial documents;

(e) Facilitating the voluntary appearance of persons as witnesses or experts before the Court;

(f) The temporary transfer of persons as provided in paragraph 7;

(g) The examination of places or sites, including the exhumation and examination of grave sites;

(h) The execution of searches and seizures;

(i) The provision of records and documents, including official records and documents;

(j) The protection of victims and witnesses and the preservation of evidence;

(k) The identification, tracing and freezing or seizure of proceeds, property and assets and instrumentalities of crimes for the purpose of eventual forfeiture, without prejudice to the rights of bona fide third parties; and

(l) Any other type of assistance which is not prohibited by the law of the requested State, with a view to facilitating the investigation and prosecution of crimes within the jurisdiction of the Court.

2. The Court shall have the authority to provide an assurance to a witness or an expert appearing before the Court that he or she will not be prosecuted, detained or subjected to any restriction of personal freedom by

the Court in respect of any act or omission that preceded the departure of that person from the requested State.

3. Where execution of a particular measure of assistance detailed in a request presented under paragraph 1, is prohibited in the requested State on the basis of an existing fundamental legal principle of general application, the requested State shall promptly consult with the Court to try to resolve the matter. In the consultations, consideration should be given to whether the assistance can be rendered in another manner or subject to conditions. If after consultations the matter cannot be resolved, the Court shall modify the request as necessary.

4. In accordance with article 72, a State Party may deny a request for assistance, in whole or in part, only if the request concerns the production of any documents or disclosure of evidence which relates to its national security.

5. Before denying a request for assistance under paragraph 1 (l), the requested State shall consider whether the assistance can be provided subject to specified conditions, or whether the assistance can be provided at a later date or in an alternative manner, provided that if the Court or the Prosecutor accepts the assistance subject to conditions, the Court or the Prosecutor shall abide by them.

6. If a request for assistance is denied, the requested State Party shall promptly inform the Court or the Prosecutor of the reasons for such denial.

7. (a) The Court may request the temporary transfer of a person in custody for purposes of identification or for obtaining testimony or other assistance. The person may be transferred if the following conditions are fulfilled:

(i) The person freely gives his or her informed consent to the transfer; and

(ii) The requested State agrees to the transfer, subject to such conditions as that State and the Court may agree.

(b) The person being transferred shall remain in custody. When the purposes of the transfer have been fulfilled, the Court shall return the person without delay to the requested State.

8. (a) The Court shall ensure the confidentiality of documents and information, except as required for the investigation and proceedings described in the request.

(b) The requested State may, when necessary, transmit documents or information to the Prosecutor on a confidential basis. The Prosecutor may then use them solely for the purpose of generating new evidence.

(c) The requested State may, on its own motion or at the request of the Prosecutor, subsequently consent to the disclosure of such documents or information. They may then be used as evidence pursuant to the provisions of Parts 5 and 6 and in accordance with the Rules of Procedure and Evidence.

9. (a) (i) In the event that a State Party receives competing requests, other than for surrender or extradition, from the Court and from another State pursuant to an international obligation, the State Party shall endeavour, in consultation with the Court and the other State, to meet both requests, if necessary by postponing or attaching conditions to one or the other request.

(ii) Failing that, competing requests shall be resolved in accordance with the principles established in article 90.

(b) Where, however, the request from the Court concerns information, property or persons which are subject to the control of a third State or an international organization by virtue of an international agreement, the requested States shall so inform the Court and the Court shall direct its request to the third State or international organization.

10. (a) The Court may, upon request, cooperate with and provide assistance to a State Party conducting an investigation into or trial in respect of conduct which constitutes a crime within the jurisdiction of the Court or which constitutes a serious crime under the national law of the requesting State.

(b) (i) The assistance provided under subparagraph (a) shall include, inter alia:

a. The transmission of statements, documents or other types of evidence obtained in the course of an investigation or a trial conducted by the Court; and

b. The questioning of any person detained by order of the Court;

(ii) In the case of assistance under subparagraph (b) (i)a:

a. If the documents or other types of evidence have been obtained with the assistance of a State, such transmission shall require the consent of that State;

b. If the statements, documents or other types of evidence have been provided by a witness or expert, such transmission shall be subject to the provisions of article 68.

(c) The Court may, under the conditions set out in this paragraph, grant a request for assistance under this paragraph from a State which is not a Party to this Statute.

Article 94
Postponement of execution of a request in respect of ongoing investigation or prosecution

1. If the immediate execution of a request would interfere with an ongoing investigation or prosecution of a case different from that to which the request relates, the requested State may postpone the execution of the request for a period of time agreed upon with the Court. However, the postponement shall be no longer than is necessary to complete the relevant investigation or prosecution in the requested State. Before making a decision to postpone, the requested State should consider whether the assistance may be immediately provided subject to certain conditions.

2. If a decision to postpone is taken pursuant to paragraph 1, the Prosecutor may, however, seek measures to preserve evidence, pursuant to article 93, paragraph 1 (j).

Article 95
Postponement of execution of a request in respect of an admissibility challenge

Where there is an admissibility challenge under consideration by the Court pursuant to article 18 or 19, the requested State may postpone the execution of a request under this Part pending a determination by the Court, unless the Court has specifically ordered that the Prosecutor may pursue the collection of such evidence pursuant to article 18 or 19.

Article 96
Contents of request for other forms of assistance under article 93

1. A request for other forms of assistance referred to in article 93 shall be made in writing. In urgent cases, a request may be made by any medium capable of delivering a written record, provided that the request shall be confirmed through the channel provided for in article 87, paragraph 1 (a).

2. The request shall, as applicable, contain or be supported by the following:

(a) A concise statement of the purpose of the request and the assistance sought, including the legal basis and the grounds for the request;

(b) As much detailed information as possible about the location or identification of any person or place that must be found or identified in order for the assistance sought to be provided;

(c) A concise statement of the essential facts underlying the request;

(d) The reasons for and details of any procedure or requirement to be followed;

(e) Such information as may be required under the law of the requested State in order to execute the request; and

(f) Any other information relevant in order for the assistance sought to be provided.

3. Upon the request of the Court, a State Party shall consult with the Court, either generally or with respect to a specific matter, regarding any requirements under its national law that may apply under paragraph 2 (e). During the consultations, the State Party shall advise the Court of the specific requirements of its national law.

4. The provisions of this article shall, where applicable, also apply in respect of a request for assistance made to the Court.

Article 97
Consultations

Where a State Party receives a request under this Part in relation to which it identifies problems which may impede or prevent the execution of the request, that State shall consult with the Court without delay in order to resolve the matter. Such problems may include, inter alia:

(a) Insufficient information to execute the request;

(b) In the case of a request for surrender, the fact that despite best efforts, the person sought cannot be located or that the investigation conducted has determined that the person in the requested State is clearly not the person named in the warrant; or

(c) The fact that execution of the request in its current form would require the requested State to breach a pre-existing treaty obligation undertaken with respect to another State.

Article 98
Cooperation with respect to waiver of immunity and consent to surrender

1. The Court may not proceed with a request for surrender or assistance which would require the requested State to act inconsistently with its obligations under international law with respect to the State or diplomatic

immunity of a person or property of a third State, unless the Court can first obtain the cooperation of that third State for the waiver of the immunity.

2. The Court may not proceed with a request for surrender which would require the requested State to act inconsistently with its obligations under international agreements pursuant to which the consent of a sending State is required to surrender a person of that State to the Court, unless the Court can first obtain the cooperation of the sending State for the giving of consent for the surrender.

Article 99
Execution of requests under articles 93 and 96

1. Requests for assistance shall be executed in accordance with the relevant procedure under the law of the requested State and, unless prohibited by such law, in the manner specified in the request, including following any procedure outlined therein or permitting persons specified in the request to be present at and assist in the execution process.

2. In the case of an urgent request, the documents or evidence produced in response shall, at the request of the Court, be sent urgently.

3. Replies from the requested State shall be transmitted in their original language and form.

4. Without prejudice to other articles in this Part, where it is necessary for the successful execution of a request which can be executed without any compulsory measures, including specifically the interview of or taking evidence from a person on a voluntary basis, including doing so without the presence of the authorities of the requested State Party if it is essential for the request to be executed, and the examination without modification of a public site or other public place, the Prosecutor may execute such request directly on the territory of a State as follows:

(a) When the State Party requested is a State on the territory of which the crime is alleged to have been committed, and there has been a determination of admissibility pursuant to article 18 or 19, the Prosecutor may directly execute such request following all possible consultations with the requested State Party;

(b) In other cases, the Prosecutor may execute such request following consultations with the requested State Party and subject to any reasonable conditions or concerns raised by that State Party. Where the requested State Party identifies problems with the execution of a request pursuant to this subparagraph it shall, without delay, consult with the Court to resolve the matter.

5. Provisions allowing a person heard or examined by the Court under article 72 to invoke restrictions designed to prevent disclosure of confidential information connected with national security shall also apply to the execution of requests for assistance under this article.

Article 100
Costs

1. The ordinary costs for execution of requests in the territory of the requested State shall be borne by that State, except for the following, which shall be borne by the Court:

(a) Costs associated with the travel and security of witnesses and experts or the transfer under article 93 of persons in custody;

(b) Costs of translation, interpretation and transcription;

(c) Travel and subsistence costs of the judges, the Prosecutor, the Deputy Prosecutors, the Registrar, the Deputy Registrar and staff of any organ of the Court;

(d) Costs of any expert opinion or report requested by the Court;

(e) Costs associated with the transport of a person being surrendered to the Court by a custodial State; and

(f) Following consultations, any extraordinary costs that may result from the execution of a request.

2. The provisions of paragraph 1 shall, as appropriate, apply to requests from States Parties to the Court. In that case, the Court shall bear the ordinary costs of execution.

Article 101
Rule of speciality

1. A person surrendered to the Court under this Statute shall not be proceeded against, punished or detained for any conduct committed prior to surrender, other than the conduct or course of conduct which forms the basis of the crimes for which that person has been surrendered.

2. The Court may request a waiver of the requirements of paragraph 1 from the State which surrendered the person to the Court and, if necessary, the Court shall provide additional information in accordance with article 91. States Parties shall have the authority to provide a waiver to the Court and should endeavour to do so.

Article 102
Use of terms

For the purposes of this Statute:

(a) "surrender" means the delivering up of a person by a State to the Court, pursuant to this Statute.

(b) "extradition" means the delivering up of a person by one State to another as provided by treaty, convention or national legislation.

PART 10. ENFORCEMENT

Article 103
Role of States in enforcement of sentences of imprisonment

1. (a) A sentence of imprisonment shall be served in a State designated by the Court from a list of States which have indicated to the Court their willingness to accept sentenced persons.

(b) At the time of declaring its willingness to accept sentenced persons, a State may attach conditions to its acceptance as agreed by the Court and in accordance with this Part.

(c) A State designated in a particular case shall promptly inform the Court whether it accepts the Court's designation.

2. (a) The State of enforcement shall notify the Court of any circumstances, including the exercise of any conditions agreed under paragraph 1, which could materially affect the terms or extent of the imprisonment. The Court shall be given at least 45 days' notice of any such known or foreseeable circumstances. During this period, the State of enforcement shall take no action that might prejudice its obligations under article 110.

(b) Where the Court cannot agree to the circumstances referred to in subparagraph (a), it shall notify the State of enforcement and proceed in accordance with article 104, paragraph 1.

3. In exercising its discretion to make a designation under paragraph 1, the Court shall take into account the following:

(a) The principle that States Parties should share the responsibility for enforcing sentences of imprisonment, in accordance with principles of equitable distribution, as provided in the Rules of Procedure and Evidence;

(b) The application of widely accepted international treaty standards governing the treatment of prisoners;

(c) The views of the sentenced person;

(d) The nationality of the sentenced person;

(e) Such other factors regarding the circumstances of the crime or the person sentenced, or the effective enforcement of the sentence, as may be appropriate in designating the State of enforcement.

4. If no State is designated under paragraph 1, the sentence of imprisonment shall be served in a prison facility made available by the host State, in accordance with the conditions set out in the headquarters agreement referred to in article 3, paragraph 2. In such a case, the costs arising out of the enforcement of a sentence of imprisonment shall be borne by the Court.

Article 104
Change in designation of State of enforcement

1. The Court may, at any time, decide to transfer a sentenced person to a prison of another State.

2. A sentenced person may, at any time, apply to the Court to be transferred from the State of enforcement.

Article 105
Enforcement of the sentence

1. Subject to conditions which a State may have specified in accordance with article 103, paragraph 1 (b), the sentence of imprisonment shall be binding on the States Parties, which shall in no case modify it.

2. The Court alone shall have the right to decide any application for appeal and revision. The State of enforcement shall not impede the making of any such application by a sentenced person.

Article 106
Supervision of enforcement of sentences and conditions of imprisonment

1. The enforcement of a sentence of imprisonment shall be subject to the supervision of the Court and shall be consistent with widely accepted international treaty standards governing treatment of prisoners.

2. The conditions of imprisonment shall be governed by the law of the State of enforcement and shall be consistent with widely accepted international treaty standards governing treatment of prisoners; in no case shall such conditions be more or less favourable than those available to prisoners convicted of similar offences in the State of enforcement.

3. Communications between a sentenced person and the Court shall be unimpeded and confidential.

Article 107
Transfer of the person upon completion of sentence

1. Following completion of the sentence, a person who is not a national of the State of enforcement may, in accordance with the law of the State of enforcement, be transferred to a State which is obliged to receive him or her, or to another State which agrees to receive him or her, taking into account any wishes of the person to be transferred to that State, unless the State of enforcement authorizes the person to remain in its territory.

2. If no State bears the costs arising out of transferring the person to another State pursuant to paragraph 1, such costs shall be borne by the Court.

3. Subject to the provisions of article 108, the State of enforcement may also, in accordance with its national law, extradite or otherwise surrender the person to a State which has requested the extradition or surrender of the person for purposes of trial or enforcement of a sentence.

Article 108
Limitation on the prosecution or punishment of other offences

1. A sentenced person in the custody of the State of enforcement shall not be subject to prosecution or punishment or to extradition to a third State for any conduct engaged in prior to that person's delivery to the State of enforcement, unless such prosecution, punishment or extradition has been approved by the Court at the request of the State of enforcement.

2. The Court shall decide the matter after having heard the views of the sentenced person.

3. Paragraph 1 shall cease to apply if the sentenced person remains voluntarily for more than 30 days in the territory of the State of enforcement after having served the full sentence imposed by the Court, or returns to the territory of that State after having left it.

Article 109
Enforcement of fines and forfeiture measures

1. States Parties shall give effect to fines or forfeitures ordered by the Court under Part 7, without prejudice to the rights of bona fide third parties, and in accordance with the procedure of their national law.

2. If a State Party is unable to give effect to an order for forfeiture, it shall take measures to recover the value of the proceeds, property or assets ordered by the Court to be forfeited, without prejudice to the rights of bona fide third parties.

3. Property, or the proceeds of the sale of real property or, where appropriate, the sale of other property, which is obtained by a State Party as a result of its enforcement of a judgement of the Court shall be transferred to the Court.

Article 110
Review by the Court concerning reduction of sentence

1. The State of enforcement shall not release the person before expiry of the sentence pronounced by the Court.

2. The Court alone shall have the right to decide any reduction of sentence, and shall rule on the matter after having heard the person.

3. When the person has served two thirds of the sentence, or 25 years in the case of life imprisonment, the Court shall review the sentence to determine whether it should be reduced. Such a review shall not be conducted before that time.

4. In its review under paragraph 3, the Court may reduce the sentence if it finds that one or more of the following factors are present:

(a) The early and continuing willingness of the person to cooperate with the Court in its investigations and prosecutions;

(b) The voluntary assistance of the person in enabling the enforcement of the judgements and orders of the Court in other cases, and in particular providing assistance in locating assets subject to orders of fine, forfeiture or reparation which may be used for the benefit of victims; or

(c) Other factors establishing a clear and significant change of circumstances sufficient to justify the reduction of sentence, as provided in the Rules of Procedure and Evidence.

5. If the Court determines in its initial review under paragraph 3 that it is not appropriate to reduce the sentence, it shall thereafter review the question of reduction of sentence at such intervals and applying such criteria as provided for in the Rules of Procedure and Evidence.

Article 111
Escape

If a convicted person escapes from custody and flees the State of enforcement, that State may, after consultation with the Court, request the person's surrender from the State in which the person is located pursuant to existing bilateral or multilateral arrangements, or may request that the Court seek the person's surrender, in accordance with Part 9. It may direct that the person be delivered to the State in which he or she was serving the sentence or to another State designated by the Court.

PART 11. ASSEMBLY OF STATES PARTIES

Article 112
Assembly of States Parties

1. An Assembly of States Parties to this Statute is hereby established. Each State Party shall have one representative in the Assembly who may be accompanied by alternates and advisers. Other States which have signed this Statute or the Final Act may be observers in the Assembly.

2. The Assembly shall:

(a) Consider and adopt, as appropriate, recommendations of the Preparatory Commission;

(b) Provide management oversight to the Presidency, the Prosecutor and the Registrar regarding the administration of the Court;

(c) Consider the reports and activities of the Bureau established under paragraph 3 and take appropriate action in regard thereto;

(d) Consider and decide the budget for the Court;

(e) Decide whether to alter, in accordance with article 36, the number of judges;

(f) Consider pursuant to article 87, paragraphs 5 and 7, any question relating to non-cooperation;

(g) Perform any other function consistent with this Statute or the Rules of Procedure and Evidence.

3. (a) The Assembly shall have a Bureau consisting of a President, two Vice-Presidents and 18 members elected by the Assembly for three-year terms.

(b) The Bureau shall have a representative character, taking into account, in particular, equitable geographical distribution and the adequate representation of the principal legal systems of the world.

(c) The Bureau shall meet as often as necessary, but at least once a year. It shall assist the Assembly in the discharge of its responsibilities.

4. The Assembly may establish such subsidiary bodies as may be necessary, including an independent oversight mechanism for inspection, evaluation and investigation of the Court, in order to enhance its efficiency and economy.

5. The President of the Court, the Prosecutor and the Registrar or their representatives may participate, as appropriate, in meetings of the Assembly and of the Bureau.

6. The Assembly shall meet at the seat of the Court or at the Headquarters of the United Nations once a year and, when circumstances so require, hold special sessions. Except as otherwise specified in this Statute, special sessions shall be convened by the Bureau on its own initiative or at the request of one third of the States Parties.

7. Each State Party shall have one vote. Every effort shall be made to reach decisions by consensus in the Assembly and in the Bureau. If consensus cannot be reached, except as otherwise provided in the Statute:

(a) Decisions on matters of substance must be approved by a two-thirds majority of those present and voting provided that an absolute majority of States Parties constitutes the quorum for voting;

(b) Decisions on matters of procedure shall be taken by a simple majority of States Parties present and voting.

8. A State Party which is in arrears in the payment of its financial contributions towards the costs of the Court shall have no vote in the Assembly and in the Bureau if the amount of its arrears equals or exceeds the amount of the contributions due from it for the preceding two full years. The Assembly may, nevertheless, permit such a State Party to vote in the Assembly and in the Bureau if it is satisfied that the failure to pay is due to conditions beyond the control of the State Party.

9. The Assembly shall adopt its own rules of procedure.

10. The official and working languages of the Assembly shall be those of the General Assembly of the United Nations.

PART 12. FINANCING

Article 113
Financial Regulations

Except as otherwise specifically provided, all financial matters related to the Court and the meetings of the Assembly of States Parties, including its Bureau and subsidiary bodies, shall be governed by this Statute and the

Financial Regulations and Rules adopted by the Assembly of States Parties.

Article 114
Payment of expenses

Expenses of the Court and the Assembly of States Parties, including its Bureau and subsidiary bodies, shall be paid from the funds of the Court.

Article 115
Funds of the Court and of the Assembly of States Parties

The expenses of the Court and the Assembly of States Parties, including its Bureau and subsidiary bodies, as provided for in the budget decided by the Assembly of States Parties, shall be provided by the following sources:

(a) Assessed contributions made by States Parties;

(b) Funds provided by the United Nations, subject to the approval of the General Assembly, in particular in relation to the expenses incurred due to referrals by the Security Council.

Article 116
Voluntary contributions

Without prejudice to article 115, the Court may receive and utilize, as additional funds, voluntary contributions from Governments, international organizations, individuals, corporations and other entities, in accordance with relevant criteria adopted by the Assembly of States Parties.

Article 117
Assessment of contributions

The contributions of States Parties shall be assessed in accordance with an agreed scale of assessment, based on the scale adopted by the United Nations for its regular budget and adjusted in accordance with the principles on which that scale is based.

Article 118
Annual audit

The records, books and accounts of the Court, including its annual financial statements, shall be audited annually by an independent auditor.

PART 13. FINAL CLAUSES

Article 119
Settlement of disputes

1. Any dispute concerning the judicial functions of the Court shall be settled by the decision of the Court.

2. Any other dispute between two or more States Parties relating to the interpretation or application of this Statute which is not settled through negotiations within three months of their commencement shall be referred to the Assembly of States Parties. The Assembly may itself seek to settle the dispute or may make recommendations on further means of settlement of the dispute, including referral to the International Court of Justice in conformity with the Statute of that Court.

Article 120
Reservations

No reservations may be made to this Statute.

Article 121
Amendments

1. After the expiry of seven years from the entry into force of this Statute, any State Party may propose amendments thereto. The text of any proposed amendment shall be submitted to the Secretary-General of the United Nations, who shall promptly circulate it to all States Parties.

2. No sooner than three months from the date of notification, the Assembly of States Parties, at its next meeting, shall, by a majority of those present and voting, decide whether to take up the proposal. The Assembly may deal with the proposal directly or convene a Review Conference if the issue involved so warrants.

3. The adoption of an amendment at a meeting of the Assembly of States Parties or at a Review Conference on which consensus cannot be reached shall require a two-thirds majority of States Parties.

4. Except as provided in paragraph 5, an amendment shall enter into force for all States Parties one year after instruments of ratification or acceptance have been deposited with the Secretary-General of the United Nations by seven-eighths of them.

5. Any amendment to articles 5, 6, 7 and 8 of this Statute shall enter into force for those States Parties which have accepted the amendment one year after the deposit of their instruments of ratification or acceptance. In respect of a State Party which has not accepted the amendment, the Court shall not exercise its jurisdiction regarding a crime covered by the amendment when committed by that State Party's nationals or on its territory.

6. If an amendment has been accepted by seven-eighths of States Parties in accordance with paragraph 4, any State Party which has not accepted the amendment may withdraw from this Statute with immediate effect, notwithstanding article 127, paragraph 1, but subject to article 127, paragraph 2, by giving notice no later than one year after the entry into force of such amendment.

7. The Secretary-General of the United Nations shall circulate to all States Parties any amendment adopted at a meeting of the Assembly of States Parties or at a Review Conference.

Article 122
Amendments to provisions of an institutional nature

1. Amendments to provisions of this Statute which are of an exclusively institutional nature, namely, article 35, article 36, paragraphs 8 and 9, article 37, article 38, article 39, paragraphs 1 (first two sentences), 2 and 4, article 42, paragraphs 4 to 9, article 43, paragraphs 2 and 3, and articles 44, 46, 47 and 49, may be proposed at any time, notwithstanding article 121, paragraph 1, by any State Party. The text of any proposed amendment shall be submitted to the Secretary-General of the United Nations or such other person designated by the Assembly of States Parties who shall promptly circulate it to all States Parties and to others participating in the Assembly.

2. Amendments under this article on which consensus cannot be reached shall be adopted by the Assembly of States Parties or by a Review Conference, by a two-thirds majority of States Parties. Such amendments shall enter into force for all States Parties six months after their adoption by the Assembly or, as the case may be, by the Conference.

Article 123
Review of the Statute

1. Seven years after the entry into force of this Statute the Secretary-General of the United Nations shall convene a Review Conference to consider any amendments to this Statute. Such review may include, but is not limited to, the list of crimes contained in article 5. The Conference shall be open to those participating in the Assembly of States Parties and on the same conditions.

2. At any time thereafter, at the request of a State Party and for the purposes set out in paragraph 1, the Secretary-General of the United Nations shall, upon approval by a majority of States Parties, convene a Review Conference.

3. The provisions of article 121, paragraphs 3 to 7, shall apply to the adoption and entry into force of any amendment to the Statute considered at a Review Conference.

Article 124
Transitional Provision

Notwithstanding article 12, paragraphs 1 and 2, a State, on becoming a party to this Statute, may declare that, for a period of seven years after the entry into force of this Statute for the State concerned, it does not accept the jurisdiction of the Court with respect to the category of crimes referred to in article 8 when a crime is alleged to have been committed by its nationals or on its territory. A declaration under this article may be withdrawn at any time. The provisions of this article shall be reviewed at the Review Conference convened in accordance with article 123, paragraph 1.

Article 125
Signature, ratification, acceptance, approval or accession

1. This Statute shall be open for signature by all States in Rome, at the headquarters of the Food and Agriculture Organization of the United Nations, on 17 July 1998. Thereafter, it shall remain open for signature in Rome at the Ministry of Foreign Affairs of Italy until 17 October 1998. After that date, the Statute shall remain open for signature in New York, at United Nations Headquarters, until 31 December 2000.

2. This Statute is subject to ratification, acceptance or approval by signatory States. Instruments of ratification, acceptance or approval shall be deposited with the Secretary-General of the United Nations.

3. This Statute shall be open to accession by all States. Instruments of accession shall be deposited with the Secretary-General of the United Nations.

Article 126
Entry into force

1. This Statute shall enter into force on the first day of the month after the 60th day following the date of the deposit of the 60th instrument of ratification, acceptance, approval or accession with the Secretary-General of the United Nations.

2. For each State ratifying, accepting, approving or acceding to this Statute after the deposit of the 60th instrument of ratification, acceptance, approval or accession, the Statute shall enter into force on the first day of the month after the 60th day following the deposit by such State of its instrument of ratification, acceptance, approval or accession.

Article 127
Withdrawal

1. A State Party may, by written notification addressed to the Secretary-General of the United Nations, withdraw from this Statute. The withdrawal shall take effect one year after the date of receipt of the notification, unless the notification specifies a later date.

2. A State shall not be discharged, by reason of its withdrawal, from the obligations arising from this Statute while it was a Party to the Statute, including any financial obligations which may have accrued. Its withdrawal shall not affect any cooperation with the Court in connection with criminal investigations and proceedings in relation to which the withdrawing State had a duty to cooperate and which were commenced prior to the date on which the withdrawal became effective, nor shall it prejudice in any way the continued consideration of any matter which was already under consideration by the Court prior to the date on which the withdrawal became effective.

Article 128
Authentic texts

The original of this Statute, of which the Arabic, Chinese, English, French, Russian and Spanish texts are equally authentic, shall be deposited with the Secretary-General of the United Nations, who shall send certified copies thereof to all States.

IN WITNESS WHEREOF, the undersigned, being duly authorized thereto by their respective Governments, have signed this Statute.

DONE at Rome, this 17th day of July 1998.

APPENDIX B

ELEMENTS OF CRIMES[1]

General introduction

1.Pursuant to article 9, the following Elements of Crimes shall assist the Court in the interpretation and application of articles 6, 7 and 8, consistent with the Statute. The provisions of the Statute, including article 21 and the general principles set out in Part 3, are applicable to the Elements of Crimes.

2.As stated in article 30, unless otherwise provided, a person shall be criminally responsible and liable for punishment for a crime within the jurisdiction of the Court only if the material elements are committed with intent and knowledge. Where no reference is made in the Elements of Crimes to a mental element for any particular conduct, consequence or circumstance listed, it is understood that the relevant mental element, i.e., intent, knowledge or both, set out in article 30 applies. Exceptions to the article 30 standard, based on the Statute, including applicable law under its relevant provisions, are indicated below.

3. Existence of intent and knowledge can be inferred from relevant facts and circumstances.

4. With respect to mental elements associated with elements involving value judgement, such as those using the terms "inhumane2 or "severe", it is not necessary that the perpetrator personally completed a particular value judgement, unless otherwise indicated.

5. Grounds for excluding criminal responsibility or the absence thereof are generally not specified in the elements of crimes listed under each crime.[2]

6. The requirement of "unlawfulness" found in the Statute or in other parts of international law, in particular international humanitarian law, is generally not specified in the elements of crimes.

---

[1] U.N. Doc. PCNICC/2000/1/Add.2 (2000).

[2] This paragraph is without prejudice to the obligation of the Prosecutor under article 54, paragraph 1, of the Statute.

7. The elements of crimes are generally structured in accordance with the following principles:

- As the elements of crimes focus on the conduct, consequences and circumstances associated with each crime, they are generally listed in that order;
- When required, a particular mental element is listed after the affected conduct, consequence or circumstance;
- Contextual circumstances are listed last.

8. As used in the Elements of Crimes, the term "perpetrator" is neutral as to guilt or innocence. The elements, including the appropriate mental elements, apply, *mutatis mutandis*, to all those whose criminal responsibility may fall under articles 25 and 28 of the Statute.

9. A particular conduct may constitute one or more crimes.

10. The use of short titles for the crimes has no legal effect.

Article 6
Genocide

Introduction

With respect to the last element listed for each crime:

- The term 'in the context of' would include the initial acts in an emerging pattern;
- The term "manifest" is an objective qualification;
- Notwithstanding the normal requirement for a mental element provided for in article 30, and recognizing that knowledge of the circumstances will usually be addressed in proving genocidal intent, the appropriate requirement, if any, for a mental element regarding this circumstance will need to be decided by the

Court on a case-by-case basis.

Article 6 (a)
Genocide by killing

Elements

1. The perpetrator killed[3] one or more persons.
2. Such person or persons belonged to a particular national, ethnical, racial or religious group.
3. The perpetrator intended to destroy, in whole or in part, that national, ethnical, racial or religious group, as such.

---

[3] The term "killed" is interchangeable with the term "caused death".

4. The conduct took place in the context of a manifest pattern of similar conduct directed against that group or was conduct that could itself effect such destruction.

Article 6 (b)
Genocide by causing serious bodily or mental harm

Elements

1. The perpetrator caused serious bodily or mental harm to one or more persons.[4]
2. Such person or persons belonged to a particular national, ethnical, racial or religious group.
3. The perpetrator intended to destroy, in whole or in part, that national, ethnical, racial or religious group, as such.
4. The conduct took place in the context of a manifest pattern of similar conduct directed against that group or was conduct that could itself effect such destruction.

Article 6 (c)
Genocide by deliberately inflicting conditions oflife calculated to bring about physical destruction

Elements

1. The perpetrator inflicted certain conditions of life upon one or more persons.
2. Such person or persons belonged to a particular national, ethnical, racial or religious group.
3. The perpetrator intended to destroy, in whole or in part, that national, ethnical, racial or religious group, as such.
4. The conditions of life were calculated to bring about the physical destruction of that group, in whole or in part.[5]
5. The conduct took place in the context of a manifest pattern of similar conduct directed against that group or was conduct that could itself effect such destruction.

---

[4] This conduct may include, but is not necessarily restricted to, acts of torture, rape, sexual violence or inhuman or degrading treatment.

[5] The term "conditions of life" may include, but is not necessarily restricted to, deliberate deprivation of resources indispensable for survival, such as food or medical services, or systematic expulsion from homes.

Article 6 (d)
Genocide by imposing measures intended to prevent births

Elements

1. The perpetrator imposed certain measures upon one or more persons.

2. Such person or persons belonged to a particular national, ethnical, racial or religious group.

3. The perpetrator intended to destroy, in whole or in part, that national, ethnical, racial or religious group, as such.

4. The measures imposed were intended to prevent births within that group.

5. The conduct took place in the context of a manifest pattern of similar conduct directed against that group or was conduct that could itself effect such destruction.

Article 6 (e)
Genocide by forcibly transferring children

Elements

1. The perpetrator forcibly transferred one or more persons.[6]

2. Such person or persons belonged to a particular national, ethnical, racial or religious group.

3. The perpetrator intended to destroy, in whole or in part, that national, ethnical, racial or religious group, as such.

4. The transfer was from that group to another group.

5. The person or persons were under the age of 18 years.

6. The perpetrator knew, or should have known, that the person or persons were under the age of 18 years.

7. The conduct took place in the context of a manifest pattern of similar conduct directed against that group or was conduct that could itself effect such destruction.

---

[6] The term 'forcibly' is not restricted to physical force, but may include threat of force or coercion, such as that caused by fear of violence, duress, detention, psychological oppression or abuse of power, against such person or persons or another person, or by taking advantage of a coercive environment.

Article 7
Crimes against humanity

Introduction

1. Since article 7 pertains to international criminal law, its provisions, consistent with article 22, must be strictly construed, taking into account that crimes against humanity as defined in article 7 are among the most serious crimes of concern to the international community as a whole, warrant and entail individual criminal responsibility, and require conduct which is impermissible under generally applicable international law, as recognized by the principal legal systems of the world.

2. The last two elements for each crime against humanity describe the context in which the conduct must take place. These elements clarify the requisite participation in and knowledge of a widespread or systematic attack against a civilian population. However, the last element should not be interpreted as requiring proof that the perpetrator had knowledge of all characteristics of the attack or the precise details of the plan or policy of the State or organization. In the case of an emerging widespread or systematic attack against a civilian population, the intent clause of the last element indicates that this mental element is satisfied if the perpetrator intended to further such an attack.

3. Attack directed against a civilian population. in these context elements is understood to mean a course of conduct involving the multiple commission of acts referred to in article 7, paragraph 1, of the Statute against any civilian population, pursuant to or in furtherance of a State or organizational policy to commit such attack. The acts need not constitute a military attack. It is understood that 'policy to commit such attack' requires that the State or organization actively promote or encourage such an attack against a civilian population.[7]

---

[7] A policy which has a civilian population as the object of the attack would be implemented by State or organizational action. Such a policy may, in exceptional circumstances, be implemented by a deliberate failure to take action, which is consciously aimed at encouraging such attack. The existence of such a policy cannot be inferred solely from the absence of governmental or organizational action.

Article 7 (1) (a)
Crime against humanity of murder

Elements

1. The perpetrator killed[8] one or more persons.

2. The conduct was committed as part of a widespread or systematic attack directed against a civilian population.

3. The perpetrator knew that the conduct was part of or intended the conduct to be part of a widespread or systematic attack against a civilian population.

Article 7 (1) (b)
Crime against humanity of extermination

Elements

1. The perpetrator killed[9] one or more persons, including by inflicting conditions of life calculated to bring about the destruction of part of a population.[10]

2. The conduct constituted, or took place as part of,[11] a mass killing of members of a civilian population.

3. The conduct was committed as part of a widespread or systematic attack directed against a civilian population.

4. The perpetrator knew that the conduct was part of or intended the conduct to be part of a widespread or systematic attack directed against a civilian population.

Article 7 (1) (c)
Crime against humanity of enslavement

Elements

1. The perpetrator exercised any or all of the powers attaching to the right of ownership over one or more persons, such as by purchasing,

---

[8] 7 The term "killed" is interchangeable with the term "caused death". This footnote applies to all elements which use either of these concepts.

[9] The conduct could be committed by different methods of killing, either directly or indirectly.

[10] 9 The infliction of such conditions could include the deprivation of access to food and medicine.

[11] The term "as part of" would include the initial conduct in a mass killing.

selling, lending or bartering such a person or persons, or by imposing on them a similar deprivation of liberty.[12]

2. The conduct was committed as part of a widespread or systematic attack directed against a civilian population.

3. The perpetrator knew that the conduct was part of or intended the conduct to be part of a widespread or systematic attack directed against a civilian population.

Article 7 (1) (d) Crime against humanity of deportation or forcible transfer of population

Elements

1. The perpetrator deported or forcibly[13] transferred,[14] without grounds permitted under international law, one or more persons to another State or location, by expulsion or other coercive acts.

2. Such person or persons were lawfully present in the area from which they were so deported or transferred.

3. The perpetrator was aware of the factual circumstances that established the lawfulness of such presence.

4. The conduct was committed as part of a widespread or systematic attack directed against a civilian population.

5. The perpetrator knew that the conduct was part of or intended the conduct to be part of a widespread or systematic attack directed against a civilian population.

---

[12] It is understood that such deprivation of liberty may, in some circumstances, include exacting forced labour or otherwise reducing a person to a servile status as defined in the Supplementary Convention on the Abolition of Slavery, the Slave Trade, and Institutions and Practices Similar to Slavery of 1956. It is also understood that the conduct described in this element includes trafficking in persons, in particular women and children.

[13] The term 'forcibly' is not restricted to physical force, but may include threat of force orcoercion, such as that caused by fear of violence, duress, detention, psychological oppression or abuse of power against such person or persons or another person, or by taking advantage of a coercive environment.

[14] 'Deported or forcibly transferred' is interchangeable with 'forcibly displaced'.

Article 7 (1) (e)
Crime against humanity of imprisonment or othersevere deprivation of physical liberty

Elements

1. The perpetrator imprisoned one or more persons or otherwise severely deprived one or more persons of physical liberty.

2. The gravity of the conduct was such that it was in violation of fundamental rules of international law.

3. The perpetrator was aware of the factual circumstances that established the gravity of the conduct.

4. The conduct was committed as part of a widespread or systematic attack directed against a civilian population.

5. The perpetrator knew that the conduct was part of or intended the conduct to be part of a widespread or systematic attack directed against a civilian population.

Article 7 (1) (f)
Crime against humanity of torture[15]

Elements

1. The perpetrator inflicted severe physical or mental pain or suffering upon one or more persons.

2. Such person or persons were in the custody or under the control of the perpetrator.

3. Such pain or suffering did not arise only from, and was not inherent in or incidental to, lawful sanctions.

4. The conduct was committed as part of a widespread or systematic attack directed against a civilian population.

5. The perpetrator knew that the conduct was part of or intended the conduct to be part of a widespread or systematic attack directed against a civilian population.

Article 7 (1) (g)-1
Crime against humanity of rape

Elements

1. The perpetrator invaded[16] the body of a person by conduct resulting in penetration, however slight, of any part of the body of the victim or of

[15] It is understood that no specific purpose need be proved for this crime.

the perpetrator with a sexual organ, or of the anal or genital opening of the victim with any object or any other part of the body.

2. The invasion was committed by force, or by threat of force or coercion, such as that caused by fear of violence, duress, detention, psychological oppression or abuse of power, against such person or another person, or by taking advantage of a coercive environment, or the invasion was committed against a person incapable of giving genuine consent.[17]

3. The conduct was committed as part of a widespread or systematic attack directed against a civilian population.

4. The perpetrator knew that the conduct was part of or intended the conduct to be part of a widespread or systematic attack directed against a civilian population.

Article 7 (1) (g)-2
Crime against humanity of sexual slavery[18]

Elements

1. The perpetrator exercised any or all of the powers attaching to the right of ownership over one or more persons, such as by purchasing, selling, lending or bartering such a person or persons, or by imposing on them a similar deprivation of liberty.[19]

2. The perpetrator caused such person or persons to engage in one or more acts of a sexual nature.

3. The conduct was committed as part of a widespread or systematic attack directed against a civilian population.

4. The perpetrator knew that the conduct was part of or intended the conduct to be part of a widespread or systematic attack directed against a civilian population.

---

[16] The concept of "invasion" is intended to be broad enough to be gender-neutral.

[17] It is understood that a person may be incapable of giving genuine consent if affected by natural, induced or age-related incapacity. This footnote also applies to the corresponding elements of article 7 (1) (g)-3, 5 and 6.

[18] Given the complex nature of this crime, it is recognized that its commission could involve more than one perpetrator as a part of a common criminal purpose.

[19] It is understood that such deprivation of liberty may, in some circumstances, include exacting forced labour or otherwise reducing a person to a servile status as defined in the Supplementary Convention on the Abolition of Slavery, the Slave Trade, and Institutions and Practices Similar to Slavery of 1956. It is also understood that the conduct described in this element includes trafficking in persons, in particular women and children.

Article 7 (1) (g)-3
Crime against humanity of enforced prostitution

Elements

1. The perpetrator caused one or more persons to engage in one or more acts of a sexual nature by force, or by threat of force or coercion, such as that caused by fear of violence, duress, detention, psychological oppression or abuse of power, against such person or persons or another person, or by taking advantage of a coercive environment or such persons or persons' incapacity to give genuine consent.

2. The perpetrator or another person obtained or expected to obtain pecuniary or other advantage in exchange for or in connection with the acts of a sexual nature.

3. The conduct was committed as part of a widespread or systematic attack directed against a civilian population.

4. The perpetrator knew that the conduct was part of or intended the conduct to be part of a widespread or systematic attack directed against a civilian population.

Article 7 (1) (g)-4
Crime against humanity of forced pregnancy

Elements

1. The perpetrator confined one or more women forcibly made pregnant, with the intent of affecting the ethnic composition of any population or carrying out other grave violations of international law.

2. The conduct was committed as part of a widespread or systematic attack directed against a civilian population.

3. The perpetrator knew that the conduct was part of or intended the conduct to be part of a widespread or systematic attack directed against a civilian population.

Article 7 (1) (g)-5
Crime against humanity of enforced sterilization

Elements

1. The perpetrator deprived one or more persons of biological reproductive capacity.[20]

---

[20] 19 The deprivation is not intended to include birth-control measures which have a non-permanent effect in practice.

2. The conduct was neither justified by the medical or hospital treatment of the person or persons concerned nor carried out with their genuine consent.[21]

3. The conduct was committed as part of a widespread or systematic attack directed against a civilian population.

4. The perpetrator knew that the conduct was part of or intended the conduct to be part of a widespread or systematic attack directed against a civilian population.

Article 7 (1) (g)-6
Crime against humanity of sexual violence

Elements

1. The perpetrator committed an act of a sexual nature against one or more persons or caused such person or persons to engage in an act of a sexual nature by force, or by threat of force or coercion, such as that caused by fear of violence, duress, detention, psychological oppression or abuse of power, against such person or persons or another person, or by taking advantage of a coercive environment or such person's or persons. incapacity to give genuine consent.

2. Such conduct was of a gravity comparable to the other offences in article 7, paragraph 1 (g), of the Statute.

3. The perpetrator was aware of the factual circumstances that established the gravity of the conduct.

4. The conduct was committed as part of a widespread or systematic attack directed against a civilian population.

5. The perpetrator knew that the conduct was part of or intended the conduct to be part of a widespread or systematic attack directed against a civilian population.

Article 7 (1) (h)
Crime against humanity of persecution

Elements

1. The perpetrator severely deprived, contrary to international law,[22] one or more persons of fundamental rights.

---

[21] It is understood that "genuine consent" does not include consent obtained through deception.

[22] This requirement is without prejudice to paragraph 6 of the General Introduction to the Elements of Crimes.

2. The perpetrator targeted such person or persons by reason of the identity of a group or collectivity or targeted the group or collectivity as such.

3. Such targeting was based on political, racial, national, ethnic, cultural, religious, gender as defined in article 7, paragraph 3, of the Statute, or other grounds that are universally recognized as impermissible under international law.

4. The conduct was committed in connection with any act referred to in article 7, paragraph 1, of the Statute or any crime within the jurisdiction of the Court.[23]

5. The conduct was committed as part of a widespread or systematic attack directed against a civilian population.

6. The perpetrator knew that the conduct was part of or intended the conduct to be part of a widespread or systematic attack directed against a civilian population.

Article 7 (1) (i)
Crime against humanity of enforced disappearance of persons[24,25]

Elements

1. The perpetrator:

(a) Arrested, detained[26,27] or abducted one or more persons; or

(b) Refused to acknowledge the arrest, detention or abduction, or to give information on the fate or whereabouts of such person or persons.

2. (a) Such arrest, detention or abduction was followed or accompanied by a refusal to acknowledge that deprivation of freedom or to give information on the fate or whereabouts of such person or persons; or

(b) Such refusal was preceded or accompanied by that deprivation of freedom.

---

[23] It is understood that no additional mental element is necessary for this element other than that inherent in element 6.

[24] Given the complex nature of this crime, it is recognized that its commission will normally involve more than one perpetrator as a part of a common criminal purpose.

[25] This crime falls under the jurisdiction of the Court only if the attack referred to in elements 7 and 8 occurs after the entry into force of the Statute.

[26] The word "detained" would include a perpetrator who maintained an existing detention.

[27] It is understood that under certain circumstances an arrest or detention may have been lawful.

3. The perpetrator was aware that:[28]

(a) Such arrest, detention or abduction would be followed in the ordinary course of events by a refusal to acknowledge that deprivation of freedom or to give information on the fate or whereabouts of such person or persons;[29] or

(b) Such refusal was preceded or accompanied by that deprivation of freedom.

4. Such arrest, detention or abduction was carried out by, or with the authorization, support or acquiescence of, a State or a political organization.

5. Such refusal to acknowledge that deprivation of freedom or to give information on the fate or whereabouts of such person or persons was carried out by, or with the authorization or support of, such State or political organization.

6. The perpetrator intended to remove such person or persons from the protection of the law for a prolonged period of time.

7. The conduct was committed as part of a widespread or systematic attack directed against a civilian population.

8. The perpetrator knew that the conduct was part of or intended the conduct to be part of a widespread or systematic attack directed against a civilian population.

Article 7 (1) (j)
Crime against humanity of apartheid

Elements

1. The perpetrator committed an inhumane act against one or more persons.

2. Such act was an act referred to in article 7, paragraph 1, of the Statute, or was an act of a character similar to any of those acts.[30]

3. The perpetrator was aware of the factual circumstances that established the character of the act.

4. The conduct was committed in the context of an institutionalized regime of systematic oppression and domination by one racial group over any other racial group or groups.

---

[28] This element, inserted because of the complexity of this crime, is without prejudice to the General Introduction to the Elements of Crimes.

[29] It is understood that, in the case of a perpetrator who maintained an existing detention, this element would be satisfied if the perpetrator was aware that such a refusal had already taken place.

[30] It is understood that "character" refers to the nature and gravity of the act.

5. The perpetrator intended to maintain such regime by that conduct.

6. The conduct was committed as part of a widespread or systematic attack directed against a civilian population.

7. The perpetrator knew that the conduct was part of or intended the conduct to be part of a widespread or systematic attack directed against a civilian population.

Article 7 (1) (k)
Crime against humanity of other inhumane acts

Elements

1. The perpetrator inflicted great suffering, or serious injury to body or to mental or physical health, by means of an inhumane act.

2. Such act was of a character similar to any other act referred to in article 7, paragraph 1, of the Statute.[31]

3. The perpetrator was aware of the factual circumstances that established the character of the act.

4. The conduct was committed as part of a widespread or systematic attack directed against a civilian population.

5. The perpetrator knew that the conduct was part of or intended the conduct to be part of a widespread or systematic attack directed against a civilian population.

Article 8
War crimes

Introduction

The elements for war crimes under article 8, paragraph 2 (c) and (e), are subject to the limitations addressed in article 8, paragraph 2 (d) and (f), which are not elements of crimes.

The elements for war crimes under article 8, paragraph 2, of the Statute shall be interpreted within the established framework of the international law of armed conflict including, as appropriate, the international law of armed conflict applicable to armed conflict at sea.

With respect to the last two elements listed for each crime:

- There is no requirement for a legal evaluation by the perpetrator as to the existence of an armed conflict or its character as international or noninternational;

---

[31] It is understood that "character" refers to the nature and gravity of the act.

- In that context there is no requirement for awareness by the perpetrator of the facts that established the character of the conflict as international or noninternational;

- There is only a requirement for the awareness of the factual circumstances that established the existence of an armed conflict that is implicit in the terms 'took place in the context of and was associated with'.

Article 8 (2) (a)
Article 8 (2) (a) (i)
War crime of wilful killing

Elements

1. The perpetrator killed one or more persons.[32]
2. Such person or persons were protected under one or more of the Geneva Conventions of 1949.
3. The perpetrator was aware of the factual circumstances that established that protected status.[33,34]
4. The conduct took place in the context of and was associated with an international armed conflict.[35]
5. The perpetrator was aware of factual circumstances that established the existence of an armed conflict.

---

[32] 31 The term 'killed' is interchangeable with the term 'caused death'. This footnote applies to all elements which use either of these concepts.

[33] This mental element recognizes the interplay between articles 30 and 32. This footnote also applies to the corresponding element in each crime under article 8 (2) (a), and to the element in other crimes in article 8 (2) concerning the awareness of factual circumstances that establish the status of persons or property protected under the relevant international law of armed conflict.

[34] With respect to nationality, it is understood that the perpetrator needs only to know that the victim belonged to an adverse party to the conflict. This footnote also applies to the corresponding element in each crime under article 8 (2) (a).

[35] The term 'international armed conflict' includes military occupation. This footnote also applies to the corresponding element in each crime under article 8 (2) (a).

Article 8 (2) (a) (ii)-1
War crime of torture

Elements[36]

1. The perpetrator inflicted severe physical or mental pain or suffering upon one or more persons.

2. The perpetrator inflicted the pain or suffering for such purposes as: obtaining information or a confession, punishment, intimidation or coercion or for any reason based on discrimination of any kind.

3. Such person or persons were protected under one or more of the Geneva Conventions of 1949.

4. The perpetrator was aware of the factual circumstances that established that protected status.

5. The conduct took place in the context of and was associated with an international armed conflict.

6. The perpetrator was aware of factual circumstances that established the existence of an armed conflict.

Article 8 (2) (a) (ii)-2
War crime of inhuman treatment

Elements

1. The perpetrator inflicted severe physical or mental pain or suffering upon one or more persons.

2. Such person or persons were protected under one or more of the Geneva Conventions of 1949.

3. The perpetrator was aware of the factual circumstances that established that protected status.

4. The conduct took place in the context of and was associated with an international armed conflict.

5. The perpetrator was aware of factual circumstances that established the existence of an armed conflict.

---

[36] As element 3 requires that all victims must be "protected persons" under one or more of the Geneva Conventions of 1949, these elements do not include the custody or control requirement found in the elements of article 7 (1) (e).

Article 8 (2) (a) (ii)-3
War crime of biological experiments

Elements

1. The perpetrator subjected one or more persons to a particular biological experiment.
2. The experiment seriously endangered the physical or mental health or integrity of such person or persons.
3. The intent of the experiment was non-therapeutic and it was neither justified by medical reasons nor carried out in such person's or persons' interest.
4. Such person or persons were protected under one or more of the Geneva Conventions of 1949.
5. The perpetrator was aware of the factual circumstances that established that protected status.
6. The conduct took place in the context of and was associated with an international armed conflict.
7. The perpetrator was aware of factual circumstances that established the existence of an armed conflict.

Article 8 (2) (a) (iii)
War crime of wilfully causing great suffering

Elements

1. The perpetrator caused great physical or mental pain or suffering to, or serious injury to body or health of, one or more persons.
2. Such person or persons were protected under one or more of the Geneva Conventions of 1949.
3. The perpetrator was aware of the factual circumstances that established that protected status.
4. The conduct took place in the context of and was associated with an international armed conflict.
5. The perpetrator was aware of factual circumstances that established the existence of an armed conflict.

Article 8 (2) (a) (iv)
War crime of destruction and appropriation of property

Elements

1. The perpetrator destroyed or appropriated certain property.

2. The destruction or appropriation was not justified by military necessity.

3. The destruction or appropriation was extensive and carried out wantonly.

4. Such property was protected under one or more of the Geneva Conventions of 1949.

5. The perpetrator was aware of the factual circumstances that established that protected status.

6. The conduct took place in the context of and was associated with an international armed conflict.

7. The perpetrator was aware of factual circumstances that established the existence of an armed conflict.

Article 8 (2) (a) (v)
War crime of compelling service in hostile forces

Elements

1. The perpetrator coerced one or more persons, by act or threat, to take part in military operations against that person's own country or forces or otherwise serve in the forces of a hostile power.

2. Such person or persons were protected under one or more of the Geneva Conventions of 1949.

3. The perpetrator was aware of the factual circumstances that established that protected status.

4. The conduct took place in the context of and was associated with an international armed conflict.

5. The perpetrator was aware of factual circumstances that established the existence of an armed conflict.

Article 8 (2) (a) (vi)
War crime of denying a fair trial

Elements

1. The perpetrator deprived one or more persons of a fair and regular trial by denying judicial guarantees as defined, in particular, in the third and the fourth Geneva Conventions of 1949.

2. Such person or persons were protected under one or more of the Geneva Conventions of 1949.

3. The perpetrator was aware of the factual circumstances that established that protected status.

4. The conduct took place in the context of and was associated with an international armed conflict.

5. The perpetrator was aware of factual circumstances that established the existence of an armed conflict.

Article 8 (2) (a) (vii)-1
War crime of unlawful deportation and transfer

Elements

1. The perpetrator deported or transferred one or more persons to another State or to another location.

2. Such person or persons were protected under one or more of the Geneva Conventions of 1949.

3. The perpetrator was aware of the factual circumstances that established that protected status.

4. The conduct took place in the context of and was associated with an international armed conflict.

5. The perpetrator was aware of factual circumstances that established the existence of an armed conflict.

Article 8 (2) (a) (vii)-2
War crime of unlawful confinement

Elements

1. The perpetrator confined or continued to confine one or more persons to a certain location.

2. Such person or persons were protected under one or more of the Geneva Conventions of 1949.

3. The perpetrator was aware of the factual circumstances that established that protected status.

4. The conduct took place in the context of and was associated with an international armed conflict.

5. The perpetrator was aware of factual circumstances that established the existence of an armed conflict.

Article 8 (2) (a) (viii)
War crime of taking hostages

Elements

1. The perpetrator seized, detained or otherwise held hostage one or more persons.

2. The perpetrator threatened to kill, injure or continue to detain such person or persons.

3. The perpetrator intended to compel a State, an international organization, a natural or legal person or a group of persons to act or refrain from acting as an explicit or implicit condition for the safety or the release of such person or persons.

4. Such person or persons were protected under one or more of the Geneva Conventions of 1949.

5. The perpetrator was aware of the factual circumstances that established that protected status.

6. The conduct took place in the context of and was associated with an international armed conflict.

7. The perpetrator was aware of factual circumstances that established the existence of an armed conflict.

Article 8 (2) (b)
Article 8 (2) (b) (i)
War crime of attacking civilians

Elements

1. The perpetrator directed an attack.

2. The object of the attack was a civilian population as such or individual civilians not taking direct part in hostilities.

3. The perpetrator intended the civilian population as such or individual civilians not taking direct part in hostilities to be the object of the attack.

4. The conduct took place in the context of and was associated with an international armed conflict.

5. The perpetrator was aware of factual circumstances that established the existence of an armed conflict.

Article 8 (2) (b) (ii)
War crime of attacking civilian objects

Elements

1. The perpetrator directed an attack.

2. The object of the attack was civilian objects, that is, objects which are not military objectives.

3. The perpetrator intended such civilian objects to be the object of the attack.

4. The conduct took place in the context of and was associated with an international armed conflict.

5. The perpetrator was aware of factual circumstances that established the existence of an armed conflict.

Article 8 (2) (b) (iii)
War crime of attacking personnel or objects involved in a humanitarian assistance or peacekeeping mission

Elements

1. The perpetrator directed an attack.

2. The object of the attack was personnel, installations, material, units or vehicles involved in a humanitarian assistance or peacekeeping mission in accordance with the Charter of the United Nations.

3. The perpetrator intended such personnel, installations, material, units or vehicles so involved to be the object of the attack.

4. Such personnel, installations, material, units or vehicles were entitled to that protection given to civilians or civilian objects under the international law of armed conflict.

5. The perpetrator was aware of the factual circumstances that established that protection.

6. The conduct took place in the context of and was associated with an international armed conflict.

7. The perpetrator was aware of factual circumstances that established the existence of an armed conflict.

Article 8 (2) (b) (iv)
War crime of excessive incidental death, injury, or damage

Elements

1. The perpetrator launched an attack.

2. The attack was such that it would cause incidental death or injury to civilians or damage to civilian objects or widespread, long-term and severe damage to the natural environment and that such death, injury or damage would be of such an extent as to be clearly excessive in relation to the concrete and direct overall military advantage anticipated.[37]

---

[37] The expression "concrete and direct overall military advantage" refers to a military advantage that is foreseeable by the perpetrator at the relevant time. Such advantage may or may not be temporally or geographically related to the object of the attack. The fact that this crime admits the possibility of lawful incidental injury

3. The perpetrator knew that the attack would cause incidental death or injury to civilians or damage to civilian objects or widespread, long-term and severe damage to the natural environment and that such death, injury or damage would be of such an extent as to be clearly excessive in relation to the concrete and direct overall military advantage anticipated.[38]

4. The conduct took place in the context of and was associated with an international armed conflict.

5. The perpetrator was aware of factual circumstances that established the existence of an armed conflict.

Article 8 (2) (b) (v)
War crime of attacking undefended places[39]

Elements

1. The perpetrator attacked one or more towns, villages, dwellings or buildings.

2. Such towns, villages, dwellings or buildings were open for unresisted occupation.

3. Such towns, villages, dwellings or buildings did not constitute military objectives.

4. The conduct took place in the context of and was associated with an international armed conflict.

5. The perpetrator was aware of factual circumstances that established the existence of an armed conflict.

---

and collateral damage does not in any way justify any violation of the law applicable in armed conflict. It does not address justifications for war or other rules related to *jus ad bellum*. It reflects the proportionality requirement inherent in determining the legality of any military activity undertaken in the context of an armed conflict.

[38] As opposed to the general rule set forth in paragraph 4 of the General Introduction, this knowledge element requires that the perpetrator make the value judgement as described therein. An evaluation of that value judgement must be based on the requisite information available to the perpetrator at the time.

[39] The presence in the locality of persons specially protected under the Geneva Conventions of 1949 or of police forces retained for the sole purpose of maintaining law and order does not by itself render the locality a military objective.

Article 8 (2) (b) (vi)
War crime of killing or wounding a person *hors de combat*

Elements

1. The perpetrator killed or injured one or more persons.
2. Such person or persons were *hors de combat*.
3. The perpetrator was aware of the factual circumstances that established this status.
4. The conduct took place in the context of and was associated with an international armed conflict.
5. The perpetrator was aware of factual circumstances that established the existence of an armed conflict.

Article 8 (2) (b) (vii)-1
War crime of improper use of a flag of truce

Elements

1. The perpetrator used a flag of truce.
2. The perpetrator made such use in order to feign an intention to negotiate when there was no such intention on the part of the perpetrator.
3. The perpetrator knew or should have known of the prohibited nature of such use.[40]
4. The conduct resulted in death or serious personal injury.
5. The perpetrator knew that the conduct could result in death or serious personal injury.
6. The conduct took place in the context of and was associated with an international armed conflict.
7. The perpetrator was aware of factual circumstances that established the existence of an armed conflict.

Article 8 (2) (b) (vii)-2
War crime of improper use of a flag, insignia or uniform of the hostile party

Elements

1. The perpetrator used a flag, insignia or uniform of the hostile party.
2. The perpetrator made such use in a manner prohibited under the international law of armed conflict while engaged in an attack.

[40] This mental element recognizes the interplay between article 30 and article 32. The term 'prohibited nature' denotes illegality.

3. The perpetrator knew or should have known of the prohibited nature of such use.[41]

4. The conduct resulted in death or serious personal injury.

5. The perpetrator knew that the conduct could result in death or serious personal injury.

6. The conduct took place in the context of and was associated with an international armed conflict.

7. The perpetrator was aware of factual circumstances that established the existence of an armed conflict.

Article 8 (2) (b) (vii)-3 War crime of improper use of a flag, insignia oruniform of the United Nations

Elements

1. The perpetrator used a flag, insignia or uniform of the United Nations.

2. The perpetrator made such use in a manner prohibited under the international law of armed conflict.

3. The perpetrator knew of the prohibited nature of such use.[42]

4. The conduct resulted in death or serious personal injury.

5. The perpetrator knew that the conduct could result in death or serious personal injury.

6. The conduct took place in the context of and was associated with an international armed conflict.

7. The perpetrator was aware of factual circumstances that established the existence of an armed conflict.

---

[41] This mental element recognizes the interplay between article 30 and article 32. The term 'prohibited nature' denotes illegality.

[42] This mental element recognizes the interplay between article 30 and article 32. The "should have known" test required in the other offences found in article 8 (2) (b) (vii) is not applicable here because of the variable and regulatory nature of the relevant prohibitions.

Article 8 (2) (b) (vii)-4
War crime of improper use of the distinctive emblems of the Geneva Conventions

Elements

1. The perpetrator used the distinctive emblems of the Geneva Conventions.

2. The perpetrator made such use for combatant purposes[43] in a manner prohibited under the international law of armed conflict.

3. The perpetrator knew or should have known of the prohibited nature of such use.[44]

4. The conduct resulted in death or serious personal injury.

5. The perpetrator knew that the conduct could result in death or serious personal injury.

6. The conduct took place in the context of and was associated with an international armed conflict.

7. The perpetrator was aware of factual circumstances that established the existence of an armed conflict.

Article 8 (2) (b) (viii)
The transfer, directly or indirectly, by the Occupying Power of parts of its own civilian population into the territory it occupies, or the deportation or transfer of all or parts of the population of the occupied territory within or outside this territory

Elements

1. The perpetrator:

(a) Transferred,[45] directly or indirectly, parts of its own population into the territory it occupies; or

(b) Deported or transferred all or parts of the population of the occupied territory within or outside this territory.

2. The conduct took place in the context of and was associated with an international armed conflict.

---

[43] Combatant purposes.in these circumstances means purposes directly related to hostilities and not including medical, religious or similar activities.

[44] This mental element recognizes the interplay between article 30 and article 32. The term 'prohibited nature' denotes illegality.

[45] The term 'transfer' needs to be interpreted in accordance with the relevant provisions of international humanitarian law.

3. The perpetrator was aware of factual circumstances that established the existence of an armed conflict.

Article 8 (2) (b) (ix)
War crime of attacking protected objects[46]

Elements

1. The perpetrator directed an attack.

2. The object of the attack was one or more buildings dedicated to religion, education, art, science or charitable purposes, historic monuments, hospitals or places where the sick and wounded are collected, which were not military objectives.

3. The perpetrator intended such building or buildings dedicated to religion, education, art, science or charitable purposes, historic monuments, hospitals or places where the sick and wounded are collected, which were not military objectives, to be the object of the attack.

4. The conduct took place in the context of and was associated with an international armed conflict.

5. The perpetrator was aware of factual circumstances that established the existence of an armed conflict.

Article 8 (2) (b) (x)-1
War crime of mutilation

Elements

1. The perpetrator subjected one or more persons to mutilation, in particular by permanently disfiguring the person or persons, or by permanently disabling or removing an organ or appendage.

2. The conduct caused death or seriously endangered the physical or mental health of such person or persons.

3. The conduct was neither justified by the medical, dental or hospital treatment of the person or persons concerned nor carried out in such person's or personsinterest.[47]

---

[46] The presence in the locality of persons specially protected under the Geneva Conventions of 1949 or of police forces retained for the sole purpose of maintaining law and order does not by itself render the locality a military objective.

[47] Consent is not a defence to this crime. The crime prohibits any medical procedure which is not indicated by the state of health of the person concerned and which is not consistent with generally accepted medical standards which would be applied under similar medical circumstances to persons who are nationals of the

4. Such person or persons were in the power of an adverse party.

5. The conduct took place in the context of and was associated with an international armed conflict.

6. The perpetrator was aware of factual circumstances that established the existence of an armed conflict.

Article 8 (2) (b) (x)-2
War crime of medical or scientific experiments

Elements

1. The perpetrator subjected one or more persons to a medical or scientific experiment.

2. The experiment caused death or seriously endangered the physical or mental health or integrity of such person or persons.

3. The conduct was neither justified by the medical, dental or hospital treatment of such person or persons concerned nor carried out in such person's or persons' interest.

4. Such person or persons were in the power of an adverse party.

5. The conduct took place in the context of and was associated with an international armed conflict.

6. The perpetrator was aware of factual circumstances that established the existence of an armed conflict.

Article 8 (2) (b) (xi)
War crime of treacherously killing or wounding

Elements

1. The perpetrator invited the confidence or belief of one or more persons that they were entitled to, or were obliged to accord, protection under rules of international law applicable in armed conflict.

2. The perpetrator intended to betray that confidence or belief.

3. The perpetrator killed or injured such person or persons.

4. The perpetrator made use of that confidence or belief in killing or injuring such person or persons.

5. Such person or persons belonged to an adverse party.

6. The conduct took place in the context of and was associated with an international armed conflict.

---

party conducting the procedure and who are in no way deprived of liberty. This footnote also applies to the same element for article 8 (2) (b) (x)-2.

7. The perpetrator was aware of factual circumstances that established the existence of an armed conflict.

Article 8 (2) (b) (xii)
War crime of denying quarter

Elements

1. The perpetrator declared or ordered that there shall be no survivors.

2. Such declaration or order was given in order to threaten an adversary or to conduct hostilities on the basis that there shall be no survivors.

3. The perpetrator was in a position of effective command or control over the subordinate forces to which the declaration or order was directed.

4. The conduct took place in the context of and was associated with an international armed conflict.

5. The perpetrator was aware of factual circumstances that established the existence of an armed conflict.

Article 8 (2) (b) (xiii)
War crime of destroying or seizing the enemy's property

Elements

1. The perpetrator destroyed or seized certain property.

2. Such property was property of a hostile party.

3. Such property was protected from that destruction or seizure under the international law of armed conflict.

4. The perpetrator was aware of the factual circumstances that established the status of the property.

5. The destruction or seizure was not justified by military necessity.

6. The conduct took place in the context of and was associated with an international armed conflict.

7. The perpetrator was aware of factual circumstances that established the existence of an armed conflict.

Article 8 (2) (b) (xiv)
War crime of depriving the nationals ofthe hostile power of rights or actions

Elements

1. The perpetrator effected the abolition, suspension or termination of admissibility in a court of law of certain rights or actions.

2. The abolition, suspension or termination was directed at the nationals of a hostile party.

3. The perpetrator intended the abolition, suspension or termination to be directed at the nationals of a hostile party.

4. The conduct took place in the context of and was associated with an international armed conflict.

5. The perpetrator was aware of factual circumstances that established the existence of an armed conflict.

Article 8 (2) (b) (xv)
War crime of compelling participation in military operations

Elements

1. The perpetrator coerced one or more persons by act or threat to take part in military operations against that person's own country or forces.

2. Such person or persons were nationals of a hostile party.

3. The conduct took place in the context of and was associated with an international armed conflict.

4. The perpetrator was aware of factual circumstances that established the existence of an armed conflict.

Article 8 (2) (b) (xvi)
War crime of pillaging

Elements

1. The perpetrator appropriated certain property.

2. The perpetrator intended to deprive the owner of the property and to appropriate it for private or personal use.[48]

3. The appropriation was without the consent of the owner.

4. The conduct took place in the context of and was associated with an international armed conflict.

5. The perpetrator was aware of factual circumstances that established the existence of an armed conflict.

---

[48] As indicated by the use of the term "private or personal use", appropriations justified by military necessity cannot constitute the crime of pillaging.

Article 8 (2) (b) (xvii)
War crime of employing poison or poisoned weapons

Elements

1. The perpetrator employed a substance or a weapon that releases a substance as a result of its employment.

2. The substance was such that it causes death or serious damage to health in the ordinary course of events, through its toxic properties.

3. The conduct took place in the context of and was associated with an international armed conflict.

4. The perpetrator was aware of factual circumstances that established the existence of an armed conflict.

Article 8 (2) (b) (xviii)
War crime of employing prohibitedgases, liquids, materials or devices

Elements

1. The perpetrator employed a gas or other analogous substance or device.

2. The gas, substance or device was such that it causes death or serious damage to health in the ordinary course of events, through its asphyxiating or toxic properties.[49]

3. The conduct took place in the context of and was associated with an international armed conflict.

4. The perpetrator was aware of factual circumstances that established the existence of an armed conflict.

Article 8 (2) (b) (xix)
War crime of employing prohibited bullets

Elements

1. The perpetrator employed certain bullets.

2. The bullets were such that their use violates the international law of armed conflict because they expand or flatten easily in the human body.

---

[49] Nothing in this element shall be interpreted as limiting or prejudicing in any way existing or developing rules of international law with respect to the development, production, stockpiling and use of chemical weapons.

3. The perpetrator was aware that the nature of the bullets was such that their employment would uselessly aggravate suffering or the wounding effect.

4. The conduct took place in the context of and was associated with an international armed conflict.

5. The perpetrator was aware of factual circumstances that established the existence of an armed conflict.

Article 8 (2) (b) (xx)
War crime of employing weapons, projectiles or materials or methods of warfare listed in the Annex to the Statute

Elements

[Elements will have to be drafted once weapons, projectiles or material or methods of warfare have been included in an annex to the Statute.]

Article 8 (2) (b) (xxi)
War crime of outrages upon personal dignity

Elements

1. The perpetrator humiliated, degraded or otherwise violated the dignity of one or more persons.[50]

2. The severity of the humiliation, degradation or other violation was of such degree as to be generally recognized as an outrage upon personal dignity.

3. The conduct took place in the context of and was associated with an international armed conflict.

4. The perpetrator was aware of factual circumstances that established the existence of an armed conflict.

---

[50] For this crime, "persons.can include dead persons" It is understood that the victim need not personally be aware of the existence of the humiliation or degradation or other violation. This element takes into account relevant aspects of the cultural background of the victim.

Article 8 (2) (b) (xxii)-1
War crime of rape

Elements

1. The perpetrator invaded[51] the body of a person by conduct resulting in penetration, however slight, of any part of the body of the victim or of the perpetrator with a sexual organ, or of the anal or genital opening of the victim with any object or any other part of the body.

2. The invasion was committed by force, or by threat of force or coercion, such as that caused by fear of violence, duress, detention, psychological oppression or abuse of power, against such person or another person, or by taking advantage of a coercive environment, or the invasion was committed against a person incapable of giving genuine consent.[52]

3. The conduct took place in the context of and was associated with an international armed conflict.

4. The perpetrator was aware of factual circumstances that established the existence of an armed conflict.

Article 8 (2) (b) (xxii)-2
War crime of sexual slavery[53]

Elements

1. The perpetrator exercised any or all of the powers attaching to the right of ownership over one or more persons, such as by purchasing, selling, lending or bartering such a person or persons, or by imposing on them a similar deprivation of liberty.[54]

2. The perpetrator caused such person or persons to engage in one or more acts of a sexual nature.

---

[51] The concept of "invasion" is intended to be broad enough to be gender-neutral.

[52] It is understood that a person may be incapable of giving genuine consent if affected by natural, induced or age-related incapacity. This footnote also applies to the corresponding elements of article 8 (2) (b) (xxii)-3, 5 and 6.

[53] Given the complex nature of this crime, it is recognized that its commission could involve more than one perpetrator as a part of a common criminal purpose.

[54] It is understood that such deprivation of liberty may, in some circumstances, include exacting forced labour or otherwise reducing a person to servile status as defined in the Supplementary Convention on the Abolition of Slavery, the Slave Trade, and Institutions and Practices Similar to Slavery of 1956. It is also understood that the conduct described in this element includes trafficking in persons, in particular women and children.

3. The conduct took place in the context of and was associated with an international armed conflict.

4. The perpetrator was aware of factual circumstances that established the existence of an armed conflict.

Article 8 (2) (b) (xxii)-3
War crime of enforced prostitution

Elements

1. The perpetrator caused one or more persons to engage in one or more acts of a sexual nature by force, or by threat of force or coercion, such as that caused by fear of violence, duress, detention, psychological oppression or abuse of power, against such person or persons or another person, or by taking advantage of a coercive environment or such person's or persons' incapacity to give genuine consent.

2. The perpetrator or another person obtained or expected to obtain pecuniary or other advantage in exchange for or in connection with the acts of a sexual nature.

3. The conduct took place in the context of and was associated with an international armed conflict.

4. The perpetrator was aware of factual circumstances that established the existence of an armed conflict.

Article 8 (2) (b) (xxii)-4
War crime of forced pregnancy

Elements

1. The perpetrator confined one or more women forcibly made pregnant, with the intent of affecting the ethnic composition of any population or carrying out other grave violations of international law.

2. The conduct took place in the context of and was associated with an international armed conflict.

3. The perpetrator was aware of factual circumstances that established the existence of an armed conflict.

Article 8 (2) (b) (xxii)-5
War crime of enforced sterilization

Elements

1. The perpetrator deprived one or more persons of biological reproductive capacity.[55]

2. The conduct was neither justified by the medical or hospital treatment of the person or persons concerned nor carried out with their genuine consent.[56]

3. The conduct took place in the context of and was associated with an international armed conflict.

4. The perpetrator was aware of factual circumstances that established the existence of an armed conflict.

Article 8 (2) (b) (xxii)-6
War crime of sexual violence

Elements

1. The perpetrator committed an act of a sexual nature against one or more persons or caused such person or persons to engage in an act of a sexual nature by force, or by threat of force or coercion, such as that caused by fear of violence, duress, detention, psychological oppression or abuse of power, against such person or persons or another person, or by taking advantage of a coercive environment or such person's or persons' incapacity to give genuine consent.

2. The conduct was of a gravity comparable to that of a grave breach of the Geneva Conventions.

3. The perpetrator was aware of the factual circumstances that established the gravity of the conduct.

4. The conduct took place in the context of and was associated with an international armed conflict.

5. The perpetrator was aware of factual circumstances that established the existence of an armed conflict.

---

[55] The deprivation is not intended to include birth-control measures which have a non-permanent effect in practice.

[56] It is understood that "genuine consent" does not include consent obtained through deception.

Article 8 (2) (b) (xxiii)
War crime of using protected persons as shields

Elements

1. The perpetrator moved or otherwise took advantage of the location of one or more civilians or other persons protected under the international law of armed conflict.

2. The perpetrator intended to shield a military objective from attack or shield, favour or impede military operations.

3. The conduct took place in the context of and was associated with an international armed conflict.

4. The perpetrator was aware of factual circumstances that established the existence of an armed conflict.

Article 8 (2) (b) (xxiv)
War crime of attacking objects or persons using the distinctive emblems of the Geneva Conventions

Elements

1. The perpetrator attacked one or more persons, buildings, medical units or transports or other objects using, in conformity with international law, a distinctive emblem or other method of identification indicating protection under the Geneva Conventions.

2. The perpetrator intended such persons, buildings, units or transports or other objects so using such identification to be the object of the attack.

3. The conduct took place in the context of and was associated with an international armed conflict.

4. The perpetrator was aware of factual circumstances that established the existence of an armed conflict.

Article 8 (2) (b) (xxv)
War crime of starvation as a method of warfare

Elements

1. The perpetrator deprived civilians of objects indispensable to their survival.

2. The perpetrator intended to starve civilians as a method of warfare.

3. The conduct took place in the context of and was associated with an international armed conflict.

4. The perpetrator was aware of factual circumstances that established the existence of an armed conflict.

Article 8 (2) (b) (xxvi)
War crime of using, conscripting or enlisting children

Elements

1. The perpetrator conscripted or enlisted one or more persons into the national armed forces or used one or more persons to participate actively in hostilities.

2. Such person or persons were under the age of 15 years.

3. The perpetrator knew or should have known that such person or persons were under the age of 15 years.

4. The conduct took place in the context of and was associated with an international armed conflict.

5. The perpetrator was aware of factual circumstances that established the existence of an armed conflict.

Article 8 (2) (c)
Article 8 (2) (c) (i)-1
War crime of murder

Elements

1. The perpetrator killed one or more persons.

2. Such person or persons were either *hors de combat*, or were civilians, medical personnel, or religious personnel[57] taking no active part in the hostilities.

3. The perpetrator was aware of the factual circumstances that established this status.

4. The conduct took place in the context of and was associated with an armed conflict not of an international character.

5. The perpetrator was aware of factual circumstances that established the existence of an armed conflict.

Article 8 (2) (c) (i)-2
War crime of mutilation

Elements

1. The perpetrator subjected one or more persons to mutilation, in particular by permanently disfiguring the person or persons, or by permanently disabling or removing an organ or appendage.

---

[57] The term "religious personnel" includes those non-confessional non-combatant military personnel carrying out a similar function.

2. The conduct was neither justified by the medical, dental or hospital treatment of the person or persons concerned nor carried out in such person's or persons' interests.

3. Such person or persons were either *hors de combat*, or were civilians, medical personnel or religious personnel taking no active part in the hostilities.

4. The perpetrator was aware of the factual circumstances that established this status.

5. The conduct took place in the context of and was associated with an armed conflict not of an international character.

6. The perpetrator was aware of factual circumstances that established the existence of an armed conflict.

Article 8 (2) (c) (i)-3
War crime of cruel treatment

Elements

1. The perpetrator inflicted severe physical or mental pain or suffering upon one or more persons.

2. Such person or persons were either *hors de combat*, or were civilians, medical personnel, or religious personnel taking no active part in the hostilities.

3. The perpetrator was aware of the factual circumstances that established this status.

4. The conduct took place in the context of and was associated with an armed conflict not of an international character.

5. The perpetrator was aware of factual circumstances that established the existence of an armed conflict.

Article 8 (2) (c) (i)-4
War crime of torture

Elements

1. The perpetrator inflicted severe physical or mental pain or suffering upon one or more persons.

2. The perpetrator inflicted the pain or suffering for such purposes as: obtaining information or a confession, punishment, intimidation or coercion or for any reason based on discrimination of any kind.

3. Such person or persons were either *hors de combat*, or were civilians, medical personnel or religious personnel taking no active part in the hostilities.

4. The perpetrator was aware of the factual circumstances that established this status.

5. The conduct took place in the context of and was associated with an armed conflict not of an international character.

6. The perpetrator was aware of factual circumstances that established the existence of an armed conflict.

Article 8 (2) (c) (ii)
War crime of outrages upon personal dignity

Elements

1. The perpetrator humiliated, degraded or otherwise violated the dignity of one or more persons.[58]

2. The severity of the humiliation, degradation or other violation was of such degree as to be generally recognized as an outrage upon personal dignity.

3. Such person or persons were either *hors de combat*, or were civilians, medical personnel or religious personnel taking no active part in the hostilities.

4. The perpetrator was aware of the factual circumstances that established this status.

5. The conduct took place in the context of and was associated with an armed conflict not of an international character.

6. The perpetrator was aware of factual circumstances that established the existence of an armed conflict.

Article 8 (2) (c) (iii)
War crime of taking hostages

Elements

1. The perpetrator seized, detained or otherwise held hostage one or more persons.2. The perpetrator threatened to kill, injure or continue to detain such person or persons.

3. The perpetrator intended to compel a State, an international organization, a natural or legal person or a group of persons to act or

---

[58] For this crime, "persons" can include dead persons. It is understood that the victim need not personally be aware of the existence of the humiliation or degradation or other violation. This element takes into account relevant aspects of the cultural background of the victim.

refrain from acting as an explicit or implicit condition for the safety or the release of such person or persons.

4. Such person or persons were either *hors de combat*, or were civilians, medical personnel or religious personnel taking no active part in the hostilities.

5. The perpetrator was aware of the factual circumstances that established this status.

6. The conduct took place in the context of and was associated with an armed conflict not of an international character.

7. The perpetrator was aware of factual circumstances that established the existence of an armed conflict.

Article 8 (2) (c) (iv)
War crime of sentencing or execution without due process

Elements

1. The perpetrator passed sentence or executed one or more persons.[59]

2. Such person or persons were either *hors de combat*, or were civilians, medical personnel or religious personnel taking no active part in the hostilities.

3. The perpetrator was aware of the factual circumstances that established this status.

4. There was no previous judgement pronounced by a court, or the court that rendered judgement was not 'regularly constituted', that is, it did not afford the essential guarantees of independence and impartiality, or the court that rendered judgement did not afford all other judicial guarantees generally recognized as indispensable under international law.[60]

5. The perpetrator was aware of the absence of a previous judgement or of the denial of relevant guarantees and the fact that they are essential or indispensable to a fair trial.

6. The conduct took place in the context of and was associated with an armed conflict not of an international character.

7. The perpetrator was aware of factual circumstances that established the existence of an armed conflict.

---

[59] The elements laid down in these documents do not address the different forms of individual criminal responsibility, as enunciated in articles 25 and 28 of the Statute.

[60] With respect to elements 4 and 5, the Court should consider whether, in the light of all relevant circumstances, the cumulative effect of factors with respect to guarantees deprived the person or persons of a fair trial.

Article 8 (2) (e)
Article 8 (2) (e) (i)
War crime of attacking civilians

Elements

1. The perpetrator directed an attack.

2. The object of the attack was a civilian population as such or individual civilians not taking direct part in hostilities.

3. The perpetrator intended the civilian population as such or individual civilians not taking direct part in hostilities to be the object of the attack.

4. The conduct took place in the context of and was associated with an armed conflict not of an international character.

5. The perpetrator was aware of factual circumstances that established the existence of an armed conflict.

Article 8 (2) (e) (ii)
War crime of attacking objects or persons using the distinctive emblems of the Geneva Conventions

Elements

1. The perpetrator attacked one or more persons, buildings, medical units or transports or other objects using, in conformity with international law, a distinctive emblem or other method of identification indicating protection under the Geneva Conventions.

2. The perpetrator intended such persons, buildings, units or transports or other objects so using such identification to be the object of the attack.

3. The conduct took place in the context of and was associated with an armed conflict not of an international character.

4. The perpetrator was aware of factual circumstances that established the existence of an armed conflict.

Article 8 (2) (e) (iii)
War crime of attacking personnel or objects involved in a humanitarian assistance or peacekeeping mission

Elements

1. The perpetrator directed an attack.

2. The object of the attack was personnel, installations, material, units or vehicles involved in a humanitarian assistance or peacekeeping mission in accordance with the Charter of the United Nations.

3. The perpetrator intended such personnel, installations, material, units or vehicles so involved to be the object of the attack.

4. Such personnel, installations, material, units or vehicles were entitled to that protection given to civilians or civilian objects under the international law of armed conflict.

5. The perpetrator was aware of the factual circumstances that established that protection.

6. The conduct took place in the context of and was associated with an armed conflict not of an international character.

7. The perpetrator was aware of factual circumstances that established the existence of an armed conflict.

Article 8 (2) (e) (iv)
War crime of attacking protected objects[61]

Elements

1. The perpetrator directed an attack.

2. The object of the attack was one or more buildings dedicated to religion, education, art, science or charitable purposes, historic monuments, hospitals or places where the sick and wounded are collected, which were not military objectives.

3. The perpetrator intended such building or buildings dedicated to religion, education, art, science or charitable purposes, historic monuments, hospitals or places where the sick and wounded are collected, which were not military objectives, to be the object of the attack.

4. The conduct took place in the context of and was associated with an armed conflict not of an international character.

5. The perpetrator was aware of factual circumstances that established the existence of an armed conflict.

---

[61] The presence in the locality of persons specially protected under the Geneva Conventions of 1949 or of police forces retained for the sole purpose of maintaining law and order does not by itself render the locality a military objective.

Article 8 (2) (e) (v)
War crime of pillaging

Elements

1. The perpetrator appropriated certain property.

2. The perpetrator intended to deprive the owner of the property and to appropriate it for private or personal use.[62]

3. The appropriation was without the consent of the owner.

4. The conduct took place in the context of and was associated with an armed conflict not of an international character.

5. The perpetrator was aware of factual circumstances that established the existence of an armed conflict.

Article 8 (2) (e) (vi)-1
War crime of rape

Elements

1. The perpetrator invaded[63] the body of a person by conduct resulting inpenetration, however slight, of any part of the body of the victim or of theperpetrator with a sexual organ, or of the anal or genital opening of the victim with any object or any other part of the body.

2. The invasion was committed by force, or by threat of force or coercion, such as that caused by fear of violence, duress, detention, psychological oppression or abuse of power, against such person or another person, or by taking advantage of a coercive environment, or the invasion was committed against a person incapable of giving genuine consent.[64]

3. The conduct took place in the context of and was associated with an armed conflict not of an international character.

4. The perpetrator was aware of factual circumstances that established the existence of an armed conflict.

---

[62] As indicated by the use of the term "private or personal use", appropriations justified by military necessity cannot constitute the crime of pillaging.

[63] The concept of "invasion" is intended to be broad enough to be gender-neutral.

[64] It is understood that a person may be incapable of giving genuine consent if affected by natural, induced or age-related incapacity. This footnote also applies to the corresponding elements in article 8 (2) (e) (vi)-3, 5 and 6.

Article 8 (2) (e) (vi)-2
War crime of sexual slavery[65]

Elements

1. The perpetrator exercised any or all of the powers attaching to the right of ownership over one or more persons, such as by purchasing, selling, lending or bartering such a person or persons, or by imposing on them a similar deprivation of liberty.[66]

2. The perpetrator caused such person or persons to engage in one or more acts of a sexual nature.

3. The conduct took place in the context of and was associated with an armed conflict not of an international character.

4. The perpetrator was aware of factual circumstances that established the existence of an armed conflict.

Article 8 (2) (e) (vi)-3
War crime of enforced prostitution

Elements

1. The perpetrator caused one or more persons to engage in one or more acts of a sexual nature by force, or by threat of force or coercion, such as that caused by fear of violence, duress, detention, psychological oppression or abuse of power, against such person or persons or another person, or by taking advantage of a coercive environment or such person's or persons' incapacity to give genuine consent.

2. The perpetrator or another person obtained or expected to obtain pecuniary or other advantage in exchange for or in connection with the acts of a sexual nature.

3. The conduct took place in the context of and was associated with an armed conflict not of an international character.

4. The perpetrator was aware of factual circumstances that established the existence of an armed conflict.

---

[65] Given the complex nature of this crime, it is recognized that its commission could involve more than one perpetrator as a part of a common criminal purpose.

[66] It is understood that such deprivation of liberty may, in some circumstances, include exacting forced labour or otherwise reducing a person to servile status as defined in the Supplementary Convention on the Abolition of Slavery, the Slave Trade, and Institutions and Practices Similar to Slavery of 1956. It is also understood that the conduct described in this element includes trafficking in persons, in particular women and children.

Article 8 (2) (e) (vi)-4
War crime of forced pregnancy

Elements

1. The perpetrator confined one or more women forcibly made pregnant, with the intent of affecting the ethnic composition of any population or carrying out other grave violations of international law.

2. The conduct took place in the context of and was associated with an armed conflict not of an international character.

3. The perpetrator was aware of factual circumstances that established the existence of an armed conflict.

Article 8 (2) (e) (vi)-5
War crime of enforced sterilization

Elements

1. The perpetrator deprived one or more persons of biological reproductive
capacity.[67]

2. The conduct was neither justified by the medical or hospital treatment of the person or persons concerned nor carried out with their genuine consent.[68]

3. The conduct took place in the context of and was associated with an armed conflict not of an international character.

4. The perpetrator was aware of factual circumstances that established the existence of an armed conflict.

Article 8 (2) (e) (vi)-6
War crime of sexual violence

Elements

1. The perpetrator committed an act of a sexual nature against one or more persons or caused such person or persons to engage in an act of a sexual nature by force, or by threat of force or coercion, such as that caused by fear of violence, duress, detention, psychological oppression or abuse of power, against such person or persons or another person, or by

---

[67] The deprivation is not intended to include birth-control measures which have a non-permanent effect in practice.

[68] It is understood that "genuine consent" does not include consent obtained through deception.

taking advantage of a coercive environment or such person's or persons' incapacity to give genuine consent.

2. The conduct was of a gravity comparable to that of a serious violation of article 3 common to the four Geneva Conventions.

3. The perpetrator was aware of the factual circumstances that established the gravity of the conduct.

4. The conduct took place in the context of and was associated with an armed conflict not of an international character.

5. The perpetrator was aware of factual circumstances that established the existence of an armed conflict.

Article 8 (2) (e) (vii)
War crime of using, conscripting and enlisting children

Elements

1. The perpetrator conscripted or enlisted one or more persons into an armed force or group or used one or more persons to participate actively in hostilities.

2. Such person or persons were under the age of 15 years.

3. The perpetrator knew or should have known that such person or persons were under the age of 15 years.

4. The conduct took place in the context of and was associated with an armed conflict not of an international character.

5. The perpetrator was aware of factual circumstances that established the existence of an armed conflict.

Article 8 (2) (e) (viii)
War crime of displacing civilians

Elements

1. The perpetrator ordered a displacement of a civilian population.

2. Such order was not justified by the security of the civilians involved or by military necessity.

3. The perpetrator was in a position to effect such displacement by giving such order.

4. The conduct took place in the context of and was associated with an armed conflict not of an international character.

5. The perpetrator was aware of factual circumstances that established the existence of an armed conflict.

Article 8 (2) (e) (ix)
War crime of treacherously killing or wounding

Elements

1. The perpetrator invited the confidence or belief of one or more combatant adversaries that they were entitled to, or were obliged to accord, protection under rules of international law applicable in armed conflict.

2. The perpetrator intended to betray that confidence or belief.

3. The perpetrator killed or injured such person or persons.

4. The perpetrator made use of that confidence or belief in killing or injuring such person or persons.

5. Such person or persons belonged to an adverse party.

6. The conduct took place in the context of and was associated with an armed conflict not of an international character.

7. The perpetrator was aware of factual circumstances that established the existence of an armed conflict.

Article 8 (2) (e) (x)
War crime of denying quarter

Elements

1. The perpetrator declared or ordered that there shall be no survivors.

2. Such declaration or order was given in order to threaten an adversary or to conduct hostilities on the basis that there shall be no survivors.

3. The perpetrator was in a position of effective command or control over the subordinate forces to which the declaration or order was directed.

4. The conduct took place in the context of and was associated with an armed conflict not of an international character.

5. The perpetrator was aware of factual circumstances that established the existence of an armed conflict.

Article 8 (2) (e) (xi)-1
War crime of mutilation

Elements

1. The perpetrator subjected one or more persons to mutilation, in particular by permanently disfiguring the person or persons, or by permanently disabling or removing an organ or appendage.

2. The conduct caused death or seriously endangered the physical or mental health of such person or persons.

3. The conduct was neither justified by the medical, dental or hospital treatment of the person or persons concerned nor carried out in such person's or persons interest.[69]

4. Such person or persons were in the power of another party to the conflict.

5. The conduct took place in the context of and was associated with an armed conflict not of an international character.

6. The perpetrator was aware of factual circumstances that established the existence of an armed conflict.

Article 8 (2) (e) (xi)-2
War crime of medical or scientific experiments

Elements

1. The perpetrator subjected one or more persons to a medical or scientific experiment.

2. The experiment caused the death or seriously endangered the physical or mental health or integrity of such person or persons.

3. The conduct was neither justified by the medical, dental or hospital treatment of such person or persons concerned nor carried out in such person's or persons' interest.

4. Such person or persons were in the power of another party to the conflict.

5. The conduct took place in the context of and was associated with an armed conflict not of an international character.

6. The perpetrator was aware of factual circumstances that established the existence of an armed conflict.

Article 8 (2) (e) (xii)
War crime of destroying or seizing the enemy's property

Elements

1. The perpetrator destroyed or seized certain property.

2. Such property was property of an adversary.

---

[69] Consent is not a defence to this crime. The crime prohibits any medical procedure which is not indicated by the state of health of the person concerned and which is not consistent with generally accepted medical standards which would be applied under similar medical circumstances to persons who are nationals of the party conducting the procedure and who are in no way deprived of liberty. This footnote also applies to the similar element in article 8 (2) (e) (xi)-2.

3. Such property was protected from that destruction or seizure under the international law of armed conflict.

4. The perpetrator was aware of the factual circumstances that established the status of the property.

5. The destruction or seizure was not required by military necessity.

6. The conduct took place in the context of and was associated with an armed conflict not of an international character.

7. The perpetrator was aware of factual circumstances that established the existence of an armed conflict.

Rules of Procedure and Evidence

Adopted by the Assembly of States Parties, First session,New York, 3-10 September 2002, Official Records ICC-ASP/1/3

Explanatory note

The Rules of Procedure and Evidence are an instrument for the application of the Rome Statute of the International Criminal Court, to which they are subordinate in all cases. In elaborating the Rules of Procedure and Evidence, care has been taken to avoid rephrasing and, to the extent possible, repeating the provisions of the Statute. Direct references to the Statute have been included in the Rules, where appropriate, in order to emphasize the relationship between the Rules and the Rome Statute, as provided for in article 51, in particular, paragraphs 4 and 5.

In all cases, the Rules of Procedure and Evidence should be read in conjunction with and subject to the provisions of the Statute.

The Rules of Procedure and Evidence of the International Criminal Court do not affect the procedural rules for any national court or legal system for the purpose of national proceedings.

In connection with rule 41, the Preparatory Commission considered whether the application of the rule would be facilitated by including a provision in the Regulations of the Court that at least one of the judges of the Chamber in which the case is heard knows the official language used as a working language in a given case. The Assembly of States Parties is invited to give further consideration to this issue.

Chapter 1
General provisions

Rule 1
Use of terms

In the present document:
– 'article' refers to articles of the Rome Statute;
– 'Chamber' refers to a Chamber of the Court;
– 'Part' refers to the Parts of the Rome Statute;
– 'Presiding Judge' refers to the Presiding Judge of a Chamber;
– 'the President' refers to the President of the Court;
– 'the Regulations' refers to the Regulations of the Court;
– 'the Rules' refers to the Rules of Procedure and Evidence.

Rule 2
Authentic texts

The Rules have been adopted in the official languages of the Court established by article 50, paragraph 1. All texts are equally authentic.

Rule 3
Amendments

1. Amendments to the rules that are proposed in accordance with article 51,

paragraph 2, shall be forwarded to the President of the Bureau of the Assembly of States Parties.

2. The President of the Bureau of the Assembly of States Parties shall ensure that all proposed amendments are translated into the official languages of the Court and are transmitted to the States Parties.

3. The procedure described in sub-rules 1 and 2 shall also apply to the provisional rules referred to in article 51, paragraph 3.

Chapter 2
Composition and administration of the Court

Section I
General provisions relating to the composition andadministration of the Court

Rule 4
Plenary sessions

1. The judges shall meet in plenary session not later than two months after their election. At that first session, after having made their solemn undertaking, in conformity with rule 5, the judges shall:

(a) Elect the President and Vice-Presidents;

(b) Assign judges to divisions.

2. The judges shall meet subsequently in plenary session at least once a year to exercise their functions under the Statute, the Rules and the Regulations and, if necessary, in special plenary sessions convened by the President on his or her own motion or at the request of one half of the judges.

3. The quorum for each plenary session shall be two-thirds of the judges.

4. Unless otherwise provided in the Statute or the Rules, the decisions of the plenary sessions shall be taken by the majority of the judges present. In the event of an equality of votes, the President, or the judge acting in the place of the President, shall have a casting vote.

5. The Regulations shall be adopted as soon as possible in plenary sessions.

Rule 5
Solemn undertaking under article 45

1. As provided in article 45, before exercising their functions under the Statute, the following solemn undertakings shall be made:

(a) In the case of a judge:

'I solemnly undertake that I will perform my duties and exercise my powers as a judge of the International Criminal Court honourably, faithfully, impartially and conscientiously, and that I will respect the confidentiality of investigations and prosecutions and the secrecy of deliberations.';

(b) In the case of the Prosecutor, a Deputy Prosecutor, the Registrar and the Deputy Registrar of the Court:

'I solemnly undertake that I will perform my duties and exercise my powers as (title) of the International Criminal Court honourably, faithfully, impartially and conscientiously, and that I will respect the confidentiality of investigations and prosecutions.'

2. The undertaking, signed by the person making it and witnessed by the President or a Vice-President of the Bureau of the Assembly of States Parties, shall be filed with the Registry and kept in the records of the Court.

Rule 6
Solemn undertaking by the staff of the Office of the Prosecutor, the Registry, interpreters and translators

1. Upon commencing employment, every staff member of the Office of the Prosecutor and the Registry shall make the following undertaking:

'I solemnly undertake that I will perform my duties and exercise my powers as (title) of the International Criminal Court honourably, faithfully, impartially and conscientiously, and that I will respect the confidentiality of investigations and prosecutions.';

The undertaking, signed by the person making it and witnessed, as appropriate, by the Prosecutor, the Deputy Prosecutor, the Registrar or the Deputy Registrar, shall be filed with the Registry and kept in the records of the Court.

2. Before performing any duties, an interpreter or a translator shall make the following undertaking:

'I solemnly declare that I will perform my duties faithfully, impartially and with full respect for the duty of confidentiality.';

The undertaking, signed by the person making it and witnessed by the President of the Court or his or her representative, shall be filed with the Registry and kept in the records of the Court.

Rule 7
Single judge under article 39, paragraph 2 (b) (iii)

1. Whenever the Pre-Trial Chamber designates a judge as a single judge in accordance with article 39, paragraph 2 (b) (iii), it shall do so on the basis of objective pre-established criteria.

2. The designated judge shall make the appropriate decisions on those questions on which decision by the full Chamber is not expressly provided for in the Statute or the Rules.

3. The Pre-Trial Chamber, on its own motion or, if appropriate, at the request of a party, may decide that the functions of the single judge be exercised by the full Chamber.

Rule 8
Code of Professional Conduct

1. The Presidency, on the basis of a proposal made by the Registrar, shall draw up a draft Code of Professional Conduct for counsel, after having consulted the Prosecutor. In the preparation of the proposal, the Registrar shall conduct the consultations in accordance with rule 20, sub-rule 3.

2. The draft Code shall then be transmitted to the Assembly of States Parties, for the purpose of adoption, according to article 112, paragraph 7.

3. The Code shall contain procedures for its amendment.

Section II
The Office of the Prosecutor

Rule 9
Operation of the Office of the Prosecutor

In discharging his or her responsibility for the management and administration of the Office of the Prosecutor, the Prosecutor shall put in place regulations to govern the operation of the Office. In preparing or amending these regulations, the Prosecutor shall consult with the Registrar on any matters that may affect the operation of the Registry.

Rule 10
Retention of information and evidence

The Prosecutor shall be responsible for the retention, storage and security of information and physical evidence obtained in the course of the investigations by his or her Office.

Rule 11
Delegation of the Prosecutor's functions

Except for the inherent powers of the Prosecutor set forth in the Statute, *inter alia*, those described in articles 15 and 53, the Prosecutor or a Deputy Prosecutor may authorize staff members of the Office of the Prosecutor, other than those referred to in article 44, paragraph 4, to represent him or her in the exercise of his or her functions.

Section III
The Registry

Subsection 1
General provisions relating to the Registry

Rule 12
Qualifications and election of the Registrar and the Deputy Registrar

1. As soon as it is elected, the Presidency shall establish a list of candidates who satisfy the criteria laid down in article 43, paragraph 3, and shall transmit the list to the Assembly of States Parties with a request for any recommendations.

2. Upon receipt of any recommendations from the Assembly of States Parties, the President shall, without delay, transmit the list together with the recommendations to the plenary session.

3. As provided for in article 43, paragraph 4, the Court, meeting in plenary session, shall, as soon as possible, elect the Registrar by an absolute majority, taking into account any recommendations by the Assembly of States Parties. In the event that no candidate obtains an absolute majority on the first ballot, successive ballots shall be held until one candidate obtains an absolute majority.

4. If the need for a Deputy Registrar arises, the Registrar may make a recommendation to the President to that effect. The President shall convene a plenary session to decide on the matter. If the Court, meeting in plenary session, decides by an absolute majority that a Deputy Registrar is to be elected, the Registrar shall submit a list of candidates to the Court.

5. The Deputy Registrar shall be elected by the Court, meeting in plenary session, in the same manner as the Registrar.

Rule 13
Functions of the Registrar

1. Without prejudice to the authority of the Office of the Prosecutor under the Statute to receive, obtain and provide information and to establish channels of communication for this purpose, the Registrar shall serve as the channel of communication of the Court.

2. The Registrar shall also be responsible for the internal security of the Court in consultation with the Presidency and the Prosecutor, as well as the host State.

Rule 14
Operation of the Registry

1. In discharging his or her responsibility for the organization and management of the Registry, the Registrar shall put in place regulations to govern the operation of the Registry. In preparing or amending these regulations, the Registrar shall consult with the Prosecutor on any matters which may affect the operation of the Office of the Prosecutor. The regulations shall be approved by the Presidency.

2. The regulations shall provide for defence counsel to have access to appropriate and reasonable administrative assistance from the Registry.

Rule 15
Records

1. The Registrar shall keep a database containing all the particulars of each case brought before the Court, subject to any order of a judge or Chamber providing for the non-disclosure of any document or information, and to the protection of sensitive personal data. Information on the database shall be available to the public in the working languages of the Court.

2. The Registrar shall also maintain the other records of the Court.

Subsection 2
Victims and Witnesses Unit

Rule 16
Responsibilities of the Registrar relating to victims and witnesses

1. In relation to victims, the Registrar shall be responsible for the performance of the following functions in accordance with the Statute and these Rules:

(a) Providing notice or notification to victims or their legal representatives;

(b) Assisting them in obtaining legal advice and organizing their legal representation, and providing their legal representatives with adequate support, assistance and information, including such facilities as may be necessary for the direct performance of their duty, for the purpose of protecting their rights during all stages of the proceedings in accordance with rules 89 to 91;

(c) Assisting them in participating in the different phases of the proceedings in accordance with rules 89 to 91;

(d) Taking gender-sensitive measures to facilitate the participation of victims of sexual violence at all stages of the proceedings.

2. In relation to victims, witnesses and others who are at risk on account of testimony given by such witnesses, the Registrar shall be responsible for the performance of the following functions in accordance with the Statute and these Rules:

(a) Informing them of their rights under the Statute and the Rules, and of the existence, functions and availability of the Victims and Witnesses Unit;

(b) Ensuring that they are aware, in a timely manner, of the relevant decisions of the Court that may have an impact on their interests, subject to provisions on confidentiality.

3. For the fulfilment of his or her functions, the Registrar may keep a special register for victims who have expressed their intention to participate in relation to a specific case.

4. Agreements on relocation and provision of support services on the territory of a State of traumatized or threatened victims, witnesses and others who are at risk on account of testimony given by such witnesses may be negotiated with the States by the Registrar on behalf of the Court. Such agreements may remain confidential.

Rule 17
Functions of the Unit

1. The Victims and Witnesses Unit shall exercise its functions in accordance with article 43, paragraph 6.

2. The Victims and Witnesses Unit shall, *inter alia*, perform the following functions, in accordance with the Statute and the Rules, and in consultation with the Chamber, the Prosecutor and the defence, as appropriate:

(a) With respect to all witnesses, victims who appear before the Court, and others who are at risk on account of testimony given by such witnesses, in accordance with their particular needs and circumstances:

(i) Providing them with adequate protective and security measures and formulating long- and short-term plans for their protection;

(ii) Recommending to the organs of the Court the adoption of protection measures and also advising relevant States of such measures;

(iii) Assisting them in obtaining medical, psychological and other appropriate assistance;

(iv) Making available to the Court and the parties training in issues of trauma, sexual violence, security and confidentiality;

(v) Recommending, in consultation with the Office of the Prosecutor, the elaboration of a code of conduct, emphasizing the vital nature of security and confidentiality for investigators of the Court and of the defence and all intergovernmental and non-governmental organizations acting at the request of the Court, as appropriate;

(vi) Cooperating with States, where necessary, in providing any of the measures stipulated in this rule;

(b) With respect to witnesses:

(i) Advising them where to obtain legal advice for the purpose of protecting their rights, in particular in relation to their testimony;

(ii) Assisting them when they are called to testify before the Court; (iii) Taking gender-sensitive measures to facilitate the testimony of victims of sexual violence at all stages of the proceedings.

3. In performing its functions, the Unit shall give due regard to the particular needs of children, elderly persons and persons with disabilities. In order to facilitate the participation and protection of children as witnesses, the Unit may assign, as appropriate, and with the agreement of the parents or the legal guardian, a child-support person to assist a child through all stages of the proceedings.

Rule 18
Responsibilities of the Unit

For the efficient and effective performance of its work, the Victims and Witnesses Unit shall:

(a) Ensure that the staff in the Unit maintain confidentiality at all times;

(b) While recognizing the specific interests of the Office of the Prosecutor, the defence and the witnesses, respect the interests of the witness, including, where necessary, by maintaining an appropriate separation of the services provided to the prosecution and defence witnesses, and act impartially when cooperating with all parties and in accordance with the rulings and decisions of the Chambers;

(c) Have administrative and technical assistance available for witnesses, victims who appear before the Court, and others who are at risk on account of testimony given by such witnesses, during all stages of the proceedings and thereafter, as reasonably appropriate;

(d) Ensure training of its staff with respect to victims' and witnesses' security, integrity and dignity, including matters related to gender and cultural sensitivity;

(e) Where appropriate, cooperate with intergovernmental and non-governmental organizations.

Rule 19
Expertise in the Unit

In addition to the staff mentioned in article 43, paragraph 6, and subject to article 44, the Victims and Witnesses Unit may include, as appropriate, persons with expertise, *inter alia*, in the following areas:

(a) Witness protection and security;

(b) Legal and administrative matters, including areas of humanitarian and criminal law;

(c) Logistics administration;

(d) Psychology in criminal proceedings;

(e) Gender and cultural diversity;

(f) Children, in particular traumatized children;

(g) Elderly persons, in particular in connection with armed conflict and exile trauma;

(h) Persons with disabilities;

(i) Social work and counselling;

(j) Health care;

(k) Interpretation and translation.

Subsection 3
Counsel for the defence

Rule 20
Responsibilities of the Registrar

Relating to the rights of the defence

1. In accordance with article 43, paragraph 1, the Registrar shall organize the staff of the Registry in a manner that promotes the rights of the defence, consistent with the principle of fair trial as defined in the Statute. For that purpose, the Registrar shall, *inter alia*:

(a) Facilitate the protection of confidentiality, as defined in article 67, paragraph 1 (b);

(b) Provide support, assistance, and information to all defence counsel appearing before the Court and, as appropriate, support for professional investigators necessary for the efficient and effective conduct of the defence;

(c) Assist arrested persons, persons to whom article 55, paragraph 2, applies and the accused in obtaining legal advice and the assistance of legal counsel;

(d) Advise the Prosecutor and the Chambers, as necessary, on relevant defence-related issues;

(e) Provide the defence with such facilities as may be necessary for the direct performance of the duty of the defence;

(f) Facilitate the dissemination of information and case law of the Court to defence counsel and, as appropriate, cooperate with national defence and bar associations or any independent representative body of counsel and legal associations referred to in sub-rule 3 to promote the specialization and training of lawyers in the law of the Statute and the Rules.

2. The Registrar shall carry out the functions stipulated in sub-rule 1, including the financial administration of the Registry, in such a manner as to ensure the professional independence of defence counsel.

3. For purposes such as the management of legal assistance in accordance with rule 21 and the development of a Code of Professional Conduct in accordance with rule 8, the Registrar shall consult, as appropriate, with any independent representative body of counsel or legal associations, including any such body the establishment of which may be facilitated by the Assembly of States Parties.

Rule 21
Assignment of legal assistance

1. Subject to article 55, paragraph 2 (c), and article 67, paragraph 1 (d), criteria and procedures for assignment of legal assistance shall be established in the Regulations, based on a proposal by the Registrar, following consultations with any independent representative body of counsel or legal associations, as referred to in rule 20, sub-rule 3.

2. The Registrar shall create and maintain a list of counsel who meet the criteria set forth in rule 22 and the Regulations. The person shall freely choose his or her counsel from this list or other counsel who meets the required criteria and is willing to be included in the list.

3. A person may seek from the Presidency a review of a decision to refuse a request for assignment of counsel. The decision of the Presidency shall be final. If a request is refused, a further request may be made by a person to the Registrar, upon showing a change in circumstances.

4. A person choosing to represent himself or herself shall so notify the Registrar in writing at the first opportunity.

5. Where a person claims to have insufficient means to pay for legal assistance and this is subsequently found not to be so, the Chamber dealing with the case at that time may make an order of contribution to recover the cost of providing counsel.

Rule 22
Appointment and qualifications of Counsel for the defence

1. A counsel for the defence shall have established competence in international or criminal law and procedure, as well as the necessary relevant experience, whether as judge, prosecutor, advocate or in other similar capacity, in criminal proceedings. A counsel for the defence shall have an excellent knowledge of and be fluent in at least one of the working languages of the Court. Counsel for the defence may be assisted by other persons, including professors of law, with relevant expertise.

2. Counsel for the defence engaged by a person exercising his or her right under the Statute to retain legal counsel of his or her choosing shall file a power of attorney with the Registrar at the earliest opportunity.

3. In the performance of their duties, Counsel for the defence shall be subject to the Statute, the Rules, the Regulations, the Code of Professional Conduct for Counsel adopted in accordance with rule 8 and any other document adopted by the Court that may be relevant to the performance of their duties.

Section 4
Situations that may affect the functioning of the Court

Subsection 1
Removal from office and disciplinary measures

Rule 23
General principle

A judge, the Prosecutor, a Deputy Prosecutor, the Registrar and a Deputy Registrar shall be removed from office or shall be subject to disciplinary measures in such cases and with such guarantees as are established in the Statute and the Rules.

Rule 24
Definition of serious misconduct and serious breach of duty

1. For the purposes of article 46, paragraph 1 (a), 'serious misconduct' shall be constituted by conduct that:

(a) If it occurs in the course of official duties, is incompatible with official functions, and causes or is likely to cause serious harm to the proper administration of justice before the Court or the proper internal functioning of the Court, such as:

(i) Disclosing facts or information that he or she has acquired in the course of his or her duties or on a matter which is *sub judice*, where such disclosure is seriously prejudicial to the judicial proceedings or to any person;

(ii) Concealing information or circumstances of a nature sufficiently serious to have precluded him or her from holding office;

(iii) Abuse of judicial office in order to obtain unwarranted favourable treatment from any authorities, officials or professionals; or

(b) If it occurs outside the course of official duties, is of a grave nature that causes or is likely to cause serious harm to the standing of the Court.

2. For the purposes of article 46, paragraph 1 (a), a 'serious breach of duty' occurs where a person has been grossly negligent in the performance of his or her duties or has knowingly acted in contravention of those duties. This may include, *inter alia*, situations where the person:

(a) Fails to comply with the duty to request to be excused, knowing that there are grounds for doing so;

(b) Repeatedly causes unwarranted delay in the initiation, prosecution or trial of cases, or in the exercise of judicial powers.

Rule 25
Definition of misconduct of a less serious nature

1. For the purposes of article 47, 'misconduct of a less serious nature' shall be constituted by conduct that:

(a) If it occurs in the course of official duties, causes or is likely to cause harm to the proper administration of justice before the Court or the proper internal functioning of the Court, such as:

(i) Interfering in the exercise of the functions of a person referred to in article 47;

(ii) Repeatedly failing to comply with or ignoring requests made by the Presiding Judge or by the Presidency in the exercise of their lawful authority;

(iii) Failing to enforce the disciplinary measures to which the Registrar or a Deputy Registrar and other officers of the Court are subject when a judge nows or should know of a serious breach of duty on their part; or

(b) If it occurs outside the course of official duties, causes or is likely to cause harm to the standing of the Court.

2. Nothing in this rule precludes the possibility of the conduct set out in sub-rule 1 (a) constituting 'serious misconduct' or "serious breach of duty' for the purposes of article 46, paragraph 1 (a).

Rule 26
Receipt of complaints

1. For the purposes of article 46, paragraph 1, and article 47, any complaint concerning any conduct defined under rules 24 and 25 shall include the grounds on which it is based, the identity of the complainant and, if available, any relevant evidence. The complaint shall remain confidential.

2. All complaints shall be transmitted to the Presidency, which may also initiate proceedings on its own motion, and which shall, pursuant to the Regulations, set aside anonymous or manifestly unfounded complaints and transmit the other complaints to the competent organ. The Presidency shall be assisted in this task by one or more judges, appointed on the basis of automatic rotation, in accordance with the Regulations.

Rule 27
Common provisions on the rights of the defence

1. In any case in which removal from office under article 46 or disciplinary measures under article 47 is under consideration, the person concerned shall be so informed in a written statement.

2. The person concerned shall be afforded full opportunity to present and receive evidence, to make written submissions and to supply answers to any questions put to him or her.

3. The person may be represented by counsel during the process established under this rule.

Rule 28
Suspension from duty

Where an allegation against a person who is the subject of a complaint is of a sufficiently serious nature, the person may be suspended from duty pending the final decision of the competent organ.

Rule 29
Procedure in the event of a request for removal from office

1. In the case of a judge, the Registrar or a Deputy Registrar, the question of removal from office shall be put to a vote at a plenary session.

2. The Presidency shall advise the President of the Bureau of the Assembly of States Parties in writing of any recommendation adopted in the case of a judge, and any decision adopted in the case of the Registrar or a Deputy Registrar.

3. The Prosecutor shall advise the President of the Bureau of the Assembly of States Parties in writing of any recommendation he or she makes in the case of a Deputy Prosecutor.

4. Where the conduct is found not to amount to serious misconduct or a serious breach of duty, it may be decided in accordance with article 47 that the person concerned has engaged in misconduct of a less serious nature and a disciplinary measure imposed.

Rule 30
Procedure in the event of a request for disciplinary measures

1. In the case of a judge, the Registrar or a Deputy Registrar, any decision to impose a disciplinary measure shall be taken by the Presidency.

2. In the case of the Prosecutor, any decision to impose a disciplinary measure shall be taken by an absolute majority of the Bureau of the Assembly of States Parties.

3. In the case of a Deputy Prosecutor:

(a) Any decision to give a reprimand shall be taken by the Prosecutor;

(b) Any decision to impose a pecuniary sanction shall be taken by an absolute majority of the Bureau of the Assembly of States Parties upon the recommendation of the Prosecutor.

4. Reprimands shall be recorded in writing and shall be transmitted to the President of the Bureau of the Assembly of States Parties.

Rule 31
Removal from office

Once removal from office has been pronounced, it shall take effect immediately. The person concerned shall cease to form part of the Court, including for unfinished cases in which he or she was taking part.

Rule 32
Disciplinary measures

The disciplinary measures that may be imposed are:

(a) A reprimand; or

(b) A pecuniary sanction that may not exceed six months of the salary paid by the Court to the person concerned.

Subsection 2
Excusing, disqualification, death and resignation

Rule 33
Excusing of a judge, the Prosecutor or a Deputy Prosecutor

1. A judge, the Prosecutor or a Deputy Prosecutor seeking to be excused from his or her functions shall make a request in writing to the Presidency, setting out the grounds upon which he or she should be excused.

2. The Presidency shall treat the request as confidential and shall not make public the reasons for its decision without the consent of the person concerned.

Rule 34
Disqualification of a judge, the Prosecutor or a Deputy Prosecutor

1. In addition to the grounds set out in article 41, paragraph 2, and article 42, paragraph 7, the grounds for disqualification of a judge, the Prosecutor or a Deputy Prosecutor shall include, *inter alia*, the following:

(a) Personal interest in the case, including a spousal, parental or other close family, personal or professional relationship, or a subordinate relationship, with any of the parties;

(b) Involvement, in his or her private capacity, in any legal proceedings initiated prior to his or her involvement in the case, or initiated by him or her subsequently, in which the person being investigated or prosecuted was or is an opposing party;

(c) Performance of functions, prior to taking office, during which he or she could be expected to have formed an opinion on the case in question, on the parties or on their legal representatives that, objectively, could adversely affect the required impartiality of the person concerned;

(d) Expression of opinions, through the communications media, in writing or in public actions, that, objectively, could adversely affect the required impartiality of the person concerned.

2. Subject to the provisions set out in article 41, paragraph 2, and article 42, paragraph 8, a request for disqualification shall be made in writing as soon as there is knowledge of the grounds on which it is based. The request shall state the grounds and attach any relevant evidence, and shall be transmitted to the person concerned, who shall be entitled to present written submissions.

3. Any question relating to the disqualification of the Prosecutor or a Deputy Prosecutor shall be decided by a majority of the judges of the Appeals Chamber.

Rule 35
Duty of a judge, the Prosecutor or a Deputy Prosecutor to request to be excused

Where a judge, the Prosecutor or a Deputy Prosecutor has reason to believe that a ground for disqualification exists in relation to him or her, he or she shall make a request to be excused and shall not wait for a request for disqualification to be made in accordance with article 41, paragraph 2, or article 42, paragraph 7, and rule 34. The request shall be made and the Presidency shall deal with it in accordance with rule 33.

Rule 36
Death of a judge, the Prosecutor, a Deputy Prosecutor, the Registrar or a Deputy Registrar

The Presidency shall inform, in writing, the President of the Bureau of the Assembly of States Parties of the death of a judge, the Prosecutor, a Deputy Prosecutor, the Registrar or a Deputy Registrar.

Rule 37
Resignation of a judge, the Prosecutor, a Deputy Prosecutor, the Registrar or a Deputy Registrar

1. A judge, the Prosecutor, a Deputy Prosecutor, the Registrar or a Deputy Registrar shall communicate to the Presidency, in writing, his or her decision to resign. The Presidency shall inform, in writing, the President of the Bureau of the Assembly of States Parties.

2. A judge, the Prosecutor, a Deputy Prosecutor, the Registrar or a Deputy Registrar shall endeavour to give notice of the date on which his or her resignation will take effect at least six months in advance. Before the resignation of a judge takes effect, he or she shall make every effort to discharge his or her outstanding responsibilities.

Subsection 3
Replacements and alternate judges

Rule 38
Replacements

1. A judge may be replaced for objective and justified reasons, *inter alia*:

(a) Resignation;
(b) Accepted excuse;
(c) Disqualification;
(d) Removal from office;
(e) Death.

2. Replacement shall take place in accordance with the pre-established procedure inthe Statute, the Rules and the Regulations.

Rule 39
Alternate judges

Where an alternate judge has been assigned by the Presidency to a Trial Chamber pursuant to article 74, paragraph 1, he or she shall sit through all proceedings and deliberations of the case, but may not take any part therein and shall not exercise any of the functions of the members of the Trial Chamber hearing the case, unless and until he or she is required toreplace a member of the Trial Chamber if that member is unable to continue attending. Alternate judges shall be designated in accordance with a procedure pre-established by the Court.

Section V
Publication, languages and translation

Rule 40
Publication of decisions in official languages of the Court

1. For the purposes of article 50, paragraph 1, the following decisions shall be considered as resolving fundamental issues:

(a) All decisions of the Appeals Division;

(b) All decisions of the Court on its jurisdiction or on the admissibility of a case pursuant to articles 17, 18, 19 and 20;

(c) All decisions of a Trial Chamber on guilt or innocence, sentencing and reparations to victims pursuant to articles 74, 75 and 76;

(d) All decisions of a Pre-Trial Chamber pursuant to article 57, paragraph 3 (d).

2. Decisions on confirmation of charges under article 61, paragraph 7, and on offences against the administration of justice under article 70, paragraph 3, shall be published in all the official languages of the Court when the Presidency determines that they resolve fundamental issues.

3. The Presidency may decide to publish other decisions in all the official languages when such decisions concern major issues relating to the interpretation or the implementation of the Statute or concern a major issue of general interest.

Rule 41
Working languages of the Court

1. For the purposes of article 50, paragraph 2, the Presidency shall authorize the use of an official language of the Court as a working language when:

(a) That language is understood and spoken by the majority of those involved in a case before the Court and any of the participants in the proceedings so requests; or

(b) The Prosecutor and the defence so request.

2. The Presidency may authorize the use of an official language of the Court as a working language if it considers that it would facilitate the efficiency of the proceedings.

Rule 42
Translation and interpretation services

The Court shall arrange for the translation and interpretation services necessary to ensure the implementation of its obligations under the Statute and the Rules.

Rule 43
Procedure applicable to the publication of documents of the Court

The Court shall ensure that all documents subject to publication in accordance with the Statute and the Rules respect the duty to protect the confidentiality of the proceedings and the security of victims and witnesses.

Chapter 3
Jurisdiction and admissibility

Section I
Declarations and referrals relating to articles 11, 12,13 and 14

Rule 44
Declaration provided for in article 12, paragraph 3

1. The Registrar, at the request of the Prosecutor, may inquire of a State that is not a Party to the Statute or that has become a Party to the Statute after its entry into force, on a confidential basis, whether it intends to make the declaration provided for in article 12, paragraph 3.

2. When a State lodges, or declares to the Registrar its intent to lodge, a declaration with the Registrar pursuant to article 12, paragraph 3, or when the Registrar acts pursuant to sub-rule 1, the Registrar shall inform the State concerned that the declaration under article 12, paragraph 3, has as a consequence the acceptance of jurisdiction with respect to the crimes referred to in article 5 of relevance to the situation and the provisions of Part 9, and any rules there under concerning States Parties, shall apply.

Rule 45
Referral of a situation to the Prosecutor

A referral of a situation to the Prosecutor shall be in writing.

Section II
Initiation of investigations under article 15

Rule 46
Information provided to the Prosecutor
Under article 15, paragraphs 1 and 2

Where information is submitted under article 15, paragraph 1, or where oral or written testimony is received pursuant to article 15, paragraph 2, at the seat of the Court, the Prosecutor shall protect the confidentiality of such information and testimony or take any other necessary measures, pursuant to his or her duties under the Statute.

Rule 47
Testimony under article 15, paragraph 2

1. The provisions of rules 111 and 112 shall apply, *mutatis mutandis*, to testimony received by the Prosecutor pursuant to article 15, paragraph 2.

2. When the Prosecutor considers that there is a serious risk that it might not be possible for the testimony to be taken subsequently, he or she may request the Pre-Trial Chamber to take such measures as may be necessary to ensure the efficiency and integrity of the proceedings and, in particular, to appoint a counsel or a judge from the Pre-Trial Chamber to be present during the taking of the testimony in order to protect the rights of the defence. If the testimony is subsequently presented in the proceedings, its admissibility shall be governed by article 69, paragraph 4, and given such weight as determined by the relevant Chamber.

Rule 48
Determination of reasonable basis to proceed
With an investigation under article 15, paragraph 3

In determining whether there is a reasonable basis to proceed with an investigation under article 15, paragraph 3, the Prosecutor shall consider the factors set out in article 53, paragraph 1 (a) to (c).

Rule 49
Decision and notice under article 15, paragraph 6

1. Where a decision under article 15, paragraph 6, is taken, the Prosecutor shall promptly ensure that notice is provided, including reasons for his or her decision, in a manner that prevents any danger to the safety, well-being and privacy of those who provided information to him or her under article 15, paragraphs 1 and 2, or the integrity of investigations or proceedings.

2. The notice shall also advise of the possibility of submitting further information regarding the same situation in the light of new facts and evidence.

Rule 50
Procedure for authorization by the Pre-Trial Chamber of the commencement of the investigation

1. When the Prosecutor intends to seek authorization from the Pre-Trial Chamber to initiate an investigation pursuant to article 15, paragraph 3, the Prosecutor shall inform victims, known to him or her or to the Victims and Witnesses Unit, or their legal representatives, unless the Prosecutor decides that doing so would pose a danger to the integrity of the investigation or the life or well-being of victims and witnesses. The Prosecutor may also give notice by general means in order to reach groups of victims if he or she determines in the particular circumstances of the case that such notice could not pose a danger to the integrity and effective conduct of the investigation or to the security and well-being of victims and witnesses. In performing these functions, the Prosecutor may seek the assistance of the Victims and Witnesses Unit as appropriate.

2. A request for authorization by the Prosecutor shall be in writing.

3. Following information given in accordance with sub-rule 1, victims may make representations in writing to the Pre-Trial Chamber within such time limit as set forth in the Regulations.

4. The Pre-Trial Chamber, in deciding on the procedure to be followed, may request additional information from the Prosecutor and from any of the victims who have made representations, and, if it considers it appropriate, may hold a hearing.

5. The Pre-Trial Chamber shall issue its decision, including its reasons, as to whether to authorize the commencement of the investigation in accordance with article 15, paragraph 4, with respect to all or any part of the request by the Prosecutor. The Chamber shall give notice of the decision to victims who have made representations.

6. The above procedure shall also apply to a new request to the Pre-Trial Chamber pursuant to article 15, paragraph 5.

Section III
Challenges and preliminary rulings under articles 17, 18 and 19

Rule 51
Information provided under article 17

In considering the matters referred to in article 17, paragraph 2, and in the context of the circumstances of the case, the Court may consider, *inter alia*, information that the State referred to in article 17, paragraph 1, may choose to bring to the attention of the Court showing that its courts meet internationally recognized norms and standards for the independent and impartial prosecution of similar conduct, or that the State has confirmed in writing to the Prosecutor that the case is being investigated or prosecuted.

Rule 52
Notification provided for in article 18, paragraph 1

1. Subject to the limitations provided for in article 18, paragraph 1, the notification shall contain information about the acts that may constitute crimes referred to in article 5, relevant for the purposes of article 18, paragraph 2.

2. A State may request additional information from the Prosecutor to assist it in the application of article 18, paragraph 2. Such a request shall not affect the one-month time limit provided for in article 18, paragraph 2, and shall be responded to by the Prosecutor on an expedited basis.

Rule 53
Deferral provided for in article 18, paragraph 2

When a State requests a deferral pursuant to article 18, paragraph 2, that State shall make this request in writing and provide information concerning its investigation, taking into account article 18, paragraph 2. The Prosecutor may request additional information from that State.

Rule 54
Application by the Prosecutor under article 18, paragraph 2

1. An application submitted by the Prosecutor to the Pre-Trial Chamber in accordance with article 18, paragraph 2, shall be in writing and shall contain the basis for the application. The information provided by the State under rule 53 shall be communicated by the Prosecutor to the Pre-Trial Chamber.

2. The Prosecutor shall inform that State in writing when he or she makes an application to the Pre-Trial Chamber under article 18, paragraph 2, and shall include in the notice a summary of the basis of the application.

Rule 55
Proceedings concerning article 18, paragraph 2

1. The Pre-Trial Chamber shall decide on the procedure to be followed and may take appropriate measures for the proper conduct of the proceedings. It may hold a hearing.

2. The Pre-Trial Chamber shall examine the Prosecutor's application and any observations submitted by a State that requested a deferral in accordance with article 18, paragraph 2, and shall consider the factors in article 17 in deciding whether to authorize an investigation.

3. The decision and the basis for the decision of the Pre-Trial Chamber shall be communicated as soon as possible to the Prosecutor and to the State that requested a deferral of an investigation.

Rule 56
Application by the Prosecutor following Review under article 18, paragraph 3

1. Following a review by the Prosecutor as set forth in article 18, paragraph 3, the Prosecutor may apply to the Pre-Trial Chamber for authorization in accordance with article 18, paragraph 2. The application to the Pre-Trial Chamber shall be in writing and shall contain the basis for the application.

2. Any further information provided by the State under article 18, paragraph 5, shall be communicated by the Prosecutor to the Pre-Trial Chamber.

3. The proceedings shall be conducted in accordance with rules 54, sub-rule 2, and 55.

Rule 57
Provisional measures under article 18, paragraph 6

An application to the Pre-Trial Chamber by the Prosecutor in the circumstances provided for in article 18, paragraph 6, shall be considered *ex parte* and in camera. The Pre-Trial Chamber shall rule on the application on an expedited basis.

Rule 58
Proceedings under article 19

1. A request or application made under article 19 shall be in writing and contain the basis for it.

2. When a Chamber receives a request or application raising a challenge or question concerning its jurisdiction or the admissibility of a case in accordance with article 19, paragraph 2 or 3, or is acting on its own motion as provided for in article 19, paragraph 1, it shall decide on the

procedure to be followed and may take appropriate measures for the proper conduct of the proceedings. It may hold a hearing. It may join the challenge or question to a confirmation or a trial proceeding as long as this does not cause undue delay, and in this circumstance shall hear and decide on the challenge or question first.

3. The Court shall transmit a request or application received under sub-rule 2 to the Prosecutor and to the person referred to in article 19, paragraph 2, who has been surrendered to the Court or who has appeared voluntarily or pursuant to a summons, and shall allow them to submit written observations to the request or application within a period of time determined by the Chamber.

4. The Court shall rule on any challenge or question of jurisdiction first and then on any challenge or question of admissibility.

Rule 59
Participation in proceedings under article 19, paragraph 3

1. For the purpose of article 19, paragraph 3, the Registrar shall inform the following of any question or challenge of jurisdiction or admissibility which has arisen pursuant to article 19, paragraphs 1, 2 and 3:

(a) Those who have referred a situation pursuant to article 13;

(b) The victims who have already communicated with the Court in relation to that case or their legal representatives.

2. The Registrar shall provide those referred to in sub-rule 1, in a manner consistent with the duty of the Court regarding the confidentiality of information, the protection of any person and the preservation of evidence, with a summary of the grounds on which the jurisdiction of the Court or the admissibility of the case has been challenged.

3. Those receiving the information, as provided for in sub-rule 1, may make representation in writing to the competent Chamber within such time limit as it considers appropriate.

Rule 60
Competent organ to receive challenges

If a challenge to the jurisdiction of the Court or to the admissibility of a case is made after a confirmation of the charges but before the constitution or designation of the Trial Chamber, it shall be addressed to the Presidency, which shall refer it to the Trial Chamber as soon as the latter is constituted or designated in accordance with rule 130.

Rule 61
Provisional measures under article 19, paragraph 8

When the Prosecutor makes application to the competent Chamber in the circumstances provided for in article 19, paragraph 8, rule 57 shall apply.

Rule 62
Proceedings under article 19, paragraph 10

1. If the Prosecutor makes a request under article 19, paragraph 10, he or she shall make the request to the Chamber that made the latest ruling on admissibility. The provisions of rules 58, 59 and 61 shall be applicable.

2. The State or States whose challenge to admissibility under article 19, paragraph 2, provoked the decision of inadmissibility provided for in article 19, paragraph 10, shall be notified of the request of the Prosecutor and shall be given a time limit within which to make representations.

Chapter 4
Provisions relating to various stages of the proceedings

Section I
Evidence

Rule 63
General provisions relating to evidence

1. The rules of evidence set forth in this chapter, together with article 69, shall apply in proceedings before all Chambers.

2. A Chamber shall have the authority, in accordance with the discretion described in article 64, paragraph 9, to assess freely all evidence submitted in order to determine its relevance or admissibility in accordance with article 69.

3. A Chamber shall rule on an application of a party or on its own motion, made under article 64, subparagraph 9 (a), concerning admissibility when it is based on the grounds set out in article 69, paragraph 7.

4. Without prejudice to article 66, paragraph 3, a Chamber shall not impose a legal requirement that corroboration is required in order to prove any crime within the jurisdiction of the Court, in particular, crimes of sexual violence.

5. The Chambers shall not apply national laws governing evidence, other than in accordance with article 21.

Rule 64
Procedure relating to the relevance or admissibility of evidence

1. An issue relating to relevance or admissibility must be raised at the time when the evidence is submitted to a Chamber. Exceptionally, when those issues were not known at the time when the evidence was submitted, it may be raised immediately after the issue has become known. The Chamber may request that the issue be raised in writing. The written motion shall be communicated by the Court to all those who participate in the proceedings, unless otherwise decided by the Court.

2. A Chamber shall give reasons for any rulings it makes on evidentiary matters. These reasons shall be placed in the record of the proceedings if they have not already been incorporated into the record during the course of the proceedings in accordance with article 64, paragraph 10, and rule 137, sub-rule 1.

3. Evidence ruled irrelevant or inadmissible shall not be considered by the Chamber.

Rule 65
Compellability of witnesses

1. A witness who appears before the Court is compellable by the Court to provide testimony, unless otherwise provided for in the Statute and the Rules, in particular rules 73, 74 and 75.

2. Rule 171 applies to a witness appearing before the Court who is compellable to provide testimony under sub-rule 1.

Rule 66
Solemn undertaking

1. Except as described in sub-rule 2, every witness shall, in accordance with article 69, paragraph 1, make the following solemn undertaking before testifying:

"I solemnly declare that I will speak the truth, the whole truth and nothing but the truth."

2. A person under the age of 18 or a person whose judgement has been impaired and who, in the opinion of the Chamber, does not understand the nature of a solemn undertaking may be allowed to testify without this solemn undertaking if the Chamber considers that the person is able to describe matters of which he or she has knowledge and that the person understands the meaning of the duty to speak the truth.

3. Before testifying, the witness shall be informed of the offence defined in article 70, paragraph 1 (a).

Rule 67
Live testimony by means of audio or video-link technology

1. In accordance with article 69, paragraph 2, a Chamber may allow a witness to give viva voce (oral) testimony before the Chamber by means of audio or video technology, provided that such technology permits the witness to be examined by the Prosecutor, the defence, and by the Chamber itself, at the time that the witness so testifies.

2. The examination of a witness under this rule shall be conducted in accordance with the relevant rules of this chapter.

3. The Chamber, with the assistance of the Registry, shall ensure that the venue chosen for the conduct of the audio or video-link testimony is conducive to the giving of truthful and open testimony and to the safety, physical and psychological well-being, dignity and privacy of the witness.

Rule 68
Prior recorded testimony

When the Pre-Trial Chamber has not taken measures under article 56, the Trial Chamber may, in accordance with article 69, paragraph 2, allow the introduction of previously recorded audio or video testimony of a witness, or the transcript or other documented evidence of such testimony, provided that:

(a) If the witness who gave the previously recorded testimony is not present before the Trial Chamber, both the Prosecutor and the defence had the opportunity to examine the witness during the recording; or

(b) If the witness who gave the previously recorded testimony is present before the Trial Chamber, he or she does not object to the submission of the previously recorded testimony and the Prosecutor, the defence and the Chamber have the opportunity to examine the witness during the proceedings.

Rule 69
Agreements as to evidence

The Prosecutor and the defence may agree that an alleged fact, which is contained in the charges, the contents of a document, the expected testimony of a witness or other evidence is not contested and, accordingly, a Chamber may consider such alleged fact as being proven, unless the Chamber is of the opinion that a more complete presentation of the alleged facts is required in the interests of justice, in particular the interests of the victims.

Rule 70
Principles of evidence in cases of sexual violence

In cases of sexual violence, the Court shall be guided by and, where appropriate, apply the following principles:

(a) Consent cannot be inferred by reason of any words or conduct of a victim where force, threat of force, coercion or taking advantage of a coercive environment undermined the victim's ability to give voluntary and genuine consent;

(b) Consent cannot be inferred by reason of any words or conduct of a victim where the victim is incapable of giving genuine consent;

(c) Consent cannot be inferred by reason of the silence of, or lack of resistance by, a victim to the alleged sexual violence;

(d) Credibility, character or predisposition to sexual availability of a victim or witness cannot be inferred by reason of the sexual nature of the prior or subsequent conduct of a victim or witness.

Rule 71
Evidence of other sexual conduct

In the light of the definition and nature of the crimes within the jurisdiction of the Court, and subject to article 69, paragraph 4, a Chamber shall not admit evidence of the prior or subsequent sexual conduct of a victim or witness.

Rule 72
In camera procedure to consider relevance or admissibility of evidence

1. Where there is an intention to introduce or elicit, including by means of the questioning of a victim or witness, evidence that the victim consented to an alleged crime of sexual violence, or evidence of the words, conduct, silence or lack of resistance of a victim or witness as referred to in principles (a) through (d) of rule 70, notification shall be provided to the Court which shall describe the substance of the evidence intended to be introduced or elicited and the relevance of the evidence to the issues in the case.

2. In deciding whether the evidence referred to in sub-rule 1 is relevant or admissible, a Chamber shall hear in camera the views of the Prosecutor, the defence, the witness and the victim or his or her legal representative, if any, and shall take into account whether that evidence has a sufficient degree of probative value to an issue in the case and the prejudice that such evidence may cause, in accordance with article 69, paragraph 4. For this purpose, the Chamber shall have regard to article 21, paragraph 3, and articles 67 and 68, and shall be guided by principles (a) to (d) of rule 70, especially with respect to the proposed questioning of a victim.

3. Where the Chamber determines that the evidence referred to in sub-rule 2 is admissible in the proceedings, the Chamber shall state on the record the specific purpose for which the evidence is admissible. In evaluating the evidence during the proceedings, the Chamber shall apply principles (a) to (d) of rule 70.

Rule 73
Privileged communications and information

1. Without prejudice to article 67, paragraph 1 (b), communications made in the context of the professional relationship between a person and his or her legal counsel shall be regarded as privileged, and consequently not subject to disclosure, unless:

(a) The person consents in writing to such disclosure; or

(b) The person voluntarily disclosed the content of the communication to a third party, and that third party then gives evidence of that disclosure.

2. Having regard to rule 63, sub-rule 5, communications made in the context of a class of professional or other confidential relationships shall be regarded as privileged, and consequently not subject to disclosure, under the same terms as in sub-rules 1 (a) and 1 (b) if a Chamber decides in respect of that class that:

(a) Communications occurring within that class of relationship are made n the course of a confidential relationship producing a reasonable expectation of privacy and non-disclosure;

(b) Confidentiality is essential to the nature and type of relationship between he person and the confidant; and

(c) Recognition of the privilege would further the objectives of the Statute and the Rules.

3. In making a decision under sub-rule 2, the Court shall give particular regard to recognizing as privileged those communications made in the context of the professional relationship between a person and his or her medical doctor, psychiatrist, psychologist or counsellor, in particular those related to or involving victims, or between a person and a member of a religious clergy; and in the latter case, the Court shall recognize as privileged those communications made in the context of a sacred confession where it is an integral part of the practice of that religion.

4. The Court shall regard as privileged, and consequently not subject to disclosure, including by way of testimony of any present or past official or employee of the International Committee of the Red Cross (ICRC), any information, documents or the evidence which it came into the possession of in the course, or as a consequence, of the performance by ICRC of its functions under the Statutes of the International Red Cross and Red Crescent Movement, unless:

(a) After consultations undertaken pursuant to sub-rule 6, ICRC does not object in writing to such disclosure, or otherwise has waived this privilege; or

(b Such information, documents or other evidence is contained in public statements and documents of ICRC.

5. Nothing in sub-rule 4 shall affect the admissibility of the same evidence obtained from a source other than ICRC and its officials or employees when such evidence has also been acquired by this source independently of ICRC and its officials or employees.

6. If the Court determines that ICRC information, documents or other evidence are of great importance for a particular case, consultations shall be held between the Court and ICRC in order to seek to resolve the matter by cooperative means, bearing in mind the circumstances of the case, the relevance of the evidence sought, whether the evidence could be obtained from a source other than ICRC, the interests of justice and of victims, and the performance of the Court's and ICRC's functions.

Rule 74
Self-incrimination by a witness

1. Unless a witness has been notified pursuant to rule 190, the Chamber shall notify a witness of the provisions of this rule before his or her testimony.

2. Where the Court determines that an assurance with respect to self-incrimination should be provided to a particular witness, it shall provide the assurances under sub-rule 3, paragraph (c), before the witness attends, directly or pursuant to a request under article 93, paragraph (1) (e).

3.(a) A witness may object to making any statement that might tend to incriminate him or her.

(b) Where the witness has attended after receiving an assurance under sub-rule 2, the Court may require the witness to answer the question or questions.

(c) In the case of other witnesses, the Chamber may require the witness to answer the question or questions, after assuring the witness that the evidence provided in response to the questions:

(i) Will be kept confidential and will not be disclosed to the public r any State; and

(ii) Will not be used either directly or indirectly against that person in any subsequent prosecution by the Court, except under articles 70 and 71.

4. Before giving such an assurance, the Chamber shall seek the views of the Prosecutor, *ex parte*, to determine if the assurance should be given to this particular witness.

5. In determining whether to require the witness to answer, the Chamber shall consider:

(a) The importance of the anticipated evidence;

(b) Whether the witness would be providing unique evidence;

(c) The nature of the possible incrimination, if known; and

(d) The sufficiency of the protections for the witness, in the particular circumstances.

6. If the Chamber determines that it would not be appropriate to provide an assurance to this witness, it shall not require the witness to answer the question. If the Chamber determines not to require the witness to answer, it may still continue the questioning of the witness on other matters.

7. In order to give effect to the assurance, the Chamber shall:

(a) Order that the evidence of the witness be given in camera;

(b) Order that the identity of the witness and the content of the evidence given shall not be disclosed, in any manner, and provide that the breach of any such order will be subject to sanction under article 71;

(c) Specifically advise the Prosecutor, the accused, the defence counsel, the legal representative of the victim and any Court staff present of the consequences of a breach of the order under subparagraph (b);

(d) Order the sealing of any record of the proceedings; and

(e) Use protective measures with respect to any decision of the Court to ensure that the identity of the witness and the content of the evidence given are not disclosed.

8. Where the Prosecutor is aware that the testimony of any witness may raise issues with respect to self-incrimination, he or she shall request an in camera hearing and advise the Chamber of this, in advance of the testimony of the witness. The Chamber may impose the measures outlined in sub-rule 7 for all or a part of the testimony of that witness.

9. The accused, the defence counsel or the witness may advise the Prosecutor or the Chamber that the testimony of a witness will raise issues of self-incrimination before the witness testifies and the Chamber may take the measures outlined in sub-rule 7.

10. If an issue of self-incrimination arises in the course of the proceedings, the Chamber shall suspend the taking of the testimony and provide the witness with an opportunity to obtain legal advice if he or she so requests for the purpose of the application of the rule.

Rule 75
Incrimination by family members

1. A witness appearing before the Court, who is a spouse, child or parent of an accused person, shall not be required by a Chamber to make

any statement that might tend to incriminate that accused person. However, the witness may choose to make such a statement.

2. In evaluating the testimony of a witness, a Chamber may take into account that the witness, referred to in sub-rule 1, objected to reply to a question which was intended to contradict a previous statement made by the witness, or the witness was selective in choosing which questions to answer.

Section II
Disclosure

Rule 76
Pre-trial disclosure relating to prosecution witnesses

1. The Prosecutor shall provide the defence with the names of witnesses whom the Prosecutor intends to call to testify and copies of any prior statements made by those witnesses. This shall be done sufficiently in advance to enable the adequate preparation of the defence.

2. The Prosecutor shall subsequently advise the defence of the names of any additional prosecution witnesses and provide copies of their statements when the decision is made to call those witnesses.

3. The statements of prosecution witnesses shall be made available in original and in a language which the accused fully understands and speaks.

4. This rule is subject to the protection and privacy of victims and witnesses and the protection of confidential information as provided for in the Statute and rules 81 and 82.

Rule 77
Inspection of material in possession or control of the Prosecutor

The Prosecutor shall, subject to the restrictions on disclosure as provided for in the Statute and in rules 81 and 82, permit the defence to inspect any books, documents, photographs and other tangible objects in the possession or control of the Prosecutor, which are material to the preparation of the defence or are intended for use by the Prosecutor as evidence for the purposes of the confirmation hearing or at trial, as the case may be, or were obtained from or belonged to the person.

Rule 78
Inspection of material in possession or control of the defence

The defence shall permit the Prosecutor to inspect any books, documents, photographs and other tangible objects in the possession or control of the defence, which are intended for use by the defence as evidence for the purposes of the confirmation hearing or at trial.

Rule 79
Disclosure by the defence

1. The defence shall notify the Prosecutor of its intent to:

(a) Raise the existence of an alibi, in which case the notification shall specify the place or places at which the accused claims to have been present at the time of the alleged crime and the names of witnesses and any other evidence upon which the accused intends to rely to establish the alibi; or

(b) Raise a ground for excluding criminal responsibility provided for in article 31, paragraph 1, in which case the notification shall specify the names of witnesses and any other evidence upon which the accused intends to rely to establish the ground.

2. With due regard to time limits set forth in other rules, notification under sub-rule 1 hall be given sufficiently in advance to enable the Prosecutor to prepare adequately and to respond. The Chamber dealing with the matter may grant the Prosecutor an adjournment to address the issue raised by the defence.

3. Failure of the defence to provide notice under this rule shall not limit its right to raise matters dealt with in sub-rule 1 and to present evidence.

4. This rule does not prevent a Chamber from ordering disclosure of any other evidence.

Rule 80
Procedures for raising a ground for excluding criminal responsibility under article 31, paragraph 3

1. The defence shall give notice to both the Trial Chamber and the Prosecutor if it intends to raise a ground for excluding criminal responsibility under article 31, paragraph 3. This shall be done sufficiently in advance of the commencement of the trial to enable the Prosecutor to prepare adequately for trial.

2. Following notice given under sub-rule 1, the Trial Chamber shall hear both the Prosecutor and the defence before deciding whether the defence can raise a ground for excluding criminal responsibility.

3. If the defence is permitted to raise the ground, the Trial Chamber may grant the Prosecutor an adjournment to address that ground.

Rule 81
Restrictions on disclosure

1. Reports, memoranda or other internal documents prepared by a party, its assistants or representatives in connection with the investigation or preparation of the case are not subject to disclosure.

2. Where material or information is in the possession or control of the Prosecutor which must be disclosed in accordance with the Statute, but disclosure may prejudice further or ongoing investigations, the Prosecutor may apply to the Chamber dealing with the matter for a ruling as to whether the material or information must be disclosed to the defence. The matter shall be heard on an *ex parte* basis by the Chamber. However, the Prosecutor may not introduce such material or information into evidence during the confirmation hearing or the trial without adequate prior disclosure to the accused.

3. Where steps have been taken to ensure the confidentiality of information, in accordance with articles 54, 57, 64, 72 and 93, and, in accordance with article 68, to protect the safety of witnesses and victims and members of their families, such information shall not be disclosed, except in accordance with those articles. When the disclosure of such information may create a risk to the safety of the witness, the Court shall take measures to inform the witness in advance.

4. The Chamber dealing with the matter shall, on its own motion or at the request of the Prosecutor, the accused or any State, take the necessary steps to ensure the confidentiality of information, in accordance with articles 54, 72 and 93, and, in accordance with article 68, to protect the safety of witnesses and victims and members of their families, including by authorizing the non-disclosure of their identity prior to the commencement of the trial.

5. Where material or information is in the possession or control of the Prosecutor which is withheld under article 68, paragraph 5, such material and information may not be subsequently introduced into evidence during the confirmation hearing or the trial without adequate prior disclosure to the accused.

6. Where material or information is in the possession or control of the defence which is subject to disclosure, it may be withheld in circumstances similar to those which would allow the Prosecutor to rely on article 68, paragraph 5, and a summary thereof submitted instead. Such material and information may not be subsequently introduced into evidence during the confirmation hearing or the trial without adequate prior disclosure to the Prosecutor.

Rule 82
Restrictions on disclosure of material and Information protected under article 54, paragraph 3 (e)

1. Where material or information is in the possession or control of the Prosecutor which is protected under article 54, paragraph 3 (e), the Prosecutor may not subsequently introduce such material or information into evidence without the prior consent of the provider of the material or information and adequate prior disclosure to the accused.

2. If the Prosecutor introduces material or information protected under article 54, paragraph 3 (e), into evidence, a Chamber may not order the production of additional evidence received from the provider of the initial material or information, nor may a Chamber for the purpose of obtaining such additional evidence itself summon the provider or a representative of the provider as a witness or order their attendance.

3. If the Prosecutor calls a witness to introduce in evidence any material or information which has been protected under article 54, paragraph 3 (e), a Chamber may not compel that witness to answer any question relating to the material or information or its origin, if the witness declines to answer on grounds of confidentiality.

4. The right of the accused to challenge evidence which has been protected under article 54, paragraph 3 (e), shall remain unaffected subject only to the limitations contained in sub-rules 2 and 3.

5. A Chamber dealing with the matter may order, upon application by the defence, that, in the interests of justice, material or information in the possession of the accused, which has been provided to the accused under the same conditions as set forth in article 54, paragraph 3 (e), and which is to be introduced into evidence, shall be subject *mutatis mutandis* to sub-rules 1, 2 and 3.

Rule 83
Ruling on exculpatory evidence under article 67, paragraph 2

The Prosecutor may request as soon as practicable a hearing on an *ex parte* basis before the Chamber dealing with the matter for the purpose of obtaining a ruling under article 67, paragraph 2.

Rule 84
Disclosure and additional evidence for trial

In order to enable the parties to prepare for trial and to facilitate the fair and expeditious conduct of the proceedings, the Trial Chamber shall, in accordance with article 64, paragraphs 3 (c) and 6 (d), and article 67, paragraph (2), and subject to article 68, paragraph 5, make any necessary orders for the disclosure of documents or information not previously disclosed and for the production of additional evidence. To avoid delay and to ensure that the trial commences on the set date, any such orders shall include strict time limits which shall be kept under review by the Trial Chamber.

Section III
Victims and witnesses

Subsection 1
Definition and general principle relating to victims

Rule 85
Definition of victims

For the purposes of the Statute and the Rules of Procedure and Evidence:

(a) 'Victims' means natural persons who have suffered harm as a result of the commission of any crime within the jurisdiction of the Court;

(b) Victims may include organizations or institutions that have sustained direct harm to any of their property which is dedicated to religion, education, art or science or charitable purposes, and to their historic monuments, hospitals and other places and objects for humanitarian purposes.

Rule 86
General principle

A Chamber in making any direction or order, and other organs of the Court in performing their functions under the Statute or the Rules, shall take into account the needs of all victims and witnesses in accordance with article 68, in particular, children, elderly persons, persons with disabilities and victims of sexual or gender violence.

Subsection 2
Protection of victims and witnesses

Rule 87
Protective measures

1. Upon the motion of the Prosecutor or the defence or upon the request of a witness or a victim or his or her legal representative, if any, or on its own motion, and after having consulted with the Victims and Witnesses Unit, as appropriate, a Chamber may order measures to protect a victim, a witness or another person at risk on account of testimony given

by a witness pursuant to article 68, paragraphs 1 and 2. The Chamber shall seek to obtain, whenever possible, the consent of the person in respect of whom the protective measure is sought prior to ordering the protective measure.

2. A motion or request under sub-rule 1 shall be governed by rule 134, provided that:

(a) Such a motion or request shall not be submitted *ex parte*;

(b) A request by a witness or by a victim or his or her legal representative, if any, shall be served on both the Prosecutor and the defence, each of whom shall have the opportunity to respond;

(c) A motion or request affecting a particular witness or a particular victim shall be served on that witness or victim or his or her legal representative, if any, in addition to the other party, each of whom shall have the opportunity to respond;

(d) When the Chamber proceeds on its own motion, notice and opportunity to respond shall be given to the Prosecutor and the defence, and to any witness or any victim or his or her legal representative, if any, who would be affected by such protective measure; and (e) A motion or request may be filed under seal, and, if so filed, shall remain sealed until otherwise ordered by a Chamber. Responses to motions or requests filed under seal shall also be filed under seal.

3. A Chamber may, on a motion or request under sub-rule 1, hold a hearing, which shall be conducted in camera, to determine whether to order measures to prevent the release to the public or press and information agencies, of the identity or the location of a victim, a witness or other person at risk on account of testimony given by a witness by ordering, *inter alia*:

(a) That the name of the victim, witness or other person at risk on account of testimony given by a witness or any information which could lead to his or her identification, be expunged from the public records of the Chamber;

(b) That the Prosecutor, the defence or any other participant in the proceedings be prohibited from disclosing such information to a third party;

(c) That testimony be presented by electronic or other special means, including the use of technical means enabling the alteration of pictures or voice, the use of audio-visual technology, in particular videoconferencing and closed-circuit television, and the exclusive use of the sound media;

(d) That a pseudonym be used for a victim, a witness or other person at risk on account of testimony given by a witness; or

(e) That a Chamber conduct part of its proceedings in camera.

Rule 88
Special measures

1. Upon the motion of the Prosecutor or the defence, or upon the request of a witness or a victim or his or her legal representative, if any, or on its own motion, and after having consulted with the Victims and Witnesses Unit, as appropriate, a Chamber may, taking into account the views of the victim or witness, order special measures such as, but not limited to, measures to facilitate the testimony of a traumatized victim or witness, a child, an elderly person or a victim of sexual violence, pursuant to article 68, paragraphs 1 and 2. The Chamber shall seek to obtain, whenever possible, the consent of the person in respect of whom the special measure is sought prior to ordering that measure.

2. A Chamber may hold a hearing on a motion or a request under sub-rule 1, if necessary in camera or *ex parte*, to determine whether to order any such special measure, including but not limited to an order that a counsel, a legal representative, a psychologist or a family member be permitted to attend during the testimony of the victim or the witness.

3. For *inter partes* motions or requests filed under this rule, the provisions of rule 87, sub-rules 2 (b) to (d), shall apply *mutatis mutandis*.

4. A motion or request filed under this rule may be filed under seal, and if so filed shall remain sealed until otherwise ordered by a Chamber. Any responses to *inter partes* motions or requests filed under seal shall also be filed under seal.

5. Taking into consideration that violations of the privacy of a witness or victim may create risk to his or her security, a Chamber shall be vigilant in controlling the manner of questioning a witness or victim so as to avoid any harassment or intimidation, paying particular attention to attacks on victims of crimes of sexual violence.

Subsection 3
Participation of victims in the proceedings

Rule 89
Application for participation of victims in the proceedings

1. In order to present their views and concerns, victims shall make written application to the Registrar, who shall transmit the application to the relevant Chamber. Subject to the provisions of the Statute, in particular article 68, paragraph 1, the Registrar shall provide a copy of the application to the Prosecutor and the defence, who shall be entitled to reply within a time limit to be set by the Chamber. Subject to the provisions of sub-rule 2, the Chamber shall then specify the proceedings

and manner in which participation is considered appropriate, which may include making opening and closing statements.

2. The Chamber, on its own initiative or on the application of the Prosecutor or the defence, may reject the application if it considers that the person is not a victim or that the criteria set forth in article 68, paragraph 3, are not otherwise fulfilled. A victim whose application has been rejected may file a new application later in the proceedings.

3. An application referred to in this rule may also be made by a person acting with the consent of the victim, or a person acting on behalf of a victim, in the case of a victim who is a child or, when necessary, a victim who is disabled.

4. Where there are a number of applications, the Chamber may consider the applications in such a manner as to ensure the effectiveness of the proceedings and may issue one decision.

Rule 90
Legal representatives of victims

1. A victim shall be free to choose a legal representative.

2. Where there are a number of victims, the Chamber may, for the purposes of ensuring the effectiveness of the proceedings, request the victims or particular groups of victims, if necessary with the assistance of the Registry, to choose a common legal representative or representatives. In facilitating the coordination of victim representation, the Registry may provide assistance, *inter alia*, by referring the victims to a list of counsel, maintained by the Registry, or suggesting one or more common legal representatives.

3. If the victims are unable to choose a common legal representative or representatives within a time limit that the Chamber may decide, the Chamber may request the Registrar to choose one or more common legal representatives.

4. The Chamber and the Registry shall take all reasonable steps to ensure that in the selection of common legal representatives, the distinct interests of the victims, particularly as provided in article 68, paragraph 1, are represented and that any conflict of interest is avoided.

5. A victim or group of victims who lack the necessary means to pay for a common legal representative chosen by the Court may receive assistance from the Registry, including, as appropriate, financial assistance.

6. A legal representative of a victim or victims shall have the qualifications set forth in rule 22, sub-rule 1.

Rule 91
Participation of legal representatives in the proceedings

1. A Chamber may modify a previous ruling under rule 89.

2. A legal representative of a victim shall be entitled to attend and participate in the proceedings in accordance with the terms of the ruling of the Chamber and any modification thereof given under rules 89 and 90. This shall include participation in hearings unless, in the circumstances of the case, the Chamber concerned is of the view that the representative's intervention should be confined to written observations or submissions. The Prosecutor and the defence shall be allowed to reply to any oral or written observation by the legal representative for victims.

3. (a) When a legal representative attends and participates in accordance with this rule, and wishes to question a witness, including questioning under rules 67 and 68, an expert or the accused, the legal representative must make application to the Chamber. The Chamber may require the legal representative to provide a written note of the questions and in that case the questions shall be communicated to the Prosecutor and, if appropriate, the defence, who shall be allowed to make observations within a time limit set by the Chamber.

(b) The Chamber shall then issue a ruling on the request, taking into account the stage of the proceedings, the rights of the accused, the interests of witnesses, the need for a fair, impartial and expeditious trial and in order to give effect to article 68, paragraph 3. The ruling may include directions on the manner and order of the questions and the production of documents in accordance with the powers of the Chamber under article 64. The Chamber may, if it considers it appropriate, put the question to the witness, expert or accused on behalf of the victim's legal representative.

4. For a hearing limited to reparations under article 75, the restrictions on questioning by the legal representative set forth in sub-rule 2 shall not apply. In that case, the legal representative may, with the permission of the Chamber concerned, question witnesses, experts and the person concerned.

Rule 92
Notification to victims and their legal representatives

1. This rule on notification to victims and their legal representatives shall apply to all proceedings before the Court, except in proceedings provided for in Part 2.

2. In order to allow victims to apply for participation in the proceedings in accordance with rule 89, the Court shall notify victims concerning the decision of the Prosecutor not to initiate an investigation or not to prosecute pursuant to article 53. Such a notification shall be given to

victims or their legal representatives who have already participated in the proceedings or, as far as possible, to those who have communicated with the Court in respect of the situation or case in question. The Chamber may order the measures outlined in sub-rule 8 if it considers it appropriate in the particular circumstances.

3. In order to allow victims to apply for participation in the proceedings in accordance with rule 89, the Court shall notify victims regarding its decision to hold a hearing to confirm charges pursuant to article 61. Such a notification shall be given to victims or their legal representatives who have already participated in the proceedings or, as far as possible, to those who have communicated with the Court in respect of the case in question.

4. When a notification for participation as provided for in sub-rules 2 and 3 has been given, any subsequent notification as referred to in sub-rules 5 and 6 shall only be provided to victims or their legal representatives who may participate in the proceedings in accordance with a ruling of the Chamber pursuant to rule 89 and any modification thereof.

5. In a manner consistent with the ruling made under rules 89 to 91, victims or their legal representatives participating in proceedings shall, in respect of those proceedings, be notified by the Registrar in a timely manner of:

(a) Proceedings before the Court, including the date of hearings and any postponements thereof, and the date of delivery of the decision;

(b) Requests, submissions, motions and other documents relating to such requests, submissions or motions.

6. Where victims or their legal representatives have participated in a certain stage of the proceedings, the Registrar shall notify them as soon as possible of the decisions of the Court in those proceedings.

7. Notifications as referred to in sub-rules 5 and 6 shall be in writing or, where written notification is not possible, in any other form as appropriate. The Registry shall keep a record of all notifications. Where necessary, the Registrar may seek the cooperation of States Parties in accordance with article 93, paragraph 1 (d) and (l).

8. For notification as referred to in sub-rule 3 and otherwise at the request of a Chamber, the Registrar shall take necessary measures to give adequate publicity to the proceedings. In doing so, the Registrar may seek, in accordance with Part 9, the cooperation of relevant States Parties, and seek the assistance of intergovernmental organizations.

Rule 93
Views of victims or their legal representatives

A Chamber may seek the views of victims or their legal representatives participating pursuant to rules 89 to 91 on any issue, *inter alia*, in relation to issues referred to in rules 107, 109, 125, 128, 136, 139 and 191. In addition, a Chamber may seek the views of other victims, as appropriate.

Subsection 4
Reparations to victims

Rule 94
Procedure upon request

1. A victim's request for reparations under article 75 shall be made in writing and filed with the Registrar. It shall contain the following particulars:

(a) The identity and address of the claimant;

(b) A description of the injury, loss or harm;

(c) The location and date of the incident and, to the extent possible, the identity of the person or persons the victim believes to be responsible for the injury, loss or harm;

(d) Where restitution of assets, property or other tangible items is sought, a description of them;

(e) Claims for compensation;

(f) Claims for rehabilitation and other forms of remedy;

(g) To the extent possible, any relevant supporting documentation, including names and addresses of witnesses.

2. At commencement of the trial and subject to any protective measures, the Court shall ask the Registrar to provide notification of the request to the person or persons named in the request or identified in the charges and, to the extent possible, to any interested persons or any interested States. Those notified shall file with the Registry any representation made under article 75, paragraph 3.

Rule 95
Procedure on the motion of the Court

1. In cases where the Court intends to proceed on its own motion pursuant to article 75, paragraph 1, it shall ask the Registrar to provide notification of its intention to the person or persons against whom the Court is considering making a determination, and, to the extent possible, to victims, interested persons and interested States. Those notified shall file with the Registry any representation made under article 75, paragraph 3.

2. If, as a result of notification under sub-rule 1:

(a) A victim makes a request for reparations, that request will be determined as if it had been brought under rule 94;

(b) A victim requests that the Court does not make an order for reparations, the Court shall not proceed to make an individual order in respect of that victim.

Rule 96
Publication of reparation proceedings

1. Without prejudice to any other rules on notification of proceedings, the Registrar shall, insofar as practicable, notify the victims or their legal representatives and the person or persons concerned. The Registrar shall also, having regard to any information provided by the Prosecutor, take all the necessary measures to give adequate publicity of the reparation proceedings before the Court, to the extent possible, to other victims, interested persons and interested States.

2. In taking the measures described in sub-rule 1, the Court may seek, in accordance with Part 9, the cooperation of relevant States Parties, and seek the assistance of intergovernmental organizations in order to give publicity, as widely as possible and by all possible means, to the reparation proceedings before the Court.

Rule 97
Assessment of reparations

1. Taking into account the scope and extent of any damage, loss or injury, the Court may award reparations on an individualized basis or, where it deems it appropriate, on a collective basis or both.

2. At the request of victims or their legal representatives, or at the request of the convicted person, or on its own motion, the Court may appoint appropriate experts to assist it in determining the scope, extent of any damage, loss and injury to, or in respect of victims and to suggest various options concerning the appropriate types and modalities of reparations. The Court shall invite, as appropriate, victims or their legal representatives, the convicted person as well as interested persons and interested States to make observations on the reports of the experts.

3. In all cases, the Court shall respect the rights of victims and the convicted person.

Rule 98
Trust Fund

1. Individual awards for reparations shall be made directly against a convicted person.

2. The Court may order that an award for reparations against a convicted person be deposited with the Trust Fund where at the time of making the order it is impossible or impracticable to make individual awards directly to each victim. The award for reparations thus deposited in the Trust Fund shall be separated from other resources of the Trust Fund and shall be forwarded to each victim as soon as possible.

3. The Court may order that an award for reparations against a convicted person be made through the Trust Fund where the number of the victims and the scope, forms and modalities of reparations makes a collective award more appropriate.

4. Following consultations with interested States and the Trust Fund, the Court may order that an award for reparations be made through the Trust Fund to an intergovernmental, international or national organization approved by the Trust Fund.

5. Other resources of the Trust Fund may be used for the benefit of victims subject to the provisions of article 79.

Rule 99
Cooperation and protective measures for the purpose of forfeiture under articles 57, paragraph 3 (e), and 75, paragraph 4

1. The Pre-Trial Chamber, pursuant to article 57, paragraph 3 (e), or the Trial Chamber, pursuant to article 75, paragraph 4, may, on its own motion or on the application of the Prosecutor or at the request of the victims or their legal representatives who have made a request for reparations or who have given a written undertaking to do so, determine whether measures should be requested.

2. Notice is not required unless the Court determines, in the particular circumstances of the case, that notification could not jeopardize the effectiveness of the measures requested. In the latter case, the Registrar shall provide notification of the proceedings to the person against whom a request is made and so far as is possible to any interested persons or interested States.

3. If an order is made without prior notification, the relevant Chamber shall request the Registrar, as soon as is consistent with the effectiveness of the measures requested, to notify those against whom a request is made and, to the extent possible, to any interested persons or any interested States and invite them to make observations as to whether the order should be revoked or otherwise modified.

4. The Court may make orders as to the timing and conduct of any proceedings necessary to determine these issues.

Section IV
Miscellaneous provisions

Rule 100
Place of the proceedings

1. In a particular case, where the Court considers that it would be in the interests of justice, it may decide to sit in a State other than the host State.

2. An application or recommendation changing the place where the Court sits may be filed at any time after the initiation of an investigation, either by the Prosecutor, the defence or by a majority of the judges of the Court. Such an application or recommendation shall be addressed to the Presidency. It shall be made in writing and specify in which State the Court would sit. The Presidency shall satisfy itself of the views of the relevant Chamber.

3. The Presidency shall consult the State where the Court intends to sit. If that State agrees that the Court can sit in that State, then the decision to sit in a State other than the host State shall be taken by the judges, in plenary session, by a two-thirds majority.

Rule 101
Time limits

1. In making any order setting time limits regarding the conduct of any proceedings, the Court shall have regard to the need to facilitate fair and expeditious proceedings, bearing in mind in particular the rights of the defence and the victims.

2. Taking into account the rights of the accused, in particular under article 67, paragraph (1) (c), all those participating in the proceedings to whom any order is directed shall endeavour to act as expeditiously as possible, within the time limit ordered by the Court.

Rule 102
Communications other than in writing

Where a person is unable, due to a disability or illiteracy, to make a written request, application, observation or other communication to the Court, the person may make such request, application, observation or communication in audio, video or other electronic form.

Rule 103
Amicus curiae and other forms of submission

1. At any stage of the proceedings, a Chamber may, if it considers it desirable for the proper determination of the case, invite or grant leave to a

State, organization or person to submit, in writing or orally, any observation on any issue that the Chamber deems appropriate.

2. The Prosecutor and the defence shall have the opportunity to respond to the observations submitted under sub-rule 1.

3. A written observation submitted under sub-rule 1 shall be filed with the Registrar, who shall provide copies to the Prosecutor and the defence. The Chamber shall determine what time limits shall apply to the filing of such observations.

Chapter 5
Investigation and prosecution

Section I
Decision of the Prosecutor regarding the initiation of an investigation under article 53, paragraphs 1 and 2

Rule 104
Evaluation of information by the Prosecutor

1. In acting pursuant to article 53, paragraph 1, the Prosecutor shall, in evaluating the information made available to him or her, analyse the seriousness of the information received.

2. For the purposes of sub-rule 1, the Prosecutor may seek additional information from States, organs of the United Nations, intergovernmental and non-governmental organizations, or other reliable sources that he or she deems appropriate, and may receive written or oral testimony at the seat of the Court. The procedure set out in rule 47 shall apply to the receiving of such testimony.

Rule 105
Notification of a decision by the Prosecutor not to initiate an investigation

1. When the Prosecutor decides not to initiate an investigation under article 53, paragraph 1, he or she shall promptly inform in writing the State or States that referred a situation under article 14, or the Security Council in respect of a situation covered by article 13, paragraph (b).

2. When the Prosecutor decides not to submit to the Pre-Trial Chamber a request for authorization of an investigation, rule 49 shall apply.

3. The notification referred to in sub-rule 1 shall contain the conclusion of the Prosecutor and, having regard to article 68, paragraph 1, the reasons for the conclusion.

4. In case the Prosecutor decides not to investigate solely on the basis of article 53, paragraph 1 (c), he or she shall inform in writing the Pre-Trial Chamber promptly after making that decision.

5. The notification shall contain the conclusion of the Prosecutor and the reasons for the conclusion.

Rule 106
Notification of a decision by the Prosecutor not to prosecute

1. When the Prosecutor decides that there is not a sufficient basis for prosecution under article 53, paragraph 2, he or she shall promptly inform in writing the Pre-Trial Chamber, together with the State or States that referred a situation under article 14, or the Security Council in respect of a situation covered by article 13, paragraph (b).

2. The notifications referred to in sub-rule 1 shall contain the conclusion of the Prosecutor and, having regard to article 68, paragraph 1, the reasons for the conclusion.

Section II
Procedure under article 53, paragraph 3

Rule 107
Request for review under article 53, paragraph 3 (a)

1. A request under article 53, paragraph 3, for a review of a decision by the Prosecutor not to initiate an investigation or not to prosecute shall be made in writing, and be supported with reasons, within 90 days following the notification given under rule 105 or 106.

2. The Pre-Trial Chamber may request the Prosecutor to transmit the information or documents in his or her possession, or summaries thereof, that the Chamber considers necessary for the conduct of the review.

3. The Pre-Trial Chamber shall take such measures as are necessary under articles 54, 72 and 93 to protect the information and documents referred to in sub-rule 2 and, under article 68, paragraph 5, to protect the safety of witnesses and victims and members of their families.

4. When a State or the Security Council makes a request referred to in sub-rule 1, the Pre-Trial Chamber may seek further observations from them.

5. Where an issue of jurisdiction or admissibility of the case is raised, rule 59 shall apply.

Rule 108
Decision of the Pre-Trial Chamber
Under article 53, paragraph 3 (a)

1. A decision of the Pre-Trial Chamber under article 53, paragraph 3 (a), must be concurred in by a majority of its judges and shall contain reasons. It shall be communicated to all those who participated in the review.

2. Where the Pre-Trial Chamber requests the Prosecutor to review, in whole or in part, his or her decision not to initiate an investigation or not to prosecute, the Prosecutor shall reconsider that decision as soon as possible.

3. Once the Prosecutor has taken a final decision, he or she shall notify the Pre-Trial Chamber in writing. This notification shall contain the conclusion of the Prosecutor and the reasons for the conclusion. It shall be communicated to all those who participated in the review.

Rule 109
Review by the Pre-Trial Chamber
Under article 53, paragraph 3 (b)

1. Within 180 days following a notification given under rule 105 or 106, the Pre-Trial Chamber may on its own initiative decide to review a decision of the Prosecutor taken solely under article 53, paragraph 1 (c) or 2 (c). The Pre-Trial Chamber shall inform the Prosecutor of its intention to review his or her decision and shall establish a time limit within which the Prosecutor may submit observations and other material.

2. In cases where a request has been submitted to the Pre-Trial Chamber by a State or by the Security Council, they shall also be informed and may submit observations in accordance with rule 107.

Rule 110
Decision by the Pre-Trial Chamber
Under article 53, paragraph 3 (b)

1. A decision by the Pre-Trial Chamber to confirm or not to confirm a decision taken by the Prosecutor solely under article 53, paragraph 1 (c) or 2 (c), must be concurred in by a majority of its judges and shall contain reasons. It shall be communicated to all those who participated in the review.

2. When the Pre-Trial Chamber does not confirm the decision by the Prosecutor referred to in sub-rule 1, he or she shall proceed with the investigation or prosecution.

Section III
Collection of evidence

Rule 111
Record of questioning in general

1. A record shall be made of formal statements made by any person who is questioned in connection with an investigation or with proceedings. The record shall be signed by the person who records and conducts the questioning and by the person who is questioned and his or her counsel, if present, and, where applicable, the Prosecutor or the judge who is present. The record shall note the date, time and place of, and all persons present during the questioning. It shall also be noted when someone has not signed the record as well as the reasons therefore.

2. When the Prosecutor or national authorities question a person, due regard shall be given to article 55. When a person is informed of his or her rights under article 55, paragraph 2, the fact that this information has been provided shall be noted in the record.

Rule 112
Recording of questioning in particular cases

1. Whenever the Prosecutor questions a person to whom article 55, paragraph 2, applies, or for whom a warrant of arrest or a summons to appear has been issued under article 58, paragraph 7, the questioning shall be audio- or video-recorded, in accordance with the following procedure:

(a) The person questioned shall be informed, in a language he or she fully understands and speaks, that the questioning is to be audio- or video-recorded, and that the person concerned may object if he or she so wishes. The fact that this information has been provided and the response given by the person concerned shall be noted in the record. The person may, before replying, speak in private with his or her counsel, if present. If the person questioned refuses to be audio- or video-recorded, the procedure in rule 111 shall be followed;

(b) A waiver of the right to be questioned in the presence of counsel shall be recorded in writing and, if possible, be audio- or video-recorded;

(c) In the event of an interruption in the course of questioning, the fact and the time of the interruption shall be recorded before the audio- or video-recording ends as well as the time of resumption of the questioning;

(d) At the conclusion of the questioning, the person questioned shall be offered the opportunity to clarify anything he or she has said and to add anything he or she may wish. The time of conclusion of the questioning shall be noted;

(e) The tape shall be transcribed as soon as practicable after the conclusion of the questioning and a copy of the transcript supplied to the person questioned together with a copy of the recorded tape or, if multiple recording apparatus was used, one of the original recorded tapes;

(f) The original tape or one of the original tapes shall be sealed in the presence of the person questioned and his or her counsel, if present, under the signature of the Prosecutor and the person questioned and the counsel, if present.

2. The Prosecutor shall make every reasonable effort to record the questioning in accordance with sub-rule 1. As an exception, a person may be questioned without the questioning being audio- or video-recorded where the circumstances prevent such recording taking place. In this case, the reasons for not recording the questioning shall be stated in writing and the procedure in rule 111 shall be followed.

3. When, pursuant to sub-rule 1 (a) or 2, the questioning is not audio- or video-recorded, the person questioned shall be provided with a copy of his or her statement.

4. The Prosecutor may choose to follow the procedure in this rule when questioning other persons than those mentioned in sub-rule 1, in particular where the use of such procedures could assist in reducing any subsequent traumatization of a victim of sexual or gender violence, a child or a person with disabilities in providing their evidence. The Prosecutor may make an application to the relevant Chamber.

5. The Pre-Trial Chamber may, in pursuance of article 56, paragraph 2, order that the procedure in this rule be applied to the questioning of any person.

Rule 113
Collection of information regarding the State of health of the person concerned

1. The Pre-Trial Chamber may, on its own initiative or at the request of the Prosecutor, the person concerned or his or her counsel, order that a person having the rights in article 55, paragraph 2, be given a medical, psychological or psychiatric examination. In making its determination, the Pre-Trial Chamber shall consider the nature and purpose of the examination and whether the person consents to the examination.

2. The Pre-Trial Chamber shall appoint one or more experts from the list of experts approved by the Registrar, or an expert approved by the Pre-Trial Chamber at the request of a party.

Rule 114
Unique investigative opportunity under article 56

1. Upon being advised by the Prosecutor in accordance with article 56, paragraph 1 (a), the Pre-Trial Chamber shall hold consultations without delay with the Prosecutor and, subject to the provisions of article 56, paragraph 1 (c), with the person who has been arrested or who has appeared before the Court pursuant to summons and his or her counsel, in order to determine the measures to be taken and the modalities of their implementation, which may include measures to ensure that the right to communicate under article 67, paragraph 1 (b), is protected.

2. A decision of the Pre-Trial Chamber to take measures pursuant to article 56, paragraph 3, must be concurred in by a majority of its judges after consultations with the Prosecutor. During the consultations, the Prosecutor may advise the Pre-Trial Chamber that intended measures could jeopardize the proper conduct of the investigation.

Rule 115
Collection of evidence in the territory of a State Party under article 57, paragraph 3 (d)

1. Where the Prosecutor considers that article 57, paragraph 3 (d), applies, the Prosecutor may submit a written request to the Pre-Trial Chamber for authorization to take certain measures in the territory of the State Party in question. After a submission of such a request, the Pre-Trial Chamber shall, whenever possible, inform and invite views from the State Party concerned.

2. In arriving at its determination as to whether the request is well founded, the Pre-Trial Chamber shall take into account any views expressed by the State Party concerned. The Pre-Trial Chamber may, on its own initiative or at the request of the Prosecutor or the State Party concerned, decide to hold a hearing.

3. An authorization under article 57, paragraph 3 (d), shall be issued in the form of an order and shall state the reasons, based on the criteria set forth in that paragraph. The order may specify procedures to be followed in carrying out such collection of evidence.

Rule 116
Collection of evidence at the request of the defence under article 57, paragraph 3 (b)

1. The Pre-Trial Chamber shall issue an order or seek cooperation under article 57, paragraph 3 (b), where it is satisfied:

(a) That such an order would facilitate the collection of evidence that may be material to the proper determination of the issues being adjudicated, or to the proper preparation of the person's defence; and

(b) In a case of cooperation under Part 9, that sufficient information to comply with article 96, paragraph 2, has been provided.

2. Before taking a decision whether to issue an order or seek cooperation under article 57, paragraph 3 (b), the Pre-Trial Chamber may seek the views of the prosecutor.

Section IV
Procedures in respect of restriction and deprivation of liberty

Rule 117
Detention in the custodial State

1. The Court shall take measures to ensure that it is informed of the arrest of a person in response to a request made by the Court under article 89 or 92. Once so informed, the Court shall ensure that the person receives a copy of the arrest warrant issued by the Pre-Trial Chamber under article 58 and any relevant provisions of the Statute. The documents shall be made available in a language that the person fully understands and speaks.

2. At any time after arrest, the person may make a request to the Pre-Trial Chamber for the appointment of counsel to assist with proceedings before the Court and the Pre-Trial Chamber shall take a decision on such request.

3. A challenge as to whether the warrant of arrest was properly issued in accordance with article 58, paragraph 1 (a) and (b), shall be made in writing to the Pre-Trial Chamber. The application shall set out the basis for the challenge. After having obtained the views of the Prosecutor, the Pre-Trial Chamber shall decide on the application without delay.

4. When the competent authority of the custodial State notifies the Pre-Trial Chamber that a request for release has been made by the person arrested, in accordance with article 59, paragraph 5, the Pre-Trial Chamber shall provide its recommendations within any time limit set by the custodial State.

5. When the Pre-Trial Chamber is informed that the person has been granted interim release by the competent authority of the custodial State, the Pre-Trial Chamber shall inform the custodial State how and when it would like to receive periodic reports on the status of the interim release.

Rule 118
Pre-trial detention at the seat of the Court

1. If the person surrendered to the Court makes an initial request for interim release pending trial, either upon first appearance in accordance with rule 121 or subsequently, the Pre-Trial Chamber shall decide upon the request without delay, after seeking the views of the Prosecutor.

2. The Pre-Trial Chamber shall review its ruling on the release or detention of a person in accordance with article 60, paragraph 3, at least every 120 days and may do so at any time on the request of the person or the Prosecutor.

3. After the first appearance, a request for interim release must be made in writing. The Prosecutor shall be given notice of such a request. The Pre-Trial Chamber shall decide after having received observations in writing of the Prosecutor and the detained person. The Pre-Trial Chamber may decide to hold a hearing, at the request of the Prosecutor or the detained person or on its own initiative. A hearing must be held at least once every year.

Rule 119
Conditional release

1. The Pre-Trial Chamber may set one or more conditions restricting liberty, including the following:

(a) The person must not travel beyond territorial limits set by the Pre-Trial Chamber without the explicit agreement of the Chamber;

(b) The person must not go to certain places or associate with certain persons as specified by the Pre-Trial Chamber;

(c) The person must not contact directly or indirectly victims or witnesses;

(d) The person must not engage in certain professional activities;

(e) The person must reside at a particular address as specified by the Pre-Trial Chamber;

(f) The person must respond when summoned by an authority or qualified person designated by the Pre-Trial Chamber;

(g) The person must post bond or provide real or personal security or surety, for which the amount and the schedule and mode of payment shall be determined by the Pre-Trial Chamber;

(h) The person must supply the Registrar with all identity documents, particularly his or her passport.

2. At the request of the person concerned or the Prosecutor or on its own initiative, the Pre-Trial Chamber may at any time decide to amend the conditions set pursuant to sub-rule 1.

3. Before imposing or amending any conditions restricting liberty, the Pre-Trial Chamber shall seek the views of the Prosecutor, the person concerned, any relevant State and victims that have communicated with the Court in that case and whom the Chamber considers could be at risk as a result of a release or conditions imposed.

4. If the Pre-Trial Chamber is convinced that the person concerned has failed to comply with one or more of the obligations imposed, it may, on such basis, at the request of the Prosecutor or on its own initiative, issue a warrant of arrest in respect of the person.

5. When the Pre-Trial Chamber issues a summons to appear pursuant to article 58, paragraph 7, and intends to set conditions restricting liberty, it shall ascertain the relevant provisions of the national law of the State receiving the summons. In a manner that is in keeping with the national law of the State receiving the summons, the Pre-Trial Chamber shall proceed in accordance with sub-rules 1, 2 and 3. If the Pre-Trial Chamber receives information that the person concerned has failed to comply with conditions imposed, it shall proceed in accordance with sub-rule 4.

Rule 120
Instruments of restraint

Personal instruments of restraint shall not be used except as a precaution against escape, for the protection of the person in the custody of the Court and others or for other security reasons, and shall be removed when the person appears before a Chamber.

Section V
Proceedings with regard to the confirmation of charges under article 61

Rule 121
Proceedings before the confirmation hearing

1. A person subject to a warrant of arrest or a summons to appear under article 58 shall appear before the Pre-Trial Chamber, in the presence of the Prosecutor, promptly upon arriving at the Court. Subject to the provisions of articles 60 and 61, the person shall enjoy the rights set forth in article 67. At this first appearance, the Pre-Trial Chamber shall set the date on which it intends to hold a hearing to confirm the charges. It shall ensure that this date, and any postponements under sub-rule 7, are made public.

2. In accordance with article 61, paragraph 3, the Pre-Trial Chamber shall take the necessary decisions regarding disclosure between the

Prosecutor and the person in respect of whom a warrant of arrest or a summons to appear has been issued. During disclosure:

(a) The person concerned may be assisted or represented by the counsel of his or her choice or by a counsel assigned to him or her;

(b) The Pre-Trial Chamber shall hold status conferences to ensure that disclosure takes place under satisfactory conditions. For each case, a judge of the Pre-Trial Chamber shall be appointed to organize such status conferences, on his or her own motion, or at the request of the Prosecutor or the person;

(c) All evidence disclosed between the Prosecutor and the person for the purposes of the confirmation hearing shall be communicated to the Pre-Trial Chamber.

3. The Prosecutor shall provide to the Pre-Trial Chamber and the person, no later than 30 days before the date of the confirmation hearing, a detailed description of the charges together with a list of the evidence which he or she intends to present at the hearing.

4. Where the Prosecutor intends to amend the charges pursuant to article 61, paragraph 4, he or she shall notify the Pre-Trial Chamber and the person no later than 15 days before the date of the hearing of the amended charges together with a list of evidence that the Prosecutor intends to bring in support of those charges at the hearing.

5. Where the Prosecutor intends to present new evidence at the hearing, he or she shall provide the Pre-Trial Chamber and the person with a list of that evidence no later than 15 days before the date of the hearing.

6. If the person intends to present evidence under article 61, paragraph 6, he or she shall provide a list of that evidence to the Pre-Trial Chamber no later than 15 days before the date of the hearing. The Pre-Trial Chamber shall transmit the list to the Prosecutor without delay. The person shall provide a list of evidence that he or she intends to present in response to any amended charges or a new list of evidence provided by the Prosecutor.

7. The Prosecutor or the person may ask the Pre-Trial Chamber to postpone the date of the confirmation hearing. The Pre-Trial Chamber may also, on its own motion, decide to postpone the hearing.

8. The Pre-Trial Chamber shall not take into consideration charges and evidence presented after the time limit, or any extension thereof, has expired.

9. The Prosecutor and the person may lodge written submissions with the Pre-Trial Chamber, on points of fact and on law, including grounds for excluding criminal responsibility set forth in article 31, paragraph 1, no later than three days before the date of the hearing. A copy of these

submissions shall be transmitted immediately to the Prosecutor or the person, as the case may be.

10. The Registry shall create and maintain a full and accurate record of all proceedings before the Pre-Trial Chamber, including all documents transmitted to the Chamber pursuant to this rule. Subject to any restrictions concerning confidentiality and the protection of national security information, the record may be consulted by the Prosecutor, the person and victims or their legal representatives participating in the proceedings pursuant to rules 89 to 91.

Rule 122
Proceedings at the confirmation hearing in the presence of the person charged

1. The Presiding Judge of the Pre-Trial Chamber shall ask the officer of the Registry assisting the Chamber to read out the charges as presented by the Prosecutor. The Presiding Judge shall determine how the hearing is to be conducted and, in particular, may establish the order and the conditions under which he or she intends the evidence contained in the record of the proceedings to be presented.

2. If a question or challenge concerning jurisdiction or admissibility arises, rule 58 applies.

3. Before hearing the matter on the merits, the Presiding Judge of the Pre-Trial Chamber shall ask the Prosecutor and the person whether they intend to raise objections or make observations concerning an issue related to the proper conduct of the proceedings prior to the confirmation hearing.

4. At no subsequent point may the objections and observations made under sub-rule 3 be raised or made again in the confirmation or trial proceedings.

5. If objections or observations referred to in sub-rule 3 are presented, the Presiding Judge of the Pre-Trial Chamber shall invite those referred to in sub-rule 3 to present their arguments, in the order which he or she shall establish. The person shall have the right to reply.

6. If the objections raised or observations made are those referred to in sub-rule 3, the Pre-Trial Chamber shall decide whether to join the issue raised with the examination of the charges and the evidence, or to separate them, in which case it shall adjourn the confirmation hearing and render a decision on the issues raised.

7. During the hearing on the merits, the Prosecutor and the person shall present their arguments in accordance with article 61, paragraphs 5 and 6.

8. The Pre-Trial Chamber shall permit the Prosecutor and the person, in that order, to make final observations.

9. Subject to the provisions of article 61, article 69 shall apply *mutatis mutandis* at the confirmation hearing.

Rule 123
Measures to ensure the presence of the person concerned at the confirmation hearing

1. When a warrant of arrest or summons to appear in accordance with article 58, paragraph 7, has been issued for a person by the Pre-Trial Chamber and the person is arrested or served with the summons, the Pre-Trial Chamber shall ensure that the person is notified of the provisions of article 61, paragraph 2.

2. The Pre-Trial Chamber may hold consultations with the Prosecutor, at the request of the latter or on its own initiative, in order to determine whether there is cause to hold a hearing on confirmation of charges under the conditions set forth in article 61, paragraph 2 (b). When the person concerned has a counsel known to the Court, the consultations shall be held in the presence of the counsel unless the Pre-Trial Chamber decides otherwise.

3. The Pre-Trial Chamber shall ensure that a warrant of arrest for the person concerned has been issued and, if the warrant of arrest has not been executed within a reasonable period of time after the issuance of the warrant, that all reasonable measures have been taken to locate and arrest the person.

Rule 124
Waiver of the right to be present at the confirmation hearing

1. If the person concerned is available to the Court but wishes to waive the right to be present at the hearing on confirmation of charges, he or she shall submit a written request to the Pre-Trial Chamber, which may then hold consultations with the Prosecutor and the person concerned, assisted or represented by his or her counsel.

2. A confirmation hearing pursuant to article 61, paragraph 2 (a), shall only be held when the Pre-Trial Chamber is satisfied that the person concerned understands the right to be present at the hearing and the consequences of waiving this right.

3. The Pre-Trial Chamber may authorize and make provision for the person to observe the hearing from outside the courtroom through the use of communications technology, if required.

4. The waiving of the right to be present at the hearing does not prevent the Pre-Trial Chamber from receiving written observations on issues before the Chamber from the person concerned.

Rule 125
Decision to hold the confirmation hearing in the absence of the person concerned

1. After holding consultations under rules 123 and 124, the Pre-Trial Chamber shall decide whether there is cause to hold a hearing on confirmation of charges in the absence of the person concerned, and in that case, whether the person may be represented by counsel. The Pre-Trial Chamber shall, when appropriate, set a date for the hearing and make the date public.

2. The decision of the Pre-Trial Chamber shall be notified to the Prosecutor and, if possible, to the person concerned or his or her counsel.

3. If the Pre-Trial Chamber decides not to hold a hearing on confirmation of charges in the absence of the person concerned, and the person is not available to the Court, the confirmation of charges may not take place until the person is available to the Court. The Pre-Trial Chamber may review its decision at any time, at the request of the Prosecutor or on its own initiative.

4. If the Pre-Trial Chamber decides not to hold a hearing on confirmation of charges in the absence of the person concerned, and the person is available to the Court, it shall order the person to appear.

Rule 126
Confirmation hearing in the absence of the person concerned

1. The provisions of rules 121 and 122 shall apply *mutatis mutandis* to the preparation for and holding of a hearing on confirmation of charges in the absence of the person concerned.

2. If the Pre-Trial Chamber has determined that the person concerned shall be represented by counsel, the counsel shall have the opportunity to exercise the rights of that person.

3. When the person who has fled is subsequently arrested and the Court has confirmed the charges upon which the Prosecutor intends to pursue the trial, the person charged shall be committed to the Trial Chamber established under article 61, paragraph 11. The person charged may request in writing that the Trial Chamber refer issues to the Pre-Trial Chamber that are necessary for the Chamber's effective and fair functioning in accordance with article 64, paragraph 4.

Section VI
Closure of the pre-trial phase

Rule 127
Procedure in the event of different decisions on multiple charges

If the Pre-Trial Chamber is ready to confirm some of the charges but adjourns the hearing on other charges under article 61, paragraph 7 (c), it may decide that the committal of the person concerned to the Trial Chamber on the charges that it is ready to confirm shall be deferred pending the continuation of the hearing. The Pre-Trial Chamber may then establish a time limit within which the Prosecutor may proceed in accordance with article 61, paragraph 7 (c) (i) or (ii).

Rule 128
Amendment of the charges

1. If the Prosecutor seeks to amend charges already confirmed before the trial has begun, in accordance with article 61, the Prosecutor shall make a written request to the Pre-Trial Chamber, and that Chamber shall so notify the accused.

2. Before deciding whether to authorize the amendment, the Pre-Trial Chamber may request the accused and the Prosecutor to submit written observations on certain issues of fact or law.

3. If the Pre-Trial Chamber determines that the amendments proposed by the Prosecutor constitute additional or more serious charges, it shall proceed, as appropriate, in accordance with rules 121 and 122 or rules 123 to 126.

Rule 129
Notification of the decision on the confirmation of charges

The decision of the Pre-Trial Chamber on the confirmation of charges and the committal of the accused to the Trial Chamber shall be notified, if possible, to the Prosecutor, the person concerned and his or her counsel. Such decision and the record of the proceedings of the Pre-Trial Chamber shall be transmitted to the Presidency.

Rule 130
Constitution of the Trial Chamber

When the Presidency constitutes a Trial Chamber and refers the case to it, the Presidency shall transmit the decision of the Pre-Trial Chamber and the record of the proceedings to the Trial Chamber. The Presidency may also refer the case to a previously constituted Trial Chamber.

Chapter 6
Trial procedure

Rule 131
Record of the proceedings transmitted by the Pre-Trial Chamber

1. The Registrar shall maintain the record of the proceedings transmitted by the Pre-Trial Chamber, pursuant to rule 121, sub-rule 10.

2. Subject to any restrictions concerning confidentiality and the protection of national security information, the record may be consulted by the Prosecutor, the defence, the representatives of States when they participate in the proceedings, and the victims or their legal representatives participating in the proceedings pursuant to rules 89 to 91.

Rule 132
Status conferences

1. Promptly after it is constituted, the Trial Chamber shall hold a status conference in order to set the date of the trial. The Trial Chamber, on its own motion, or at the request of the Prosecutor or the defence, may postpone the date of the trial. The Trial Chamber shall notify the trial date to all those participating in the proceedings. The Trial Chamber shall ensure that this date and any postponements are made public.

2. In order to facilitate the fair and expeditious conduct of the proceedings, the Trial Chamber may confer with the parties by holding status conferences as necessary.

Rule 133
Motions challenging admissibility or jurisdiction

Challenges to the jurisdiction of the Court or the admissibility of the case at the commencement of the trial, or subsequently with the leave of the Court, shall be dealt with by the Presiding Judge and the Trial Chamber in accordance with rule 58.

Rule 134
Motions relating to the trial proceedings

1. Prior to the commencement of the trial, the Trial Chamber on its own motion, or at the request of the Prosecutor or the defence, may rule on any issue concerning the conduct of the proceedings. Any request from the Prosecutor or the defence shall be in writing and, unless the request is for an *ex parte* procedure, served on the other party. For all requests other than those submitted for an *ex parte* procedure, the other party shall have the opportunity to file a response.

2. At the commencement of the trial, the Trial Chamber shall ask the Prosecutor and the defence whether they have any objections or observations concerning the conduct of the proceedings which have arisen since the confirmation hearings. Such objections or observations may not be raised or made again on a subsequent occasion in the trial proceedings, without leave of the Trial Chamber in this proceeding.

3. After the commencement of the trial, the Trial Chamber, on its own motion, or at the request of the Prosecutor or the defence, may rule on issues that arise during the course of the trial.

Rule 135
Medical examination of the accused

1. The Trial Chamber may, for the purpose of discharging its obligations under article 64, paragraph 8 (a), or for any other reasons, or at the request of a party, order a medical, psychiatric or psychological examination of the accused, under the conditions set forth in rule 113.

2. The Trial Chamber shall place its reasons for any such order on the record.

3. The Trial Chamber shall appoint one or more experts from the list of experts approved by the Registrar, or an expert approved by the Trial Chamber at the request of a party.

4. Where the Trial Chamber is satisfied that the accused is unfit to stand trial, it shall order that the trial be adjourned. The Trial Chamber may, on its own motion or at the request of the prosecution or the defence, review the case of the accused. In any event, the case shall be reviewed every 120 days unless there are reasons to do otherwise. If necessary, the Trial Chamber may order further examinations of the accused. When the Trial Chamber is satisfied that the accused has become fit to stand trial, it shall proceed in accordance with rule 132.

Rule 136
Joint and separate trials

1. Persons accused jointly shall be tried together unless the Trial Chamber, on its own motion or at the request of the Prosecutor or the defence, orders that separate trials are necessary, in order to avoid serious prejudice to the accused, to protect the interests of justice or because a person jointly accused has made an admission of guilt and can be proceeded against in accordance with article 65, paragraph 2.

2. In joint trials, each accused shall be accorded the same rights as if such accused were being tried separately.

Rule 137
Record of the trial proceedings

1. In accordance with article 64, paragraph 10, the Registrar shall take measures to make, and preserve, a full and accurate record of all proceedings, including transcripts, audio- and video-recordings and other means of capturing sound or image.

2. A Trial Chamber may order the disclosure of all or part of the record of closed proceedings when the reasons for ordering its non-disclosure no longer exist.

3. The Trial Chamber may authorize persons other than the Registrar to take photographs, audio- and video-recordings and other means of capturing the sound or image of the trial.

Rule 138
Custody of evidence

The Registrar shall retain and preserve, as necessary, all the evidence and other materials offered during the hearing, subject to any order of the Trial Chamber.

Rule 139
Decision on admission of guilt

1. After having proceeded in accordance with article 65, paragraph 1, the Trial Chamber, in order to decide whether to proceed in accordance with article 65, paragraph 4, may invite the views of the Prosecutor and the defence.

2. The Trial Chamber shall then make its decision on the admission of guilt and shall give reasons for this decision, which shall be placed on the record.

Rule 140
Directions for the conduct of the proceedings and testimony

1. If the Presiding Judge does not give directions under article 64, paragraph 8, the Prosecutor and the defence shall agree on the order and manner in which the evidence shall be submitted to the Trial Chamber. If no agreement can be reached, the Presiding Judge shall issue directions.

2. In all cases, subject to article 64, paragraphs 8 (b) and 9, article 69, paragraph 4, and rule 88, sub-rule 5, a witness may be questioned as follows:

(a) A party that submits evidence in accordance with article 69, paragraph 3, by way of a witness, has the right to question that witness;

(b) The prosecution and the defence have the right to question that witness about relevant matters related to the witness's testimony and its reliability, the credibility of the witness and other relevant matters;

(c) The Trial Chamber has the right to question a witness before or after a witness is questioned by a participant referred to in sub-rules 2 (a) or (b);

(d) The defence shall have the right to be the last to examine a witness.

3. Unless otherwise ordered by the Trial Chamber, a witness other than an expert, or an investigator if he or she has not yet testified, shall not be present when the testimony of another witness is given. However, a witness who has heard the testimony of another witness shall not for that reason alone be disqualified from testifying. When a witness testifies after hearing the testimony of others, this fact shall be noted in the record and considered by the Trial Chamber when evaluating the evidence.

Rule 141
Closure of evidence and closing statements

1. The Presiding Judge shall declare when the submission of evidence is closed.

2. The Presiding Judge shall invite the Prosecutor and the defence to make their closing statements. The defence shall always have the opportunity to speak last.

Rule 142
Deliberations

1. After the closing statements, the Trial Chamber shall retire to deliberate, in camera. The Trial Chamber shall inform all those who participated in the proceedings of the date on which the Trial Chamber will pronounce its decision. The pronouncement shall be made within a reasonable period of time after the Trial Chamber has retired to deliberate.

2. When there is more than one charge, the Trial Chamber shall decide separately on each charge. When there is more than one accused, the Trial Chamber shall decide separately on the charges against each accused.

Rule 143
Additional hearings on matters relatedto sentence or reparations

Pursuant to article 76, paragraphs 2 and 3, for the purpose of holding a further hearing on matters related to sentence and, if applicable, reparations, the Presiding Judge shall set the date of the further hearing. This hearing can be postponed, in exceptional circumstances, by the Trial Chamber, on its own motion or at the request of the Prosecutor, the defence or the legal representatives of the victims participating in the proceedings pursuant to rules 89 to 91 and, in respect of reparations hearings, those victims who have made a request under rule 94.

Rule 144
Delivery of the decisions of the Trial Chamber

1. Decisions of the Trial Chamber concerning admissibility of a case, the jurisdiction of the Court, criminal responsibility of the accused, sentence and reparations shall be pronounced in public and, wherever possible, in the presence of the accused, the Prosecutor, the victims or the legal representatives of the victims participating in the proceedings pursuant to rules 89 to 91, and the representatives of the States which have participated in the proceedings.

2. Copies of all the above-mentioned decisions shall be provided as soon as possible to:

(a) All those who participated in the proceedings, in a working language of the Court;

(b) The accused, in a language he or she fully understands or speaks, if necessary to meet the requirements of fairness under article 67, paragraph 1 (f).

Chapter 7
Penalties

Rule 145
Determination of sentence

1. In its determination of the sentence pursuant to article 78, paragraph 1, the Court shall:

(a) Bear in mind that the totality of any sentence of imprisonment and fine, as the case may be, imposed under article 77 must reflect the culpability of the convicted person;

(b) Balance all the relevant factors, including any mitigating and aggravating factors and consider the circumstances both of the convicted person and of the crime;

(c) In addition to the factors mentioned in article 78, paragraph 1, give consideration, *inter alia*, to the extent of the damage caused, in particular the harm caused to the victims and their families, the nature of the unlawful behaviour and the means employed to execute the crime; the

degree of participation of the convicted person; the degree of intent; the circumstances of manner, time and location; and the age, education, social and economic condition of the convicted person.

2. In addition to the factors mentioned above, the Court shall take into account, as appropriate:

(a) Mitigating circumstances such as:

(i) The circumstances falling short of constituting grounds for exclusion of criminal responsibility, such as substantially diminished mental capacity or duress;

(ii) The convicted person's conduct after the act, including any efforts by the person to compensate the victims and any cooperation with the Court;

(b) As aggravating circumstances:

(i) Any relevant prior criminal convictions for crimes under the jurisdiction of the Court or of a similar nature;

(ii) Abuse of power or official capacity;

(iii) Commission of the crime where the victim is particularly defenceless;

(iv) Commission of the crime with particular cruelty or where there were multiple victims;

(v) Commission of the crime for any motive involving discrimination on any of the grounds referred to in article 21, paragraph 3;

(vi) Other circumstances which, although not enumerated above, by virtue of their nature are similar to those mentioned.

3. Life imprisonment may be imposed when justified by the extreme gravity of the crime and the individual circumstances of the convicted person, as evidenced by the existence of one or more aggravating circumstances.

Rule 146
Imposition of fines under article 77

1. In determining whether to order a fine under article 77, paragraph 2 (a), and in fixing the amount of the fine, the Court shall determine whether imprisonment is a sufficient penalty. The Court shall give due consideration to the financial capacity of the convicted person, including any orders for forfeiture in accordance with article 77, paragraph 2 (b), and, as appropriate, any orders for reparation in accordance with article 75. The Court shall take into account, in addition to the factors referred to in rule 145, whether and to what degree the crime was motivated by personal financial gain.

2. A fine imposed under article 77, paragraph 2 (a), shall be set at an appropriate level. To this end, the Court shall, in addition to the factors referred to above, in particular take into consideration the damage and injuries caused as well as the proportionate gains derived from the crime by the perpetrator. Under no circumstances may the total amount exceed

75 per cent of the value of the convicted person's identifiable assets, liquid or realizable, and property, after deduction of an appropriate amount that would satisfy the financial needs of the convicted person and his or her dependants.

3. In imposing a fine, the Court shall allow the convicted person a reasonable period in which to pay the fine. The Court may provide for payment of a lump sum or by way of instalments during that period.

4. In imposing a fine, the Court may, as an option, calculate it according to a system of daily fines. In such cases, the minimum duration shall be 30 days and the maximum duration five years. The Court shall decide the total amount in accordance with sub-rules 1 and 2. It shall determine the amount of daily payment in the light of the individual circumstances of the convicted person, including the financial needs of his or her dependants.

5. If the convicted person does not pay the fine imposed in accordance with the conditions set above, appropriate measures may be taken by the Court pursuant to rules 217 to 222 and in accordance with article 109. Where, in cases of continued wilful non-payment, the Presidency, on its own motion or at the request of the Prosecutor, is satisfied that all available enforcement measures have been exhausted, it may as a last resort extend the term of imprisonment for a period not to exceed a quarter of such term or five years, whichever is less. In the determination of such period of extension, the Presidency shall take into account the amount of the fine, imposed and paid. Any such extension shall not apply in the case of life imprisonment. The extension may not lead to a total period of imprisonment in excess of 30 years.

6. In order to determine whether to order an extension and the period involved, the Presidency shall sit in camera for the purpose of obtaining the views of the sentenced person and the Prosecutor. The sentenced person shall have the right to be assisted by counsel.

7. In imposing a fine, the Court shall warn the convicted person that failure to pay the fine in accordance with the conditions set out above may result in an extension of the period of imprisonment as described in this rule.

Rule 147
Orders of forfeiture

1. In accordance with article 76, paragraphs 2 and 3, and rules 63, sub-rule 1, and 143, at any hearing to consider an order of forfeiture, Chamber shall hear evidence as to the identification and location of specific proceeds, property or assets which have been derived directly or indirectly from the crime.

2. If before or during the hearing, a Chamber becomes aware of any bona fide third party who appears to have an interest in relevant proceeds, property or assets, it shall give notice to that third party.

3. The Prosecutor, the convicted person and any bona fide third party with an interest in the relevant proceeds, property or assets may submit evidence relevant to the issue.

4. After considering any evidence submitted, a Chamber may issue an order of forfeiture in relation to specific proceeds, property or assets if it is satisfied that these have been derived directly or indirectly from the crime.

Rule 148
Orders to transfer fines or forfeitures to the Trust Fund

Before making an order pursuant to article 79, paragraph 2, a Chamber may request the representatives of the Fund to submit written or oral observations to it.

Chapter 8
Appeal and revision

Section I
General provisions

Rule 149
Rules governing proceedings in the Appeals Chamber

Parts 5 and 6 and rules governing proceedings and the submission of evidence in the Pre-Trial and Trial Chambers shall apply *mutatis mutandis* to proceedings in the Appeals Chamber.

Section II
Appeals against convictions, acquittals, Sentences and reparation orders

Rule 150
Appeal

1. Subject to sub-rule 2, an appeal against a decision of conviction or acquittal under article 74, a sentence under article 76 or a reparation order under article 75 may be filed not later than 30 days from the date on which the party filing the appeal is notified of the decision, the sentence or the reparation order.

2. The Appeals Chamber may extend the time limit set out in sub-rule 1, for good cause, upon the application of the party seeking to file the appeal.

3. The appeal shall be filed with the Registrar.

4. If an appeal is not filed as set out in sub-rules 1 to 3, the decision, the sentence or the reparation order of the Trial Chamber shall become final.

Rule 151
Procedure for the appeal

1. Upon the filing of an appeal under rule 150, the Registrar shall transmit the trial record to the Appeals Chamber.

2. The Registrar shall notify all parties who participated in the proceedings before the Trial Chamber that an appeal has been filed.

Rule 152
Discontinuance of the appeal

1. Any party who has filed an appeal may discontinue the appeal at any time before judgement has been delivered. In such case, the party shall file with the Registrar a written notice of discontinuance of appeal. The Registrar shall inform the other parties that such a notice has been filed.

2. If the Prosecutor has filed an appeal on behalf of a convicted person in accordance with article 81, paragraph 1 (b), before filing any notice of discontinuance, the Prosecutor shall inform the convicted person that he or she intends to discontinue the appeal in order to give him or her the opportunity to continue the appeal proceedings.

Rule 153
Judgement on appeals against reparation orders

1. The Appeals Chamber may confirm, reverse or amend a reparation order made under article 75.

2. The judgement of the Appeals Chamber shall be delivered in accordance with article 83, paragraphs 4 and 5.

Section III
Appeals against other decisions

Rule 154
Appeals that do not require the leave of the Court

1. An appeal may be filed under article 81, paragraph 3 (c) (ii), or article 82, paragraph 1 (a) or (b), not later than five days from the date upon which the party filing the appeal is notified of the decision.

2. An appeal may be filed under article 82, paragraph 1 (c), not later than two days from the date upon which the party filing the appeal is notified of the decision.

3. Rule 150, sub-rules 3 and 4, shall apply to appeals filed under sub-rules 1 and 2 of this rule.

Rule 155
Appeals that require leave of the Court

1. When a party wishes to appeal a decision under article 82, paragraph 1 (d), or article 82, paragraph 2, that party shall, within five days of being notified of that decision, make a written application to the Chamber that gave the decision, setting out the reasons for the request for leave to appeal.

2. The Chamber shall render a decision and shall notify all parties who participated in the proceedings that gave rise to the decision referred to in sub-rule 1.

Rule 156
Procedure for the appeal

1. As soon as an appeal has been filed under rule 154 or as soon as leave to appeal has been granted under rule 155, the Registrar shall transmit to the Appeals Chamber the record of the proceedings of the Chamber that made the decision that is the subject of the appeal.

2. The Registrar shall give notice of the appeal to all parties who participated in the proceedings before the Chamber that gave the decision that is the subject of the appeal, unless they have already been notified by the Chamber under rule 155, sub-rule 2.

3. The appeal proceedings shall be in writing unless the Appeals Chamber decides to convene a hearing.

4. The appeal shall be heard as expeditiously as possible.

5. When filing the appeal, the party appealing may request that the appeal have suspensive effect in accordance with article 82, paragraph 3.

Rule 157
Discontinuance of the appeal

Any party who has filed an appeal under rule 154 or who has obtained the leave of a Chamber to appeal a decision under rule 155 may discontinue the appeal at any time before judgement has been delivered. In such case, the party shall file with the Registrar a written notice of discontinuance of appeal. The Registrar shall inform the other parties that such a notice has been filed.

Rule 158
Judgement on the appeal

1. An Appeals Chamber which considers an appeal referred to in this section may confirm, reverse or amend the decision appealed.

2. The judgement of the Appeals Chamber shall be delivered in accordance with article 83, paragraph 4.

Section IV
Revision of conviction or sentence

Rule 159
Application for revision

1. An application for revision provided for in article 84, paragraph 1, shall be in writing and shall set out the grounds on which the revision is sought. It shall as far as possible be accompanied by supporting material.

2. The determination on whether the application is meritorious shall be taken by a majority of the judges of the Appeals Chamber and shall be supported by reasons in writing.

3. Notification of the decision shall be sent to the applicant and, as far as possible, to all the parties who participated in the proceedings related to the initial decision.

Rule 160
Transfer for the purpose of revision

1. For the conduct of the hearing provided for in rule 161, the relevant Chamber shall issue its order sufficiently in advance to enable the transfer of the sentenced person to the seat of the Court, as appropriate.

2. The determination of the Court shall be communicated without delay to the State of enforcement.

3. The provisions of rule 206, sub-rule 3, shall be applicable.

Rule 161
Determination on revision

1. On a date which it shall determine and shall communicate to the applicant and to all those having received notification under rule 159, sub-rule 3, the relevant Chamber shall hold a hearing to determine whether the conviction or sentence should be revised.

2. For the conduct of the hearing, the relevant Chamber shall exercise, *mutatis mutandis*, all the powers of the Trial Chamber pursuant to Part 6 and the rules governing proceedings and the submission of evidence in the Pre-Trial and Trial Chambers.

3. The determination on revision shall be governed by the applicable provisions of article 83, paragraph 4.

Chapter 9
Offences and misconduct against the Court

Section I
Offences against the administration of justice under article 70

Rule 162
Exercise of jurisdiction

1. Before deciding whether to exercise jurisdiction, the Court may consult with States Parties that may have jurisdiction over the offence.

2. In making a decision whether or not to exercise jurisdiction, the Court may consider, in particular:

(a) The availability and effectiveness of prosecution in a State Party;

(b) The seriousness of an offence;

(c) The possible joinder of charges under article 70 with charges under articles 5 to 8;

(d) The need to expedite proceedings;

(e) Links with an ongoing investigation or a trial before the Court; and

(f) Evidentiary considerations.

3. The Court shall give favourable consideration to a request from the host State for a waiver of the power of the Court to exercise jurisdiction in cases where the host State considers such a waiver to be of particular importance.

4. If the Court decides not to exercise its jurisdiction, it may request a State Party to exercise jurisdiction pursuant to article 70, paragraph 4.

Rule 163
Application of the Statute and the Rules

1. Unless otherwise provided in sub-rules 2 and 3, rule 162 and rules 164 to 169, the Statute and the Rules shall apply *mutatis mutandis* to the Court's investigation, prosecution and punishment of offences defined in article 70.

2. The provisions of Part 2, and any rules there under, shall not apply, with the exception of article 21.

3. The provisions of Part 10, and any rules there under, shall not apply, with the exception of articles 103, 107, 109 and 111.

Rule 164
Periods of limitation

1. If the Court exercises jurisdiction in accordance with rule 162, it shall apply the periods of limitation set forth in this rule.

2. Offences defined in article 70 shall be subject to a period of limitation of five years from the date on which the offence was committed, provided that during this period no investigation or prosecution has been initiated. The period of limitation shall be interrupted if an investigation or prosecution has been initiated during this period, either before the Court or by a State Party with jurisdiction over the case pursuant to article 70, paragraph 4 (a).

3. Enforcement of sanctions imposed with respect to offences defined in article 70 shall be subject to a period of limitation of 10 years from the date on which the sanction has become final. The period of limitation shall be interrupted with the detention of the convicted person or while the person concerned is outside the territory of the States Parties.

Rule 165
Investigation, prosecution and trial

1. The Prosecutor may initiate and conduct investigations with respect to the offences defined in article 70 on his or her own initiative, on the basis of information communicated by a Chamber or any reliable source.

2. Articles 53 and 59, and any rules there under, shall not apply.

3. For purposes of article 61, the Pre-Trial Chamber may make any of the determinations set forth in that article on the basis of written submissions, without a hearing, unless the interests of justice otherwise require.

4. A Trial Chamber may, as appropriate and taking into account the rights of the defence, direct that there be joinder of charges under article 70 with charges under articles 5 to 8.

Rule 166
Sanctions under article 70

1. If the Court imposes sanctions with respect to article 70, this rule shall apply.

2. Article 77, and any rules there under, shall not apply, with the exception of an order of forfeiture under article 77, paragraph 2 (b), which may be ordered in addition to imprisonment or a fine or both.

3. Each offence may be separately fined and those fines may be cumulative. Under no circumstances may the total amount exceed 50 per cent of the value of the convicted person's identifiable assets, liquid or realizable, and property, after deduction of an appropriate amount that

would satisfy the financial needs of the convicted person and his or her dependants.

4. In imposing a fine the Court shall allow the convicted person a reasonable period in which to pay the fine. The Court may provide for payment of a lump sum or by way of instalments during that period.

5. If the convicted person does not pay a fine imposed in accordance with the conditions set forth in sub-rule 4, appropriate measures may be taken by the Court pursuant to rules 217 to 222 and in accordance with article 109. Where, in cases of continued wilful non-payment, the Court, on its own motion or at the request of the Prosecutor, is satisfied that all available enforcement measures have been exhausted, it may as a last resort impose a term of imprisonment in accordance with article 70, paragraph 3. In the determination of such term of imprisonment, the Court shall take into account the amount of fine paid.

Rule 167
International cooperation and judicial assistance

1. With regard to offences under article 70, the Court may request a State to provide any form of international cooperation or judicial assistance corresponding to those forms set forth in Part 9. In any such request, the Court shall indicate that the basis for the request is an investigation or prosecution of offences under article 70.

2. The conditions for providing international cooperation or judicial assistance to the Court with respect to offences under article 70 shall be those set forth in article 70, paragraph 2.

Rule 168
Ne bis in idem

In respect of offences under article 70, no person shall be tried before the Court with respect to conduct which formed the basis of an offence for which the person has already been convicted or acquitted by the Court or another court.

Rule 169
Immediate arrest

In the case of an alleged offence under article 70 committed in the presence of a Chamber, the Prosecutor may orally request that Chamber to order the immediate arrest of the person concerned.

Section II
Misconduct before the Court under article 71

Rule 170
Disruption of proceedings

Having regard to article 63, paragraph 2, the Presiding Judge of the Chamber dealing with the matter may, after giving a warning:

(a) Order a person disrupting the proceedings of the Court to leave or be removed from the courtroom; or,

(b) In case of repeated misconduct, order the interdiction of that person from attending the proceedings.

Rule 171
Refusal to comply with a direction by the Court

1. When the misconduct consists of deliberate refusal to comply with an oral or written direction by the Court, not covered by rule 170, and that direction is accompanied by a warning of sanctions in case of breach, the Presiding Judge of the Chamber dealing with the matter may order the interdiction of that person from the proceedings for a period not exceeding 30 days or, if the misconduct is of a more serious nature, impose a fine.

2. If the person committing misconduct as described in sub-rule 1 is an official of the Court, or a defence counsel, or a legal representative of victims, the Presiding Judge of the Chamber dealing with the matter may also order the interdiction of that person from exercising his or her functions before the Court for a period not exceeding 30 days.

3. If the Presiding Judge in cases under sub-rules 1 and 2 considers that a longer period of interdiction is appropriate, the Presiding Judge shall refer the matter to the Presidency, which may hold a hearing to determine whether to order a longer or permanent period of interdiction.

4. A fine imposed under sub-rule 1 shall not exceed 2,000 euros, or the equivalent amount in any currency, provided that in cases of continuing misconduct, a new fine may be imposed on each day that the misconduct continues, and such fines shall be cumulative.

5. The person concerned shall be given an opportunity to be heard before a sanction for misconduct, as described in this rule, is imposed.

Rule 172
Conduct covered by both articles 70 and 71

If conduct covered by article 71 also constitutes one of the offences defined in article 70, the Court shall proceed in accordance with article 70 and rules 162 to 169.

Chapter 10
Compensation to an arrested or convicted person

Rule 173
Request for compensation

1. Anyone seeking compensation on any of the grounds indicated in article 85 shall submit a request, in writing, to the Presidency, which shall designate a Chamber composed of three judges to consider the request. These judges shall not have participated in any earlier judgement of the Court regarding the person making the request.

2. The request for compensation shall be submitted not later than six months from the date the person making the request was notified of the decision of the Court concerning:

(a) The unlawfulness of the arrest or detention under article 85, paragraph 1;

(b) The reversal of the conviction under article 85, paragraph 2;

(c) The existence of a grave and manifest miscarriage of justice under article 85, paragraph 3.

3. The request shall contain the grounds and the amount of compensation requested.

4. The person requesting compensation shall be entitled to legal assistance.

Rule 174
Procedure for seeking compensation

1. A request for compensation and any other written observation by the person filing the request shall be transmitted to the Prosecutor, who shall have an opportunity to respond in writing. Any observations by the Prosecutor shall be notified to the person filing the request.

2. The Chamber designated under rule 173, sub-rule 1, may either hold a hearing or determine the matter on the basis of the request and any written observations by the Prosecutor and the person filing the request. A hearing shall be held if the Prosecutor or the person seeking compensation so requests.

3. The decision shall be taken by the majority of the judges. The decision shall be notified to the Prosecutor and to the person filing the request.

Rule 175
Amount of compensation

In establishing the amount of any compensation in conformity with article 85, paragraph 3, the Chamber designated under rule 173, sub-rule 1, shall take into consideration the consequences of the grave and manifest miscarriage of justice on the personal, family, social and professional situation of the person filing the request.

Chapter 11
International cooperation and judicial assistance

Section 1
Requests for cooperation under article 87

Rule 176
Organs of the Court responsible for the transmission and receipt of any communications relating to international cooperation and judicial assistance

1. Upon and subsequent to the establishment of the Court, the Registrar shall obtain from the Secretary-General of the United Nations any communication made by States pursuant to article 87, paragraphs 1 (a) and 2.

2. The Registrar shall transmit the requests for cooperation made by the Chambers and shall receive the responses, information and documents from requested States. The Office of the Prosecutor shall transmit the requests for cooperation made by the Prosecutor and shall receive the responses, information and documents from requested States.

3. The Registrar shall be the recipient of any communication from States concerning subsequent changes in the designation of the national channels charged with receiving requests for cooperation, as well as of any change in the language in which requests for cooperation should be made, and shall, upon request, make such information available to States Parties as may be appropriate.

4. The provisions of sub-rule 2 are applicable *mutatis mutandis* where the Court requests information, documents or other forms of cooperation and assistance from an intergovernmental organization.

5. The Registrar shall transmit any communications referred to in sub-rules 1 and 3 and rule 177, sub-rule 2, as appropriate, to the Presidency or the Office of the Prosecutor, or both.

Rule 177
Channels of communication

1. Communications concerning the national authority charged with receiving requests for cooperation made upon ratification, acceptance,

approval or accession shall provide all relevant information about such authorities.

2. When an intergovernmental organization is asked to assist the Court under article 87, paragraph 6, the Registrar shall, when necessary, ascertain its designated channel of communication and obtain all relevant information relating thereto.

Rule 178

Language chosen by States Parties under article 87, paragraph 2

1. When a requested State Party has more than one official language, it may indicate upon ratification, acceptance, approval or accession that requests for cooperation and any supporting documents can be drafted in any one of its official languages.

2. When the requested State Party has not chosen a language for communication with the Court upon ratification, acceptance, accession or approval, the request for cooperation shall either be in or be accompanied by a translation into one of the working languages of the Court pursuant to article 87, paragraph 2.

Rule 179

Language of requests directed to States not party to the Statute

When a State not party to the Statute has agreed to provide assistance to the Court under article 87, paragraph 5, and has not made a choice of language for such requests, the requests for cooperation shall either be in or be accompanied by a translation into one of the working languages of the Court.

Rule 180

Changes in the channels of communication or the languages of requests for cooperation

1. Changes concerning the channel of communication or the language a State has chosen under article 87, paragraph 2, shall be communicated in writing to the Registrar at the earliest opportunity.

2. Such changes shall take effect in respect of requests for cooperation made by the Court at a time agreed between the Court and the State or, in the absence of such an agreement, 45 days after the Court has received the communication and, in all cases, without prejudice to current requests or requests in progress.

Section II
Surrender, transit and competing requests under articles 89 and 90

Rule 181
Challenge to admissibility of a Case before a national court

When a situation described in article 89, paragraph 2, arises, and without prejudice to the provisions of article 19 and of rules 58 to 62 on procedures applicable to challenges to the jurisdiction of the Court or the admissibility of a case, the Chamber dealing with the case, if the admissibility ruling is still pending, shall take steps to obtain from the requested State all the relevant information about the *ne bis in idem* challenge brought by the person.

Rule 182
Request for transit under article 89, paragraph 3 (e)

1. In situations described in article 89, paragraph 3 (e), the Court may transmit the request for transit by any medium capable of delivering a written record.

2. When the time limit provided for in article 89, paragraph 3 (e), has expired and the person concerned has been released, such a release is without prejudice to a subsequent arrest of the person in accordance with the provisions of article 89 or article 92.

Rule 183
Possible temporary surrender

Following the consultations referred to in article 89, paragraph 4, the requested State may temporarily surrender the person sought in accordance with conditions determined between the requested State and the Court. In such case the person shall be kept in custody during his or her presence before the Court and shall be transferred to the requested State once his or her presence before the Court is no longer required, at the latest when the proceedings have been completed.

Rule 184
Arrangements for surrender

1. The requested State shall immediately inform the Registrar when the person sought by the Court is available for surrender.

2. The person shall be surrendered to the Court by the date and in the manner agreed upon between the authorities of the requested State and the Registrar.

3. If circumstances prevent the surrender of the person by the date agreed, the authorities of the requested State and the Registrar shall agree upon a new date and manner by which the person shall be surrendered.

4. The Registrar shall maintain contact with the authorities of the host State in relation to the arrangements for the surrender of the person to the Court.

Rule 185
Release of a person from the custody of the Court other than upon completion of sentence

1. Subject to sub-rule 2, where a person surrendered to the Court is released from the custody of the Court because the Court does not have jurisdiction, the case is inadmissible under article 17, paragraph 1 (b), (c) or (d), the charges have not been confirmed under article 61, the person has been acquitted at trial or on appeal, or for any other reason, the Court shall, as soon as possible, make such arrangements as it considers appropriate for the transfer of the person, taking into account the views of the person, to a State which is obliged to receive him or her, to another State which agrees to receive him or her, or to a State which has requested his or her extradition with the consent of the original surrendering State. In this case, the host State shall facilitate the transfer in accordance with the agreement referred to in article 3, paragraph 2, and the related arrangements.

2. Where the Court has determined that the case is inadmissible under article 17, paragraph 1 (a), the Court shall make arrangements, as appropriate, for the transfer of the person to a State whose investigation or prosecution has formed the basis of the successful challenge to admissibility, unless the State that originally surrendered the person requests his or her return.

Rule 186
Competing requests in the context of a Challenge to the admissibility of the case

In situations described in article 90, paragraph 8, the requested State shall provide the notification of its decision to the Prosecutor in order to enable him or her to act in accordance with article 19, paragraph 10.

Section III
Documents for arrest and surrender under articles 91 and 92

Rule 187
Translation of documents accompanying request for surrender

For the purposes of article 67, paragraph 1 (a), and in accordance with rule 117, sub-rule 1, the request under article 91 shall be accompanied, as appropriate, by a translation of the warrant of arrest or of the judgement of conviction and by a translation of the text of any relevant provisions of the Statute, in a language that the person fully understands and speaks.

Rule 188
Time limit for submission of documents after provisional arrest

For the purposes of article 92, paragraph 3, the time limit for receipt by the requested State of the request for surrender and the documents supporting the request shall be 60 days from the date of the provisional arrest.

Rule 189
Transmission of documents supporting the request

When a person has consented to surrender in accordance with the provisions of article 92, paragraph 3, and the requested State proceeds to surrender the person to the Court, the Court shall not be required to provide the documents described in article 91 unless the requested State indicates otherwise.

Section IV
Cooperation under article 93

Rule 190
Instruction on self-incrimination accompanying request for witness

When making a request under article 93, paragraph 1 (e), with respect to a witness, the Court shall annex an instruction, concerning rule 74 relating to self-incrimination, to be provided to the witness in question, in a language that the person fully understands and speaks.

Rule 191
Assurance provided by the Court under article 93, paragraph 2

The Chamber dealing with the case, on its own motion or at the request of the Prosecutor, defence or witness or expert concerned, may decide, after taking into account the views of the Prosecutor and the witness or expert concerned, to provide the assurance described in article 93, paragraph 2.

Rule 192
Transfer of a person in custody

1. Transfer of a person in custody to the Court in accordance with article 93, paragraph 7, shall be arranged by the national authorities concerned in liaison with the Registrar and the authorities of the host State.

2. The Registrar shall ensure the proper conduct of the transfer, including the supervision of the person while in the custody of the Court.

3. The person in custody before the Court shall have the right to raise matters concerning the conditions of his or her detention with the relevant Chamber.

4. In accordance with article 93, paragraph 7 (b), when the purposes of the transfer have been fulfilled, the Registrar shall arrange for the return of the person in custody to the requested State.

Rule 193
Temporary transfer of the person from the State of enforcement

1. The Chamber that is considering the case may order the temporary transfer from the State of enforcement to the seat of the Court of any person sentenced by the Court whose testimony or other assistance is necessary to the Court. The provisions of article 93, paragraph 7, shall not apply.

2. The Registrar shall ensure the proper conduct of the transfer, in liaison with the authorities of the State of enforcement and the authorities of the host State. When the purposes of the transfer have been fulfilled, the Court shall return the sentenced person to the State of enforcement.

3. The person shall be kept in custody during his or her presence before the Court. The entire period of detention spent at the seat of the Court shall be deducted from the sentence remaining to be served.

Rule 194
Cooperation requested from the Court

1. In accordance with article 93, paragraph 10, and consistent with article 96, *mutatis mutandis*, a State may transmit to the Court a request for cooperation or assistance to the Court, either in or accompanied by a translation into one of the working languages of the Court.

2. Requests described in sub-rule 1 are to be sent to the Registrar, which shall transmit them, as appropriate, either to the Prosecutor or to the Chamber concerned.

3. If protective measures within the meaning of article 68 have been adopted, the Prosecutor or Chamber, as appropriate, shall consider the views of the Chamber which ordered the measures as well as those of the relevant victim or witness, before deciding on the request.

4. If the request relates to documents or evidence as described in article 93, paragraph 10 (b) (ii), the Prosecutor or Chamber, as appropriate, shall obtain the written consent of the relevant State before proceeding with the request.

5. When the Court decides to grant the request for cooperation or assistance from a State, the request shall be executed, insofar as possible, following any procedure outlined therein by the requesting State and permitting persons specified in the request to be present.

Section V
Cooperation under article 98

Rule 195
Provision of information

1. When a requested State notifies the Court that a request for surrender or assistance raises a problem of execution in respect of article 98, the requested State shall provide any information relevant to assist the Court in the application of article 98. Any concerned third State or sending State may provide additional information to assist the Court.

2. The Court may not proceed with a request for the surrender of a person without the consent of a sending State if, under article 98, paragraph 2, such a request would be inconsistent with obligations under an international agreement pursuant to which the consent of a sending State is required prior to the surrender of a person of that State to the Court.

Section VI
Rule of speciality under article 101

Rule 196
Provision of views on article 101, paragraph 1

A person surrendered to the Court may provide views on a perceived violation of the provisions of article 101, paragraph 1.

Rule 197
Extension of the surrender

When the Court has requested a waiver of the requirements of article 101, paragraph 1, the requested State may ask the Court to obtain and provide the views of the person surrendered to the Court.

Chapter 12
Enforcement

Section I
Role of States in enforcement of sentences of imprisonment and change in designation of State of enforcement under articles 103 and 104

Rule 198
Communications between the Court and States

Unless the context otherwise requires, article 87 and rules 176 to 180 shall apply, as appropriate, to communications between the Court and a State on matters relating to enforcement of sentences.

Rule 199
Organ responsible under Part 10

Unless provided otherwise in the Rules, the functions of the Court under Part 10 shall be exercised by the Presidency.

Rule 200
List of States of enforcement

1. A list of States that have indicated their willingness to accept sentenced persons shall be established and maintained by the Registrar.

2. The Presidency shall not include a State on the list provided for in article 103, paragraph 1 (a), if it does not agree with the conditions that such a State attaches to its acceptance. The Presidency may request any additional information from that State prior to taking a decision.

3. A State that has attached conditions of acceptance may at any time withdraw such conditions. Any amendments or additions to such conditions shall be subject to confirmation by the Presidency.

4. A State may at any time inform the Registrar of its withdrawal from the list. Such withdrawal shall not affect the enforcement of the sentences in respect of persons that the State has already accepted.

5. The Court may enter bilateral arrangements with States with a view to establishing a framework for the acceptance of prisoners sentenced by the Court.

Such arrangements shall be consistent with the Statute.

Rule 201
Principles of equitable distribution

Principles of equitable distribution for purposes of article 103, paragraph 3, shall include:

(a) The principle of equitable geographical distribution;

(b) The need to afford each State on the list an opportunity to receive sentenced persons;

(c) The number of sentenced persons already received by that State and other States of enforcement;

(d) Any other relevant factors.

Rule 202
Timing of delivery of the sentenced person to the State of enforcement

The delivery of a sentenced person from the Court to the designated State of enforcement shall not take place unless the decision on the conviction and the decision on the sentence have become final.

Rule 203
Views of the sentenced person

1. The Presidency shall give notice in writing to the sentenced person that it is addressing the designation of a State of enforcement. The sentenced person shall, within such time limit as the Presidency shall prescribe, submit in writing his or her views on the question to the Presidency.

2. The Presidency may allow the sentenced person to make oral presentations.

3. The Presidency shall allow the sentenced person:

(a) To be assisted, as appropriate, by a competent interpreter and to benefit from any translation necessary for the presentation of his or her views;

(b) To be granted adequate time and facilities necessary to prepare for the presentation of his or her views.

Rule 204
Information relating to designation

When the Presidency notifies the designated State of its decision, it shall also transmit the following information and documents:

(a) The name, nationality, date and place of birth of the sentenced person;

(b) A copy of the final judgement of conviction and of the sentence imposed;

(c) The length and commencement date of the sentence and the time remaining to be served;

(d) After having heard the views of the sentenced person, any necessary information concerning the state of his or her health, including any medical treatment that he or she is receiving.

Rule 205
Rejection of designation in a particular case

Where a State in a particular case rejects the designation by the Presidency, the Presidency may designate another State.

Rule 206
Delivery of the sentenced person to the State of enforcement

1. The Registrar shall inform the Prosecutor and the sentenced person of the State designated to enforce the sentence.

2. The sentenced person shall be delivered to the State of enforcement as soon as possible after the designated State of enforcement accepts.

3. The Registrar shall ensure the proper conduct of the delivery of the person in consultation with the authorities of the State of enforcement and the host State.

Rule 207
Transit

1. No authorization is required if the sentenced person is transported by air and no landing is scheduled on the territory of the transit State. If an unscheduled landing occurs on the territory of the transit State, that State shall, to the extent possible under the procedure of national law, detain the sentenced person in custody until a request for transit as provided in sub-rule 2 or a request under article 89, paragraph 1, or article 92 is received.

2. To the extent possible under the procedure of national law, a State Party shall authorize the transit of a sentenced person through its territory and the provisions of article 89, paragraph 3 (b) and (c), and articles 105 and 108 and any rules relating thereto shall, as appropriate, apply. A copy

of the final judgement of conviction and of the sentence imposed shall be attached to such request for transit.

Rule 208
Costs

1. The ordinary costs for the enforcement of the sentence in the territory of the State of enforcement shall be borne by that State.

2. Other costs, including those for the transport of the sentenced person and those referred to in article 100, paragraph 1 (c), (d) and (e), shall be borne by the Court.

Rule 209
Change in designation of State of enforcement

1. The Presidency, acting on its own motion or at the request of the sentenced person or the Prosecutor, may at any time act in accordance with article 104, paragraph 1.

2. The request of the sentenced person or of the Prosecutor shall be made in writing and shall set out the grounds upon which the transfer is sought.

Rule 210
Procedure for change in the Designation of a State of enforcement

1. Before deciding to change the designation of a State of enforcement, the Presidency may:

(a) Request views from the State of enforcement;

(b) Consider written or oral presentations of the sentenced person and the Prosecutor;

(c) Consider written or oral expert opinion concerning, *inter alia*, the sentenced person;

(d) Obtain any other relevant information from any reliable sources.

2. The provisions of rule 203, sub-rule 3, shall apply, as appropriate.

3. If the Presidency refuses to change the designation of the State of enforcement, it shall, as soon as possible, inform the sentenced person, the Prosecutor and the Registrar of its decision and of the reasons therefore. It shall also inform the State of enforcement.

Section II
Enforcement, supervision and transfer under articles 105, 106 and 107

Rule 211
Supervision of enforcement of sentences and conditions of imprisonment

1. In order to supervise the enforcement of sentences of imprisonment, the Presidency:

(a) Shall, in consultation with the State of enforcement, ensure that in establishing appropriate arrangements for the exercise by any sentenced person of his or her right to communicate with the Court about the conditions of imprisonment, the provisions of article 106, paragraph 3, shall be respected;

(b) May, when necessary, request any information, report or expert opinion from the State of enforcement or from any reliable sources;

(c) May, where appropriate, delegate a judge of the Court or a member of the staff of the Court who will be responsible, after notifying the State of enforcement, for meeting the sentenced person and hearing his or her views, without the presence of national authorities;

(d) May, where appropriate, give the State of enforcement an opportunity to comment on the views expressed by the sentenced person under sub-rule 1 (c).

2. When a sentenced person is eligible for a prison programme or benefit available under the domestic law of the State of enforcement which may entail some activity outside the prison facility, the State of enforcement shall communicate that fact to the Presidency, together with any relevant information or observation, to enable the Court to exercise its supervisory function.

Rule 212
Information on location of the person for enforcement of fines, forfeitures or reparation measures

For the purpose of enforcement of fines and forfeiture measures and of reparation measures ordered by the Court, the Presidency may, at any time or at least 30 days before the scheduled completion of the sentence served by the sentenced person, request the State of enforcement to transmit to it the relevant information concerning the intention of that State to authorize the person to remain in its territory or the location where it intends to transfer the person.

Rule 213
Procedure for article 107, paragraph 3

With respect to article 107, paragraph 3, the procedure set out in rules 214 and 215 shall apply, as appropriate.

Section III
Limitation on the prosecution or punishment of other offences under article 108

Rule 214
Request to prosecute or enforce a sentence for prior conduct

1. For the application of article 108, when the State of enforcement wishes to prosecute or enforce a sentence against the sentenced person for any conduct engaged in prior to that person's transfer, it shall notify its intention to the Presidency and transmit to it the following documents:

(a) A statement of the facts of the case and their legal characterization;

(b) A copy of any applicable legal provisions, including those concerning the statute of limitation and the applicable penalties;

(c) A copy of any sentence, warrant of arrest or other document having the same force, or of any other legal writ which the State intends to enforce;

(d) A protocol containing views of the sentenced person obtained after the person has been informed sufficiently about the proceedings.

2. In the event of a request for extradition made by another State, the State of enforcement shall transmit the entire request to the Presidency with a protocol containing the views of the sentenced person obtained after informing the person sufficiently about the extradition request.

3. The Presidency may in all cases request any document or additional information from the State of enforcement or the State requesting extradition.

4. If the person was surrendered to the Court by a State other than the State of enforcement or the State seeking extradition, the Presidency shall consult with the State that surrendered the person and take into account any views expressed by that State.

5. Any information or documents transmitted to the Presidency under sub-rules 1 to 4 shall be transmitted to the Prosecutor, who may comment.

6. The Presidency may decide to conduct a hearing.

Rule 215
Decision on request to prosecute or enforce a sentence

1. The Presidency shall make a determination as soon as possible. This determination shall be notified to all those who have participated in the proceedings.

2. If the request submitted under sub-rules 1 or 2 of rule 214 concerns the enforcement of a sentence, the sentenced person may serve that sentence in the State designated by the Court to enforce the sentence pronounced by it or be extradited to a third State only after having served the full sentence pronounced by the Court, subject to the provisions of article 110.

3. The Presidency may authorize the temporary extradition of the sentenced person to a third State for prosecution only if it has obtained assurances which it deems to be sufficient that the sentenced person will be kept in custody in the third State and transferred back to the State responsible for enforcement of the sentence pronounced by the Court, after the prosecution.

Rule 216
Information on enforcement

The Presidency shall request the State of enforcement to inform it of any important event concerning the sentenced person, and of any prosecution of that person for events subsequent to his or her transfer.

Section IV
Enforcement of fines, for feature measures and reparation orders

Rule 217
Cooperation and measures for enforcement of fines, forfeiture or reparation orders

For the enforcement of fines, forfeiture or reparation orders, the Presidency shall, as appropriate, seek cooperation and measures for enforcement in accordance with Part 9, as well as transmit copies of relevant orders to any State with which the sentenced person appears to have direct connection by reason of either nationality, domicile or habitual residence or by virtue of the location of the sentenced person's assets and property or with which the victim has such connection. The Presidency shall, as appropriate, inform the State of any third-party claims or of the fact that no claim was presented by a person who received notification of any proceedings conducted pursuant to article 75.

Rule 218
Orders for forfeiture and reparations

1. In order to enable States to give effect to an order for forfeiture, the order shall specify:

(a) The identity of the person against whom the order has been issued;

(b) The proceeds, property and assets that have been ordered by the Court to be forfeited; and

(c) That if the State Party is unable to give effect to the order for forfeiture in relation to the specified proceeds, property or assets, it shall take measures to recover the value of the same.

2. In the request for cooperation and measures for enforcement, the Court shall also provide available information as to the location of the proceeds, property and assets that are covered by the order for forfeiture.

3. In order to enable States to give effect to an order for reparations, the order shall specify:

(a) The identity of the person against whom the order has been issued;

(b) In respect of reparations of a financial nature, the identity of the victims to whom individual reparations have been granted, and, where the award for reparations shall be deposited with the Trust Fund, the particulars of the Trust Fund for the deposit of the award; and

(c) The scope and nature of the reparations ordered by the Court, including, where applicable, the property and assets for which restitution has been ordered.

4. Where the Court awards reparations on an individual basis, a copy of the reparation order shall be transmitted to the victim concerned.

Rule 219
Non-modification of orders for reparation

The Presidency shall, when transmitting copies of orders for reparations to States Parties under rule 217, inform them that, in giving effect to an order for reparations, the national authorities shall not modify the reparations specified by the Court, the scope or the extent of any damage, loss or injury determined by the Court or the principles stated in the order, and shall facilitate the enforcement of such order.

Rule 220
Non-modification of judgements in which fines were imposed

When transmitting copies of judgements in which fines were imposed to States Parties for the purpose of enforcement in accordance with article 109 and rule 217, the Presidency shall inform them that in enforcing the fines imposed, national authorities shall not modify them.

Rule 221
Decision on disposition or allocation of property or assets

1. The Presidency shall, after having consulted, as appropriate, with the Prosecutor, the sentenced person, the victims or their legal representatives, the national authorities of the State of enforcement or any relevant third party, or representatives of the Trust Fund provided for in article 79, decide on all matters related to the disposition or allocation of property or assets realized through enforcement of an order of the Court.

2. In all cases, when the Presidency decides on the disposition or allocation of property or assets belonging to the sentenced person, it shall give priority to the enforcement of measures concerning reparations to victims.

Rule 222
Assistance for service or any other measure

The Presidency shall assist the State in the enforcement of fines, forfeiture or reparation orders, as requested, with the service of any relevant notification on the sentenced person or any other relevant persons, or the carrying out of any other measures necessary for the enforcement of the order under the procedure of the national law of the enforcement State.

Section V
Review concerning reduction of sentence under article 110

Rule 223
Criteria for review concerning reduction of sentence

In reviewing the question of reduction of sentence pursuant to article 110, paragraphs 3 and 5, the three judges of the Appeals Chamber shall take into account the criteria listed in article 110, paragraph 4 (a) and (b), and the following criteria:

(a) The conduct of the sentenced person while in detention, which shows a genuine dissociation from his or her crime;

(b) The prospect of the resocialization and successful resettlement of the sentenced person;

(c) Whether the early release of the sentenced person would give rise to significant social instability;

(d) Any significant action taken by the sentenced person for the benefit of the victims as well as any impact on the victims and their families as a result of the early release;

(e) Individual circumstances of the sentenced person, including a worsening state of physical or mental health or advanced age.

Rule 224
Procedure for review concerning reduction of sentence

1. For the application of article 110, paragraph 3, three judges of the Appeals Chamber appointed by that Chamber shall conduct a hearing, unless they decide otherwise in a particular case, for exceptional reasons. The hearing shall be conducted with the sentenced person, who may be assisted by his or her counsel, with interpretation, as may be required. Those three judges shall invite the Prosecutor, the State of enforcement of any penalty under article 77 or any reparation order pursuant to article 75 and, to the extent possible, the victims or their legal representatives who participated in the proceedings, to participate in the hearing or to submit written observations. Under exceptional circumstances, this hearing may be conducted by way of a videoconference or in the State of enforcement by a judge delegated by the Appeals Chamber.

2. The same three judges shall communicate the decision and the reasons for it to all those who participated in the review proceedings as soon as possible.

3. For the application of article 110, paragraph 5, three judges of the Appeals Chamber appointed by that Chamber shall review the question of reduction of sentence every three years, unless it establishes a shorter interval in its decision taken pursuant to article 110, paragraph 3. In case of a significant change in circumstances, those three judges may permit the sentenced person to apply for a review within the three-year period or such shorter period as may have been set by the three judges.

4. For any review under article 110, paragraph 5, three judges of the Appeals Chamber appointed by that Chamber shall invite written representations from the sentenced person or his or her counsel, the Prosecutor, the State of enforcement of any penalty under article 77 and any reparation order pursuant to article 75 and, to the extent possible, the victims or their legal representatives who participated in the proceedings. The three judges may also decide to hold a hearing.

5. The decision and the reasons for it shall be communicated to all those who participated in the review proceedings as soon as possible.

Section VI
Escape

Rule 225
Measures under article 111 in the event of escape

1. If the sentenced person has escaped, the State of enforcement shall, as soon as possible, advise the Registrar by any medium capable of delivering a written record. The Presidency shall then proceed in accordance with Part 9.

2. However, if the State in which the sentenced person is located agrees to surrender him or her to the State of enforcement, pursuant to either international agreements or its national legislation, the State of enforcement shall so advise the Registrar in writing. The person shall be surrendered to the State of enforcement as soon as possible, if necessary in consultation with the Registrar, who shall provide all necessary assistance, including, if necessary, the presentation of requests for transit to the States concerned, in accordance with rule 207. The costs associated with the surrender of the sentenced person shall be borne by the Court if no State assumes responsibility for them.

3. If the sentenced person is surrendered to the Court pursuant to Part 9, the Court shall transfer him or her to the State of enforcement. Nevertheless, the Presidency may, acting on its own motion or at the request of the Prosecutor or of the initial State of enforcement and in accordance with article 103 and rules 203 to 206, designate another State, including the State to the territory of which the sentenced person has fled.

4. In all cases, the entire period of detention in the territory of the State in which the sentenced person was in custody after his or her escape and, where sub-rule 3 is applicable, the period of detention at the seat of the Court following the surrender of the sentenced person from the State in which he or she was located shall be deducted from the sentence remaining to be served.

APPENDIX C

RESOLUTION RC/RES.6

Adopted at the 13th plenary meeting, on 11 June 2010, by consensus RC/Res.6

The crime of aggression

The Review Conference,

Recalling paragraph 1 of article 12 of the Rome Statute,

Recalling paragraph 2 of article 5 of the Rome Statute,

Recalling also paragraph 7 of resolution F, adopted by the United Nations Diplomatic Conference of Plenipotentiaries on the Establishment of an International Criminal Court on 17 July 1998,

Recalling further resolution ICC-ASP/1/Res.1 on the continuity of work in respect of the crime of aggression, and *expressing its appreciation* to the Special Working Group on the Crime of Aggression for having elaborated proposals on a provision on the crime of aggression,

Taking note of resolution ICC-ASP/8/Res.6, by which the Assembly of States Parties forwarded proposals on a provision on the crime of aggression to the Review Conference for its consideration,

Resolved to activate the Court's jurisdiction over the crime of aggression as early as possible,

1. *Decides* to adopt, in accordance with article 5, paragraph 2, of the Rome Statute of the International Criminal Court (hereinafter: "the Statute") the amendments to the Statute contained in annex I of the present resolution, which are subject to ratification or acceptance and shall enter into force in accordance with article 121, paragraph 5; and *notes* that any

State Party may lodge a declaration referred to in article 15 *bis* prior to ratification or acceptance;

2. *Also decides* to adopt the amendments to the Elements of Crimes contained in annex II of the present resolution;

3. *Also decides* to adopt the understandings regarding the interpretation of the abovementioned amendments contained in annex III of the present resolution;

4. *Further decides* to review the amendments on the crime of aggression seven years

after the beginning of the Court's exercise of jurisdiction;

5. *Calls upon* all States Parties to ratify or accept the amendments contained in annex I.

! See Depositary Notification C.N.651.2010 Treaties-8, dated 29 November 2010, available at

Annex I
Amendments to the Rome Statute of the International Criminal Court on the crime of aggression

1. Article 5, paragraph 2, of the Statute is deleted.
2. The following text is inserted after article 8 of the Statute:

Article 8 *bis*
Crime of aggression

1. For the purpose of this Statute, "crime of aggression" means the planning, preparation, initiation or execution, by a person in a position effectively to exercise control over or to direct the political or military action of a State, of an act of aggression which, by its character, gravity and scale, constitutes a manifest violation of the Charter of the United Nations.

2. For the purpose of paragraph 1, "act of aggression" means the use of armed force by a State against the sovereignty, territorial integrity or political independence of another State, or in any other manner inconsistent with the Charter of the United Nations. Any of the following acts, regardless of a declaration of war, shall, in accordance with United Nations General Assembly resolution 3314 (XXIX) of 14 December 1974, qualify as an act of aggression:

(a) The invasion or attack by the armed forces of a State of the territory of another State, or any military occupation, however temporary, resulting from such invasion or attack, or any annexation by the use of force of the territory of another State or part thereof;

(b) Bombardment by the armed forces of a State against the territory of another State or the use of any weapons by a State against the territory of another State;

(c) The blockade of the ports or coasts of a State by the armed forces of another State;

(d) An attack by the armed forces of a State on the land, sea or air forces, or marine and air fleets of another State;

(e) The use of armed forces of one State which are within the territory of another

State with the agreement of the receiving State, in contravention of the conditions provided for in the agreement or any extension of their presence in such territory beyond the termination of the agreement;

(f) The action of a State in allowing its territory, which it has placed at thedisposal of another State, to be used by that other State for perpetrating an act of aggression against a third State;

(g) The sending by or on behalf of a State of armed bands, groups, irregulars or mercenaries, which carry out acts of armed force against another State of such gravity as to amount to the acts listed above, or its substantial involvement therein.

3. The following text is inserted after article 15 of the Statute:

Article 15 *bis*
Exercise of jurisdiction over the crime of aggression (State referral, *proprio motu*)

1. The Court may exercise jurisdiction over the crime of aggression in accordance with article 13, paragraphs (a) and (c), subject to the provisions of this article.

2. The Court may exercise jurisdiction only with respect to crimes of aggression committed one year after the ratification or acceptance of the amendments by thirty States Parties.

3. The Court shall exercise jurisdiction over the crime of aggression in accordance with this article, subject to a decision to be taken after 1 January 2017 by the same majority of States Parties as is required for the adoption of an amendment to the Statute.

4. The Court may, in accordance with article 12, exercise jurisdiction over a crime of aggression, arising from an act of aggression committed by a State Party, unless that State Party has previously declared that it does

not accept such jurisdiction by lodging a declaration with the Registrar. The withdrawal of such a declaration may be effected at anytime and shall be considered by the State Party within three years.

5. In respect of a State that is not a party to this Statute, the Court shall not exercise its jurisdiction over the crime of aggression when committed by that State's nationals or on its territory.

6. Where the Prosecutor concludes that there is a reasonable basis to proceed with an investigation in respect of a crime of aggression, he or she shall first ascertain whether the Security Council has made a determination of an act of aggression committed by the State concerned. The Prosecutor shall notify the Secretary-General of the United Nations of the situation before the Court, including any relevant information and documents.

7. Where the Security Council has made such a determination, the Prosecutor may proceed with the investigation in respect of a crime of aggression.

8. Where no such determination is made within six months after the date of notification, the Prosecutor may proceed with the investigation in respect of a crime of aggression, provided that the Pre-Trial Division has authorized the commencement of the investigation in respect of a crime of aggression in accordance with the procedure contained in article 15, and the Security Council has not decided otherwise in accordance with article16.

9. A determination of an act of aggression by an organ outside the Court shall be without prejudice to the Court's own findings under this Statute.

10. This article is without prejudice to the provisions relating to the exercise of jurisdiction with respect to other crimes referred to in article 5.

4. The following text is inserted after article 15 bis of the Statute:

Article 15 *ter*
Exercise of jurisdiction over the crime of aggression (Security Council referral)

1. The Court may exercise jurisdiction over the crime of aggression in accordance with article 13, paragraph (b), subject to the provisions of this article.

2. The Court may exercise jurisdiction only with respect to crimes of aggression committed one year after the ratification or acceptance of the amendments by thirty States Parties.

3. The Court shall exercise jurisdiction over the crime of aggression in accordance ce with this article, subject to a decision to be taken after 1 January 2017 by the same majority of States Parties as is required for the adoption of an amendment to the Statute.

4. A determination of an act of aggression by an organ outside the Court shall be without prejudice to the Court's own findings under this Statute.

5. This article is without prejudice to the provisions relating to the exercise of jurisdiction with respect to other crimes referred to in article 5.

5. The following text is inserted after article 25, paragraph 3, of the Statute:

3 *bis*. In respect of the crime of aggression, the provisions of this article shall apply only to persons in a position effectively to exercise control over or to direct the political or military action of a State.

6. The first sentence of article 9, paragraph 1, of the Statute is replaced by the following sentence:

1. Elements of Crimes shall assist the Court in the interpretation and application of articles 6, 7, 8 and 8 *bis*.

7. The chapeau of article 20, paragraph 3, of the Statute is replaced by the following paragraph; the rest of the paragraph remains unchanged:

3. No person who has been tried by another court for conduct also proscribed under article 6, 7, 8 or 8 *bis* shall be tried by the Court with respect to the same conduct unless the proceedings in the other court:

Annex II
Amendments to the Elements of Crimes

Article 8 *bis*
Crime of aggression

Introduction

1. It is understood that any of the acts referred to in article 8 *bis*, paragraph 2, qualifyas an act of aggression.

2. There is no requirement to prove that the perpetrator has made a legal evaluation as to whether the use of armed force was inconsistent with the Charter of the United Nations.

3. The term "manifest" is an objective qualification.

4. There is no requirement to prove that the perpetrator has made a legal evaluation as to the "manifest" nature of the violation of the Charter of the United Nations.

Elements

1. The perpetrator planned, prepared, initiated or executed an act of aggression.

2. The perpetrator was a person1 in a position effectively to exercise control over or to direct the political or military action of the State which committed the act of aggression.

3. The act of aggression – the use of armed force by a State against the sovereignty, territorial integrity or political independence of another State, or in any other manner inconsistent with the Charter of the United Nations – was committed.

4. The perpetrator was aware of the factual circumstances that established that such a use of armed force was inconsistent with the Charter of the United Nations.

5. The act of aggression, by its character, gravity and scale, constituted a manifest violation of the Charter of the United Nations.

6. The perpetrator was aware of the factual circumstances that established such a manifest violation of the Charter of the United Nations.

1 With respect to an act of aggression, more than one person may be in a position that meets these criteria.

Annex III
Understandings regarding the amendments to the Rome Statute of the International Criminal Court on the crime of Aggression

Referrals by the Security Council

1. It is understood that the Court may exercise jurisdiction on the basis of a Security Council referral in accordance with article 13, paragraph (b), of the Statute only with respect to crimes of aggression committed after a decision in accordance with article 15 *ter*, paragraph 3, is taken, and one year after the ratification or acceptance of the amendments by thirty States Parties, whichever is later.

2. It is understood that the Court shall exercise jurisdiction over the crime of aggression on the basis of a Security Council referral in accordance with article 13,paragraph (b), of the Statute irrespective of whether the State concerned has accepted the Court's jurisdiction in this regard.

Jurisdiction *ratione temporis*

3. It is understood that in case of article 13, paragraph (a) or (c), the Court may exercise its jurisdiction only with respect to crimes of aggression committed after a decision in accordance with article 15 *bis*, paragraph 3, is taken, and one year after the ratification or acceptance of the amendments by thirty States Parties, whichever is later.

Domestic jurisdiction over the crime of aggression

4. It is understood that the amendments that address the definition of the act of aggression and the crime of aggression do so for the purpose of this Statute only. The amendments shall, in accordance with article 10 of the Rome Statute, not be interpreted as limiting or prejudicing in any way existing or developing rules of international law for purposes other than this Statute.

5. It is understood that the amendments shall not be interpreted as creating the right or obligation to exercise domestic jurisdiction with respect to an act of aggression committed by another State.

Other understandings

6. It is understood that aggression is the most serious and dangerous form of the illegal use of force; and that a determination whether an act of aggression has been committed requires consideration of all the circumstances of each particular case, including the gravity of the acts concerned and their consequences, in accordance with the Charter of the United Nations.

7. It is understood that in establishing whether an act of aggression constitutes a manifest violation of the Charter of the United Nations, the three components of character, gravity and scale must be sufficient to justify a "manifest" determination. No one component can be significant enough to satisfy the manifest standard by itself.

BIBLIOGRAPHY

Abdulai Napoleon (ed.), Genocide in Rwanda, Africa Research & Information Centre (1994).

Abtahi Hirad and Gideon Boas (eds.), The Dynamics of International Criminal Justice - Essays in Honour of Sir Richard May (2005).

Ackerman John E. and Eugène O'Sullivan, Practice and Procedure of the International Criminal Tribunal for the Former Yugoslavia; with selected material from the International Criminal Tribunal for Rwanda (2000).

Adelman Howard and Astri Suhrke (eds.), The Path of a Genocide: The Rwanda Crisis, from Uganda to Zaire (1999).

Akande D., International Law Immunities and the International Criminal Court, American Journal of International Law 407-433 (2004).

—. The jurisdiction of the International Criminal Court over Nationals of Non-Parties: Legal Basis and Limits, Journal of International Criminal Justice 618-650 (2003).

Akehurst Michael, Jurisdiction in International Law, 1972-1973 BYIL 145.

Aksar Yusuf, Implementing International Humanitarian Law: From the Ad Hoc Tribunals to a Permanent International Criminal Court (2000).

—. Implementing International Humanitarian Law: From the Ad Hoc Tribunals to a Permanent International Criminal Court (2004).

Alebeek Rosanne van, From Rome to the Hague: Recent Developments on Immunity Issues in the ICC Statute, 13 Leiden Journal of International Law 485 (2000).

Allmand Warren, The International Criminal Court and the Human Rights Revolution, 46 (1) McGill Law Journal (2000).

Alston and Steiner (eds.), International Human Rights in Context (2000).

Alter R.T., International Criminal Law: A Bittersweet Year for Supporters and Critics of the International Criminal Court, The International Lawyer 541-550 (2003).

Amann D.M. and M.N.S. Sellers, The United States of America and the International Criminal Court, American Journal of Comparative Law 381-404 (2002).

Ambion Bienvenido C., Organization of a Court of International Criminal Jurisdiction, 29 Philoppine Law Journal 345 (1954).

Amnesty International, The International Criminal Court: Making the Right Choices-Part V (1998).

Anderson Benedict, Imagined Communities: Reflections on the Origin and Spread of Nationalism (rev.ed.1991).

Anderson Perry, Arguments within English Marxism (1980).

Andreasen Scott W., The International Criminal Court: Does the Constitution Preclude Its Ratification By the United States? 85 (2) *Iowa Law Review* (2000).

Andreopoulos George J. and Mark R. Shulman (eds.), The Laws of War: Constraints on Warfare in the Western World (1994).

Annan Kofi, Advocating for an International Criminal Court, 21 Fordham International Law Journal 363 (1997).

Aref Mohamed, La Cour Pénale Internationale: une Nouvelle Perspective Pour le Continent Africain, 1 International Law Forum Du Droit International 30 (1999).

Arend Anthony C. and Robert J. Beck, International Law and the Use of Force: Beyond the U.N. Charter Paradigm (1993).

Armstead J. Holmes., The International Criminal Court: History, Development and Status, 38 Santa Clara Law Review 745-835 (1998).

Arnaut Damir, When in Rome? The International Criminal Court and Avenues for U.S. Participation, 43 (2) Virginia Journal of International Law (2003).

Arsanjani Mahnoush H., The Rome Statute of the International Criminal Court, 93 American Journal of International Law 22-43 (1999).

Askin Kelly Dawn, Crimes within the Jurisdiction of the International Criminal Court, 10 (1) Criminal Law Forum 33 (1999).

—. War Crimes against Women: Prosecution in International War Crimes (1997).

Austin John, The Province of Jurisprudence Determined and the Uses of the Study of Jurisprudence (1954).

Ayissi Anatole and Robin-Edward Pulton (eds.), Bound to Cooperate, Conflict, Peace and People in Sierra Leone (2000).

Bachrach Michael, The Permanent International Criminal Court: An Examination of the Statutory Debate, 5 ILSA Journal of International and Comparative Law 139 (1998).

—. The Protection and Rights of Victims under International Criminal Law, 34 (1) The International Lawyer (2000).

Badar Mohamed Elewa and Nora Karsten, Current Development at the International Criminal Tribunals, 8 International Criminal Law Review 353-380 (2008).

Badar Mohamed Elewa, The Mental Element in the Rome Statute of the International Criminal Court: A Commentary from a Comparative Criminal Law Perspective, 19 Criminal Law Forum (2008).

Baez Jose A., An International Crimes Court: Further Tales of the King of Corinth, 23 Georgia Journal of International and Comparative Law 289 (1993).

Balkin J.M., Understanding Legal Understanding: The Legal Subject and the Problem of Legal Coherence, 103 Yale Law Journal 105 (1993).

Ball H., Prosecuting War Crimes and Genocide: The Twentieth Century Experience (1999).

Banton Michael, West African City: A Study of Tribal Life in Freetown (1957).

Barboza Julio, International Criminal Law, 278 Recueil Des Cours 9-200 (1999-2000).

Barnett Michael N., Eyewitness to a Genocide: The United Nations and Rwanda (2002).

Barron Anne, (Legal) Reason and its "Others": Recent Development in Legal Theory, in Introduction to Jurisprudence and Legal Theory: Commentary and Materials 1038-63 (Penner, Schiff and Nobles, eds., 2002).

Barry Brian, Justice as Reciprocity, in Justice (Eugene Kamenka and Alice Erh-Soon Tay, eds., 1979).

Bass Gary Jonathan, Stay the Hand of Vengeance: The Politics of War Crimes Tribunals (2000).

Bassiouni M. Cherif (ed.), International Criminal Law (2d ed. 3 vols., 1999).

—. (ed.), International Criminal Law (3 vols. 1986).

—. (ed.), International Criminal Law (3d ed. 3 vols., 2008).

Bassiouni M. Cherif and Benjamin B. Ferencz, The Crime Against Peace and Aggression: From Its Origins to the ICC, in International Criminal Law, vol I, 207-242 (M. Cherif Bassiouni, ed. 2008).

Bassiouni M. Cherif and Christopher L. Blakesley, The Need for an International Criminal Court in the New International World Order, 25 Vanderbilt Journal of Transnational Law 151 (1992).

Bassiouni M. Cherif and Daniel Derby, Final Report on the Establishment of an International Criminal Court for the Implementation of the Apartheid Convention and Other Relevant Instruments, 7 Hodstra Law Review 523 (1981).

Bassiouni M. Cherif and Edward M. Wise, Aut Dedere, Aut Judicare: The Duty to Extradite or Prosecute in International Law (1995).

Bassiouni M. Cherif and P. Manikas, The Law of The International Criminal Tribunal for The Former Yugoslavia (1996).

Bassiouni M. Cherif and Ved P. Nanda (eds.), A Treatise on International Criminal Law: Crimes and Punishment (2 vols. 1973).

Bassiouni M. Cherif, Protection of Collective Victims in International law, New York Law School Human Rights Annual (1985).

—. A Comprehensive Strategic Approach on International Cooperation for the Prevention, Control and Suppression of International and Transnational Criminality, Including the Establishment of an International Criminal Court, 15 Nova Law Review 353 (1991).

—. A Draft International Criminal Code and Draft Statute for an International Criminal Tribunal (2nd rev. ed. 1987).

—. Combating Impunity for International Crimes, 71 University of Colorado Law Review 409 (2000).

—. Crimes against Humanity in International Criminal Law (1999).

—. Crimes Against Humanity, in International Criminal Law, vol I, 437-492. (M. Cherif Bassiouni, ed. 2008).

—. Crimes Against Humanity: The Need for a Specialized Convention, 31 Columbia Journal of Transnational Law 457 (1994).

—. Draft Statute International Criminal Tribunal, 9 Nowellese Tudes Penaes (1993).

—. Enforcing Human Rights through International Criminal Law and through an International Criminal Tribunal, in Human Rights: An Agenda for the Next Century 524 (Louis Henkin & John Lawrence Hargrove, eds., 1994).

—. Establishing an International Criminal Court: Historical Survey, 149 Military Law Review (1995).

—. From Versailles to Rwanda in Seventy-Five Years: The Need to Establish a Permanent International Criminal Court, 10 Harvard Human Rights Journal 11 (1997).

—. International Recognition of Victims' Rights, 6(2) Human Rights Law Review 203-279 (2006).

—. International Recognition of Victims' Rights, in International Criminal Law, vol III, 635-701 (M. Cherif Bassiouni, ed. 2008).

—. Introduction to International Criminal Law (2003).

—. Introduction to International Humanitarian Law, in International Criminal Law, vol I,269-292 (M. Cherif Bassiouni, ed. 2008).

—. Introduction to Transfer of Criminal Proceedings, in International Criminal Law, vol II 515-519 (M. Cherif Bassiouni, ed. 2008).

—. Issues Pertaining to the Evidentiary Part of International Criminal Law, in International Criminal Law, vol III, 581-602 (M. Cherif Bassiouni, ed. 2008).
—. Law and Practice of the United States, in International Criminal Law,vol II, 269-341 (M. Cherif Bassiouni, ed. 2008).
—. Mixed Models of International Criminal Justice, in International Criminal Law, vol III, 155-194 (M. Cherif Bassiouni, ed. 2008).
—. Negotiating the Treaty of Rome on the Establishment of an International Criminal Court, 43 (2) Correll International Law Journal (1999).
—. Nuremberg Forty Years After, 64 Proc ASIL, 1986.
—. Observation Concerning the 1997-98 Preparatory Committee's Work, 29 Denver Journal of International Law and Policy 397 (1997);.
—. Observations Concerning the Structure of the (Zutphen) Consolidated Text, 13 bis Novelles Etudes Penales 5 (1998).
—. Policy Perspectives Favouring the Establishment of the International Criminal Court, 52 Journal of International Affairs 795-810 (Spring 1999).
—. Principles of Legality in International and Comparative Criminal Law, in International Criminal Law,vol. I, 73-105 (M. Cherif Bassiouni, ed. 2008).
—. The Discipline of International Criminal Law, in International Criminal Law, vol I 3-40 (M. Cherif Bassiouni, ed., 2008).
—. The Duty to Prosecute and/or Extradiate: Aut Dedere Aut Judicare, in International Criminal Law, vol. II, 35-45 (M. Cherif Bassiouni, ed. 2008).
—. The International Criminal Court: Observations and Issues before the 1997-98 Preparatory Committee, and Administrative and Financial Implications (Toulouse: Chicago: Érès; International Human Rights Institute, DePaul University, 1997) (Nouvelles Études Pénales 13) (Joint project of: International Association of Penal Law, International Human Rights Law Institute, DePaul University, International Institute of Higher Studies in Criminal Sciences, International Law Association, American Branch, Committee on ICC).
—. The Making of the International Criminal Court, in International Criminal Law, vol III, 117-154 (M. Cherif Bassiouni, ed. 2008).
—. The Modalities of International Cooperation in Penal Matters, in International Criminal Law, vol II, 3-34 (M. Cherif Bassiouni, ed. 2008).

—. The Normative Framework of International Humanitarian Law: Overlaps, Gaps and Ambiguities, 8 Transnational Law and Comparative Problems 199 (1998).
—. The Normative Framework of International Humanitarian Law: Overlaps, Gaps and Ambiguities, in International Criminal Law, vol I, 493-531 (M. Cherif Bassiouni, ed. 2008).
—. The Ratione Materiae of International Criminal Law, in International Criminal Law,vol. I, 129-203 (M. Cherif Bassiouni, ed. 2008).
—. The Regulation, Control, and Prohibition of the Use of Certain Weapons in the Context of War, in International Criminal Law, vol I, 377-401 (M. Cherif Bassiouni, ed. 2008).
—. The Statute of the International Criminal Court: a Documentary History (1998).
—. The Statute of the International Criminal Court and Related Instruments: Legislative History, 1994-2000 (2001).
—. The Subjects of International Criminal Law: Ratione Personae, in International Criminal Law, vol I, 41-70 (M. Cherif Bassiouni, ed., 2008).
—. The Time Has Come for an International Criminal Court, 1 Indiana International and Comparative Law Review 1-43 (1991).
—. Universal Jurisdiction for International Crimes: Historical Perspectives and Contemporary Practice, in International Criminal Law, vol II 153-199 (M. Cherif Bassiouni, ed. 2008).
Baum L. M., Pursuing Justice in a Climate of Moral Outrage: An Evaluation of the Rights of the Accused in the Rome Statute of the International Criminal Court, 19 Wisconsin international law journal 197 (2001).
Behrens Hans-Jörg, Investigation, Trial and Appeal in the International Criminal Court Statute (Parts V, VI, VIII), 6 European Journal of Crime, Criminal Law and Justice 113 (1998).
Bellamy Alex J., Paul D. Williams and Stuart Griffin (eds.), Understanding Peacekeeping (2004).
Bellot Hugh H.L., Draft Statute for the Permanent International Criminal Court, International Law Association, Report of the Thirty-Third Conference Held at the Riddarhuset and at the Riksdaghust, Stockholm September 8th to 13th, 1924 75 (1925).
Benedetti Fanny and John L. Washburn, Drafting the International Criminal Court Treaty: Two Years to Rome and an Afterword on the Rome Diplomatic Conference, 5 Global Governace 1 (1999).

Benison Audrey I., International Criminal Tribunals: Is There a Substantive Limitation on the Treaty Power? 37 Stanford Journal of Internaitonal Law 75 (2001).

—. War Crimes: A Human Rights Approach to a Humanitarian Law Problem at the International Criminal Court, 88 Georgetown Law Journal 141-176 (1999).

Benton Barbara, Soldiers for Peace: Fifty Years of United Nations Peacekeeping (1996).

Berber F.J., Some Thoughts on the Laws of War and the Punishment of War Crimes, in Essays on International Law (M. K. Nawaz, ed., 1976).

Beresford Stuart and Hafida Lahiouel, The Right to be Defended in Person or Through Legal Assistance and the International Criminal Court, 13 Leiden Journal of International Law 949 (2000).

Berg Bradley E., The 1994 ILC Draft Statute for an International Criminal Court: A Principled Appraisal of Jurisdictional Structure, 28 Case Western Reserve Journal of International Law 221 (1996).

Bergsmo Morten, Occasional Remarks on Certain State Concerns about the Jurisdictional Reach of the International Criminal Court, and Their Possible Implications for the Relationship between the Court and the Security Council, 69 Nordic Journal of International Law 87-113 (no.1, 2000).

Berman Franklin, The Relationship Between the International Criminal Court and the Security Council, in Reflections on the international criminal court: Essays in Honour of Adriaan Bos, 173-80 (Herman von Hebel, Johan G. Lammers and Jolien Schukking, eds. 1999).

Bermann et al George A.., Cases and Materials on European Community Law (1993).

Berry John A. and Carol Pott Berry (eds.), Genocide in Rwanda (1999).

Best Geoffrey, Peace Conferences and the Century of Total War: The 1899 Hague Conference and What Came After, 75 (3) International Affaris (1999).

Bickley L. S., US Resistance to the International Criminal Court: Is the Sword Mightier than the Law, 14 Emory International Law Review 159 (2000).

Black Donald, The Behavior of Law (1976).

Blackesley Christopher L., Obstacles to the Creation of a Permanent War Crimes Tribunal, 18 Fle tcher Forum of World AFF. 77 (1992).

—. Extraterritorial Jurisdiction, in Intrnaitonal Criminal Law, vol II, 85-152 (M. Cherif Bassiouni, ed. 2008).

Bleich Jeffrey L., Complementarity, 13 Nouvelles Etude Penalles 231 (1997)-.

—. Cooperation with National Systems, 13 Nouvelles Etude Penalles 245 (1997).
Bloxham Donald, Genocide on Trial: War Crime Trials and the Formation of Holocaust History and Memory (2001).
Boas Gideon and William A. Schabas (eds.), International Criminal Law Developments in the Case Law of the ICTY (2003).
Boed Roman, The Effect of a Domestic Amnesty on the Ability of Foreign States to Prosecute Alleged Perpetrators of Serious Human Rights Violations, 33 Cornell Internaitonal Law Journal 297 (2000).
—. The International Criminal Tribunal for Rwanda, in International Criminal Law, vol III, 103-116 (M. Cherif Bassiouni, ed. 2008).
Boister Neil, The Exclusion of Treaty Crimes from the Jurisdiction of the Proposed International Criminal Court: Law, Pragmatism, Politics, 3 Journal of Armed Conflict Law 27-43 (No.1, June 1998).
Bolton John R., Courting Danger: What's Wrong with the International Court, No. 54 The National Interest 60-71 (Winter 1998).
Boot Machteld, Genocide, Crimes against Humanity, War Crimes: V. 12: Nullum Crimen Sine Lege and the Subject Matter Jurisdiction of the International Criminal Court (2002).
Bosly Henri D., Actualité du Tribunal International Pénal, 1-2 h's.4Les De Droit Lowain 3 (1995).
Bottigliero Ilaria, Redress for Victims of Crimes under International Law (2004).
Bourdon William, La Cour Pénal Internationale (2000).
Boyle James D.A. (ed.), Critical Legal Studies (1992).
Brackman Arnold C., The Other Nuremberg (1987).
Braeckman Colette, Rwanda: Histoire d'un Génocide (1994).
—. Terreur Africaine. Burundi, Rwanda, Zaïre: Les Racines de la Violence (1996).
Brandon Ben (ed.), The Prosecution of International Crimes: a Practical Guide to Prosecuting ICC Crimes in Commonwealth States (2005).
Brilmayer Lea, American Hegemony: Political Morality in a One-Superpower World (1994).
Broomhall Bruce, International Justice and the International Criminal Court: Between Sovereignty and the Rule of Law (2003).
—. Looking Forward to the Establishment of an International Criminal Court: Between State Consent and the Rule of Law, 8 Criminal Law Forum 317 (1997).
Brown Bartram S., Primacy or Complementarity: Reconciling the Jurisdiction of National Courts and International Criminal tribunals, 23 Yale Journal of Internaitonal Law 383 (1998).

Browning Christopher, The Path to Genocide: Essays on Launching the Final Solution (2002).
Brownlie Ian, International Law and the Use of Force by States (1963).
—. Principles of Public International Law (5th, ed. 1998).
—. Principles of Public International Law (6th, ed. 2003).
Burns Peter, An International Criminal Tribunal: The Difficult Union of Principle and Politics, 5 Criminal Law Forum 341 (1994).
Butz Arthur R., The Hoax of the Twentieth Century: A Case Against the Presumed Extermination of Europe Jewry (2003).
Byron Christine and David Turns, The Preparatory Commission for the International Criminal Court, 50 International and Comparative Law Quarterly 420 (2001).
Caflisch Lucius, The Rome Statute and the European Convention on Human Rights, 23 Human Rights Law Journal 1 (2002).
Cairns Huntington, Plato's Theory of Law, 56 Harvard Law Review 359 (1942).
Capaldo Giuliana Ziccardi and Michele Nino, Globalization of International Law Enforcement Mechanisms: Issues of Legality and Legitimacy, in International Criminal Law, vol II, 47-70 (M. Cherif Bassiouni, ed., 2008).
Carey John and John R. Pritchard (eds.), International Humanitarian Law: Origins, Challenges and Prospects (2000).
Carjeu Pierre, Projet D'une Juridiction Pénales Internationale (1953).
Carpenter A.C., The International Criminal Court and the Crime of Aggression, 64 Nordic Journal of International Law 223 (1995).
Cassese Antonio and Albin Eser (eds.), The Rome Statute of the International Criminal Court: A Commentary (2002).
Cassese Antonio, Albin Eser, Giorgio Gaja and Robert E. Conor, Justice at Nuremberg (1980).
Cassese Antonio, On the Current Trends Towards Criminal Prosecution and Punishment of Breaches of International Humanitarian Law, 9 European Journal of Internaitonal Law 2 (1998).
—. Reflections on International Criminal Justice, 61 Modren Law Review 1 (1998).
—. The Statute of the International Criminal Court: Some Preliminary Reflections, 10 European Journal of International Law 158 (1999).
Castonguay, Jacques Les Casques Bleus au Rwanda (1998).
Choate Joseph H., The Two Hague Conferences (1913).
Chrétien Jean Pierre, Le Défi de l'Ethnisme: Rwanda et Buruni, 1990 - 1996 (1997).
—. The Great Lakes of Africa: Two thousand years of history (2003).

Chryssikos Demostenes, Commentary on the United Nations Draft Model Law on Extradition, in International Criminal Law, vol II, 377-382 (M. Cherif Bassiouni, ed. 2008).

Clark Roger S., The Crime of Aggression and the International Criminal Court, in International Criminal Law, vol, I243-265. (M. Cherif Bassiouni, ed. 2008).

—. The Mental Element in International Criminal Law: The Rome Statute of the International Criminal Court and the Elements of the Offences, 12 *Criminal Law Forum* 291 (2001).

—. The Proposed International Criminal Court: Its Establishment and Its Relationship with the United Nations, 8 Criminal Law Forum 411 (1997).

Combs Nancy Amoury, Plea Bargains in International Criminal Prosecutions, in International Criminal Law, vol III 561-579 (M. Cherif Bassiouni, ed. 2008).

Concannon B. Jr., Beyond Complementarity: The International Criminal Court and National Prosecutions, A View from Haiti, 32 Columbia Journal of Human Rights Law Review 201 (2000).

Copelon Rhonda, Gender Crimes as War Crimes: Integrating Crimes against Women into International Criminal Law, 46 Mcgill Law Journal 217 (2000).

Crane David M., The Special Court for Sierra Leone, in International Criminal Law, vol III 195-218 (M. Cherif Bassiouni, ed. 2008).

Crawford James, Prospects for an International Criminal Court, 48 Current Legal Problems 303 (1995).

—. The ILC's Draft Statute for an International Criminal Tribunal, 88 American Journal of International Law 140 (1994).

Cryer Robert and Neil Boister (eds.), Documents on the Tokyo International Military Tribunal: Charter, Indictment and Judgments (2008).

Cryer Robert, Prosecuting International Crimes: Selectivity and the International Regime (2005).

—. The Doctrinal Foundations of International Criminalization, in International Criminal Law,vol I, 107-128 (M. Cherif Bassiouni, ed. 2008).

Damaska Mirjan, Structures of Authority and Comparative Criminal Procedure, 84 Yale Law Journal 480 (1974).

David Eric and Pascale Heirman., Code de Droit International Pénal 2009 (2e edition, 2009).

David Eric, The Belgian Experience, in International Criminal Law, vol III, 359-383 (M. Cherif Bassiouni, ed. 2008).

—. Principes de Droit des Conflits Armés (2nd ed. 1999).
Davis Melton S., Who Defends Rome (1972).
Davis Michael C., Wolfgang Dietrich, Bettina Scholdan and Dieter Sepp, International Intervention in the Post-Cold War World: Moral Responsibility and Power Politics (2003).
Detmold M.J., The Unity of Law and Morality: A Refutation of Legal Positivism (1984).
Dickinson Laura A., Mercenarism and Private Military Contractors, in International Criminal Law, vol I, 355-375 (M. Cherif Bassiouni, ed. 2008).
Dickson Julie, Evaluation and Legal Theory (2001).
Diehl Paul F., International Peacekeeping (1993).
Dinstein Yoram, International Criminal Law, 20 *Israel Law Review* 206 (1985).
—. Laws of War (1983).
Döhrmann Knut, Preparatory Commission for the International Criminal Court: The Elements of War Crimes, 82 International Review of The Red Cross 771 (2000).
—. The First and Second Sessions of the Preparatory Commission for the International Criminal Court, 2 Yearbook of International Humanitarin Law 283 (1999).
—. Elements of War Crimes under the Rome Statute of the International Criminal Court: Sources and Commentary (2003).
Douzinas Costas, Peter Goodrich and Yifat Hachamovitch, Politics, Postmodernity and Critical Legal Studies (1994).
—. Understanding Criminal Law (1998).
Driscoll W. (ed.), The International Criminal Court: Global Politics and the Quest for Justice (2004).
Dupuy René-Jean (ed.), Manuel sur les Organisations Internationales (1988).
Durch William J. (ed.), Peacekeeping, American Politics and the Uncivil Wars of the 1990s (1996).
—. (ed.), The Evolution of UN Peacekeeping: Case Studies and Comparative Analysis (1993).
Eser Albin, "For Universal Jurisdiction: Against Fletcher's Antagonism", Vol.39, no.4 *Tulsa Law Review* (2004), pp.955-978.
—. "Towards an International Criminal Court: Genesis and Main Feature of the Rome Statute", *Vol.20, n.1 University of Tasmania Law Review (2001),* pp.1-28.
Evered Timothy C. An International Criminal Court: Recent Proposals and Concerns American, 6 Pace International Law Review 121 (1994).

Ewald F., Unger's Philosophy: A Critical Legal Study, 5 Yale Law Journal 665 (1988).
Feld Werner, The Court of the European Communities: New Dimension in International Adjudication (1964).
Ferencz Benjamin B., An International Criminal Court, A Step Toward Peace: A Documentary History (2 vols 1980).
—. Defining International Aggression: The Search for World Peace - A Documentary History and Analysis (1975).
—. An International Criminal Code and Court: Why They Stand and Where They're Going, 30 Columbia Journal of Transnational Law 375 (1992).
Fife Rolf Einer, Penalties in The International Criminal Court: The making of the Rome statute 470 (Roy S. Lee, ed., 1999).
Finnis John (ed.), Natural Law (1991).
—. Aquinas: Moral, Political and Legal Theory (1998).
—. Fundamentals of Ethics (1983).
—. Natural Law and Natural Rights (1980).
Franck Thomas M., Fairness in International Law and Institutions (1997).
—. The Power of Legitimacy Among Nations (1990).
—. Who Killed Article 2(4): Changing Norms Governing the Use of Force by States, 64 American Journal of International Law 809 (1970).
Friedlander Robert A., The Foundations of International Criminal Law: A Present-Day Inquiry, 15 Case Western Reserve Journal of International Law 13 (1983).
Friedman Thomas L., The Lexus and the Olive Tree: Understanding Globalism (1999).
Friman H., Rights of Persons Suspected or Accused of a Crime, in The International Criminal Court: The Making of the Rome Statute: Issues, Negotiations, and Results, 247-62 (Roy S. Lee, ed. 1999).
Fuller Lon Luvios, The Morality of Law (2nd ed 1969).
Fuller S., Playing Without a Full Deck: Scientific Realism and the Cognitive Limits of Legal Theory, 97 Yale Law Journal 549 (1988).
Garcia-Mora M. R., Crimes Against Peace, 34 *Fordham Law Review* (1965).
Gardam Judith G. and Michelle J. Jarvis, Women, Armed Conflict and International Law (2001).
Garkawe Sam, The Victim-Related Provisions of the Statute of the International Criminal Court: A Victimology Analysis, 8 International Review of Victomology 284 (2001).

Garraway Charles, Superior Orders and the International Criminal Court: Justice Delivered or Justice Denied, 836 International Review of the Red Cross 785 (1999).

Gavison Ruth (ed.), Issues in Contemporary Legal Philosophy: The Influence of H.L.A. Hart (1987).

Gavron Jessica, Amnesties in the Light of Developments in International Law and the Establishment of the International Criminal Court, 51 International Law and Comparative Quarterly 111 (2002).

George Robert P., Natural Law Theory: Contemporary Essays (1994).

—. (ed.), The Autonomy of Law: Essays on Legal Positivism (1995).

Ginsburgs George and V.N. Kudriavtsev (eds.) The Nuremberg Trial and International Law (1990).

Glaser Stefan, Droit International Pénal Conventionnel (2 vols 1970).

—. Droit International Pénal: son Origine, son État Actuel et son Développement, L'indice Pénale (1968).

—. Infraction Internationale (1957).

—. Introduction à L'étude du Droit International Pénal (1954).

Gleck Sheldon, By what Tribunal shall War Offenders be Tried? 56 *Harvard Law Review* 1059 (1942-3).

—. The Nuremberg Trial and Aggressive War (New York, 1946).

Goldstone Richard J., For Humanity: Reflections of a War Crimes Investigator (2000).

Golsan Richard J. (ed.), Memory and Justice on Trial: The Papon Affair (2000).

Gomaa Mohammed M., The Definition of the Crime of Aggression and the ICC Jurisdiction over that Crime, in International Criminal Court and the Crime of Aggression (Mauro Politi and Guiseppe Nesi eds., 2004).

Goodrich Peter, Languages of Law (1990).

—. Reading the Law: A Critical Introduction to legal Method and Techniques (1986).

Government Commissioner of the General Tribunal of the Military Government for the French Zone of Occupation in Germany v. Roechling (Roechlingcase), vol. 14 (Trials), 1950.

Gowlland-Debbas Vera, The Relationship Between the Security Council and the Projected International Criminal Court, 3 Journal of Armed Conflict Law 97 (1998).

Green Leslie C., The Contemporary Law of Armed Conflict (2nd ed. 2000).

Greenberg Michael D., Creating an International Criminal Court, 10 Boston University International Law Journal 119 (1992).

Gully-Hart Paul, The European Approach to Extradition, in International Criminal Law, vol II, 343-376 (M. Cherif Bassiouni, ed. 2008).

Hacker P.M.S. and J. Raz, (eds.), Law, Morality and Society: Essays in Honour of H.L.A. Hart (1977).

Hall Christopher Keith, The Fifth Session of the UN Preparatory Committee on the Establishment of an International Criminal Court, 92 American Jorunal of International Law 331-339 (1998).

—. The First Proposal for a Permanent International Criminal Court, 322 international review of the red cross 75-74 (1998).

—. The First Two Sessions of the UN Preparatory Committee on the Establishment of an International Criminal Court, 91 American Journal of International Law 177 (1997).

Hanna Michael Wahid, An Historical Overview of National Prosecutions for International Crimes, in International Criminal Law, vol. III, 297-328 (M. Cherif Bassiouni, ed. 2008).

Harris David, Progress and Problems in Establishing an International Criminal Court, 3 Journal of Armed Conflict Law 1 (1998).

Harris J.W., Legal Philosophies (2nd edn. 1997).

Hart H.L.A., Essays in Jurisprudence and Philosophy (1983).

—. The Concept of Law, (P.A. Bulloch and J. Raz, ed 1994).

—. The Concept of Law (1961).

Haye Eve La, The Jurisdiction of the International Criminal Court: Controversies over the Preconditions for Exercising Its Jurisdiction, 46 Netherlands International Law Review 1-25 (No. 1, 1999).

Hayner Priscilla B., Unspeakable Truths: Confronting State Terror and Atrocity (2001).

Hazan Pierre, Justice in a time of War, the true story behind the International Criminal Tribunal for the Former Yugoslavia (James Thomas Snyder, translator, 2004).

Hegler Alfred, Prinzipiendes Internationalen Strafrechts (1906).

Henzelin Marc, Le Principle de l'Universalité en Droit Pénal International (2000).

Hetesy Z., The Making of the Basic Principles of the Headquarters Agreement, 25 Fordham International Law Journal 625 (2002).

Higgins Rosalyn, Problems and Process: International Law and How We Use It (1994).

Hirsch Johan L., Sierra Leone: Diamonds and The Struggle For Democracy (2001).

History of the United Nations War Crimes Commission and the Development of the Laws of War (1943).

Holmes John T., The Principle of Complementarity, in The International Criminal Court: The Making of the Rome Statute 470 (Roy S. Lee, ed., 1999).
Huet André and Renée Koering-Joulin, Droit Pénal International (1994).
Hughe G., Validity and the Basic Norm, 59 California Law Review 695 (1971).
Hull William I., The Two Hague Conferences and their Contributions to International Law (1908).
Human Rights Watch, Commentary to the Preparatory Commission on the International Criminal Court, Elements of Crimes and Rules of Evidence and Procedure (June 2000).
Huntington Samuel P., The Clash of Civilizations and the Remarking of World Order (1996).
Hurd Heidi, Challenging Authority, 100 Yale Law Journal 1611 (1991).
Hurlock William L., The International Court of Justice: Effectively Providing a Long Overdue Remedy for Ending State-Sponsored Genocide (Bosnia-Herzogovina v. Yugoslavia), 12 American University Journal of International Law and Policy 299 (1997).
Hussain Farah, A Functional Response to International Crime: An International Justice Commission, ST. John's Law Review (1996).
Ilias Bantekas and Susan Nash, International Criminal Law (2007, 3ed.).
Ingadottir T. (ed.) The International Criminal Court: Recommendations on Policy and Practice: Financing, Victims, Judges, and Immunities (2003).
International Military Tribunal, Trial of the Major War Criminals before the International Military Tribunal in Nuremberg (1947).
Jackson Robert H., Forward the Nürenberg Trial Becomes a Historical Precedent, 20 Temple L.Q (1946-7).
Janis Mark W. (ed.), International Courts for the Twenty-First Century (1992).
Jescheck Hans-Heinrich, Die Verantwortlichkeit der Staatsorgane nach Völkerstrafrecht (1952).
Johannes Christoph and Maria Safferling, Towards an International Criminal Procedure (2001).
Jones Adam (ed.), Genocide, War Crimes and the West History and Complicity (2004).
Jones John R.W.D., The Practice of the International Criminal Tribunals for the Former Yugoslavia and Rwanda. (2nd edn 2000).
Jori Mario (ed.), Legal Positivism (1992).
Joyner Christopher and Christopher C. Posteraro, The United States and the International Criminal Court: Rethinking the Struggle Between

National Interest and International Justice, 10 Criminal Law Forum 359 (1999).
Kahan Dan M., The Secret Ambition of Deterence, 113 Harvard Law Review 414 (1999).
Kairys David, (ed.), The Politics of Law: A Progressive Critique (1982).
Kamenka Eugene, What is Justice? in Justice (Eugene Kamenka and Alice Erh-Soon Tay, eds., 1979).
Kandic Natasa, The ICTY Trials and Transnational Justice in Former Yugoslavia, 38:3 Cornell International Law Journal 789 (2005).
Katzenstein Suzanne, Hybrid Tribunals: Searching for Justice in East Timor, Harvard Human Rights Journal 245-278 (2003).
Kaul Hans-Peter and Claus Kress, Jurisdiction and Cooperation in the Statute of the International Criminal Court: Principles and Compromises, 2 Yearbook of International Humanitarian Law 143 (1999).
Kaul Hans-Peter, Special Note: The Struggle for the International Criminal Court's Jurisdiction, 6 European Journal of Crimes, Criminal Law and Criminal Justice 48 (1998).
Kelman Mark, A Guide to Critical Legal Studies (1987).
Kelsen Hans, Peace Through Law (1973).
—. Pure Theory of Law, (transl Maz Knight 1967).
—. What is Justice? Justice, Law, Politic in the Mirror of science (1957).
—. Will the Judgement of the Nürenberg Trial Constitute a Precedent in International Law, 1 INT'L L.Q 153 (1947).
Kennedy D., Law and Ideology, 3 TIKKUN (1988).
Kerr Rachel R., The International Criminal Tribunal for the Former Yugoslavia: an exercise in law, politics and diplomacy (2004).
Kim Y. S., The Preconditions to the Exercise of the Jurisdiction of the International Criminal Court: With Focus on Article 12 of the Rome Statute, 8 Journal of International Law and Practice 47 (1999).
King Henry T. Jr., and T.C. Theofrastous, From Nuremberg to Rome: A Step Backwards for US Foreign Policy, 31 Case Western Reserve Journal of International Law 47 (1999).
Kirsch Philippe and John T. Holmes, The Rome Conference on an International Criminal Court: The Negotiating Process, 93 American Journal of International Law 2 (1999).
Kirsch Philippe and V. Oosterveld, Negotiating an Instrument of the Twenty-First Century: Multilateral Diplomacy and the International Criminal Court, 46 McGill Law Journal 1141 (2001).

Kirsch Philippe and V. Oosterveld, The Preparatory Commission for the International Criminal Court, 25 Forhham International Law Journal 563 (2002).

Kirsch Phillipe, Alain Pellet and Bert Swart (eds.), International Criminal Law for an International Criminal Court (2001).

Kittichaisaree Kriangsak, International Criminal Law (2005).

Klein Fannie andDaniel Wilkes, United Nations Draft Statute for an International Criminal Court: An American Evaluation, in International Criminal Law 526 (Gerhard O.W. Mueller &Edward M. Wise eds., 1965).

Knoops Geert-Jan G.J., Defenses in Contemporary International Criminal Law (2001).

Kohler Josef, Internationales Strafrecht (1917).

Krapp Peter, Amnesty: Between an Ethics of Forgiveness and the Politics of Forgetting, 6 German Law Journal (2005).

Krohne S. W., The United States and the World Need an International Criminal Court as an Ally in the War Against Terrorism, 8 Indiana International Comparative law review 159 (1997).

Kup P., A History of Sierra Leone 1400-1787 (1961).

Larry May, Aggresion and Crimes Against Peace (2008).

Larsen Laurence Burgorgue (ed.), La Répression Internationale du Génocide rwandais, (2003).

Lattanzi Flavia and Valeria Santori (eds.), Essays on The Rome Statute of The International Criminal Court (2004).

Lawyers Committee for Human Rights, Report Issues of Jurisdiction and Admissibility in the Rules of Procedure and Evidence (2000).

—. The Accountability of an Ex Officio Prosecutor (Feb. 1998).

—. The International Criminal Court Trigger Mechanism and the Need for an Independent Prosecutor (July 1997).

Lee Roy S. (ed.), The International Criminal Court: The Making of The Rome Statute—Issues, Negotiations, Results (1999).

Leeb United States v. von (High Commandcase), Trials of War Criminals before the Nuremberg Military Tribunals under Control Council Law No. 10, vol. 11 (Trials), 1950.

Leigh Monroe, The United States and the Statute of Romc, 95 AJIL 124 (2001).

Leila Sadat Wexler, Panel Discussion, Association of American Law School Panel on the International Criminal Court, 36 American Journal of Law Review 223 (1999).

Levi Nino, Diritto Penale Internationale (1949).

Linton Suzannah, East Timor and Accountability for Serious Crimes, in International Criminal Law, vol III, 257-282 (M. Cherif Bassiouni, ed. 2008).

—. Indonesia and Accountability for Serious Crimes in East Timor, in International Criminal Law, vol III, 399-406. (M. Cherif Bassiouni, ed. 2008).

Lippman Matthew, Genocide, in International Criminal Law, vol I, 403-435 (M. Cherif Bassiouni, ed. 2008).

Lloyd of Hampstead, Lord Introduction to Jurisprudence (4th ed. 1979).

Lombois Claude, Droit Pénal International (1971).

—. Droit Pénal International (1979).

Ludwig von Bar, Das Internationale Private- und Strafrecht, (1862).

MacCormack G., Hägerström on Rights and Duties, Juridical Review 59 (1970).

MacGoldrick Dominic (ed.), The Permanent International Criminal Court: Legal and Policy Issues (2004).

MacIntyre Alasdair, After Virtue: A Study in Moral Theory (1982).

Malcolm Helen and Rodney Dixon (eds.), International Criminal Law Reports (2000).

Malekian Farhad, Armenian Genocide and the Questions of Responsibility of the Turkish Government (House of Commons Conference on the Armenia Genocide, Nor Serount Publications, 2007).

—. Condemning the Use of Force in the Gulf Crisis (1st ed., 1992), (2nd, 1994).

—. Confessing the International Rights of Children: The Basic documents with Analysis (Farhad Malekian, Kerstin Nordlöf, Cambridge Scholars Publishing, 2012).

—. Documents on the Principles of International Human Rights (2007).

—. Emasculating the Philosophy of International Criminal Justice in the Iraqi Special Tribunal, 38(3) Cornell International Law Journal (2005).

—. International Criminal Law: The Legal and Critical Analysis of International Crimes, 2 volumes (1991).

—. International Criminal Responsibility in, International Criminal Law, Crimes (M. Cherif Bassiouni, ed.) (2nd ed. 1999).

—. International Criminal Responsibility of States: A Study on the Evolution of State Responsibility with Particular Emphasis on the Concept of Crime and Criminal Responsibility (1985).

—. International Legal Status of Children in the Encyclopaedia of Criminology & Criminal Justice (Jay S. Albanese, editor), contribution by Farhad Malekian and Kerstin Nordlöf (3300 words) forthcoming soon by Wiley-Blackwell (5 volumes, 2013).

—. Islamic Criminal Justice Systems in the Encyclopaedia of Criminology & Criminal Justice (Jay S. Albanese, editor), (contribution after invitation, 3400 words) forthcoming soon by Wiley-Blackwell (5 volumes, 2013).

—. Judging International Criminal Justice in the Occupied Territories, International Criminal Law Review (Brill, Martinus Nijhoff Publishers, 2012), pp.827–869.

—. Principles of Islamic International Criminal Law, A Comparative Search (2011).

—. Mutilating the Philosophy of Justice in the Time of Armed Conflicts, Contemporary Journal of International Criminal Law (2007).

—. Prohibition Governing Child Soldiers Constituting an Integral Part of Jus Cogens and Obligatio Erga Omnes, XVII World Congress of the International Association of Youth and Family Judges and Magistrates, Belfast, Northern Ireland, 27 August – 2 September (2006).

—. Prohibition of Sexual Exploitation of Children Constituting Obligation *Erga Omnes* (Farhad Malekian, Kerstin Nordlöf,Cambridge Scholars Publishing, 2013).

—. The Functions of International Criminal Law and the Problem of Positivism and Neutralism Philosophy, Contemporary Journal of International Criminal Law (2007).

—. The Homogeneity of International Criminal Court with the Islamic Jurisprudence, 9 International Criminal Law Review (2009).

—. The Miserable Wedding of Naturalism into Positivism, 2 ID EST Journal (2009).

—. The Monopolization of International Criminal Law in the United Nations, A Jurisprudential Approach (1st ed., 1993), 2nd ed. (1995).

—. Prohibition of Sexual Exploitation of Children Constituting Obligation *Erga Omnes* (Farhad Malekian, Kerstin Nordlöf,Cambridge Scholars Publishing, 2013).

—. The Sovereignty of Children in Law (Farhad Malekian “chief editor”, Kerstin Nordlöf, Cambridge Scholars Publishing, 2012).

—. The System of International Law: Formation, Treaties, Responsibility (1987).

Malekian Farhad and Nordlőf Kerstin, *International Legal Status of Children,* in Encyclopaedia of Criminology and Criminal Justice (Albanese, Jay S. ed., Wiley- Blackwell, New York, 2014).

Maogoto Jackson Nyamuya, State Sovereignty and International Criminal Law: Versailles to Rome (2003).

Mario Jori (ed.), Legal Positivism (1992).

Marler M. K., The International Criminal Court: Assessing the Jurisdictional Loopholes in the Rome Statute, 49 Duke Law Journal 825 (1999).

Marquardt Paul D., Law Without Borders: The Constitutionality of an International Court, 33 Columbia Journal of Transnational Law 73 (1995).

May Larry, Crimes Against Humanity: A Normative Account (2004).

May Richard and Marieka Wierda, International Criminal Evidence (2002).

May Richard, David Tolbert, John Hocking, Ken Roberts, Bing Bing Jia, Daryl Mundis and Gabriel Oosthuizen, Essays on ICTY Procedure and Evidence in Honour of Gabrielle Kirk McDonald (2000).

McCormack Timothy L.H.and Gerry J. Simpson (eds.), The Law of War Crimes: National and International Approaches (1997).

McDonald Gabrielle Kirk and Olivia Swaak-Goldman, Substantive and Procedural Aspects of International Criminal Law: Commentary (2000).

McDonald Gabrielle Kirk, Olivia Swaak-Goldman (eds.), Substantive and Procedural Aspects of International Criminal Law: The Experience of International and National Courts, Documents 3 vols. (2002).

McGregor Lorna, Individual Accountability in South Africa: Cultural Optimum or Political Facade? 95 American Journal of International Law 32 (2001).

Meili Friedrich, Lehrbuch des Internationalen Strafrechts und Strafprozessrechts (1910).

Merryman John Henry, The Civil Law Tradition (1969).

Merton Thomas, The Normative Impact on International Law of the International Tribunal for the Former Yugoslavia, Israel Yearbook on Human Rights, 163-82 (1994).

Minow Martha, Between Vengeance and Forgiveness: Facing History After Genocide and Mass Violence (1998).

Moir Lindsay, Non-International Armed Conflict and Guerrilla Warfare, in International Criminal Law, vol I, 323-354 (M. Cherif Bassiouni, ed. 2008).

Mueller G.O.W and E.M. Wise (eds.), International Criminal Law (2 vols. 1965).

Murphy Avray, UN peacekeeping in Lebanon, Somalia and Kosovo: Operational and Legal Issues in Practice (2007).

Murphy John P., The Quivering Gulliver: US Views on a Permanent International Criminal Court, 34 International Lawyer (2000).

Murungi Betty Kaari, Implementing the International Criminal Court Statute in Africa, International Legal Practitioner 87 (2001).

Neier Aryeh, Waiting for Justice: The United States and the International Criminal Court, 15 World Policy Journal 33 (Fall 1998).

Nordlöf Kerstin, Straffprocessuella Tvångsmedel: Gripande, Anhållande och Häktning (1987).

—. 'Economic Raison d'être of Trafficking in Children' *in Rätten i den Ekonomiska Krisen* (2012).

—. Argumentation i Nordisk Straffrätt (2013).

—. *En rättsstridig presumtion om uppsåt vid allvarlig psykisk störning hos unga lagöverträdare*, in Festskrift till Anna Hollander, Norstedts Juridik AB, 2012, pp 359-374.

—. *International Principles and Rights of Children in Criminal Cases*, Contemporary Journal of International Criminal Law, Institute of International Criminal Law, 2007.

—. *International Principles and Rights of Children in Criminal Cases,* Juridicum Årsboken 2010, Örebro University, 2011.

—. *Oskuldspresumtionen – en utopi för minderåriga barn misstänkta för brott*, in Argumentation i Nordisk Straffrätt, pp 168-199.

—. Straffrättens Processer för Unga Lagöverträdare (1991).

—. The Legal Philosophy of Protecting a Suspect Child, Journal of the XVII World Congress of the International Association of Youth and Family Judges and Magistrates in Belfast, Northern Ireland, 27 August – 1 September 2006.

—. Unga Lagöverträdare i Social, Straff- och Processrätt (2005).

—. See also Malekian.

O'Connor Gerard E., The Pursuit of Justice and Accountability: Why The United States Should Support the Establishment of an International Criminal Court, 27 (4) Hofstra Law Review (1999).

Oehler Dietrich, Internationales Strafrecht (2nd ed. 1983).

Olivecrona Karl, Law as Fact (1939).

—. Law as Fact (2nd edn. 1971).

Oliver et al Covey T., The International Legal System (4th ed. 1995).

Orentlicher Diane F., Politics by Other Means: The Law of the International Criminal Court, 32 Cornell International Law Journal 489 (1999).

—. Settling Accounts: The Duty to Prosecute Human Rights Violations of a Prior Regime, 100 Yale Law Journal 2537 (1991).

Osiel Mark J., Modes of Participation in Mass Atrocity, 38:3 Cornell International Law Journal 791-822 (2005).

—. Obeying Orders: Atrocity, Military Discipline and the Law of War, 86 California Law Review 939 (1998).

—. Why Prosecute? Critics of Punishment for Mass Atrocity, 22 Human Rights Quarterly 118 (2000).

—. Mass Atrocity, Collective Memory, and the Law (1997).

P. Fitzpatrick (ed.), Dangerous Supplements: Resistance and Renewal in Jurisprudence (1991).

Palmisano Giuseppe, Co-operation by Non-States Parties, in the international criminal court: Comments on the draft statute 339-66 (Flavia Lattanzi, ed., 1998).

Patterson Dennis (ed.), Postmodernism and Law (1994).

Pejic Jelena, Creating a Permanent International Criminal Court: The Obstacles to Independence and Effectiveness, 29 Collombia Human Rights Law Review 291 (1998).

—. The International Criminal Court and the Human Rights Revolution, 34 International Lawyer 65 (2000).

Pella Vespasian V., Fonctions Pacificatrices du Droit Pénal Supranational et Fin du Système Traditionnel des Traités de Paix, Le Droit International Public 1 (1947).

—. La codification du droit pénal international, 56 Revuse Generale de Driot International Public 337 (1952).

—. Plan for World Criminal Code, 17 Revue Intenationale de Droit Penal (1946).

—. Plan d'un Code Répressif Mondial, 6 Revue International de Droit Penal 1948 (1935).

—. Towards an International Criminal Court, 44 AJIL 37 (1950).

Penrose Mary Margaret, It's Good to be the King!: Prosecuting Heads of State and Former Heads of State Under International Law, 39 columbia journal of transnational law 193 (2000).

Perelman C., The Idea of Justice and the Problem of Argument (1963).

Pfanner Toni, The Establishment of a Permanent International Criminal Court: ICRC Expectations of the Rome Diplomatic Conference, 322 International Review of the Red Cross 21 (1998).

Phillimore Lord, An International Criminal Court and the Resolutions of the Committee of Jurists, 1922-23 british yearbook of international law 79.

Phillips Paul, Marx and Engels on Law and Laws (1980).

Plawski Stanislaw, Etude des Principes Fondamentaux du Droit International Pénal (1972).

Politi Mauro and Guiseppe Nesi (eds.), The International Criminal Court and The Crime of Aggression (2004).

Politi Mauro and Guiseppe Nesi (eds.), The Rome Statute of the International Criminal Court: a Challenge to Impunity (2004).

Postema Gerald J., Bentham and the Common Law Tradition (1986).

Pound Roscoe, Jurisprudence (1959).

Pradel Jean, Droit Penal Comparé (1995).

—. Procedure Pénale (1997).

Preece Jennifer Jackson, Ethnic Cleansing as an Instrument of National-State Creation: Changing State Practices and Evolving Legal Norms, 20 Human Rights Quarterly 817 (1998).

Pritchard R.J. (ed.), The Tokyo Major War Crimes Trial: The Records of thc International Military Tribunal for the Far East with an Authorized Commentary and Comprehensive Guide (1998-2005, 124 volumes).

Quintano-Ripolles Antonio, Tratado de Derecho Penal Internacional e Internacional Penal (2 vols. 1955-1957).

Rabkin Jeremy, Global Criminal Justice: An Idea Whose Time Has Passed, 38:3 Cornell International Law Journal 753 (2005).

Rakate P. K., An International Criminal Court for a New Millennium – The Rome Conference, 23 South Africa Yearbook of International Law 217 (1998).

Randell Kenneth C., Universal Jurisdiction under International Law, 66 Texas Law Review 785 (1988).

Rao S. Rama, Financing of the Court, Assembly of States Parties and the Preparatory Commission, in TInternational Criminal Court: The making of the rome statute 470 (Roy S. Lee, ed., 1999).

Ratner Steven R. and Jason S. Abrams (eds.), Accountability for Human Rights Atrocities in International Law: Beyond the Nuremberg Legacy (2001).

Ratner Steven R. and Jason S. Abrams, Accountability for Atrocities in International Law (1997).

Rawls John, A Theory of Justice (1971).

—. A Theory of Justice (1999).

Rayfuse Rosmary, The Draft Code of Crimes Against the Peace and Security of Mankind: Eating Disorders at the International Law Commission, 8 Criminal Law Forum 43 (1997).

Raz Joseph, Practical Reason and Norms (1999).

—. The Authority of Law (1979).

—. The Concept of Legal System: An Introduction to the Theory of Legal System (2nd ed. 1980).

—. The Morality of Freedom (1986).

Reisman W. Michael (ed.), The Definition of Aggression and the ICC (2002).

—. Legal Responses to Genocide and Other Massive Violations of Human Rights, 59 Law and Contemporary Problems 75 (1996).

Retico Vincenzo, The Trial of First Instance before the International Criminal Court, in the international criminal court: Comments on the draft statute 193-208 (Flavia Lattanzi, ed., 1998).

Rhodes Richard, The Making of the Atomic Bomb (1995).

Rifatt Ahmed M., International Aggression: A Study of the Legal Concept: Its Development and Definition in International Law (1979).

Roberge Marie-Claude, The New International Criminal Court: A Preliminary Assessment, 325 International Review of the Red Cross 671 (1998).

Robertson Geoffrey, Crimes Against Humantiy: The Struggle for Global Justice (2000).

—. Ending Impunity: How International Criminal Law Can Put Tyrants on Trial, 38:3 Cornell International Law Journal 649-671 (2005).

Robinson Darryl, Defining 'Crimes Against Humanity' at the Rome Conference, 93 American Journal of International Law 43-57 (1999).

Roggemann Herwig and Petar Šarčević, National Security and International Criminal Justice (2002).

Röling B.V.A. and Antonio Cassese, The Tokyo Trial and Beyond (1993).

Rorty Richard, Philosophy and the Mirror of Nature (1990).

Rotberg Robert I. and Dennis Thompson (eds.), The Morality of Truth Commissions: Truth v. Justice (2000).

Roth-Arriaza Naomi (ed.), Impunity and Human Rights in International Law and Practice (1995).

Rubin Alfred P., Challenging the Conventional Wisdom: Another View of the International Criminal Court, 52 Journbal of International Affairs 783 (1999).

Rydberg Å., The Protection of the Interests of Witnesses – The ICTY in Comparison to the Future ICC, 12 Leiden Journal of International Law 455 (1999).

Sadat Leila Nadya and S. Richard Carden, The New International Criminal Court: An Uneasy Revolution, 88 Georgetown Law Journal 381 (2000).

Sadat Leila Nadya, Competing and Overlapping Jurisdictions, in International Criminal Law, vol II 201-229 (M. Cherif Bassiouni, ed., 2008).

—. Custom, Codification and Some Thoughts about the Relationship Between the Two: Article 10 of the ICC Statute, 49 Depaul Law Review 909 (2000).

—. The French Experience, in International Criminal Law, vol III 329-358 (M. Cherif Bassiouni, ed., 2008).
—. The International Criminal Court and the Transformation of International Law: Justice for the New Millenium (2002).
—. Universal Jurisdiction and National Amnesties, Truth Commissions and Other Alternatives to Prosecution: Giving Justice a Chance, Princeton Project on Universal Jurisdiction (Princeton University, 2001).
Sands P. (ed.), From Nuremberg to The Hague: the future of international criminal justice (2003).
Sarooshi Danesh, The Statute of the International Criminal Court, 48 International and Contemporary Law Quarterly 387 (1999).
Satzger Helmut, German Criminal Law and the Rome Statute – A Critical Analysis of the German Code of Crimes Against International Law, 2 international criminal law review 261 (2002).
Scaliotti Massimo, Defences Before the International Criminal Court: Substantive Grounds for Excluding Criminal Responsibility – Part 1, 1 International Criminal Law Review 111 (2001).
—. Defences Before the International Criminal Court: Substantive Grounds for Excluding Criminal Responsibility – Part 2, 2 International Criminal Law Review 1 (2002).
Schaack Beth van, The Crime of Political Genocide: Repairing the Genocide Convention's Blind Spot, 106 Yale Law Journal 2259 (1997).
Schabas William A., An Introduction to the International Criminal Court (2001).
—. An Introduction to the International Criminal Court (2nd 2004).
—. Complementarity in Practice: Creative Solutions or a Trap for the Court in The Rome Statute of the International Criminal Court: A Challenge to Impunity (Mauro Politi and Federica Gioia, eds., 2001).
—. Genocide in International Law, the Crime of Crimes (2000).
—. Justice, Democracy and Impunity in Post Genocide Rwanda: Searching for Solutions to Impossible Problems, 7 Criminal Law Forum 523 (1996).
—. Ramesh Thakur and Edel Hughes (eds.), Atrocities and International Accountability: Beyond Transnational Justice (2007).
—. Sentencing by International Tribunals: For a Human Rights Approach, 7:2 Duke Journal oof Comparative & International Law 461 (1997).
—. The Abolition of the Death Penalty in International Law (2002 and 2003).
—. The UN International Criminal Tribunals: the former Yugoslavia, Rwanda and Sierra Leone (2006).

—. War Crimes, Crimes Against Humanity and the Death Penalty, 60:3 Albany Law Review 733 (1997).

Scharf Michael P., Results of the Rome Conference for an International Criminal Court, ASIL INSIGHT (Aug. 1998).

Scheffer David J., The United States and the International Criminal Court, 93 American Journal of International Law 12-22 (1999).

Scheffer David, The Extraordinary Chambers in the Courts of Cambodia, in International Criminal Law, vol III 219-255 (M. Cherif Bassiouni, ed., 2008).

Schutter Bart de (ed.), La Belgique et le Droit International Pénal (1975).

Schwarzenberger Georg, The Frontiers of International Law 181-209 (1962).

—. The Problem of an International Criminal Law, 3 Current Legal Problems 263 (1950).

Schwelb Egon, Crimes Against Humanity, 1946 British Yearbook of International Law 178.

Segal David R. and Mady W. Segal, Peacekeepers and Their Wives: American Participation in the Multinational Force and Observers (1993).

Selden Kyoko, Mark Selden and Robert Jay Lifton (eds.), The Atomic Bombs: Voices From Hiroshima and Nagasaki (Japan in The Modern World) (1997).

Sewall Sarah B. & Carl Kaysen (eds.), The United States and the International Criminal Court: National Security and International Law (2000).

Shabtai Rosenne, The World Court: What it is and how it works (1989).

Shah S.B., The Oversight of the Last Great International Institution of the Twentieth Century: The International Criminal Court's Definition of Genocide, 16 Emory International Law Review 351 (2002).

Sharp P., Prospects for Environmental Liability in the International Criminal Court, 18 Virgina Enviromental Law Journal 217 (1999).

Shaw Malcolm N., The International Criminal Court – Some Procedural and Evidential Issues, 3 Journal of Armed Conflicts Law 65 (1998).

Shelton Dinah (ed.), International Crimes, Peace and Human Rights: The Role of the International Criminal Court (2000).

Sheng Ada Y., Analyzing the International Criminal Court Complementarity Principle Through a Federal Courts Lens, Bepress Legal Series paper 1249, 30 (2006).

Shklar Judith, Legalism: Law, Morals and Political Trials (1964).

Shotton Anna, A Strategy to Address Sexual Exploitation by U.N. Peacekeeping Personnel, 39 Cornell Law Review 97 (2006).

Shukri Muhammed Aziz, Will Aggressors Ever be Tried Before the ICC?, in the International Criminal Court and the Crime of Aggression 41 (Mauro Politi and Guiseppe Nesi, eds., 2004).

Siegert K., Grundlinien des Völkerstrafprozessrechts (1953).

Silvia D'Ascoli., Sentencing in International Criminal Law: the UN ad hoc Tribunals and Future Perspectives for the ICC (2011).

Sliedregt Elies van, The Criminal Responsibility of Individuals for Violations of International Humanitarian Law (2003).

—. The Surrender of War Criminals to the International Criminal Court, 25 Loy. L.A. Int'l & Com. L. Rev. 605-51 (2003).

Smidt M. L., The International Criminal Court: An Effective Means of Deterrence?, 167 Military Law Review 156 (2001).

Smith Alison, Child Recruitment and the Special Court for Sierra Leone, 2 Journal of International Criminal Justice 1141-1153(2004).

Soh Pierre, The Dynamics of International Criminal Tribunals: Perspectives on Achieving Effective Human Rights Protection, 67: 2 Nordic Journal of International Law 139 (1998).

Sowilet A., The Problem of the Creation of a Permanent International Criminal Court (1951).

Spieker Heike, The International Criminal Court and Non-International Armed Conflicts, 13 Leiden Journal of International Law 395 (2000).

Sternberg Mark R. von, A Comparison of the Yugoslav and Rwandan War Crimes Tribunals: Universal Jurisdiction and the Elementary Dictates of Humanity, 22 Brooklyn Journal of International Law, 111 (1966).

Stimson Henry L., The Nuremberg, Trial, Landmark in Law, 25 Foreign Affaris 179 (1946-7).

Stoelting David, Status Report on the International Criminal Court, 3 Hofstra Law and Policy Symposium 233 (1999).

Stone Julius and Robert Woetzel, Toward a Feasible International Criminal Court (1970).

Sugarman David (ed.), Legality, Ideology and the State (1983).

Swart Bert, The European Union and the Schengen Agreement, in International Criminal Law, vol II 243-265 (M. Cherif Bassiouni, ed., 2008).

Sweets John F., The Politics of Resistance in France (1976).

Sypnowich C., The Concept of Socialist Law (1990).

Talbee J. L., A Call to Arms Declined: The United States and the International Criminal Court, 14 Emory International Law Review 105 (2000).

Tamanaha Brian, A General Jurisprudence of Law and Society (2001).

Taylor Telford, The Anatomy of the Nuremberg Trials (1992).

The Judgment of the International Military Tribunal for the Trial of German Major War Criminals, Nuremberg 1946, H.M. Stationary Office Cmd. 6964.

Tisci G. (ed.), La Corte Penale Internazionale (2003).

Tochilovsky Vladimir, Rules of Procedure for the International Criminal Court: Problems to Address in Light of the Experience of the Ad Hoc Tribunals, 46 Netherland International Law Review 343 (1999).

Tomuschat Christian, Crimes Against the Peace and Security of Mankind and the Recalcitrant Third State, 24 Isreal Yearbook on _International Human Rights 41 (1994).

Travers Maurice, Le Droit Pénal International et sa Mise en Oeuvre en Temps de Paixet en Temps de Guerre (5 vols. 1920-1922).

Trials of War Criminals Before the Nuremberg Military Tribunals under Control Council Law No. 10 (Nuremberg, 1946-1949).

Trials of War Criminals before the Nuremberg Military Tribunals under Control Council (1951).

Triffterer O. (ed.), Commentary on the Rome Statute of the International Criminal Court (1999).

Tucker Robert W., The International Criminal Court Controversy, 18 World Policy Journal 71 (2001).

Unger R., The Critical Legal Studies Movement, 96 Harvard Law Review 561 (1983).

Uvin Peter, Difficult Choices in The New Post-Conflict Agenda: The International Community in Rwanda After The Genocide, 22: 2 Third World Quarterly 177-189 (2001).

Vabres H. Donnedieu de, Introduction à L'étude du Droit Pénal International (1922).

—. Les Principes Modernes du Droit Pénal International (1928).

Vagts Detlev F., The Hague Conventions and Arms Control, 94 AJIL 31 (2000).

Verdirame Guglielmo, The Genocide Definition in the Jurisprudence of the ad hoc Tribunals, The International and Comparative Law Quarterly, Vol. 49, No. 3 578-598 (Jul., 2000).

Verweij H., The International Criminal Court: Alive, Still Kicking, 25 Fordham International _Law Journal 737 (2002).

Vetter Greg, Command Responsibility of Non-Military Superiors in the International Criminal Court (ICC), 25 Yale Journal of International Law 89 (2000).

Vierucci L., The First Steps of the International Criminal Tribunal for the Former Yugoslavia, 6 European Journal of International Law 134 (1995).

Vincenzo Militello, The Personal Nature of Individual Criminal Responsibility and the ICC Statute, 5 Journal of International Criminal Justice 941-952 (Number 4. 2007).

Vyver Johan D. van der, Personal and Territorial Jurisdiction of the International Criminal Court, 14 Emory International Law Review 1 (2000).

Wainhouse David W., International Peace Observation: A History and Forecast (1986).

—. International Peacekeeping at the Crossroads: National Support? Experience and Prospects (1973).

Waluchow W.J., Inclusive Legal Positivism (1994).

Ward A., Breaking the Sovereignty Barrier: The United States and the International Criminal Court, 41 Santa Clara Law Review 1123 (2001).

Ward Ian, An Introduction to Critical Legal Theory (1998).

Washburn John, The Negotiation of the Rome Statute for the International Criminal Court and International Lawmaking in the 21st Century, 11 Pace International Law Review 361 (1999).

Webster Paul, France Denies Arming Hutus for Genocide, Guardian Weekly, London, 3 (18.1.1998).

Wedgewood Ruth, Address to the Cornell International Law Journal Symposium: Milosevic & Hussein on Trial, 38:3 Cornell International Law Journal 779 (2005).

—. The International Criminal Court: An American View, 10 European Journal of International Law 93 (1999).

Wexler Leila Sadat (ed.), Model Draft Statute for the International Criminal Court Based on the Preparatory Committee's Text to the Diplomatic Conference, Rome, June 15 – July 17, 1998 (Association Internationale de Droit Pénal, Nouvelles Études Pénales No. 13ter) (1998).

Wexler Leila Sadat, A First Look at the 1998 Rome Statute for a Permanent International Criminal Court: Jurisdiction, Definition of Crimes, Structure and Referrals to the Court, in International Criminal Law Vol. III 655-91 (M. Cherif Bassiouni, ed., 1999).

—. International Law Association (American Branch) Committee on a Permanent International Criminal Court, First Committee Report on Jurisdiction, Definition of Crimes and Complementarity, 25 Denver Journal of International Law and Policy 221 (1997).

—. The Proposed Permanent International Criminal Court: An Appraisal, 29 Cornell International Law Journal 665, no 75 (1996).

Wexler Sadat Leila and M. Cherif Bassiouni (eds.), Observations on the Consolidated ICC text before the final session of the Preparatory Committee (1998).

Williams Derek, The Reach of Rome (1988).

Williams Sharon A., The Rome Statute on the International Criminal Court: From 1947-2000 and Beyond, 38 OSGOOD Hall Law Journal 297 (2000).

Williamson Jamie A., Command Responsibility in the Case Law of the International Criminal Tribunal for Rwanda, 13 (3) Criminal Law Forum, Official Journal of the Society for the Reform of Criminal Law 365-384 (2002).

Willis James F., Prologue to Nuremberg: The Politics and Diplomacy of Punishing War Criminals of the First World War (1981).

Wippman David, Atrocities, Deterrence, and the Limits of International Justice, 23 Forham International Law Journal 473 (1999).

Wise Edward M., International Crimes and Domestic Criminal Law, 38 Depaul Law Review 923 (1989).

Witschel G., Financial Regulations and Rules of the Court, 25 Forham International Law Journal 665 (2002).

Wladimiroff Michail, The Assignment of Defence Counsel before the International Criminal Tribunal for Rwanda, 12 (4) Leiden Journal of International Law 957-968 (1999).

Wright Quincy, Proposal for an International Criminal Court, 46 AJIL 60 (1952).

—. The Law of the Nuremberg Trial, 41 AJIL 38 (1947).

—. The Scope of International Criminal Law: A Conceptual Framework, 15 VJIL (1975).

Wright W. F., Limitations on the Prosecution of International Terrorists by the International Criminal Court, 8 Jornal of International Law and Practice 139 (1999).

Yengejeh S. M., Rules of Procedure of the Assembly of States Parties to the Rome Statute of the International Criminal Court, 25 Fordham International Law Journal 674 (2002).

Young S. N. M., Surrendering the Accused to the International Criminal Court, 71 British YearBook of International Law 317 (2000).

Zagaris Bruce, United States Treaties on Mutual Assistance in Criminal Matters, in International Criminal Law, vol II 385-402 (M. Cherif Bassiouni, ed., 2008).

Zahnd Patrick, How the International Criminal Court Should Help Implement International Humanitarian Law, in International crimes,

Peace and human rights: The Role of the international criminal court 35-42 (Dinah Shelton, ed., 2000).
Zaid Mark S., The U.S. War Crimes Act of 1966, inInternational Criminal Law, vol III 407-419 (M. Cherif Bassiouni, ed., 2008).
Zappalà Salvatore, Human Rights in International Criminal Proceedings (2003).
Ziegler David W., War, Peace and International Politics (7th ed 1997).